AMERICAN POLITICS
AND THE
PARTY SYSTEM

McGRAW-HILL SERIES IN POLITICAL SCIENCE

ADRIAN State and Local Government

ADRIAN AND PRESS Governing Urban America

BONE American Politics and the Party System

CHRISTENSON AND McWILLIAMS Voice of the People: Readings in Public Opinion and Propaganda

DRUKMAN Community and Purpose in America

EASTON AND DENNIS Children in the Political System: Origins of Political Legitimacy

GERBERDING United States Foreign Policy

HARMON Political Thought: From Plato to the Present

McCANDLESS Urban Government and Politics

McCLOSKY AND TURNER The Soviet Dictatorship

MILLETT Government and Public Administration

MILLETT Management in the Public Service

NEUMANN European Government

POOL Contemporary Political Science: Toward Empirical Theory

PRITCHETT The American Constitution

PRITCHETT American Constitutional Issues

SHUMAN International Politics

WILSON Police Administration

HUGH A. BONE

Professor of Political Science
University of Washington

AMERICAN POLITICS AND THE PARTY SYSTEM

FOURTH EDITION

McGRAW-HILL BOOK COMPANY

New York   San Francisco   St. Louis   Düsseldorf   Johannesburg
Kuala Lumpur   London   Mexico   Montreal   New Delhi   Panama
Rio de Janeiro   Singapore   Sydney   Toronto

This book was set in Baskerville by
Applied Typographic Systems and printed on
permanent paper and bound by The Maple Press
Company. The designer was Janet Bollow;
the drawings were done by Robert Bausch and
Judith McCarty. The editors were Robert P. Rainier
and Eva Marie Strock. Charles A. Goehring
supervised production.

AMERICAN POLITICS AND THE PARTY SYSTEM

Printed in the United States of America.

Library of Congress catalog card number: 79-133806

234567890   MAMM   7987654321

06487

091829

TO MY WIFE

PREFACE

A number of changes have taken place in the mood of American politics and the college curriculum since the appearance of the last edition. Instead of an updating, therefore, at least three-fourths of this edition has been completely rewritten with a thorough revision of the remainder, including new chapters dealing with American state- and foreign-party systems and protest politics.

There are several other changes in this edition. In the first chapter the student is immediately taken into the various theories and ways of looking at political parties. With these concepts as background, he is then directed toward the genesis and development of American parties, their characteristics, and their tripartite character represented in the organizational activists, public office holders, and electoral bases. Some of the newer approaches to recruitment and to campaigns follow. The individual in politics and political participation through voting and political organizations receives greater attention than before. The final section of the book reviews the nature of the American pluralist society and the traditional means of access to government. The concluding chapter analyzes the challenges to this society emanating from the wide-spread use of forceful techniques and violence and the protests against the "system" as currently operated. At this concluding point the general lines of the "new politics" approach are considered. It is believed that the several changes in both emphasis and data will contribute to the student's search for "relevant" explanations and considerations in the politics of the seventies.

The literature on American politics, parties, state political sys-tems, campaigning, interest groups, and voting behavior continues to increase rapidly. Most of these works are empirical in character, testing hypotheses on the basis of evidence gleaned through polling, interview-ing, and new analyses of data. More than ever, undergraduate and graduate students are making studies of political life in their own com-munities and comparing their data with those gathered elsewhere. The present-day student, therefore, has a better opportunity to obtain political information and insight.

I have chosen to use a wide variety of monographs and articles representing many points of view. Citations relevant to the particular subject appear in each chapter, with several additional references for further reading at the end of each chapter. Because of the hundreds of articles appearing during the last decade it is of course impossible to cite every useful item. Although acknowledging the heavy debt owed by myself and the profession to the Michigan Survey Research Center and the Inter-University Consortium in Political Research, I have drawn from many other studies of voting behavior and made extensive use of studies conducted at the subnational level.

Hugh A. Bone

CONTENTS

PART ONE THE THEORY AND DEVELOPMENT OF PARTIES

CHAPTER 1 POLITICAL PARTIES AND POLITICAL THEORY   1
CHAPTER 2 DEVELOPMENT OF THE AMERICAN PARTY SYSTEM   27

PART TWO PARTY SYSTEMS

CHAPTER 3 THE NATIONAL TWO-PARTY SYSTEM   63
CHAPTER 4 OTHER PARTY SYSTEMS   98

PART THREE PARTY OF THE ACTIVISTS

CHAPTER 5 STATE AND LOCAL PARTY ORGANIZATION   131
CHAPTER 6 NATIONAL PARTY ORGANIZATION   160

PART FOUR PARTY IN THE GOVERNMENT

CHAPTER 7   EXECUTIVE PARTIES AND POLITICS   195
CHAPTER 8   THE PARTY IN LEGISLATURE AND JUDICIARY   226

PART FIVE NOMINATIONS AND ELECTIONS

CHAPTER 9   RECRUITMENT OF CANDIDATES   255
CHAPTER 10   PRESIDENTIAL NOMINATIONS   286
CHAPTER 11   CAMPAIGN ORGANIZATIONS AND STRATEGY   322
CHAPTER 12   CAMPAIGN TECHNIQUES   360
CHAPTER 13   FINANCING CAMPAIGNS AND PARTIES   391

PART SIX POLITICAL SOCIALIZATION AND SUFFRAGE

CHAPTER 14   POLITICAL SOCIALIZATION   423
CHAPTER 15   SUFFRAGE PROBLEMS   446

PART SEVEN VOTING BEHAVIOR AND PARTICIPATION

CHAPTER 16   PSYCHOLOGICAL INFLUENCES ON VOTING   475
CHAPTER 17   SOCIAL DIFFERENTIATION AND VOTING
              PREFERENCES   501
CHAPTER 18   POLITICAL PARTICIPATION AND ALIENATION   536

PART EIGHT THE INTEREST-GROUP SOCIETY

CHAPTER 19   THE AMERICAN PLURALIST SOCIETY   569
CHAPTER 20   THE TACTICS OF INTEREST GROUPS   603
CHAPTER 21   THE CHALLENGE OF PROTEST POLITICS   645

AUTHOR INDEX   671
SUBJECT INDEX   681

x

PART ONE THE THEORY AND DEVELOPMENT OF POLITICAL PARTIES

Self-government demands a free circulation of
"individual's" impulses. This calls for a varied network
throughout the social structure. Disciplined parties,
clearly differentiated, result in a hardening
of these arteries.

E. P. HERRING

Party government is the democratic and liberal
solution of reconciling authority and liberty; they can
manage interests without becoming oppressive.

E. E. SCHATTSCHNEIDER

CHAPTER 1 POLITICAL PARTIES AND POLITICAL THEORY

That much sought-after man in the street seldom theorizes about politics and democracy. His vote, his consent, and his money are wooed by the politician in the name of "public opinion," "democracy," "politics," "conservatism," "liberalism," "the middle of the road," and "the will of the people." Although the American citizen is usually not a politically philosophical person, he regards himself as dedicated to political democracy and at least has a hunch that public opinion is necessary to his system and that it works wonders.

Three of the most frequently used terms in the political vocabulary are *democracy, politics,* and *public opinion.* These have provoked a fair measure of semantic trouble, for their meanings vary from person to person. Carl Becker was moved to write that *democracy* is a word "which connotes different things to different people, a kind of conceptual Gladstone bag which, with a little manipulation, can be made to accommodate almost any collection of social facts we may wish to carry about in

1

it."[1] This may be said for *politics, public opinion,* and many other terms as well.

There has indeed been a tyranny surrounding these political terms, a tyranny that often confuses more than it clarifies. This book is about political parties and, secondarily, about special-interest groups as institutions through which operate their democracy and their politics. In this opening chapter, it is appropriate to consider briefly some of the issues and concepts associated with these closely related terms. Definitions do not fully explain how democracy, politics, and public opinion work in real life, but they do state the principles, propositions, and references from which we can start to analyze and view man in his political relationships.

WHAT IS DEMOCRACY?

Varied Uses. The several connotations of the word *democracy* have arisen because it is used in diverse political, economic, social, psychological, legal, institutional, and ideological senses. Each user fits it to his own needs, and it is often impregnated with ethical values. It is said that political parties and pressure groups should be "democratically" operated or that groups should be operated in a "democratic" way. The label *democratic* may be used to describe people's behavior and their attitude toward life.

The term *democracy* is used in a social sense to describe a degree of access to public accommodations and recreational facilities irrespective of sex, race, national origin, or interest. To those striving for economic betterment, job opportunity becomes a cherished principle of democracy. Persons refused membership in fraternities, societies, and clubs may call restrictive membership standards undemocratic.

Democracy is frequently associated with forms or mechanisms of government. The term is used to distinguish dictatorships from governments resting on free, periodic elections of public officials who are responsible to voters who can remove them at the next election. In the latter political society, it is assumed that the people have the right of freedom of association, assembly, press, and speech. Among the classical writers, popular sovereignty was the essence of the democratic system. In this sense, democracy is an ideology associated with equality and concerned with recognizing the common people and not just the privileged class as the source of power.

The new Afro-Asian nations are carefully studying the forms of governments, and many have adopted systems which, on paper at least, carry the form of democracy. Here again, democracy may be a form of government, but not any one *specific* form such as unitary, federal, presidential, or parliamentary with a hereditary monarch. To look only at the

[1] *Modern Democracy*, Yale University Press, New Haven, Conn., 1941, p. 4.

mechanism is to run the risk of missing the essential features of democracy—a fact experienced by the peoples of some of the developing nations.

A considerable amount of disagreement over the term concerns what the *central* principle or principles of democracy are. Is there one more indispensable and essential than all the others? Are there several that must be present and mutually complement one another? What follows are descriptions of the essential doctrines of the American political democracy that are of particular significance to the subjects of this volume. Some of them have constitutional and legal sanction; but all are rooted in custom, general acceptance, and faith. Controversy surrounds their operation. Democracy, in these terms, is both a theory and a reality. It is not yet and probably never will be fully achieved; but it is the goal, the ideal, to which the American people have committed themselves.

Popular sovereignty and majority rule have provoked extensive comment in the writings of democratic theorists. In briefest compass, what is meant is that the ultimate ruling power resides in the people. This requires neither that all the people meet face to face and arrive at decisions nor that they may not delegate the exercise of authority to someone else. It does mean that those who govern must do so in response to an orderly set of rules and procedures and in accordance with an expressed popular will.

Those who would govern must first attain office by accepted legitimate means. More is involved than simply the avoidance of force and violence to win public office. Nomination and election must be accomplished in prescribed ways. All interested parties are expected to operate on the assumption that persuasion shall play a decisive role in the selection of rulers and that attempts to win over the voter shall take place in open and free public discussion. In the American polity there is much flexibility in the methods of nomination and in the conduct of elections. Even so, there are laws against bribery and the use of force, and there is considerable regulation of nominating and electing procedures.

"Consent of the governed" also indicates that public men have the duty to consult their constituencies and to seek the maximum of voluntary cooperation from them in furthering the government's programs. Educating the governed by explaining methods and purposes is a part of the process of effective consultation and of leadership itself. Political leaders are concerned with the public's attitudes and opinions not only in terms of their own reelection but also in terms of accomplishing certain goals while in office. The ability to persuade and to lead public opinion becomes the hallmark of the successful public man.

In a democracy a public action presumably requires the consent of the majority. When two or more policy alternatives are before the legislature, we say that the opinion of the larger group—theoretically one-half plus one—shall prevail. It is not argued that the majority is right and that the minority is wrong but that the majority opinion is to be accepted. Majority rule is convenient and clear-cut. In contrast, if minority rule were to prevail, there would always be the question of which minority.

The principle of majority rule in elections is accepted, but it does not always prevail. Several American Presidents have been elected without a majority of the popular vote, but with the majority electoral vote required by the Constitution.

The plurality principle is used in single-member district elections for the legislature. Third-party entries may result in the election of a nominee who failed to receive a majority vote but polled more votes than any other single candidate. In direct primary elections, a plurality victory may result in a choice not necessarily acceptable to the majority of the party voters. In most Southern states, where nomination in the Democratic party primary is virtual assurance of election, provision is made for a runoff primary. If no candidate gets a clear majority in the first primary election, the two highest run in a second one, thus ensuring that the winning candidate is acceptable to a majority of party voters. These examples will suffice to show that the application of majority rule raises problems both for those who wish to assure it and for those who would circumvent the decisions of a simple majority.

An important corollary of majority rule is the protection of minority rights. Many limitations on government are written into constitutions to protect the right of minorities. The majority must comply with certain rules of the game, observe certain procedures, and operate within certain restraints and limitations. The minority has the right to be heard, to vote, and to be represented when it does elect its candidate. The legislative bodies in most democratic countries include officially recognized minority leaders. Although the minority must acquiesce in the decision of the majority, the minority remains free to criticize the majority and to resort to constitutional and legitimate means to change it. The right to opposition remains a basic characteristic of a democratic system.

There appears to be conflict in the basic theory of majority-minority rule. From one point of view, the political system should be a *responsible* one that reflects the majority will, backed up by instruments such as party government that assure that rulers are held accountable for their decisions. From another viewpoint, the task of political leaders is to promote, to use Walter Lippmann's phrase, "the public philosophy"; that is, there are ultimate, higher truths that the majority may not see or subscribe to, and if its will prevailed, the result could be a tyrannical majority. In both cases the theorists are unlikely to be enthusiastic about compromise: on the one side because it would thwart the will of the majority, on the other because it would overemphasize the importance of one's own interests and weaken restraints on the power-oriented man and group. The group theorist is content to worry less about the alleged bad effects of compromise and to insist that group competition resulting in accommodation and compromise is both efficient and realistic. These conflicting theories will appear many more times as we analyze parties, voters, and groups.

The term *political equality* means that each citizen is entitled both to equality before the law and to equal political rights. In a democracy, this equality and the dignity of the individual are the ideal, but in practice they are often not obtained. In a democracy, the facts that each man is worthy and that institutions may exist to make life better for him are recognized. He has the right to pursue a private life and to enjoy the fruits of his talents and labor. The state makes certain requirements of him such as military service, payment of taxes, and obedience to the law. Beyond this, he is permitted the opportunity to pursue his own private interests.

The concept of equality is also undergoing expansion in the area popularly known as civil rights. Controversy has raged, particularly since World War II, over discrimination against minorities in housing, education, recreation, public facilities, and the ballot box. Underneath the great political turmoil over these issues is the view that man is entitled to the good things in life which he can earn by his talent and that these are not to be denied by artificial barriers of race, national origin, or religion.

Very closely related to equality is a fourth basic article of democratic faith: the opportunity for each person to participate in the determination of public policy and in the exercise of control over his government. A considerable portion of this book is devoted to the various means of participation and the problems associated with it. Major subjects include how citizens organize and operate political parties and political interest groups, how they exercise the franchise, and how money and communications media influence politics.

Four principles of the democratic creed—consent of the governed, majority rule, political equality, and participation—have been singled out for brief mention. Each of these requires the existence of other basic principles, such as freedom, consultation, and persuasion. There is disagreement among political theorists and practitioners of government on how each of the postulates should and does operate. Some would place tighter limits on discussion and advocacy than others. Internal security problems have caused some persons to assert that the state must set limits on freedom of speech and on group membership to a greater extent than heretofore. These issues must be left to other writers except as they become particularly relevant to some of the topics discussed later.

POLITICS

Nature of Politics.   Harold Lasswell has stated that politics is "the science of who gets what, when, and how." For him the study of politics is the "study of influence and the influential." D. W. Brogan attaches a "value" and sees politics as "the study of the means whereby liberty and authority may be best combined, whereby the dignity of the free man is made compatible with the highest and richest forms of cooperation."[2] From these definitions, politics would not be limited exclusively to the governmental relationships of man but would embrace activities within one's sorority, club, league, trade union, or other group.

Our major concern is with the relation between the governors and the governed. In this context, politics is a struggle for power or an attempt to influence the course of public policy and public decision. It means, as Max Weber said, "striving to share power or striving to influence the distribution of power, either among states or among groups within the state."[3] Power is the capacity to produce results and indicates the possession of some control or command over some person or some thing.

Persons and groups have certain expectations and often remain discontented with the degree to which their hopes have been fulfilled; power is sought to help fulfill such desires. Some people want power and influence in order to bring about reform and changes in a governmental program; others seek power and influence to prevent innovation and to bring about stability or a freezing of the status quo. Power is sought by some individuals for its own sake; others may wish to use power to enhance their prestige or economic well-being; still others may be motivated by an overriding desire to promote the good of a special group or of the general will and general welfare. To quote Weber again, "He who is active in politics strives for power either as a means in serving other aims, ideal or egoistic, or as 'power for power's sake,' that is, in order to enjoy the prestige feeling that power gives."[4]

Politics is rather frequently used interchangeably with the term *political system.* A political system in turn is defined by Robert A. Dahl as

[2] *The Study of Politics*, Cambridge University Press, London, 1946, p. 7.
[3] *From Max Weber: Essays in Sociology*, edited and translated by H. H. Gerth and C. Wright Mills. Copyright 1946 by Oxford University Press, Inc., p. 78. Reprinted by permission.
[4] *Ibid.*

TABLE 1-1 Actors in public decision making

Individuals	Private agencies	Public agencies	
Citizens) Voters)	Political parties) Interest groups) Citizens associations)	Legislative) Executive) Administrative) Judiciary)	Public policy
	←————————————Feedback ←————————		

"any persistent pattern of human relationships that involves, to a significant extent, power, rule and authority."[5] Although we use this general definition, our major concern is with the political behavior, political techniques, and relationships among groups in our society seeking governmental power and influence. From an individual's point of view we are interested in analyzing why and how he "throws his political weight around." One of the advantages of a representative democracy is the many opportunities it affords the citizen to engage in politics—indeed politics becomes every citizen's business if he chooses to make it so.

Pattern of American Politics. The essence of politics is the shaping of public policy. In the United States, policies are evolved through a diversity of ways and processes rather than through one or two institutions. Table 1-1 shows the complex of factors and agencies that can be brought to bear on public policy. Any table attempting to depict the public decision-making process is bound to be an oversimplification, for it fails to give an accurate picture of the interaction among the various public institutions and among the voters, parties, and interest groups and, in turn, their interaction with the public agencies. The table also does not show that constitutional amendments, proposed by the legislatures and ratified by the people (or federal amendments proposed by Congress and ratified by the states), have paved the way for public policies profoundly affecting the political, social, and economic order. But the table does indicate the fragmented, atomized sources of policy.

To this may be added the decentralization of decision making brought about by a federal system that provides for policy determination at the local, state, and national levels. Great battles continue over which decisions are most appropriately made at each level and which must be joint enterprises. Expediency as well as principle enters into questions of whether separate municipal governments or an overall metropolitan government should perform a given function. Metropolitics has brought an additional area of politics to the historic struggles

[5] *Modern Political Analysis*, Prentice-Hall, Inc., Englewood Cliffs, N.J., 1963, p. 6.

over home rule, states' rights, and federal prerogative. Decentralization is another basic characteristic of the American polity: Both operationally and as a part of the belief system *power is and must be diversified.*

The proliferation of political organization and activity and the decentralization and diversity of policy-making agencies present a confusing picture to those seeking the pattern of American politics. On the surface, the pattern seems an absence of pattern, with as many variations as rules. We see, for example, great concentrations of economic power, yet the real locus of power in our great trade union federations, farm associations, and political parties often rests with the locals. Persons of great power in a community do not necessarily hold official high positions in the city government, and the same may be true of power holders in a legislative body. The mosaic of decision making in Florida, Pennsylvania, and Montana, for example, does not follow a common pattern. Even so, the student of government is dedicated to the detection of patterns and uniformities in the operation of politics, both at the national and at the local levels.

Party and Pressure-group Politics. Two great sets of groups wield informal or essentially nonlegal power – political parties and political interest groups. In a few instances, political organizations may exercise legal functions, such as recommending persons to fill temporary vacancies in a public office or to serve on government boards. In the main, however, they function outside the constitutional framework of government. The often amorphous and inchoate group that we call a political party selects candidates for public office and tries to get them elected. Party members in the legislature, acting as a party group, organize the leadership and committees of the assembly. From the welter of individual ideas and interests, the party formulates some general principles and policies that it hopes will be honored by the persons it nominates and helps to elect. The winning party attempts to maintain public support for its program, while the losers endeavor to offer an opposition to provide an avenue for the expression of discontent.

Sometimes the alpha and omega of political activity and power struggles appear to be largely carried on by political parties. Such an impression is erroneous, for parties are not the only or necessarily the most important groupings in the political arena. Various social, fraternal, ethnic, and economic interests use their organizations to extend their influence into the political life of the community. The large occupational, professional, and citizens associations are growing in importance as institutions for molding and expressing public opinion; and millions of persons find in them one of their best opportunities for political self-expression.

Political parties and interest groups that have political goals invite comparison. Both are associations of persons organized to influence constituents and government and to seek power. Both are interested in public policy and at times resemble each other. However, there is this important distinction: The two major political parties in the United States seek to capture control of government through elective processes; private political organizations—often called pressure groups—do not seek to exercise legal power except in a few cases in which they may be called upon to share in administering a program. Membership in the interest group is more clearly defined, and the program of the group is narrower. In other words, parties encompass the interests of pressure groups but have had to accommodate these interests and certain other larger party interests as well. Interest groups try to attain status and favor with all branches of the government and usually at all levels of the government.

Political parties do not monopolize the aggregating of political influence. They are in competition with economic and social groups, civic associations, and diverse nonparty campaign organizations for all kinds of resources—manpower, money, ideas, and public support and sympathy. Parties also have much competition within their own ranks for power and influence.

POLITICAL PARTIES AND DEMOCRATIC THEORY

Political parties in a free society are expected to relate themselves to the democratic concepts of popular sovereignty, majority rule, and political equality and to such other principles as responding to public opinion and working for consensus. What this relationship should be is a moot point among philosophers and practitioners. Some would remove parties entirely from certain operations of government or at least from participation in the choice of leaders, as witness the judiciary, some of the executive bureaucracy, and nonpartisan municipal government. Some of the older Progressives wanted direct participation of citizens without intervention of parties and to this extent were antiparty. Others wish some but not too much of a role for parties as instruments of majority rule and popular sovereignty. Finally, supporters of full-blown party government see parties as mechanisms for expressing majority rule and accomplishing change. These points of view may be considered as we search for a theory and definition of political parties.

What Is a Political Party? The meaning of a political party is varied and differs in time and in place. Political parties have been defined in state statutes and empirically in several different ways, and one has his choice of a wide range of definitions and interpretations. (Many of these will be found in the references at the end of the chapter.) Some have tried to encompass in their explanations the single party in totalitarian nations, others see parties as presupposing a democratic state, philosophy, and climate. E. E. Schattschneider avers that "political parties created democracy and modern democracy is unthinkable save in terms of parties." Edmund Burke saw parties as a body of men united to promote the national interest, but others see them as promoting private interest. Some definitions stress the structure of parties—who belongs to the party, who votes for its candidates, and its composition of alliances of interests or combinations of groups. Maurice Duverger viewed present-day parties throughout the democratic world as distinguished less by programs and class of membership "than by the nature of their organization." Party has a psychological meaning for many persons.

The explanations of party generally agree that in organizational structure and behavior, American political parties are semipublic, decentralized, multigroup associations. Functionally as well as organizationally, each party is made up of several egos, and this is the basis of much of the confusion. The identities are a *voters'* party, a *structural* party, and a *government* party. Quantitatively, the bulk of a party consists of the ticket voters and mass of loyal partisans. This description of a party seems vague or incomplete to others who argue that parties are not associations of voters who support the party's candidates but rather associations of the organization activists and party workers. Thus the heart of the question consists in limiting party membership to those who make some contribution to the party in addition to simply voting for its nominees. A party exists only when its members are in one degree or another consciously associated and organized. The party is composed of people who are aware of its end of seeking popular support and who act to achieve it.

Whatever its precise composition, the party-in-the-electorate is mobilized largely by an army (often undisciplined) of political committeemen and working politicians who strive with party and nonparty groups to elect the party's nominees to public office—from the lowest town or county office to the Presidency of the United States. Depending on party rules, traditions, and public law, the party organization participates in varying degrees in nominating candidates for office. In some states the function of nomination is actually performed by party delegates in a convention or by a group of party executives, as in New York City, where party voters can, but seldom are able to, defeat the organization slate in the direct primary. Irrespective of the degree of influence in the nominating process, the prime purpose of the party-in-the-electorate and organizational activists is to win elections in order to control the government and to exercise governmental power.

Once elected, the officeholders tend to become in fact, if not in law, a party group, often designated nationally as the congressional parties and the presidential parties. Although party officials and voters may regard the government groups as simply segments of the party with responsibility to them for election and policy, the public men are likely to view the matter differently. James M. Burns argues provocatively that these parties-in-the-government are not wings of the main party but separate entities with their own lines of power, communication, aims, and polities.[6] Whether this overstates the case or not, the President and the national committee tend to speak for the executive wing. When a party does not control the Presidency, the legislative wing asserts itself and often purports to speak for the party-in-the-government and is likely to dominate what is loosely viewed as the executive wing. These two wings frequently come into conflict in the following national convention and have rivals for the presidential nomination.

Interrelatedness of Party Functions. The electoral party, which is bent on winning power, ties the much less politically motivated social groups to the political system. As the large secondary groups undergo change, so must the party if it is to be successful. A major party wishes to serve as a reference for as many groups as possible, and a party's factions are helpful in making contacts and alliances with subgroups and factions within the various social groups. Conservative party members, for example, are a bridge to conservative nonparty groups, liberals to liberal groups, and so on. This helps foster both stability and change.

Survey data on voting behavior and political perceptions point to opportunities and limitations for party managers. The data show that parties cannot be content with winning over and strengthening the commitment only of members of secondary groups, such as blacks, businessmen, and Catholics. Persons also belong to categoric groups, such as an age level or the college educated, which have no conscious group identifications or political goals but nonetheless have some distinctive voting behavior. These persons may be moved by a candidate or a program to vote a certain way, without taking a cue from a secondary group. When this fact is added to the psychological factors of party identification, candidate, and issue orientation and perception, it becomes obvious that flexibility and versatility are required in the waging of campaigns.

Basically, the parties must function within and cater to a broad-center model. They must assume that the great block of voters are neither to the far right nor to the far left in political desires. Accordingly, campaign appeals must be directed more toward the center and the moderates. To move radically right or left, unless there is evidence that

---

[6] *The Deadlock of Democracy: Four Party Politics in America*, Prentice-Hall, Inc., Englewood Cliffs, N.J., 1963.

the political mean is also moving sharply, invites loss of followers, if not defeat. But, as observed above, a major party can tolerate and actually benefit by having a few of its activists and officeholders well to the right or the left of the party's political center.

Third parties have historically served to voice the protests of substantial elements of society when their grievances are overlooked or are not satisfactorily accommodated by the major parties. Sometimes people turn to third parties while in transition of their party faith. Nonpartisan leaguers embraced the La Follette Progressives, then went on to the Republicans. Some Southern Democrats found it convenient to become Dixiecrats in 1948, and four years later they became Eisenhower Republicans. In short, third parties may provide a haven for regional, social class, or ideological interests that are momentarily (or sometimes permanently) outside the mainstream of American politics. The strength of minor parties, at least in part, is a clue to the success of the major parties in satisfying diverse political interests by proposing attractive candidates and programs. Third parties thrive in a class-structured society or where there are deep ideological cleavages. This has made it easier to construct a theory of third parties in the Western democracies than a theory for the two-party system.

The party activists, who constitute the core of the electoral party, function as a vast communications network to link groups, interests, and ideologies to the government. This intermediary role has long been recognized. It helps make both aspirants to public office and officeholders conscious of what is necessary for consensus and what is required for winning and maintaining power. The party organization gives the citizen a frame of reference, a "Republican viewpoint," a "Democratic outlook." This educational function is better performed as communication among all wings of the party and nonparty groups is improved.

An electoral party facilitates citizen participation and recruitment of persons for public office. It helps certain party activists attain some of their goals, such as public office, policy objectives, or recognition. Persons with ambitions of this kind who are outside the structure very often find the party a mechanism for accomplishment and indeed may find their objectives achievable only by becoming active in the party.

Active partisans in the constituencies make much of the *party* policy, and the party's officeholders, as will be seen in the next section, formulate the party's *public* policy. The two policies differ, leading to conflict between the electoral and government parties. Party policy concerns itself with recruitment, selection, nomination, and organizational matters. It follows through with campaign management and the raising and disbursing of campaign funds and, to some degree, with election administration, including challenges where fraud is suspected, the demanding of recounts, or the facilitating of absentee voting. Party policy is also concerned with what resources are to be allocated to registering voters and what conferences (such as "how to do it" or "issues" seminars for party workers or potential recruits) are to be held. Drafting platforms, holding conventions, and relations with the press and with nonparty group leaders also become policy questions for the leaders. There is, therefore, a large area of party policy that is strongly influenced, if not fully controlled, by the party leaders as distinct from the party's officeholders. The latter participate in many of these party decisions but are often content to leave most of them to the active political agents in the party organization. The success of the party-in-the-electorate is to be judged in terms of how well it performs the functions of maintaining an effective organization and acting wisely on party matters.

Concern with Public Policy. During campaigns, all wings and subgroups of the party are united in an effort to capture or retain as many public offices as possible. For a great many, but by no means all, of the rank-and-file members of the party-in-the-electorate, public policy, as distinct from internal party policy, is a crucial nexus with the party-in-the-government. This is often a great annoyance for the public officeholders who wish to be free to negotiate with pressure-group leaders and many others in the shaping of public policy. Party leaders in Congress do not wish to be encumbered by policy declarations emanating from their fellow partisans (who helped elect them) outside the government. The legislative officeholder feels that he must listen to his constituents and to his state delegation and not merely to a national party declaration of policy. There are a growing number of amateurs active in political party clubs and some in precinct positions who are strongly oriented toward the discussion and formulation of party positions on foreign and domestic problems. They are dissatisfied with what they see as an exclusive emphasis on the politics of personality and the election of the so-called best man, irrespective of his party and position on issues. They can point out with logic that split-ticket voting is encouraged when party differences are blurred and candidates' stands are kept ambiguous. They are convinced that issueless parties make it difficult to persuade voters during campaigns that there are meaningful party differences and approaches logically calling for support of the presidential and congressional candidates and the gubernatorial and state legislative candidates of the same parties.

Legislative candidates are not totally unmindful of the importance of talking about some issues in the campaign, and most are willing to give a very general endorsement of the party platform. But the members of the government party, in one degree or another, do not wish the party program to be initiated, after the election, by those party members outside the halls of government. In the controlling party, much of the initiation of policies comes from the executive wing of the party, with the congressional wing endorsing, modifying, or refusing to accept the individual parts of the program. The executive frequently attempts to mobilize the support of the local organizations and clubs behind his program with the hope that they will convince their legislators that it is in the interest of the party, the public, and the lawmaker himself.

The situation is somewhat different for the opposition. Nearly every national chairman of the party not controlling the White House or the Congress has, of his own volition or under pressure from party leaders in the states, suggested the need for policy statements updating the national platform. Party workers argue that the party needs issues upon which to wage the next campaign and to guide the party's congressmen as they try to build a record on which the party may hope to take over control of the government. These suggestions are invariably opposed by the leaders of the congressional party who feel that they alone must decide what position, if any, the party shall take on great national and international issues. They see their approach to issues as realistic and more likely to win a majority for the party than issues and positions originating in party organizations and clubs throughout the land and brought together by some broadly composed representative group within the party.

Politicians in and out of government further defend their position by pointing out that they are generally reflective of the values and interests held by the loose groupings of voters supporting the party. Each party has certain core elements, and those elected know and appreciate their needs. At the same time, officeholders must cater to other than the core strength, for it alone is not likely to be sufficient to assure reelection. Hence flexibility is needed in the formulation of programs that the peripheral (but electorally indispensable) voters may demand. In the very nature of the party system, practitioners note that policy making is facilitated because each party seeks to capture both the executive and legislative positions, a highly desirable condition for the enactment of a program.

Party Response to Social Change. The theory and practice of the American party system must be considered in the context of a rapidly changing social order despite the static nature of the constitutional structure. Although the legal setting rarely changes, the political climate does. Durable parties are those that adapt themselves to the times. During the last generation, striking changes have taken place in the political society, changes that are not yet fully analyzed or evaluated but nonetheless are

affecting every unit of the party system. There is an imperative need for
a strong President, especially on matters of foreign policy, national defense, and civil rights. Presidents, as well as governors in many states, are
being called upon to negotiate racial demands and in some cases to utilize armed forces to quell disturbances. The expanding role of the federal
government in such areas as labor-management, agriculture, poverty,
social security, and conservation have called for an expansion of the
presidential role.

Electoral competition between the parties since 1940 has shown
a dramatic increase. There are fewer one-party states, one-party delegations in Congress, and one-party congressional districts. The national
committees have greatly expanded their efforts in the midterm elections.
At the same time, an increasing number of voters seem to be splitting
their tickets, suggesting the importance of candidate image projected by
television and new public relations techniques.

At the local level, the old-style political boss and machine have
almost passed from the scene, bringing about shifts in the community
power structure. An increasing number of cities are adopting the city-
manager plan, and the nonpartisan ballot is widely used for the election
of many local officials. Public relations men are assuming a larger role in
campaign management. Private public opinion polls are now widely used
and can greatly influence election campaigns for good or bad. The pressures for reapportionment brought by judicial decisions are profoundly
affecting the balance of power between urban and rural areas and the
political pattern in many states. The threat of force and the use of violence in recent years pose a challenge to established party structure and
the older means of accomplishing change through persuasion, voting,
and peaceful activism (this development is considered in Chapter 21).
These events by no means complete the list of forces that the party elites
are being called up to face, but they illustrate the conditions necessitating party adaptation if not dramatic change.

PARTY GOVERNMENT

Broadly conceived, responsible party government is a method of implementing majority rule. Under this system each party evolves and formulates a set of coherent policy alternatives with active partisans as well as
the party's public officeholders participating in formulating the platforms and programs. These programs for public action are placed
before the electorate. Moreover, and most important, a party's candidates commit themselves to the policies and assume, if elected, a collective responsibility for enacting them. This would necessitate a measure
of party discipline over those elected to the legislature.

The party activists accept the responsibility for managing the campaign and presenting its alternatives to the voters. Voters, if the arrangement is to result in the adoption of one of the alternatives, must understand the program and vote for a candidate first because the candidate believes in the approach recommended by his party and only second because of the nominee's personal qualities.[7]

Arguments for Ideologically Unified Parties. Supporters of the ideal of congressional party government usually begin by criticizing the existing system. First, they argue that present practices are weak and ineffective. The winning party often fails to deliver, by votes in Congress, on its platform promises and dogma. The independence of congressmen often leads them, so it is alleged, to disregard campaign pledges and the party platform and even to vote with the opposition party. In 1946, former Vice President Henry A. Wallace said: "I say it is a fraud upon the voters when a candidate says, 'I stand in full agreement with President Truman' if he then votes in Congress against the forward-looking program enunciated by Harry S. Truman. Unless a member of the majority in Congress votes in favor of major issues upon which he and his party were elected the legislative branch of our government ceases to function."[8] This was reminiscent of a statement in Calvin Coolidge's Inaugural Address:

> There is no salvation in a narrow and bigoted partisanship. But if there is to be responsible party government, the party label must be something more than a mere device for securing office. Unless those who are elected under the same party designation are willing to assume sufficient responsibility and exhibit sufficient loyalty and coherence, so that they can cooperate with each other in the support of the broad general principles of the party platform, the election is merely a mockery, no decision is made at the polls, and there is no representation of the popular will.

Critics assert that the existing system encourages drift and dangerous inaction resulting in compensation by overextending the Presidency. Unless the two parties develop "alternative programs that can be executed, the voter's frustration and the mounting ambiguities of national policy might also set in motion more extreme tendencies to the political left and political right."[9] By implication, at least, the lack of effective ideological parties will have a splintering effect leading to sev-

---

[7] For an excellent overall discussion of party government and an extensive bibliography both for and against the proposal, see Austin Ranney, *The Doctrine of Responsible Party Government: Its Origin and Present State*, The University of Illinois Press, Urbana, 1962. The report of the Committee on Political Parties of the American Political Science Association stimulated much discussion of the policy role of parties. Under the title *Toward a More Responsible Two-party System*, the committee made recommendations to correct the weaknesses it saw. (Published as a supplement to *The American Political Science Review*, vol. 44, 1950.)

[8] *The New York Times*, Apr. 23, 1946.

[9] *Toward a More Responsible Two-party System*, p. 95.

eral smaller parties. Other critics, including Walter Lippmann, express the fear that the crucial role of the United States in world affairs will be weakened by chaos in party positions on foreign policy. In short, the failure to deliver a majority party vote on great national and international issues can lead to instability, weaken the hand of the Secretary of State, and lead to vacillating leadership by the United States.

On the positive side, proponents of stronger, more unified legislative parties maintain that each party should espouse definite policies and programs and discipline officeholding members who fail to support the party program. In this way the parties will keep faith with the voters and will become effective instruments for enabling the government to cope with the problems of society in a more definite and positive manner. A responsible system is seen as providing a meaningful and purposeful range of choice and as giving the public an opportunity to express an effective preference for a particular government program. In the words of E. E. Schattschneider, party responsibility would perform the function of the "simplification of alternatives." [10] Collective responsibility would be substituted for individual responsibility.

Advocates also see party government as focusing more attention on policies and programs, which in turn will give more meaning to party labels. This would activate and energize both the party adherents and the general public. It would help reduce inertia and broaden the range of public opinion. The legislative process, now so fragmented and complex, would be simplified and more easily understood. Government as a whole would become responsible to the people as a whole.

Proponents of stronger congressional party government have evolved proposals from relatively mild changes to fundamental constitutional changes. The latter would call for constitutional amendments looking toward parliamentary government or arrangements calling for a legislative cabinet or a joint executive-legislative cabinet responsible for preparing a legislative program. These would imply concentration of power in the congressional political party in contradistinction to the presidential party.

The Committee on Political Parties recommends the building of a strong national organization capable of providing leadership between national conventions and the strengthening of party leadership in Congress. A party council drawn from all groups within the party would provide current interpretations of the party platform, make recommendations with respect to congressional candidates and "conspicuous departures from general party decisions by state or local party organizations." Such a council is seen as capable of harmonizing, synthesizing,

---

[10] E. E. Schattschneider, *Party Government*, Holt, Rinehart and Winston, Inc., New York, 1942, offers one of the best statements for responsible party government.

and integrating the various centers of power (local political bosses, pressure groups, and the party members in office) in the national interest. Repeatedly recalcitrant members of Congress, according to strong party advocates, would be disciplined by withdrawal of patronage or removal from coveted committee assignments. Some of the more zealous supporters of party government would use the purge in the party primaries where other measures fail. There are, incidentally, numerous instances in which incumbents presumably have been defeated for renomination by groups of party voters who became incensed with a voting record too frequently in opposition to the party's majority. (It will always be a moot point whether the voters in a primary retired an incumbent mainly for such reasons.)

Opposition to Party Government. The essence of party government is that a party's members in Congress can be bound to vote in conformity with the decisions of the party leadership. In practice, this means the use of the caucus or conference to decide party policies. This implies a high degree of ideological unity among the party's members in the legislature, a condition rare in our history. The concept of party government is opposed by many persons in and out of the legislatures for a wide variety of theoretical and practical reasons. The proposal is seen as unrealistic and impractical because the present loose party system is viewed as the natural consequence of the nation's structure of government. As will be seen subsequently, parties arise from and reflect the cultural, social, and legal context of the society in which they operate. It follows, then, that political behavior is not going to change simply by reorganizing parties. Party councils are ineffective in the absence of ideologically unified and disciplined parties and hence are regarded by opponents as gadgetry.

Some scholars fear on philosophical grounds and some local politicians fear on practical grounds that centralization would quench the individualism of state and local organizations by requiring congressmen to accept the dictates of a central office. They stress the virtue of the independent party member in Congress who is in a position to criticize and vote against a special interest. The disciplined man cannot do this if the program of a special interest becomes incorporated into his party's program. Congressmen want to be free to support measures benefiting their own districts.

A number of writers praise the present lack of intraparty agreement on policies and programs. A highly disciplined, homogeneous party in power might adopt sharp changes of policy bitterly opposed by a large segment of the electorate. A party dominated by labor might ram through legislation detrimental to farmers and businessmen. The ideological congressional party might interfere with what many if not most

Americans regard as the consensus rule. Consensus means building majorities by combining major groups within each party. No one group is able to have its way or muster a majority unless it can carry substantial factions of other important groups. Presidents and majority party leaders are forced to work for concurrent majorities by attempting to conciliate most or all classes and to work out compromises with minorities on both sides of the aisles. In this system, sectional, local, party, and other interests are protected.

Defenders of the present decentralized party system see its value in avoiding sharp swings to either the right or the left. Moderates and those in the center can more easily formulate solutions which, although not satisfying to all, are enduring and acceptable. Interparty shifts and conflicts, friction between the President and Congress, bipartisan coalitions, and bargaining and maneuvering between interests are all a part of the process of building consensus. These processes, often deplored, are unavoidable. Supporters of the present system believe that the parties have met the programmatic test, however blundering and muddling they may be at times. They have come through in emergencies and have done what is needed to keep the nation healthy and reasonably well unified. American congressional parties are what they are because they are appropriate to the kind of government people want. Research shows that large numbers of voters are not ideologically oriented, and it is therefore hardly surprising that they have not demanded ideologically oriented parties.

Finally, there are those who argue that the legislative parties do present clear alternatives to the voters and show distinct differences in voting behavior in Congress and in many state legislatures. They cite a number of roll-call votes in which the two major parties differed significantly and are satisfied that the two major parties have become about as bipolarized over issues as is desirable or safe. Party leaders show greater difference in ideological preferences than do the rank and file. The elite within each party tend to see their party as presenting an alternative view of government. They proceed on the assumption that there are significant party differences—this is most important to the operation of the system.

Although not always appreciated, the philosophical issue underlying much of the American argument over the theory of parties centers around the question of *unlimited majority rule*. Strongly disciplined parties implement the will of the electoral majority, and the individual congressman must accept the party position if he is to use his party's resources to obtain and exercise public power. A large majority of Americans and their political leaders, on the other hand, are concerned with the preservation of minority rights and local interests and do not want full-blown majority rule. They regard independence from party as a virtue and, although often critical of weak parties and the inability of Congress to act on public issues, prefer the present system. Perhaps a majority of the students of government and the party activists at some time or other have, with some impatience, suggested that parties should stand more definitely for principles and certain programs and have called for more effective leadership and party unity. But there is disagreement over means and degree.

The empirical approach suggests that, very broadly speaking, a citizen's specific public programmatic needs are best enhanced in the United States at the moment by pressures exerted in his behalf by private interest organizations that are ever alert to finding new as well as existing resources to take his case to some point in the government. A person's concern with the quality of men and women elected to public office is best served by his playing an active role in political parties. Parties are not insensitive to issues, but their primary purpose is to select the personnel of government. They use policies to achieve electoral objectives. Pressure groups, in the first instance, originate policies and are less involved with getting certain persons elected. Political parties are seldom constructive innovators of policies, but they nevertheless influence policies. Parties are primarily occupied with who shall rule and stay in power. Pressure groups and political parties in a real sense complement each other, each providing different emphases in the political system. Both serve to integrate and to advance different, but not mutually exclusive, interests of the citizenry. At times, parties and private groups are competitors, but to date neither has seriously threatened the survival of the other. Both are necessary adjuncts of popular control of government.

Attitudes toward Parties: Overview. In summary, the welter of attitudes toward parties may be placed in four fairly distinct patterns and options. The differences stem quite largely from one's *normative* or *empirical* outlook, and center around the perceived capabilities of American parties and the desirability of unlimited majority rule. Each relates parties to democratic theory in somewhat different ways.

First, party-government proponents are convinced that parties can coordinate government and enhance majority rule and that they ought to do so. Through party discipline, policy programs, electoral mandates, and centralized leadership, the majority preferences can become effective through clear-cut government actions. When its advocates talk of party reform they appear basically concerned with making parties more ideological. Fundamental changes would be necessary to bring about full-blown party government including much greater leadership control of nominations and political finance, sharp modification of the seniority system in Congress, and a willingness at the constituency level to have representatives bound to a party program.

A second group believes in party reform and greater party responsibility but is not prepared to go all the way with party government. There are naturally degrees of desired responsibility within this group, with some going considerably farther than others. Parties are viewed as capable of providing more innovation in the realm of policy and of integrating and coordinating government to a greater degree than is currently the case. Advocates of party reform would improve mechanisms for evolving party policies (party councils, for example) and would involve more persons in party decisions and activities. Many of the 1968 supporters of Sens. Robert F. Kennedy and Eugene J. McCarthy referred to this practice as participatory democracy. They would also make parties more competitive everywhere. A long list of reforms has been advanced over the years by those wishing more party responsibility, such as a shorter ballot, abolition of the Electoral College, a four-year term for United States representatives, tighter primary laws, more stable party finance, expanded year-round headquarters operations, more attention to party positions on policies, and perhaps some modification of seniority in Congress. The general basic party structure, however, is regarded as suitable; and complete party government carries too great a cost and, moreover, is not necessary to making parties responsive to citizen needs and demands.

A third group would maintain the present party system as is, with only small incremental changes from time to time. In so doing, concurrent majorities would remain the operative rule, with minorities protected from possible majority tyranny. Conflict is seen as better managed this way, resulting also in moderate, compromise public policy. Supporters of the present system also see it as keeping open channels of recruitment to public office, while providing adequate means for registering protest. Current partisan allegiances in legislative bodies are sufficient to provide adequate organization and coordination for proper functioning, with capability from time to time of bringing forth a party program despite heterogeneous composition of the electoral party. Advocates of the status quo generally fear the overall results of radical changes in the direction of more centralized, unified parties.

A fourth attitudinal classification includes those who are essentially indifferent to parties or are nonparty if not antiparty. As far as municipal government is concerned, this outlook is quite prevalent and operates under the nonpartisan label. Its proponents wish to keep partisan labels and considerations out of elections and from city council decision making. Further, the judiciary and school and other officials should be removed from party politics. The nonpartisans do not believe party labels are necessary for the organization of local government bodies. Nonpartisans stress consensus rather than majority rule. Although they might admit that parties could coordinate government, two-party competition would be undesirable because it might heighten conflict and result in radical innovation. Many nonpartisans undoubtedly recall the old days of boss rule and patronage politics with the concern that party politics might bring a return of this system. Nonpartisans argue that there is not a Democratic or Republican way to clean or light streets; these are technical questions best resolved by professionals unfettered with party goals.

The old Progressives of the early twentieth century were highly critical of political parties and their influences on legislatures. They championed reforms that restricted party organizations in their nominating influences and regulated their activities and structures. On the positive side, they sought direct popular participation to influence public leaders to enact progressive social and economic measures. The system of initiative, referendum, and recall was used to buttress the concept of an enlightened citizenry at the state and local levels. Many of their remedies remain intact and are accepted by those who wish to preserve the status quo and by many who would make parties more responsible. There is, therefore, an overlapping of some of the four viewpoints toward parties.

Notwithstanding the contentious questions of degree of party government, there is virtual unanimity among all on the essentiality of parties to democratic government at the national level. Few advocate nonpartisan elections for President and for Congress. In this arena, parties have become indispensable.

National parties provide legitimate means for persons to seek public office and are a vital part of the rules of the game for those wishing to exercise power. One of the functions of parties in this context is the polarizing of issues. Electoral parties reduce complex issues to a point where voters may make a choice—a choice between the "ins" and the "outs." This function is often rather badly performed. But without a party system (implying more than one effective party), those in charge of the government would have no effective method of securing the consent of the governed—and this is highly important to their own effectiveness! On the other side, voters would lack an efficient means of turning out their governors should they be dissatisfied.

Political parties provide a competitive political system. They give the voters an alternative group of policy makers as well as an alternative program stated in general terms. The party in power bids with the voters for a vote of confidence for its candidates, its record, and its promises for the future. The opposition party's role is to subject the controlling party to merciless surveillance of its record, both in the areas of policies adopted and in their administration. An opposition political party provides an instrument for an *overall* evaluation of everything the controlling party is doing. Granted that its criticism is rarely detached and objective, it does have the advantage of broadness and is in a position to make an electoral challenge and a contest in Congress, where it can introduce rival measures and exercise protest on roll calls.

Another basic function of party, especially evident in the United States, is to soften sectional, group, economic, and other tensions. A major party brings great diversities under its umbrella. Accommodation is made in the interests of the larger objective of control of government. By being flexible, paralyzing deadlocks are avoided and compromises are worked out.

THE STUDY OF POLITICAL PARTIES

One of the most significant developments in modern political science is the utilization of a wide variety of rather disparate types of political analysis. In addition to new approaches, the new, more sophisticated methodologies have at their disposal instruments capable of yielding and storing enormous amounts of data. The random-sample, standardized, and often lengthy schedules of interviews permit the investigator not only to gather information but to make comparisons across boundaries such as counties, states and even nations. Scholars and professional public opinion polling agencies are not alone in conducting surveys; undergraduates are busy asking questions of precinct committeemen and county chairmen, legislators, county commissioners, and mayors and, of course, John Q. Citizen himself. Results may be put on cards, fed to computers, stored, and later retrieved for diverse purposes!

In addition to surveys, social scientists use participant observation, election statistics, structures, laws, and other sources of data for analysis. The scientist is, of course, limited by the availability of data, and his theories and insights are enlarged as he secures more information. Meanwhile, he can utilize the existing data to construct more imaginative models and approaches. These, in turn, show up gaps that lead to seeking of new data to fill them. It is not surprising that there is no universally accepted theory of parties, nor is there one approach which is used to the exclusion of all others.[11]

The reader of today's professional works in political science is met with such terms as *game theory, role theory, simulation, systems analysis,*

---

[11] Literature on methodology is both extensive and scattered. Many of those contributing to specific aspects of parties are found in the footnotes and reference lists throughout this book. Two general works deserve special mention here: Charles G. Mayo and Beryl L. Crowe, *American Political Parties: A Systematic Perspective,* Harper & Row, Publishers, Incorporated, New York, 1967, and William N. Chambers and Walter D. Burnham, *The American Party Systems,* Oxford University Press, Fair Lawn, N.J., 1967.

functionalism, structural-functional framework, decision-making analysis, political development theory, communications models, behavioralism, psychiatric analysis, power structure, and dozens of subheads such as *eclectic functionalism* and *empirical functionalism*.[12] Here our major interest is contemporary American political parties and the political interest groups with which they interact. At this point, brief attention is called to various ways of analyzing and thinking about parties.

David Easton's systems analysis impelled political scientists to focus on the major dependent variable, the "authoritative allocation of values," and to consider other variables as they affect the process of allocation.[13] He urges the study of inputs in the form of demands and supports and the outputs of the system in the form of decisions and policies. Public opinion, voting, and political groups could be studied as independent variables having an impact on the authoritative allocation of values. Parties could be viewed to the extent that they are significant in affecting outputs. This framework is helpful in identifying relevant variables and components and the functions of political activities for society and its publics. It differentiates the object of study from its environment, but it also directs attention to the interaction of subsystems in the environment. Concisely, parties need to be looked at within the framework of the political system. This calls for analysis of how, why, and when parties influence and affect the political system and where the system with its laws, contributions, and cultures has its impact on the parties.

A whole series of approaches not necessarily rooted in the continuum of time or in the system per se are used to understand parties. One is a search for a definition. Ideologically this looks at the values and principles of those embracing a party label in accordance with Edmund Burke's definition that party is "a body of men united for promoting by their joint endeavors the national interests upon some particular principle on which they are all agreed." As observed above, American scholars for the most part have not found this an apt description of the Democratic and Republican parties. Rather, parties are looked at in terms of three interrelated but somewhat separate identities; an electorate party; the hierarchical body of activists; and the party in the government, the elected officeholders who are tied together by a common label.

Parties can be examined in terms of organization. Concerns here are the studies of party structures, recruitment, and socialization of its activists. For example, what are the incentives and the career goals of

---

[12] One recent volume explaining these terms and providing an extensive bibliography is that of James C. Charlesworth (ed.), *Contemporary Political Analysis,* The Free Press, New York, 1967. As the editor notes in his introduction, "approaches to the study of political science are where you find them, and how you find them."

[13] See his *The Political System: An Inquiry Into the State of Political Science,* Alfred A. Knopf, Inc., New York, 1953, and *A Systems Analysis of Political Life,* John Wiley & Sons, Inc., New York, 1965.

those active in the organization? How do parties organize and raise money to accomplish their ends? With the decline of the old-style political boss and machine there is much to be learned about modern party organization in terms of replacement of patronage systems and campaign techniques, social characteristics and skills of current bodies, and the growth of alternative competitive nonparty organizations.

An extensive literature of American parties surveys their functions and activities. This terminology has troubled specialists as it is not always clear how a function differs from an activity. William Mitchell believes that "functional analysis attempts to ascertain the relationships of the part to the whole through an analysis of the contributions which the part makes to the functioning of the more inclusive system."[14] In the 1940s, Robert R. Merton wrote that "functions are those observed consequences which make for the adaption or adjustment of a given system; and dysfunctions, those observed consequences which lessen the adaption or adjustment of the system."[15] In many writings, parties are seen as functioning to propose candidates for public office, contest elections, and attempt to organize the decision makers after election. The host of activities required to fulfill these goals includes registering and canvasing voters, raising money, and taking issues to the electorate. There are, of course, numerous latent and indirect functions and activities, such as dispersing patronage, providing opposition, research, educating the membership and the voters, winning converts, expanding the size of attentive publics, and increasing the salience of issues for them.

In summary, parties may be thought of in a variety of ways. They can be looked at from the standpoint of the organizational theory and the myriad problems incident to their composition and structure. Their roles can be analyzed together with their activities. Parties may be viewed as a subsystem of the larger political system with attention in turn on their interrelated but separate egos in the electorate and in the government. All of these and other aspects will be treated in subsequent pages.

A developmental analysis — which looks at parties over a period of time, noting changes, trends, and transformations — has interested the political historian. This is a major concern of the following chapter. Students of today's developing nations as well as of early America find the genesis and establishment of a party system within the framework of nation building an intriguing subject.[16]

[14] Mayo and Crowe, *op. cit.*, page 39.

[15] *Social Theory and Social Structure*, The Free Press, New York, 1949, p. 50. For a general treatment of the subject, see Don Martindale (ed.), *Functionalism in the Social Sciences*, American Academy of Political and Social Science Monograph 5, Philadelphia, 1965.

[16] A general comparative developmental analysis work is that of Joseph La Palombara and Myron Weiner, *Political Parties and Political Development*, Princeton University Press, Princeton, N.J., 1966.

FOR FURTHER READING

Bailey, Stephen K.: *The Condition of Our National Parties*, 1959.

Downs, Anthony: *An Economic Theory of Democracy*, 1957.

Fenton, John H.: *People and Parties in Politics*, 1966.

Greenstein, Fred J.: *The American Party System and the American People*, 1963.

Harris, Seymour: *The Economics of the Political Parties*, 1962.

Herring, E. Pendleton: *The Politics of Democracy*, 1940.

Holcombe, Arthur N.: *Our More Perfect Union*, 1950.

James, Judson L.: *American Political Parties: Potential and Performance*, 1969.

Leiserson, Avery: *Parties and Politics*, 1958.

McDonald, Neil A.: *The Study of Political Parties*, 1955.

Ranney, Austin, and Willmoore Kendall: *Democracy and the American Party System*, 1956.

Sindler, Allen P.: *Political Parties in the United States*, 1966.

Sorauf, Frank J.: *Political Parties in the American System*, 1964.

Out of the conquest of the resources of the continent
emerged new social institutions peculiar to
America, among which none is more nearly
unique than the political interest group
combinations that constitute our national
political parties.

WILFRED E. BINKLEY

CHAPTER 2 DEVELOPMENT OF THE AMERICAN PARTY SYSTEM

STAGES IN AMERICAN PARTY DEVELOPMENT

Factions and groups reach back into antiquity, but political parties as we know them today are one of man's newest political institutions. Contests between the Tories and Whigs in eighteenth-century England highlighted divisions in emphasis of the Crown and the rights of the people. Many of these feuds came to the New World with the colonists. Soon new issues arose between business and working classes, creditors and debtors, large and small land interests, and between the frontier and the older settlements. They contained ingredients for polarization of thought and aspiration and for local parties.

William N. Chambers divided American political party development into three major stages.[1] The first is represented by the genesis and

[1] William N. Chambers, *Political Parties in a New Nation: The American Experience, 1776–1809*, Oxford University Press, Fair Lawn, N.J., 1963, and his "Party Development and the American Mainstream" in his work co-edited with Walter D. Burnham, *The American Party System: Stages of Political Development*, Oxford University Press, Fair Lawn, N.J., 1967. The former volume contains an extensive annotated bibliography. Both books are recommended for conceptualization through developmental analysis.

invention of parties in the 1790s and again in the 1820s and 1830s following a more or less party interregnum during the administrations of James Monroe and John Quincy Adams. The next stage, called by one writer the second party system, is demarked by the solid establishment of two national parties from Andrew Jackson's Presidency to the Civil War.[2]

The third period, since 1860, has been more directive than creative, with incremental changes but with the basic form and substance retained. In turn, historians have found it useful to subdivide the third stage into three eras. First the post-Civil War period to 1896, which saw the rise of political machines and expansion of the male electorate. The Progressive Movement followed, with new approaches to democratizing the party and the electoral system; it had run its course by 1921. The current period, beginning with the New Deal, has been associated with a great nationalization of politics and modern alignments.

Surprisingly, the movement for independence failed to generate parties, probably because the Revolutionary leaders did not need parties to mobilize support outside the government. Many of them were government leaders who could work through established institutions of government without dependence upon mass movements to organize resistance.

Before the adoption of the Constitution, it was difficult to establish national parties because of so many diversities and the loose assemblage of thirteen states. Each state had its own contenders for power. Politics were factional and nonparty, with a swirl of leaders, interests, and opinions. Parties did not spring up naturally, but leaders after the inauguration of Washington found it necessary to assemble national groupings out of widely scattered state and local materials. State party systems of a kind had emerged in Pennsylvania, and there were some embryonic forms elsewhere. The materials for a party were found in a variety of subgroupings, in the emergence of more democratic modes of life, and in a growing feeling that some political structure would be helpful to attain political objectives and provide opposition. When a national arena of popularly elected House of Representatives and an indirectly but partially popularly chosen Senate and President came into being, a long stride toward the foundation of a national party was taken.

FEDERALISTS AND REPUBLICANS

Although regular two-party contests for the Presidency did not begin until 1832, the basis for party struggle was present in the 1780s.[3] Issues at the Constitutional Convention itself and over the adoption of the Constitution served to encourage the formation of political organiza-

[2] See Richard P. McCormick, *The Second American Party System: Party Formation in the Jackson Era*, University of North Carolina Press, Chapel Hill, 1966.

[3] Our treatment of party history is necessarily brief. Many volumes are available on specific periods of history. The best general work for students of party politics is Wilfred E. Binkley, *American*

tions of persons who wished to control government policies. Hamilton and Jefferson articulated rival philosophies. Hamilton believed that the wealth and security of the nation depended on "the prosperity of its manufactures" and supported a tariff, a national banking system, and the assumption of debts by the national government. He favored a strong national government, feared the "turbulent" masses, and would give the rich and well-born the "destined, permanent share in the government."

Thomas Jefferson voiced opposition to many of these ideas that became associated with the Federalists. He felt the farmers to be the most valuable citizens and dreamed of an agrarian America. He upheld states' rights, majority rule, and frequent rotation in office. Hamiltonian and Jeffersonian principles are found in each of the major parties today; the country has adopted some of the policies of each and has rejected others, and the two major parties have changed sides on some great issues. The conservatives no longer advocate a strong national government, and the party tracing its origin to Jefferson has come to support greater national powers.

The Federalists were the proponents of the Constitution. Ironically they grew into a political party, although opposed to political parties and to creation of effective national and state party organization. As such, the Federalists perfected no outward organization of grass-roots precinct and county committees. Congressional and state legislative caucuses selected candidates and performed the functions of a party. The Federalists attempted to keep what organization they had a secret and soundly condemned their opponent's organizational activities. The Federalist partisans launched the new government and controlled it until 1801. But its role as a party was short-lived, and in 1816 the party nominated its last presidential candidate, Rufus King.

Even before the Revolutionary War, Virginia had a democratic party under the leadership of Patrick Henry. It consisted of back-country small farmers, land-hungry squatters, tobacco growers, Western trappers, and diverse unorganized small proprietors and slave owners. Opposed to the ratification of the Constitution, the party came to be called Anti-Federalists, who challenged the coastal communities supporting the Constitution. The Anti-Federalists were not coordinated into a national party but offered the potential of protest especially against Alexander Hamilton's financial policies. Late in Washington's first term, Thomas Jefferson quietly began to mobilize this group of loosely federated local parties. Hamilton's whisky tax further enraged the Western

Political Parties, 4th ed., Alfred A. Knopf, Inc., New York, 1962. Voting statistics and the party composition of various Congresses will be found in T. W. Couzens, *Politics and Political Organizations in America*, The Macmillan Company, New York, 1942. On the Federalist period an especially useful work is Richard Hofstadter, *The Idea of a Party System: The Rise of Legitimate Opposition in the United States, 1780–1840*, University of California Press, Berkeley, 1969.

frontiersmen, and his financial policies alienated many Southern planters who had supported the Constitution. By 1800, Jefferson had molded this protest group into a combination (of Republicans) large enough to win the Presidency.

In retrospect it seems somewhat surprising that any national parties could be formed. Each state had its own diversities and contenders for power. Party rivalry was suspect, and Washington warned against its "baneful effects" in his Farewell Address. In a way, leaders were building parties without fully realizing that they were doing so. Party building was, as Chambers says,

> . . . an endeavor of pragmatic adaptation and inventiveness under necessity, guided at the beginning by immediate purposes or a general desire to prove the republican experiment, informed only later by a conception of party as a goal. The problems of establishing the republic and of establishing party overlapped, and in a sense they all involved the practical fulfillment of the national and democratic promise of the Declaration of Independence.[4]

Jefferson's popularity, the democratic image of Republicans, and the Federalist's own mistakes, such as the Hartford Convention and belief in a partyless government, undoubtedly contributed to the rapid demise of the Federalist party. Jefferson in office continued most of the policies acceptable to the Federalists, which won them over; and the Madison and Monroe administrations continued this course.[5]

President Monroe was unopposed in 1820, and the country was treated to a no-party or one-party rule. It became fashionable to downgrade parties; and even Andrew Jackson, later to embrace strong partisanship, wrote Monroe in 1816 that it was time to "exterminate the monster called party spirit." Two-party organization and feelings were not yet strong enough to result in a permanent establishment. However, within a few years, "Old Hickory's" administration brought with it new and successful alliances, both for and against him. These set the nation on a firm two-party footing, never again to see an "era of good feeling" of partyless government. The unplanned institution of political parties henceforth was accepted as necessary to the American scheme of government.

DEMOCRATS AND WHIGS

So dedicated were most voters to the cause of the Jeffersonian Republicans from 1816 to 1828 that they saw no need for a two-party rivalry. John Quincy Adams and Henry Clay regarded themselves as National

---

[4] Chambers, *op. cit.*, pp. 10-11.

[5] Presidential electoral and popular vote statistics from 1789 through 1960 may be found in Svend Petersen, *A Statistical History of the American Presidential Elections*, Frederick Ungar Publishing Co., New York, 1963. The work also contains state-by-state votes as well as total votes for all major-party and minor-party candidates. Tables 2-1 and 2-2 contain election statistics for the modern period 1932 through 1968.

Republicans, and Andrew Jackson and his followers were happy to be Democratic Republicans. In a short time, each took parts of the old Republican aggregation to form a separate party. Jackson's assault on the national bank and his financial policies offended bankers and merchants, and business interests and sugar planters wanted more protection than he was inclined to give. Jackson's executive "tyranny" offered a rallying point for those opposed to him. Into this Whig group came a motley assortment of heterogeneous and often contradictory interests. Many Westerners were attracted to Henry Clay's nationalism as were the followers of John Quincy Adams with whom Jackson had bitter rivalry in the elections of 1824 and 1828. Nativists and antislavery people also felt that the Whigs would be better spokesmen for their views.

The period from 1832 to 1856 was in several respects the most significant in terms of party development. During this time, the parties became institutionalized and adopted many of the forms, procedures, and outward trappings so characteristic of parties today. For example, the procedure for presidential and vice presidential nominations was established, and the broad general rules for governing the national conventions were developed. The Democratic National Committee was organized in 1848 as an outgrowth of a central committee appointed in 1844 to aid in the election of Polk and Dallas. On the deathbed of their party in 1852 the Whigs created their national committee. These antecedents helped the Republicans begin their national organization in more advanced form in 1856.

The practice of appointing electors by state legislatures gave way to selection by popular vote, and the practice of casting all the electoral votes in a given state for the candidate receiving the most popular votes became crystallized. With only a few exceptions, electoral votes have been cast en bloc, and the stakes in carrying the large states have been enhanced.

The Whig-Democratic era was marked by much effort at building state and local organization, and patronage aided this objective. Suffrage was radically broadened, and longer ballots and rotation in office encouraged many to be potential officeholders. Politics became the business of a much larger number of citizens. Longer ballots in turn required more campaign organization. Although the ballot has been reduced in many communities since 1900, the legacy of the Jacksonian period is still much in evidence.

Of great significance was the firm establishment and recognized legitimacy of the two-party system during the era of the second party system. The first party system had deteriorated after 1815. Although the second party system had its origin in the 1824 contest, its full dimensions were not reached until 1840. Thereafter there was never to be another party interregnum. In war and in peace, the minority party was to wage a campaign, regardless of basic differences or issues. The campaign might emphasize, as it so often did under the Whigs and Democrats, demagoguery, spurious issues, and inconsequentials, but nonetheless it was waged.

DEVELOPMENTAL PATTERNS OF AMERICAN PARTIES

The Whig-Democratic era offers an opportunity to draw some generalizations about parties which have had validity over the years. One obvious fact is the heterogeneity of composition. That the Whig party with its highly diversified makeup could hold together for twenty years is a remarkable demonstration of the binding force of negativism, protest, and the hope for patronage. Jefferson's party was also a conglomeration. Binkley says of the Federalist party, "To dismiss it as merely a group of aristocrats would be as grotesque an oversimplification as to assume that the present Republican party is simply an aggregation of capitalists."[6] Black voters in New York, for example, were almost all Federalists, as were New England fishermen.

The Federalists' neglect of inland agrarian interests, however, was fatal and illustrates that no one sizable interest can be ignored by a major party. A party that possesses the greater cohesion among its interests and can avoid enervating factionalism and internal warfare is likely to be the winner.[7] This was evident for the Jeffersonian Republicans and for the Democrats during the Jackson and Franklin D. Roosevelt periods.

Parties that remain in power are those that adapt themselves to change and whose programs are pragmatic and flexible. A party that confines itself too strictly to principle in the face of changing times runs the risk of losing a following. When a new majority assumes control, it retains much of the program of its predecessor that was popular. Jefferson did not abandon much of the Federalist program and, as some writers have suggested, "out-federalized the Federalists." Eisenhower Republicans did not repeal the New Deal, and neither Cleveland nor McKinley attempted sharp breaks when their administrations represented party changes.

In retrospect, two other observations may be mentioned. One of these is the importance — or lack of it — of strong presidential leadership. Popular and powerful figures attract voters to the party and help forge an alliance that often outlasts the tenure of the President. Dynamic leadership helps to personalize the party and the government. The man himself provides a rallying point for the partisans and for the "antis." Jefferson, Jackson, Lincoln, and the two Roosevelts illustrate successful

---

[6] Binkley, *op. cit.*, p. 43.
[7] Ivan Hinderaker has shown the applicability of this point for all periods of American party history in *Party Politics*, Holt, Rinehart and Winston, Inc., New York, 1956, chaps. 10–13.

presidential-party leadership. All were able to cement conglomerations that survived their own terms. Woodrow Wilson during his first term likewise rehabilitated the Democrats and made them into a majority. However, the backwash of the war and reaction to him quickly dissipated his party's strength in 1920.

Henry Turner has noted that nationally power has not tended to rotate between the two parties at fairly even intervals. Rather, one party has remained in control for considerable periods of time broken only by sporadic victories for the opposition party.[8] The domination by one party is undoubtedly due in part to the advantage of initial presidential leadership and political flexibility. But it is also due to more materialistic factors such as the attraction of success. New talent, ambitious for a career, tends to follow the party that offers chance for victory. Patronage, favors, preferments, and government contracts strengthen the party in power at the state and local as well as national levels.

The American value system became much evident during the Democratic-Whig period and was articulated in one way or another by the parties. One of the most enduring and dominant of the beliefs and aspirations has been equalitarianism. The Jacksonians emphasized upward mobility and believed the common man competent to perform the tasks of government. Pre-Civil War European travelers noted that the fight for free public schools had been won. Other closely related values were strong emphasis on achievement and the inevitability of progress. Education became an instrument for both. It followed that citizenship training and participation were of high importance. Parties and political interest groups for more than a hundred years have been forced to adjust their platforms, organizational arrangements, and procedures to these values and belief systems if they wished to have widespread influence.

The period was not only one of elaborating an organizational structure for competition at all levels of government. The many new states extended the spatial dimension for operating parties. Strong sectional biases were reduced, and the parties were more national in scope than in earlier days. (Notwithstanding this, the parties were unable to cope with the sectional conflicts in the late 1850s.) The first minor parties were created, and one or more of them has been evident on the political landscape to the present. This also enlarged opportunities for political participation.

Before the Civil War and continuing after it, changes in ethno-cultural concerns were to affect voting divisions at the local level, with some impact on the national level as well. Evangelical Protestantism brought in such issues as prohibition, nativism, and antislavery; and

[8]"National Politics: Eras of One-party Control," *Social Science*, vol. 28, pp. 137–143, 1953.

many of this persuasion voted Republican. The Democrats received support from Catholics, German Lutherans, and nonevangelical Protestant, native-born Americans who opposed the evangelicals.[9] Some nativist groups were successful in securing laws prohibiting instruction in a foreign language in schools below the college level, and immigrants of both major parties combined to try for repeal.

The two major parties have always been conscious of the need for putting together sectional fragments, agrarians, ethnics, town artisans, cliques of officeholders, and innumerable other interests. Each major party has its minor contradictions and cannot be reduced to a simple formula. As the student studies the political development of the nation and its parties, he should look for generalizations of this kind and for departures from these patterns.

FROM LINCOLN TO McKINLEY

During the 1850s the Whigs and Democrats, confronted with the burning issue of slavery, were unable to hold together their combinations of voters. Compromises and conciliation no longer proved durable enough to avoid a war between the states, a war destined to break up the old parties and forge new party alliances. The seeds of disintegration are familiar — bitter differences over abolition, transportation routes, sectional advantages, cotton traffic, aliens, and immigration. Evidence of the strife was seen in third-party candidates in every presidential election after 1832 under the banner of Liberty or Free Soil. The influx of aliens stirred a strong native American movement which crystallized into a political party in 1856. With former President Millard Fillmore as its candidate, the party polled more than 20 percent of the popular vote. Buchanan, the last Democrat to be elected for more than a quarter of a century, polled less than half of the popular vote but managed to beat Frémont, the first Republican nominee, by half a million votes.

The 1860 election revealed how badly rent were the two major parties. Lincoln was saved by the electoral vote of most of the Northern states but received only 39.9 percent of the popular vote. Stephen A. Douglas as the regular Democrat polled only 10 percent less than Lincoln but carried only Missouri and a few stray electors. Vice President Breckenridge, the Southern Democratic nominee, and John Bell, appearing as a Constitutional Union candidate, polled between them almost a third of the national popular vote. The Civil War broke up the Constitutional Union party, and its border-state members moved into

[9] See Seymour M. Lipset, "Religion and Politics in the American Past and Present," in Robert Lee and Martin E. Marty (eds.), *Religion and Social Conflict*, Oxford University Press, New York, 1964, and Clifford S. Griffin, *Their Brothers' Keepers*, Rutgers University Press, New Brunswick, N.J., 1960.

the Republican party. The Civil War shook party coalitions to their foundations and resulted in new alignments, some of which have remained for a century. The Douglas Democrats supported Lincoln and the Union cause, and in 1864 the Republicans, to emphasize unity, nominated Andrew Johnson of Tennessee as Vice President. The South, humiliated by the loss of the war and irritated by carpetbaggers and Reconstructionists, formed the backbone of the Democratic party, and Republicans "waved the bloody shirt" in political campaigns for many years.

To the new Republican party fell the responsibility for mobilizing the Union effort. It sought the support of Democratic leaders both formally and informally and used each election to try to nationalize the war. The 1862 midterm elections were held as usual, with Republicans pressing the citizenry for commitment to the national cause. Although failing to capture a majority of the House seats in 1858, the Republicans mustered a large enough coalition to elect a Speaker and in 1860 and 1862 easily won both houses because many Southern states failed to hold elections for Congress.

The Republicans in 1864 seemed far from certain to win the Presidency and in an effort to dramatize unity and the breadth of appeal called themselves the Union party. This proved a successful device for detaching Democrats from their regular party loyalties, but the Democrats maintained their regular organizations. As a result of maintaining their structure from the start of the war, the Democrats did well in many state legislatures and actually picked up seats in Congress in 1862. However, in 1864 with Lincoln's comfortable margin of reelection, the Democrats lost heavily in Congress. Lincoln's reelection was also accompanied by the restoration of Republican majorities to every state legislature, congressional delegation and governorship. The Confederacy held its own elections but little importance seemed attached to them.[10]

From 1860 to 1932, the Republicans were in the ascendancy, especially in presidential elections, a winning streak interrupted only by the elections of Cleveland and Wilson, neither of whom was successful in forming an alignment capable of providing Democratic successors. On numerous occasions the Democrats were able to capture one house of Congress thanks to sweeping Southern congressional seats, but they were unable to carry the huge Northern electoral blocs essential for success in presidential contests. Republicans controlled appointments to the Supreme Court, a power as important in many respects as control of Congress.

The Republican party's strength rested upon diverse support. Newly enfranchised blacks felt indebted to support the party of the

[10]A useful work on the politics of the Civil War and its aftermath is Wood Gray, *The Hidden Civil War: The Story of the Copperheads*, The Viking Press, Inc., New York, 1942.

"Great Emancipator." Until the time of McKinley the Northern soldiers, organized as the Grand Army of the Republic, received beneficent legislation from Republican administrations. The fact that the Democrat Cleveland vetoed many veterans' pensions was cited by Republican workers as indicative that their party was the party for Northern veterans.

Powerful Western interests including cattle, lumber, land, and mineral barons attached themselves to the Republican party, which was glad to bestow on them portions of the public domain. Homestead legislation helped the more humble and adventurous, and they, too, appreciated the federal beneficence. President Lincoln's administration created the first Department of Agriculture, and farmers appreciated this friendly recognition of their interests. The very considerable transportation industry voted for a party willing to subsidize a railroad to the Pacific Ocean, a link between the West and the East.

Much has been made of the backing of Republicans by the banking, manufacturing, and commercial interests from 1860 to the present. In the period after the Civil War the financial community remained grateful for the reestablishment of the national banking system and for the Republican bulwark against easy money, greenbacks, and bimetallism.

Notwithstanding the great interests that tended toward the Republican party after the Civil War, there was much protest and discontent from farmers with heavy mortgages, from unemployed workers, and from those horrified at corruption and the excesses of the "robber barons." Many of them joined the Democrats, and in 1876 Samuel J. Tilden actually polled a majority of the popular vote but failed to carry the Electoral College. The Democrats followed with a very respectable vote in 1880 and won with Cleveland in 1884 and 1892.

During the same years antimonopoly politics and easy-money demands led to a flurry of third-party candidates. In 1892 these groups felt that Cleveland would not provide the answer and followed the Populist James B. Weaver who called for increased government ownership and free and unlimited coinage of silver. His popular vote of more than a million frightened both major parties and set the stage for the great battle of 1896.

Each major party had a silver wing, but the Republicans succeeded in nominating William McKinley, a gold-standard supporter. William Jennings Bryan captured the Democratic nomination and ran on a bimetal plank. Since Bryan had stolen their thunder on silver, the Populists elected to support him rather than to split the vote.

The campaign of 1896 was one of the most colorful in American history. Tons of literature were distributed. McKinley, as "the advance agent of prosperity," waged a "front porch" campaign from his home in Canton, Ohio. Business and commercial interests heavily subsidized his campaign to prevent the "anarchist" Bryan from being elected. More than $7 million was collected for the Republican coffers, largely from frightened capitalists. Bryan received liberal help from the silver miners, but only about $1 million was raised. He stumped the country from one end to the other as the "defender of the poor and the protector of the oppressed" and identified his campaign as an economic crusade in "the cause of humanity."

Besides the unprecedented financing, the campaign was notable for its emotional appeals of mass against class and for its sectional sentiment. The outcome of the election also reflected these appeals. The Eastern and North Central states were carried by McKinley, and the Solid South and most of the Western silver-mining states went for Bryan.

For the student of government the election would be classed a critical one because the immensity of the Democratic defeat was so thorough that the party was unable to put together a significant realignment until Wilson's reelection in 1916.[11]

The Democratic-Populist strategy of class appeals to workers and farmers showed that control of the party was in different hands than it was under Cleveland, who had been able to carry a sizable Eastern commercial vote. Although Bryan was for the "common man," he was not successful in carrying Eastern wage workers with him. The Republicans were able to unite most business interests through promise of seeking new foreign markets, preserving sound money, and continuing the protective tariff. They were able to sell the workers on these programs with the promise of employment and greater security. The ideas, moreover, sounded plausible to workers unemployed as a result of the recession following the panic of 1893. Furthermore, McKinley had dealt fairly with organized labor, and industrial laborers believed that his slogan of "a full dinner pail" would pay better dividends than the Populist Bryan's assault on financial capitalism. Although the McKinley election was a victory for conservative financing over easy money, the Republican coalition was strengthened by substantial margins over the Democrats from 1900 through 1908. Bryan carried many Western states in 1896 but only three in 1908 in his third presidential campaign. Alton B. Parker, the 1904 Democratic standard bearer, carried only the South.

THE PROGRESSIVE ERA

The political environment underwent rapid change during the last half of the nineteenth century. Organized interest groups in business, labor, and agriculture, which were developing on a national scale, sought to influence planks in the party platforms. But because parties were

[11] See V. O. Key, Jr., "A Theory of Critical Elections," *Journal of Politics*, vol. 17, pp. 3–18, 1955.

broadly based in geography they would not speak with clear-cut positions on specific issues of interest to many groups. The interest groups found themselves turning to their own types of political action outside the parties. Many group leaders rejected working through political parties. The National Farmers Union and the Federation of Organized Trades disavowed partisan politics and adopted policies of supporting or opposing legislators irrespective of party, judging them in terms of their commitment to legislation favorable to labor and farmers respectively. Parties were to become competitors with interest-group political action in both administrative and legislative arenas. The economic groups were interested in new systems of decision making.

Machine control of some of the urban party organizations was corrupt and came under attack both from those involved in the newer forms of decision making and from critics with rather high community and literary status, including municipal voters' leagues and chambers of commerce. Nonpartisanship in local government was seen as better than partisan government. The way was being paved to make changes in the political system certain to have far-reaching effects on major American parties.

A broad-gauge attack on economic and political practices was led by groups of writers, Populists, Socialists, and reformers. They denounced the corrupt alliances of business and politics, municipal boss rule, the sordidness of urban life, the evils of big business, exploitation of women and children, and the materialism of the acquisitive society in general. During the administrations of Theodore Roosevelt, Taft, and Wilson, a remarkable amount of legislation was passed designed to curb speculation and corruption. The cries of the Socialists and Populists for a graduated income tax, shorter working hours, control of monopoly, and public regulation of transportation and parts of the economy bore some fruit. The Federal Reserve banking system, the Clayton Act, the Federal Trade Commission, food and drug inspection, and the creation of a separate labor department were some of the answers that the government provided to the protests of the humanitarians. Although the Socialists (who began proposing presidential candidates in 1896) joined in the protests, the wellspring of the progressive movement came from those believing in private enterprise and reform within the capitalistic framework. The movement cut across party lines and had no one plan or reform. Actually it was a series of many reforms, led by many leaders in many directions, often contradictory.

The progressives' political reforms had a lasting impact on political parties, and an institutionalization and democratization of parties comparable to the pre-Civil War era took place. Political reformers were largely motivated by a feeling that there were few evils that could not be cured by more democracy. One step was to take nominations out of the hands of caucuses and conventions and place them, by law, in the hands of registered voters. The direct primaries were also extended in many states to the choice of delegates to national conventions. Party leaders nonetheless turned their attention, with some success, to controlling the primaries. Prominent leaders of both political parties endorsed the direct election of senators, and the Seventeenth Amendment was ratified in 1913. Shortly thereafter, the parties found it necessary to create a separate national committee to work for senatorial candidates. Universal woman suffrage, becoming effective in 1920, prompted the parties to constitute their committees with female "co-leaders" and vice-chairmen. The primaries and woman suffrage increased the costs of elections and required new considerations in campaign strategy. Corrupt practices laws placed limitations on campaign contributions from banks and corporations.

Several other political innovations not directly related to parties nonetheless influenced them. Popular control through the initiative, referendum, and recall meant interest-group participation in elections on behalf of propositions. Money expended by interests to pass or defeat ballot measures was often that much less to be donated to parties. Parties thereafter were often challenged to take positions on these measures or run the risk of embarrassment for "dodging issues." The ballot was also lengthened by "direct legislation."

The replacement of weak mayor systems by commission and city-manager plans and the extension of nonpartisan elections in many municipalities deprived the parties of a certain amount of patronage and influence on local policies. Party organizations had to be discreet and circumspect about supporting candidates in these nonpartisan primaries and elections. The extension of the federal merit system also reduced the number of jobs available to the parties.

These reforms, which appeared far-reaching on the surface, failed to reduce boss and machine rule as much as their advocates had hoped. Longer ballots confused the voters, and political machines mobilized their followers to take advantage of the confusion. Clearly, the progressive reforms demonstrated a fundamental political truth that party organizations adapt to their environment. Political bosses could not be destroyed by primaries, direct legislation, and exhortation. A far more basic change, which came a generation later, was necessary to reduce the old-style machine. From a long-run point of view, however, woman suffrage, the great renaissance of interest in politics, and the formation of large numbers of nonpartisan political and economic interest groups between 1900 and 1920 profoundly affected the political system.

There were many Republican reformers and Republicans op-posing reforms; Democrats likewise were far from unanimous in their support of change. Overall, however, greater support for reforms came from Democratic than from Republican congressmen. Democrats in particular from 1910 to 1912 were anxious to make a progressive record that could be taken to the voters in 1912. Insurgent, reform-minded Republicans and progressive Democrats frequently exchanged brick-bats but often ended up voting together. The articulate character of the progressive Republicans such as Robert M. La Follette and the crusading Theodore Roosevelt probably made more of an impression than the numbers of Republican reformers would seem to warrant. It should be further observed that progressive Republicans (and Democrats, for that matter) were also not invariably united on foreign policy issues. In the American system it has not been unusual for ardent progressives in domestic matters to oppose change in foreign policy. Until more recent times, some of the most vigorous advocates of domestic reform were isolationist or noninterventionist in foreign affairs.

The Republicans in 1912 faced a disastrous schism. When an in-cumbent party suffers a serious enough erosion to have a sizable seg-ment split off and nominate a ticket of its own, it is inviting defeat if the opposition party can unify itself behind a popular candidate. The Taft-Roosevelt split was not sectional or strongly ideological. Internal contro-versy over the conservation of natural resources, inept leadership, and insurgency in Congress led to the disintegration of the powerful Re-

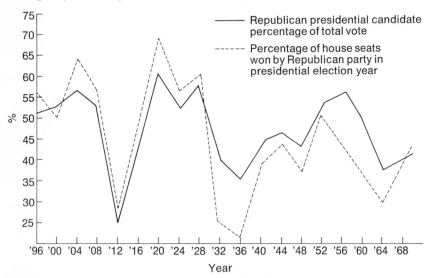

FIGURE 2-1 Percentage of Republican House seats won in the presidential election years 1896–1968.

publican combination left to Taft in 1909. Theodore Roosevelt stepped into the breach with his "new nationalism" and passionate crusaders. He received much support from dairymen and grain growers and miners but failed to obtain the necessary vote from industrial labor. Wilson, an erstwhile conservative "second Cleveland," sensed the waves of public opinion and promised a "new freedom." When the votes were counted, Wilson had carried all the South and most of the East and West. Taft won only Utah and Vermont; Roosevelt carried Pennsylvania, Michigan, Minnesota, South Dakota, Washington, and most of California.

The Progressive party rapidly disintegrated after much of its program was enacted by the Democratic administration. Roosevelt declined the Progressive's renomination in 1916, and the party accepted the Republican nominee, Charles Evans Hughes. The Democratic record generally satisfied the agrarians and labor, and Wilson was reelected on the slogan "He kept us out of war" in one of the closest elections in history. But the outcome raised serious doubts as to whether a durable Democratic alliance had been formed. Notwithstanding the remarkable record of social legislation enacted during Wilson's first term, Hughes carried virtually all the East and Midwest, and Republican candidates for Congress received several hundred thousand more votes than their opponents. The 1916 victory was a tribute to Wilson's personal leadership rather than a portent of party realignment.

In 1920 the Republican candidate, Sen. Warren G. Harding of Ohio, an "unpromising" dark horse, won a sweeping victory. The Democratic candidate, James M. Cox of Ohio, carried only Kentucky and ten Southern states. The Republicans captured Tennessee, the first Southern state to go Republican since the Reconstruction. Harding's popular vote majority was almost 2 to 1 over his Democratic opponent and was the largest shift of votes from one party to another since the Civil War. Republicans similarly showed strength in their congressional party, carrying the House 303 to 131 seats, the largest majority in the party's history. Although Harding was supported by the Old Guard wing of the party, he appears to have profited immensely by a sharp shift of Progressives, who had supported Wilson in 1916, back to the Republicans. The political climate had turned against progressivism.[12]

REPUBLICAN HEGEMONY

The Roaring Twenties are often portrayed as an unprogressive, cynical, politically barren period, a decade that Americans like to forget. From the standpoint of party development, its contributions are few compared

[12]On the 1920 contest, see Wesley M. Bagby, *The Road to Normalcy: The Presidential Campaign and Election of 1920*, The Johns Hopkins Press, Baltimore, 1962.

with many others. Even so, this period, dominated mostly by conservative Republicanism, is of interest to students of politics. In the first place, several patterns of political behavior were manifest. Insecurities, frustrations, and hatreds cropped up publicly, as they do after a major war. Civil liberties were restricted and the nation went through a witch-hunting phase against left-wingers, and the Ku Klux Klan grew rapidly in numbers. Scandals in high places did not result in defeat of the party in power any more than they did after the Civil War. Very little reform was attempted or presumably wanted, and strong presidential leadership was not regarded as desirable. Conservatism was the order of the day. In 1924, after a bitter convention fight over the mounting prohibition issue, the Democrats nominated John W. Davis, a conservative lawyer and the antithesis of Bryan and Wilson. Robert M. La Follette of Wisconsin broke with the Republican party and ran for President as a Progressive. His action failed to split the Republican party as in 1912 but gave some Progressives a place to go.

At least two developments during the twenties were to have longrun significance. One of these was the advent of radio, which at the outset hurt the Democrats. In 1924 the public was given an opportunity to listen to their convention, which defeated by one vote a resolution denouncing the Klan. The boisterous fight between William G. McAdoo, representing the rural, Protestant, dry wing of the party, and Alfred E. Smith, epitomizing the urban, Catholic, wet wing, signaled the deep split in the party and ruined what little chance it had to attack Republican scandals and win the election.

A second development was the laying of the groundwork, unforeseen at the time, for a Democratic resurgence that was to be built into a majority. Smith made tremendous inroads in the urban vote, carrying a number of the largest cities. Undoubtedly Smith's humble background, Catholicism, and advocacy of repeal of prohibition helped him in the urban areas. Herbert Hoover's stand for the "noble experiment" (prohibition) appears to have been the more popular one in 1928 but four years later was to become a minority view. Smith's candidacy appealed to underprivileged urban minorities and was useful subsequently in the Democratic contention that it was the party of the little man and the underdog.

Economic recession results in protest, and protest is an important characteristic of voting behavior. Reactions against the panic of 1893 and World War I helped the Republicans regain power. The Great Depression during the Hoover administration brought a violent reaction against the Republicans and a dramatic revival of the Democratic party strength in 1933. It caused the most far-reaching realignment since the

TABLE 2-1   Presidential election statistics, 1932–1948

Year	Candidate	Party	Popular vote	Number of states carried	Electoral vote
1932	Franklin D. Roosevelt	Democrat	22,809,638	42	272
	Herbert Hoover	Republican	15,758,901	6	59
	Norman Thomas	Socialist	885,314		
	William Foster	Communist	102,991		
	William Upshaw	Prohibition	81,869		
	William Harvey	Liberty	53,425		
	Verne Reynolds	Socialist Labor	33,275		
	Jacob Coxey	Farmer-Labor	7,294		
1936	Franklin D. Roosevelt	Democrat	27,478,945	46	523
	Alfred M. Landon	Republican	16,674,665	2	8
	William Lemke	Union	882,479		
	Norman Thomas	Socialist	187,720		
	Earl Browder	Communist	80,159		
	D. Leigh Colvin	Prohibition	37,487		
1940	Franklin D. Roosevelt	Democrat	26,890,401	38	449
	Wendell L. Willkie	Republican	22,321,018	10	82
	Norman Thomas	Socialist	116,796		
	Roger Babson	Prohibition	57,812		
	Earl Browder	Communist	48,610		
	John Aiken	Socialist Labor	14,881		
1944	Franklin D. Roosevelt	Democrat	25,602,505	36	432
	Thomas E. Dewey	Republican	22,006,278	12	99
	Norman Thomas	Socialist	80,518		
	Claude Watson	Prohibition	74,758		
	Edward Teichert	Socialist Labor	45,336		
1948	Harry S. Truman	Democrat	24,105,695	28	303
	Thomas E. Dewey	Republican	21,969,170	16	189
	J. Strom Thurmond	States' Rights Democratic	1,169,021	4	39
	Henry A. Wallace	Progressive	1,156,103		
	Norman Thomas	Socialist	139,009		
	Claude Watson	Prohibition	103,216		
	Edward Teichert	Socialist Labor	29,061		
	Farrell Dobbs	Socialist Workers	13,613		

Note: Minor-party candidates polling fewer than 8,000 popular votes not included.

Civil War and gave the Democrats an opportunity to become the new majority party.

By 1932, Union veterans were no longer a significant voting bloc. Many business, transportation, financial, and commercial interests who had always supported the Republican party voted for a change in administration in 1932, and some even stayed with the Democrats in

1936. Negroes who suffered heavily as jobless left the party of the Great Emancipator. The New Deal measures brought agrarians, labor, many professionals, and young people into the Democratic party. The party of protest soon became a cohesive combination dedicated to a New Deal and to FDR as a personality.

POLITICAL SIGNIFICANCE OF THE NEW DEAL

President Franklin D. Roosevelt is often cited as the prototype of the strong President and party leader. Possessed of an engaging personality and prepossessing appearance, he was able to inspire confidence and loyalty of large masses of people. Few reacted neutrally to "that man in the White House"; he was loved or hated. He maintained contact with the people through successful "fireside chats" over the radio and many dramatic public appearances. He went before Congress in person not only to give his annual State of the Union messages but also on other occasions. So successful was his revival of the annual personal appearance that his successors continued the practice. Roosevelt turned the press conference into a significant instrument of popular leadership. Many electrifying announcements as well as consistent front page news came from the conferences. He used patronage effectively and during the war years brought Republicans into important posts to assure bipartisan cooperation. The success of Roosevelt's party leadership also lay in his ability to muster great support from private interest groups which in turn brought pressure to bear on reluctant Democrats to support the President's program. Roosevelt became not only the Chief Executive but also the "Chief Legislator." New ideas, proposals, and policies emanated from the White House so rapidly from 1933 to 1936 that Congress could scarcely keep up with them. Executive initiative became the rule, while hostile groups dubbed Congress the President's "rubber stamp."

Policy Changes. The age of Roosevelt was a turning point in American history. It ushered in positive government. In the words of the President, "new instruments of public power" were forged and placed "in the hands of a people's government." This power was "to assist the development of an economic declaration of rights, an economic constitutional order." In his second Inaugural Address, President Roosevelt said: "The essential democracy of our nation and the safety of our people depend not on the absence of power, but upon lodging it with those whom the people can change or continue at stated intervals through an honest and free system of elections." Concisely, the government was to control power possessed by private groups in order to make "private office a public trust."

Another basic policy of profound significance was the gradual reversal of American foreign policy from nonintervention to active participation in international affairs. This was achieved in the face of organized hostility toward aiding the Allies and reluctance on the part of Republican congressional leaders to intervene prior to Pearl Harbor. After involvement, Roosevelt led his party and the nation in dedicating the United States to cooperation in international organization and world leadership.

These broad policies were brought into effect by means of thousands of laws and executive orders, by unprecedented federal expenditures, and through a huge increase in the executive establishment. They required the mobilization of public opinion on a grand scale, the support of the masses associated with powerful organized minorities, and vigorous party leadership. Like Andrew Jackson and Theodore Roosevelt, Franklin D. Roosevelt assumed personal leadership of his party and the government. Many of his actions and methods were tradition-shattering and spectacular and resulted in strengthening and maintaining a hold on some segments of the population, and at the same time incurring an abiding hatred and enmity from other groups.

Recent political history may be viewed in terms of the struggle to achieve economic security for the individual and his family and national security for the United States in the world. The politics of the New Deal became the politics of security to a greater extent than in any other period of our history. An underlying concept of the New Deal, as enunciated in its earlier days, was that the people had been made less secure because they were "regimented into the service of the privileged few." By curbing these few, the Rooseveltian philosophy held, greater freedom, liberty, and security for the average man would result. This social pioneering, the President stressed, would bolster, not weaken, private initiative and enterprise and help promote competition.

Third Term. The rise and fall of the third-term tradition provoked several volumes and much controversy. After Roosevelt had been elected for a third and fourth time, a large number of Republicans were determined to place a two-term limitation in the federal Constitution. When substantial Republican majorities came into control of Congress in 1947, the proposal became immediate business. Few believed that three-fourths of the legislatures would accept the Twenty-second Amendment. Within a few years, however, the Republican state legislatures of the North and West and the Southern state legislatures, disgruntled with the

Truman Fair Deal, ratified the amendment. By February, 1951, it was ratified by thirty-six states and became effective.

From the standpoint of a major political party, the amendment was objected to on the grounds that a President's control over his party during the latter part of his second term would be reduced. His party's congressmen, it was argued, would be less inclined to follow his leadership. Moreover, his popular control over public opinion and public affairs would diminish. Rifts in the President's party would be aggravated, for candidates would vie for nomination soon after his second inauguration instead of waiting until late in his term. Eisenhower's second term was characterized by Democratic majorities in Congress, so tension between the President and Republican congressmen was not easily apparent. The third-term limitation, however, did aid Nixon in his plan to capture the 1960 nomination years in advance without embarrassing Eisenhower.

"Bipartisan" Foreign Policy. Beginning in 1944, the leaders of the two parties pledged themselves to a "bipartisan" foreign policy. This term remains ill defined and has not always been honored subsequently. Nonetheless, the controlling party has found it necessary to consult the opposition on foreign policy, and both parties endorsed the principle of presenting a united national posture to the outside world, particularly toward communism. This was a practice far different from the one existing from 1918 to 1920 and from 1940 to 1942, when bitter party differences were aired publicly. Although foreign policy has not been removed from the arena of party politics, debate takes place in a different context.

PARTY BATTLES, 1936–1948

Roosevelt's Reelections. In 1936 a group of "Jeffersonian Democrats" including Alfred E. Smith bolted and announced their support for Gov. Alfred M. Landon, the Republican nominee. The American Liberty League and a number of big business men warned the nation of disaster if Roosevelt were reelected. They supported Landon, although he was not as conservative as they wished. In spite of the enormous popularity of the Roosevelt program and of the President himself, the election stirred considerable interest. The *Literary Digest* poll predicted a landslide for Landon, and the great majority of Northern newspapers supported him. In spite of this support, Landon carried only Maine and Vermont, and Republicans were disastrously defeated in the congressional election, winning only eighty-nine House and eighteen Senate seats.

The Republicans were to take heart shortly after inauguration when Roosevelt proposed reorganization of the Supreme Court, including the addition of a judge for each one over seventy who had not retired. The Supreme Court had declared a number of important New Deal laws unconstitutional, and several cases were pending before the Court to test other New Deal legislation. All members of the Court had been appointed by previous Presidents, and Roosevelt believed that they were out of step with the political policies overwhelmingly voted by the people. Moreover, a number of the Court's actions were split decisions. Opponents dubbed Roosevelt's proposal "packing the Court." Conservatives of both parties used the measure to weaken the leadership of the President by charges that his recommendation smacked of dictatorship. The same argument was used to defeat the plan to give the President power to reorganize the executive branch. Although the Court plan was soundly defeated by Congress, the President in effect lost the battle but won the war because the Court in effect reformed itself. As one scholar quipped, "A switch in time saved nine."

On the heels of these reverses, the President was rebuffed in several 1938 primaries where he urged voters to defeat Democratic congressmen who had opposed his program. Republicans and the press felt that this heralded an anti-Roosevelt revolt. Although this was premature, these actions widened the gap between liberal and conservative Democrats and virtually brought to an end innovation in social legislation. Further, the President suffered a decline in prestige.

A new chapter began in the field of foreign policy as war broke out in Europe in 1939. Sharp differences between the parties were manifest as an overwhelming majority of Republicans opposed revision of the neutrality laws, selective service, lend-lease, and the arming of merchant ships. Wendell Willkie, the Republican presidential candidate in 1940, gave general approval to Democratic foreign policy objectives but late in the campaign became more critical of them, the Democrats argued that in troubled times an experienced pilot should not be dropped for a person who had never held public office. Republicans inveighed against a third term and against much of the New Deal domestic program but to little avail. Willkie carried the Dakotas, Colorado, Kansas, Nebraska, Iowa, Indiana, and Michigan as well as Maine and Vermont but ran 4.5 million votes behind Roosevelt.

By 1940 and again in 1944, it was obvious that the Democratic alliance was weakening in spots but gaining in others. Farmers returned to the Republican party in large numbers, as did Italian- and German-Americans, but pro-British and numerous Eastern financial interests supported the foreign policy program of the Democrats. Moreover, the

Republicans were badly split over foreign policy between so-called interventionists and isolationists. Willkie was roundly denounced as a "oneworlder," and Governor Dewey and Sen. Arthur Vandenburg, who were also of the internationalist wing of the party, were regarded by Old Guard Republicans as little better.

Seasoned observers were reasonably certain that the nation would reelect its wartime President in 1944. Governor Thomas E. Dewey attacked the administration as "tired and quarrelsome" and subservient to political and labor bosses. He emphasized the need for change. Democrats meanwhile could raise essentially the same appeals as in 1940 and warn against a change in leadership in the midst of war. Dewey reduced the proportion of popular vote for Roosevelt and won twelve states, keeping all those won by Willkie except Michigan and adding Wyoming, Wisconsin, and Ohio. Although the Democratic delegates did not know it, they were nominating a new President when they dropped Vice President Henry Wallace, an anathema to the South, and chose Sen. Harry S. Truman of Missouri. Truman became President in April, 1945, less than three months after Roosevelt's inauguration.

The Truman Administration. The termination of the war in 1945 presaged a Republican comeback. Popular unrest over strikes, the slowness of reconversion in some lines, and shortages especially of meats and foods plus skyrocketing prices led to strong reaction against the party in power. The clever slogan "Had enough? Vote Republican!" symbolized to millions of voters a method of ending wartime controls and war weariness and sweeping away the backwash of the war. Republicans registered substantial gains and won control of both houses of Congress. It appeared that the New Deal alliance had cracked and that the 1946 midterm election was the harbinger of a new party majority comparable to those of 1894 and 1918.

President Truman's quarrels with Congress during 1947 and 1948 provided further eivdence for those who foresaw the end of the Democratic cycle. A number of Southerners bolted and nominated a states' rights candidate, Strom Thurmond. Left-wingers who were dissatisfied with the bipartisan foreign policy ran Henry Wallace at the head of the Progressive party. Republicans were reasonably united around Governor Dewey and what seemed to be another 1860, with the prospect of a dissipated Democratic vote.

To the astonishment of almost everyone except Harry S. Truman and pollster Louis Bean, Truman won, even though he lost New York and the Middle Atlantic states and four Southern states. Where Roosevelt had lost strength among farmers in 1944, notably in Colorado, Iowa, Ohio, Wisconsin, and Wyoming, Truman was victorious. Truman kept the labor vote and most of the big-city and minorities vote. The New Deal under President Truman was given a new lease on life, and presumably a Democratic majority remained in existence. A number of Democratic Senate seats were lost in the 1950 midterm elections, but the party kept control of both houses of Congress. With this usual midterm erosion of majority party strength and the declining popularity of President Truman, the Republicans looked hopefully to 1952. Congressional investigating committees were making headlines on "influence peddling," tax fixing, and the acceptance of gratuities for government contracts, all of which gave Republicans a battle cry of "corruption." Relations with the Soviet Union worsened, and definitive victory was not forthcoming in the Korean conflict. Senator Joseph McCarthy, Republican from Wisconsin, charged that numerous federal employees either were Communists or had been one-time sympathizers. President Truman's removal of Gen. Douglas MacArthur from command in Korea and the general's rousing reception when he returned to the United States further highlighted the unpopularity of the Truman regime. The Democratic assets of a fair degree of prosperity and a successful twenty-year voting coalition were to be offset by the Republican charge of "crime, Korea, and communism."

EISENHOWER INTERLUDE

The Republican convention in 1952 passed up such well-known office-holders as Gov. Earl Warren of California and Sen. Robert A. Taft of Ohio, who was affectionately called "Mr. Republican." A great many delegates who wanted Taft to be nominated voted against him because they felt that he could not win because of his unpopularity with labor unions and his public image as an isolationist in foreign affairs. The convention chose "nonpartisan" Gen. Dwight D. Eisenhower, who was reported never to have voted in a Republican primary. Eisenhower was unfamiliar with the exigencies of party politics, and his views on public questions were essentially unknown. In the context of the times, these were assets that added to his already immense personal popularity. People had confidence in his ability to handle foreign affairs, and his nonpartisan background enabled him to capture millions of Democratic and independent votes. Governor Adlai Stevenson of Illinois, the Democratic nominee, was a fresh personality possessed of wit and excellent speech but was relatively unknown outside his own state. He attracted an enthusiastic following among intellectuals and liberals but was unable to hold the votes of organized labor, farmers, and various ethnic-religious minorities (except the Negroes) to the same extent as Roosevelt and Truman.

In other words, the turn to Eisenhower was due not to a sharp movement of one or more groups from the Democratic party to the Republican party but to a general decay of Democratic strength across most of the political spectrum, including congressional races, and Republicans won control of both houses by razor-thin margins. The usual midterm decline of the party in office in 1954, however, was enough to return control of both houses to the Democrats. As with most Presidents winning a second term beginning with Lincoln, the Eisenhower popular vote victory in 1956 was larger than the first.[13]

The selection of Eisenhower and the record of his administration were unusual in several respects. For the first time in three-quarters of a century, the nation chose a professional military man as its Chief Executive. Moreover, his inexperience in elective public office was virtually without parallel in the nation's history. These two issues were raised by some of the opposition but left a majority of the electorate unimpressed. The nomination and election of Eisenhower was a demonstration of the flexibility of recruitment in the American system. When suitable personnel within the party appear to be unavailable, delegates and voters look elsewhere.

The President himself repeatedly stated his intentions to decentralize controls over the economic order and to revitalize states' rights by diminishing federal control and activity. But the movement toward the so-called welfare state was hardly arrested. Coverage under the Social Security Act was substantially expanded, and the President recommended certain extensions of federal aid to education. He signed a civil rights bill and sent forces to Little Rock, Arkansas, as a demonstration of federal intention to stop interference with court-ordered desegregation in public schools. Despite Eisenhower's economy drive when he took office, federal expenditures in subsequent years increased, and "big government" remained. Concisely, the Eisenhower administration did not repeal the New Deal, or Fair Deal, but consolidated it. Eisenhower himself exalted the political center and used the middle class as a nationalizing force. Both the middle class and the political center underwent radical expansion during the Eisenhower years.

The President himself often assumed the stance of nonpartisanship and being above politics. He did not find party politics appealing and delegated much of the leadership of party matters to Vice President Nixon and to Republican National Chairman Leonard Hall. The President did campaign during the congressional elections of 1954 and 1958

[13]Cleveland received a majority of the popular vote in seeking a second term but failed to win in the electoral college. Taft and Hoover offer conspicuous deviations of the tendency of incumbents to be elected a second time.

TABLE 2-2 Presidential election statistics, 1952–1968

Year	Candidate	Party	Popular vote	Number of states carried	Electoral vote
1952	Dwight D. Eisenhower	Republican	33,824,351	39	442
	Adlai Stevenson	Democrat	27,314,987	9	89
	Vincent Hallinan	Progressive	133,608		
	Stuart Hamblen	Prohibition	73,768		
	Eric Haas	Socialist Labor	29,333		
	Darlington Hoopes	Socialist	18,322		
	Douglas MacArthur	Christian Nationalist	16,949		
	Farrell Dobbs	Socialist Workers	8,956		
1956	Dwight D. Eisenhower	Republican	35,589,471	41	457
	Adlai Stevenson	Democrat	26,035,504	7	73
	T. Coleman Andrews	Constitution	176,887		
	Harry F. Byrd	States' Rights	134,132		
	Eric Haas	Socialist Labor	44,443		
	Enoch A. Holtwick	Prohibition	41,937		
1960	John F. Kennedy	Democrat	34,227,096	23	303
	Richard M. Nixon	Republican	34,107,646	26	219
	Harry F. Byrd	*	440,298	1	15
	Eric Haas	Socialist Labor	46,478		
	Rutherford L. Decker	Prohibition	46,220		
	Orval Faubus	National States' Rights	44,967		
	Farrell Dobbs	Socialist Workers	39,541		
	Charles L. Sullivan	Constitutional	18,169		
1964	Lyndon B. Johnson	Democrat	43,126,233	45†	486
	Barry Goldwater	Republican	27,174,989	6	52
	Eric Haas	Socialist Labor	42,642		
	Clifton DeBerry	Socialist Workers	22,249		
	Earle H. Munn	Prohibition	22,962		
1968	Richard M. Nixon	Republican	31,785,480	32	301
	Hubert H. Humphrey	Democrat	31,275,165	14	191
	George C. Wallace	American Independent	9,906,473	5	45
	Eldridge Cleaver	Peace and Freedom	195,134		
	Dick Gregory	Peace and Freedom	148,622		
	Henning A. Blomen	Socialist Labor	51,962		
	Fred Halstead	Socialist Workers	38,011		
	Earle H. Munn	Prohibition	14,987		

Note: Minor-party candidates polling fewer than 8,000 popular votes not included.
*Unpledged electors in Alabama and Mississippi cast their ballots for Senator Byrd.
†Including District of Columbia. In Alabama the Independent Democratic electors polled 210,732 votes.

but between elections tended to remain aloof from the hurly-burly of party politics. Nixon's role as a top leader in the party virtually assured his nomination in 1960. Rarely does a President permit his Vice President to assume so dominant a role in party leadership.

The Eisenhower years were significant also for an emphasis on "personality politics" and split-ticket voting. The split between voter support for Eisenhower and for his congressional Republican compatriots indicated that many preferred Eisenhower but not his party. Although he strongly pleaded for a Republican Congress in 1954, 1956, and 1958, the voters elected increasing Democratic majorities to Congress. Consequently, 1958 was a particularly disastrous year for Republican congressmen; the overwhelming Democratic majorities in Congress were reminiscent of the early days of the New Deal.

THE DEMOCRATIC MAJORITY

The elections of Dwight Eisenhower failed to bring about any substantial party realignment. While the President talked sporadically about "modern Republicans" and remaking the party into one with strong voting appeal, he failed to stir this image at the grass roots. Although he could siphon several million votes from the Democratic coalition for himself, he could not get them for congressional candidates and very often not for Republican gubernatorial candidates. His dream of a Republican successor was shattered in 1960 when Nixon polled more than a million fewer votes than Eisenhower in 1956, and Kennedy received 9.5 million more votes than Stevenson did in his second effort.

The fact that Nixon barely lost the popular vote majority demonstrates, however, that the Republican party remained strong at the presidential level but weak as a congressional party. If Nixon had been elected by a small switch of votes in a very few close states such as Illinois and Michigan, the Democrats would have remained in control of Congress. Nixon outpolled Republican candidates for the House of Representatives by well over 5 million votes, and Democratic House candidates outpolled Kennedy by more than 600,000 votes. House Democratic candidates held a 1 million plurality over their Republican opponents in 1956, 6 million in 1960, and 2.5 million in 1962.

Analysis of the figures of the 1960 election will occupy students of elections for many years. Kennedy was elected by 303 electoral votes in twenty-three states to 219 votes for Nixon in twenty-six states. One state, Mississippi, was carried by a slate of eight independent electors, with seven other Southern electors voting for Sen. Harry F. Byrd of Virginia. Kennedy's popular vote margin was but 119.450 over Nixon. Thirteen minor-party candidates and unpledged electors collectively

TABLE 2-3 Congressional party lineup, 1961–1971*

Year	House		Senate	
	Democrat	Republican	Democrat	Republican
1961–1963	263	174	64	36
1963–1965	259	176	68	32
1965–1967	295	140	68	32
1967–1969	247	188	64	36
1969–1971	243	192	57	43

*Figures often fluctuate slightly during a congressional session because of vacancies, which are sometimes filled with persons of the opposite party.

drew about a half million votes. Religion was obviously important in voting behavior, with Kennedy running well in Catholic areas and Nixon in Protestant areas. Yet Kennedy received from 38 to 46 percent of the Protestant vote.

The Kennedy victory appeared to reinstate the Democratic presidential majority. The alliance of big-city voters, labor, ethnic minorities, and Southern whites was, at least on the surface, reestablished. He failed to win a majority of the farm votes which had gone to Truman and then to Eisenhower. Eisenhower had failed, unlike Lincoln and Roosevelt, to realign forces to produce a durable Republican majority capable of remaining intact after his departure from office. At the same time there was an uneasy restiveness of Southerners in the Democratic coalition, and the Kennedy vote from another point of view could hardly be called formidable. Kennedy's 49.7 percent popular vote was only slightly better than that for Truman. Further, unlike Truman, he was not handicapped by two formidable third-party threats from erstwhile Democrats who captured well over 2.25 million votes between them. The narrow Kennedy victory was not the strong reassertion of the majority coalition evidenced by the McKinley victory in 1896 and that of Harding in 1920.

President Kennedy campaigned vigorously in 1962 for Democratic congressional candidates until interrupted by the crisis brought on by the discovery of Russian missiles in Cuba. The outcome of the midterm election, as with most elections, gave both sides something to be jubilant about. Democratic losses in Congress were spectacularly less than the majority usually suffers. Richard Nixon lost his bid for the governorship of California, weakening his chances to win the nomination of his party in 1964. Republicans, however, obtained a majority of the votes cast for gubernatorial candidates. They won important contests for governor in Ohio, Michigan, and Pennsylvania. Governor Nelson Rockefeller of New York was reelected and became the leading Republican presidential aspirant until his divorce and remarriage in 1963. As his cause slumped on public opinion polls, Sen. Barry Goldwater's rose, and by November when President Kennedy was assassinated, he was referred to in the press as the leading GOP candidate.

Superb Goldwater organization and the weaknesses and lack of effort by other potential contenders led to Senator Goldwater's capture of the Republican nomination. Johnson continued throughout the campaign to lead Goldwater by a wide margin on all national public opinion polls. Goldwater's strong appeals to conservatives and against socialism, centralization, and immorality failed to impress an electoral majority, resulting in a Johnson landslide of forty-four states and the District of Columbia. The President's percentage of the popular vote slightly exceeded that for Roosevelt in 1936; but Democrats in Congress did not hold as many seats as in the Roosevelt landslide, although they increased their majorities in both houses. For the first time in many years, congressional Republicans demonstrated greater popular vote strength than presidential Republicans.

President Johnson substantially reinforced the Democratic majority and showed great strength across the entire political spectrum including the business and professional classes. Goldwater's "Southern strategy" of strong appeals to states' rights and opposition to the federal civil rights laws of 1964 paid off to the extent that he carried the hard-core states won by J. Strom Thurmond in 1948 — Alabama, Louisiana, Mississippi, and South Carolina — and added Georgia. But he ran worse than Nixon in most other Southern and Border States. Goldwater barely won his home state of Arizona, running far behind Nixon's popular vote percentage in that state. Illustrative of the upheaval caused by the Goldwater nomination was a sharp defection of many Republicans to Johnson, and more than half of the newspapers making endorsements supported Johnson. Some Southern newspapers that had never before supported a Republican presidential nominee came out for Goldwater.

For the first time in its history, the Republican presidential party appeared stronger in the South than in any other section of the nation. It lost heavily in the Midwest and in New England where it usually had been strong. The party was faced with rebuilding along lines having greater appeal to moderates and to voters in the broad political center or with becoming the voice of the right to the far right. Election returns indicated that the majority of voters were unwilling to support a candidate who espoused doctrines or at least had the image of championing causes considerably to the political right of Dewey, Eisenhower, and Nixon.

The Democrats made spectacular gains in both houses of Congress enabling President Johnson to get a massive output of social legislation through Congress including medical care for the elderly, federal aid to education, poverty measures, and civil rights. Republicans picked up four Senate seats in the 1966 midterm election but netted forty-eight in the House. Nevertheless, at the beginning of 1967 the Democrats looked forward opitmistically to 1968, with expectations of retaining the Democratic majority. Shortly thereafter the Democratic coalition began to crumble under the weight of an unpopular Vietnam war, domestic troubles, and the President's loss of prestige.

The size of the Goldwater defeat in 1964 removed him from any chance for renomination. Governor George Romney of Michigan led the polls for the Republican nomination, but he lost ground in his campaign. Meanwhile, Gov. Nelson Rockefeller vacillated and neither he nor Romney was very popular with large numbers of potential Republican delegates to the national convention. By the time of the New Hampshire primary in 1968, it was generally believed the presidential contest would be between Richard Nixon, who was available to fill the Republican vacuum, and President Johnson. Johnson, however, withdrew on March 31, leaving a three-way contest for the Democratic nomination among Vice President Hubert Humphrey and Sens. Eugene McCarthy and Robert Kennedy. The assassination of Senator Kennedy in June threw Democratic politics into further confusion. After a turbulent national convention, Mr. Humphrey emerged with the nomination and at the head of a very badly divided party. Every public opinion poll showed Humphrey well behind. The outcome was further placed in doubt by what appeared to be a serious third-party bid by former Gov. George Wallace of Alabama. Some polls showed him taking more than 20 percent of the vote. His name appeared on the ballots of all fifty states and the problem for campaign managers was whether he would siphon off more votes from Nixon or from Humphrey.

The narrow Nixon victory was quite comparable with his narrow defeat of 1960. In the West, he lost only Washington and Hawaii, whereas he lost Hawaii, New Mexico, and Nevada in 1960; he carried most of the Midwest both times. Highly important in the victory was his ability to carry the Carolinas, Illinois, New Jersey, and Missouri, which he had lost in 1960. As Kennedy had done in 1960, Humphrey carried most of the Eastern industrialized states and Michigan. In the South, Humphrey lost all but Texas (see Table 2-4), the poorest showing for that area made by a Democratic presidential candidate in the twentieth century. Governor Wallace carried five Southern states; Nixon carried four plus Kentucky and Tennessee. Only 500,000 popular votes, however, separated Nixon from Humphrey nationally. Wallace with 13.6 percent of the national vote had made the most formidable third-party bid since Robert La Follette, Sr., in 1924.

The Nixon victory was the first time since 1844 that an incoming President failed to bring in majorities of his own party in both houses of Congress. Because the Wallace party was mainly presidential it contested

TABLE 2-4 Southern and Border-state votes for President, 1968

State	Nixon	Humphrey	Wallace	Others
Alabama	14.1%	18.6%	66.0%	1.3%
Arkansas	31.0	30.3	38.7	
Florida	40.5	30.9	28.6	
Georgia	29.7	27.0	43.3	
Kentucky	43.8	37.6	18.3	0.3
Louisiana	23.5	28.2	48.3	
Mississippi	13.5	23.0	63.5	
North Carolina	39.5	29.2	31.3	
South Carolina	38.1	29.6	32.3	
Tennessee	37.8	28.1	34.1	
Texas	39.9	41.1	19.0	
Virginia	43.4	32.5	23.6	0.5

few congressional seats. The weakness of the Republican congressional party again showed itself. It gained only four seats in the House and five in the Senate. [14] The Democratic congressional majority remained stable, losing one seat each to Republicans in Virginia and North Carolina but winning one seat each from them in West Virginia and Missouri. Clearly, sizable majorities of Southern Democratic voters were disaffected with the choice of the Democratic National Convention but were reasonably content to stay with the party's congressional candidates. Republicans found little encouragement in the support for their Southern congressional nominees.

Democratic presidential support, though insufficient to win the Presidency, nonetheless remained rather largely intact. There was general slippage across the political spectrum, as in the case of Adlai Stevenson, but without substantial realignment between the two major parties. Humphrey retained a very strong hold on Jewish, Negro, and Puerto Rican voters and retained a majority of the Catholic vote though many shifted to Nixon. [15] He received a sizable plurality among those under thirty and a smaller plurality from those in the thirty to forty-nine age bracket. As in the past, Nixon did better than his opponent with those over fifty. He also kept the white-collar, college, and Protestant vote. Lyndon Johnson had done well with farmers and independents, but there was substantial defection of these two groups to Nixon in 1968. Nixon received most of the hard-core Republican vote and a considerable number of Republicans who had deserted to Johnson in 1964 returned to the fold. The Gallup Poll estimated that 14 percent of those who classified themselves as Democrats voted for Wallace while only 5

[14] Table 2-3 shows a Republican gain of seven Senate seats between 1967 and 1969. Two of these resulted from the deaths of Democratic Sens. Robert F. Kennedy of New York and E. L. Bartlett of Alaska. Both states had Republican governors, who appointed Republicans to the Senate.

[15] See Table 17-2 for vote by groups for President.

percent of the Republicans did so.[16] Concisely, the Democrats retained their national congressional majorities but saw in the ranks of support for their presidential nominee erosion that would have to be recouped to establish presidential majorities. The Republicans also controlled thirty governorships including those of nearly all the large states. By capturing two more governorships from Democrats in 1969, the Republicans began the 1970s in control of thirty-two state houses.

SYNOPTIC VIEW

Elections Differentiated. A historical survey of elections shows each possessing different characteristics. Yet there are discernible types which one group of scholars sees as *realigning, maintaining, deviating* and *reinstating.*[17] Rarely do extensive shifts of voter preferences from one party to the other take place. When they do, as in the 1860s and 1930s, realignments occur that persist for quite some time. The majority of elections maintain the same party, keeping it in power for a long time. Short-term circumstances and a popular opposition candidate such as Eisenhower may lead many voters to defect momentarily from the majority; 1952 and 1956 afford examples of deviating elections. Serious trouble within the major party leading to a third-party challenge has also resulted in deviation, as in 1912 and 1968. After the deviation, the dominant majority has reinstated itself as in 1896, 1920, and 1960.

There is a perceptible short-term tendency for the party in power to suffer a loss of seats in Congress in midterm elections.[18] The election of 1934 is the sole example in modern times in which the party controlling the Presidency and Congress augmented its majorities in both houses of Congress in midterm.

Until more extensive study has been made, we shall have to be content with recognizing that shifts of power between the national parties and changes of party preference and identification on the voter's part which are so important in bringing it about are complex. Prosperity, depression, political protest, wars and international tensions, and attractive, charismatic candidates are contributory. Influences such as the political activities of organized labor, public relations, power to purchase mass-communication publicity, reapportionment, and patronage may also extend or shorten longevity of dominance of a national or state party. A party's rule ends when its support deteriorates to a point at which enough voters are attracted to the opposition party to enable it to win the Presidency (or the governorship in the case of a state party). The challenge to the student of government is to ascertain the reasons

[16]See figures in *The New York Times*, Dec. 8, 1968.
[17]See Angus Campbell, Philip E. Converse, Warren E. Miller, and Donald E. Stokes, *The American Voter*, John Wiley & Sons, Inc., New York, 1960, chap. 19.
[18]A table and elaboration of this point if found in Chap. 18.

for the loss of strength, the causes of factionalism, and the loss of popularity that lead to the breakup of the majority party.

Since the 1830s, the two-party system has been so thoroughly established that only infrequently is it unable to crowd out minor parties. The two parties in presidential races have averaged between them about 95 percent of the total vote. However, on occasions the two major parties have not been able to accommodate a bloc of voters, and they defected to a third party.

Reform Tradition in America. The Nixon victory in 1968, as the Eisenhower triumph in 1952, appeared to bring to an end another reform period under an activist Democratic President. The reform tradition in this century has carried along the legacy of William Jennings Bryan who brought populism to the Democratic party in 1896. Although he was a loser's loser, having been thrice nominated and defeated for President, he had an enormous impact on the Democratic party and the nation and saw many of his proposed reforms enacted. Theodore Roosevelt and his supporters captured the Republican party and between 1902 and 1908 moved toward progressivism, with Mr. Roosevelt having the effect of forcing Wilson to move further left toward the urban reform movement.

The only time in this century that the progressive wing has controlled a Republican presidency was under Theodore Roosevelt and, to a lesser extent, William Howard Taft who, in Roosevelt's view, betrayed the cause. The presidencies of Harding, Coolidge, Hoover, and Eisenhower represented moratoriums or periods of consolidation rather than innovation. Wilson, Franklin Roosevelt, Harry S. Truman, John F. Kennedy, and Lyndon B. Johnson carried on the reform tradition with innovative proposals designed to meet the demands of urban reformers.

The progressive tradition in American is a deep-seated one and has made its greatest strides in this century under strong presidential leadership. In general, progressives have chosen to function through one of the two parties, more often the Democrats. They have been willing to use the powers of government to aid the underprivileged, to fight monopoly, to obtain greater social security, and to regulate those who appear to be abusing private power. A small group of Marxists function as a wing of reform and choose the course of minor-party politics. Unlike the majority of progressives, they advocate radical change in or the abolition of existing institutions. Most reformers have accepted the general societal values and work to modify existing institutions rather than to substitute socialism for capitalism or to champion radical governmental reorganizations.

Nationalization of American Politics. In concluding this review of basic forces in American politics, we think it imperative to mention the movement toward nationalization. Although this trend has been evident since the beginning of the Republic, the pace has been faster at some times than at others. Nationalization has crumbled the old sectionalism without completely dispelling it as a force for political cleavage and socialization. The growing industrialization and urbanization that began in the nineteenth century fostered a more national outlook. Improved transportation and the great migrations and redistributions of populations brought new viewpoints to all sections. Labor unionism and the increasingly higher standard of living and level of education were antagonistic to viewpoints based on geography alone. Although sectionalism helps pull class interests together, class interests cut across and soften sectional lines. In a word, the older separatisms caused by sectional viewpoints are giving way to class and ethnic divisions. Many problems formerly handled by local politics have been transferred to the national government or to a nation-state settlement.

The causes of this nationalization are manifold. Foreign affairs plunged the United States into leadership of the free world, and it required a great allocation of national resources to fight the world wars and to wage a cold war from South Vietnam to Korea to Berlin. The race into space has placed very heavy demands on the federal government. The great increase in the social as well as geographic mobility of the population made such explosive issues as civil rights a national problem in which great contenders for power sought national solutions from the President, the Congress, and the federal courts. Pressure groups created national headquarters, adopted national programs and industry-wide proposals, and sought federal intervention for programs believed to be of benefit to their members.

The technological revolutions in communications such as the mass newspaper, syndicated news columnists, and network radio and television helped nationalize information and opinions. The great increase in the number of automobiles brought demands for more and better superhighways, with the national government appropriating billions for road building. Congress found itself involved with legislation on crime, kidnapping, reclamation, building high dams, labor-management relations, public health, farm surpluses, federal aid to education, and medical care for the aged — to mention but a few of the great issues.

The moving of political issues into the federal battleground has been due also to an inability or an unwillingness of the states to cope with local problems. As states could not handle relief and welfare problems, groups looked elsewhere, usually to national authority. City officials are found bypassing the state legislatures, which they may consider unrepresentative of their interests, and going directly to the national government.

Despite the pressures for increased federal power or federal-state coordinate effort, the struggle over states' rights will continue, as in the past, to provide the opportunity for much oratory in and outside the government. People often exhibit a strong pride in their immediate area of residence, and they value freedom of local action. The theme of localism has constantly recurred since 1800, and there is no diminution in sight for the historic debates in the American polity over state versus national activity.

From this brief analysis of the background of American politics we look at the operation of the party system.

FOR FURTHER READING

There are scores of political biographies of Presidents and works on individual elections which shed much light on the historical development of political parties and cleavages.

Agar, Herbert: *The Price of Union*, 1945.
Blum, John M.: *The Republican Roosevelt*, 1967.
Bowers, Claude: *The Party Battles of the Jackson Period*, 1922.
Burdette, Franklin L.: *The Republican Party: A Short History*, 1968.
Chambers, William N.: *The Democrats: 1789–1964*, 1964.
Glad, Paul W.: *The Trumpet Soundeth: William Jennings Bryan and His Democracy, 1896–1912*, 1960.
Goldman, Ralph: *The Democratic Party in American Politics*, 1966.
Graham, Otis L.: *An Encore for Reform: The Old Progressives and the New Deal*, 1967.
Hofstadter, Richard: *The Age of Reform*, 1955.
Hollingsworth, J. R.: *The Whirligig of Politics: The Democracy of Cleveland and Bryan*, 1963.
Jones, Charles O.: *The Republican Party*, 1965.
Joyner, Conrad: *The Republican Dilemma*, 1963.
Mayer, George H.: *The Republican Party*, 1964.
Moos, Malcolm: *The Republicans*, 1956.
Nichols, Roy F.: *The Invention of American Political Parties*, 1967.
Porter, K. A., and D. B. Johnson: *National Party Platforms, 1840–1960*, 1961.

PART TWO **PARTY SYSTEMS**

CHAPTER 3 **THE NATIONAL TWO-PARTY SYSTEM**

A familiar refrain of this volume is that American major parties are multipurpose and multifunctional and operate within the context of a highly pluralistic society. In serving democratic government, parties provide a channel through which citizens can influence the course of public policy and are the basic instrument in furnishing the personnel for the great decision-making positions in government. The party-sponsored legislators and popularly elected executives select judges and administrators and at times are influenced by party patronage considerations.

The two large parties are simultaneously agents of change and agents of preservation. They serve the American penchant for stability in the midst of change. At one time, one party is dominant and the other at low ebb; at another time there is a reversal of positions. The majority party assumes the responsibility for putting public policies into effect.

In democratic societies, the majority is often helped by the minority party in this endeavor. At other times, the minority refuses to accept the majority's proposals and forces a public debate and discussion of the proposals and of the record of the party in office. The defeated party then performs the function of surveillance over the holders of public office and has the power to give or to refuse approbation to the majority's actions.

The minority party may not be able, by opposition, to stop the enactment of the majority's program, but the latter cannot be defended as consensus but as the majority's position. The degree of approval of the minority party (assuming the high unity of the majority) represents in effect the degree of consensus.

With the exception of the 1860s, party officeholders in Congress have been able to manage conflict and bring about political change with a minimum of violence. Parties are instruments whereby citizens may influence, if not control, the actions of their leaders. The American major parties are great aggregations of interests useful among other things in building consensus. They afford one means of connecting and relating the individual to his government. In addition to proposing candidates for public office and trying to elect them, parties do other things in varying degrees with varying success. They contribute to political socialization and transmit political values and information. They symbolize political points of view and help establish rules of the game for completion and for the political system.

Because of the congeries of activities and functions performed by diverse groups known as parties in various countries on various levels, the conceptualization and definition of parties is not always so easily defined as one might expect. As observed in Chapter 1, there may be more than one criterion, and a given party may not fulfill all the criteria. One element characteristic of all groups that scholars designate as political parties is the putting forth of candidates for elective public office. Some European writers place a further limitation by saying a group must compete for election of members to a legislature. The definition would rule out many minor parties in the United States, because they contest only the Presidency. The broader definition, therefore, meets our definitional need better.

Conceptualization is further complicated by the fact that parties have several egos and in nearly every country at least three are discernible: the party-in-the-country, the party of the activists, and the party officeholders. In the United States, the party-in-the-government is further divided into a legislative and an executive unit. The bureaucracy and the judiciary are also influenced by parties in various ways. Despite the tripartite character and necessary interrelationships of all these party egos, convenience dictates that each be treated separately. This chapter examines the general components of the national party system in the United States and the role of minor parties. Chapter 4 examines state parties and, for purposes of comparison, parties under other systems of government. Subsequent sections will review the party as represented by its organization and in the government.

ENVIRONMENTAL INFLUENCES ON PARTIES

General context. Parties operate within a context of a social environment and a political system. If they are to survive and be effective they must recognize and adjust to a climate of politics and the temper of the times within which they must exist. American major parties have learned that they must be flexible, essentially nondoctrinaire and pragmatic, ever sensitive to changing conditions and to historic processes and issues. Unless they adapt to these realities, they invite defeat.

The knowledgeable party leaders are aware of the public's general ambivalence in attitude toward parties. People combine favorable and unfavorable norms and impressions about political parties. One study, for example, found that only about 13 percent of the respondents were strongly supportive of the present party system.[1] More than half believed parties confused more than clarified issues and that they created conflict more often than not when none had existed. A majority opposed the idea of tax deductions for political contributions and cohesive, responsible parties. At the same time, a great majority rejected the idea of making all elections nonpartisan by removing party labels from the ballot and felt that democracy "works best" when there is "strong party competition."

Public attitudes of this kind are important to parties in formulating campaign strategies, seeking financial support, and in the recruiting of party personnel. Many local environments are more friendly (or hostile) to party activity than others; this appears especially true in suburbs.

Parties are competitors with other political organizations such as interest groups, special election groups, civic leaders, and various local political elites. They are rivals for all kinds of political resources including manpower, skills, support from communications media, and, very importantly, money. They compete for public favor or good will. During legislative sessions interest groups press the party's lawmakers for support for certain policies that may or may not be favored by large numbers of the general supporters of the party. As a result of the pluralistic system, horizontal linkages with nonparty political organizations and elites must be established. In addition, the parties must develop vertical

[1] Jack Dennis, "Support for the Party System by the Mass Public," *American Political Science Review*, vol. 60, pp. 600–615, 1966.

linkages and communications arrangements between the various levels of their own structures.

If parties are to be viable and long-lived, they must function within an imposed political framework, even while they may be trying to alter the outward forms of the framework. British parties must live under a unitary government, and Canadians must function in a federal system. Norwegian and Italian parties operate within a parliamentary system whereas American and Mexican parties live with a presidential framework. Government structure modifies and tends to mold the patterns of party organization, leadership, and activity. Although the general role and purposes of political parties resemble each other in all free societies, their character and emphasis show much variation from nation to nation.[2]

Constitutional Framework. When the fathers of the Constitution decided on a federal system, they in effect provided for many arenas for the contesting for power — national, state, congressional, county, judicial, and diverse municipal and local constituencies. In thirty-five states, governors are chosen during nonpresidential election years. City elections are often held at different times from those for the state legislature and cover different constituencies as well. As a result, party organizations perforce must constantly prepare for some election from the sheriff or county commissioner up to the President. Further, in each election the ballot is likely to be long, calling for the election of candidates for from ten to as many as fifty public offices. Many of the offices, moreover, are remote from national issues and struggles.

The federal system is composed of fifty different sets of state parties that are independent alliances of local interests. The Constitution accentuates a politics of fragmented, decentralized power and organization. Congressmen and senators are products of local group alliances and parties. Their reelection depends in varying degrees on the strength of their local alliances with groups and the party whose name they bear. Their initial election is rarely dependent on the activities of the national party organization. In addition, the issues that provide a national party identity may not be very consequential to a candidate in his own congressional district. National issues, moreover, may be without appeal in local party circles. Congressmen are therefore often highly independent of the national party organization and at times of their county and town organizations as well.

---

[2] Literature on party systems is extensive. Three useful general works showing many different bases of parties throughout the world are Maurice Duverger, *Political Parties*, John Wiley & Sons, Inc., New York, 1954; Joseph La Palombara and Myron Weiner (eds.), *Political Parties and Political Development*, Princeton University Press, Princeton, N.J., 1966; Sigmund Neumann (ed.), *Modern Political Parties*, The University of Chicago Press, Chicago, 1956.

Division of authority into executive, legislative, and judicial sections, at both national and state levels, further complicates and atomizes the party system. Bicameralism adds complexity for the political system both in Congress and in the state legislatures. In a number of states, members of the two houses are chosen from different constituencies or for different terms. With different constituencies for the executive, the representative, and the senate, proliferated party organization becomes virtually imperative. Multiple organization capable of concentrating on the particular needs of the diverse constituencies is required. Manifestly, if a party is to operate harmoniously in campaigns, cooperation, coordination, and liaison must exist among the organizational units. In many states, judges are chosen on a partisan ballot, and parties are most anxious to elect their men in order to obtain judicial patronage. At the local level, therefore, the court positions become involved in partisan politics, and in some states there are party conventions and organizations whose primary effort is the nomination and electing of judges.

Because the Constitution has widely distributed power and because state and local governments in turn insist on placing so many offices and propositions on the ballot, the voter is required to focus his attention on a wide range of elections and problems. He takes less interest in the election of state and local officers whose duties appear to be administrative and custodial. Great policy decisions made at the national level captivate his interest. Important decisions are made at the local level, too, but it is not easy for the citizen to separate the trivia from the important, and the significance of a single election is obscured because there are multiple elections. State and local party organizations are forced to combat this diffusion of the voters' attention and interest in diverse offices and elections.

A most important mission for parties under a separation of powers system is to seek control of both executive and legislative branches of the government in order to avoid potential deadlock. It is their function to try to integrate the programs of these two branches of the government by furnishing personnel who, at least in label, are of the same political faith. Bicameral legislative bodies can be better integrated if a single party captures a majority in both houses, but a party winning the Presidency often fails to win or retain control of Congress. In this century, Presidents Taft, Wilson, Hoover, Truman, Eisenhower, and Nixon faced, during a part of their terms, a Congress dominated by the opposition.

Although political parties arose outside specific constitutional sanction, laws and constitutions have had profound effects on the operation, activity, and function of parties. Three constitutional amendments lifting restrictions on black and female suffrage and calling for direct election of United States senators resulted in substantial broadening of party organization and activities. The Twenty-second Amendment limited the president to two terms, thereby forcing a change in leadership in the party office. Congress has had before it many proposals for changing the system of electing the President.

Congress has left national conventions and party organization unregulated but has recognized and regulated parties in other ways. The Hatch Act prohibits federal employees from engaging actively in partisan affairs. Limitations on the amount of money spent by political committees and by individual candidates for Congress have been imposed. Corrupt practices legislation dates back to the beginning of the century with the prohibition of political contributions by corporations. This ruling was later extended to include labor unions. Congress also has required the independent regulatory commissions to be bipartisan. Congress perennially conducts investigations and publishes reports on campaign donations, expenditures, and practices.

It was well into the nineteenth century before the states embarked on the regulation of parties. The first measures were designed to prevent fraud and manipulation of nominating conventions. Mandatory direct primary laws were enacted after 1900, greatly influencing the nominating process. Most states also enacted corrupt practices legislation to cover state and local elections. In most states today laws specify how certain party officials such as precinct committeemen are to be elected. State laws usually prescribe biparty election boards and require party committees to make recommendations for the filling of public offices prematurely vacated. Parties are permitted to prescribe their own rules and in general are recognized in law as semipublic institutions. Yet a great deal of party activity remains unregulated. Legislatures have tended to follow a laissez-faire attitude toward parties, believing that they can function best if unfettered by statutory controls.

The courts, particularly the federal ones, have opened the way for statutory control by reversing earlier decisions that held that parties were essentially *private*, not official agencies. Southern legislatures had treated parties as private clubs reserving the right to exclude blacks and others from the party and from participation in the primaries. Beginning in 1944, the Supreme Court held that when a state permits a party to conduct a primary, it makes the party action a state or public one.[3] In 1947 a circuit court recognized that at one time a party may have been a private aggregation of individuals, "but with the passage of years, political parties have become state institutions, governmental agencies through which sovereign power is exercised by the people."[4]

[3] *Smith v. Allwright*, 321 U.S. 649 (1944).
[4] *Rice v. Elmore*, 165 F. 2d 387 (1947).

To conclude, the Constitution forced the parties into a geographic–electoral unit pattern of organization. In order to approximate effective control of government, a party must capture both houses of Congress as well as the Presidency. Public law, both national and local, has established the framework and has even prescribed many of the details for party contests for power. Although the Constitution has had its impact on the party system, the parties in turn have had their influence on the operation of the Constitution. Parties drastically changed the system envisaged for the election of the President, without the necessity of amending the Constitution. Through their organization of Congress, parties strongly influence the legislative process. Many Presidents have used their party as an instrument of vigorous leadership. To a considerable extent, our major parties are what they are because of the Constitution. Conversely, the constitutional system is in part what it is because of energies and goals of the major parties. The party system in any modern democratic society cannot be fully understood without reference to the constitutional-legal basis of the nation; similarly, the parties are agents providing meaning and vitality to the laws and to the constitutional arrangements of the political society. E. E. Schattschneider likened American parties to "the river of American politics" and the Constitution to the "river bed." The latter is the "firm land whose contour shapes the stream." Although the river is "the prisoner of the land" through which it flows, the river nonetheless "can transform the landscape."[5]

CAUSES OF DUALITY

Even more conspicuous than the extraconstitutional character of the American party system is its national bipartisan nature. Starting with the Democratic-Whig era, there have always been minor parties in the United States, but usually they have been very small and unimportant. On the rare occasions when a minor party achieved substantial strength, it seldom survived one or two elections. Although conditions have radically changed as have party alignments, American bimodal arrangements at the national level have never been seriously threatened. The electoral system, custom, and psychology have contributed to the origin and maintenance of two major coalitions.

The Electoral System. Congressional representation is based largely on the single-member, geographical district. Whoever wins a plurality (more votes than anyone else) is elected; he need not poll a majority to win. This tends to crowd out the smaller parties since they are unable to get representation in proportion to the votes polled for their candidates. Third parties generally find that if they are to get any of their

[5] *Party Government*, Holt, Rinehart and Winston, Inc., New York, 1942, p. 124.

candidates into public office, they will have to follow one of two courses. One is to merge with one of the two major parties as the Farmer-Laborites did in Minnesota; the other is to retain independent identity but to be satisfied with endorsing one of the major-party candidates.

By the same logic, the Electoral College system of electing the President has a bipolarizing effect. Under the general-ticket, winner-take-all arrangement, one presidential nominee gets all a state's votes.[6] Minor-party candidates, therefore, have little chance to poll a plurality of popular votes and win a state's electoral votes. Numerous Southerners have advocated an unpledged electoral system which would leave electors free to vote for a minor-party candidate or swing behind the major-party candidate most congenial to their views. The present general-ticket method leads strategists to think of carrying combinations of states that will give them a majority of electoral votes. Change in the electoral strategy would undoubtedly result from alteration of the present system. Dissatisfaction is periodically expressed with the Electoral College, leading Congress to study changes that would avoid the possibility of the choice being made by the House of Representatives.

A major argument against changing the general-ticket pledged-elector system is that it would tend to splinter combinations seeking the Presidency.[7] Four major proposals for reform are widely discussed and have their proponents in Congress—the automatic system, proportional plan, the district system, and direct popular vote. The automatic system would keep the winner-take-all practice but would abolish the actual office of elector so that a state's popular plurality would be translated into a unanimous electoral vote from the state thus removing the chance of an elector voting for someone who did not carry the state. This reform is the least radical and could still result in a person being elected President without carrying a majority or plurality of the nation's popular vote. A 40 percent electoral plurality for election would avoid in most cases the probability of placing the decision in the hands of the House of Representatives. Campaign strategy under this change would be altered but little from past practice.

Under a proportional plan, a split-state electoral vote would be made in proportion to the state's popular vote, with a 40 percent plurality of the national electoral vote sufficient to elect a President. A high-water mark of support for this plan (known as the Lodge-Gossett

[6] Occasionally an elector will decide to cast his ballot for someone other than the winner of state's popular vote. One elector broke the pledge to Truman, one to Stevenson (1956), and one to Nixon in both 1960 and 1968.

[7] Literature on alternative systems for electing the President is very extensive and only brief summary treatment is included here. For an extensive analysis of alternatives, arguments for and against each, and discussion of problems in specific elections of the past, see Neal R. Peirce, *The People's President: The Electoral College in American History and the Direct-Vote Alternative*, Simon and Schuster, Inc., New York, 1968.

amendment) came in 1950 when it received more than a two-thirds majority in the Senate. The plan had much support from Democrats and most moderate Republicans but was opposed by conservative Republicans.

A plan more to the liking of conservatives in Congress is the district plan, which provides for the choice of one elector in each congressional district with the remainder of a state's allotment chosen at large. Conservatives, so the argument goes, would win in many districts in small states and frequently might win more electors in large states than their percentage of the statewide vote would justify. Malapportioned congressional districts would, of course, have their effect. States as units would probably cease to be targets of special campaign efforts to a lesser extent than under the other two plans. Because the system appears to favor small-state, rural conservatism, it would dilute big-state, urban liberalism. Peirce estimates that in 1960 "Nixon would have been the clear winner under a district system—278 electoral votes to 245."[8]

Although hundreds of amendments have appeared in Congress since 1876 favoring direct popular vote for President, the greatest interest and support for it has been since 1960. This was partly due to the close elections of 1960 and 1968 and to the possibilities of potential disparities between popular and electoral votes of those plans retaining the electoral vote in some form. Undoubtedly campaign strategies would undergo revision with a direct popular system in which states would not be treated as separate voting blocs. A direct popular election amendment passed the House of Representatives in 1969 and President Nixon announced he would accept the plan.

Changing the system of electing the President has been slowed because Congress has been unable to reach the large agreement necessary for proposing a constitutional amendment. The plans are viewed in terms of whether they give advantage to the small or large states, liberalism or conservatism, small-town or big-city interests, favor Republicans or Democrats, or disturb too greatly the calculations of managers of presidential campaigns. Whether the threat is real or fancied, there are congressmen who fear "reform" will be to the advantage of third parties and to the detriment of two-party presidential politics.

Psychological Factors.   The electoral structure is not the only factor working in favor of limiting the major parties to two in number. In many state legislative districts two or more representatives are chosen at the same election, yet third parties have not fared well in these multimembered constituencies. However, the election goes to those polling the highest number of votes. If a system of proportional representation were used,

[8]*Ibid.,* p. 163.

third parties would probably be more encouraged to try for the election of one of their members in some constituencies.

The biparty system in the United States is strongly rooted in history, custom, and psychology. Colonists were for or against the Declaration of Independence and then for or against the ratification of the Constitution. Rivalry followed between Jefferson and Hamilton, the Anti-Federalists and the Federalists, and two-party contests took place from 1796 through 1816. With the Whig-Democratic struggles, the bimodal habit patterns became well established, and the nation and party system survived the multiparty split of 1860. The aftermath of the Civil War further solidified the nation into two major political camps.

The lack of a sharp class consciousness and attachment to the doctrine of the separation of church and state tended to discourage class and religious parties. Voters have not taken kindly to agrarian and labor parties. The two-party habit is so entrenched now that voters tend to regard support of a minor-party candidate as throwing their vote away. Millions of voters with middle-class outlooks and values consider minor parties radical, extremist, and fringe. They see the major parties as best representing the principles, goals, and stability of the vast majority of the citizenry. Two parties appear to satisfy the voters as offering a moderate liberalism or a moderate conservatism as needed at a particular time.

There are intensely practical considerations which militate against the building of a large, durable, and successful minor party. During the past generation there have been attempts, often with much fanfare, to launch a new national party. Immediately sponsors were confronted with raising the millions of dollars necessary to conduct campaigns and operate parties. Practical men asked what chance the new party had and what payoff might be expected for donors. Third parties have a problem of attracting talent. Where can it find well-known men and women of good repute to become its organizational activists or who will run for office under its label? Persons aspiring to a political career tend to become Republicans or Democrats as the most likely if not the only road to election. Those expecting rewards in terms of jobs or other benefits are unlikely to find incentives in working for a new or third party. The two-party legislatures are interested in perpetuating the values and election laws that preserve the status quo and keep serious third-party challenges from possible success. Third parties find that state laws make it difficult for their candidates to get on the ballot.

The broad consensus of Americans over the prevailing social, economic, and political values and institutions is believed important in keeping out strong third parties bent on fundamentally changing the private enterprise economy and the constitutional arrangement for separation of powers and federalism. Contests occur between the "ins" and the "outs" and the two-party "we-they" choices seem sufficient most of the time to bring about changes in public policy without resort to third-party politics. All of these factors—electoral, ideological, cultural, and pragmatic—conspire to retain the two-party system as the national pattern. Similar factors favor duality in the great majority of the states, though a few function with essentially one-party or multiparty arrangements.

PARTY MEMBERSHIP AND FACTIONALISM

Universality of Membership. In a two-party system each party must make the widest possible appeal. All shades of economic and political opinion and persons from all walks of life are found in each party, although not in equal proportions. The American major parties are mass rather than elite parties and broadly middle class rather than narrowly occupational or religious. Policies are important to Republicans and Democrats in attracting new constituents. It is hoped that, once attracted, the new adherents will become permanent members, even though the party's leaders, organization, and policies undergo change.

Once established, party images can be used and exploited for years—an example of the social lag one finds in political society. Democrats since the Depression have traded on their party's image of helping the poor, bringing about better times, and being the party of the "little man." Republicans have employed for years the image of hard money, balanced budget, and sound policies in managing and encouraging the economy. Yet each party appeals to every segment of the voting public (save the Communists), insisting that it can best fulfill the desire for peace and prosperity. A party can retain its membership by old war cries and shibboleths, while developing new policies and emphases. New members may also be obtained by appealing to the past as well as by holding certain prospects for the future.

Where there is competition between the parties, the leaders and candidates desire to expand their followings and broaden their coalitions. Membership begets membership; members recruit friends and relatives into the party. Many people are attracted to a party because of the popularity of its leaders and candidates. Parties are multipurpose, and people become affiliated with them not only because of issues and policies but also because of personal loyalty and tradition and for reasons of conviviality and friendship.

There are no accepted criteria of what constitutes party membership. Does it refer to the voting coalition on election day? Is there a distinction between loyal party membership and mere affiliation? Is membership limited to those within the ranks who are active in party activities? "Legal" membership is necessary for voting in the party's primary in those states using the closed primary system, but in about one-fourth of the states there are no such tests for affiliation. In some states one is required to take an oath when he registers that he will support the party's nominees at the next general election. One may become a Democrat or Republican by attending meetings, caucuses, or social functions. He may become a Republican or Democrat by doing none of the above but by simply proclaiming himself to be one.

In a word, party affiliation is a casual affair consisting more of an attitude than a formal act. Voters do not apply for membership, pay no dues except perhaps to a party club, and are not expected to carry a membership card. Even in those states that require party enrollment in order to vote in the primary, there is no way to compel voters to refrain from supporting candidates of the opposite party in the general election. Millions of people fail to register for the primary, and large numbers so registered have so little interest in the party's nominees that they fail to participate in the primary. Except for racial barriers in some areas, it is easy to enter into political party life and easy to leave it and to go over to the opposition party if one wishes. Many persons are sporadic in their affiliation and activity.

Categories of Membership. The composition of a party is not a completely ambiguous matter, however. If we think of a party as a coalition at election time, the membership can be broadly categorized. There are four major groups, three of which constitute the party-in-the-electorate. The first group can be thought of as the inner core—the party politicians, the leaders and subleaders, who in their official capacities give the time, effort, and often considerable money to run the organization between as well as during campaigns. A subgroup within the inner core is composed of the party's officeholders who hold the responsibility for the party's record in government and consequently for much of the party's future. Even though a party's officials and its public officeholders are to some extent two different groups, both have the common objective of winning the next election, and both regard themselves as the wielders of power central to decision making within the party. Powerful officeholding incumbents sometimes remain aloof from the party organization and as such are neither party activists nor necessarily members of the elite circle.

A second group may be designated as the loyal partisans who, although not active party workers, are strongly oriented toward a given party. A third group, numerically larger, are those who have a weak or nominal party identification. These often split their party tickets and can be lured away from their party faith by an attractive opposition candidate or by an issue of deep significance to them. Finally, there are the so-called independents who publicly avow no reasoned or emotional involvement with either party but vote for the best man. Many self-classified independents privately have a party faith, and the true independents devoid of party attachment are probably a good deal smaller in number than is popularly believed.

Factions. The various constitutional, pluralistic, and psychological factors in American politics contribute to the growth of factions. Factionalism is found at one time or another in most political interest groups but is especially persistent in political parties. Where parties are concerned, the term *faction* applies to a group or an element within a party organization which appears to have a set of interests distinguishing the group from other groups. Some factions are permanent, others transient and fleeting; some want to capture control of the party, others are content merely to try to influence the party by making their voices heard and concerns known. There are several types and causes of factions.

One type of factionalism is more or less inherent in the constitutional division of powers between the national government and the states and in the separation of powers in both levels of government. We have seen that in the electoral process a member of Congress, in the final analysis, owes his power and election to the people in his own district and not to such an amorphous group as a national party. The President, on the other hand, has a national constituency, and his strength is built on great combinations of voters and interests. Some interest groups call for national action, while others demand states' rights. The former are apt to cluster around the President, hoping that he will by patronage, prestige, and other methods push their programs through Congress. Opposing forces find that the congressional and local parties are potentially effective agencies in opposing centralization. The presidential and congressional wings of the party serve as bases for potential factional struggles. Governors and the members of their party in the state legislature frequently provide a similar setting for intrastate party factions.

We find great sectional conflicts at the national level, such as that between the Northern and Southern Democrats and the less pronounced but nonetheless evident Midwest-East factionalism within the Republican party. In both parties the struggles break out in nearly every national convention and are ameliorated in compromises over planks in the platform and in nominations for President and Vice President. Sectional factionalism also manifests itself at times on congressional roll calls and in battles over party leadership.

James Madison in *The Federalist* saw "the various and unequal distribution of property" as "the most common and durable source of factions." Madison's observation holds true today, although it would be stated in somewhat different terms. Ideology and shared values of some of the members lead them to act together both formally and informally in an effort to translate their goals into party policy. The familiar left and right wings and liberals and conservatives serve as a basis for splits. Intellectuals, businessmen, and working-class leaders are among those who have an affinity of interest and program and seek to make their influence felt within the party. Sometimes they concentrate only on platforms and programs; at other times they take an active interest in candidates and seek to win places for them in the primaries and elections.

A great deal of factionalism cannot be explained in clear-cut terms such as ideology, program, boss rule, personal devotion, and geography. A host of psychological factors fused with these contributes to factions. Personality clashes and dissatisfaction over patronage distribution may be rationalized as differences due to principle. Where one group has ruled for a long time and has naturally made some enemies, it may be dubbed the Old Guard. Old Guard Republicanism, however, is freely associated with conservatism and, whatever the reason, is subject to challenge by the Young Turks. Although not often publicly acknowledged, ethnic, racial, and religious backgrounds provide a bond for groups within the party. These have come to demand recognition either in patronage or on the ticket if not both. Timing between the gradualists and those demanding "socialism in our time" caused sharp quarrels in the British Labour party. Less severe strife has occurred over timing within American politics, but it has nonetheless occasionally appeared.

Finally, the tripartite nature of American parties leads to factionalism. Organizational activists and the party's public officials are often in disagreement over prerogatives, strategies, public policies, and leadership. Factions have existed within the various segments of the government party since the inception of parties, and, they sometimes seriously threaten the party's program or electoral successes. One recalls the Hamilton war Federalists and the Adams peace Federalists, Radicals in Lincoln's administration, the Bull Moose Republicans, the McCarthy "dove" Democrats as a few examples.

Whatever the causes and rationalizations for intraparty rivalries, it is the function of professional politicians and often of the middle-of-the-roaders to seek conciliation and adjustments in order to promote unity—especially during campaigns. They may need to go to interest groups or prominant members in the electorate party for help in promoting cohesion or to minimize the strength of a debilitating group that especially threatens the party's fortunes. Much factionalism is discontinuous; it is ephemeral and disappears after successful mediation or with the passage of certain personalities from the scene. Power and authority within the party may be redistributed, thereby disposing of the claims of one faction but sowing the seeds for another. Factionalism is not *ipso facto* harmful to a party. It is inevitable and a consequence of universality of membership. If multifactionalism were impossible within the major parties, the only recourse might be the creation of multiple parties. Factionalism is a logical attribute of a two-party system. Even within the multiple small parties with restricted membership, factions arise.

PROGRAMMATIC CONSEQUENCES OF A TWO-PARTY SYSTEM

Opinion surveys indicate that countless Americans are not only unsophisticated but also uninformed and indifferent about the way their constitutional system operates and often lack understanding of specific substantive issues. They are relatively satisfied with their lots and, unlike their European brothers, have not been consigned to a class. Most citizens are usually pragmatic without realizing it. Politicians believe that the voters possess a common set of values and outlooks, which most are wont to see as a euphoric Americanism. These attitudes make so-called consensus or a common body of agreement easier than if the reverse or the absence of them were true. Negatively, there is the appearance of consensus when there is an absence of widespread, articulate disagreement over the norms that presumably almost everyone accepts. Politicians assume that the electorate shares many beliefs, opinions, and ways of thinking — or what is rather imprecisely called a common ideology. It is not surprising, therefore, that both parties purport to embrace it and appeal to it.

President Franklin D. Roosevelt once spoke of his views as "a little left of center." President Dwight D. Eisenhower styled himself a "moderate" and spoke of steering his administration "a little right of center." Both men were enormously popular as personalities, but it is also highly probable that substantial numbers of adherents agreed with each Presidents' perceived location on the political spectrum at the time he held office. Opposition oratory to the contrary, Roosevelt did not lead the nation into socialism and public ownership of the means of production any more than Eisenhower set the nation on the road to sharp decentralization or dark reaction. In retrospect, both men catered to the broad center, one somewhat to the left, the other somewhat to the right. In so doing, they reflected the reality of the distribution of voter attitudes in a political society characterized by a high degree of ideological agreement.

The Broad Center Model.   We may think of American political attitudes, preferences, and values as the model shown in Figure 3-1. At the extreme left are only a comparatively few voters, and the same with the extreme right. (The extreme left and extreme right, however, need not balance each other and probably never do.) As one moves from the right toward the center or from the left toward the center, the number of voters increases. The bulk of voters are to be found between numbers 2 and 4, and further away from center the number declines. Obviously, if a party wishes to win, it needs to appeal to the large center since there are many fewer votes to be won or lost either at the extreme left or at the extreme right. If the curve were different and showed the big bulge not near the center but well toward the right or left side or if the curve were inverted and indicated two huge voting blocs, one to the left, the other to the right, then the appeals of the two parties would be profoundly affected. In the first case both parties would feel that they would have to move sharply left or sharply right to bid for votes. If the second supposition were true, then one party would likely be strongly leftist, and the other strongly rightist. But since the bulge is in the center, if they are to win, the two major parties must orient their ideology and appeals toward the center. Unless there is a sharp shift in public sentiment toward the right or the left, the major parties would find it risky to direct their appeals strongly in either direction.

The task for each party is to try to make a bid to those between 2 and 4 and, if possible, to get some votes between 0 and 2 and between 4 and 6 or at least to keep such voters from forming a third party, which might siphon some votes from those who are between 2 and 4 on the spectrum. At the national level the Democrats have found that extreme leftists are as unhappy with them as the extreme rightists are with the Republicans. Some of the prominent members of each party at times

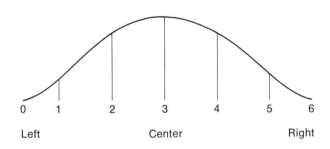

FIGURE 3-1   Distribution of voters by ideological preferences

make statements that please one or the other of the poles. This may help to preserve bimodal voting by persuading the extremists to decide to stay with the party and vote for its candidates rather than refrain from voting or vote for a third-party candidate. Statements of right-wing Republicans and left-wing Democrats, in other words, help keep the more extreme voters in their respective parties, however restive they may be with the moderates who are in the majority in both parties.

Models of this kind are never perfect, and care must be taken that they are not oversimplified. We cannot, for example, precisely define "center" or what is a "little left" or a "little right" of it, nor can we easily define "ultraliberal" or "radical right." It is also next to impossible to determine very accurately the numbers of voters in each of the categories used. Even so, the diagram helps show the pressures toward and the probable results of a bimodal system of parties.

Two parties offer voters only two effective choices, neither of which may give voters at the far ends of the spectrum what they want in the way of ideology. But they give them a chance to support someone who can legitimately exercise political authority. On the other hand, a scattergram distribution of voters shows density around the political center and sparseness toward the peripheries. As long as this propensity for the center exists, the two parties will tend to converge in their ideologies, although the convergence is never complete and need not be so in order to maintain stability of the political order.

Wideness and Ambiguity of Program. In terms of public policies, each major party casts longing eyes toward all major voting groups—farmers, laborers, businessmen, senior citizens, ethnic and religious groups, and veterans. Both platforms promise something to each group, although what is offered is not necessarily the same. One party may promise more to a given group than another at a given time, but both parties are likely to invade the other's territory with blandishments for votes. One party may be stationed slightly to the left of center, and the other to the right, and in fact, this is likely to be the case. Yet each party will cross the center line well over to the other's side and at times make a special effort to get the votes of some extremists. Both parties are quite likely to agree with any position that a majority of citizens strongly favors, although they may phrase the position in different words. The parties take different routes into and out of the center. At times the routes may virtually touch each other and at other times may appear to be far apart. But on an average they are not too distant, for they must stay close to where the majority of constituents are located—the great middle. Obviously, party leaders will talk in generalities and be intentionally vague and ambiguous in their programs. Occasionally, however, candidates and platforms are forced to be specific in order to sell the voter on the idea that there is a difference. When a specific stand is taken, it must be shown to be in harmony with the cherished fundamental principle on which the leaders presume there is consensus. If the stand is on a controversial issue, then it may well be couched in equivocal terms. Party and public officials are wary that a too categorical and forthright position will lead some voters to desert to the opposition. Democrats from conservative areas take on the attitudes and policies of the dominant groups and must do so in order to be elected. Republicans from liberal areas do the same. Workers from a heavily industrialized area look to their congressman, regardless of his label, to support prolabor measures, and this is also the case with other interests. An advantage of this system is that it makes each party the home for widely different points of view and values. Critics see this as interfering with the welding of party cleavages on a national scale, upsetting party lines in many if not in most states, and often preventing parties from taking a stand on controversial proposals. Far from providing a haven for nearly everyone, the ideological purists agree that neither the Democrats nor the Republicans are capable of providing a political homeland for those who want a party to articulate a specific stand on the great issues. These tendencies toward convergence cause a reduction in a party vote, and legislative leaders must therefore work for a majority vote composed of members from both parties.

Voters alone do not force certain similarities of viewpoints on the two parties. The parties help mold the preferences of the voters. Platforms and candidates reflect the views of political leaders who tend to share certain common values and goals. To illustrate, Republican and Democratic leaders today overwhelmingly favor social security, public education, membership in the United Nations, and private enterprise. There is, in a word, a biparty agreement on the desirability of retaining these policies, and appeals to voters will be in terms of strengthening the effectiveness of all four of them. The presumption is that the voters favor them or, if not, that they should. The two parties then attempt to build up and reinforce membership. These and other causes may be supported by both parties but for somewhat different reasons. Very few responsible Republican or Democratic organizations will call for the abolition of private enterprise, social security legislation, public education, or withdrawal of the United States from the United Nations. Some Southerners may see the Supreme Court as subverting public education, and a few, thoroughly disillusioned with the United Nations, favor nonparticipation in it, but it would take a major upheaval in events for one of the two parties to champion radical institutional change in the Court or withdrawal from the UN. If the situation were severe enough to cause one party to advocate so drastic a change, the other would probably soon follow the same course!

IS THERE A DIFFERENCE?

The student frequently asks whether there are real differences between the Democratic and Republican parties. If he reads party platforms and listens to the speeches of presidential nominees, he can detect some political distance between the opposing parties. Generally these indexes are not very reliable, although one might be able to obtain an impression of dissimilarity of approach to some problems.

Congressional Roll Calls. Scholars seek a more objective standard. One widely used technique is the analysis of party cleavages on congressional roll calls. Users readily recognize the limitation of this yardstick of party loyalty. Any interpretation of roll calls is difficult because on many bills there is a high degree of absenteeism, and it is necessary to understand which of a series of roll calls on a given proposal is the crucial one. If, for example, a motion to "recommit" is defeated, many opponents of a bill will vote for it on final passage, realizing that the cause is lost and that they might as well get credit with certain constituents for its passage. The vital party vote therefore was on "recommitment," not on the passage. This is especially true of foreign aid and various domestic appropriation bills. Representatives, especially those who are uncommitted to their local districts on a matter, may vote out of obligation or friendship for a fellow legislator rather than out of party loyalty. Roll-call records tell how Republicans and Democrats voted but not necessarily why they voted as they did. Finally, what constitutes a party vote? A bare majority? Seventy-five percent? Ninety percent? Even though these limitations are recognized, roll calls help indicate the center of gravity of each party and show the general degree to which a majority of one party finds itself in opposition to the other on controversial measures.

With very rare exceptions, a unanimous party vote takes place on internal organizational matters such as selection of the Speaker of the House, committee appointments, and chairmanships. The actual selections are made in each party caucus and are subsequently ratified by the legislative body along strict party lines. Party unity, however, does not extend to programmatic questions, for on these there is usually a significant number of dissenters in each party.

Table 3-1 gives four examples on which the two parties divided; each is illustrative of a type of party unity. The vote over raising the national debt limit produced a very sharp cleavage between the two parties; such party unity in opposition to each other is most unusual. The natural gas vote is opposite in that both parties had substantial internal splits with more than one-third of each splitting off from its own majority. The Peace Corps measure brought high Democratic unity with low Republican unity, and the Tidelands Oil Bill resulted in high Republican and low Democratic unity.

TABLE 3-1 Types of party unity, United States House of Representatives

Measure	Percentage yea		Percentage nay	
	Democrats	Republicans	Democrats	Republicans
National debt limit increase (1963)	73	1	12	98
Peace Corps Act (1961)	78	47	11	39
Tidelands Oil Act (1953)	46	83	42	8
Exempt natural gas from federal control (1956)	60	37	33	59

In Tables 3-2 and 3-3, party divisions by percentages are shown on several important national and international measures spanning Republican and Democratic voting under several Presidents.[9] In support of social and labor legislation and civil rights, a majority of Republicans often vote with a majority of Democrats, but Republican margins tend to be less, showing somewhat less internal cohesion. After 1939, Southern Democrats parted company with Northern Democrats on social legislation and have kept their party from being united on measures favoring labor unions and civil rights. A larger number of Republicans than Democrats have been willing to impose regulations on labor unions.

On two other issues, agriculture and foreign policy, time is also shown to be important. Before 1933, the farm bloc showed great strength across party lines and, in effect, virtually nullified hope of a party vote. After 1933, the farm program became more and more one of partisan cleavage; and, during the Eisenhower administration, Democrats stood for high price supports, whereas Republicans tended to favor "flexible" ones. Republicans were once very stanchly protectionist in tariff battles and opposed Democrats in close party-line votes. Under Eisenhower, the Republican party majorities accepted the reciprocal trade agreements. Meanwhile Southern Democrats became less enthusiastic for them. On foreign policy in general the differences between the parties have been much less sharp since World War II. Before that time, Republicans tended to vote, often by big margins, against revision of the neutrality laws, selective service, and measures to aid the Western European allies. In general, Eisenhower continued the Truman foreign policy.

For some time the *Congressional Quarterly* has found that there is a marked difference between congressional Republicans and Democrats

[9] *Congressional Quarterly* regularly compiles roll-call votes on all crucial issues in Congress. It generally records the number in each party voting for and against a bill. The student is invited to make his own analysis from these figures. The figures in our tables are computed into percentages of the total Republican and Democratic membership voting yes or no. This also shows that there is often considerable absenteeism on a given roll call.

TABLE 3-2 Party voting on national legislation

	House of Representatives				Senate			
	% yea		% nay		% yea		% nay	
Measure	Dem.	Rep.	Dem.	Rep.	Dem.	Rep.	Dem.	Rep.
First AAA (1933)	88	33	8	62	80	40	8	43
TVA (1933)	91	15	1	76	N*	N	N	N
Social Security Act (1935)	90	75	4	17	87	56	1	20
National Housing Act (1937)	72	27	11	55	73	37	11	50
Wage-Hour law (1938)	78	52	17	46	66	13	19	87
Taft-Hartley bill (1947)	55	88	35	5	38	73	33	4
Natural gas amendment (1950)	37	46	44	33	52	38	30	52
High farm price supports (1956)	81	23	10	71	71	31	8	65
Civil Rights bill (1957)	42	84	45	10	59	90	37	0
National defense education (Eisenhower "must," 1958)	59	36	12	27	75	63	14	17
Public works appropriation (Spending measure, 1959)	94	30	1	58	89	52	1	41
Federal airport construction (1959)	86	20	9	71	80	35	8	50
Public housing, urban renewal (1959)	78	12	18	82	75	24	12	68
Agricultural Act (1962)	76	17	14	69	67	11	14	78
Civil Rights bill (1964)	60	76	36	19	69	62	31	15
Tax cut (1964)	85	61	8	35	80	63	15	30
Federal aid to education (1965)	77	25	19	68	81	56	6	44
Medicare (1965)	80	50	16	48	84	40	10	53
Open housing (1968)	60	53	35	44	66	80	26	8
10% tax surcharge (1968)	62	60	31	33	34	86	50	8

Source: Figures are taken from various compilations appearing in The New York Times and the Congressional Quarterly and computed into percentages by the author. Paired votes are not included.
*N denotes a voice, not a roll-call vote; not recorded.

in voting for a larger federal role. Compiling the votes on measures that would make for increased federal activity between 1959 and 1964, 73 percent of the Senate Democrats and 75 percent of the House Democrats supported the larger federal role, and Republican support respectively was 33 and 27 percent. In the late 1960s, the Democratic percentages remained approximately the same; Republican percentages for a larger role increased somewhat but were still well behind those for the Democrats. There is abundant evidence that congressional Democrats can get majority votes for spending easier than Republicans can.[10]

During the Johnson administration there were several important measures on which Senate Republicans sharply deviated from House Republicans with the latter voting in the negative. Senate Republicans overwhelmingly supported open-housing legislation and their House members voted 106 to 77 against accepting the Senate bill without

[10]Additional aspects of party as a variable in congressional voting are noted in Chap. 8. A useful general work is that of D. R. Mayhew, *Party Loyalty among Congressmen: The Difference between Democrats and Republicans, 1947–1962,* Harvard University Press, Cambridge, Mass., 1966.

TABLE 3-3   Party votes on foreign policy roll calls

| | House of Representatives | | | | Senate | | | |
| | % yea | | % nay | | % yea | | % nay | |
Measure	Dem.	Rep.	Dem.	Rep.	Dem.	Rep.	Dem.	Rep.
Mandatory arms embargo (1939)	23	89	63	4	17	52	65	39
Revision of neutrality laws (1939)	85	11	11	83	78	35	17	65
Selective Service (1940)	81	31	13	66	72	35	25	43
3-year trade agreement extension (1940)	80	2	8	87	59	0	22	87
Truman Doctrine (1947)	85	52	7	38	71	69	16	31
Korean aid (1950)	70	25	16	58	N	N	N	N
Mutual Security Act (1952)	71	39	9	45	80	53	2	19
Mutual Security (1954)	67	54	20	38	61	25	14	54
Reciprocal trade extension (1958)	79	66	16	29	81	67	12	25
Foreign aid (1959)	60	58	28	32	N	N	N	N
Foreign assistance (1963)	67	30	25	68	60	50	10	21
Test Ban Treaty (1963)	...	...	...	...	82	76	17	24

change. However, on the final roll when it was apparent the bill would pass, 53 percent of the House Republicans voted for it. Conversely 70 House Republicans voted for Medicare and 68 opposed while Senate Republicans opposed the measure 17 to 13. A majority of Senate Republicans favored federal aid to education but only 25 percent of their party in the House was favorable.

In conclusion, for those who require 100 percent unity as evidence of a party vote, cohesion is rare. But if we are willing to settle for smaller majorities, there is a good deal of truth in Julius Turner's contention of a significant party cohesion when one compares the vote distribution in one party with that of the other on single issues.[11] The approach of the majorities (of various sizes) of the two parties on legislation concerning business, labor, agriculture, medical care, and social reform has shown an overall divergency. Since the advent of the New Deal, party labels have stood for something different, but the difference is easily exaggerated. Nevertheless, roll-call votes give evidence that program is not a meaningless thing in the American biparty system.

The existence of national party differences is also demonstrated by one examination of the opinions of Democratic and Republican leaders which showed them to be "distinct communities of co-believers who diverge sharply on many important issues."[12] The sample was taken

[11] *Party and Constituency: Pressures on Congress*, The Johns Hopkins Press, Baltimore, 1951. *Congressional Quarterly* makes annual computations of "party unity votes," i.e., the percentage of the time a Republican or Democrat votes with his party majority in disagreement with the other party's majority, and like Turner, has found enough unity within each party to permit a student to conclude that on a large number of controversial issues, most Democrats vote in opposition to most Republicans.

[12] Herbert McCloskey, Paul J. Hoffman, and Rosemary O'Hara, "Issue Conflict and Consensus among Party Leaders and Followers," *American Political Science Review*, vol. 54, pp. 406–427, 1960.

from the party hierarchy as well as from governors and senators. Their disagreements tended to be similar to those observed in congressional roll calls. Rank-and-file members of the two parties were noticeably less divided over issues than their leaders.

In reviewing the often contradictory data on party loyalty on public policy in Congress, notice has been taken of discernible party differences, yet executives very often need the help of votes from the minority party. These votes from "both sides of the aisle" are essential to the building of consensus—the familiar principle of concurrent majority. Sectionalism, parochial considerations, heterogeneous party membership, and a philosophy of responsibility to local constituencies interfere with the welding of party unanimity in the legislatures. Group representation manifests itself across party lines. Party solidarity builds slowly and often not at all. Legislative leaders may find themselves having to piece together the majority vote from both parties rather than just from the majority party.

MINOR PARTIES

As observed earlier, many forces have deterred the development of American third parties as a formidable threat to the two parties or as a political homeland for large segments of the population. In European countries, workers found themselves in a common class, whereas in the United States, rigid status groups were virtually nonexistent, and one could move from one class to another. Some working-class bodies and those who advocated a socialist economy through labor unions found great difficulty in nurturing a political consciousness among American workers. Agrarians, businessmen, laborers, and professionals were usually intensely pragmatic and regarded it as folly to try to build a party based primarily on their own membership. Moreover, a high level of prosperity and absence of widespread economic protest have stolen the thunder of economic malcontents. Fear and hatred of Communists have hurt the extreme left-wing parties. The strength of partisan attachments and the weakness of the American electorate's ideological interests also make the going difficult for those who would build a permanent third party.

Often overlooked is the fact that third parties continually suffer internal weaknesses, particularly in the matter of formal organization, which is necessary for survival if support is to be obtained. Their leaders tend to overemphasize policy at the expense of organization. Minor parties in the United States usually pour their meager resources into presidential politics and neglect to recruit candidates for state and congressional offices. A number of small parties have been torn asunder by their own sectarianism.

Categories. Although differences in minor parties are readily observed, it is not easy to classify them. Some are permanent, others are fleeting and transient; some are centered in ideology, others have practical goals.[13] One minor party may confine itself to one state or a section, while another attempts to function nationally. For purposes of analysis, third parties may be classified as doctrinal-ideological and splinter-secessionist. The lines between these two are often blurred; a splinter group from a major party may have a strong ideological basis.

For example, George Wallace's American Independent Party of 1968 is difficult to categorize. Although Mr. Wallace was a former Democratic Governor in Alabama and numerous Southern Democrats worked for it, the party could not be said to be secessionist. It polled fairly heavily among Republicans as well as Democrats. Its ideology of state control o :r civil rights and opposition to federal government and its emphasis on "law and order" had strong appeal to many right-wing elements and to others alarmed over demonstrations by blacks and students. Wallace's protest movement, therefore, appealed across party lines; but his greatest vote came from the deep South, where discontent with the national Democratic party felt by Southern Democrats has been considerable since the 1940s. The Wallace party, on its own admission, was dedicated to changing the direction of the policy orientations of the major parties. In contrast, the small permanent Marxist groups remain independent of the major parties and give the impression that they are not trying to influence their actions but rather to offer an ideological alternative.

Three clear-cut "bolter" parties are to be found in the "Gold Democrats" movement of 1896, the Bull Moose secession from the Republican party in 1912, and the States' Rights Democratic revolt in 1948. In each case, the seceding party operated during only one election, and a majority or very large bloc of its members returned to the fold at the following election. The National Democrats of 1896 broke away over the Democratic bimetallist platform and campaigned with meager success under the banner of "pro-gold standard." Progressives in the Republican party wished to block the renomination of President Taft in 1912 and nominated Theodore Roosevelt. Under the third-party label, Roosevelt succeeded in outpolling Taft, but divided the Republican vote-and made it possible for Wilson to win with 42 percent of the popular vote.

A 1948 Southern Dixiecrat revolt was precipitated by President Truman's active support of a strong civil rights program and the adoption of a national civil rights plank at the Democratic National Con-

[13]General accounts of minor parties include Howard P. Nash, Jr., *Third Parties in American Politics*, Public Affairs Press, Washington, D.C., 1959, and W. B. Hesseltine, *Third Party Movements in the United States*, Van Nostrand Reinhold Company, New York, 1962.

vention. A states' rights conference convened in Birmingham a short time later and adopted a strong states' rights-anti-Truman platform. The conference designated J. Strom Thurmond of South Carolina as the Democratic nominee. A battle ensued in the Southern states between the regular Democrats who were loyal to the national party and the Dixiecrats. In four states, the latter succeeded in placing on the ballot electors pledged to Thurmond as the head of the official Democratic ticket and in each case won. Where Truman ran as the Democratic candidate in the South, he won.

Few of the third parties in the United States over the years may be regarded as ideological parties. *Ideology* implies a coherence of attitudes, beliefs, or ideas which gives meaning to a wide scope of social, economic, and political matters, and perhaps other matters as well. Ideology assumes a set of relationships and helps the adherent "understand" or "make sense" out of events. It can provide him with a course of action. The Marxist parties are strongly ideologically oriented, so much so that there are several different Marxist groups, each purporting to be the "true" one. Another ideological group, the Prohibitionists, began placing presidential candidates before the electorate in 1872. They were a single-issue party until fairly recently, but now their platforms contain statements on many social and economic problems.

A large number of short-lived, episodic minor-party movements have been rooted in economic discontent and protest. The leaders in many cases undoubtedly possessed, in varying degrees, an ideology, but their mass followings had little clear-cut ideological comprehension. More often they were disgusted with the major parties and wished to protest and demanded "better times." They blamed Wall Street bankers, plutocrats, monopoly grain-elevator companies, foreigners, or some segment of society, without attacking the overall economic and social system, as did the socialist parties.

Two sizable national parties of protest made creditable showings at the polls—the Populists in 1892 and the Progressive party of 1924. Both parties directed their appeals to discontented laborers and agrarians, had by far their greatest strength in the West, and ran popular presidential candidates from the Midwest. Both advocated a miscellaneous set of reforms and embraced some of the proposals espoused by the Socialists, but neither called for a socialist society. Whereas socialism was barely getting established in 1892 when the Populists made their bid with James B. Weaver of Iowa, it was a widely discussed doctrine in 1924; and the Socialist party endorsed Robert M. La Follette of Wisconsin, rather than nominate a candidate of its own. In voting strength, the Progressive party was of negligible influence in the South, while Populism was significant in the 1890s, especially in Alabama, Texas, and Louisiana.

The Progressive party concentrated on the Presidency and had little time, manpower, and money to build organizations to campaign for many congressional seats. However, two Socialists and three Farmer-Laborites were elected to the House, and one Farmer-Laborite secured a Senate seat. Considering the handicaps involved in a third-party presidential bid, the La Follette candidacy showed that progressivism and protest were by no means dead. La Follette won the electoral vote in Wisconsin and ran second in eleven states; one of every six persons in the country voted for him. After the election, the Socialists tried to keep the party together, but the spokesmen for unions and farmers associations deserted the cause. Many of the old-timers remembered the defeat of the Populists, and two unsuccessful third-party efforts within a generation convinced them that protest must find a better channel. In retrospect, most of their proposals in 1924 were mild, calling for collective bargaining and vigorous labor unions, popular election of judges, opposition to the sales tax, extension of federal credit to farmers, businessmen, and homebuilders, and public ownership of the nation's water power and railroads.

THE MARXIST PARTIES

Socialist Labor Party. A Socialist Labor party (SLP) was formed during the 1870s as an outgrowth of the Social Democratic Workingmen's party. It was German in origin and clung to its German heritage. Its early meetings were conducted in German, and the party was reinforced by new waves of German immigrants exiled from their country under the Bismarck regime. Because of its alien origin, it never became a significant part of the American labor movement.[14] Daniel De Leon took the group into a dual unionism venture by founding the Socialist Trade and Labor Alliance, with a view to supplanting the American Federation of Labor (AFL), which was unresponsive to the idea of politically supported socialism. De Leon envisaged unions as a framework for a socialist society. He attacked geographic representation and called for it to be replaced by occupational representation by trades, which he felt would eliminate conflicting interests in the capitalistic society. The SLP refused to temporize with a reform group such as the Populists and ran its own presidential candidate. The poor showing of only 21,000 votes in 1892 did not discourage it from running a candidate in every subsequent election; its showing at the polls has always been meager.

The Socialist Laborites have remained more theoretical, doctrinaire, and visionary than the Socialist party. They refused to compromise with capitalism and have advocated the overthrow of the state and replacing it with a large industrial union. The SLP has vigorously as-

---

[14] See O. M. Johnson and H. Kuhn, *Socialist Labor Party during Four Decades: 1890–1930*, Labor News, New York, 1931; and H. H. Quint, *The Forging of American Socialism: Origins of the Modern Movement*, University of South Carolina Press, Columbia, 1953.

serted that it is "the only party with a truly Marxist program." It bitterly attacked the Socialist party as a "fraud" and accused it of playing "capitalist politics." Eric Haas, its 1952 presidential candidate, boasted, "We'll dance a fandango on the grave of the Socialist party."

Socialist Party. Many Socialists would not accept De Leon's leadership and flocked to the banner of the Social Democrats in 1898; the Socialist label was taken in 1901 and prevailed thereafter. The Socialists zealously attacked capitalism, supported social ownership, and sought a Socialist order through parliamentary methods rather than through revolution. At times they have been opportunistic and dealt with contemporary economic and social issues as they arose.[15] Because of its dedication to peaceful reform and emphasis on education and progressivism, white-collar workers and intelligentsia were attracted to the party when it was led by Norman Thomas from 1928 to 1952.

Under the colorful leadership of Eugene V. Debs and Norman Thomas from 1900 to 1948, the Socialist party was usually able to poll at least 100,000 votes and came close to the million-vote mark on three occasions.[16] After 1948, Thomas argued that the party should not spend its meager funds on presidential campaigns but should limit itself to education and criticism, except where it might have a chance to win in a local race. The Socialist convention would not accept the Thomas viewpoint, and the party polled a meager 20,000 votes in 1952. After a pitiful perfomance of less than a thousand votes in three states in 1956, the Socialists gave up campaigns and no presidential candidate has appeared subsequently. In retrospect, however, many reforms advocated by the Socialists have been accepted without a revolution.

It is an interesting paradox that the SLP, which has shown little virility, has continued to live, while the Socialist party, once possessed of great vitality, has passed from the scene. Although most other Western democracies boast a socialist party, the movement in the United States never really caught the imagination of great masses of voters. There are many explanations for the failure of the Socialists as a party. The ethnic heterogeneity led workers to identify themselves more with the aspirations of their racial and nationalist group than with their class. Workers and distressed classes were pragmatic and wanted immediate, tangible results. Ironically, the Socialist attempt to build a third party with a labor base received more support from rural and mining areas than from urban labor.

[15] There are a number of works on the Socialist party including several by Norman Thomas. A basic work which contains an exhaustive and annotated bibliography is that of David A. Shannon, *The Socialist Party of America: A History,* The Macmillan Company, New York, 1955.

[16] The Socialist party was able to attract votes considerably beyond its membership. In 1912, it was estimated that the Socialist party reached its peak of 115,000 dues-paying members, yet Eugene V. Debs polled about 920,000 votes. The SLP likewise has attracted more votes than it has members.

Added to this was the party's slight interest in local and state affairs. Its emphasis was on national and international matters. When Milwaukee Socialists offered a local program, they had much success.

> The Socialist Party never fully decided whether it was a political party, a political pressure group, a revolutionary sect, or a political forum. It tried to play all these roles at the same time. One of the first rules of American politics is to build strong local and state organizations. Outside of a few places, notably Milwaukee and Oklahoma, the Socialists failed to establish political machines. Indeed, they usually did not even try to build them.[17]

All Socialist groups have suffered from the inability to communicate with the voters; Marxist dialectics and language were just not understood by most people. Finally, the Socialist party was handicapped, as have been all minor parties, by its inability to attract competent leadership and to meet the legal and other obstacles that face a third party's electoral efforts.

No study has been made of the interaction between the various Socialist and other minor parties. During the first quarter of the present century, it appears, nonetheless, that the Socialist and Progressive movements reacted beneficially with one another. The Socialist party stimulated the Progressive movement, and the growth of the Progressive movement swelled the vote for Debs. This was due more to accident than to design, since the farmer-labor coalition on the one side and the Socialists on the other agreed mainly on the fact that change was needed. Although they were able to get together on a few prescriptions such as public ownership of the railroads and collective bargaining, Farmer-Labor protests did not encompass the radical socioeconomic dogma of the Socialists.

The Communists. Division split the Socialist party after the success of the Bolsheviks in Russia. The left wing demanded a change from reform to the overthrow of the government and capitalism. Several leftist members were expelled and, with others who left voluntarily, organized the Workers' party which became the Communist party. The latter refused to go along with the La Follette group and ran its own candidate for President for the first time in 1924 and continued to do so through the 1940 election. Characteristically, the SLP would have no truck with either the Communists or the Socialists and put up its own candidate. Also characteristically, the Communists had their own sectarian fight and threw out the Trotskyites in 1928. This group became the Socialist-Workers party which lent further gaiety to the Socialist movement by putting forth a presidential candidate beginning in 1948. Its high-water mark was 39,000 votes in 1960.

[17] Shannon, *op. cit.*, p. 258.

Writers about American political parties remain puzzled about the Communist party. It hardly fits the pattern and certainly not the norm of a democratic political system. Communists differ sharply from other Socialist groups (except the Socialist Workers) and from the minor and major parties in the acceptance of physical force to overthrow the bourgeois state. Their history is a fantastic story of intrigue, expediency, and sharp reversals of policy.[18] The party has been alternately pacifistic and prowar. Its policy shifts appear to be inspired by the foreign policies of the Soviet Union, and disclosures have satisfied most Americans and their agencies of government that the party has functioned as a conspiratorial group as an instrument of the official policies of the Moscow regime.

Despite its small numbers, the Communist movement in the United States has profoundly affected domestic politics.[19] Rigid discipline, hard work, and shrewd tactics enabled it to infiltrate for a time the leadership councils of some interest groups. Several local labor unions were expelled from national unions when this was discovered, and the Congress of Industrial Organizations (CIO) won a decisive victory over the Communist party.[20] During the battle, however, the problem of communism in labor unions was one filled with bitterness and dissension. After they no longer ran candidates under their own label, the Communists tended to back American Labor party candidates in New York and nationally infiltrated the Progressive party in 1948, when Henry Wallace was its candidate. Leftist minor parties were undoubtedly discredited by the activities of the Communists and were called subversive by many persons.

American communism has had numerous other effects. Investigations turned up the names of many fairly prominent Americans as onetime members or supporters who voted Communist as a protest (as did many who voted Socialist). Some of these were attracted during the Depression by the Communists' vigorous championship of the underdog and by the Soviet effort against nazism and fascism. Many of these people were apparently unaware of the conspiratorial character of the party. Nonetheless, a number lost their jobs and careers, even though they had left the party long before exposure. A spate of loyalty oaths were used

[18] There is an enormous volume of literature on American communism in congressional hearings and in general works. For an analysis of the social composition of the movement, as well as an annotated bibliography, see Nathan Glazer, *The Social Basis of American Communism*, Harcourt, Brace & World, Inc., New York, 1961. The history of the party to 1957 is reviewed and analyzed by Irving Howe and Lewis Coser in *The American Communist Party: A Critical History*, Beacon Press, Boston, 1957. For legal aspects, see Kathleen L. Barber, "The Legal Status of the American Communist Party: 1965," *Journal of Public Law*, vol. 15, pp. 94–121, 1966.

[19] Estimates of membership were 70,000 in 1947, 22,000 in 1954, and 13,000 in 1968.

[20] See Max Kampleman, *The Communist Party vs. the C.I.O.: A Study in Power Politics*, Frederick A. Praeger, Inc., New York, 1957.

by legislatures as a tool for ferreting out allegedly disloyal teachers and public employees. The fight against Communists was employed by some to repress dissent by non-Communists including pacifists, one-worlders, and world federalists. Many ultraright-wing groups continue to use anti-communism to attack political liberalism, progressives, and reformers.

A few very small parties of the right have appeared in some recent elections with such labels as "Christian Nationalist," "Constitution," or "States' Rights." In 1960 the National States' Rights party ran a presidential candidate in four states, and the "Conservative" and "Constitution" labels each appeared in one state. Their emphasis has been against "big government" and the "welfare state." They have expressed concern that both major parties are "soft on communism." Except for the Wallace party in 1968, the right-wing movement in the United States, unlike the Marxist groups, has expended little energy in third-party activity. Rather it has put money and effort into nonparty group activity and has often endorsed major-party candidates for Congress whose views are to its liking. (Right-wing movements are covered in Chapter 19.)

EFFECTS OF MINOR PARTIES ON THE SYSTEM

It is not easy to conceptualize minor parties and it is difficult to find uniformities in their organization functions and roles. Some of the transient ones have only a momentary effect on the major parties; other doctrinal, less-permanent groups provide a political haven for a tiny group of the populace. Minor parties are hardly comparable with the major ones as they tend not to compete for control of the total system but only for a few offices. Some groups call themselves parties even after they no longer propose candidates for public office — a criterion we are applying if a group is to call itself a party. Minor parties nonetheless have had consequences on the nation's political life.

Voting strength. Although no third-party candidate has won the Presidency, five times in our history — 1892, 1912, 1924, 1948, and 1968 — a single minor-party candidate polled more than 2 million votes and at times may have changed the electoral outcome. In 1860, two "splinter" nominees together polled more than Democrat Stephen Douglas. The close electoral and popular vote in 1968 gave rise to much speculation on the influence of the Wallace third party; he received more than 13 percent of the popular vote and the electoral vote in five states. The results in many non-South states were close, with Humphrey or Nixon winning by a plurality rather than a majority vote. This is not to suggest that the final national verdicts of some presidential elections would have necessarily been altered by the redistribution of the minor-party votes; the anomaly of the Electoral College is the crucial point.

TABLE 3-4 Third-party and other minor-party votes, 1900–1968 (percentages of national total vote)

Year	Name of third party*	Third-party vote	Other minor-party vote	Total minor-party vote
1900	...	...	2.83%	2.83%
1904	Socialist	2.98	3.03	6.01
1908	Socialist	2.83	3.03	5.38
1912	Progressive (Roosevelt)	27.42		
	Socialist	5.99	1.58	34.99
1916	...	...	...	...
1920	Socialist	3.43	1.12	4.55
1924	Progressive (La Follette)	16.60	0.53	17.13
1928	...	...	...	...
1932	...	...	2.94	2.94
1936	...	...	2.66	2.66
1940	...	...	0.47	0.47
1944	...	...	0.71	0.71
1948	States' Rights Democrats	2.40		
	Progressive (H. Wallace)	2.38	0.59	5.37
1952	...	...	0.49	0.49
1956	...	...	0.65	0.65
1960	...	...	1.21	1.21
1964	...	...	0.47	0.47
1968	American Independent (G. Wallace)	13.49	0.56	14.05

*The third parties named here are the ones most significant.

In this century, minor-party candidates have collectively averaged about 5 to 6 percent of the popular vote. They failed to poll this percentage, however, in many elections. The American Independent party in 1968 was one of the very few third parties to have its candidate's name appear on the ballots of all states. Failures of the minor parties to poll more than 5 percent have usually signified that voters are reasonably satisfied with the two major-party choices. In other words, such failures have usually occurred in times of tranquility without great social ferment and protest, and the major parties were able to field candidates of wide accommodation and appeal. Voters tend to respond in larger numbers to a minor party that has grown out of a policy split within one of the major parties, as in 1912, 1924, 1948, and 1968. In this sense, the new parties are a means of registering dissatisfaction with the major parties.

Despite discouragement and often inept leadership, third parties have won some state and local offices. The Socialist party's greatest electoral successes were in municipal elections in which it captured the mayorality in Milwaukee, Wisconsin; Bridgeport, Connecticut; and Reading, Pennsylvania. In the stormy history of New York City's multiparty politics, a Liberal party candidate was elected president of the city council in 1953, and numerous candidates of the fleeting as well as the permanent minor parties have been elected to the city council.[21] Mayor John Lindsay was denied renomination in the Republican primary in 1969 but won reelection on the Liberal party ticket.

With a few exceptions, minor parties have been more successful in attracting votes for their presidential candidate than for the lesser offices on the same ticket. Even the limited support for a minor presidential nominee seems not transferable to other levels such as the legislature since most poll less than the top of the ticket. (This is not necessarily true in a state party situation.) It might be theorized that citizens would see less at stake and be more willing to support a minor party for offices lower than the presidency, but this is generally not the case.

Purveyors of Program and Protest. The presence of minor parties is felt in three ways — as exponents of dissent, champions of change, and critics of the major parties. Farmer-labor and socialist parties serve as voices of protest. In years past, they criticized the Eastern moneyed interests, financial capitalism, monopoly, and specific groups such as the railroads and mortgage companies. Small parties of the right in recent years have inveighed against the graduated income tax, "big labor," the United Nations, and "Communists in the government." The major opposition party may object to many of the same things as the minor parties but often does so in terms too mild and too general for the more zealous of the protesters.

Although their dissents are vociferous, third parties have not contented themselves with a purely negative program of being against existing public policies. A general characteristic of most minor parties is the profession of an ideology, a program, or a counterprogram. In fact, the presentation of policy alternatives is necessary for third parties since they seldom can match the major parties in offering well-known candidates. The abolitionist parties took a clear-cut stand on slavery, and the Greenbackers and Populists came up with panaceas on monetary questions. The Prohibitionists took a position on the manufacture and sale of alcoholic beverages, which the major parties supported only briefly for the duration of the Eighteenth Amendment.

Minor-party candidates were calling for railroad regulation, a graduated income tax, federal youth programs, unemployment insur-

[21] Charles Garrett has woven minor parties into the history of New York City's political system in his *The La Guardia Years: Machine and Reform Politics in New York City*, Rutgers University Press, New Brunswick, N.J., 1961. See also Hugh A. Bone, "Political Parties in New York City," *The American Political Science Review*, vol. 40, pp. 272–282, 1946.

ance, direct primaries, and popular election of senators well in advance of their acceptance by major-party candidates. Often measures of this kind were discussed by nonparty groups at the same time, so that it would be hard to prove that Democrats and Republicans embraced the causes belatedly as a result of minor-party agitation. After some of the policies were enacted by the major parties, however, the minor parties tended to lose support and membership. Many proposals of third parties never gain support and are relegated to the limbo of defeated issues; repeated and disastrous defeats.

Effects on Major Parties. The influence of small parties, both ideological and splinter, on the major parties is not easy to measure or to document, yet it is broadly evident on occasions. A large minor-party vote is something of a fever chart of the times. It may well be a reflection of the degree to which major parties, through their programs and candidates, have failed to accommodate the frustrations, desires, and anxieties of segments of the electorate. In 1932, Farmer-Labor and Marxist parties attracted more than a million votes or about three times as many as in 1928. Clearly, many persons were not satisfied with the Hoover policies and felt that Roosevelt would not bring the country out of the disastrous Depression. There were still many discontented voters in 1936 who registered their protest by voting for minor parties.

The bitter battle over civil rights at the 1948 Democratic convention resulted in the States' Rights party. The defection produced such a close election that the lesson was not fully lost on the Northern Democrats; they worked for compromise and conciliation with the South in subsequent conventions. Some Northern state delegations could hardly swallow the selection of Lyndon Johnson as vice presidential candidate in 1960 but realized, as had Stevenson, that concessions had to be made to the Southern wing. Although Roosevelt could have been elected without the South, it would be needed for electoral success of Stevenson and Kennedy.

The threat of a third-party or independent or uninstructed elector system remains in the South and figures in the calculations of both major parties. In Alabama, insurgent Democrats put up a slate of Thurmond electors in 1948 and uninstructed electors in 1964; consequently, voters had no opportunity to cast their ballots for Truman or for Johnson. In 1948 the supporters of Thurmond and in 1968 Wallace partisans expressed the desire that their nominees would muster enough electoral muscle to throw the election into the House of Representatives, permitting the region to bargain with the two major parties for federal actions more congenial to the South.

Of older vintage is the strain of populism and progressivism. When the Populists joined the Democratic party in supporting William

Jennings Bryan in 1896, many conservatives left the party; and differences between the two major parties were sharpened in that election. Theodore Roosevelt and Woodrow Wilson attracted the support of most old-line progressives, but the Socialists went their own way. Reaction set in after World War I, and progressiveness breathed third-party fire again in 1924, when it could not find a satisfactory expression in either major party.

Although the Republican party has always had a progressive wing, it has been in the minority. With one or two conspicuous exceptions, however, it has forced the nomination of middle-of-the-road presidential candidates. Beginning with Franklin Roosevelt, progressives for the most part have chosen to stay with the Democratic party. As long as the Democrats are able to identify themselves with the aspirations of the most discontented agrarians, urban laborers, and ethnic groups, third-party farmer-labor progressive revolt seems improbable.

The Democrats face a bolting threat from some intellectuals, youth, and others over foreign policy. Senator Eugene McCarthy of Minnesota was pressed to head a third party featuring an anti-Vietnam foreign policy in 1968 but refused. A few of his supporters voted for diverse "peace" candidates.

In retrospect, the dissonant minorities who have chosen the channel of small parties for their operations may have unintentionally strengthened the two-party system. They are usually on the fringe of the mainstream of politics. When their proposals attracted wide support, the major parties often responded by remedial action in one form or another. Where the major parties fail to act, the minor groups continue to provide a channel of protest. They constitute attacks by outsiders against the ruling elites of both parties. The larger minor-party protests have been precursors of changes and realignments within the major parties; such protests were made by the Free Soilers in the 1840s, the Populists in the 1890s, and the La Follette Progressives in the 1920s. It may well be that the party of George Wallace will profoundly affect the major parties during the 1970s.

FOR FURTHER READING

Allardt, Erik: *Cleavages, Ideologies, and Party Systems*, 1964.
Downs, Anthony: *An Economic Theory of Democracy*, 1957.
Goldwin, Robert A. (ed.): *Political Parties, U.S.A.*, 1964.
Herring, E. P.: *The Politics of Democracy*, 1940.
Hofstadter, Richard: *The Age of Reform*, 1955.
Leiserson, Avery: *Parties and Politics: An Institutional and Behavioral Approach*, 1958.

Ranney, Austin, and Willmoore Kendall: *Democracy and the American Party System*, 1956.
Rossiter, Clinton: *Parties and Politics in America*, 1960.
Stedman, Murray S., and S. W. Stedman: *Discontent at the Polls*, 1950.
Sorauf, Frank J.: *Party Politics in America*, 1968.

See also references at the end of Chapter 1.

Groups of men contend for control of state government. Although state parties are intertwined with national parties and politics, in varying degrees the skirmishes for control of state governments are fought out on different issues and to some extent by different cliques of leaders than those involved in the federal battle.

V. O. KEY, JR.

CHAPTER 4 OTHER PARTY SYSTEMS

STATE PARTIES

Until recently, writings about American political parties tended to concentrate on the national party system on the one hand and municipal organizational politics on the other. Somehow the functioning and problems of the state parties other than their relationship to the national and big city governments did not receive widespread attention. This gap is now being rapidly filled as scholars find the politics of individual states and comparative state politics an exciting area for testing hypotheses and studying the effect of environment on political parties.[1]

[1] Today one finds articles if not books on parties and politics on each state as well as a number of volumes on regional politics. Duane Lockhard has compiled a state-by-state bibliography of state and urban politics in *The Politics of State and Local Government*, The Macmillan Company, New York, 1963, pp. 544–558. See also Herbert Jacob and Kenneth N. Vines (eds.), *Politics in American States: A Comparative Analysis*, Little, Brown and Company, Boston, 1965; Frank Munger (ed.), *American State Politics: Readings for Comparative Analysis*, Thomas Y. Crowell Company, New York, 1966; and Robert C. Crew, Jr., *State Politics: Readings on Political Behavior*, Wadsworth Publishing Co., Belmont, Calif., 1968.

As at the national level, state parties seek to build coalitions to try to control the government. They adopt platforms, assist in recruiting and electing candidates, organize the legislature (a few exceptions), and provide opposition. But state parties are not simply the national Democratic and Republican parties writ small. The variations among the states are striking, making comparative analysis a challenging but difficult undertaking. Party structures are very different, as are nominating procedures. Descriptive nomenclature is not even the same! The formation of party primary slates in Pennsylvania is called endorsement, in New York this is a designation, and in Virginia it is termed the nod. The term *the organization* is commonly used in Pennsylvania but not in Texas or California. Georgians call a polling place an election district, Oregonians speak of a precinct and Texans refer to it as a box. As always reformers see their group as an organization and the opponents in control as a machine. One is a ward leader in Chicago but a district leader in Seattle. Differences in local terminology often reflect reality and possibly the tenor of political conflict.

The precise meaning of *party* causes problems for scholars and the layman not only in the United States but also in nations throughout the world. Generically, the term is used to describe both the government party and the electorate party that was organized to elect the public officeholders. In some localities, *the party* is loosely used to mean the leaders and organizational hierarchy.

Because America has a two-party system, it may appear that a similar arrangement obtains throughout the local political systems. At the state and community levels, there are numerous instances of a competitive two-party conflict; but a great many areas, for all practical purposes, function under a one-party system. In many areas, party organization is fragmentary, and there is virtually no party system at all. Even though we think of Congress as biparty in character, a majority of seats are generally quite safely Republican or safely Democratic with control of Congress turning on elections in 100 to 125 districts. Two-thirds of the time since 1933 the Republicans have held from 162 to 245 seats in the House. Similarly during the days of Republican hegemony the Democrats managed to hold no less than 132 seats and usually had in excess of 165 seats. One-party Democratic districts have tended to offset one-party Republican strongholds, with the decisive contests for control waged in one-fifth to one-fourth of the districts. Within many states there are deep pockets of strength for each party with control of the state legislature centered in well under half of the districts. County offices are not infrequently dominated by one party for long periods of time.

Quite a number of congressional seats go uncontested by Republicans. In 1966 and 1968 there were no Republican candidates in 52 districts. Democrats failed to contest only four seats in 1966 and nine seats in 1968. The great majority of seats going to the Democrats by default are in the Southern states. As shown in Figure 4-1, Republicans also fail to capture a percentage of House seats comparable to their national popular vote for congressional candidates. It is rare that a Senate seat is unopposed. In 1968 only Aiken of Vermont and Russell of Georgia were reelected without a contest.

State party arrangements show great variation even though every state has a Democratic and a Republican party organization of some form. In a number, but probably not a majority, of states, the two parties compete with each other on quite even terms. Control of offices rotates fairly frequently and the opposition, if it has a good candidate, always has a chance. In a large number of states, a single party dominates the government, with the minority capturing executive and numerous legislative posts only infrequently. In one-party states the minority party seldom if ever wins the major contests and elects few members of the legislative body. New York State now has two active minority (third and fourth) parties, the Conservatives and Liberals, which can make a difference in the outcome in certain electoral contests. When the Liberals ran their own candidate for governor in 1966, Nelson Rockefeller, the Republican candidate, was able to win a third term by capturing 44.6 per-

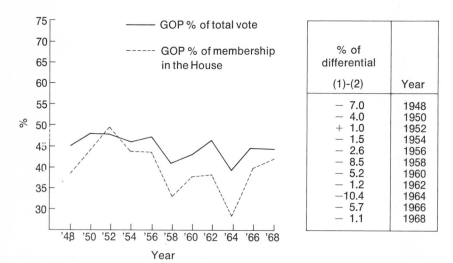

FIGURE 4-1   Republican percentage of the total House vote compared to the Republican percentage of the House membership, 1948–1968.

cent of the votes. During the 1930s, Minnesota and Wisconsin operated under a three-party combination. Therefore, we find one-party, two-party, and multiparty states in the American experience.[2]

THE POLITICAL SETTING

A political system must respond to the environment within which it operates; political parties as a subsystem of the larger system are influenced by many factors, legal and nonlegal. Physical and geographical features differ considerably among the states and have consequences for those states. Mountain ranges that split some states create very different kinds of regions within the states and the differences influence legislators. Copper in Montana, oil in Texas, water in the Southwest and waterpower in Maine affect the states' politics, especially of interest groups. The size and availability of a state's natural resources and its transportation system have their effect, since the presence or absence of such leads to demands and requests for protection or enhancement.

Historical and Socioeconomic Considerations. The Civil War resulted in setting up regional voting habits in a considerable number of states. Southern and Border States became strongly Democratic in state and national elections, and states in the Deep South became one-party states. Persons ambitious to hold elective office tended to embrace the Democratic label as the preferred if not the only channel to elective office. This tended to perpetuate Democratic dominance and the party could always attract better talent than the opposing party.

Effects of the Civil War were not significant in the historical dominance of the Republican party in Maine, Vermont, and New Hampshire. For long periods, voters have been rather overwhelmingly Republican in several of the Midwestern states but GOP candidates could be upset at times by popular Democratic candidates at the state level. Although by no means fully descriptive, such states as Iowa, Nebraska, the Dakotas, Kansas, and Wisconsin were often referred to as traditionally Republican before 1932. An erosion of the traditional voting habits has tended in the direction of split-ticket voting. In the 1960s, for example, Democratic governors were elected in Maine, Vermont, Minnesota, New Hampshire, and Kansas, and Republican governors in Arkansas, Florida, Oklahoma, Rhode Island, and South Carolina.[3]

[2] On state party systems see Lockhard, *op. cit.*, pp. 544–558, and Jacob and Vines, *op. cit.*, pp. 61–99.

[3] Survey data indicate that about 70 percent of the electorate voted straight tickets for state and local offices in 1956, with a decline to 50 percent in 1966. Further aspects of split-ticket voting are covered in Chap. 17.

There is recognizable diversity in the political culture among the states.[4] Certain Southern states are considerably more moderate than others in attitudes toward black voter registration and school desegregation. Ideologies differ from state to state; some states are strongly conservative while others are liberal. Concentrations of Mormons in Utah, Catholics in Louisiana and Massachusetts, Protestants in several Border and Midwestern states give denominational leaders the right to be heard if not to exercise informal political power.

Public attitudes toward political parties have not been studied on a state-by-state basis, but evidently they vary widely. Direct primary laws may broadly reflect public attitudes toward party organizations. Westerners are quick to proclaim that they do not want bosses "like they have back East." Partisan municipal elections prevail in some states; in other states city governments are nonpartisan. It is probably not coincidence that no Eastern or Southern state operates under an open primary system and that the greatest experimentation with direct primary systems has occurred in the Far West. Party discipline in the state legislatures shows much variation. Parties have often but not always divided on such issues as government participation in various programs, use of lotteries to raise public funds, sales taxes, conservation, public welfare, and liquor regulation.

Although not fully studied, socioeconomic characteristics often influence interparty competitiveness. The two-party system is usually found in highly urbanized states, while the one-party or modified one-party system prevails in nonurban states.[5] Urban states have the highest median income and the highest percentage of labor force engaged in manufacturing, and the lowest in agriculture. Republican states tend to be the most agricultural, except in the South. A higher percentage of first- and second-generation immigrants are found in the two-party states and a larger proportion of Roman Catholics. The ecological basis of the local party systems is not yet fully established; however, there is evidence of some relationship between an area's structure and the structure of its party system. In Ohio, urban county structures have been conducive to more competitive party systems with transition to more competition as urbanization progresses. This was not found to be true in Iowa, however.[6]

Constitutional-Legal Arrangements. The state and local parties must function within state constitutions and statutes, which in turn influence the

[4] Considerable literature points to the importance of political culture and styles in various nations. Although of less importance in the American states, it is a factor to be recognized. See Gabriel Almond and Sidney Verba, *The Civic Culture,* Princeton University Press, Princeton, N.J., 1963.

[5] See table in Jacob and Vines, *op. cit.,* p. 69.

[6] See Heinz Eulau, "The Ecological Basis of Party Systems: The Case of Ohio," *Midwest*

OTHER PARTY SYSTEMS
103

organization and operation of the parties. Constitutions prescribe the
state and usually the county elective offices as well as length of term for
all branches of the government. In Alaska and New Jersey among other
states, the governor possesses the authority to choose his own department heads. At the other extreme, in some states more than a dozen
state officials are popularly elected. The great majority of states have a
plural executive; thus an opposition party can gain a toehold in the state
politics by capturing a lesser office, such as secretary of state or treasurer.
State constitutions determine the size and method of election of state
legislatures and usually fix the number of judicial positions and method
of selection. Constitutions not only determine which offices shall be
elective, therefore influencing opportunity levels for party control, but
also fix the term of office; and a number of states limit the governor to
one or two terms. Some state constitutions provide for a consolidated
ballot so that the governor is assured a lieutenant governor of his own
party.

Partisanship or nonpartisanship of elective offices is also usually
determined by the state constitution. The fundamental law often provides for nonpartisan election of the state superintendent of education
and judges, thus removing certain amounts of patronage from the party
organization, and in many states elections are nonpartisan.

Largely in response to scandals and charges of corruption, state
legislatures began in the nineteenth century to regulate political parties.
The first laws were designed to prevent fraud and manipulation of nominating conventions. Mandatory direct primary laws were enacted after
1900, greatly affecting the relationship of party organizations to the
nominating process. Nearly all states regulate to some extent, usually
ineffectually, party finance. Statutes usually specify how certain party
officials are to be elected and their term of office and generally prescribe
biparty election boards and registration requirements. Some state laws
authorize party committees to recommend persons to fill public offices
prematurely vacated. The state law usually specifies the conditions an
organization must meet to qualify as a political party. In closed primary
states, the qualifications for the right to vote in the primary are stipu-
lated. The body of state law pertaining to parties indicates that they are
regarded as at least semipublic institutions, yet a great deal of party activity remains unregulated. Except for state laws providing for the direct
primary, parties in most states are permitted much latitude in determining their own organizations and affairs.

Journal of Political Science, vol. 1, pp. 125–135, 1957, and David Gold and John R. Schmidhauser,
"Urbanization and Party Competition: The Case of Iowa," *Midwest Journal of Political Science*, vol. 4,
pp. 62–75, 1960. For a study involving ten states, see Phillips Cutright, "Urbanization and Competitive
Party Politics," *Journal of Politics*, vol. 25, pp. 552–564, 1963.

CLASSIFICATION OF STATE PARTY SYSTEMS

Because of the great variations in the party system from state to state, and even within the same state from time to time, it is difficult to classify the party systems found in the several states. Party strength tends to be cyclical in character, and observation for one period may be inapplicable a few years later. One party may be dominant for a rather long time only to give way to a long reign by the opposition party. The extent of interparty contests varies for different offices. In recent years, there has usually been greater interparty competition for the Presidency than for the governorship and the state legislature. The governorship is frequently more competitive than the lesser statewide offices such as auditor, treasurer, and attorney general.

By Office. It is noteworthy that neither party has been able to capture the electoral votes of any one of the states in every election since 1952. Although Republican presidential candidates have done well in Deep South states during this period, the party has in these states been hopelessly outnumbered in the state legislatures, the county courthouses, and governorships.

TABLE 4-1 Five indexes showing the ten most competitive states*

Jewell-Patterson	Dawson-Robinson	Ranney	Schlesinger	Munger-Weber
Washington	Washington	Washington	Washington	Iowa
Indiana	Illinois	Hawaii†	Inidana	Indiana
Massachusetts	Massachusetts	Massachusetts	Ohio	South Dakota
Delaware	Delaware	Delaware	...	Nebraska†
Colorado	...	Colorado	Colorado	Vermont
Montana	Montana	Montana	...	North Dakota
Utah	Utah	Alaska†	...	Utah
...	Idaho	Missouri	Idaho	Idaho
Oregon	...	...	Oregon	Kansas
Pennsylvania	Pennsylvania	Nevada	Nevada	...
California	...	...	Wyoming	Wyoming
...	Connecticut	...	Connecticut	...
...	Rhode Island	Rhode Island	...	...

Sources: Malcolm E. Jewell and Samuel C. Patterson, *The Legislative Process in the United States,* Random House, Inc., New York, 1966, pp. 141–146; Richard E. Dawson and James A. Robinson, "Inter-Party Competition, Economic Variables, and Welfare Policies in the American States," *Journal of Politics,* vol. 25, pp. 265–289, 1963; Austin Ranney, "Parties in State Politics," in Herbert Jacob and Kenneth N. Vines (eds.). *Politics in American States: A Comparative Analysis,* Little, Brown and Company, Boston, 1965, pp. 63–67; Joseph A. Schlesinger, "A Two-Dimensional Inter-Party Competition," *American Political Science Review,* vol. 49, pp. 1120–1128, 1955; and Robert E. Weber and Frank J. Munger, "Party identification and the Classification of State Party Systems," paper presented to the annual meeting of the American Political Science Association, September, 1968.
*Not listed in order of competitiveness but in frequency of appearance on two or more indexes.
†By reason of time, unicamerical body, or nonpartisan legislature, this state was not rated on all five indexes. Schlesinger rated only nine instead of ten states but found New York, Utah, and West Virginia, which do not appear on his list, as "cyclically competitive."

If one chooses the state legislatures and/or governorships as a measure of interparty competition, the successes of each major party throughout the country are substantially equal over a period of years, despite the dominance of one party in many states. In 1970, Democrats controlled both houses in twenty states and the Republicans controlled both houses in twenty states. In eight states, each party controlled one house; Minnesota and Nebraska use a nonpartisan ballot to elect their legislators. As further evidence of the division of party strength, only half of the Republican governors (sixteen) had a legislature controlled by their party and only twelve of the eighteen Democratic governors had a legislative majority of their party. In many states, however, one-party dominance of the legislature is the rule. In 1970, the Alabama and Louisiana legislatures included only one Republican serving in each, and the Mississippi legislature had none. Only a handful of Republicans were elected to other Deep South state legislatures. Republican control was one-sided in Kansas, the Dakotas, New Jersey, and Vermont.

Time base period used as well as offices considered make considerable differences in results of analyses. Table 4-1 shows the classifications of the ten most competitive states using five different sets of criteria; all except Munger-Weber are based on competition for state office.[7] Only Washington was found on all of these. Indiana, Massachusetts, Delaware, Colorado, Montana, Utah, and Idaho make the top on three of the five studies.

The office of governor offers a basis for classification because it is the most visible and likely to be the most competitive of all state offices. Using this basis, Schlesinger found a low rate of alternation in the office between 1870 and 1950 with more than half the states giving it to one party in 70 percent or more of the elections.[8]

One of the more complete categorizations has been prepared by Austin Ranney for the period 1946–1963.[9] Calculations were made on the basis of (1) the average percentage of the popular vote won by the Democratic gubernatorial candidates; (2) the average number of seats held by the Democrats in the state house and in the state senate; and (3) the percentage of all terms for governor, senate, and house in which

[7] Limitations of space preclude analysis of the criteria for classification and a listing of states appearing in each. The student may wish to do this for himself from footnote citations. Jewell and Patterson used party competition of the state legislatures between 1947 and 1966. Malcolm E. Jewell and Samuel C. Patterson, *The Legislative Process in the United States*, Random House, Inc., New York, 1966, pp. 141–146. Seven different categories are used to provide refinement. Two-party states were designated as those where neither party predominated and party control approximated control of the governorship.

[8] Joseph A. Schlesinger, "A Two-Dimensional Inter-Party Competition," *American Political Science Review*, vol. 49, pp. 1120–1128, 1955.

[9] See his analysis in Jacob and Vines, *op. cit.*, pp. 63–67.

the Democrats had control. Using this measure Alabama, Arkansas, Florida, Georgia, Louisiana, Mississippi, South Carolina, and Texas were classified as one-party Democratic. Next were the modified one-party states of Arizona, Kentucky, Maryland, New Mexico, North Carolina, Oklahoma, Tennesee, Virginia, and West Virginia. There were no one-party Republican states, but Iowa, Kansas, Maine, New Hampshire, North Dakota, South Dakota, Vermont, and Wisconsin were found to be modified one-party Republican. The remaining twenty-five states were placed in varying degrees of two-party politics.[10]

Dawson and Robinson ranked the states according to percentage of the two-party vote for the predominant party governor and percentage of seats held by the predominant party in each of the two houses in the state legislature. Results were not precisely but generally in the same direction as Ranney's.[11]

By Party Identification or Other Bases. By moving from party success in capturing elective offices to party identification of eligible or participating electorates, individual states might be placed in a different category. Robert E. Weber and Frank J. Munger utilized a vote-type methodology to classify the fifty states.[12]

One might also utilize nonelectoral bases to ascertain the varieties of parties. Such a base might be the degree of organizational development, with a range from highly organized ones as in Pennsylvania and Connecticut to active and viable but very loosely organized parties in California and the Democratic party in Texas. Many Southern Republican parties have been little more than agencies to receive patronage whenever their party controlled the White House. This situation is changing as Republican parties in the South, like Democratic parties in the New England, are attracting more activists and are becoming increasingly more viable.

In summary, none of the numerous classifications describes a state's party strength with precision and the endeavor at times seems more interesting than rewarding.[13] Yet, if one will omit federal offices,

[10] Gubernatorial elections were used as measures in Minnesota and Nebraska because of their nonpartisan legislatures; Alaska and Hawaii were included only from the dates of their statehood in 1959.

[11] Richard E. Dawson and James A. Robinson, "Inter-Party Competition, Economic Variables, and Welfare Policies in the American States," *Journal of Politics*, vol. 25, pp. 265–289, 1963. Time period was 1938–1958.

[12] See their paper "Party Identification and the Classification of State Party Systems," presented to the annual meeting of the American Political Science Association, September, 1968.

[13] A useful critique and review of attempts to classify state party systems is provided by David G. Pfeiffer, "The Measurement of Inter-Party Competition and Systemic Stability," *American Political Science Review*, vol. 61, pp. 457–467, 1967. Two other useful works are Herbert Jacob and Michael Lipsky, "Outputs, Structure, and Power: An Assessment of Changes in the Study of State and Local Politics," *Journal of Politics*, vol. 30, pp. 510–538, 1968, and Thomas R. Dye, *Politics, Economics and the Public: Policy Outcomes in the American States*, Rand McNally & Company, Chicago, 1966.

the various state office indexes tend to come up with the same broad political coloration for all except six to ten states that appear in different categories as the criteria are changed. Scholars are agreed that frequent reevaluation is needed because changes and realignments are constantly taking place with modified one-party states becoming much more two-party in character.

TYPES OF STATE POLITICAL FACTIONALISM

In contrast to interparty competition, which is often absent or weak, intraparty struggles are omnipresent at all levels of government. Factional struggles over the leadership and programs between subgroups within a party are a vital part of the democratic process, though usually denounced by leaders of the dominant faction as sacrificing the overall party good for factional interests. Factionalism, according to this view, should be avoided and those responsible for it are to be criticized if not suspect.

The term faction is sometimes used to cover amorphous situations but is more useful when applied to a definite identifiable personnel and leadership, possessing enough organization to provide the subgroup with at least a rudimentary structure and cohesion. Cohesion requires the presence of at least some common objectives. Further, a faction is best recognized when there are identifiable rivals and opponents. Outsiders should perceive the faction as a subgroup. These components of faction, of course, are fulfilled in varying degrees.

Factions arise from many different sources. Religious, ethnic, and racial ties are often present in party factional groups, although such bases for factional groups are often criticized. Ideology and program form a long-recognized basis for intraparty division. Often faction is traceable to personal ambitions and centers around a candidate or party leader. Often state and local party chiefs and many congressmen have positions of power that thrive on personal followings. Disunited parties are likely to provide more upward routes of mobility than tightly disciplined ones. The forming of factions to attain ends for those seeking higher party or public office is to be expected. Social class and contests among leaders of different geographic areas afford other bases for factions. Ideological factionalism is likely to be the most bitter form and least subject to accommodation.

Patterns. Factionalism is generally quite transitory without continuity in program, leadership, direction, and voter loyalty. Patterns of bifactionalism, trifactionalism, and multifactionalism may be found in the hundreds of county and state parties. Generally, the more fragmented,

decentralized, and autonomous the party apparatus, the more dispersed will be its factions.

Louisiana is cited as a more or less classic example of a fairly
durable structured bipolarization between the Long and the anti-Long
forces.[14] Their contests are settled in the Democratic primaries. The
bifactional loyalties of the voters and the personal followings together
with the "ticket system" helped to form a cohesive base. Statewide slates
for each side are formed in the nature of a balanced ticket, which in
reality is a gubernatorial ticket. There is the further attempt to get candidates for local offices to affiliate with the state ticket. This arrangement
gives the state candidates a grass-roots organization and the parish
candidates receive support from the top and some financial assistance in
their campaigns.

Trifactional politics is found in several states and requires some
participation from the weak second party. Texas affords one of the best
illustrations. Conservative Democrats, liberal Democrats, and Republicans have well-defined political contenders and officeholders and all
three factions utilize the Democratic primary to attain their ends.
Liberals try to win nomination for their candidates; if they lose, they
attempt to defeat the conservative Democrat in the general election. If
the liberals win, the Republicans try to get conservative Democrats to
vote Republican. If conservatives win the Democratic nomination, the
Republicans try to persuade liberal Democrats to vote Republican.
Senator John Tower, a Republican, has been able to win elections because of the factionalism in the Democratic party. Trifactionalism is
nurtured in a state moving from a one-party to a two-party system.

Even in states with two competitive parties, trifactionalism may
appear, as it has in New York and Pennsylvania. Because of a closed
primary system, Republican voters cannot participate in Democratic
primaries but disgruntled Democrats may vote Republican or at least
give no help to the Democratic candidates in the general election.

It is not uncommon for each of the two major parties to have a
sharp bipolarization resulting in four and even more factions within the
overall state party system. In California, the California Democratic
Council (CDC), which is more liberal than the regular Democratic organization, has in the past endorsed candidates and conducted preprimary
campaigns for them; but its control over party nominations has weakened in recent years. In 1964, the then Assembly speaker, Jess Unruh,
organized CDC dissidents and others into his own support auxiliary, the

[14]See especially Allan P. Sindler, "Bifactional Rivalry as an Alternative to Two-Party
Competition in Louisiana." *American Political Science Review*, vol. 49, pp. 641–662, 1955. Sindler found
the state's bifactionalism "considerably inferior to the two-party politics."

Democratic Volunteers Committee. The California Republican Assembly has come under control of ultraright groups that are often anathema to moderate Republicans. The Republican Assembly lost some of its former power in a further right-wing split through a new auxiliary called the United Republicans of California. Another disarray in the ranks, more liberal in orientation, led to a California Republican League. Such proliferation has made the numerous auxiliaries in both parties more or less candidate organizations.[15]

Minor-Party Factions. In New York State, and especially in New York City, minor parties are an important part of the political system. The Marxist groups are separate parties but the larger, more important ones exemplified by the American Labor, Liberal, and Conservative parties originated in factionalism and function more or less in that role though officially recognized in law as separate parties. The American Labor party (ALP) was founded in 1936 by Labor's Nonpartisan League and trade unions to work for the reelection of President Franklin D. Roosevelt since the Tammany Hall organization showed little enthusiasm for him. He received his margin of victory, as did Mayor La Guardia and others, on the ALP line. The right wing bolted in 1944 and formed the Liberal Party. The ALP abandoned its supporting role for the Democrats and ran its own candidate for governor in 1950 and 1954. The venture was a disastrous one and the party lost its legal status for failure to poll enough votes.

John F. Kennedy carried New York in 1960 with a plurality of 386,000, receiving 406,000 votes as the Liberal candidate. The New York victories of Johnson and Humphrey did not depend on the Liberal vote but it greatly augmented their pluralities. In almost every congressional election in the state, the Liberals have provided the decisive margin for one or more Democrats. On the occasions when the Liberals have run their own candidate for a state or local office, the Democrats have suffered more than the Republicans, occasionally permitting the Republican to obtain a plurality. In 1968, the Liberals ran Humphrey for President and went over to nominate Republican Jacob Javits for reelection to the United States Senate. This was one of the comparatively few times the Liberals have supported a Republican candidate. Mayor John Lindsay won reelection in New York City in 1969 at the head of the Liberal party ticket after he failed to get a renomination from the Republicans. Liberals run their own candidates frequently

[15]On California party factionalism, see Totton J. Anderson, "California: Enigmatic Eldorado of National Politics," in Frank H. Jonas (ed.), *Politics in the American West*, University of Utah Press, Salt Lake City, 1969, pp. 93–101.

enough that the threat of such action is more than an idle one as far as the Democrats are concerned.

In a sense, the Liberal party is a party within a party, tending to be a satellite of the Democratic party and performing a *supportive* role for it. The Non-Partisan League in the Dakotas and the Progressives in Wisconsin afford examples of parties that once functioned as satellites of the Republican party and exerted influence on its candidates and programs.

Dismayed with the liberal cast that Gov. Nelson Rockefeller was giving New York's Republican party, a group within the party formed a Conservative party in 1962. The Conservatives sought to have a greater voice in the Republican party, more or less comparable to that of the Liberals with the Democrats. This called for underpinning Republican nominations with Conservative endorsement where the candidate merited such support. It also hoped to head off "deals" in which some Republican congressional candidates showed a tendency to run also on the Liberal ticket. The Conservatives also wanted to give New Yorkers of their political persuasion a chance to vote for a nonliberal candidate. It ran journalist William Buckley for mayor of New York when it could not accept John M. Lindsay as the Republican candidate in 1965. Conservatives also ran their own candidate for governor in 1966. Conservatives also could not accept Senator Javit's renomination in 1968 and ran their own candidate, who polled a surprising 1,140,000 votes, the largest of any minor-party candidate in history. In contrast, the Liberals polled only 459,000 votes for Javits. The independent course taken by the Conservatives poses problems for the Republican party and makes them a formidable third party force in the state. The Conservative party sought to run Republican presidential electors in 1968 to aid Nixon. The Republican state organization feared the consequences of a Conservative endorsement of Nixon and denied permission.

The separate party status of the Conservatives and Liberals in New York points up the problems of a dissonant minority trying to affect the electoral process. One can stay with a majority and try to affect its policies and nominations. To do so has meant for many liberals in New York the support of old line, if not Tammany Hall, candidates; for many conservatives staying with the Republicans has meant support of the "big spending" Rockefeller forces. By following the independent minor party course, candidates close to one's own ideology can be supported and a warning given to the "establishment" that they can expect defection or additional support according to how well they accommodate to the minority. But this style of small-party activity runs the risk of dispersing resources and votes and electing the opposition.

NATIONAL AND STATE PARTIES

Paradoxically, American major parties function as both decentralizers and nationalizers. The national ego, functioning through the presidential party, may find itself held back if not opposed by the state parties operating through the congressional wing. Local leaders and influential groups may pressure their congressmen to maintain a stand of states' rights on one problem but on another occasion may agree with the President that a national solution is needed and urge their congressmen to follow the Chief Executive. Presidents and governors often must vie with the legislative wings of their own parties. A President cannot rely on the national chairman to rally congressional support for his program; governors are in an analogous position. Executives must try to build up their own political support—some of it from within the party and some from outside. Similarly, powerful congressmen will attempt to mobilize power both within and outside the party in their contest with the executive. In 1958 the then House Congressional Committee Chairman Richard M. Simpson advised incumbent Republicans that they should feel free to make known their disagreement with the President when campaigning for reelection.[16]

The vote cast for party candidates for state and local offices may vary widely from that cast for its candidates for national offices. Local organizations may be much more successful in mobilizing their electorate for President than for Congress or vice versa. Since 1952, for example, the Republican vote for President in Florida and Virginia has been strong while its vote for state legislative candidates was almost nonexistent. Elsewhere in the South since the end of World War II, the Republican strength has been largely in the presidential race, with occasional support for a Republican candidate for Congress. However, Republicans are making gains in the state and local contests.

Many voters who register as members of one of the two major parties often vote for candidates of the opposite party. In most states, a voter who regards himself as an independent nevertheless must register as a member of a party in order to qualify to vote in primary elections, and for this reason party registration is a poor guide to party strength. Apparently split-ticket voting is increasing. Since 1936, the Democratic party in California has held a registration edge of almost 60 percent of registered voters, yet only one Democratic candidate for governor was elected, and in 1952, 1956, 1960, and 1968, the Republican candidate for President carried the state. In the state of Washington only once in the period from 1948 through 1968 did candidates for President and

[16] See Hugh A. Bone, *Party Committees and National Politics*, University of Washington Press, Seattle, 1958, pp. 160–161.

for governor of the same party win. Many other states have shown similar anomalies.

Within a state there may be pockets of highly independent voting strength in the midst of classical ticket voting. In New York City, the boroughs of Brooklyn and Manhattan run strongly Democratic both in registration and in voting. In Queens the Democrats are favored in registration by about 2 to 1, but did not carry the borough for the Democratic candidate for President between 1936 and 1960. The borough also has tended to favor the Republican candidate for governor, but consistently votes Democratic in municipal elections.

The national party system functions with decentralized state party systems. The parties strive for national unity during campaigns, but their elected officeholders often become decentralizers in the halls of the legislature. Social science analysis has not fully answered the question of why voters regard party labels as more important for some offices than for others. Later, however, we shall look more closely at what has been learned about the voting behavior of the American citizen.

The graph in Figure 4-2 shows the percentages of United States House seats and governorships held by Democrats and the percentage of popular vote for the party's Presidential candidates. Before 1952, one party tended in general to gain or to lose in all three areas. This pattern

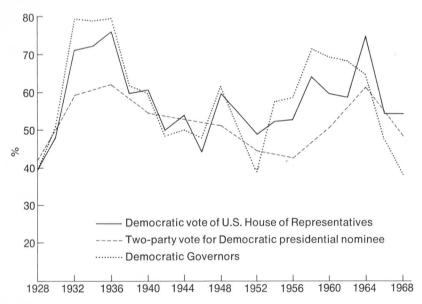

FIGURE 4-2 Democratic percentage of the total vote in the election for House of Representatives, Governors, and Presidents, 1928–1968.

was present in 1964 but was followed much less closely in the other elections. In the thirty-four gubernatorial contests in 1966, Republicans substantially outpolled their Democratic opponents (53.8 percent) but Republicans mustered only 48.7 percent of the House vote. Republicans polled 53 percent for their gubernatorial and 48.9 percent for their House candidates in 1968. The Wallace movement greatly reduced Mr. Nixon's popular vote in 1968, and Republicans made spectacular increases in the governorships but with very slight gains in the House.

Apparently, two opposite influences are at work in national and state politics. State parties are insulated from national politics by election laws and traditions. Further, many states hold their statewide elections in midterm years. Under the decentralized system, state and local chiefs and congressmen often have powers that they could not hope to have if parties were centralized nationally. At the same time, two-party politics is well established in most industrial states, and they are not fully resistant to the tides of national policies. This tends to tie the two together and, in so doing, helps to modify fragmenting tendencies in the states.

The minority party within a state often draws strength from a strong national ticket. National party trends undoubtedly affect the political fortunes of party in most states. Republican candidates for governor and other state offices undoubtedly benefited from having Eisenhower at the head of the ticket. Republican governors in 1952 were particularly instrumental in the Eisenhower nomination because of their belief that he would aid the party candidates in their states. Although congressmen build their own alliances and may have bases of strength different from that of their statewide party, they often profit immeasurably from a strong presidential candidate. The Michigan Survey Research Center's sample of Southern Eisenhower voters showed that those who also voted for Republican congressional candidates rose from 21 percent in 1952 to 46 percent in 1956.[17] The reverse may also be true, for strong local candidates appeared to help President Truman in 1948 and were of some aid to Kennedy in 1960.

For many years students of government have registered concern over the role of states in the federal system with the rise of nationalization of politics. The competence of state governments to handle the overshadowing problems of the day has been questioned. The relationship of the states to the federal system is not merely a structural matter, it is a political one as well. State parties are faced not only with finding candidates for local offices but with recognizing that so many problems

[17]Angus Campbell and Warren Miller, "The Motivational Basis of Straight and Split Ticket Voting," *American Political Science Review*, vol. 51, p. 296, 1957.

cross state boundary lines and political party lines. Variety is a common attribute of state parties. What is true of a party in one state is not necessarily true in an adjacent state and two parties within the same state may function in a dissimilar way. Nevertheless a political party is a useful vehicle in all states for providing leadership, articulating interests, and focusing attention on state affairs.

LOCAL PARTIES

Politics is a system of activities with the various segments constantly relating to each other. What has been said of the national and state parties is generally applicable to their local segments. They do not stand alone but must relate to other party units and to interest groups and are influenced by their political environment and rules of the game. Their structures are often prescribed by law. They face factionalism and the need for money and manpower. Patterns of politics vary enormously among the separate regions and cities. The courthouse politics of the Byrd organization in Virginia is well disciplined in contrast to county politics in Maine and Colorado. Why old-style politics continues to persist in some settings and not in others is not certain any more than why there are so many varieties of urban politics. The older patterns continue in some degree in situations that gave rise to strong local partisan politics, as in some Eastern cities. Changes in the social composition of cities are bringing changes in the East as well as elsewhere. The spread of non-partisanship and the entry of a new class of amateur democrats and reformers has also changed urban political styles.

Two aspects of local politics have been extensively researched. One is the study of the old-style municipal boss and political machine, their function and general demise.[18] The others are the numerous analyses of community power structures and local decision making. In many of the local power studies, party leaders receive little attention because they are found to be comparatively unimportant in decision making. In other communities, party leaders are regularly consulted and participate actively in the making of policy.

City and county parties, like the state and national parties, exist to win elections; therefore, their structures run parallel to the governmental structure. However, their environment has certain differences from those of the state parties. In many areas, there are overlapping county and city governments as well as thousands of townships and special districts. In most states the county is the basic and highly significant political party unit. Nearly all counties use the partisan ballot for their elective offices. Counties are the electoral units not only for county offices

---

[18] Machine politics and analyses of local party organization are covered in Chap. 5.

but often for state judges, state legislators, and sometimes for Congress. Many counties have resisted extensive civil service inroads and have sizable amounts of patronage at the disposal of the winning party.

Partisanship and Nonpartisanship. The county parties in this century were unable to prevent the great movement for nonpartisan elections in municipal government. More than 60 percent of cities with populations more than 5,000 have nonpartisan local elections and cities with the council-manager form of government almost invariably elect the members of the council in nonpartisan elections. In many cities, elections are nonpartisan in fact as well as form and the two parties do not enter candidates for city offices. In other communities the local party organizations support candidates in one way or another and voters associate candidates with party labels.

In some cities where the national parties do not function through local units in municipal elections, local parties have arisen. They operate under such labels as Commonwealth, Fusion, Charter, Good Government, or the colorful nomenclature New Order of Cincinnatus. Several of these local parties are only semipermanent. Candidates or groups of them may form temporary electoral alliances with ties into business, labor, civic, and various minority groups. Such groups do not take on the full attributes of a local political party and rival groups for office are the "blues" against the "yellows." Local politics in numerous places are carried without anything resembling a party.

In some American cities the two parties conduct full-blown contests for their elective offices. In Connecticut, nonpartisanship has not made significant inroads, and candidates for local office run under a party label. Robert A. Dahl reports the importance of local parties in New Haven and that they are used as an instrument to obtain public policies.[19] It might be observed that nonpartisan elections, though found in all sections, are less used in the New England and Middle Atlantic areas. In general, parties are more highly organized in the concentrated urban areas than in the rural and suburban parts. There is, of course, a significant difference in the effectiveness and strength of political organization from one city to another.

Where nonpartisan elections are required by law, municipal parties bearing the national two-party labels have problems of being. In some cases, notably Chicago, the nominal nonpartisan is actually partisan. Voters associate candidates with parties, and one has little chance of winning unless so identified. Parties in this environment function as in partisan elections. Other nonpartisan cities tolerate at least some degree

[19] Robert A. Dahl, *Who Governs?*, Yale University Press, New Haven, Conn., 1961.

of open campaigning by parties, but party organizations are more circumspect than in partisan elections. In a large number of nonpartisan cities, local groups take the lead in organizing slates and campaigning for them. "Self-starters" organize their own supporters outside the party system. Regular party organizations have little to do with the local campaign because voters are indifferent, if not outright hostile, to their efforts.

National and Local Parties. The electoral strength of municipal and county parties compared with their state and national units has not received overall examination. For example, in some cities Democratic mayors and councilmen appear to have lost votes because of statewide victories for Republican governors and Presidents. But in Chicago, Philadelphia, New York, and Cleveland, to mention only a few cities, Democratic municipal officials have resisted national and state Republican tides. This can be deceptive, however, if it is assumed that huge numbers of voters in big cities invariably prefer Democratic mayors but split their ballots to support Republicans nominees for governor and President. Democratic city pluralities for Democratic presidential nominees and very often for governor are commonplace. Statewide Republican successes are often due to huge outstate Republican pluralities.

In his analysis of the relationship between the large cities holding partisan local elections and presidential politics between 1928 and 1960, Charles E. Gilbert found that more cities were locally competitive between Republicans and Democrats in the 1920s and 1930s than was true in 1960. Further "partisan cities have become *more* closely competitive in general elections despite the oft-remarked erosion of the bases of 'machine' politics since that time. All of the cities that have become less competitive since the nineteen-thirties have tended in a Democratic direction and, in contrast to the period of the nineteen-twenties none of the partisan large cities today is normally Republican, and only one or two are closely contested with any frequency."[20]

"It thus appears that, in the long run, local electoral behavior in the partisan cities has been heavily influenced by national electoral behavior and attitudes—that 'party identifications' previously rooted in national politics have resulted in Democratic dominance locally and have reduced the incident of local party competition."[21] Local scandals resulting in campaigns to "throw the rascals out," racial and religious conflict, strength of the political organization, and economic recession were found to be factors in the local successes (or failures) of the Demo-

[20]Charles E. Gilbert, "National Political Alignments and the Politics of Large Cities," in Philip B. Coulter (ed.), *Politics of Metropolitan Areas: Selected Readings,* Thomas Y. Crowell Company, New York, 1967, pp. 452–465.
[21]*Ibid.,* p. 454.

crats, but the Gilbert study gives evidence that the influence of national politics was decisive during the period studied.

Although most central cities are Democratic and suburbs tend to be Republican, there are many exceptions. Contests for county offices as a rule are conducted by local Democratic and Republican organizations. Because of cleavages over such issues as law enforcement, welfare, transportation, blight and pollution, party differences are often blurred. One finds great differences in degrees of competitiveness between the parties in different communities.[22]

One thesis holds that rural areas have the least party competition, with competitiveness increasing as urbanization increases; but a study of Iowa's counties found some tendency of greater competition to be associated with less urbanization. The problem has been to separate urbanization as a factor in competitiveness from other ecological considerations such as industrialization, religious affiliation, income, and occupation. It is obvious that much remains to be learned about the causes of competitiveness and noncompetitiveness at all levels and in other nations.

FOREIGN PARTY SYSTEMS

Political party systems vary widely in different countries.[23] Sociological conditions, degree of national development, governmental structure, and disposition of power in the community profoundly affect the nature of various parties and systems within which they operate. As members of the British Commonwealth of Nations, Australia and Canada might be expected to have essentially similar party systems, but the variations between the Canadian and the Australian arrangements are marked. Australia, for example, has a Country party that defends the interests of both big and small farmers. The Labour party is based upon trade unions and farm workers, and the Liberal party, which is the most to the right is a "town capital" party of professionals, businessmen, and the middle class. Australian parties, largely because of historical factors, have distinct class bases; there is much less class voting in the national parties in Canada. Great Britain also has no counterpart of the Country party. Party systems are not readily exportable because they rest upon their own cultures. Some devices and techniques, however, may be transported and may prove useful.

[22]A summary and critique of the various findings is provided by Philip Coulter and Glen Gordon, "Urbanization and Party Competition: Critique and Redirection of Theoretical Research," *Western Political Quarterly*, vol. 21, pp. 274–288, 1968.

[23]A wealth of material is found on parties in the individual nations and in a comparative context. A few of the newer major works in the latter category are R. R. Alford, *Party and Society: The Anglo-American Democracies*, Rand McNally & Company, Chicago, 1963; S. M. Lipset and Stein Rokkan (eds.), *Party Systems and Voter Alignments: Cross National Perspectives*, The Free Press, New York, 1967; Sigmund Neumann (ed.), *Modern Political Parties*, University of Chicago Press, Chicago, 1956.

Classification: No one has successfully classified the world's party systems. Maurice Duverger has had some success in broadly typing the older parties according to their structures and memberships.[24] Another work sees three main bases—pragmatic, doctrinal, and interest.[25] Pragmatic parties are not mainly concerned with doctrine and ideology. Their programs change with the times. The two major American parties and the Conservative party of Great Britain and Canada are examples of pragmatic parties. Ideological foundations characterize the socialist and some labor parties in various countries. The German Christian Democratic Union, the Mizrachi Party (Israel), and the Christian Historical Union in the Netherlands exemplify parties with religious attachments. The Dutch party system is especially interesting because there are systems of both secular and religious parties. Interest parties differ from the doctrinal ones in that they are strongly dominated by a single interest, such as the Irish and South African Nationalists, the Swiss Farmers' party and the Swedish People's party in Finland.

The problem with these categories is that they do not satisfactorily encompass developments in the emerging states. Goals and sources of support are envisaged but not their interrelationships within the political framework. The use of one-party, biparty, and multiparty classifications also may not tell us too much about the internal workings of the system even though rather definite attributes can be found in each style. Almond and Coleman classify party systems as competitive two-party, competitive multiparty, dominant nonauthoritarian, and authoritarian party systems.[26]

The Single-Party System.   Following the Almond categories, single parties are found within both totalitarian and nonauthoritarian political frameworks. In the former, rival groups are outlawed or very severely restricted, and the one party becomes the source as well as the agent of political authority. Admission to the ranks is a privilege and usually involves acceptance of rigid discipline and often oppressive obligations. Party membership may well be the only channel to career opportunities in government. Unflagging loyalty to the party's rulers is required. The totalitarian single party with its use of force as a political technique stands outside the democratic mold because it can tolerate nothing short of the monopolization of political power. It can hardly be treated as

[24] Maurice Duverger, *Political Parties,* John Wiley & Sons, Inc., New York, 1954. He notes such types as "mass" and "cadre" parties and deals with articulation, linkages, and direct and indirect structure.

[25] Dell G. Hitchner and Carol Levine, *Comparative Government and Politics,* Dodd, Meade & Company, Inc., New York, 1967, chap. 5.

[26] Gabriel A. Almond and James S. Coleman (eds.), *The Politics of Developing Areas,* Princeton University Press, Princeton, N.J., 1960, pp. 40–43.

comparable to a nontotalitarian party, for even the state itself is an instrument of the monolithic party. Several of the Eastern European states, the Soviet Union, and Communist China afford examples of one-party totalitarian systems.

Although many African states are single-party, *authoritarian* is more descriptive than *totalitarian* because the degree of full control does not yet approximate the Communist party in either Asia or Eastern Europe. There are also quite different degrees of authoritarianism and differences in party ideologies in the emerging African states. Even some Communist nations in Europe are becoming polycentric with regard to local policies and are deviating from the "one" single truth of the U.S.S.R. Communist party. The Soviet Union, however, has established a point beyond which it will not tolerate resistance, as evidenced by its occupation and restriction on reforms in Czechoslovakia in 1968.

One-party domination exists in some nations within a nonauthoritarian context. In some cases minor parties exist but present no real challenge to the main official party. A state may be emerging from a dictatorship or colonial rule and may not yet have polarized its politics into two or more great parties. This pattern is found in some of the developing nations in Africa and Asia.

Mexico has been controlled by one party, the PRI (Partido Revolucionario Institucional), for a long time, and the regime has been reasonably stable and moderate with little serious challenge from an opposition. It is almost synonymous with the government and has played an important role in social and economic reforms. Another example is the Congress party in India, which operated without effectual opposition until 1967 when it received some setbacks though maintaining a majority in parliament.

Competitive Systems. The two-party system characterizes the politics of dual divisions uncommon outside the United States, Canada, and Great Britain; Uruguay, Colombia, the German Federal Republic, and New Zealand function politically with two parties. Canada has not only two major parties but also two vigorous minor parties, the Social Credit and the New Democratic parties, which are capable of winning control in some of the provincial elections; but neither minor party has offered a serious challenge in national elections to the dominant Liberal and Conservative parties.[27] As in the United States, Canadian parties must operate in a federal system requiring a local, provincial, and national

---

[27] The New Democratic and Social Credit parties in recent years often either controlled or served as official opposition party in Alberta, British Columbia, Manitoba, Ontario, and Saskatchewan. Since World War I, every province except New Brunswick and Prince Edward Island has been governed at one time or another by a third party.

organization but within a framework of cabinet instead of presidential leadership. To control the national government, a party must carry at least two sections, and these geographical considerations have helped to foster a two-party system at the national level. Although using British names, Canadian parties are more like American parties, for they are coalitions of regional, ethnic, and economic interest groups. National parties are, in effect, federations of provincial parties.

Like American politics, Canadian politics has often been characterized by the dominance of a single party for long periods of time. Since World War I, a variety of minor parties have disturbed the old two-party system. The minor parties, unlike those in the United States, have shown remarkable strength in provincial elections. It is not at all unusual (and at times seems almost the rule) for Canadian voters to elect provincial officials differing in party affiliation from the party controlling the national Parliament. Cabinet government requires disciplined political parties, and notwithstanding the viability of minor parties, the two-party system is dominant in national parliamentary politics.

The British party system presents many contrasts to that of the United States. Parties in Great Britain are highly nationalized, centralized, and disciplined. They are able to get a "party vote" in Parliament. A British member of Parliament is not free to vote as he likes but is compelled to follow the decisions of the party council or run the risk of being disciplined if he opposes the party position too often. This cohesion is by no means due to unanimity over doctrine, although ideology is of some importance in the Labour party. The concept of party loyalty or responsibility undoubtedly has nonideological foundations. A legislative majority is needed in order to gain control of the executive. Lack of unity runs the risk of "no confidence" and loss of the executive. The British member of Parliament who is interested in a political career seeks to be appointed to one of the ministerial positions when his party is in power. This provides a strong personal incentive for members to demonstrate their party loyalty. The member of Parliament, moreover, is not dependent on the good wishes of his constituents. He need not even be a resident of his district. Britain is a unitary rather than a federal state, and politics is nationalized to a greater extent than in the United States. The legislator, therefore, is freed from many of the vicissitudes of localism and regionalism; moreover, local interests historically have not expected their members of Parliament to be subservient to them. They expect them to support the national party leadership. Attitude, therefore, is important in cohesion.

It is difficult to generalize about the multiple-party systems in Europe because political programs and strengths are both changing and deceptive. Parties are implements through which contending forces struggle for power. Religious schisms, nationalism, pro- and anti-European alliance, neutralism in the cold war, socialism, liberalism, communism, and agrarianism, ultraconservatism are among the movements often finding expression through political parties. These forces are rarely integrated into two major parties but express themselves through multiple parties variously based on ideology, status differentiation, and sometimes pragmatism.

Under the multiparty system, parties aim to win the greatest possible electoral support from a limited base, knowing that their chances of obtaining a majority are likely to be thin. They need not make the compromises that are required by a two-party system and hence can stress ideological conflicts and differences. Their commitments are not to the entire electorate but to a particular group.

Coalition government is necessary in multiple systems, and election results may not significantly affect the composition of the government. A group of two or more parties, led usually by the one having the most seats, becomes the ministerial party, while the remainder constitute the opposition parties. In France and Italy, where the Communists are strong, the government coalition seeks to neutralize the Communists and to keep them out of the ministerial coalition.

Americans hear much of cabinet crises and instability in the multiparty systems, but they overlook the fact that many European countries boast stability. The Swiss and Scandinavians have kept stable governments, notwithstanding their multiple-party systems. Some think this is due to homogeneity of population and a high degree of social stability; others attribute it to political arrangements. In the Scandinavian countries, the economic system has accommodated both capitalist and socialist enterprises, which have led to a fair degree of prosperity. Their parties fall somewhat naturally into two blocs. Swiss conservatives and progressives have shown a willingness to make concessions, and they know that a national referendum will be used to invalidate their proposals if they depart from the popular will. Experience in these and some other nations indicates that multiparty systems do not *ipso facto* result in unstable governments. Other factors seem to mitigate tendencies toward fragmentation.

The one great virtue of a national biparty arrangement is the provision of fairly consistent parliamentary majorities. With the great necessity for compromise among the large interests composing each party, permanent, if imperfect, unity is given to a nation. Electoral success comes from votes, and this forces the parties to pass legislation favoring group interests and to balance and harmonize these interests. Spoils alone cannot keep a party in control forever; sooner or later it must support programs demanded by the large constituency. Where the multiple parties may reflect the varied currents of social thought, they may accentuate community splits. The two-party system tries to work out an overall average of group interests by playing down the shades and nuances within its ranks. As Sir Ernest Barker says, "The system of two parties leaves room for a margin of imprecision, or an area of incalculability, which is a safety-valve in the working of a democratic state."

ELECTION SYSTEMS AND PARTY STRENGTH

The reasons for the existence of two or a number of parties have provoked speculation. One group sees the electoral system as the most important influence on the number of parties. Maurice Duverger attempts to demonstrate the causal effect of electoral systems and concludes that "the party system and the electoral system are two realities that are indissolubly linked, and even difficult sometimes to separate by analysis."[28] Others assert that the number as well as the character of parties emanates from the social cleavages, rigid status groups, and deep-seated interests in a nation, cleavages that find expression through multiple parties. If this is the case, then the type of electoral system would have little effect on the number of parties.

Where a two-party system exists, there is almost invariably an electoral system that minimizes, if not eliminates, representation in the legislature of those parties incapable of winning a plurality of votes in a single-member geographical district. As with so many generalizations, there are exceptions. If a party is particularly strong in one region, it may obtain more than a mere handful of national representatives even in a plurality system. This has happened in some European countries where Socialists captured some working-class constituencies. As mentioned earlier, some third parties in rural Canadian provinces have dominated numerous constituencies.

Every country using proportional representation has several parties represented in the legislature. Multiple-party systems usually require coalitions in order to obtain a governing majority. In a few nations, including Ireland, Norway, and Sweden, one party has frequently been able to win absolute parliamentary majorities. Norway has six main parties, but the Labor party dominated before 1965. The structure of Norwegian politics is largely in terms of party representation of class interests; there is a polarization between class status and party preference.[29]

The ratio of proportionality of voting strength to seats in the legislature is likely to be strongly influenced by the electoral system. The

---

[28] Duverger, *op. cit.*, p. 204.

[29] On this point, see Angus Campbell and Henry Valen, "Party Identification in Norway and the United States," *The Public Opinion Quarterly*, vol. 25, pp. 505–525, 1961.

TABLE 4-2 Voting strength and parliamentary strength in three PR elections

Austria, 1959			Switzerland, 1955			Netherlands, 1959		
Party	Votes	Seats	Party	Votes	Seats	Party	Votes	Seats
Austrian			Radical			Catholic		
People's	42.0	47.9	Democrats	23.3	25.5	People's	31.6	32.7
Socialist	46.0	47.3	Social			Labor	30.4	32.0
Freedom	9.0	4.8	Democrats	27.0	27.0	Freedom	12.2	12.7
			Catholic Con-			Anti-Revolu-		
			servatives	23.2	24.0	tionary	9.4	9.3
			Peasants					
			et al.	12.1	11.2			

Note: Only highest parties shown. The figures are percentages.

d'Hondt and variations of list systems of proportional representation are widely used in Europe and are designed to relate popular votes to seats.[30] The Hare system of the single transferable vote used in Eire and formerly in New York City also attempts to give each element in the voting population representation closely corresponding to its numerical strength. On occasions, the leading group in Eire, Fianna Fáil, has been able to win a majority of seats without polling a majority of votes. But generally correlation between voting strength and seats has been remarkably close, as it was in New York when the Hare system was used.[31]

Proportional representation (PR) requires multimember constituencies, and sometimes the whole nation comprises one constituency with seats assigned according to relative voting strength. In the 1959 election in Israel, there were ten parties, and the whole country functioned as one constituency. Each party received a percentage of legislative seats within a few decimal points of the percentage of votes. In Table 4-2, the votes and seats of the highest parties in different European countries are shown as evidence of the comparatively high correlation between representation and electoral strength. Under the d'Hondt list system, a party list with a large number of votes may obtain several seats before a list with a small number of votes gains its first seat.[32] It is a fair generalization to say that the proportionality between seats and votes is directly related to the size of the constituency; the ideal proportionality arises whenever the entire nation comprises a single constituency. The correlation is higher and the percentage of wasted votes is lower where

[30] The formulas used in diverse systems and the process of allocating seats under proportional representation are complicated. The details and mechanics of operating the proportional representation systems are beyond the scope of this book. A concise but adequate explanation of both the operations and results of proportional representation in Europe will be found in Wolfgang Birke, *European Elections by Direct Suffrage*, A. W. Sythoff, Leyden, Netherlands, 1961. See chap. 1 for methods of distributing seats in parliament under the various systems.

[31] On party representation during this period, see Belle Zeller and Hugh A. Bone, "The Repeal of Proportional Representation in New York City: Ten Years in Retrospect," *American Political Science Review*, vol. 42, pp. 1122–1148, 1948.

[32] See Birke, *op. cit.*, pp. 62ff.

more seats are to be filled; PR will be more proportional as a rule when ten seats are to be filled rather than five.

The smallest degree of proportionality is to be found in electoral systems in which only one party obtains seats in a constituency. In three-cornered fights among Conservatives, Labour, and Liberals, where each approximates the strength of the other, the outcome can be a matter of chance. In 1959, British Conservatives won 58.1 percent of the seats with 49.4 percent of the votes; in 1951, they got 48.0 percent of the votes compared to Labour's 48.8 but won 51.3 percent of the seats in the House of Commons. The Liberals in 1959 polled 6 percent of the votes but won only 0.8 percent of the seats.

Further discussion of proportional and other systems of representation is beyond our scope except to repeat that the party system and legislative representation are strongly influenced by the election system. Proportional representation may not necessarily cause (although some argue it does) multiple parties, but it encourages them and facilitates their representation in legislatures. Single-member constituencies work hardships on the lesser parties. For example, the abandonment of PR in New York City councilmanic elections resulted in immediate loss of representation by minor parties and even hurt the Republicans. At the first election after the repeal of PR, the old familiar pattern of one-party dominance returned with a council of twenty-four Democrats and one Republican. To win in single-member systems, a candidate must appeal very broadly to those within his electoral units, particularly the "great middle" of the district. A multiparty system with proportional representation uses a specific interest or ideological group in lieu of a territorial unit as the basis of representation. This tends to reduce the effect of geography as a basis of election.

In summary, representation in legislative bodies under any system is biased. It favors some of the population over the other. Proportional representation gives minorities representation in parliament, and the system helps preserve declining parties and facilitates the growth of new ones. Minor parties tend to support, if not cling tenaciously to, proportional representation since seats in parliament help to give them a forum and public identity. Without the identity or some semblance of a legislative party, the small party finds it difficult to keep constituents happy and to build a durable party-in-the-electorate. Coalitions of parties are likely to be needed if there is to be an effective majority. The single-member plurality method forces minor parties to merge with a major one if they want to get into the national legislature and, in so doing, may cause them to lose their identity. If they are unwilling to do this, they must be content to function outside parliament and be satisfied to run candidates for purposes of education and perhaps to win occasional victories in local governments.

USES OF PARTIES

The diverse types of parties and party systems throughout the world are related to a myriad of factors including the very origin of the parties themselves. In the older Western nations the development of parties is generally associated with the rise of parliaments and the growth of suffrage. Members of parliament needed a group to act together to attain ends within the institution. Party in this context meant parliamentary party. Legislators also needed support to mobilize the expanding electorates. In a sense, parliamentary groups were created first, then electoral committees were organized and finally links were established between the government party and electoral party.[33]

Parties also emerged from outside of government to challenge the ruling group. An expanding suffrage gave impetus to such objectives; but ideology, anticolonialism, nationalistic emotions also gave rise to parties. Socialist parties in Western Europe, agrarian parties in Scandinavia, and religious groups in Belgium and Germany afford examples of parties essentially created outside legislative assemblies: In some colonial regimes, parties were formed by groups that wished to influence the colonial government, increase opportunities for members to obtain administrative posts, and to enable citizens to voice their aspirations.

In the new, developing nations, parties are used for many purposes.[34] A number of parties were patterned after those in the West, including the Communist party. Such parties serve as agencies for national integration, attaining legitimacy for rulers or would-be rulers, managing conflict, crushing opposition, and for political socialization. They are used by the rulers as direct links with the masses to bring about so-called integration and modernization without the intermediary of traditional tribal authority. In Africa, parties help to create an effective tie at times between the new and the traditional elites.[35] There has been a strong tendency toward the one-party system with the rationale that national goals are better achieved by a single party. With nation building as the top priority, so the argument goes, several parties would be divisive if not subversive and would interfere with its attainment. With a low level of political sophistication, the function of a loyal opposition might not be properly performed. Many scholars have questioned whether in practice the new single party in the states effectively bottles

---

[33] See Maurice Duverger, *Political Parties*.

[34] A basic work on this subject containing an extensive bibliography is Joseph La Palombara and Myron Weiner, *Political Parties and Political Development*, Princeton University Press, Princeton, N.J., 1966.

[35] W. J. Foltz writes, for example, concerning Africa: "The mass party becomes the framework within which ethnic, caste, and regional differences among the population at large could be submerged in the search for a common goal. It both embodied and promoted a preliminary sense of national unity and identity." Cited in *ibid.*, p. 297n.

up conflicts, avoids or reduces tensions, and eliminates diversity or sub-ordinates it to the prime goal of political unity.

In the authoritarian states and in many new states, the single party is concerned with winning and maintaining support while molding and changing public attitudes in the direction of goals established by the rulers. The uses of a party in such instances differs in emphasis from those of matured, democratic nations with two or more parties whose great concern is to win elections and less with day-to-day political socialization of the people. In a sense, a single party is trying to develop a popular support without providing at the same time for full political participation and opportunity for dissent.

In summary, parties in both totalitarian and democratic systems and in both developed and developing nations connect the citizen to his government by allowing him to participate in the recruitment of public officials or by controlling him and rallying him behind national goals without benefit of significant electoral choice. Parties are a major way of aggregating claims of citizens by formulating policies in which interests are accommodated and represented. Parties play a role in providing stable and legitimate government. They are useful in cultivating national identification and in many if not most countries are instruments for expressing local views as well. Generically, they may have been created for one purpose but later abandoned it for new purposes without abandoning the label or the original image.

The single party in totalitarian states and in many of the new states has prompted speculation about the extent to which parties are causes and prime movers of events and shape the views of citizens and the extent to which they are the consequence of their environment. Are parties the cause or the effect? Are they independent or dependent variables?[36] Certainly one can find examples where parties play an independent role and where they simply reflect or react to other factors in the political society. In the single party states, they appear in the main as a causative force in directing and remaking society. Where there are competing parties in a pluralistic society this is much less the case. Parties have nonparty competitors and must adapt to them. They do not have full power to bring about changes in and of themselves because the circumstances are not the same—wide electoral participation, loyal oppositions, powerful organizations, and a free press impose some limitations on what the majority party can do. For the scholar this makes difficult the comparison of one-party systems with two-party or multiple-party systems. In most one-party systems, open contests for legislative

---

[36]One writer who sees American parties as reflecting basic factors in the society is Morton Grodzins, "American Political Parties and the American System," *Western Political Quarterly*, vol. 13, pp. 974–998, 1960.

seats (or executive offices) is not a major characteristic; in democratic societies this is a major reason for the existence of parties. It perhaps provides a challenge to find a separate nomenclature for what is currently labeled a one-party system.

FOR FURTHER READING

Literature on state parties is vast, with materials on almost every state. Titles have been compiled state by state in James Herndon, Charles Press, and Oliver P. Williams, *A Selected Bibliography of Materials in State Government and Politics*, Bureau of Government Research, University of Kentucky, Lexington, 1963. Works on foreign party systems are also very numerous.

Banfield, Edward C.: *Big City Politics*, 1965.
Cotter, Cornelius P. (ed.): *Practical Politics in the United States*, 1969.
Davis, S. R., et al.: *The Australian Political Party System*, 1954.
Dye, Thomas R.: *Politics in States and Communities*, 1969
  and Brett W. Hawkins (eds.): *Politics in the Metropolis*, 1967.
Engelmann, F. C., and M. A. Schwartz: *Political Parties and the Canadian Social Structure*, 1968.
Fenton, John H.: *Politics in the Border States*, 1957.
Goodwin, George, Jr. (ed.): *Party Politics in the New England States*, 1968.
Jonas, Frank (ed.): *Politics in the American West*, 1969.
Katz, Valery H., and D. Katz: *Political Parties in Norway*, 1964.
Lockhard, Duane: *New England State Politics*, 1959.
McKenzie, A. T.: *British Political Parties*, 1955.
Michels, Robert: *Political Parties*, 1959.
Rustow, Dankwart: *The Politics of Compromise*, 1955.
Thorburn, Hugh G. (ed.): *Party Politics in Canada*, 1963.
Williams, E. J.: *Latin American Christian Democratic Parties*, 1967.
Zolberg, A.: *Creating Political Order: The Party States of West Africa*, 1966.

PART THREE PARTY OF THE ACTIVISTS

More public works have resulted from the efforts of precinct
leaders than from all the efforts of reform movements,
taxpayers' leagues and newspaper crusades.

SENATOR HUGH SCOTT

CHAPTER 5 STATE AND LOCAL PARTY ORGANIZATION

Organization and collective activity are basic attributes of modern life.
People organize in order to carry out better certain plans and aspirations.
The functions of a political party have become so varied that, as with
pressure groups, there is an imperative demand for a network of organizations. Organization is needed to arrange and manage the periodic
conventions from the caucus on up through districts or wards, counties,
and states to the national level. In numerous states, specific functions
are imposed by law, such as making nominations for statewide offices
and submitting names of persons to fill public offices prematurely
vacated.

The management of a campaign requires a veritable army of
workers, both line and staff. Money must be raised, and campaign literature must be designed and distributed. Charges against the party or its
members need to be answered, and the party name must be kept before

the public between campaigns. Some groups of officials must determine party policies between the meetings of party conventions. A permanent headquarters and staff are needed to provide continuity and to serve the party throughout the year. Finally, the promotion of party interests demands organization. Patronage positions have to be filled, factional quarrels mediated, and prospective members recruited into the ranks. Building the membership and promoting party harmony require the touch of the specialist—the professional politician.

BASIC ASPECTS OF PARTY ORGANIZATION

The Study of Party Organization. A large number of works on American national, state, and local party organizations are available. They look at structures and recruitment of activists and examine the social backgrounds and incentives of the men and women who are party officeholders. There is much organizational theory about both party and nonparty organizations; yet there is no simple well-developed theory of parties as organizations. "Organizational theory," as James G. March says, "is a collection of incongruous elements."[1] One theory starts with announced goals and views organizations as instruments for realizing them. It begins with examining the purposes and functions of parties and analyzes the organizational arrangements for fulfilling them. The efficiency of an organization could be evaluated in terms of how well it performed in contributing to the attainment of the overall missions.

Another model assumes that the alleged goals of the organization are not exclusive and that nongoal functions such as service and custodial activities are a part of the system. It is concerned as well with functions not necessarily publicly proclaimed or different from those officially announced. Both of these are useful and each has its limitations.[2] Before we turn to consideration of specific aspects of American party organization, a few summary characteristics may be mentioned. By carefully studying organization in his own state and county, the student can note the extent to which they resemble or differ from those elsewhere. One must start from the assumption that there are enormous variations in the functions and structures of party organizations. Failure to recognize this leads to the overgeneralization that all parties

[1] "Some Recent Substantive and Methodological Developments in the Theory of Organizational Decision-Making," in Austin Ranney (ed.), *Essays in the Behavioral Study of Politics*, The University of Illinois Press, Urbana, 1962, p. 192.

[2] Two recent works are recommended for a general theoretical background: William J. Crotty (ed.), *Approaches to the Study of Party Organization*, Allyn and Bacon, Inc., Boston, 1968, and Joseph A. Schlesinger, "Political Party Organization," in James G. March (ed.), *Handbook of Organizations*, Rand McNally & Company, Chicago, 1965, pp. 764–801. The older "classics" are still useful as well: Maurice Duverger, *Political Parties*, John Wiley & Sons, Inc., New York, 1954; and Robert Michels, *Political Parties*, The Free Press, New York, 1949.

perform similar functions to the same degree. Also there is often a failure to distinguish between what parties *actually do* and what they *may do*.

Some General Characteristics. Party organizations have an outer, external life with publicly acknowledged goals. They also have an inner, private life that is often not visible and whose struggles break into print only infrequently as factional, personal, or other contests. They are not directly related to the organization's public objectives. Though perhaps not admitted by the leadership, public and private goals may be contradictory. An organization and its leaders are concerned with survival. Realization of this goal as well as of the functioning of a party within a larger political system are necessary to the understanding of organizational theory and practice.

American major party organizations are office-motivated. When a party is able to compete favorably with its opposition, the public officeholders tend to try—often successfully—to dominate the party organization to achieve their office goals. This sets up tension between public officeholders and the nonofficeholder activists who may not wish to serve the ambitions of the officeholders. In other words, the activists' objectives are different in a degree, and sometimes a large degree, from those in elective positions.

Powerful, well-entrenched public men may control the organization so that it is more of a *candidate* than a *party* organization. Candidates come and go, but organizations continue; the latter's objectives and functions vary over time. For this reason, a given organizational system needs periodic evaluation in light of new personalities and change in policy and status.

Considerable change is usually forced when the in-party becomes the out-party. Consequently, party organizational arrangements and functions vary between the majority and minority party. In Chapter 4 we noted the existence of many variations in party competition. The degree of competition affects operation and functions of the parties. Often the actual structure of the two sets of party committees differs in a single state or county and the activities and operation of their headquarters staffs are quite dissimilar. This is especially the case when one party is strongly dominant. The strength and resources of a party organization, of course, may affect the division of party votes at the polls. There is a complex interplay between organizational activity and party competition.[3]

[3] For empirical evidence and elaboration of theory on this point see Crotty, *op. cit.*, chap. 7. He notes that "the strength of the majority party's local organization in any given locality is positively correlated with the competition provided by the minority party" (p. 293).

General Pattern.   Party structure is lacking in cohesion and is highly decentralized and dispersed. In most states there are several party organizations in addition to the party organization in the government. One of these is the official or formal organization, with lines of authority neatly drawn from precinct leader to district, county, state, and national committees. State and local committees are often prescribed by law.[4] The party gradually evolved from an informal, amorphous, caucus organization to a more definite, regular framework which today is recognized by statute and custom as *the* party committee system. But the power structure of the party is seldom portrayed by the formal structure.

The functions of the network of committees and the auxiliaries that constitute the official party hierarchy are often imprecisely defined: some are imposed by law; others appear in the bylaws of the party; and still others are the result of custom and tradition. California law, for example, is silent on precinct organization, whereas many other states have detailed laws on the nomination, election, and composition of precinct and county committees. Minnesota law lodges final legal authority over the affairs of each political party in the state convention; between conventions the state central committee, "subject to control of the convention," is vested with power over a party's affairs. Illinois law provides for a municipal central committee which becomes important where municipal elections are partisan.

The organizational pattern of the major parties is predicated on the assumption that a party committee is needed for each electoral unit. In addition to the national, state, and county committees, there are many other committees, such as congressional, state legislative district, judicial, probate, village, educational district, and village or township committees. These are semipermanent in character and are mainly used to aid in election campaigns.

Committees are often paper organizations whose members seldom if ever meet and perform few functions, but party leaders of imagination and ability may make them effective instruments in the political struggle. Power centers within the local groups vary from state to state, but more often than not, the county central committee is the key to strength or weakness of organization.

A second type of organization is the hierarchy of conventions paralleling the committee system. These conventions, which usually meet biennially, perform certain nominating functions, adopt resolutions, ratify decisions of executive committees, serve as a general forum for the party, and sometimes choose party officials such as the state

---

[4] For a summary of the types of regulation see L. R. Gaitskill, *State Regulation of Political Parties*, Legislative Research Commission, Frankfort, Ky., 1962. The student should also consult the statutes of his own state, for regulation varies considerably from state to state.

chairman and national committeemen. Conventions are often regarded as the sovereign body, with authority to make the rules for the party that are to be executed by the party committees and their chairmen. Because of the infrequency of conventions and shortness of their meetings, they cannot provide the day-to-day leadership of the party, a function appropriately left to party officers and the party's public officeholders. Conventions are useful as a safety valve in airing, testing, and settling factional disputes.

A third "organization" is not easily charted, for it is entirely informal and composed of certain influential leaders who may hold no position whatsoever in the party hierarchy and indeed may never attend conventions as delegates. These may be officeholders, such as mayors, county commissioners, congressmen, or even governors; or they may be influential citizens or prominent businessmen or labor leaders. The former boss and machine organization has, in many areas, been superseded by a group of elective officeholders who dominate and control personnel, patronage, and party policies. They are able to do this by influencing friends on the regular committee, exploiting their prestige, moving into the vacuum left by inept committee leadership, and using to advantage the necessity for committeemen to respect the wishes of their public officeholders. They are sometimes regarded as *the* party organization because they are the moving forces of power in the organization.

Autonomy characterizes the individual units requiring communication and linkages between them and the nonparty political organization. Relationship and degrees of control show much variation. Vertical linkages are necessary to tie together the organizations from precincts to the national committee in the interests of victory for the ticket as well as for separate candidates. Horizontally, a county committee, for example, needs to cooperate and coordinate with local nonparty groups and with auxiliary party associations in the same area who share common electoral or other goals. Some of the most valuable leaders are those who facilitate connective liaison relationships.

Autonomy brings problems of control. To what extent may a state committee control a county committee's fund raising or campaign strategies? How much control does a county chairman have over a district leader and in turn a district leader over a precinct committeeman? The sources and bases of control differ from unit to unit.[5] The

[5] Samuel J. Eldersveld has applied the concept of "stratarchy," the diffusion of power prerogative and power exercise, to political parties, observing that "although authority to speak for the organization may remain in the hands of their top elite nucleus, there is great autonomy in operations at the lower strata or echelons of the hierarchy, and control from the top is minimal and formal." *Political Parties: A Behavioral Analysis*, Rand McNally & Company, Chicago, 1965, pp. 99–100.

level of agreement among party officials differs over public policy, operational arrangements, and strategies. Organizations for a period of time enjoy consensus in particular matters only to lose it.

Unity and cohesion are in a fluid state most of the time; and, as observed earlier, factionalism is a common attribute of party groups. There is seldom a monolithic ideological structure within party organizations.

COMMITTEE STRUCTURE

County and Local Committees. The composition and selection of county, district, and state committees follow no uniform pattern, but the major variations may be summarized. In a number of states, party voters choose the precinct leaders at the primary election for two- or four-year terms, and the committeemen so selected constitute the county committee and choose its offices. In large counties, the committee becomes ridiculous in size — more than 2,700 members, for example, in one county in New York City. Some of the county committees in Southern states and in Hawaii are elected by the county conventions. Democratic county committees in Alabama are elected from beats (districts); its members are called beat committeemen! In Texas, the county party executive is elected by the qualified voters of the entire county. In Chicago, ward committeemen, who are elected at the primary and collectively from the city committee, appoint the precinct captains. In Cook County, outside Chicago, township chairmen appoint the precinct captains. In Michigan, candidates for county and state legislative offices constitute the executive committee of the county committee; they number half of the full committee. The other half are selected by the county convention. The executive committee chooses the officers of the county committees.

There are places where ward or district committeemen are popularly elected and are powerful or influential in party matters. In Massachusetts, the ward committeemen collectively constitute the city committee and choose the city chairman. Brooklyn district leaders may replace a county leader at any time. A contrasting pattern is found in metropolitan Seattle, where the Republican county chairman appoints the district leaders. Elected New York County Democratic committeemen choose their chairmen, but the leader of Tammany Hall, who may also be the county chairman, is elected by an executive committee of sixty-six members, and the leader is invested with top authority.

State Committees. Practices differ so much that there are scarcely any dominant patterns for composing state central committees; several references to practices throughout the nation will serve to illustrate the makeup of these committees.[6] Two state committeemen are elected from each assembly district in New York. In Minnesota, the state central committee is composed of the major leadership of the party, such as the national committeeman and committeewoman, the county executives, chairman of party auxiliaries—men's, women's and youth clubs—and representatives of the party's nominees for major state and federal offices, making a committee of 200 to 300 members.

One man and one woman from each senatorial district in Massachusetts are elected to the state committee by the party members in the district. Each county convention in the state of Washington selects one man and one woman as state committeemen. In Kansas, the state party committee is composed of the chairmen and vice-chairmen of the county committees. Each congressional district selects one man and one woman to the Iowa state central committee. Michigan gives the state convention the power to choose the state committeemen and chairman but requires the committee to be composed of two men and two women from each congressional district.

The California state committee numbers more than 800 members; each member of the state convention is a member of the committee and, in addition, appoints three to nine other persons to serve on the committee. The committee meets only once in two years for the exclusive purpose of electing its officers; an executive committee exercises the few functions accorded the state committee.

The "in-between" committees—larger than one county but smaller than the state—such as certain congressional committees, are chosen in diverse ways but are often composed of county chairmen and committeemen of the counties in the district plus other members. Many of these committees are much less permanent and more amorphous than the county and state bodies. Most of them are active only in political campaigns and seldom have a permanent headquarters. Candidates for the state legislature often find it necessary to form their own campaign committees because of the ineffectiveness or inaction of the official party organization. Candidates' committees usually disappear after the election.

Dispersal of Power. The centers of power in the party organization vary from state to state and are not necessarily indicated by the statutory provisions governing the selection of committee members and chairmen. In some states the county chairman is a powerful figure, but in other states he is a figurehead. In some cities the ward or district leaders wield great power but not in others. Seldom do party committees exercise

---

[6] Richard S. Childs compiled the laws and procedures of all states under the title *State Party Structure and Procedures*, National Municipal League, New York, 1967. The work also covers county and local committees.

much power, and in some states they rarely meet, and when they do, they merely ratify the decisions of the party leaders. In the city of Chicago the ward leader is the real power and hard core of the organization. The precinct captains, whom he appoints, tend to work hard and have a great stake in the organization.[7] In most states, however, the county chairmen are the leading local party officers.

Despite neat organizational charts, there is no line of hierarchical authority in the state and local organization. The hierarchies are selected by different processes, and consequently the state party organization has little control over the county or local organizations. The state chairman is seldom the real head of the party in the state. Each committee is autonomous in its own bailiwick, manages the conventions and campaigns within its own political boundaries, and cooperates with the rest of the hierarchy when expedient to do so. At times a powerful candidate, officeholder, or leader may dominate the organization. Public officeholders usually prefer party committees that take orders rather than give them. Conversely, party committees do not wish to become lackeys of the party's officeholders.

With very few exceptions, official state and local committees are too large and unwieldy to determine party policies. The leadership of the party is usually provided by executive committees composed of a few members and presided over by the chairman. Executive committees are likely to make the major decisions that are later ratified by the full committee or the conventions. In the larger states and cities there is a trend for the parties to use a professional paid staff. Several Republican state chairmen receive compensation, but only a few Democratic chairmen are paid a salary.

AUXILIARY ORGANIZATIONS

American major parties have numerous extrahierarchical and semiofficial groups that not only serve part of the membership but even purport to speak for the party in some matters. These organizations may be chartered and operated under party sponsorship but are distinguished from the regular committees by the absence of legal recognition as the official party agencies. Unlike a pressure group, the extraparty organization acknowledges itself to be composed of persons of only one party and presses its viewpoints only on that party. Some of these groups are established by the regular organizations; a few are created by members who wish to concentrate on policy questions; others evolve from dissatisfaction with the regular organization; still others are, practically speaking, created by persons to further political ambitions. Since motivation for organizing the miscellaneous groups varies, they have different

[7] See Harold F. Gosnell, *Machine Politics: Chicago Model*, The University of Chicago Press, Chicago, 1937.

relationships with the regular organizations and usually perceive their roles as differing from one another.

Party-created Groups. Young Republicans, Young Democrats, the National Federation of Republican Women, and the Pennsylvania Republican United Finance Committee are examples of party-sponsored and chartered groups. They are created to raise money, sponsor social and party events, appeal to certain classes of voters, and serve the regular party membership in diverse ways. Many of these groups provide like-minded young people, men, or women, with opportunities to get together socially. They also render assistance and leg work that would not be forthcoming without the organization. They may find themselves kept in a state of anemia by the regular organization because it does not want them to threaten its leadership. Youth groups sometimes insist on making pronouncements on public issues that are embarrassing to their seniors. Youngsters frequently become discouraged with their own party clubs, for they find that the regulars do not want to give them what they feel to be meaningful authority and functions. The regular organization is likely to take the view that it should control all other party organizations and is reluctant to permit auxiliary organizations to carry on significant activities. The regular party is often shortsighted and rigid in its attitudes and fails to draw on the enthusiasm and potential of party-sponsored clubs.

Ward or district clubs are found in some urban areas. Clubs in New York City are prominent in the life of the Democratic party and of the district organization. A resourceful leader can weld the club into a powerful vote-getting and service institution. He may attach doctors, lawyers, judges, and others to provide free advice to those in need. An assembly district leader's power depends on his ability to get persons to work effectively, and the assembly district club is a useful tool for this purpose.

Although not acknowledged officially, the local political club is often a breeding ground for political candidates and a springboard for personal ambition. Clubs themselves are sometimes formed around a leader or candidate, and their own viability rises or falls with the fortunes of that person. A number of clubs dedicate their entire effort during a campaign to the election of one of their own to a local or state legislative position.

Ideological Clubs. Another category of organization, unlikely to be established by the regular hierarchy, concerns itself mainly with issues. These groups are usually composed of liberals or conservatives who are unhappy with the regular organization's preoccupation with patronage and personnel matters and who believe that a major function of parties is to take positions on public policy questions. The Democrats of Texas club represents the liberal faction in the party and holds its own state conventions and supports various party programs and candidates. In practice, it is virtually a second Democratic party in Texas.

Perhaps best known of unofficial organizations are the California Republican Assembly and the California Democratic Council (CDC). The former organization was founded in 1934 by insurgents dissatisfied with the conservative leadership of the party. They instituted programs to improve the party and to encourage political education. In 1964, the right wing captured control of the Republican Assembly and subsequently endorsed ultraconservative candidates. In so doing, it spoke much less for the party as a whole than previously.[8] The California Democratic Council was formed as an analogous group in 1953 to strengthen the party and provide workers in campaigns. Similar to its Republican counterpart, the CDC and its local clubs have as a major function the endorsement of candidates before primary elections and take a leading part in campaigns. However, other activities of the councils have become very important, more notably the year-around program of forums, panel discussions, and social activities. Membership leans heavily to business and professional people and university graduates. It is not particularly representative of the rank and file. In the 1960s, the CDC amateurs and the Democratic pros engaged in many disputes both on ideology and candidates, often to the detriment of party unity.

In Wisconsin, one-time dissident groups have continued to exist beside the regular organization. The conservative wing of the Wisconsin Republicans in the 1920s formed an extralegal party organization to support its own candidates in primaries. When Progressives left the party to form their own group, the regulars continued to operate as a volunteer group. In 1948, a Democratic Organizing Committee, later to call itself the Democratic Party of Wisconsin, revolted against the party's conservative leadership. In time both groups proved to be more effective bases of operations than the cumbersome statutory party structure.

Still another form of organization arises from persons so dissatisfied with the leadership that they attempt to organize more or less formally to capture and reform the official committee. The Committee for Democratic Voters, a reform, anti-Tammany group in New York City, successfully contested many assembly district posts in 1961. District reform clubs have continued to press for intraparty democracy and a reorientation of older-style organization politics to ideological concerns. Thus organizations and movements occasionally crop up but are usually

---

[8]See Joseph P. Harris, *California Politics*, 4th ed., Chandler Publishing Company, San Francisco, 1967, chap. 2, and Frances Carney, *The Rise of Democratic Clubs in California*, Holt, Rinehart and Winston, Inc., New York, 1958. See chap. 4 for other aspects of the California groups.

short-lived because they are defeated or, having won control of the party, no longer have a reason for existence. Another weakness of unofficial organizations is that they may be taken over by extremists who are unrepresentative of the rank-and-file party voters.

THE RATIONALE OF MULTIPLE ORGANIZATIONS

Criticisms of Existing Systems. At first blush, there is much to criticize both in the regular party hierarchy and in the almost unbelievable proliferation of volunteer auxiliary associations. The paper committee system often gives way to real control by bosses and leaders, many of whom hold no membership on the committees. Legal provisions or party rules for committees are often ambiguous. The proliferation of party organization leads to overlapping, duplication of effort, fragmentation of control, diffusion of strength, and the numerous autonomous units bring problems of administration and liaison. The existence of so many organizations within a single geographic area implies a criticism of the regular machinery. If the statutory committees were satisfactorily performing the functions that the party membership believes they should perform, there would be no need for multiplication of organization.

A fairly general characteristic of local party organization is its loose structure and low level of activity and organization. Millions of Americans have never been visited by a precinct captain. A great many precinct positions in both rural and urban areas are unfilled except in the weeks just preceding an important election. The statutory parties fail to attract energetic workers in numerous precincts even in competitive districts at election time.

The function of the party organization, other than campaigning, is not clearly defined and the role perceptions of the leadership show little agreement. In the Detroit area, the lower party echelons (district and precinct leaders) were unable to articulate a goal for their party; and others saw their purposes variously as "vote mobilizers" and "socioeconomic welfare promoters."[9] In St. Louis, some 27 percent admitted to not performing any significant amount of political electioneering tasks, and the same has been true in other communities.[10] Communication between the top and lower strata within the same county and between state and local organizations is often poor if not nonexistent. Chairmen frequently do little indoctrination of fellow workers in their organization.

[9] Eldersveld, *op. cit.*, chap. 10.
[10] See Robert H. Salisbury, "The Urban Party Organization Member," *Public Opinion Quarterly*, vol. 29, p. 558, 1965–1966, and Lewis Bowman and G. R. Boynton, "Activities and Role Definition of Grassroots Party Officials," *Journal of Politics*, vol. 28, pp. 132–133, 1966.

Eldersveld found precinct leaders holding their posts though anathema to the top leadership and the latter could not obstruct upward mobility despite ideological nonconformity. "From the bottom to the top, the party welcomes, and rewards, the ideological deviant."[11] Rarely do party groups participate in developing policies on municipal transportation, parking, health, education, and the host of problems of a burgeoning suburbia and megalopolis. These problems are community-wide, while a party's organization follows election district lines. No party group exists for developing policies associated with metropolitanism, and there is only infrequent formal informed consultation on these matters. This leaves much of the study and proposals of solutions on civic issues to nonpartisan leaders. Although this approach to handling metropolitan problems is pleasing to some, others fault the parties for failing to plunge into the major issues of local government.

Utility of Multiple Organization. Statutory controls of the official party organization are partially responsible for the proliferation of unofficial organizations. Laws often require huge committees, making them too unwieldy to perform party functions. In most states, the official party committees are debarred from taking sides in direct primaries and hence are prohibited from making preprimary endorsements of candidates. Where endorsement in a competitive primary is forbidden by law, party groups outside the hierarchy are formed to make endorsements. If primary elections are hotly contested, the official party organization may find it unwise to endorse either of the competing candidates, fearing that preprimary endorsements would lead to ill feeling, debilitation of the party, and alienation of potential supporters. Many party leaders are satisfied to have law or custom impose neutrality upon them. Much the same might be said for policies and programs. Official committees and conventions seek to avoid pronouncements on controversial issues that would split the party. As a result, their policy pronouncements may be so general as to be meaningless and innocuous. But this many be the better part of wisdom!

Given this situation, the host of party associations outside the regular hierarchy makes sense as desirable and necessary adjuncts of party life. Concisely, the extraparty agencies perform the historic party functions that the official organization either cannot do by law or finds inexpedient to do. Not everyone in the party is agreed on the mission of the party, and the several groups can perform missions in accordance with their interests. Preprimary endorsement and support may be necessary to recruit able talent for certain offices. The volunteer groups in California and Wisconsin breathed new life and vigor into their parties

[11] Eldersveld, *op. cit.*, p. 219.

through candidate support and assistance in the primary. A number of reformers, intellectuals, and strongly oriented right- and left-wing members are often homeless in the officialdom of the party and believe that the official party committees are insufficiently interested in policies and issues. Through various auxiliary groups they may find a place in the party where they can discuss issues and offer, in a partially official way at least, public policy suggestions.

A more efficient bureaucratization might call for replacing the multiple clubs and associations with a single organic organization in each county or congressional district. But this would be counter to the present attitudes of party members. Existing arrangements help attract large numbers of people into party life, where everyone can find a niche in which he can function and participate in line with his inclinations. His interest may be largely social, or it may run to education and policy issues. He may wish to participate in organizational matters, enjoy the excitement of campaigning, raise funds, assist in preparing a newsletter, join in candidate endorsement, or further a political ambition. Whatever the interest, he can find an institution through which to express it.

Dispersion of organization affords a chance for specialization and particularization. It is difficult for a single organization to give sufficient attention to the individual needs of the party's officeholders and candidates and to utilize effective available talent in the community to promote the diverse interests of the party. Diffused party organization can be rationalized in terms of the American pluralistic society in which each major party is composed of widely differing groups. Multiple organization reflects the objective of the open society in the American democracy by providing easier access and more opportunity to influence government and politics. It gives political entrepreneurs several channels for advancement. It may help the official party become sensitive to the need for change. Youth groups, campus clubs, auxiliaries, and ancillaries also can add much incremental strength and vitality to the electoral party.

"Modernization" of State and Local Parties. Periodically demands arise for more viable parties, representative party structure, and participatory democracy. But when specific arrangements are advanced to realize these objectives they are seldom adopted. Organizational theory suggests that the way a party structures itself should be related to what it is expected to do and its perceived role in the political society. Because both active partisans and the general public are not agreed on priorities or saliency of functions, changes in party organization are difficult to bring about. In other words, a "representative party organization" for whom to do what? Opinion falls far short of unanimity in the local

parties on such questions. The task in modernizing state party structures is to find an organizational arrangement that will encompass the diverse expectations, hopes, and attitudes. Differences in the political life styles and cultures remain so varied as to constitutional frameworks that common arrangements for statewide party organization are next to impossible.

Political benefits from change rarely come without political or other costs—there is likely to be a ripple effect. For example, if county chairman should become regular or ex officio members of the state control committee, integration of the party throughout the state would be strengthened. But in states with a large number of counties of radically different sizes, such a practice would make the state committee dysfunctional in terms of a representative, effective working body. If party committees were organized and mandated to designate candidates for public office would this keep open adequate opportunities for those seeking public office, especially young people and black citizens? Reorganization seldom benefits everyone. Choices between options must be made after analysis of the reciprocal effect of forces at work.

There is no simple formula applicable to all states for restructuring the parties or standardizing the functions of party organizations. Changes are best made in each state after an evaluation of the state's political system and needs, including an analysis of cause and effect. Parties, moreover, will not be made to play a more vital role simply by restructuring them; such a view deals with gadgetry. A few arrangements, some of which are now operative in one degree or another, might be helpful in some states.[12] The state headquarters should be operated year-round, with a salaried chairman and permanent staff and with responsibility for maintaining an effective liaison with the national committee, the county chairmen, and congressional district organizations where they exist. The state committee is critical in the vertical linkage among the local level organizations, national committees, and the comparatively new regional associations, such as the Republican Midwest Conference and Western States Democratic Conference. Republicans place on their national committee the chairmen of states voting for Republican presidential electors, a Republican governor, or a majority of the congressional delegation. An alternative tie-in would co-opt the national committeeman and committeewoman on the state central committee to make it into a more vital communication mechanism.

Parties seem not to have fully tapped nonareal strategies for recruiting persons of certain social, economic, and other diverse group-

[12]An elaboration will be found in Hugh A. Bone, "No Simple Formula," *National Civic Review*, vol. 58, pp. 148–153, 1969. See Charles E. Schutz, "Bureaucratic Political Staffing," *Midwest Journal of Politics*, vol. 8, pp. 127–142, 1964.

ings into the party. In such cases, area-based organizations that currently underlie most party structure would be augmented by arrangements reaching across territorial boundaries and attempting to bring social workers, intellectuals, writers, and minorities of all kinds into the party organizations. In some communities, an institutionalized link is forged through chartering or by providing for membership on official party committees for youth, men's, women's, and other groups. Representation in county and state conventions has also been extended in some places. A horizontal nexus with ad hoc auxiliaries may (though by no means is it assured) improve communication and better contain conflicts that so often arise among the diverse elements. A few states have amended bylaws to permit eighteen-year-olds to attend caucuses and to be eligible for election to party conventions.

Because the more or less autonomous egos of the party need aggregation, expression, and integration in the interests of its continuing life, a member of the legislative party and the governor might also be placed on the state committee ex officio to attend at their pleasure to keep the committee informed firsthand on the government party's program. In the main, the popular election in the primaries of a majority of the state committee members seems preferable to ex officio status or appointment by lower party bodies. A state committee, if kept small, could function as a working body without having to devolve all its functions on an executive committee.

As parties develop mechanisms for studying local problems and formulating approaches, more amateur democrats and college faculty and professional people are likely to be attracted to their ranks. The state committee should assume responsibility for working out arrangements and seeking support for party research and analysis of voting habits and political profiles.

PARTY LEADERSHIP

Precinct Leaders. To a considerable degree, the effectiveness of a political party in getting voters registered and to the polls and in bolstering a party's general fortunes rests in the "unit cell of the party structure," that is, the precinct or voting district. Presumably, the precinct functionaries work year-round in the interest of the party—discussing campaign issues; explaining voting propositions on the ballot; distributing literature; serving as sources of intelligence at the grass roots; and, in those states where they are held, presiding over precinct conventions. Beyond these routine jobs connected with elections, the precinct position is likely to be what one makes of it. In some larger cities, the leader functions as a broker between the citizen and his government. Voters go to him with complaints about tax assessments, street repairs, traffic citations, waste collections, recreational facilities, and so on, and he provides information about how to contact city officials. Diverse other activities include providing bail and counsel, securing physicians for those in need of medical care, aiding aliens, handling nonpatronage job requests, furnishing travel information, and interceding with school authorities on behalf of a "misunderstood" student. It is doubtful that more than a small percentage of the precinct committeemen perform these many functions in any sustained way. But these are the "goals" set by the party hierarchy or the organization for the small-fry cogs.

In the absence of a comprehensive study of the backgrounds of the hundreds of thousands of precinct leaders, generalization is difficult. The fragmentary studies show much diversity.[13] Local party activists are stratified and the characteristics differ somewhat as between the top elite such as county chairmen and the leaders at the lowest level. There are middle-range leaders in a secondary cadre status composed of ward leaders and diverse district chairmen. Additionally, volunteers help with fund raising, registration, office work, and campaign activity without benefit of an official position in the party structure. Our consideration is limited mainly to the precinct committeemen and chairmen. A 1960 study of precinct committeemen in Manhattan shows important variations from the older studies of political activists in other cities.[14] The committeeman of the 1960s was better educated than his predecessor; two-thirds had attended college. Many young people and women are now found in the ranks. Catholics are being displaced by Protestants and Jews, with the last-mentioned occupying about two-thirds of the positions. The majority of committee members have incomes greater than the national average.

Socioeconomic background or class appears less important in the differentiation of each party's committeemen than their ideas and ideology. All three New York political parties recruited workers largely from the middle class, but the committeemen differed along party lines in their attitudes toward people, minorities, policies, and politics.

---

[13] Profiles of precinct leaders of a generation ago showed that they were persons of social attributes quite different from those who have functioned since 1950. A comprehensive analysis of the data on precinct leaders and other activists before 1960 is provided by Robert Lane, *Political Life: Why People Get Involved in Politics*, The Free Press, New York, 1959. Studies in specific areas include Paul Bartholomew, *Profile of a Precinct Committeeman*, Oceana Publications, Dobbs Ferry, N.Y., 1968 (Indiana); Eldersveld, *op. cit.*, (Detroit); Hugh A. Bone, *Grass Roots Party Leadership*, Bureau of Governmental Research and Services, University of Washington, Seattle, 1952 (Seattle). Several other references will be found in the footnotes to follow. A number of graduate student dissertations and books on specific state political systems have investigated local party executives.

[14] See Robert S. Hirschfield, Bert E. Swanson, and Blanche D. Blank, "A Profile of Political Activists in Manhattan," *Western Political Quarterly*, vol. 15, pp. 489–506, 1962. The study is based on a random sample of 409 Democratic, Republican, and Liberal party precinct leaders.

Liberal party committeemen appeared to be well-named; Republicans were noticeably conservative, and Democrats were in between but differed significantly from Republicans in attitudes toward governmental power and policies. In the matter of ideas and attitudes, there is clearly a differentiation between the committeemen of the three parties, and the labels are meaningful.

The Manhattan Democratic committeemen as members of the dominant party occupy the broad center on nearly every dimension — demographic background, policy, and political activity. They show a deeper commitment to professionalism, and more of them are active in issues of local concern. Liberal party committeemen, as might be expected, were considerably more interested in public policies and less involved with practical political activity than either Republicans or Democrats. Liberal committeemen visit their political clubs much less often than do those of the major parties.

Most precinct studies show that local-level leaders tend to have had rather long residence in their communities, even where there was an influx of newcomers. As might be expected, surveys of precinct leaders in earlier days showed more professional and business-managerial classes manning Republican precinct posts than Democratic posts. Today both parties appear to be attracting more white-collar and professional workers.

In Los Angeles, with its loose, diffused party organization, volunteer campaign workers perform many of the functions expected of precinct leaders in New York. The Los Angeles party workers come largely from the middle class, in contrast with those who worked for earlier big-city machines, which drew heavily from lower classes. Furthermore, the party activists are interested in ideology and issues and generally see a meaningful difference between Republicans and Democrats. Accounts of party organization in other states suggest trends in the same direction in many cities.

The results of recent empirical studies suggest that one-time assumptions that political organizations are largely composed of hacks need reappraisal. Many additional surveys are required before the student of government can make comfortable generalizations about the political activists in party organizations. It is probably safe to conclude, however, that workers are expected to have unflagging loyalty to their party. While the higher-ups in the party supply the strategy and brainwork, the real success of the grass-roots politician is apt to be measured by his legwork. Precinct leaders have tended to reflect the dominant ethnic, nationalistic, and religious composition of their districts. They are politicians and as such mirror the aspirations and prejudices of their districts. In a study of organization in an urban community, the authors observed that "what stands out is the importance of the precinct committeeman's being a part of the social organization of his neighborhood. Where the committeeman has many friends among his neighbors and actually canvases his constituents, the party fares very well at the polls. Nor need his efforts be directed specifically at persuasion; his presence as a member of the informal neighboring circles counts more than his proselytizing efforts."[15]

County Chairmen. The key figure in the local organization is usually the county chairman; in many states he represents the county on the state central committee. If his party is in power, the county chairman serves as the clearinghouse for many patronage positions. He is important in the party's councils and often directs the campaign in the county. In some cities where a boss, mayor, county commissioner, or other person may be the real party leader, the chairman must be content with titular leadership.

An active rural county chairman regularly visits the county's officeholders and local leaders and can personalize politics to a greater extent than his urban colleague; in this respect he resembles a city precinct captain. In many counties, the chairman has authority to fill precinct vacancies. It is his job to see that all positions are filled during campaigns and to work out appropriate relationships among the county organization and the many candidates and nonparty campaign committees. The chairmanship is a position calling for tact, persistency, resourcefulness, and organizing ability.

A county chairman's role is, of course, determined by his own perception of it and the expectations of the party members in his area. Although he is expected to be the liaison between his organization and the state and national organization, he usually ties himself to the party's cause in his county. Almost everywhere the chairman is oriented toward organizational matters: urging precinct leaders on to party activities, keeping harmony within the organization, and helping candidates. Some leaders are more oriented toward policies—managing campaigns and formulating campaign issues—and toward trying to find candidates for public office. But customs within the party and prerogatives of powerful figures and public officeholders in the party may circumscribe chairmen disposed to these kinds of activities. Further, the role of a chairman in a one-party district may be different from that of one in a strong competitive district or from that of a strongly dominant majority party and that of the minority. Many chairmen, therefore, often find their functions difficult to define and frustrating in operation.

[15] Peter H. Rossi and Phillips Cutright, "The Impact of Party Organization in an Industrial Setting," in Morris Janowitz (ed.), *Community Political Systems*, The Free Press, New York, 1961, p. 115.

TABLE 5-1 Occupations of county chairmen in four states

Occupation	Republican				Democratic			
	Okla.	Wis.	Wash.*	Ohio	Okla.	Wis.	Wash.*	Ohio
Business-managerial	20	45	55	32	22	17	53	32
Lawyer	12	30	17	19	24	19	9	18
Farmer	25	3	17	20	19	16	9	6
Manual worker	5	0	0	6	5	24	9	11
Educator	18*	3	0	4*	15*	5	5	3*
Sales-clerical	13	8	3	3	10	8	0	4
Public official	0	0	0	†	2	2	9	†
Other	7	11	8	16	3	9	6	26

Note: Figures are in percentages rounded to even numbers. Patterson's categories of occupations of county chairmen in Kansas are not quite analogous to those in this table but show interstate differences attributable to the political structure and characteristics of the states. See Samuel C. Patterson, "Characteristics of Party Leaders," *Western Political Quarterly*, vol. 16, pp. 339–340, 1963.
*Washington figures supplied by author; others supplied by Patterson.
†Other professions counted in with educators.
‡Counted in "other" category.

Notwithstanding the importance of the office, there are few published studies giving demographic data on county chairmen. Such materials that have been gathered indicate that large numbers of chairmen first served the party as precinct or district leaders, club presidents, secretaries, financial directors, or in comparable capacities. Rarely is a chairman recruited entirely from the outside. Leon Epstein found in 1956 that close to half of Wisconsin's chairmen had run for a public office and that others intended or desired to do so.[16] County chairmen come from the higher-status vocations, although there are sharp variations both between states and within states (see Table 5-1). They are men of fairly high educational attainment and incomes who have achieved political and social success. Pomper found that a majority of chairmen in New Jersey held an elective or appointive office along with their party position.[17] In many other states such is not the case. Also in New Jersey, there were distinctions between majority and minority leaders, with the former tending to be recruited from more prestigious groups. Crotty found this in North Carolina where the Democratic party was strongly dominant and

the minority party is in the unenviable position of molding a coalition of out-group interests. . . . The weaker party in the electorate must draw its organizational activists from the fringe elements in the society—represented here by the more recent arrivals,

[16]*Politics in Wisconsin*, The University of Wisconsin Press, Madison, 1956, pp. 86–90, and tables, pp. 185–187. Samuel C. Patterson found that a considerably smaller number of Oklahoma county leaders had political aspirations and in both states minority-party chairmen registered a higher degree of aspiration than majority chairmen. "Characteristics of Party Leaders," *Western Political Quarterly*, vol. 16, pp. 332–352, 1963.

[17]Gerald Pomper, "New Jersey County Chairmen," *Western Political Quarterly*, vol. 18, pp. 186–197, 1965.

those with less education or occupational achievement, and, inferentially, those with less community standing or influence.[18]

Most chairmen have served a period of apprenticeship before assuming the position. More than 40 percent of the Oklahoma party leaders previously held party office. In New Jersey, 5 percent had attended a national convention, and 71 percent had been in politics ten or more years. The median years for party work for Wisconsin Republican chairmen was twenty-one and only ten years for the Democrats, but the corresponding figures for the state of Washington respectively were twelve and fifteen. Women frequently serve as vice-chairmen and do much of the routine headquarters work; they are becoming increasingly important in party activities in the country.

As in many other states, county chairmen and secretaries in Ohio were found to be groups of like-minded men and women who were not neutrals on issues.[19] The interparty differences are not attributable to differences in social background between Republicans and Democrats. Their attitudes were fairly consistent with those of their respective national leaders. Succinctly, the county party functionaries have definite policy preferences, which are likely to affect their strategies both during and between elections.

Incentives and Motivations. "Men and women are drawn into politics by a combination of motives," writes Stimson Bulitt; "these include power, glory, zeal for contention or success, duty, hate, oblivion, hero worship, curiosity, and enjoyment of the work."[20] Why people go into politics is a fascinating subject and is under extensive investigation. Persons may become precinct leaders for one reason but may remain in politics for different reasons, and goal perspectives both for themselves and their parties undergo change.

Activists have tended to ascribe their initial recruitment to reasons other than "self-starting." In an Indiana congressional district, about 20 percent ran for a precinct post on their own initiative; most said they were asked to take the position or were appointed by party leaders by default since no one wanted the position.[21] Other studies likewise show the number of self-starters under 30 percent and many could not recall why they took the step. External forces included succumbing to the urging of family, friends, and party leaders.

[18] William J. Crotty, "The Social Attributes of Party Organizational Activists in a Transitional Political System." *Western Political Quarterly,* pp. 669–681, 1967. An extensive bibliography of attributes of activists is found in this article.
[19] Thomas A. Flinn and Frederick M. Wirt, "Local Party Leaders: Groups of Like-Minded Men," *Midwest Journal of Politics,* vol. 9, pp. 77–98, 1965.
[20] *To Be a Politician,* Doubleday & Company, Inc., Garden City, N.Y., 1959, p. 42, chap. 2, is devoted to "incentives" and is recommended for its summary of motivations for political activity.
[21] Bartholomew, *op. cit.,* p. 23. See Eldersveld, *op. cit.,* chap. 6, for career origins in Detroit.

Before World War II, most urban party workers hoped to obtain concrete economic rewards by entering precinct politics, and in some cities more than 75 percent of the precinct leaders were public employees. With the steady shrinking of patronage positions, this inducement is much less important, and in only a few cities today would one find as many as half simultaneously holding local party leadership and public employment positions. However, some material, economic arrangements have remained, such as selling goods or services to the government, securing business preferment or other favors, and making contacts that could result in benefits.

Party chairmen originally rationalized patronage as essential to strengthening the parties. Jobs provide incentives for service in the party and help enforce party discipline. Parties will remain sensitive to the public's wishes, so the contention goes, because the army of jobholder wants to remain in power. Without patronage a sufficient number of activists could not be found to run vigorous campaigns and fulfill party functions.

Today many party chairmen find the distribution of patronage a distasteful business and complain that it causes more party rifts than it heals. It takes time that might better be devoted to other activities, and spoils in the old days often tended to corrupt the parties. Preoccupation with jobs directed attention from other important functions and sometimes encouraged the buildup of unofficial party groups at the expense of the regular organization. With the decline of patronage incentives, social, psychological, and noneconomic personal motivations gain importance.

For persons ambitious for elective office, the holding of a party position may be a desirable if not required prelude. Biographies of public officeholders note that a number of them began their careers as precinct committeemen. Although there is no ladder to becoming a city official, state legislator, or congressman, party work is an important initial step for large numbers, especially where keen competition between the parties exists. Where high-echelon party officials exercise considerable control over nominations one is expected to serve the party in some capacity before getting the nod. Outsiders are likely to find winning the primary difficult. Even where this is not the case, activity in a party club or in the precincts is most helpful in building an image of party loyalty and making acquaintances, with subsequent payoff when one enters the primaries.

A complexity of political, social, and psychological rewards attracts persons to party work. Some toilers in the precinct vineyards hope to be rewarded sometime with a trip as delegate, usher, or whatnot to the national convention. They may have strong ideological motivations and may use parties as a way to try to realize them. Sometimes called a new type of politician or amateur democrats, they see the political world in terms of ideas, principles, and sets of policies and goals.[22] Generally the amateur of this type is primarily interested in programmatic activities of parties and in policy commitments for them. He believes intraparty democracy is essential and uses club politics on behalf of this and policy ends. This provides incentive for some people to become active in a party, but for party candidates trying to win elections it can create difficulties because issues are too greatly sharpened. Tension between the ideologists and professionals may result because the latter see parties in terms of catering to individual constituents, winning elections, raising money, and keeping their own positions intact.

Social and psychic satisfactions alone may attract people to parties, or they may be combined with the seeking of political goals. Almost 10 percent of a selected group of Indiana precinct committeemen reportedly were in politics "for fun." Others formulated their rewards as "being a part of the action" or a "feeling of accomplishment." Some motivations are stated in clichés such as "to promote Americanism," "to save private enterprise," "a sense of public duty," and "to practice good citizenship." Such intangible benefits as belonging to a collegial body with the occasional excitement of meeting prominent men, receiving friendship, and adding to one's identity answer perhaps unrecognized psychological needs. Housewives and many others find social satisfaction in giving coffee hours and attending social events sponsored under a party label.

There is little doubt that many people are lured into politics by admiration for an Eisenhower or a Goldwater, a Stevenson or a Kennedy. Some are induced to remain in or enter the regular party organizations after the election. In this sense citizens groups provide some new talent for the permanent parties—but many fail to find compatible colleagues in the parties and drop out. Some members of labor unions and "cause" associations enter party groups because they feel an opportunity will be provided to work for policies—many of these drop out in disillusionment.

To a certain extent, the viability of the precinct as the core unit is open to question. Radio and television, the importance of great world and national issues, and mobility from central cities to suburbs are forcing changes in personnel needs of the parties and candidates. The party hierarchy is being pressed into a modus vivendi that incorporates adjustment to the influx of public relations firms and nonparty and citizen's political actions groups. Party organizations now have serious

---

[22] On this point see James Q. Wilson, *The Amateur Democrats: Club Politics in Three Cities*, The University of Chicago Press, Chicago, 1962. Wilson adds to his description of club activists in New York, Chicago, and Los Angeles much evaluation and theory of party organizations.

competition as satisfiers of personal needs, and the affluent society has made parties less useful to the immigrants and poor in moving up the social ladder. When party leaders have no influence in choosing candidates, some see a nonrelevance to party activity. Campaign managers often bypass party structures on the ground that the regular organizations have poor personnel. In turn, how does one attract persons interested in campaigning if the organization has no activity?

URBAN MACHINES

A spate of novels, plays, motion pictures, television shows, and biographies have immortalized machine politics and political bosses.[23] The one-time boss of the Bronx, Edward J. Flynn, was less certain of this and saw the matter as largely one of semantics. "It is only the 'leader' you don't like who is a 'boss'; and the 'organization' you don't like that is a 'machine.'" Though the terms are sometimes used synonymously, *organization* and *machine* generically represent different bodies, though there is overlapping. In the broadest sense, the organization consists of the committee hierarchy and the gamut of workers from the bottom to the top who are assisting the party as a whole. The machine usually connotes a smaller group within the organization that is in actual control and is bent upon the perpetuation of its own power within the organization. The machine may have an extralegal basis, with its leaders holding neither public nor party office. It often has private goals considered less respectable than those generally associated with the public life of the party.

Bosses and machines are seen by some as historical phenomena to be treated in the past tense. Undoubtedly many of the old-style urban machines have faded but remnants and fragments linger on. Edward F. Costikyan, a self-styled reform Democrat and leader of the party's New York County organization during part of Mayor Robert F. Wagner's term, has written a candid account of the functioning of the county's politics during the 1960s.[24] He shows how a modern "boss" operates in keeping the organization going; the role of patronage; and the factors, maneuvers, and deals in candidate selection. The Daley machine in

---

[23] There is a huge volume of scholarly and journalistic writing as well. A selected, annotated bibliography of nonfiction was prepared by James S. Ottenburg, "Political Reform: 'Machines' and Big City Politics: 1950-1960s," in the New York Public Library's *Municipal Reference Notes*, vol. 36, pp. 153–157, 1962.

[24] *Behind Closed Doors: Politics in the Public Interest*, Harcourt, Brace & World, Inc., 1966. A number of accounts of the functions and mechanisms within local parties are brought together by Paul Tillett (ed.), *Cases on Party Organization*, McGraw-Hill Book Company, New York, 1963. For machines in the modern setting, see "City Bosses and Political Machines," in *The Annals of the American Academy of Political and Social Science*, vol. 353, May, 1964.

Chicago, the O'Connell machine in Albany, and vestiges in some other cities indicate that some of the older practices are far from extinct.[25]

Some Characteristics and Styles. Both the older and newer urban machines should be thought of as representative of the extremes in the variety of party organization. In contrast to the loose, undermanned organization, the relatively few urban machines are tightly disciplined with control over nominations and much else in the city's life. The erstwhile machine was based largely on motivation for personal gain and little, if at all, on ideology. It was a source of jobs for many of the poor and underprivileged. Its incentive system was one of material and economic rewards. Petty favors were provided for those in the lower echelons and often great riches for those at the top. Most machines were wasteful and expensive, if not corrupt; there was rarely a financially poor boss.[26]

Bosses, old or new style, defy typing. There were marked differentiations between the Tammany Hall bosses and Boss Ruef of San Francisco, who was allied with labor interests.[27] Boies Penrose of Pennsylvania and Abe Ruef of San Francisco were highly talented college men, but most of the old-line bosses were not academic men. William Hale "Big Bill" Thompson, mayor of Chicago for twelve years between 1915 and 1931, was blustery and vociferous and engaged in fabulous buffoonery. As a rabid Anglophobe, he promised to "kick the snoot of King George out of Chicago." He thrived on publicity, whether good or bad. When one of his opponents called him a hoodlum, he yelled to his audiences, "Come on out, hoodlums, and bring another hoodlum with you to the polls!" While Thompson attracted the people's attention with these antics, his political associates were engaged with spoils politics, gangster alliances, and scandals in public contracts.

Richard J. Daley, who became mayor of Chicago in 1955, has been called the last dinosaur of the old-time bosses. He is quiet, intense, and rather colorless but enjoys respectability, even though his Democratic machine is often called corrupt. Daley worked his way through

[25] In Chicago, the Daley machine was found to have awarded nearly $500,000 of city insurance business, without bidding, to a machine-picked park commissioner. The murder of a Negro alderman two days after his reelection in 1963 had earmarks of a syndicate job. See Hal Bruno, "Chicago Ain't Ready for Reform," *The Reporter,* March 28, 1963, pp. 41–43, and Alfred Balk, "The Last Dinosaur Wins Again," *Saturday Evening Post,* May 11, 1963, pp. 72–73.

[26] Quite interesting contrasts are found in Edward C. Banfield's pungent essays on politics in several cities in the 1960s. *Big City Politics,* Random House, Inc., New York, 1965.

[27] There is a profusion of works on particular bosses, such as Huey Long, Tom Pendergast, Frank Hague and various Tammany Hall leaders. A newer approach to one of the most famous is that by Seymour J. Mandelbaum, *Boss Tweed's New York, New York,* John Wiley & Sons, New York, 1965. A different, psychological approach is found in Alex Gottfried's *Boss Cermak of Chicago,* University of Washington Press, Seattle, 1962.

DePaul University Law School with a night job in the stockyards and enjoyed long apprenticeship in politics, beginning as a precinct captain and moving on to become a city council secretary, county clerk, state representative, and senate floor leader. He is a career politician, and opponents concede his political craftsmanship. When a scandal touches his administration, he makes concessions to good government and some excellent appointments. The press reports that he rules the city council with an iron hand and that few councilmen dare to oppose him. A major reason for this is that he handpicks candidates for the position and has let it be known that he disapproves of men who try to run without his blessing.

These brief references suffice to show that there was no distinct species or typical urban boss. Temperaments differed widely, but many if not most of the bosses were generous (usually with other people's money) to the poor, possessed a flair and love for the game of politics, and were loyal to their henchmen. Most bosses showed both a remarkable ability to withstand the onslaughts of reformers and the resiliency to make a comeback if defeated. A number of bosses were unseated not by an aroused electorate but by the courts. "Nocky" Johnson of Atlantic City and Arthur Samish, the liquor lobbyist once called the secret boss of California, had their careers terminated by the federal government because of income tax evasion.

Financial Income. Money was oil to the machine in its drive for self-perpetuation. It was needed to wage campaigns, to pay party workers on election day, sometimes to purchase votes outright, and to reimburse the leader and his henchmen. Money was garnered from a host of sources. In earlier days rake-offs were common on public works contracts, city purchases, deposits of public money in banks, and other sources. Special interests paid the machine to block harmful legislation; corporations desiring franchises and licenses to operate were required to pay the machine for them. Gambling interests and slot machines and pinball companies were usually ready to help the machine, provided that they in turn were permitted to do business. A corrupt alliance between business and the machine prevailed in most large cities.

Tammany District Leader George Washington Plunkitt earned immortality and a place in political science textbooks through his distinction between "honest graft and dishonest graft." He admitted he got rich on "honest graft." He said, in part,

> I'm gettin' richer every day, but I've not gone in for dishonest graft—blackmailin' gamblers, saloonkeepers, disorderly people, etc.—and neither has any of the men who have made big fortunes in politics.
>
> There's an honest graft, and I'm an example of how it works. I might sum up the whole by sayin': I seen my opportunities and I took 'em.

> Just let me explain by examples. My party's in power in the city, and it's going to undertake a lot of public improvements. Well, I'm tipped off, say, that they're going to lay out a new park at a certain place.
>
> I see my opportunity and I take it. I go to that place and I buy up all the land I can in the neighborhood. Then the board of this or that makes its plan public, and there is a rush to get my land, which nobody cared particular for before.
>
> Ain't it perfectly honest to charge a good price and make a profit on my investment and foresight? Of course it is. Well, that's honest graft.[28]

The assessment and kickback of municipal employees yielded large funds to numerous big-city machines. A study by the municipal auditor of Jersey City found that during the last two years of the Democratic Hague machine, 1948 to 1949, employees paid collectors in their departments campaign contributions on the basis of 3 percent of their annual salaries.[29] Some party organizations still raise campaign funds through systematic percentage levies, but it would be difficult for any segment of the party to receive so huge a percentage of the total raised and for the party treasury itself to receive so little as in the days of Hague. Assessments today are more likely to be "voluntary" and for dinner tickets, not regular monthly collections for the machine.

Protection and Service. Machines received healthy donations from a myriad of interests who wished protection in the form of nonenforcement of Sunday or other closing laws and various nuisance ordinances and inspections. Strict interpretations of ordinances and building codes could force enterprises out of business, and they were willing to contribute in order to be free from strict enforcement. Some street-corner businesses were willing to pay exorbitant license fees in order to avoid a narrow construction of an ordinance that would put them out of business. Sometimes machines ordered policemen to overlook the operation of illegitimate businesses. Tax assessors under control of the machine exercised their discretion in evaluating property for tax purposes. Assessors could either carefully probe or overlook tangible and personal property, and sizable contributions to the party could lead assessors to be more lenient toward the owner. In most cities, the machine was geared in with industry, finance, and often labor. Machines inclined to be antireform, and groups fearful of "good government" frequently made alliances to keep the reformers from controlling the city.

The machine's services to immigrants, Thanksgiving baskets, theater parties for the kiddies, free clothing to needy families, and so on,

[28] This extract taken from W. L. Riordan, *Plunkitt of Tammany Hall* (introduction by Roy V. Peel), Alfred A. Knopf, Inc., 1948, pp. 3–4, 6–7.
[29] *The New York Times*, June 23, 1950.

are too well known to need retelling. All added up to the fact that thousands of voters or their friends or relatives received services or something that made them willing to tolerate the machine and vote for its candidates. On one occasion, the Daley machine in Chicago was charged with fixing half a million traffic tickets. The investigation evaporated when the machine "misplaced" the evidence. When things got too bad, many machines were not above the use of force on election day and the spoilation of ballots or a fraudulent count. After the 1960 election, some 600 election workers were charged with fraud, but only one was convicted.

THEORIES OF MACHINE RULE

Why the boss system? A favorite subject of speculation has turned to the reasons for boss and machine rule in American cities while similar political controls were absent in the great European cities. Antidemocratic theorists attributed the system to the incapacity of citizens for self-government. The muckrakers believed that the sordid aspects of the acquisitive society fostered corrupt boss rule. Henry Jones Ford, writing in 1904, thought that separation of powers and defects in the organization of government, not its popular character, contributed to bad government. Other writers thought that the influx of aliens and the burgeoning urbanization were the cause of machines.

Since the decline of the old-style machines, we have additional perspective on them[30] The machine was first of all a political interest group, a group often distinct from the political party whose name it bore. It thrived on patronage and distribution of favors, managed prerequisites of office, elected its slate in the primaries and general elections, and had the support, for highly diverse reasons, of powerful groups in the city. In a city, decentralization of power can lead to inaction, difficulty of decision, and confusion. The boss could give leadership, direction, and centralization more easily through an unofficial structure than through the official governmental structure. Further, the ward heelers and political bosses "humanized" government by befriending the lowly who needed help. A machine's workers could cut through red tape and provide assistance not only to those on the lower rung of the economic ladder but also to business and professional people seeking privileges of one kind or another.

[30] There are still very effective "submachines" such as the Negro political organization in Chicago. This machine, led by Congressman William L. Dawson, is sustained by the tangible objectives of patronage, election of its men, and its commitment to the Democratic party. It is unfettered, according to James Q. Wilson, by strong attachment to principle and is "issue free." Four of its six Negro councilmen during the 1960s were also ward committeemen, which makes for a close tie between the party and the city council. See James Q. Wilson, *Negro Politics*, The Free Press, New York, 1960, chap. 3.

Robert K. Merton has suggested also that the machine provided alternative channels of social mobility for those otherwise excluded from the more conventional avenues for personal advancement.[31] Subgroups including immigrants gained control or influence in the machine and used it as a means of social mobility. Illegitimate as well as some legitimate businesses likewise could use the machine to gain ends not realizable through 'respectable' channels. In the social context of the times, the machine provided services and functions, albeit expensively, for its patrons. The accomplishment of certain piecemeal changes by reform administrations was so often short-lived because of an inability to alter the social structure sufficiently. The political machine returned because it had a place in the scheme of things.

But the old-line bosses and machines declined when basic changes took place in the municipal society. The extension of the merit system and the decline of patronage and favors available to machines dealt them a severe blow; as people moved from the city to the suburbs, new ones moved in, some with different values. This disturbed the social structure under which the bosses had flourished. It is perhaps too early to suggest that the values and interests of the political clubs, once so important to the machine, are undergoing change. But a survey of New York City Democratic clubs in 1959 brought the astonishing discovery that poker tables were being replaced by art.[32]

The growing literacy, the increase in both education and economic and social well-being, and the independence of the first generation of immigrants and of the underprivileged native-born also weakened the hold of the machine. In 1935, the social security system began to provide welfare services through an official agency to recipients as a matter of law. This deprived the machine of a function which had given it a powerful hold on many groups within the electorate. In addition to a national program leading to the professionalization of welfare services, a number of structural changes in the organization of cities reduced the power of the machine.

Future Prospects. It may be speculated that chronic unemployment and the movement of the more economically affluent to the suburbs might set the stage in some cities for a revival of boss rule. Some features of the old rings might spring up again, but there are significant forces operating against them. Government responsibility for welfare and the merit system are unlikely to be abandoned. The great new pressing problems are those of governing metropolitan areas and intercity cooperation in transportation, education, and services. It seems doubtful that the

[31] See *Social Theory and Social Structure*, The Free Press, New York, 1957, pp. 71–81.
[32] See article by Wayne Phillips in *The New York Times*, Oct. 16, 1959.

middle-class leadership of much of suburbia would permit their communities to be engulfed by a Hague or a Pendergast or whether the federal government would tolerate boss interference with national programs in the cities. Machines, large and small, played a tremendous part in our history, and certain familiar features of them still crop up now and then. A fundamental change has taken place in municipal politics, and the governors, mayors, and elected local leaders have built up influence in certain areas and provide some of the centralization of power which the boss did in his day. The need for political leadership and direction is as great as ever, but that leadership and direction will be supplied in a manner different from that of the older-style boss. Many cities are now relying on nonpartisan leaders to manage municipal problems. A new breed of politicians, generally well educated and highly motivated, operating through auxiliaries of the party organization, also constitutes a formidable barrier in some cities to the resurgence of bossism.

FOR FURTHER READING

See references at the end of Chapter 6.

CHAPTER 6 NATIONAL PARTY ORGANIZATION

American political parties, at both the national and local levels, illustrate the fact that an institutionalization of an interest is usually preceded by informal organization. Committees of correspondence were, in a general way, precursors of unified party action. The letter writing and other activities of Alexander Hamilton and Thomas Jefferson provided informal presidential campaign organization. President Jackson's Kitchen Cabinet acted as a center of campaign direction. Formal national organization was not perfected until after the national conventions came into use in the 1830s and after the need arose to link one convention with another and to coordinate intraparty communication during campaigns.

NATIONAL COMMITTEES

Development and Composition. The Democratic National Committee was organized in 1848 as an outgrowth of a "central committee" appointed in 1844 to "promote the election of Polk and Dallas." The Whigs, on their deathbed, created a national committee in 1852. These antecedents helped the Republicans to begin their national organization in a more advanced form. They created their committee by a resolution at their 1856 national convention.

Until 1920, the national committees were composed of one man from each state and territory. With the ratification of the Nineteenth Amendment, one woman was added from each area. Republicans made a further change in 1952 (rule 22), permitting a state chairman to serve on the national committee if at the preceding presidential election his state had cast its vote for Republican electors or if the state had elected a Republican governor or sent a Republican majority of the state's delegation to Congress. The size of the committee was increased because it was felt by many within the party that the Southern states, which up to that time rarely gave the party any electoral votes, were overrepresented. At the same time, the Taft forces believed that the rule would give Midwest Republican state officials a stronger voice in the national councils. Southern party leaders opposed the change, which they foresaw would lessen their influence in the national committee, but Republican victories in the presidential elections in the South since 1952 have increased the number of Southern members on the national committee.

Women are rarely elected as state chairmen, and their representation on the Republican committee is reduced considerably from the original 50 percent. Some national committeemen observe privately that the rule makes an already too large committee even more unwieldy. Others see a diminution of the unique position possessed by a committeeman as intermediary between his state party and Washington. Many state chairmen devote more attention to national party problems then before.

The members of the national committee are chosen every four years by the national convention. In practice, however, the convention ratifies the choice previously made by each state at the state convention or by a vote of the state's delegation to the national convention or of the state central committee; a few states select their committeemen in the party primary. With wholly separate processes of selection in the various states, the national committee in a sense is more a list of persons than a group. Vacancies are filled by the respective state central committees.

National committeemen tend to be older than state chairmen, with 60 percent in both parties between forty-six and sixty-five years of age at the time they come into office, and about 10 percent over sixty-five.[1] National committeemen come from the higher socioeconomic strata. From 1932 to the present, the proportion of lawyers has remained more or less constant at 40 to 45 percent; businessmen were second in occupation. Very few national committeemen come from the ranks of skilled or unskilled working classes. Over 60 percent of the men claim to have at least one college degree. About 86 percent of the Republican and 65 percent of the Democratic committeemen are Protestants. There are large numbers both of housewives and of career women among the committeewomen. One of the most striking characteristics of persons in office is that about 90 percent of them held a party or governmental position and thus had something of a power base in their states.

National committees presumably are creatures of the national conventions and subordinate to their control and direction. They exercise such powers and functions as are delegated by the conventions. Both parties have compiled their rules, but these are brief and limited to the more obvious duties, such as those in connection with the national conventions. Operation of the committees is left to custom and the discretion of the chairman and his staff. This lack of institutionalization permits each chairman "to run his own show" with a good deal of flexibility and change from chairman to chairman.

Role of Individual Committeeman. In operation today, the national committee has three separate egos: its chairman, its self, and its staff. Committeemen have a dual capacity: to serve as functionaries in their own states and to operate collectively with more than a hundred others who compose the national committee per se. Republican National Chairman Mark Hanna (1896-1904) made the committeeman a most important cog in the party organization, both during and between campaigns. He used committeemen as political agents and expected the county chairmen to report their needs to the state chairman, who turned to the national committeeman, and on up to the national chairman himself. The newly elected committeemen and committeewomen today soon learn that there is no formal list of duties describing their role in the state. They must inquire of others and learn by trial and error.

National committeemen are usually expected to be involved with fund raising and obtaining the state quota for the national committee. Some committeemen work to enhance the cause of a certain

---

[1] Data in this paragraph are taken from Cornelius P. Cotter and Bernard G. Hennessy, *Politics without Power: The National Party Committees*, Atherton Press, New York, 1964, chap. 3. This is the definitive work on national committees. A somewhat shorter account covering the committee, its headquarters staff, and operation from 1954 to 1958 is found in Hugh A. Bone, *Party Committees and National Politics*, University of Washington Press, Seattle, 1958 (third printing, 1968).

presidential contender; in other states by tradition they remain neutral. The Republican national committeeman and committeewoman are frequently but not invariably delegates to the national convention; Democrats give each state two votes for its committeemen. Commonly the committeewomen handle guest tickets for the convention. Committeemen are expected to be involved with the presidential and vice presidential campaigns in their own states, but this function is widely shared with other party leaders and citizen campaign groups.

Historically, the national committees handle patronage, but there are exceptions. As is customary, a new patronage division was established in the Republican National Committee when Richard Nixon became President. Two persons were sent at the outset to the White House to establish closer liaison with the executive. Ostensibly, the national committeeman is a major channel for dispensing patronage. In practice, powerful congressmen are likely to deal directly with the White House, often to the chagrin of the national committeemen. Notwithstanding, many committeemen remain in fact the initial appropriate channels for seeking noncivil service appointments.

Individually the committeemen are local agents and spokesmen of the national party in their states. It is their job to interpret the committee's activities to the people at home and vice versa and to serve as a liaison between the national and state parties and to some extent between the congressmen and the state. Committeemen able to build the prestige of their state in national party councils obtain more for their state in terms of party services.

National committeemen and committeewomen are charged with obtaining prominent out-of-state speakers for dinners and fund-raising occasions. They frequently assist in planning the itinerary for the party's presidential and vice presidential candidates when they come through their state. The committeemen are contact persons for obtaining campaign literature and other publicity items from the national committee. They serve as sources of intelligence for the fieldmen sent out by the national committee.

The degree of influence a committeeman has in his home state is conditioned in part by the strength of the local leaders. Where a vacuum exists because of changes in local leadership or incompetence, the committeeman may have a chance to step in and wield a good deal of influence. The individual's own prestige and standing in the state is the main determinant of his ability to exercise power and influence. There is a paradox in the amount of influence a committeeman exerts. On the one hand, there seem to be few major struggles in most states for control of these national posts, suggesting that the office is not of great importance. On the other hand, Cotter and Hennessy found that in ratings by informants in the states, about 90 percent of the national committee*men* were regarded as being in the top twenty-five party leaders in their state, although fewer than 50 percent were placed in the top half dozen party leaders.[2] The national committee*woman*, however, was found in many states to enjoy very little power but nevertheless was as influential as the female party leaders in her state.

Regional associations such as the Republican Midwest Conference and the Western States Democratic Conference have become important bodies for the national committeemen and committeewomen who compose them. These associations frequently draft policy statements, which are carried to national officeholders. In turn the President may use the regional groups of his own party to obtain local support for the administration's program.

MALADIES OF THE NATIONAL COMMITTEE

The national committees have operated under several major handicaps. First, there has been a high turnover in the national chairmanship. From 1940 to 1970 the Republicans had 16 chairmen, and the Democrats 13.[3] Four-year terms are uncommon, and eight-year terms highly exceptional. Party chairmen gain competence and wide acquaintances only to be replaced with new chairmen who usually have to start from the beginning. Although turnover may reflect political reality and the party's sensitivity to change, it tends to be upsetting in the national office.

Until 1892, chairmen of both parties were selected from among the committee members. Suggestions for going outside for a leader were objected to on the sole ground that the chairman should be a committee member. Since that time, only about one-third of the chairmen have been elected from the ranks of the committee. Paul Butler (1955–1960), John M. Bailey (1961–1968), Meade Alcorn (1957–1959), and Ray C. Bliss (1965–1969) are the only chairmen in recent years to come from the committee's ranks. Persons elected from the committee's membership to the top position in the party have an acquaintance with the national party hierarchy, some appreciation of the staff work done in the headquarters, and an awareness of the place and role of the national committee.

A second problem of the committee is the base — or lack of it — of its own existence. Its place in the state party organization is undefined, and the committeemen often do not participate in party decisions at the local level. Committeemen are frequently selected on the basis of financial contribution or in recognition of their "elder statesmen"

---

[2] *Op. cit.,* p. 57.
[3] For a list of chairmen and their terms of office to 1968, see Bone, *op. cit.,* pp. 241–243.

status in the party rather than because of their influence in the state organization. Committeemen and committeewomen as a rule pay their own expenses to committee meetings, a fact accounting in part for the position's being filled by persons able to spend money on party affairs.

A case can be made that membership on the national committee should include representation from the power centers exemplified by (1) private interest groups; (2) institutions of government including mayors, governors, and congressmen; and (3) state and local party leaders. Some representation of this type is found on the committee, but this is by chance and not by design. Geographic rather than functional representation is the rule in nearly all regular party committee organization.

The success of the Republican practice of adding many state chairmen to the committee has not yet been evaluated, but it has the virtue of giving the national party organization some root in the state and of familiarizing the top state party leader with the problems of the national-level organization. There is evidence in some states of bickering between the state chairmen and the other two committeemen. The latter also may become concerned that the state chairmen's position in the party will become enhanced at the expense of their own.

During campaigns and sometimes between campaigns the national chairman appoints or organizes advisory or similarly designated committees composed of a broad cross section of the party to render advice and assistance. All these efforts to alter or strengthen the national committee were the results of some dissatisfaction in both parties with the way the national committee is constituted.[4]

Obviously it is impossible for a national committee as a collegial body of more than a hundred persons to function as a working group. Accordingly, each party has an executive committee of eleven to fifteen persons selected with geographic representation in mind. These executive committees meet frequently and are often in telephonic communication with the national chairman.

A third difficulty encountered by the national committee is the lack of a constitution or bylaws that clarify the powers of the committee. Cannon's *Democratic Manual* summarizes some powers or duties in addition to those conferred by the convention. It asserts that no convention "has authorized the formulation of proposals which might be construed to be in the nature of platform declarations." Despite this, a few chairmen have tried to bring about the adoption of policy statements by the national committee, an action invariably bringing criticism from some groups within the party.

[4] Cotter and Hennessy recommend the abolition of the offices of national committeeman and committeewoman in favor of national committees composed of the state chairmen and vice-chairmen. *Op. cit.*, p. 234.

The relationships between the national committees and the party committees in the House and Senate are nowhere defined. The latter are not an organic part of the national committee, yet they are national party organizations united in the common purpose of controlling the national government. In the absence of bylaws prescribing jurisdiction or coordination, all party agencies must operate according to precedents and expediency. In the national committee there is much "playing by ear," trial and error, and advance and withdrawal of activity and program. This lack of formalization has provided the chairman and his lieutenants with considerable freedom of action. For students of national committees, this situation has meant that descriptions of their functioning must be rewritten for each new chairman.

As the local organization, the national committee must contend with diverse nationally organized dissident groups that would work changes in the party's structure or its ideologies. The Ripon Society, founded in 1962 by a group of liberal Republicans, is trying to change the conservative image of the party to one associated more with new ideas; it has appealed to Republican intellectuals. The New Democratic Coalition was formed after the 1968 elections, with branches in about three-fourths of the states. The group seeks changes in the party's position on Vietnam and build-up of military installations and tries to get control of local Democratic organizations.

THE NATIONAL CHAIRMAN

In practice, the national chairman is named by the party's nominee for President, and the choice is ratified by the national committee. A chairman stays in office only if he is *persona grata* to the President. A defeated presidential candidate does not have the same prerogative. Barry Goldwater saw his chairman, Dean Burch, pushed out in 1965 and replaced by a skilled technician, Ray C. Bliss. Vice President Humphrey prevailed upon Lawrence O'Brien, a Kennedy and Johnson man, to accept the chairmanship. O'Brien wished to leave early in 1969; Humphrey stated his preference for Sen. Fred R. Harris of Oklahoma and the national committee respected his wishes. However, after Harris' resignation in 1970 O'Brien was persuaded to return to the chairmanship.

It is not easy to generalize about either the career lines or the factors in the selection of national chairmen.[5] Republicans have called

[5] Ralph M. Goldman finds that most of them, at the time of their first designation, were forty-five to forty-nine years old and tended to be resident in their state of birth rather than transients from other states. Most chairmen held bachelor's degrees or high school diplomas and most had worked their way up through ranks of party agencies. The most numerous religious affiliation among Democratic chairmen has been Catholic; among the Republicans, Presbyterian. *The Democratic Party in American Politics*, The Macmillan Company. New York, 1966, p. 130.

on many congressmen to serve in a dual role. Most recently, Rogers C. B. Morton, representative from Maryland, replaced Ray C. Bliss after Mr. Nixon's inauguration. Senator Harris was only the third man from the Congress in modern times to become Democratic national chairman.[6] Harris at age 38 was one of the youngest to hold office, and Jackson was one of the few Protestants to hold the office. Harris is an attorney; Representative Morton is a farmer-businessman. Chairmen coming from Congress bring to the position personal acquaintance with the national lawmakers and a recognition of the need for coordinating campaigns for both the Presidency and Congress.[7] At the same time, a congressman has much difficulty in finding time to perform effectively as national chairman. Republican Chairman William E. Miller (1961– 1964) was criticized by some in the national committee as a part-time leader who failed to maintain effective operational control; some factions within the party called for his replacement largely for this reason. Yet historically it has often been a part-time job and one that few men have aspired to or have been qualified to fill.

With few exceptions the men picked for the chairmanship have the reputation of being "regulars," and a large number held positions in state and party politics. In addition, many chairmen previously were in public office. Democratic National Chairman James A. Farley (1932– 1940) had a genius for organization, a remarkable memory for names, and enjoyed immense popularity from one end of the nation to the other. He was succeeded by Edward J. Flynn (1940–1943), long-time political boss of the Bronx and a practical politician schooled in the rough and tumble of urban politics. Stephen Mitchell (1952–1954) and Paul Butler (1955–1960), on the other hand, were loyal partisans but not powerful leaders in their own states. Mitchell was lacking in political experience. Republican Chairman Leonard Hall (1953–1957) was extraordinarily competent in the public relations aspects of politics and was nicknamed by some as "the Barnum of the GOP." Like Mark Hanna, Hall wielded much power, but Guy Gabrielson (1949–1952) who succeeded the ousted Hugh Scott, Jr., avowed his role as "an impartial presiding officer." A number of Democratic chairmen have received a salary; few Republicans have been salaried. The national chairmanship rarely is a step toward nomination for federal office, William Miller being a conspicuous exception when selected by Senator Goldwater as his running mate.

[6] The other two were Sens. Henry M. Jackson and J. Howard McGrath.

[7] Joseph W. Martin, Jr., dissents from the viewpoint favoring combination of the chairmanship with a congressional position. He writes, "I think it is, generally speaking, a mistake for a member of Congress, whether he be a Democrat or a Republican, to accept the role of national chairman of his party, although I did so reluctantly myself. The positions he may have to take on national issues may conflict disastrously with the interests of his own state or district." *My First Fifty Years in Congress*, McGraw-Hill Book Company, New York, 1960, p. 247.

All chairmen, in the words of Mr. Farley, are required to "promote harmony, teamwork, and united action in the interests of party
success at the November balloting." Originally a major function of the
chairman was to raise money. Although still important, fund raising is
being delegated more and more to the treasurer and to special finance
groups in order to free the chairman for his other ever-increasing burdens.

Of mounting importance for the modern chairman is his role as
the public relations man for the dominant faction of the party. Paul
Butler once told the American Society of Newspaper Editors that he did
little of his work in a smoke-filled room but that he was in the communications business and "about the most unhidden persuader in the
political arena." Butler in 1958 "traveled 72,911 miles to attend 194
party meetings; made sixty-one formal speeches and eighty-four informal speeches; appeared on forty-six network and local programs;
held fifty-one press conferences and filmed fifty-nine spot interviews
for television news shows."[8] In public appearances and through press
releases, the national chairman blisters the opposition and defends and
extols his own party. Sometimes called a "hatchet man," he is usually less
inhibited in criticizing the opposition than his party's public officials.
Chairmen need a keen sense of timing and publicity.

One of the tasks of a national chairman is to take patronage
requests to the President, a function especially difficult and onerous in
the first year of a new President. As a practical matter, the chairman is
frequently the arbiter in patronage controversies because he is the person who places endorsements and recommendations on the President's
desk. Deserving party workers expect him to obtain large numbers of
fair-paying jobs without appearing to be sacking the merit system, a job
indeed calling for legerdemain.

The national chairman is called upon as a troubleshooter.
Former Chairman Hugh D. Scott, Jr., spoke of the chairman as the
"thousand-fingered Dutch boy" of American politics, forever traveling
about plugging the holes in the party's election hopes. He talks with
state and local leaders, helping them to mend political fences and healing breaches within the party's ranks caused by heated primaries, personal factionalism, and disputes over patronage. Chairmen keep their
ears to the ground for reaction of public opinion and party leaders to
the administration in power.

The chairman's role is a hard one and requires ambivalence. He
must be an agent of the President but give the impression that he is
subordinate to the congressional leadership of his party. He must get

[8] David S. Broder, "Changing Face of the Party Chairman," *The New York Times Magazine*,
Oct. 18, 1959, p. 101.

money from the rich but keep up the appearance that his party is financially poor and operating on the basis of small contributions from large numbers of people. He is expected to fire his listeners with oratory and state his party's policies in black and white terms but not become a prima donna or take the spotlight from the President or important bigwigs in Congress. He is often called upon to tell where his party stands on issues and must phrase his answers to avoid irritating powerful sectional and local supporters. The role of the chairman of the party controlling the White House differs markedly from that of the chairman of the out-party. In fact, the in-party, out-party chairmanship is a most useful conceptual framework for studying the role and functions of the national chairman and his headquarters staff. When all is said and done, the in-party chairman must satisfy the President and serve his personal wishes. He may be a political adviser to the President, a "fall guy," used to send up "trial balloons," and any number of other things.[9] The chairman must not take headlines from the President while serving as what amounts to staff assistant to the President for partisan political matters. Because of his long-time interest in partisan politics, President Nixon maintains a close liaison with his national chairman and committee.

The out-party chairman shares his leadership with and must show deference to the defeated presidential candidate. He is a special liaison with his party's congressional leaders. To some extent he fills the vacuum of national party leadership, and image building falls to him in the absence of presidential leadership. He usually has greater personal opportunity than his counterpart for focusing attention on the national party. Both chairmen are expected to assume a negotiating role between dissident elements of the party.

THE HEADQUARTERS BUREAUCRACY

After his defeat in 1924, Franklin D. Roosevelt commented that the national organization was "a farce." "The headquarters," he remarked, "consisted of two ladies occupying one room in a Washington office building." After the defeat of Alfred E. Smith in 1928 and of Alfred Landon in 1936, the respective parties opened full-time offices, and each headquarters now has a sizable payroll and staff.

As shown in Table 6-1, the rise and fall in the number of staff give a periodic flavor to life in the national offices. The radical changes result in confusion and job insecurity for the majority of employees.

[9] For a thoughtful, analytical account, see Joel M. Fisher, "The Role of the National Party Chairman," paper delivered to meeting of American Political Science Association, September, 1969. Fisher classifies the chairman's functions as those of "continuity," "stabilization," "relational," "service," "financial," and the maintenance of communications with the public.

TABLE 6-1   Paid staffs of Republican and Democratic National Committees

Date	Republicans	Democratic
1952	386	251
1953	98	59
1954	107	77
1956	250	201
1957	85	74
1960	352	375
1961	89	75
1962	100	107
1963	124	70
1964	618	302
1965	117	85
1966	116	92
1967	138	85
1968	184*	317
1969	191	87

Note: Figures supplied either by national committees or compiled from treasurer's reports to the House of Representatives. Figures are for October because it is usually the month of maximum campaign activity and the year's high point in employment.

* In 1968 Republicans had an office in New York as well as in Washington, with a total employment of 484. All other figures in the table for both parties refer to Washington, D.C., operations only and do not include the congressional campaign committee staffs.

Financial supporters of the party are unwilling to see a big headquarters payroll after an election, and many excellent staff people are let out with some rehired a year or so later for the next campaign — a dysfunctional practice in many respects. Notwithstanding this personnel fluctuation, both parties retain a small core of more or less permanent, well-trained, experienced, and highly competent staff members. They help provide continuity and compensate in part for the frequent turnover of national chairman.

Democratic national chairmen do not commit their organizational arrangements to a chart, and the national office is a rather loose congeries of groups with interrelationships commonly blurred or indistinct. Republican National Chairman Leonard Hall (1953–1957) published an organization chart, and his successors have retained most of the major divisions but regrouped them and altered some lines of authority.[10] Although not an official chart, Figure 6-1 shows the variety of

[10] Charts of Hall's regular and 1956 campaign organizations are reproduced in Bone, *op. cit.*, pages 43 and 61.

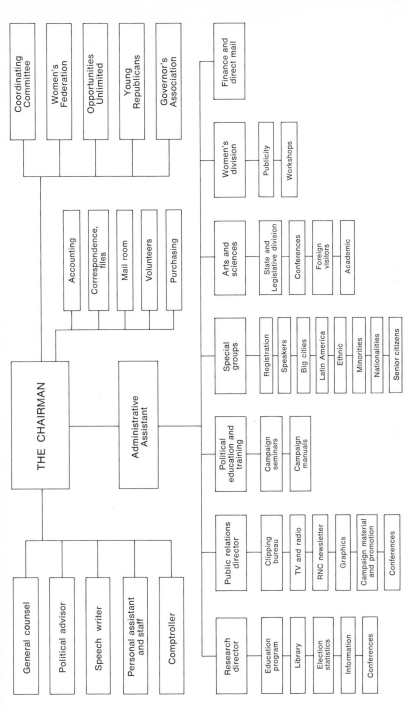

FIGURE 6-1 Organization chart of Republican National Headquarters under Ray C. Bliss, 1969.

agencies and presumed lines of responsibility in chairman Bliss' last year (1968-1969).[11]

Both national headquarters house other groups. The Young Republican National Federation, created in 1935, and the Young Democratic Clubs of America, formed in 1932, operate as official youth auxiliaries; and the chairman of the former group serves ex officio on the Republican National Committee. Both groups help integrate the hundreds of youth clubs throughout the state and college campuses. Women's divisions are devoted to stressing the "woman's angle," preparing materials for coffee hours and giving special assistance to the party's female officeholders. The national vice-chairman, always a woman, oversees women's activities. In the 1960s the expansion and financing of the Republican Governor's Association was undertaken by the national committee and given office space in the headquarters building. For many years the Republicans have maintained a more highly developed headquarters and larger staffs then the Democrats.

Major Activities. The major efforts of the national headquarters go into research, publicity, service, and attention to ethnic and religious minorities.[12] These functions are interrelated, and the distinction, for example, between research and publicity is often unclear. Democrats issue fewer materials and give less emphasis to public relations per se than do Republicans.

Since the 1930s, the Republicans have had a well-developed research division, with several persons employed to operate a library containing more than 8,000 volumes and files of newspaper clippings. The Democrats manage with a much smaller staff, and at times the research section all but disappears. Research and publicity divisions compile voting statistics, analyze election returns, monitor articles from the press and periodicals. In 1968, Republicans installed a microfilm retrieval system containing more than 30,000 items for the campaign. Their electronic data processing was used to project long- and short-term trends by counties and provide technical services to state and local organizations.

---

[11] As expected, when Rep. Rogers C. B. Morton became Republican national chairman in 1969, considerable regrouping took place; but the major change was coordination through Deputy Chairman Harry Dent in order to permit Mr. Morton to continue his congressional duties.

[12] It would take a small volume to cover these activities. For details of these operations see Bone, *op. cit.,* chaps. 2–4, Cotter and Hennessey, *op. cit.,* chaps. 6–8. Ray Bliss prepared an especially comprehensive report for 1968: *The Chairmen's Report—1968 to the Republican National Committee,* Republican National Committee, Washington, D.C., January, 1969. See the account of national headquarters prepared by Charles O. Jones, *The Republican Party in American Politics,* The Macmillan Company, New York, 1965, chap. 2. Considerable information on the Democratic National Committee is found in the *Congressional Quarterly,* May 27, 1966, pp. 1074–1080, and Jan. 17, 1969, p. 100.

Research and publicity units handle three types of data and information. Analysis of the voting records and "misdeeds" of the opposition is made available to candidates challenging incumbents. A number of state and congressional district political and voter "profiles" also aid individual candidates. Some issue materials are evolved to provide data for campaign use on foreign policy, urban problems, agriculture, inflation, and many other topics. Finally, materials on diverse types of operations are featured in "fact books" on campaign techniques, registration, voter laws, precinct activity, and various headquarters manuals. Reams of "know-how" materials advise candidates on the most effective use of radio, television, and newspapers. Publicity kits, public relations seminars, posters, and biographical sketches are especially helpful for nonincumbents. Generally, national committee research efforts are designed to provide information on national issues for all in the party rather than highly detailed information on specific congressional districts. When requests are received for help of this kind, they are usually turned over to the congressional campaign committees.

Publicity divisions prepare news releases attacking the opposition and extolling their own record and prepare insertions for the *Congressional Record*. The development of high-powered publicity divisions is one of the most significant developments in party organization in this century. Such a unit is imperative for the minority party, which cannot command the great facilities of the executive branch of the government. It receives less continuous publicity than the "in" party, although its members in Congress can and do make news. The President often finds his party's headquarters useful for advice, information, and the release of data provided by the Chief Executive.

Although a political party press has never been popular in the United States, as it is in many other nations, several state organizations and the national committees sporadically publish magazines and newsletters. (Federal law forbids national committees to sell campaign literature.) Most party publication ventures are costly, and the mortality rate is high, as party managers believe that scarce resources should be allocated elsewhere.

Both national party organizations are aware that the stakes of urban politics are very high. For this reason, the national committees keep more or less permanent divisions in operation under such titles as "All-Americans," "Heritage," "Nationalities," or "Minorities" divisions.[13]

---

[13] On the date and theories of these activities as applied in the early 1960s, see Frances E. Rourke, "Urbanism and the National Party Organizations," *Western Political Quarterly*, vol. 18, pp. 149–163, 1965. See also Charles E. Gilbert, "National Political Alignments and the Politics of Large Cities," *Political Science Quarterly*, vol. 79, pp. 25–81, 1964.

Because the Democrats have been much the greater beneficiaries of ethnic, religious, and racial groups in the big cities, their approach has been different from that of the Republicans who face an uphill battle. High-ranking Democrats in the cities are given responsibility for using their local organization to mobilize the minority vote even though a unit is maintained in the national office. Republicans have a larger staffed office in Washington, D.C., for this purpose and usually set up district units for various ethnics and for blacks. As must always be pointed out, the percentage of vote one gets from minorities may bear little relationship to organizational strength, but the party officials nonetheless stress the necessity for units to give particular attention to specific groups.

In both parties, there are many other specialized divisions devoted to maintaining contact with and getting the votes of farmers, senior citizens, labor, and others. Since 1960, the Republicans have experimented with an arts and sciences division designed to mobilize the support and skills of Republican-oriented professors and "recruit uncommitted college students with leadership abilities into the Republican party." Its director works with a state legislative division to assist Republican state legislative candidates.

Fieldmen from various divisions in the headquarters travel about the country meeting with local party and group leaders. This is a useful two-way intelligence system for taking information out to the country and bringing back information useful to the national office. The fieldmen render advice when asked and help to obtain services from the national headquarters for the local agencies.

THE CAPITOL HILL COMMITTEES

National party organization is further proliferated and decentralized by a campaign committee in each house of Congress and a Senate policy committee for good measure.[14] Dispersion of power in the White House, the Senate, and the House encourages multiplication of organization. That these interests are served by several autonomous committees meets the test of pragmatism for party leaders.

Congressional and Senatorial Committees. According to Clarence Cannon, historian for the Democratic party's national conventions, the congressional committee was born in 1842 as a joint House-Senate committee to publish "a declaration of principles for General Harrison's administration." Republicans had a joint committee of congressional Republicans to assist their candidates during Lincoln's first administration. Both

[14] The policy committees and other aspects of Congressional party organization are covered in chap. 8.

parties adopted a permanent organization in 1866. It is uncertain when the congressional committees began to operate on a year-round basis. Ostrogorski observed that in 1900 they were active between campaigns. In 1916 when senators began to be popularly elected, both parties established separate senatorial campaign committees.

The National Republican Congressional Committee is composed of one member of the House of Representatives from each state having one or more Republican representatives. Each member is selected biennially by his respective state delegation, subject to the approval of the Republican conference. The committee selects its own chairman and other officials. The Democratic National Congressional Committee is similarly constituted. The full committees meet sporadically and may operate through subcommittees. The Democratic staff seldom exceeds a half-dozen and is crowded into a room in the House Office Building. By contrast, the Republican staff continues around thirty between campaigns and is considerably larger during campaigns. Its staff members consist of well-trained specialists in art, writing, publicity, photography, and fieldwork. Republican expenditures have been larger than those of the Democrats.

The Senate Office Building houses both the Republican and Democratic senatorial campaign committees. The Democratic leader of the Senate appoints the Democratic chairman, who in turn appoints the remainder of the five- to nine-member committee. Republican chairmen are generally selected by the Republican conference. The committee usually numbers around eight, one member from each geographic area. Each group has a staff of four or five.[15] The work of the senatorial committees is less extensive than that of the House committees because only a third of the Senate seats are up for election at a given time, and many of these are from "safe" states.

The goal of the House and Senate campaign committees is to reelect incumbents and, when possible, to assist nonincumbents where prospects appear good enough to justify staff help and financial assistance. Money is likely to be given according to "need" and prospect for success. The allocation of funds sometimes leads to criticism and disaffection with the committees. Quite complete legislative histories and roll-call voting records of opponents are compiled, and the staff usually prepares materials useful for campaign speeches. A major function of the committees is to arrange for party speakers to go into the states and districts to speak on behalf of colleagues who are up for reelection.

[15] The reported size of the committee staffs may be misleading, since staff members are transferred from one payroll to another, and many congressional secretaries and staff members of standing committees may be "on loan" to help the campaign committees.

The House Republican committee is a big operation.[16] It conducts extensive publicity operations through news releases and newsletters and has become a press agent for Republican congressmen. They are supplied with a wide range of services, such as being photographed while engaged in legislative business or with constituents who come to Washington to visit them. On request, a congressman will be helped in designing his campaign literature and drafting his local newsletter and will be given technical aid in preparing radio and television programs. The House Democrats provide very few of the same services and expend almost no money for public relations.

Since 1953, the House Republicans have had a full-time field service coordinated with the national and senatorial committees. Fieldmen are assigned to a regional area and visit local party chairmen and officeholders with a view to stimulating local organizations by discussing leadership and management problems and by stressing the importance of the district in terms of party control of Congress. The field representatives act as "needlers" and catalysts and try to get the local organization men to complete precinct analysis forms useful for subsequent campaigns. Fieldmen try to build up a knowledge of each district, evaluate the leadership, and observe the voting behavior and demography in each district.

The efforts of all Capitol Hill committees are largely limited to the marginal district broadly defined as having been won by 55 percent or less of the vote. This is likely to consist of only 90 to 150 districts. Aid of course will be given to others where the win-loss ratio is as high as 60 to 40 or even higher if there are other indications of a turnover. Republicans have picked up some seats in the South by taking a gamble on somewhat longer odds.

Intercommittee Relations. The decentralization of national party functions into the hands of three separate committees provides no model of efficiency. There is no organic relationship among the committees, and the relationships are ill defined, resulting in considerable duplication and overlapping of effort in research and publicity. There is often dissatisfaction with financial allocations among the committees, and each has at times been critical of the work of others. The party committees on Capitol Hill remain jealous of their independence and are quick to

---

[16] For a more comprehensive analysis of the Republican as well as other Capitol Hill committees, see Hugh A. Bone, "Some Notes on the Congressional Campaign Committees," *Western Political Quarters*, vol. 9, pp. 116–137, 1956, and Guy B. Hathorn, "Congressional and Senatorial Campaign Committees in the Mid-term Election Year 1954," *Southwestern Social Science Quarterly*, vol. 37, pp. 207–221, 1956. A short but informative account of how the Hill and national committees assist the congressman in campaigns is found in Charles L. Clapp, *The Congressman: His Work as He Sees It*, The Brookings Institution, Washington, D.C., 1963, pp. 351–366.

resist encroachment by the national committees. Republican National Chairman Guy Gabrielson in 1951 proposed some consolidation of the committees' staff work in research and publicity. Congressional groups immediately vetoed the idea, and his proposal for coordinating meetings of staffs of the different committees was not well received. Congressional leaders want the national committee to confine itself to raising money and rendering service, leaving them to operate as they see fit. Congressmen and national committeemen are too preoccupied and perhaps too remote for fruitful joint committee meetings. There is, however, a considerable amount of informal coordination by the chairmen and their staffs.

Many congressmen consider the main purpose of the national committee to be the election of a President. At the other level, the state and local committees show a strong tendency to work for their own particular tickets. In this situation, the congressman finds he is a party orphan. His district often does not coincide with county lines, and few areas have full-fledged congressional district organizations. A congressman, who is away from his district more than half the time, cannot hope to maintain the close contact with the local organization that a state legislator or county commissioner can. The congressional committee takes care of some of the congressman's needs during campaigns, in his constituent relations and in his work in the House. These needs are not fully served by either the national or the local committees.

Congressmen are often in disagreement with policies supported by the national committee. In a remarkable statement to Republican state leaders in New York, the congressional committee chairman Rep. Richard M. Simpson counseled his party's candidates to forget Eisenhower's coattails in the 1958 elections and make known to voters their disagreement with the President's policies.[17] The speech exemplified the lack of party unity and the dispersion of power within the party organization. It illustrates the point that although a national chairman is expected to be loyal to his President's program, the congressional chairman need not be associated with the President's wing of the party. Simpson served notice that aid to those expressing disagreement with Eisenhower's policies would not be denied.

Congressional committees, like the national committees, are regarded as service agencies. Although they give financial aid and other assistance, they cannot impose discipline or wield power in policy matters. Party platform and program are subordinate to organization. A congressman or senator can be for or against rigid farm price supports,

---

[17] *The New York Times*, Oct. 21, 1958. Hathorn says that the Capitol Hill groups "symbolized the desire of congressional leaders to protect their interests when they believe these interests to be counter to the ambitions of the national party organization." *Op. cit.*, p. 208.

or he may be a nationalist or an internationalist, an ultraliberal or an ultraconservative; but as long as he wears the party label, asks for help, and presumably needs it, he will be given at least a minimum amount of assistance. In other words, he who pays the fiddler cannot call the tune. Some congressmen, however, may be able to receive some extra help by being friendly to the legislative leaders and by pointing to their record on party roll calls.

The maintenance of Capitol Hill committees on a year-round basis rests on several other factors. There appears to be a significant increase in split-ticket voting in recent years, and congressional committees recognize that many congressmen are reelected for reasons not directly associated with the degree of their party loyalty or their record in Congress. Appeals by local committees to vote a straight ticket may be of insufficient help to a congressman or senator. The Capitol Hill committees give incumbent lawmakers financial and tailor-made assistance helpful in bolstering their own causes.

Many lawmakers have never been inside their own national committee headquarters. In contrast, the congressional committees are in convenient proximity to legislative offices. They are composed of members of their "own club," who presumably have greater understanding of a congressman's needs than has the national committee. The committees on the Hill help freshman congressmen learn their way around Washington and give them assistance in various ways. During presidential years congressmen feel, with some reason, that the national committee neglects them. Former Speaker and Republican National Chairman Joseph W. Martin, Jr. wrote:

> In 1952 and 1956 a disproportionate amount of money for television and other campaign activities was directed to the presidential race at the expense of the Congressional campaign. Candidates for the Senate and House were largely neglected. The Madison Avenue crowd that has attached itself to this administration (Eisenhower) has displayed little interest in electing a Congress. It's the presidency they are concerned about.[18]

Evaluation. During the present century, the party controlling the White House has tended to suffer losses in congressional strength in the midterm elections. Presidents Taft, Wilson, Hoover, Truman, and Eisenhower saw loss of their party's control of Congress. During a presidential election, the candidate can help accommodate factionalism and build unity within his party in the larger interest of electing party candidates. During the midterm battle, attention cannot be centered around a presidential personality, and each congressman runs on his own platform. Moreover, neither party has responded favorably to the suggestion of a

[18] Martin, *op. cit.*, p. 228.

biennial national convention or the drafting of a midterm platform which might serve to highlight issues for the congressional election.

Republicans have controlled Congress only twice since 1930 and have viewed the congressional and senatorial committees as devices for bolstering their electoral strength both in presidential and in midterm elections. However, the expansion of these committees' activities and Eisenhower's active intervention did not result in Republican control of Congress in 1954 and 1958. This experience suggests that the midterm problem is not exclusively one of organizational efforts, but the assistance given by the congressional party committees is nonetheless helpful to many incumbents facing serious challenges in their districts.

Despite the obvious advantages of greater coordination and closer integration of the activities between the national party committee and the two congressional party committees and their respective staffs, a proposal to unify them would scarcely get a hearing on Capitol Hill because of jealousy and the well-entrenched independence of the lawmakers' committees. The diffusion of the national party headquarters is another instance in which an outwardly illogical form possesses, at least to party practitioners, certain recognizable virtues. The executive-legislative strife leading to the formation of campaign committees in Congress has disappeared, but the committees remain because new needs for them have arisen and because they have become far more than sporadically active campaign committees.

National committees, even in midterm elections, as a rule deal with national issues; the congressional and senatorial committees serve the needs of members of Congress in their own states and districts. National committees in midterm elections work for the whole party and attack the opposition en masse. They defend or attack the President and answer the charges of the opposition leaders. Congressional committees, although interested in the overall record of the party, are more interested in the individual voting record and activities of the senator and congressman; their object is more narrow and pinpointed than that of the national committees, which must defend an unpopular President or policy. When expedient, the Hill committees may remain silent on these matters and emphasize the incumbent's record. This approach may not promote party unity, but it shows a practicality so characteristic of American party politics. The congressional and senatorial committees are fully established and are assured survival—a testimony to the fact that they have found a niche for themselves.

Although the sphere of influence has not yet been systematically studied, the United States senator himself may, if he wishes, be an effective link between the national and state party organizations. Only a few senators have simultaneously held positions as national committeemen, but many senators actively participate in state organizational matters and intervene in the selection of a state chairman. This affords another example of the tendency of parties to be dominated by officeholders who use party organizations to achieve their office goals.

THE NATIONAL COMMITTEE AS A CENTER OF POWER

In a study of the history of the Republican organization, Gordon Klee-berg wrote in 1911 that the initiators of the first executive committee did not foresee that they were "establishing a party organ which would arrogate to itself at times almost unlimited powers and supreme control of the national party machinery."[19] Yet a generation later, the widely experienced columnist Thomas L. Stokes depreciated the committee, saying, "A national committee never nominated anybody, never elected anybody, never established party policy."[20] Since the power of the national committee has varied from time to time, its strength has often been a moot point. Originally, the prime purpose of the committee was to arrange for the holding of the national convention and, to some extent, to serve as an agent for carrying out the convention's instructions. Over the years, the committee has been called upon to assume many additional roles; we shall summarize these before analyzing the question of power. Unless otherwise noted, we shall use *committee* broadly to refer to the chairman or the national office as well as the individual committeemen.

Functions. Today the committee is the largest single collector, allocator, and spender of the party's financial resources. The national office estimates the financial needs of the party and works out the basic design for obtaining and expending the money. In raising funds, the national chairman works closely with the chairmen of the senatorial and congressional committees.

It has long been a function of the national committee to distribute patronage. The committee is likewise recognized as the clearinghouse and secretariat for the party; staff members speak of the headquarters as the housekeeper of the national party's business. To a considerable extent, it is the custodian of the party's platform. The research and publicity divisions try to relate the platform to new developments. An out-party is a watchdog of the opposition and scrutinizes and criticizes the record of the controlling party. Its chairman is quick to point out where the majority deviates from its own platform and the virtue of his

[19]"The Formation of the Republican Party as a National Political Organization," Ph.D. dissertation, Columbia University, 1911; privately printed, p. 200.
[20]Syndicated column, *Chicago Sun-Times*, Aug. 9, 1949.

own party's platform. With considerable latitude in their research, public relations, and speechmaking activities, the committeemen and headquarters staffs may play up or play down certain parts of their own party's and opponent's records. It is not unusual for the committee to be a catalytic agent both in organizational matters and in policy, and it was the spirit behind the development of the new regional associations.

As a source of intelligence on matters of party concern, the national committee has become increasingly important. Its members are listening posts and sounding boards year in and year out and are useful to campaign strategists for consultation purposes. Facts, warnings, and suggestions go from committeemen to the White House, to Congress, and to the party's officialdom. The committee is a vital publicity link with the public.

In national elections, the chairman and his lieutenants usually participate to some extent in the determination of campaign strategy. In recent elections, the campaign has been run by a person chosen by the President or the presidential nominee, and the committee collectively has had little or no voice in this selection or in the campaign. Individual committeemen are expected to carry out the master plan, determined by the nominee's entourage, in their own states.

Although committeemen are often disappointed in the role accorded them in campaigns, their year-round functioning has provided a valuable channel of communication between the local party committeemen and certain national party leaders. Through the committee's efforts, party enthusiasts in the states are drawn, however infrequently, into thinking about the party as a national entity. The very existence of the national committee serves as a reminder to the local hierarchy that there is a national party that requires its support.

Exercise of Power within Party. The degree of influence of an individual committeeman in his own state can usually be ascertained by a study of the state's politics. In the performance of its diverse duties noted above, the national committee is bound to be of some but not of major influence. The role and influence of the national committee are affected particularly by the interest and attitude of the President and national chairman. Many Presidents have kept control over party affairs and have dominated the committee and its chairman. President Eisenhower was content to let Republican national chairmen, particularly Leonard Hall, handle the party's politics, and Hall became a highly influential force within the national party. Newspapermen generally credited Hall with overriding opposition to the renomination of Vice President Nixon in 1956 and with keeping up pressure for Eisenhower's renomination after his heart attack. "When the President was stricken," wrote Walter Lippmann, "the whole future of the party was in doubt. It was at that time that Hall, obviously a strong man who knows his own mind, took command. He decreed that Eisenhower and Nixon must run again. He put the President under pressure to agree to run again. And he put the party under pressure to accept Nixon again."[21]

Another area in which the committee has exercised power is in preparation for the national convention. At times the committee, in maneuvers before the convention, may play favorites in the race for the nomination. In selecting speakers and sites for the convention, the committee has appeared to favor one faction over another. In general, the national convention has exhibited little control over the national committee. But the committees have influenced the convention. On numerous occasions, national committees have recommended changes in party rules and requested and obtained ratification from the convention. The 1960 Democratic convention vested authority in the national committee to prescribe the formula for the allocation of delegates for future conventions.

To some extent, a struggle for control of the party apparatus of the party out of power takes place in the national committee. A study of the Republican National Committee activities and professional personnel in 1963 by the *Congressional Quarterly* staff found "conservatively oriented Goldwater forces in numerous key posts and in effective control of major policy decisions."[22] Several 1964 Republican convention appointments were also in the hands of Goldwater people. Historically, the temper and focus of the national committee are often that of the dominant faction within the party.

As a result of the clash between "dissident Democrats" and the Johnson-Humphrey wing of the party, the 1968 Democratic National Convention directed the appointment of a reform commission to recommend alterations for 1972. In one of his first major acts as Democratic national chairman, Senator Harris appointed Sen. George McGovern, who had been a stand-in for the Kennedy faction at the convention, and Sen. Harold Hughes, a McCarthy supporter, as chairman and vice-chairman respectively of a Commission on Party Structure and Delegate Selection. Representative James G. O'Hara, a Humphrey supporter and former leader of the Democratic Study Group of the House of Representatives, was appointed chairman of the Committee on Party Structure. Harris' choice of leaders and designation of a broad-gauge membership were designed to promote party unity and head off bitter quarrels over the composition of and procedures at the 1972

[21] *Seattle Times*, Aug. 23, 1956.
[22] See "Goldwater Supporters Hold Key Professional GOP Posts," in issue of Oct. 11, 1963, pp. 1770–1774. This article also includes an analysis of the Republican headquarters activities and organizational activities under Chairman Miller.

Democratic convention.[23] Hearings were held around the nation to elicit ideas for the better operation of the national convention. The convention itself, as in the past when the committee recommended rule changes, has sole authority to accept or reject committee proposals.

The congressional wing of the party at times (but by no means invariably) gets control over the national committee and is able to name one of its own as chairman or to strongly influence the choice of the person. But as soon as a presidential candidate is nominated, and especially if he is elected, the national committee is regarded as an adjunct of the presidential party.

Since the major concern of the national committee is the election of a President, it has tried to do everything within its power to see that the electors chosen in a state support the nominees of the national convention. There is no provision in federal law or in the Constitution requiring an elector to support his party's candidates. Only a few states so compel their electors. Thus it is left largely to moral obligation or to persuasion. A North Carolina elector in 1968 voted for George C. Wallace instead of for Nixon who carried the state. Similarly in 1948 a Democratic Tennessee elector voted for Strom Thurmond even though the state gave its popular vote to Truman.[24]

In an effort to avoid situations like this and the bitter quarrel over a convention-imposed loyalty oath, Democratic National Chairman Stephen Mitchell in 1954 appointed a Special Advisory Committee on Rules and Regulations chosen from all sections of the party. This group proposed that the state Democratic parties, when selecting delegates to the national convention, undertake to assure that the convention's nominees would be placed on the ballot with electors pledged to them.[25] Further, every member of the Democratic National Committee was to declare affirmatively for the convention's nominees and failure to do so would be to declare his seat vacant. These rules were adopted by the convention in 1956 and accepted again in 1960. These rules in principle said that the state parties, in sending delegates to the national convention, assumed responsibility for permitting voters to cast ballots for nominees of the convention under Democratic party electors. By sending

[23] Memberships of the two commissions are found in the *Congressional Quarterly*, Feb. 14, 1969, p. 250. See also *U.S. News & World Report*, May 26, 1969, pp. 46–48.

[24] In 1952 the Alabama Democratic Executive Committee, exercising power delegated to it by the legislature, was overruled by the Alabama courts when it tried to remove an elector from the ballot who refused to be bound to the candidate of the Democratic National Convention. The United States Supreme Court reversed this decision in *Ray v. Blair*, 343 U.S. 214 (1952). The Supreme Court of Texas has held that electors must vote for the party's candidates. State laws and court decisions show many discrepancies in these matters.

[25] A useful analysis of this development has been prepared by Abraham Holtzman, "Party Responsibility and Loyalty: New Rules in the Democratic Party," *Journal of Politics*, vol. 22, pp. 485–501, 1960, and *The Loyalty Pledge Controversy in the Democratic Party*, McGraw-Hill Book Company, New York, 1960.

delegates to the national convention, the state party signifies its intention to affiliate with the national party.

The national committee and convention can decree regulations but have no real power to enforce them. In 1958 and 1959, Alabama, Georgia, and Arkansas passed laws freeing electors from supporting nominees of a national convention. All the Kennedy-pledged electors fulfilled their obligations in 1960, although strong efforts were made in many Southern states to get them to defect. In Mississippi, an unpledged slate was elected over the Democratic one by a margin of about 8,000 votes, and it was decided to cast Mississippi's eight votes for Sen. Harry F. Byrd of Virginia.

The Democratic National Committee is empowered to expel members for cause and has expunged from its rolls on several occasions since 1896 members actively opposing the election of the party's presidential nominee. In 1958, Louisiana expelled a national committeeman for his opposition to segregation. National Chairman Butler refused to recognize the action as binding on the national committee. The committee sustained Butler and would not seat the new selectee from Louisiana. Over the years, the Democrats have tried to establish rules defining the nebulous relationship of the national committees and conventions to state committees and to the electoral college. States' rights is strongly entrenched in political party thinking, and it is not easy for the national agency to develop the power to bring bolting state organizations into line.

POWER OVER PARTY PROGRAM

As is true of state and local committees, the most controversial issue concerning the power of the national committee is in the realm of policy formulation. When a party does not control the Presidency, its national committee is frequently involved in bitter quarrels over whether the committee itself should state party positions or convene a group to do so. A great many rank-and-file members clamor for a statement on "what the party stands for" and ask, with some logic, whether the party can hope to win the next election without policies and programs. They note that the majority party gets the headlines and that the President in effect formulates its program. It seems sensible to them that the minority should likewise have a central program. But they soon learn that the congressmen of their party will discourage such a practice. Moreover, the congressmen feel that they alone should be free to make the party's record and resent statements on legislative programs by any group within their party. Although staking out this position for itself, the congressional party rarely takes a public position on policy or attempts to enforce party-line voting (see Chapter 8). For party committees and volunteer workers, therefore, the party role in making policy is a frustrating business. A few illustrations will demonstrate this point.

Experiences with Policy Statements. During the regimes of Franklin D. Roosevelt and Harry S. Truman, several Republican chairmen attempted to outline official party programs, and various conferences were called with a view toward evolving a statement. In every instance, Republican congressmen objected, and only a few would participate. In one or two instances, the national committee endorsed a policy statement. Generally, however, such policy declarations as were made emanated from outside the committee, although some of its members and even the chairman had a prominent part in the enterprise.

In 1962, former President Eisenhower called an all-Republican conference at his Gettysburg farm. Many Republican congressmen were restive about it; others publicly opposed it; and the group was not reconvened. But it led in 1963 to the establishment of a Republican Critical Issues Council of twenty-three members, backed by the President's brother, Milton S. Eisenhower. The announced purpose of the group was "to articulate a Republican citizens' position on the great problems that face our people and our government." The group said that it would cooperate with both the Republican National Committee and Republican congressmen but that its positions would be "those of a citizens' organization and not those of a particular elected official or group." Many of the persons on the council were former cabinet officials in the Eisenhower administration; a few were former congressmen. Significantly, current members of the Republican National Committee and the party's congressmen were omitted from the membership.[26]

Republican National Chairman Ray C. Bliss made the most ambitious modern attempt to unite the various segments of the national party by the creation in 1965 of a Republican Coordinating Committee composed of thirty-six members, including the party's former Presidents, congressional leaders, representatives of the Republican governors' and legislative associations and with himself as chairman. Its stated purpose was to work out party positions in advance of the 1968 convention.[27] After nearly four years of work and many

[26] For an extensive account of the Republican National Committee and its policy committees since 1920, see Cotter and Hennessy, *op. cit.*, chap. 10. An account of numerous council activities was published by the Republican National Committee under the title *The Development of National Party Policy between Conventions*, Washington, D.C., 1966.

[27] For summary of the work of this group, see Bliss, *The Chairman's Report*, pp. 1–9. Mr. Bliss stated that the group was created "for the specific purpose of promoting Party unity and providing the Party a broadly based, representative leadership group which would seek solutions to mounting crises in foreign and domestic affairs" (p. 3).

formal work sessions about seventy-five position papers and statements on foreign and domestic affairs were issued and later distributed to Republican candidates as a book under the title *Choice for America*. Mr. Bliss claimed that about 90 percent of the subject matter of the convention's platform came from the recommendations of the Coordinating Committee. Mr. Bliss's approach was oblique enough so that it did not arouse the ire of congressmen nor did the Committee purpose to state official party positions.

The most extensive attempt of Democrats as an out-party was under Paul Butler's chairmanship from 1956 to 1961.[28] Called the National Democratic Advisory Council, it was composed of several prominent state and local party officials and public officeholders, a few United States senators, Harry S. Truman, and Adlai Stevenson, as well as several national committeemen. It issued a large number of liberally oriented policy statements. The committee invited Speaker Sam Rayburn and Senate Majority Leader Lyndon Johnson and other congressmen to become council members, but they refused and never recognized the council as a body entitled to speak for the party.

It is perhaps remarkable that the National Democratic Advisory Council was sanctioned by the Democratic National Convention in 1960 and that it survived the wrath of a number of congressmen for four years. After Kennedy was inaugurated, the council was disbanded on the grounds that, with Democratic control of the Presidency and the Congress, a national party council was no longer needed, for policy would be determined by the party's elected officeholders.

At the urging of Vice President Humphrey, the Democratic National Committee voted unanimously early in 1969 to create a Democratic Policy Council—composed of nationally prominent leaders—that would speak for the party during the next four years and would give to states without Democratic governors and United States senators "a voice in the determination of basic party policy." Congressional Democrats were reported in opposition to its creation. In a rather unusual move for the out-party, Chairman Harris selected the party's titular leader, Hubert Humphrey, as chairman of the council.

Experiences with out-party councils illustrate the characteristics of American party life. They usually irritate many congressmen, who in turn ignore the policy pronouncements; and they seem to have little perceptible effect on the Senate policy committees. The officeholders' attitudes toward it show that the national committee is likely to be impotent and ineffective in providing leadership in the area of policy. It has competitors not only on Capitol Hill but among powerful gover-

---

[28] For an account of the council, see Cotter and Hennessy, *op. cit.*, chap. 11, and Bone, *op cit.*, pp. 214–233.

nors, who also make policy statements on national positions. On occasions, however, governors give strong support to policy councils in opposition to congressmen. Council publications are widely distributed to local clubs and provide the basis for "issues" discussions, perhaps serving a good purpose for the noncongressional wings of the party.

When both national committees made pronouncements on the Cuban and Berlin crises, columnist William S. White wrathfully called on leaders of both parties to tell the "national political committees to get out and stay out of foreign policy." "National committees," he wrote, "are strictly political megaphones and bear no iota of responsibility for public policy. Their stuff is loud, but rarely good. And no national committee is or can be really informed on matters of this sort. Any national committee thus will inevitably utter not only a good deal of nonsense, but often nonsense which may be harmful to its own party's presidential aspirants."[29]

A national committee finds itself in the hapless position of being criticized if it takes no interest in public policy and of being lambasted if it makes a public pronouncement. In terms of recruitment of informed and able men and women for positions on the national committee, the views of Mr. White—shared by many other journalists and congressmen—are likely to be discouraging. Persons interested in policy may decide that serving in the national party hierarchy is not worth their time.

Who Should Formulate Policy? The American party system offers a contrast to that of most European parties, whose central offices or executive group within the party formulate manifestos, resolutions, and policies. As such, these executive agencies are important power centers within the party. Yet even in the party structures in Europe with tighter-knit parties, more policy-oriented than in the United States, a strict definition of roles between the party-in-the-country and the party-in-the-government is maintained. The British Labour party, for example, adopts general programs that make the party meaningful, but it does not tell its parliamentary members how to vote on measures or participate in parliamentary struggles. Unlike the executive party committees in some other nations, American committees cannot nominate or suspend members of Congress from party membership.

National committees can and do make organizational roles for themselves but party policies are made by many different people and agencies, and the national committee is very rarely an important center of power in terms of drafting the party's legislative program and exercising authority over its candidates and public officeholders. The President is the recognized spokesman for the party in power. But the party

[29] See White's column, *Seattle Times*, Oct. 5, 1961.

not in control of the Presidency is less fortunately situated. It has no one national-level executive unit fully representative of, and therefore capable of speaking for, the party's national ego. The national committee must be respectful of and work with other national units, particularly the congressional and senatorial committees and the Senate policy committees. The committees have no effective sanctions to secure compliance with their decisions. Philip S. Wilder, Jr., who served in one of the committee offices, has told his fellow political scientists that "for the foreseeable future, the national committee must operate without enough tools to do the jobs for which it, as the central office of the party, can logically be held responsible." National chairmen of the party not controlling the White House are generally frustrated, for they feel that, by focusing attention on party programs, they can keep the party before the public and pave the way for victory; yet their own party's lawmakers are unwilling to accord such a role to the committee. Succinctly, the party hierarchy is expected to show imagination in devising new techniques and methods for the manipulation of mass opinion but avoid innovation, if not maintain silence, in realms of party policy.

In summary, party committees at every level come in for sharp criticism in their policy role—or lack of it. The dissatisfaction arises in part from the pretensions of some members of the committees that they are expected to determine both party policy and legislative program. It is due also to the fact that the unsophisticated do not understand how the system works and expect committees and party conventions to formulate policies that are binding on the party's elected officeholders. Others appreciate that the party organizations do not exercise this function but insist that they should.

From a legislator's point of view, when his party does not control the executive branch, he regards it as his prerogative to determine party policy and does not take kindly to usurpation of the function by a party committee or any other body. He contends that such bodies cannot understand the complexities of modern issues and that he has greater knowledge and responsibility for dealing with them. He wants the freedom to be flexible and uncommitted to a program or line. Although he may not like to admit it, his objection to statements emanating from a party group may well be that he finds them at variance with his own views.

THE ROLE OF PARTY ORGANIZATION

Among party activists as well as students of government the role of party organizations in the system is not clearly defined because of the disagreement over what the appropriate functions for the committees, their leaders, and their staffs are — the familiar controversy over what *is* and what *ought* to be. The point has been made and will reappear several times subsequently that there is no single organization or agency for determining policies within a political party. This is attributable to many causes. The organizations themselves are often not so representative of the broad coalitions within the party as seems desirable. A federal form of government, division of authority among the branches of government, different processes of nomination, degrees of competition between the parties in different localities, and the pluralistic society itself work to decentralize the formulation of a party program. The President becomes the central figure for determining and coordinating the policy of his party, but local policies of his own party as well as all levels of the opposition party's program are not favored with such an integrating or unifying force.

In the party struggle, the organizations and their auxiliaries have the prime function of *service*. This involves the responsibility for conducting research, obtaining publicity to keep the party before the public, assisting in speech writing, supplying speakers and materials to both party and nonparty groups, and in general serving as the secretariat for the party. In performing these functions, party workers try to crystallize and reinforce the concept of party voting among the faithful and to win converts. In these activities they may at times have the opportunity of molding the views of some voters. Party organizations are further expected to discover and interest new talent and bring it into activity on behalf of the party. Registration, managing rallies, telephoning, and doorbell ringing as well as locating potential sources of campaign contributions are well-established roles for party workers and committeemen. Party organizations per se are best judged on the effectiveness with which they perform these functions. The jobs are not consistently exciting but need not be downgraded. They are indispensable aspects of party life, and it is fortunate that many find these activities rewarding and satisfying.

As to participation in policy making, the contention really centers around the unwillingness of numerous party activists to accept a *supportive* and *suggestive* rather than a *formulative* role. At the outset this involves acceptance of the principle that it is not the function of national, state, and local party committees and related groups to formulate specific legislative programs that are binding on the elective officials of the party. In the American pluralist society, the loose coalitions we call political parties do not elect persons who have near unanimity on public issues. To insist that they vote a certain way is to invite their defeat and to alienate prospective party supporters in their districts. But the supportive role does not mean that party organizations must eschew entirely policies and issues; it involves publicizing, upholding, and reinforcing the general policy declarations adopted by the party conventions; it means that the function of formulating a specific position (and of course voting) on legislative issues is left to elective public officeholders and that the elected executives put forth programs in the name of the party.

Merely ratifying what one's public officeholders do is unlikely to satisfy the more imaginative, policy-oriented persons in the organizations. They believe that party organizations devoid of interest in issues are a farce. There must be room in the party's program for them to concern themselves in a more positive way with issues. This function is facilitated by serving on the resolutions committees of the county, state, and national conventions. It is furthered by state and local committees and political clubs fostering issues conferences where comprehensive discussion is given to carefully prepared papers on the important policy questions before the community. Irrespective of whether the party's legislators, mayors, or governors like it, there is no reason why the conclusions of these conferences should not be made public, provided that it is made clear that they are not the official party position. The statements then are suggestive but not incumbent upon those who have the responsibility for formulating public policy. An example of the possibilities of influencing and to some extent formulating policy is the regional association. What is more, a number of congressmen have welcomed the assistance of these conferences in mobilizing support for certain bills.

Many seasoned officeholders recognize that they themselves are not the only ones interested in programs and that their party will fail to attract active, talented adherents if its activists are deprived of the heady enthusiasm associated with discussing and taking stands on public issues. A large number of new-style amateur democrats are moving into both the regular and auxiliary party organizations. Their emphasis is on issues rather than personalities, and they demand intraparty democracy and full participation in party activities. This development is certain to guarantee continued controversy over the role of the party, both in formulating policy and in the management of party affairs.

Although American party organization is hierarchical on paper we have seen that it does not so operate in practice. What we call parties are myriads of official and extralegal committees and conventions and individuals in partisan roles. What is easily overlooked is that the organizations noted in the last two chapters help to tie together the many subsystems into a loosely connected party system. Although official electorate organizations can hardly be said to cement the party units into a system they nevertheless assist in integrating (sometimes better than others) party activities and help provide a public image of party. But the student of government recognizes that the legal committee system very often does not accurately portray the distribution of influence within the parties.

To this point, attention has been focused on the nature of the party as it functions in the electorate. Before looking at how party organizations relate themselves to nominations and elections an examination will be made of the other party egos—those surrounding the executive, legislative, and judicial branches. The pieces though separately treated nevertheless fit together and react on one another as a part of a huge system.

FOR FURTHER READING

A state-by-state bibliography of books and articles on state organization, leadership, and politics has been prepared by James Herndon, Charles Press, and Oliver P. Williams, *A Selected Bibliography of Materials in State Government and Politics*, Bureau of Government Research, University of Kentucky, Lexington, 1963.

Bailey, Stephen K.: *The Condition of Our National Parties*, 1959.

Banfield, Edward C.: *Political Influence*, 1961.

———— and James Q. Wilson: *City Politics*, 1963.

Burns, James M.: *The Deadlock of Democracy*, 1963.

Calkins, Fay: *The CIO and the Democratic Party*, 1952.

Cotter, Cornelius P.: *Practical Politics in the United States*, 1969.

Dahl, Robert A.: *Who Governs?* 1962.

Davies, James C.: *Human Nature in Politics: The Dynamics of Human Behavior*, 1963.

Downs, Anthony: *An Economic Theory of Democracy*, 1957.

Duverger, Maurice: *Political Parties*, 1954.

Farley, James A.: *Behind the Ballots*, 1938.

Gouldner, A. W. (ed.): *Studies in Leadership*, 1950.

Lasswell, Harold: *Psychopathology and Politics*, 1930.

Ostrogorski, M.: *Democracy and the Organization of Political Parties, II*, 1902.

Redding, Jack: *Inside the Democratic Party*, 1958.

Wilder, Philip S., Jr.: *Meade Alcorn and the 1958 Election*, 1959.

Wilson, James Q.: *Negro Politics*, 1960.

PART FOUR PARTY IN THE GOVERNMENT

CHAPTER 7 EXECUTIVE PARTIES AND POLITICS

The American Presidency developed both from authority resting in the
Constitution and from sources outside. It has been shaped by the forces
of American history and culture, and the men who have held the office
operated it in quite different ways. The President performs many functions and holds several positions; in each he exercises numerous kinds
of power. He is the chief of state, the major formulator and director of
foreign policy, and the head of the Armed Forces. The Constitution
emphasizes his role as Chief Executive and administrator. The executive is often called the Chief Legislator although his constitutional
authority appears to be limited to messages, vetoes, and calling special
sessions of Congress. The President is the spokesman for the American
people and a leader of public opinion and at times is referred to as a
leader of the free world. His responsibility for the preparation of the
budget and as director of many economic programs was scarcely envisaged even a hundred years ago. Finally the President is the leader and

symbol of his party and is at the center of American politics. He must relate his party role to his other and sometimes contradictory responsibilities. In this chapter we are concerned with the President's role as party leader, Chief Legislator, and influencer of national opinion—all of which are of course interrelated.

THE NATIONAL CONSTITUENCY

President Grover Cleveland is reputed to have asserted that "the President and the President alone represents all of the people." The President's constituency is composed of fifty different states and the District of Columbia, and he is generally elected by popular vote. With only a few exceptions (the last in 1876) popular vote majority or plurality and electoral vote majorities have gone together, although the total Electoral College vote usually distorts the strength of candidates in terms of the popular votes they received. A man elected to the Presidency is expected to be, in the words of Harry S. Truman, "a lobbyist for all the people."

As the nation has become more urbanized, the successful candidate for President under the general-ticket system must reflect the urban and large-state interests far more than candidates for Congress in which rural areas and small states are overrepresented in relation to population; this trend seems destined to continue. The urban areas, moreover, show greater interest in social legislation and in measures designed to benefit the urban dweller. Broadly speaking, the urban electorate is more progressive in terms of what it wants from government. National convention delegations chosen on a state basis and roughly in accordance with population tend to select candidates who appeal to the voters in the great metropolitan centers. The influence of the large urban states on the presidential election is greatly increased by the practice of giving the entire electoral vote of each state to the candidate who receives the highest vote in the state. Various proposals to change the method of electing the President were discussed in Chapter 3.

Presidential parties, if they are to be successful, are national parties, which in turn are coalitions and confederations of state and local parties, clusters of interest groups, and followings of personal candidates. During the past fifty years the President has usually been the leader of his party, but earlier, presidential leadership was the exception rather than the rule. Sectional interests, internal party dissension, the lack of qualities of leadership in the President, congressional dominance, and even the mood of the country have interfered with the nation's being consistently led by a Jackson or a Roosevelt. The electorate has not invariably wanted a strong President and legislative leader, and the national conventions have frequently failed to offer it one.

As seen in an earlier chapter, when strong, popular candidates were elected President, they were important in the forging of alliances that provided the backbone for the majority party. A number of these coalitions originated in the politics of protest and in opposition. In bringing together a party capable of unseating the Federalists and maintaining itself in power for more than two decades, Thomas Jefferson appealed to backwoodsmen, frontier and interior elements, and immigrants. His strength was enhanced by the Louisiana Purchase. Andrew Jackson's coalition included similar elements, non-English stock, agrarians, and antimonopolists. His war on the national bank was popular with the rank-and-file Democrats.

The new party, which under Lincoln bore success, was able to capitalize on discontented elements within the Democratic party and on its violent internal disagreements over slavery. But the skillful Lincoln was able to add Democrats of Northern and Border States under a Union party appeal, and many Border-State Democrats were glad to have their states exempted from the Emancipation Proclamation. Working classes, Negroes, and homesteaders were attracted to the party for diverse reasons, and business appreciated the restoration of the national bank and the Republican opposition to easy money. When the alliance was weakened late in the century, President McKinley, although not a strong President in the usual sense of the term, was able to keep the working classes from being won over by Bryan and the Populists. Theodore Roosevelt was particularly effective in projecting a popular image of the party and in combining Eastern business support with Western interests and labor. Woodrow Wilson was unable, partly because of the reaction to World War I, to bring into being a new Democratic majority; it remained for Franklin D. Roosevelt, capitalizing on economic discontent and a program of social legislation, to do so.

Whether a President is regarded as strong or weak, he alone represents the national party and the national constituency. He leads and tries to unite it. He is, by reason of holding the office, the most visible person in the party and in the electorate. His constituency is different from that of a congressman and it is not unusual for him to be in conflict with individual congressmen or groups of congressmen from his own party. The defeated presidential candidate who may be the most visible person in the party and its titular leader usually has little influence with members of his party in Congress who have their own leaders and is not able to provide leadership for the party comparable to that provided by the President. The out-party rarely has an effective single spokesman. Although their constituencies are different, both the opposition party's national chairman and its congressional leaders attempt in some ways to speak for it.

The fact that the successful presidential nominee has a national constituency is probably of some but rather indeterminate help in strengthening his own party's congressional delegation. With Richard Nixon in 1968 and Eisenhower in his reelection bid as the only exceptions in this century, the man winning the Presidency has gone into office with a party majority in Congress. But a built-in midterm adjustment takes place with the President losing some of the congressional party support he gained in the year of his own election (see Table 18-2). Generally, districts in which a President runs ahead of his party's candidates for United States representatives are more likely than others to be lost in the ensuing midterm election.[1] In effect, this means that the greatest midterm losses by the President's party have usually been experienced after elections of largest presidential pluralities. For this reason, a President wishes to get as much of his program as possible passed during the first two years when he has a "honeymoon" period and more of his own party's supporters in Congress than he may have in the last two years of his term.

PRESIDENTIAL LEADERSHIP IN LEGISLATION

Institutionalization of the Chief Executive's role in the legislative process has evolved through his duty to recommend legislation and his veto power. His messages command wide public attention and by their content and timing establish priorities for legislative action. A large staff assists the President in preparing his messages to Congress, the most important ones usually being delivered in person. They are tangible evidence of the President's participation in the legislative process.

At first glance the veto appears to be a negative tool, but it is useful at times in protecting the executive against legislation that is out of harmony with his program. The threat of a veto increases the power of the President in bargaining with congressmen for the enactment of his measures. A careful study of the use of veto by Presidents indicates how it has been used to support their programs.[2] Franklin D. Roosevelt, who averaged fifty-two vetoes per year, second only to President Cleveland's seventy-two per year, outlawed many private pension and relief bills in an effort to hold appropriations to what he considered more

[1] See Barbara Hinckley, "Interpreting House Midterm Elections: Toward a Measurement of the In-Party's Expected Loss of Seats," *American Political Science Review*, vol. 61, pp. 694–700, 1967. Other pertinent works are Charles O. Jones, *Every Second Year: Congressional Behavior and the Two-Year Term*, The Brookings Institution, Washington, D.C., 1967, and Malcolm Moos, *Politics, Presidents, and Coattails*, The Johns Hopkins Press, Baltimore, 1952.

[2] See Carlton Jackson, *Presidential Vetoes 1792–1945*, University of Georgia Press, Athens, 1967.

central spending. He, like others, often threatened to veto measures unless Congress put them in a form he could approve. Vetoes were used also to get support and sympathy from the larger public.

General Aspects. Extraconstitutional devices are of greater significance in Presidential leadership and each President is free to develop his own leadership and his own relationship to Congress.[3] Great variations exist in the type of legislative leadership exercised by Presidents. With the increase in population of the nation and with the growth and increasing complexity of national problems, the functions of the federal government have multiplied, and the country and Congress inevitably look to the President to present a program of needed legislation. Much more institutionalization and bureaucratization of the executive office of the President became necessary, but each man gave his administration much of its personality and direction. That they were able to do so illustrates the flexibility of the American system.

During the first century of the Republic, Presidents tended to operate in practice, if not in theory, in one of three ways: (1) close to the Constitution, (2) according to the Whig concept, and (3) in line with party government. Hamilton and Jefferson argued over how strong a President should be. Jackson chose the role of the strong party President. An opposite position was taken by the Wade-Davis manifesto in 1864 warning Lincoln against executive usurpation and asserting that the duty of the President was "to obey and execute, not to make laws." Since 1900, the President has tended to provide leadership in legislation, and the nation appears to expect him to do so.

The two Adamses and Monroe saw the President as the leader of the entire country, not simply as a party leader or spokesman for a particular faction. Some later Presidents, facing hostile majorities in Congress, were forced to follow a similar course.

Other Presidents have recognized the importance of parties as desirable if not essential instruments in the passage of legislation, but for diverse reasons they were content to remain nominal leaders and to leave the major initiative for formulating a legislative program to powerful congressional leaders such as a Henry Clay. This dependency on congressional rather than Presidential leadership in policy formation is sometimes called the Whig concept of the Presidency. To some extent this fits in well with a President's lacking political skill in leading his party in Congress.

[3] There is a vast amount of literature on presidential-congressional relations, including rich anecdotal material in various memoirs. For a succinct, highly relevant discussion of presidential approaches to Congress see A. N. Holcombe, "Presidential Leadership and the Party System," *The Yale Review*, vol. 43, pp. 321–335, 1954.

Jackson and Van Buren put themselves at the head of their parties and exercised vigorous party leadership to win support for their legislative programs in Congress. Lincoln, the two Roosevelts, Wilson, Kennedy, Johnson, and Nixon exploited agencies of public opinion as well to strengthen their hands both in party leadership and with Congress. They made every effort to use organized partisan support, and they placed emphasis on party responsibility for the formulation of public policy. This type of leadership can be regarded as presidential party government even though success in enactment depends on discipline and the holding of party lines in Congress.

Not every incumbent in the White House can be neatly fitted into one of these three categories. Some inclined to one approach but found themselves forced by opposition control of Congress or by the times into taking another approach. Cleveland, Wilson, Truman, and Eisenhower, for example, all lost control of Congress in midterm and had to resort to the veto and other devices to try to influence legislators. They were forced into bargaining with the opposition. Truman was later rescued when his party recaptured control of Congress but ran afoul of Southern Democrats.

Dwight D. Eisenhower affords an example of a Chief Executive who operated in each of the three ways at different times during his administration. He admittedly cared little for partisan politics and was without experience in it when he became President. Senator Robert A. Taft, a long-time partisan and Eisenhower opponent for the nomination, became floor leader and with Speaker Joseph Martin in the House became the director of the party's program in Congress much in the tradition of responsibility under the Whig approach. The President ran the Cabinet and the administration and let Taft assume much of the legislative initiative. Taft's death during the first session of Congress left a serious gap in this leadership. The Democrats won control of Congress in 1954 and retained it for the balance of Eisenhower's eight years. Faced with the necessity of securing support of the opposition party to pass his program, Eisenhower tended to remain aloof from party politics between elections. He preferred to be "nonpartisan." In the last two years of his second term he took more interest in partisan politics. He participated vigorously in the midterm election of 1958, vowed that he wanted to remake the image of the party into one of "Modern Republicanism," and became very much concerned with being succeeded by a Republican. But his party leadership both of the electorate and of Congress came late, and many felt that his actions were out of character.

The duality of role and interest that bothered Eisenhower and other Presidents grows out of the recognition that the person holding the office must be a national and world leader and that in the performance of these duties, powerful interests may have to be offended. Eisenhower was elected by votes of independents and Democrats, not just Republicans. He, like other Presidents, had to have support from members of the opposition in Congress, a case of building a concurrent majority or a coalition of concurrent minorities. If a President is too ardent a partisan, he invites partisanship in the opposition without necessarily carrying all the members of his own party; he may thereby lose his voting majority. It takes skill for an executive to make the greatest possible use of party leadership without destroying the image that he is President of all the people. Party leadership is but one weapon in the arsenal of the Chief Executive, and appeals to party loyalty must be blended with many other techniques.

Legislative Clearance. The Bureau of the Budget is an agency that has not attracted much publicity, particularly for its work in legislative clearance. Proposals of individual congressmen and of administrative agencies are reviewed in the Bureau to see whether they are in conflict with the President's legislative program.[4] Departments are required to secure the approval of the President before seeking legislation. In the preparation of the budget, the Bureau in effect establishes priorities and separates the items submitted to it into those that are on the President's program but not yet enacted, those calling for increases in expenditures, and so on.

Closely related to these functions of the Budget Bureau was the emergence under Presidents Franklin D. Roosevelt, Truman, and Eisenhower of the concept of a presidential legislative program to be presented annually to Congress. White House relations with Congress were formalized by the appointment of liaison officers who report to either the President or a top aide and work with persons on Capitol Hill for the President's program. These officers in no way replace the highly important meetings of the President with the legislative leaders in Congress, meetings that are always important sources of information for both the President and the leaders. They help focus on the areas of agreement and disagreement, reveal something of what is in the mind of each, and may show the way to possible action. Both the Budget Bureau's operations and the liaison with the Hill are sources of intelligence and a consequent aid to the Chief Executive in marshaling his forces.

Patronage. There has been much discussion over the amount of patronage and its importance to the Chief Executive. There are not nearly so many positions to be awarded as formerly, thanks to civil service. In

[4]See Richard E. Neustadt, "Presidency and Legislation: The Growth of Central Clearance," *American Political Science Review*, vol. 48, pp. 641–671, 1954, and "Presidency and Legislation: Planning the President's Program," *American Political Science Review*, vol. 49, pp. 980–1021, 1955.

1962, it was estimated that the governorship of Pennsylvania carried with it more than 50,000 jobs in a state of 11 million population. The Presidency proportionately carries considerably fewer jobs. Presidents can use jobs to reward those who have helped them get elected and thus strengthen their personal if not party support. Other jobs, given through senators and congressmen, may also be useful to the President in winning support for his legislative proposals. Our concern here is with the use of patronage as a resource by the President in his dealings with Congress.

Patronage does not always strengthen the President in securing congressional approval of his program. Disputes over appointments have often incurred the enmity of influential members; after his initial appointments, the President's influence gained through patronage may decline. If the President gives choice appointments in order to win over doubtful members, those who are steadfast supporters of his program are likely to resent it. The job of the Chief Executive, therefore, will be to placate his friends by showing them why the favors had to go to the uncommitted. If he cannot do this, he may lose the enthusiasm of his loyal followers. On balance, he may actually have failed to strengthen himself with these followers even though his favors won the margin of victory among the doubtfuls. Senatorial courtesy also modifies the President's unrestricted use of patronage because senators accept, and insist on, the right to name or approve Presidential appointees in their states, except postmasterships, which traditionally are approved by representatives.

A number of Presidents have turned patronage matters over to their national chairmen who in turn deal directly with party leaders in the states. Two days after his inauguration, President Kennedy served notice that patronage was to be funneled through Democratic National Chairman John M. Bailey in order to remove the White House and the agencies from political pressures. However, the President or someone on his staff handles positions used to muster support in Congress; moreover, congressmen usually prefer to deal directly with the Chief Executive or his aide rather than through the national chairman. In the latter part of the Truman administration, liaison officers were appointed for both the House and Senate to be mainly concerned with patronage and favors for legislators. This fitted in with the Eisenhower staff system and was expanded so that nearly half a dozen men were assigned to Capitol Hill to handle legislative and personal relations. Kennedy merged the functions performed by these men into one job held by a special assistant for congressional affairs and personnel.

Patronage is considerably more than the giving of jobs to a congressman in return for his vote. In broader context, it involves any favor that can be bestowed by the executive at any level of government.

On the national level, such favors may be giving a defense contract to a firm in the legislator's district, a missile site, a new post office, an item in the budget, help in a campaign, a reclamation project, or any number of other public works. The mores of giving and receiving favors usually dictate that they be done privately and remain as invisible as possible and that the *quid pro quo* be understood and not demanded. Sometimes these benefits constitute a "promissory note" that is to be collected at some future time. Legislators and executives, when confronted with need for support on a vital matter, resort to the collection of these IOUs.

In observing the question of patronage, we should remember that the President (or a governor) is only one of many traders in the market.[5] Legislators are constantly trading with each other on public works (sometimes irreverently called pork barrel bills) and other measures. On a number of bills, the legislator's vote is committed and therefore not negotiable in dealing with the executive. But his support may be marketable if it appears to be useful in bringing a benefit to himself or to his constituency. The demand for favors by a legislator from the executive therefore varies considerably. Availability of patronage is limited in time, place, and kind and is consequently an uncertain instrument for the executive.

A President is always faced with the problem of the value and timing of his patronage resources. If a situation is favorable on the floor but doubtful in a committee, then a few crucial committee people must be reached. Seniority may be such that some of the committee people cannot be reached by anything the executive can offer. Also fewer persons are involved than in a floor vote, and it is not easy to mobilize sizable numbers on the committee, but the power of a committee to report a bill favorably, before floor action can be taken, places it in a crucial position. A vote to discharge a bill from a committee is rare, and the Chief Executive and his allies in the House must try to get the committee to bring out the bill itself. Potentially, patronage at the committee stage of the bill is costly.

At least one other factor to be recognized is the degree of importance of a bill and the amount of support for it in the legislature irrespective of executive preference. President Kennedy in a press conference stated this tersely by saying, "You can water bills down and get them by, or you can have bills which have no particular controversy to them and get them by. But important legislation, medical care for the aged and these other bills, farm programs, they are controversial, they involve great interest, and they are much more difficult."[6] Although we have

[5] On the President's market position, see the concise but cogent analysis by Stanley Kelley, Jr., "Presidential Legislative Leadership: The Use of Patronage," paper presented to the American Political Science Association, September, 1962.

[6] June 28, 1962.

little empirical evidence, it is probable that congressmen are less easily moved by "trading" with the President on major legislation than on measures of medium or minor importance.

In summary, patronage in the widest sense of the word is a complicated and subtle executive resource in dealing with the legislature. It contains numerous pitfalls and is an uncertain asset. For lesser positions outside the mores of senatorial courtesy, it may strengthen the President's hand. In important appointments such as Cabinet secretaries the President may find that by giving the position to a well-known member of the opposition, he may be able to get bipartisan goodwill if not support for certain foreign policy and defense proposals. Knowledge of legislators' preferences and what they might be interested in obtaining from the President is helpful, and good staff work in this connection facilitates the judicious use of patronage. Extension of courtesies to legislators and the explanation to one's friends of the realities of the situation are also a part of the process of the successful use of the patronage market. Negatively, the withholding of favors may give a President leverage. He often can use discretion in ordering certain expenditures and in interpreting the administration of laws. Refusals to grant audiences, to dedicate a project in a local district, to sign a private bill, or to go along with amendments desired by a legislator are also part of the process by which a President can strengthen his hand. If the Chief Executive can create a legislative need or demand for these, he will improve his position as a "seller."

Party Leadership. The functions of party chieftain and leader of public opinion also involve the President in the legislative process. Although the roles of party chief and chief legislator are closely connected, they are nonetheless separable, and one is never completely absorbed by the other. The former role places a President at the head of his party-in-the-electorate, a useful resource for' marshaling support for his party in Congress. As leader of the electorate, few limitations save common sense, custom, and discretion are imposed on him, and he is free to use techniques and talents helpful in retaining popular support and securing renomination and election. A strong popular basis causes congressmen to give the President a respectful hearing and strengthens him with those who are beneficiaries of the same voting support as the President's. The President can and does appeal to many members on the basis of party. Party then is a useful tool for bringing the Chief Executive and the legislature together and for effecting a working arrangement between them.

When he runs for office, a presidential candidate is expected to render assistance to the party's nominees for Congress. It has always

been a question whether the head of the ticket should give blanket endorsement to all those running under his own party's label. Of President
Eisenhower's assertion that he would support every Republican for
every office national as well as local, Arthur Krock commented in *The
New York Times* that "if this is to be settled policy it is a peril-taken notice
to all Republicans that they will not forfeit his partisan endorsement by
opposing his programs. He didn't want to go that far, but neither did
some of his predecessors."[7] It would be difficult to determine what
effect, if any, campaigning by the President has had on obtaining support of members of his party for his legislative measures at the ensuing
session of Congress. But campaigning dramatizes national party goals
and the President's desire for his party to control Congress. It is useful
to the President in building party morale and gaining support of state
and county party leaders who, in turn, will urge congressmen to support
his program. Congressmen of the President's party always want to win a
majority in each House so that they will enjoy the perquisites and power
accorded majority members. This fact has been helpful to Democratic
Presidents in restraining would-be bolters among conservative Southerners, who also have been reminded that without the election of liberal
Northern Democrats they will not continue to hold their committee
chairmanships.

American Presidents and governors find parties a resource to
help them in their leadership problems. They have the help of their
respective national and state party committees and may speak of their
programs as their party's programs. But being a partisan, though useful,
is not invariably an asset. Party activities and internal quarrels may demand an executive's attention to the neglect of other duties. Some
Republican leaders and congressmen grumbled in 1969 that President
Nixon was not partisan enough in his appointments and appointed his
personal friends and confidants rather than party men to important
positions on his staff. He was also criticized for being too slow in moving
out "Johnson's men."

Press Conference. Another instrument of both party and popular leadership is the President's press conference. This unique political institution
amazes foreign leaders and newspaper correspondents, for they are
unaccustomed to such a give-and-take discussion. Although Presidents
Cleveland and McKinley on infrequent occasions met with a few carefully chosen correspondents, Theodore Roosevelt is credited with the
introduction of the press conference. He invited journalists to the barber
shop and, while being shaved, fascinated reporters by expounding his

[7] See his column, *The New York Times*, Oct. 30, 1953.

views with gestures. President Wilson was the first to make the conference a weekly affair by receiving correspondents in his private office. Presidents Harding, Coolidge, and Hoover continued the conferences with less success because they required the journalists to submit written questions in advance.

Beginning with Franklin D. Roosevelt the press conference underwent a metamorphosis and became an established institution. Roosevelt, who enjoyed the camaraderie with newsmen, made the press conference exciting and usually informative. He held 998 while in office, Truman held 324, Eisenhower 192, Kennedy 63 and Johnson 134. Eisenhower permitted the conferences to be televised and later broadcast in whole or in part. President Kennedy expanded the practice by allowing live telecasts and broadcasts. Citizens can now hear and see the President instead, as in the days of Roosevelt, of reading an interpretation by newsmen of what the President said. Televised news conferences inevitably make the President more visible and afford greater opportunity for showmanship on the part of both the inquiring correspondent and the President.

In terms of leadership in legislation the press conferences enable the President to comment on actions or contemplated actions of Congress. Presidents are very often queried about presidential recommendations and proposals before Congress. Friendly reporters are often asked to raise questions that the Presidents want to answer. Sometimes the President opens the conference with an important policy statement leading reporters to follow up with questions. Reporters also ask him pointed questions about party matters, campaigns, and electoral results. Queries often result in "no comment" but sometimes bring retorts indicating the President's thinking. Conferences are now broad-gauge affairs, giving the President a forum to comment not only on foreign affairs and domestic problems but also on legislative matters, personalities, and party problems. The use of these opportunities calls for a high degree of skill and discretion.

Modern Presidents utilize radio and television to focus attention on legislative proposals. President Kennedy on nationwide television called for enactment of his Medicare program, and President Johnson did the same for civil rights and income tax deduction. President Nixon made special Vietnam peace proposals and appeals by television. Television and radio give the President instantaneous means to influence on public opinion in contrast to the slower process of speech making and newspaper coverage such as President Wilson had to rely on for his ill-fated peace plans. But television requires judicious use. The Chief Executive must avoid overexposure and expending large amounts of personal prestige in trying to rally the public on behalf of a legislative cause only to lose it.

ADMINISTRATIVE LEADERSHIP AND ROLES

The majority party must control the administrative apparatus if it is to realize its overall program. A legislature commonly makes compromises in a way that leaves decisions on policy to be made during the process of administration. The agencies possess much discretion and through action or inaction can forward or hinder a party's conception of the public interest. Many businessmen, for example, were greatly interested in the Nixon administration's control of the vast administrative establishment as something of an antidote to Democratic control of Congress. The administration is ordinarily subject to political control by the Chief Executive, and hence the politics of administration is closely identified with that of the President. However, on occasions the bureaucracy or a part of it may overtly or covertly oppose Presidential policies and advance its own interests. In general, however, the Chief Executive finds the administration a great resource in his party and in his legislative leadership. The degree to which a President or a governor can direct the policies and activities of administrative agencies depends in part on his qualities of leadership and his authority over agencies of the executive branch.

Uses to President. Collectively the role of the administrative agencies and staffs in the legislative process includes (1) initiating and preparing either in outline or in detail bills relating to strengthening, expanding, or sponsoring programs in their respective areas; (2) rendering expert advice to the President and to Congress; (3) presenting testimony and using lobbying devices to influence the passage (or defeat) of a bill. A large number of questions and programs handled by the administrative branch do not touch on party policy. On the other hand, a number of items are the direct outgrowth of the party program, such as certain Democratic requests for federal activity in the field of health. Still other matters under consideration by administrative agencies only indirectly or incidentally bear upon party policy. In this category would be measures of interest to certain groups that would have a degree of party identification.[8] Several business, farm, labor, and Negro organizations have interests of this kind. These groups may seek support for their positions from persons in the lower of middle echelons, then from the department head, and ultimately from the President.

The bureaucracy is helpful to the President in the initiation of ideas for modifications and improvements of old programs and for new ones. Some of the most able persons in the administrative establishment devote their efforts to Presidential legislation. These activities include

[8] The relationship of administrative agencies to private interest groups is considered in chap. 20.

not only the formulation of new programs but also, and perhaps even more important, the filling out of details of a stated general policy and the ways of implementing it. Preparing statements for presentation at committee hearings and submitting data are most significant activities. Administrative officials are customarily requested by Congress to testify on administration-sponsored bills. A reading of the list of witnesses appearing before congressional committees commonly shows half or more of them to be spokesmen of the executive establishments. Many administrators other than Cabinet officers develop personal friendships on the Hill, and Presidents may tap them for support.

In addition to providing formidable technical assistance to the President for his campaign speeches and messages to Congress and to the public, the administrative agencies become something of a public relations arm for the executive. They prepare many bulletins, press releases, materials for films, radio, and television, and answers to thousands of requests from citizens for information. In a subtle way, these may build up goodwill for a Presidential program and help to counteract criticism.

Limitations. Numerous restrictions on the federal bureaucracy limit its usefulness to the President in his role of party chief and chief legislator. Because of criticisms of administrative publicity, Congress passed a statute in 1913 prohibiting spending for "publicity agents" unless an appropriation was specifically designated for such a purpose. Later a law forbade spending any appropriations for purposes of influencing legislation except on the request of a congressman or through official channels. The administrations of both Democratic and Republican Presidents are perennially accused of violating that statute. The subjects on which it appears legitimate for the government to issue releases remain a moot point. Congressional threats of an investigation and public criticism, both by the lawmakers and by the public, have a modifying and deterring effect on the public relations activities of administrators.

Hundreds of thousands of federal civil service employees have been politically neutralized by the Hatch acts of 1939 and 1940. A number of unclassified employees remained unaffected and are free to engage in political activities. Specially classified employees, that is, those who are within the civil service and who are appointed on the basis of merit, are "hatched" in the following way. It is unlawful for them to (1) take any active part in a political campaign, (2) use their official authority to affect the nomination or election of candidates for a federal office, (3) promise a public job or benefit as a reward for a political activity, (4) solicit or receive any political contributions from persons benefiting from federal relief programs. The law also extends to state and local employees who are administering activities subsidized in whole or in part by the federal government. The last provision has provoked outcries that it violates states' rights and has embroiled the United States Civil Service Commission, which issues implementing orders, in controversies with local politicians. Generally speaking, employees covered by the Hatch acts may attend political rallies and, of course, vote; but they are not expected to speak at rallies, hold office in a party or one of its clubs, solicit campaign funds, run for office on a partisan ballot, or serve as delegates to a nominating convention. Accordingly, classified employees under civil service are not directly helpful to the party in power during campaigns.

It goes without saying that non-civil service employees are often very active in parties both during and between campaigns; this is particularly the case with state and local employees who are not under restrictive laws. Election outcomes may vitally affect their positions, and they and their families frequently constitute not only a voting bloc but a source of personnel for party activities; they often serve as fund raisers, secretaries in party headquarters, speech writers, and researchers.

The strength and independence of department administrators due to their alliances outside government limit the President or governor. Executive agencies, particularly those that serve organized clienteles, often become so politically powerful that they are largely independent of control by their administrative superiors.

Finally, the amount of a Chief Executive's authority over the personnel and functions of the administrative establishment varies; hence his influence is uneven. Some agencies are traditionally — and even in law — more partisan than others. The Cabinet secretaries and sub-secretaries, for example, are quite close to the President and owe their appointments to him; the White House establishment is even closer to the President, and most of the top staff do not require senatorial confirmation. The independent regulatory commissions are farther removed from the President, as are proprietary corporations. Although the executive departments and agencies and their employees are broadly termed the administration, it is necessary to examine their political roles separately.

THE CABINET

Department heads are appointed by the President with the consent of the Senate and serve at his pleasure as political officers concerned with policy as well as with administration.[9] Although the Secretaries are

[9] For an overall analysis of the Cabinet set in a political context see Richard F. Fenno, Jr., *The President's Cabinet*, Harvard University Press, Cambridge, Mass., 1959.

advisors to the President, they do not function as a party collegial body
nor do they all necessarily represent the President's wing of the party.
Lincoln's cabinet was composed of rivals.

Composition. The Nixon Cabinet illustrates the various considerations
involved in its selection; most of the same considerations influenced his
predecessors in choosing their Cabinets. Every section of the country
was represented, with two members each from Illinois and New York
and one each from Alabama, Alaska, Nebraska, California, Maryland,
Michigan, Massachusetts and Wisconsin. Maurice H. Stans, appointed as
Secretary of Commerce, claimed three state residences as owner of
businesses in Chicago, New York, and Los Angeles. Other businessmen
were appointed to Treasury (David M. Kennedy), Post Office (Winton
M. Blount), and Interior (Walter J. Hickel). A personal friend and lawyer, William P. Rogers, became Secretary of State; and another friend,
Robert H. Finch, lieutenant governor of California, received the Health,
Education, and Welfare (HEW) secretaryship. An attorney, John N.
Mitchell, who became the Attorney General, was likewise a long-term
friend and a law partner. Two governors, John A. Volpe of Massachusetts and George Romney of Michigan, left their positions to assume
the leadership of the Departments of Transportation and of Housing
and Urban Development (HUD) respectively. Interior Secretary Hickel
had been elected Governor of Alaska just two years before his appointment and, unlike Governors Volpe and Romney, had not had long experience in politics. The Labor secretaryship went to labor economist
George P. Schultz, and the Agriculture post went to the chancellor of the
University of Nebraska, Clifford M. Hardin. In deviation from usual
practice for preceding Cabinets, Secretaries Schultz and Hardin did not
offer direct ties to labor unions and farm organizations. The highly
important Defense position went to Congressman Melvin Laird, a
pragmatic conservative who had previously supported Goldwater for
President and had spoken favorably of Gov. Nelson Rockefeller for the
1968 presidential nomination. However, he had not actively worked for
Rockefeller. This appointment of a congressman was unusual, as
Defense had tended to be dominated by financiers and business executives. Two Catholics and two Mormons were in the Cabinet.

Quite frequently, new Presidents appoint one or two members
of the opposition party to the Cabinet; but Mr. Nixon appointed no
Democrats, although he offered the post of Secretary of Defense to
Sen. Henry M. Jackson who declined. Secretaries Finch, Laird, Hickel,
Romney, and Volpe had previously been officeholders but only one or
two of the others had had any experience in politics. Most of the members of the Cabinet were drawn from business or had been associated
with business; and most, like Nixon, were moderate conservatives in

outlook. Except for an unexpected outburst by some Senate conservationists about Governor Hickel, the men were noncontroversial and presumably were not chosen to placate Rockefeller or Reagan supporters or the more militant interest groups. Conservatives were happy with the Treasury and Commerce appointments; and liberals could accept the Transportation, HEW, and HUD appointments. Since Dr. Hardin was essentially uncommitted on farm programs, his appointment avoided at the outset the sharp contentions over agricultural policies.

Political Uses. Presidents have used appointments to the cabinet to placate factions, head off insurgency, or pay off political debts. The positions may be used to build strength with various groups. Appointees are helpful to the President in his role as party leader and legislative leader. They are usually expected to engage in political campaigns and speak at fund-raising dinners. Secretaries of State, since the advent of so-called bipartisan foreign policy, tend to remain aloof from partisan activity.

Cabinet secretaries aid the Chief Executive in developing major policies and securing public and legislative support for them. They often speak for the administration on matters within their jurisdiction. In his *Memoirs*, Harry S. Truman writes: "When a cabinet member speaks publicly, he usually speaks on authorization of the President, in which case he speaks for the President. If he takes it upon himself to announce a policy that is contrary to the policy the President wants carried out, he can cause a great deal of trouble."[10] Truman and other Presidents have at times been embarrassed by statements of their Cabinet officers and had to "correct" them.

Some Cabinet members have constituencies of their own and may be of help to the President in the job of building and holding the support of subpublics. Luther Hodges of North Carolina was useful as a tie for President Kennedy to the South. Ezra Benson, as Eisenhower's Secretary of Agriculture, came under increasing attack by some farm organizations for his conservative policies but gained support for the President from conservative groups. By appointing William Jennings Bryan, thrice the Democratic presidential nominee, as Secretary of State, Woodrow Wilson made an open bid for the support of Bryan Democrats. Bryan subsequently embarrassed Wilson's administration and resigned over differences in foreign policy, illustrating the hazard of appointing a potential rival to the Cabinet. Martin Durkin, the head of a national trade union, was appointed by Eisenhower as Secretary of Labor to gain support of labor but was of little value to the President in dealing with the labor constituency. Very often the Cabinet officers are

[10]Doubleday & Company, Inc., Garden City, New York, 1955, vol. I, p. 329.

not top leaders or prestigious among their constituencies and therefore bring little substantial strength or power to the President in his national constituency.

Much the same situation appears in Cabinet help in the President's leadership in legislation. James A. Farley and Cordell Hull enjoyed excellent and cordial relations with Congress. Hull had been a member of Congress and was very useful to Franklin Roosevelt in getting foreign policy programs through Congress. Legislators trusted Hull, and for a Cabinet officer, he was remarkably immune from criticism. Congressman Laird was likewise popular on Capitol Hill and useful to the Nixon administration in defense matters. A Secretary who has cordial relations with Congress may spare the President sharp criticism as well as obtain the passage of legislation. Unpopular Secretaries, however, may turn out to be serious liabilities because of attack by members of Congress. One of the first requirements of a successful Secretary of a department is to get along with Congress.

As Fenno concludes, "The political help which the President receives comes not from the group but from individual cabinet members, who can and do augment the President's effectiveness in his leadership roles. It would be a serious mistake not to emphasize the possibilities for crucial assistance by individuals. But probably most striking is the fact that the possibilities for such assistance are very frequently negated by the number of limitations which surround them."[11] In addition to the political limitations, a Cabinet officer is not responsible exclusively to the President but to Congress as well. Congress creates the departments, outlines their functions, and appropriates money for their operation. As a result, a Secretary must be concerned with keeping goodwill in Congress for his own department and avoiding congressional investigations of its activities.

INDEPENDENT REGULATORY AGENCIES

There are more than forty agencies functioning independently of the Cabinet Departments, but many of these are not regarded as a part of the President's political team. Most of the regulatory agencies, for example, the Interstate Commerce Commission, the Federal Power Commission, the Federal Communications Commission, the Federal Reserve Board, the Civil Aeronautics Board, and the National Labor Relations Board, exercise authority over policy matters of concern to a President and his party supporters. Among the substantive areas of the economy coming under the jurisdiction of the agencies are all forms of public transportation and communication; hydroelectric development; water resources; stock markets; unfair trade practices in industry, commerce,

[11] *Op. cit.*, p. 247.

and labor; credit policies; and interstate transportation of natural gas. Congress gave the regulatory commissions a status independent from the executive (therefore free from partisan turnover) because they performed quasi-legislative and judicial functions and operated in an experimental field where policy was in need of gradual development. The formula was to establish a plural body with five to eleven members selected on a bipartisan basis with staggered terms of longer than four years so that a President in his first term at least could not name all the commissioners or board members. The law also provides for limitations on removal.

The independent regulatory commissions, notwithstanding their philosophical justification, are hardly independent of politics. The agencies are caught, as can be expected, in a network of pressures from private interest groups. The appointment of the commissioners and board members themselves is not free from political considerations — partisan and otherwise. There is executive review of commission budgets and of course congressional control of appropriations. Further, Congress has not been reluctant to investigate the agencies, sharply criticize the commissioners themselves, and revamp the organization and jurisdiction of the agencies. The whole concept of independent establishments has been under study and provoked debate, but our concern must be limited to the effect of the system on the presidential party program.

In 1949 Leland Olds, an incumbent member of the Federal Power Commission (FPC), was reappointed by President Truman. As commissioner, Olds had been an able and effective advocate of federal regulation of the prices charged to consumers of natural gas. The oil and gas interests, who have strong bipartisan influence in the Senate, rolled up their big guns with the result that the Senate refused to confirm him.[12] The Truman administration favored the policy position of Olds, and the action therefore denied the opportunity of continuing on the FPC a vigorous exponent of its views.

The Eisenhower administration's power program varied considerably from those of its predecessors. It emphasized "partnership" between the federal government, the states, and private power companies in developing electric power. The FPC is given the authority to survey water resources and pass on applications to establish hydroelectric projects along navigable waters and public lands. Eisenhower's program depended to a considerable extent on the willingness of the FPC to grant permits to private companies and to the states. Early in his administration, the new Secretary of the Interior, Douglas McKay, withdrew his Department's support (adopted by the Truman administration)

---

[12]On this informative case of politics, see Joseph P. Harris, "The Senatorial Rejection of Leland Olds: A Case Study," *American Political Science Review*, vol. 45, pp. 674–692, 1951.

for the construction of a huge multipurpose dam at Hell's Canyon on the Snake River and its opposition to the proposal of Idaho Power Company, a private power firm, for permission to build a series of smaller dams. Eisenhower took the opportunity to appoint some new commissioners, including the chairman and those persons largely oriented toward private power. In this instance, a Republican Secretary of the Interior plus control of the Federal Power Commission facilitated the adoption of a party program. Many Presidents, however, have had difficulties in bringing commissions and party policies into successful working arrangements. Yet unless the President can integrate the policies of the independent commissions with those of his administration, he will be unable to carry out his program.

In staffing the independent agencies, an administration is faced with the necessity of influencing policy but retaining the necessary technical impartiality. In effect, the commissions are given authority to deal with important economic problems, yet at the same time Congress does not wish to place control in the Cabinet, where the policies would be under direct authority of the President. Although it has not been established by study, it seems a fair assumption that commissioners do not view their positions as "political" in the same sense as those of the Cabinet secretaries. Nevertheless many if not most of the policy matters with which the regulatory agencies deal are legitimate issues for parties and indeed are often reflected in a general way in their platforms. Yet it is only under fortuitous circumstances that a President can shape the views and decisions of the agencies if he finds, after being inaugurated, that they conflict with his program. The commissioners have no established channels to the executive that are analogous to the Cabinet's. Overlapping terms of the board members often retain persons from previous administrations whose views are difficult if not impossible to change. This dilemma caused by Presidential responsibility for program and legalistic independence of the regulatory commissions is likely to become more aggravated as the need for coordination of the nation's economic life grows.

THE PERSONAL TOUCH

Added to these resources for leadership are several inherent advantages of the office itself. The position helps a President overcome the fact that he is not the leader of his congressional party and that large numbers of his own party in Congress are elected without his help and are thus considerably independent of him. A President is in a better position than Congress to assume the initiative in proposing policies. He has more information at his disposal, and information is a potential source of power in dealing with those who are less well informed. He is able to

command the great resources of the executive departments in formulating and mustering public support for his legislative proposals. A
President can make up his mind in private and emerge with a statement
perhaps carrying the public impression of strong leadership. Congress
in committee hearings and in floor debates often gives the impression
of bickering, quarreling, and vacillating in making up its mind. The
President assumes the initiative in preparing and presenting a legislative program and functions as a centripetal force and as an agent for
coherence.

Despite the great resources available to him, the President does
not push a button and see things done. Executives have ordered and
asked, but they have found that their requests are not always carried
out. This brings us to a final and crucial aspect of presidential leadership—the man himself and how he mobilizes and combines the available
power sources. Each President has his own style and gives his own touch
to the office.[13] The mood of the nation is always important in determining what the President tries to do in the exercise of his power. The interaction of the President with the realities of a situation both inside and
outside the government depends on his appraisal of the situation and on
his style of handling it.

Some Presidents greatly enjoyed the personal power of the office
and used it to the hilt. Franklin D. Roosevelt was such a man. In a sense
he acted as if the job of being President was synonymous with being
Franklin D. Roosevelt. He relished the give-and-take with reporters in
press conferences and in meetings with individuals. Many callers leaving
his office were persuaded by him and believed that he agreed with them.
In running the Presidency, he seemed to sense that his own power was
extracted in part from other people by getting them to realize that their
own self-interest was similar to his. He lived in a time of great social
ferment and international change and had the ability, as do most successful Presidents, to identify himself publicly with the times. Although the
New Deal was not a carefully thought-out ideology, FDR moved in the
direction of change. His relationship with the public was personal, in
sharp contrast to Hoover's, and he used the radio fireside chat and
widespread personal appearance to develop popular support. Roosevelt
enjoyed politics, party and otherwise, and immersed himself in it.
Arthur M. Schlesinger, Jr., has observed that FDR successfully used a
"competitive theory of administration" which kept "grants of authority
incomplete, jurisdictions uncertain, charters overlapping."[14] This kept

[13] Using case studies and illustrations, Richard E. Neustadt has provided a cogent analysis
of the Presidency from the standpoint of personal power. See *Presidential Power: The Politics of Leadership*, John Wiley & Sons, Inc., New York, 1960. Abundant literature and presidential biographies exist
relating how individual Presidents have operated.

[14] *The Age of Roosevelt*, vol. 2, *The Coming of the New Deal*, Houghton Mifflin Company, Boston,
1959, p. 528.

the power of decision with the President and also in effect forced the President to make decisions, thus keeping pressure on himself. He used the same competitive practices to obtain and to cross-check information.

Dwight D. Eisenhower's operation and viewpoint of the Presidency came close to being the antithesis of Roosevelt's. His background with the Army isolated him from the mainstream of politics, which had been so valuable to Roosevelt before 1933. Repeatedly, Eisenhower said that he did not want to get "involved in personalities" and made no secret of the fact that he did not care for politics or regard politicians very highly. During much of his term he tried to remain "above the battle" and the hurly-burly of practical politics. As a general he had been accustomed to giving orders and seeing them carried out. As President he found that this was insufficient, for many requests are not self-enforcing. The President must persuade and cajole. Mr. Eisenhower brought a staff system without parallel to the White House. The Cabinet was institutionalized with a secretary and a prepared agenda. Eisenhower himself preferred that as many decisions as possible be made at lower echelons and that only when they failed to agree would he become involved. He desired less of the competition on which Roosevelt thrived. Neustadt concludes that "Roosevelt was a politician seeking personal power. Eisenhower was a hero seeking national unity. He came to crown a reputation, not to make one. He wanted to be arbiter, not master. His love was not for power but for duty — and for status. Naturally, the thing he did not seek he did not often find."[15] But the Eisenhower image was not dimmed for the public, and they gave him an enormous vote of confidence in 1956. Many appeared attracted to him because, like Hoover, he was "not a politician." Moreover, he symbolized unity and tranquility after an age of domestic quarrels and international upheavals.

Harry S. Truman's image of the Presidency, an office he never sought and never expected to have, differed from both his predecessor's and his successor's. He created a more elaborate staff system than Roosevelt, yet worked around it when he thought it necessary and was most accessible to politicians and to his staff. This plus his avid interest in reading helped information to get through to him, and he was not as isolated as Eisenhower. Because of his background, he had deference toward Congress but was quick to protect executive prerogatives. Few Presidents have resorted to less deviousness and circumlocution than Truman. Although Roosevelt, Eisenhower, and Kennedy were often content to speak in generalities, Truman spoke in specifics. He once spoke of the Senate as having "too many Byrds in it," referring to the conservative Virginia Senator. He would comment on a bill bottled up

[15] Neustadt, *op. cit.*, p. 165.

in a committee and name the chairman. His blunt talk sometimes enraged certain congressmen, but there were constituents who applauded his courage for calling a spade a spade. But often he took fixed positions on legislation, leaving himself no exit. Again this sometimes embarrassed him with Congress but made him a hero with those whose causes he so forthrightly championed.

Truman's biographers have not attributed to him the seeking of power but note that he was never above the political struggle or a fight. Mr. Truman, unlike some Presidents, appeared to like to make decisions and never shrank from performing what he thought was his duty. Intimates often remarked that he was guided by the reminder on his desk, "Buck-passing stops here." Despite criticisms that he was insensitive if not intransigent on many issues, Truman did back down when he was convinced that a losing fight would risk disaster in more vital areas.[16] He was fiercely loyal to the Democratic party and to his subordinates in government. He separated his role of party leadership from that of President and lambasted Republicans, even while soliciting their support for legislation. No other President in modern times talked as much about "party responsibility," and he urged his party's legislators to be loyal to the Democratic party; yet he was to find that exhortation alone did not produce Democratic congressional majorities. The distinction in his own mind of the various roles of the President was a real one, and he often seemed to operate on the assumption that different roles called for different behavior.

John F. Kennedy was the first President to come directly from the Senate since Warren G. Harding. His comparative youth and narrow electoral victory brought him into the White House with less prestige than Eisenhower or Roosevelt. He lost the skillful services of the two Texans, Lyndon Johnson and Sam Rayburn, who had long led the Democrats in Congress (Speaker Rayburn died at the end of the first session of Congress in 1961); and their successors were less experienced and less effective. Kennedy was therefore inclined to feel his way and be cautious. Before acting in the Cuban situation and before sending federal troops into Mississippi in connection with that state's opposition to an integration order, Kennedy telephoned the former Presidents Hoover, Truman, and Eisenhower to gain support for his action. He was particularly careful to consult Republican leaders on foreign policy. Because of his unusual facility in the English language, he was able to state and defend his policies and goals with great eloquence. He made many speeches before highly diverse groups, and public opinion

---

[16] Louis W. Koenig has provided an interesting analysis of the Truman style in handling this measure and aid to Yugoslavia in Alan F. Westin (ed.), *The Uses of Power*, Harcourt, Brace & World, Inc., New York, 1962, chap. 2.

polls reported him to be enormously popular. He tended to speak in generalities rather than in Trumanesque specifics. Because of his experience in Congress, Kennedy was able to appraise the balance of forces and moved boldly when victory seemed assured; but during his first year he backed off from pressing issues when defeat was in prospect. This was sometimes done by redefining the issue. His opponents criticized his leadership as one of "words rather than deeds." After his first year, Kennedy displayed a good deal more self-confidence; and, instead of ducking such issues as a Department of Urban Affairs and Medicare, on which he presumably lacked the votes in Congress, he fought for them. Even though defeated on both, he probably strengthened himself with groups within the electorate and perhaps paved the way for future enactment. One correspondent spoke of Kennedy as having the "most strongly marked presidential style in the twentieth century."

Lyndon B. Johnson's style was strikingly different from Kennedy's. He showed great sensitivity to the Kennedy goals in the months after the assassination and vigorously championed them. At once he resorted to the tactics and devices that were successful during his years as a Senate floor leader. Mr. Johnson not merely acceded to the Presidency but seized it with unexcelled energy and gave the impression that he enjoyed every minute of being President and the game of politics itself—resembling Franklin Roosevelt in this respect. He saw large numbers of people every day and made a huge number of personal telephone calls to leaders in and out of government and hosted many in the White House. He preferred and skillfully used personal negotiation. Although showing great deference to Congress and resourcefulness in gluing coalitions together on certain bills, he nonetheless spoke vigorously for his legislative objectives and did not emphasize publicly a willingness for compromise.

Johnson concentrated on personal talks with leaders, but he never forgot the importance of public opinion. Johnson made much less use of the live televised press conference, which Kennedy employed so successfully; but he called the press together very frequently on short notice to brief them and to answer questions. Often these conferences were held on Saturday, making much front-page news for the Sunday newspapers. President Johnson was much more homespun and less sophisticated than Kennedy in speech, manner, and wit, but both men made many public appearances and enjoyed crowds.

Johnson's relations with Congress showed the greatest contrast with his predecessor even though both came from the Senate. The former was a wielder of power as floor leader and an insider, while Kennedy was in effect an outsider and never was powerful in the Senate. Kennedy dealt with Congress through aides and at a distance; and, in personal conversations with congressmen, he lacked the warmth and hail-fellow manner of Johnson, who treated legislators as old friends and was not above appealing to sentiment and emotion when he wanted their support. Probably no other President became as intimately involved with Congress in pressing for measures such as federal aid to education. In this instance, he virtually set the legislative tactics, masterminded procedure, and made known to handlers of the legislation that he wanted a "closed rule," in order to avoid amendment on the floor.

The Johnson approach was pragmatic, practical, and nonideological; but he was quick to appeal to sentiment, patriotism, brotherhood, and compassion in support of his requests for legislation he believed would aid the underprivileged or would promote equality of opportunity and world peace. He used the same tactics with disputant parties in a threatening railroad strike and in other cases of conflict. His consensus emphasized the duty of the President to develop the common interests of all sections and groups. He often gave ground on appropriations rather than risk alienating members of Congress; and, unlike Mr. Truman, he avoided last-ditch fights. His emphasis on the role of negotiator and pacificator brought charges that he was a "wheeler and dealer." An unpopular war in Vietnam and allegations by the press and others that he was not being candid about the war permitted his opponents to charge him with a "credibility gap." These factors damaged his national image and led to his retirement from the presidential area without seeking another term.

During the 1968 campaign, Richard Nixon said, "The days of a passive Presidency belong to a simpler past. . . . [The] President must take an activist view of his office. He must articulate the nation's values, define its goals, and marshal its will." He took office after a traumatic year of assassinations, riots, protests, and national divisiveness. During the first two years, his style was in his own words "to lower his voice," follow a low-key posture of avoiding conflict with Congress, trying to heal intergroup strife, and playing down Republican partisanship in Congress. At the same time, the President, as before his inauguration, took great interest in Republican party affairs; delivered campaign speeches for Republican candidates; and, with the help of Vice President Agnew, sought to strengthen himself and his party in the South. During 1969, Mr. Nixon devoted much time to world affairs and assumed a more cautious, consolidating policy in domestic affairs; but in 1970 he moved vigorously into domestic affairs and seized initiative from the Democrats in the environmental field by taking over many of the reform positions they had held. Meanwhile, Mr. Nixon's highly successful live telecasts and press conferences blunted the peace issues; and, with appeals to the "silent majority," he proved himself an artful politician. He followed a zig-zag course that appealed at one time to the political right, then to the political left, but retained his image of broad appeal to the center.

He carried public opinion somewhat more successfully than Congress, partly because he took public stands on fewer roll-call votes than did his predecessors. In 1969, he won on 74 percent of the roll calls that presented clear-cut tests of support for his views. Congressional backing during the first year in office for President Eisenhower was 89 percent, 81 percent for President Kennedy, and a huge 93 percent for President Johnson in the first year after election in his own right (1965). President Nixon, however, had a Congress controlled by the opposition and felt also that he must concentrate on building a firm foundation with the majority of the people—a strategy dictated by his capturing only 43 percent of the popular vote in 1968.

Full analysis of Mr. Nixon's manner of operation must await the conclusion of his term in office, for all Presidents change their modus operandi with Congress over time, and it is easy to overgeneralize about presidential styles and techniques. Experience demonstrates what works and what does not. Times change, new problems and personalities arise, new resources must replace exhausted ones, and an executive must be flexible in the way he employs his personal and institutional powers. Roosevelt assumed a somewhat different posture when he became a war President, and there is some truth in the observation that a "new Eisenhower" was emerging late in his term. No matter what tactics are used, the great personal resource of a Chief Executive is his ability to persuade. Our brief excursion into some of the techniques of six Presidents since 1933 has been designed to emphasize that the Presidency like other political institutions can be better understood by looking at each occupant as an individual as well as in the formal context of the office itself.

All modern Presidents must rely heavily on their party's congressional floor leaders, so they meet regularly with them. The functional interdependence works the other way as well. Floor leaders need the help of the executive in their legislative aspirations. The President is an outside source of leverage for the floor leader. An important tie between the Chief Executive and his floor leader is the party label, even though each may come from a different wing of the party. But both are concerned with the success of their own party and with reelection. This has a mediating effect, provides an impetus for collaboration, and provides a common objective.

STATE ADMINISTRATIVE PARTIES

Electoral Variations. Many of the generalizations about the President and the executive branch hold true for the state governors and their administrative establishments. Governors and their department heads and staffs are active in the legislative and electoral processes. However, state administrative organizational and constitutional requirements show marked variations among the states, as do their laws governing the merit system, patronage, and political activities of public employees. Administrative politics therefore takes on a different flavor in each state. One of the most marked variations is in the practice of designating the major officials. In Alaska and New Jersey, for example, the governor possesses the authority to choose his own department heads. At the other extreme, many state officials are elected. In some states, the legislature chooses certain administrative officers.

Several new state constitutions have reduced the number of elected state officials, but a large number of states still have a plural executive system. In several states, the superintendent of public instruction is chosen on a nonpartisan ballot. This has usually effectively removed the office from partisan politics, but this is not invariably the case. In one instance a "nonpartisan" superintendent groomed himself to challenge an incumbent Democratic governor. The superintendent won the Republican primary and almost defeated the governor in the election. Depending upon voting habits and traditions, there are potential administrative parties rivaling the governor even in his own party.

South Dakota is illustrative of one style of voting pattern where one party is considerably stronger at the state level than the other. There are eight elective officers chosen on a partisan ballot, and in the fifteen elections from 1932 through 1960 the Republicans carried all of them eleven times; the Democrats swept the positions only twice; and in two elections the parties split. It is obvious that there is a strong tendency for the voters to view a party's candidates as a slate and to support its nominees for the lesser offices.[17] In other words, the gubernatorial candidate and his seven colleagues are likely to rise or fall together. In Illinois likewise a party slate usually wins even though some officials are elected during presidential years and others at the midterm.

Massachusetts presents a far different picture; a party seldom wins all the state offices. In only three of the sixteen biennial elections from 1932 to 1962 did the same party sweep the field. Although seven Republicans were elected governor during this period, Democrats controlled the office of state auditor in all but two years. Washington's voting patterns are quite similar, with many candidates for lesser office

[17]Alan L. Clem's study of voting behavior in thirty-seven South Dakota elections found that in the great majority of them the differential between the vote for the Republican candidate for governor and that for the lowest office on the ticket did not exceed 5 percent. *South Dakota Political Almanac*, Governmental Research Bureau, State University of South Dakota, Vermillion, 1962, pp. 18–23.

on the same ticket averaging a 10 to 20 percent greater plurality than that for governor.

In periods of discontent, distress, or national trends, the governor in many states is more likely to be defeated than his colleagues because he is marginal. The governor is the most visible of the state officers and more in the public eye. He is likely, therefore, to bear the brunt of discontent, barring a major scandal, which sometimes occurs in one of the lesser offices. In the Eisenhower sweeps of 1952 and 1956, several Democratic governors lost by narrow margins, although a number of Democrats entrenched in the lesser state offices survived. With some exceptions, the lieutenant governor is the most closely associated with the governor in the minds of the voters, and some states have provided for the lieutenant governor to be chosen in the manner of the Vice President, that is, by a joint ballot. Where separate ballots are cast, the lieutenant governor more often than not is swept out of office with the governor.

In states in which the party electing the governor usually captures the rest of the offices, the "cabinet" may be presented as a party team with a unified front. Party ties are obviously strong, and the slate-makers have made selections designed to strengthen the ticket. A governor may find his colleagues helpful in his party and legislative roles in a manner somewhat analogous to Cabinet officers, even though the governor does not have the power of removal. This latter fact may be an important difference. If an attorney general or secretary of state becomes *persona non grata* to the governor, the governor can only hope to see the man defeated at the next primary, try to get party leaders to put pressure on him, or get him to see the error of his ways.

A governor may be aided by a popular auditor if the voters identify the two as personally friendly, cooperative, and complementary. The lesser officers may give the governor additional ties to interest groups and to the legislature. On the other hand, even if the officer is willing to use his prestige to speak vigorously for the governor in campaigns and to his friends in the legislature, American experience has shown that it is difficult for one public man to transfer his popularity to another. Moreover, many elected state officials have pretty small empires and could not be very helpful to the governor even if they wished.

Rivalries. A President seldom appoints Cabinet secretaries who are likely to rival him for nomination or who are even eager to be his successor. President Coolidge's Secretary of Commerce went on to the Presidency. But this must be regarded as exceptional, since the Cabinet is not generally regarded as an immediate stepping-stone to the office of Chief Executive. A similar situation exists in many states. Offices such as auditor, treasurer, various commissioners, and members of a board of regents are seldom regarded as steps on the road to the governorship;[18] they are "careers" in themselves and are so viewed by the voters, although they have little knowledge of the efficiency and performance level of these officeholders. Long-time holders of these offices become virtually nonpartisan in the mind of the electorate.

On the other hand, the lieutenant governor, attorney general, and secretary of state not infrequently use their offices for building themselves into gubernatorial candidates. Those of the governor's own party wait for him to retire, to run for the Senate, or to be appointed to federal office. This situation demands that they maintain contacts with party leaders and the party's voters (since they must win nomination) and, if the governor is not overly popular, that they have as little association with him as possible so far as voters are concerned. In California, as in many other states, statewide candidates of the same party are inclined to run their own campaigns and pay little attention to teamwork, except to sit on the same platform with the governor when a national figure speaks at a rally.

In states where the same party seldom carries all state offices, campaigning is frequently atomistic and decentralized. Each man realizes that he will stand or fall largely on his own campaign efforts, and he builds his own organization and raises much of his own money. If elected and if his own party's gubernatorial candidate fails, he constructs something of his own administrative party and may have some patronage to dispense. If the gubernatorial nominee wins, the administrator may become a potential rival of the gubernatorial party; if not, he is at least not a member of the executive's political team. An elected state official may clash with the governor over the recommended budget for his department. (This sometimes also happens where the governor and the officer wear the same party label.) A governor therefore has flanks exposed to persons in his own cabinet, and they are of no resource to him and are not expected to be so.

In summary, the gubernatorial party, unlike that of the President, may not be the only executive party in the state; there may be one or more small administrative parties headed by popular elected figures. Some of these men are content to seek no higher office and constitute a nimbus of indirect assistance to the gubernatorial party that, although not easy to measure, is not to be depreciated. Others, although

---

[18] There are, of course, conspicuous exceptions. In 1962 in Ohio, State Auditor James A. Rhodes defeated the incumbent governor, Michael V. DiSalle.

not threatening the party, become in effect entrenched "nonpartisans" who help the party but little. In still other cases, the elected administrators are potential or actual threats to the governor and may provoke an enervating rivalry to the state party and weaken its unity. The existence of plural elected offices in a state where party organization can draw up or influence the slate permits the balancing of tickets in terms of big-city and outstate, and of ethnic and religious considerations. This may assist in invigorating the state party and is one of the reasons why party organizations fight proposals to shorten the ballot.

Elective administrative offices serve as beachhead and bridgehead for the opposition party. By capturing an office or two, the party has at least some foothold in the state government and provides a place for a person to develop name familiarity that is later useful in running either for governor or for the United States Senate. A number of senators served in statewide executive offices, an obvious help in becoming known. If an opposition state administrative officer is unlikely to seek the governorship, he may still be valuable to his party as a symbol of state party and as a focal point around which, to one degree or another, it is represented in the government. In New York, State Controller Arthur Leavitt, a Democrat, survived the Rockefeller sweeps for governor and was frequently at public odds with the Governor on tax programs. Leavitt enjoyed the advantage of speaking from the forum of a state office on fiscal matters rather than from outside the government.

The Governor in the System. From the foregoing review, it is obvious that a governor is not "a little President"; his position is quite different from that of the President. He enjoys less power and influence. He has less freedom to appoint and instruct his executive heads and is less able to attract public attention. A governor has at least two strong competitors for attention, the two United States senators. One-fourth of the states forbid governors a second successive term. Where there is no limitation, many incumbents seeking a third term find it difficult in attainment. Unlike a President, the governor is frequently ambitious for a career in politics after he leaves the governorship and may aspire to the United States Senate, a federal appointment, or even the Presidency. He is tempted to conduct his official and party role with this desired future in mind and to forge alliances that will help him.

At the same time, a number of governors possess resources that are not available to the President. One is the item veto. Comparatively more patronage is available to some governors. Often this patronage goes through the county chairmen, who may impose some restrictions on the governor's appointments but through whom the executive has a lever and some tie-in with the local party organization. In Illinois under the Democrats, the patronage administrator is an administrative assistant to the governor; and county chairmen frequently go to Springfield to deal directly with him.[19] County chairmen at times appeal over his head directly to the governor.

The governorship of a state, even with its limitations, is a position of distinction and considerable power, even though the governor must share his power with other participants in the system—the legislature, the courts, the bureaucracy, the opposition party, and pressure groups. Governors are generally more urban oriented than their legislative parties and must make a record attractive to urban voters who in turn are a source of strength for them. Like the President, the governor's success will depend on his style and his abilities to mobilize resources available to him. In many states, but by no means all of them, the political party that he heads gives him a potent instrument for achieving his policy goals and his personal ambitions should he seek higher office. At times his party leadership responsibilities may be a heavy burden.

FOR FURTHER READING

Binkley, Wilfred: *The Man in the White House,* 1959.
_____: *President and Congress,* 1947.
Brown, Stuart Gerry: *The American Presidency: Leadership, Partisanship, and Popularity,* 1966.
Burns, James M.: *Presidential Government,* 1965.
Hargrove, Erwin C.: *Presidential Leadership,* 1966.
Hyman, Sidney: *The American President,* 1954.
Koenig, Louis: *The Invisible Presidency,* 1960.
McConnell, Grant: *The Modern Presidency,* 1968.
Pollard, James E.: *The Presidents and the Press,* 1947.
Ransone, Coleman B., Jr.: *The Office of Governor in the United States,* 1956.
Rossiter, Clinton: *The American Presidency,* 1956.
Schlesinger, Joseph: *How They Became Governor,* 1957.

[19] On this patronage system, see Joseph P. Tucker, "The Administration of a State Patronage System: The Democratic Party in Illinois," *Western Political Quarterly,* vol. 22, pp. 79–84, 1969. The data suggests that "the patronage coming from the state party serves primarily to satisfy local expectations and aspirations, not necessarily to promote directly the state party organization" (p. 84).

The congressional party . . . is a loose cluster of men,
sharing a common concept of the public interest,
convinced that they are protecting the nation against
radicalism, benefiting from and in turn protecting a set
of rules that bolster their own power, and the product
of local political patterns. These men deal with one
another by bargaining and accommodation rather than
by direction and command.

JAMES M. BURNS

CHAPTER 8 THE PARTY IN LEGISLATURE AND JUDICIARY

In the majority of legislative struggles in Congress and in the state legislatures, the parties are little more than observers and are often content
to play a neutral role. Very large numbers of proposals are noncontroversial and nonpartisan and pass without opposition; many others
provoke only a few dissenting votes that are based on local considerations. On some very important measures, however, there are sharp
cleavages, many of which cut deeply across party lines. Some provoke
sharp contentions between the two major parties. Students of the American political system have long debated the role of party in legislation.
Some admirers of the Western parliamentary systems would like to see
a greater degree of party unity, cohesion, and discipline in matters of
public policy in the American legislatures. The present system is
criticized as chaotic and irresponsible; it is defended by those who feel

that it works as well as can be expected. At this point we shall discuss what influences the men who make up the legislative party and the instruments of leadership in American lawmaking bodies.

HOW DOES A LEGISLATOR MAKE UP HIS MIND?

The neophyte legislator learns soon after his election—if he did not know it before—that he is the object of much pressure and that the legislative process is more complex than he realized. Pressures impinge on him from every direction. His political decisions are made neither in a vacuum nor on the basis of pure objectivity or party label. A student of government who is fortunate enough to secure an internship with a congressman soon observes many of the influences that go into the making of a legislative decision. Even with a good rapport, however, the intern will not see many of the subsurface factors at work.[1]

Influences on Legislators. There are at least seven sources of pressure that can influence a legislator and that to varying degrees help determine the legislator's decisions: (1) the constituency as a whole, (2) special-interest forces from a segment of the constituency, (3) internal influences from the legislative chamber, (4) executive and administrative agencies, (5) attitudes of other members of one's own state delegation, (6) one's own predispositions and attitudes, and (7) political party pressures. Party influences therefore conflict with many other interests for the legislator's vote.

Very briefly, senators and representatives represent their own states and districts and regard service to them as matters of top priority. Their votes are conditioned in one degree or another by their own images and perceptions of their district. Polls, mail from constituents, communications with leaders in the district, and various impressionistic devices are used to ascertain the wishes and desires of constituents. A legislator from a one-party district can ignore many minorities even within his own party as long as he can continue to win in the primary. But as his margin of victory narrows in the primary or general election and as his district becomes competitive, a lawmaker must give more attention to actual and potential opposition and serve those particularly important to his reelection.

Few, if any, legislators pursue their jobs in total disregard of political interest groups. The legislative function is one calling for the adjustment, accommodation, and conciliation of group demands. The

[1]An interesting autobiographical account is presented by the late Congressman Clem Miller, *Member of the House*, Charles Scribner's Sons, New York, 1962, chap. 2.

viewpoint of the legislator himself is important in the amount of group influence on him. Some legislators are friendly to certain groups and see their role as facilitating group demands. Others may be hostile to the same groups and may be determined to resist their legislative objectives; still other legislators may be indifferent or professed neutrals in the controversy. In each major legislative issue there are usually persons strongly committed to one or the other of two positions. There are others who are much less involved and perhaps uncommitted; they will mediate the dispute and may be the determining factor on the legislative roll calls. When legislative leaders have worked out compromises satisfactory to rival groups, many legislators who were not involved tend to go along with them without feeling the need to know about the bargains and arrangements that were made. A study of Vermont legislators showed a rather surprisingly low level of recognition among many of them of interest-group activity.[2] Those who were more policy and program oriented saw more organized group activity than those who were more faction oriented and who did not view the legislature as an arena of rival interests. This study further emphasizes the point that there is a good deal of differential in the roles that legislators see themselves playing and in an awareness of the activities of organized groups.

Internal influences, pressures for conformity, rules of the game, and legislative norms also affect the behavior of representatives. Personal friendships have never been sufficiently analyzed but are often instrumental in obtaining votes on measures where one is indifferent or uncommitted. Similarly, reciprocity (owing a vote to someone) and prestige may influence those who are neutral. In a measure where commercial and savings and loan banks are rivals, there may be a large number of representatives who are neutral in the fight. On these occasions, the psychological and personality factors play an important part in supplying cues to others in their social group.[3]

On measures involving a federal program of direct value to a state, such as a defense establishment or a reclamation or public works project, all the Democratic and Republican members of the state's delegation may act in concert to get the measure through Congress. On issues not directly related to one's state, the party delegation in each state serves as a mechanism for supplying cues. The influence of the

[2] Oliver Garceau and Corinne Silverman, "A Pressure Group and the Pressured: A Case Report," *American Political Science Review*, vol. 48, pp. 672–691, 1954. Fuller attention is given to lobbying and pressure-group activity in chap. 20 below.

[3] Alan Fiellin notes that Congress is unstructured and that subgroups are useful not only for exchanging views and information but even at times in bloc voting. See "The Function of Informal Groups in Legislative Institutions," *Journal of Politics*, vol. 24, pp. 72–91, 1962.

delegation is not the same from state to state or from issue to issue because of the many other forces operating on a congressman. David Truman in his analysis of twenty-three state delegations in the Eighty-first Congress found that in general the issues most sharply dividing the parties in the House of Representatives did not set up comparable cleavages within the state delegations.[4] He also found that issues dividing a party as a whole did not split the state delegation or at least not so widely. The most apparent influence of the state delegation was on votes of relatively low party cohesion that were often either highly controversial within the party or relatively trivial. In these cases the state delegations seemed to provide guidance and reassurance to the individual representative. In terms of reelection and relations "back home" there is defensive value if not logic in legislators from the same area presenting a united front on questions tending to divide the national congressional party.

Finally, of course, members of the legislative branch are influenced by the position of the Chief Executive. Members of the majority party may go along with the governor or the President, out of personal as well as party loyalty. Opposition party members may be guided by the President's position on matters concerning foreign policy. Indeed, this may provide their public rationalization, for they can point to the need for "national unity" and "standing by the President."

Three theories or explanations of legislative voting in Western democracies have been propounded. One is that there is a popular will that manifests itself through political party programs and through persons and groups in the district. The legislator is mandated to follow this will as it is understood and ascertained. Proponents of party voting particularly emphasize the obligation of a legislative party to follow the dictates of a program drawn up by representatives of the party. A second approach to legislative decision making doubts that there is an easily definable popular will. Proponents of this approach believe that the lawmaker must be free to adjust conflicts according to his concept of the public interest and in a manner necessary to his own reelection. Opportunism, appropriately, is necessary if not desirable. Between the "rationalist" and the "realist" theories of voting behavior is the third type, that of the "idealist" whose duty is to seek the public interest by using his own judgment and conscience. In American legislatures, followers of these three types are often dubbed the "party hack," the "opportunist,"

---

[4] David Truman, *The Congressional Party: A Case Study,* John Wiley & Sons, Inc., New York, 1959, pp. 249–269. See also Duncan MacRae, Jr., *Dimensions of Congressional Voting,* University of California Press, Berkeley, 1958, pp. 269–270. In his work treating all the leadership groups in the House, Randall B. Ripley notes the influences of state delegations, *Party Leadership in the House of Representatives,* The Brookings Institution, Washington, D.C., 1967, pp. 169–175.

and the "independent." Much of the time, explaining behavior in any one of these exclusive terms is an oversimplification. Many if not most legislators at one time or another have been influenced by all three considerations in making legislative decisions. This is understandable because of a public man's reaction to the power and force of so many variables. From these somewhat less tangible but nonetheless significant influences that affect the reality of a legislative party—or lack of it—we shall turn our attention to how party leadership is exercised in Congress.

CONGRESSIONAL LEADERSHIP

General Characteristics. Congressional parties are called upon to manage legislation through two houses, a process involving more than a score of steps. Leadership is dispersed and exercised by numerous legal and extralegal mechanisms. Leadership instruments serve as forces both for dispersion and for integration. There are numerous leaders elected by the members of the respective parties in both houses—the floor leader, whips, and caucus, campaign committee, and patronage chairmen. The majority party chooses the Speaker of the House and the President Pro Tem of the Senate. Republicans elect a House policy committee chairman, and both parties have Senate policy committees.[5]

Another class of leaders exercises power according to seniority—the chairmen and the ranking minority members of the standing committees. These are not chosen by their partisans at the beginning of each session of Congress but automatically receive their positions by virtue of length of service on the same committee, and of course they have enjoyed long unbroken strings of reelections.[6] Standing-committee chairmen are older than their colleagues; 60 percent of the House and Senate chairmen are more than sixty years of age. When Democrats control Congress, the Southern and Border States obtain a lion's share of the chairmanships; the Midwest is the most favored when the Republicans control. In the Ninety-first Congress the distribution of House chairmanships by section was South, eight; Border, six; East, three; and two each from the Midwest and Far West; Senate distributions were South, ten; Border, two; and Far West, four. From 1947 to 1959, more than half of the Democratic chairmen came from one-party or modified

[5] Congressional party leadership is covered in detail in many works on Congress. See especially Randall B. Ripley, *Party Leadership*, and his *Majority Party Leadership in Congress*, Little, Brown and Company, Boston, 1969. Bibliography is found on pages 213–215 of *Majority Party Leadership* and in the most complete reference list prepared by Ripley and Charles O. Jones, *The Study of Congress: A Bibliography and Research Guide*, University of Arizona Institute of Government Research, Tucson, 1966.

[6] For a comprehensive discussion of seniority and its implications, see George Goodwin, Jr., "The Seniority System in Congress," *American Political Science Review*, vol. 53, pp. 412–436, 1959.

one-party states.[7] However, more than half of the Republican chairmen came from two-party states. If we use congressional districts in the House and states in the Senate as criteria, the rural areas tended to control more chairmanships than the urban areas; Republican chairmen, however, were more likely than Democrats to come from urban states and districts.

The basic unit of party control in each house is the caucus or conference. Before 1917, the caucuses generally formulated their party's position on leadership and organization and enforced the party will on them. Before being shorn of his power in 1910, the Speaker, working with the caucus, enforced party discipline and undoubtedly controlled many votes on party policy positions. During President Wilson's first term, the Democratic caucus was a powerful instrument in pushing through the party's legislative program. Both parties have fairly elaborate caucus rules, but the caucuses themselves are of little importance today in laying down and enforcing a party line.

Caucuses and conferences, although no longer important in policy positions, are fundamental to each party in determining party positions on leadership, organization, and personnel matters. Most party leaders have found that divisional issues cannot be resolved in the party conference but that differences may actually be exacerbated. At times in both parties, the conference has been used for the discussion of carefully selected issues on which it is believed that the party can be united, but it is rare for the conference to adopt a formal statement embodying a party stand. A steering committee is a subgroup within a caucus designed to serve as an executive committee for the larger group and has not been very important in recent years. In 1949, the Republicans in the House converted their steering committee into a House Republican Policy Committee. In many state legislatures the caucuses are effective operating instruments of party control in matters of policy as well as organization. In legislative bodies the caucuses, composed of all the party membership, are potential and often actual forces for party unity and help to reinforce the party by the very fact that they make the legislative party visible to the membership.

Floor Leaders. Around the end of World War I, each party in Congress selected a floor leader to serve as an agent to enhance the position of the party. These leaders devote their efforts to tying together the loose, incongruous alliances that compose each political party and attempt to marshal majorities large enough to pass or defeat bills. Floor leaders are parliamentary tacticians who often assume responsibility for guidance of bills on the floor by making numerous motions and engaging in debate.

[7] *Ibid.*, p. 425.

Majority floor leaders have much influence in the scheduling of debate. The floor leader is not an officer of the House but fills an extralegal position; and, when his party is in the majority, he is second in importance to the Speaker. In the Senate, the majority leader has no peer, as neither the Vice President nor the President Pro Tem exercises the authority of the Speaker.

Floor leaders have differed in their views of their role as a spokesman for the President. Senator Alben Barkley, long-time Democratic leader, argued that the majority leader is expected to be the legislative spokesman of the administration, assuming that they are of the same party.[8] He is expected to confer with the President on the latter's recommendations to Congress and to report and interpret the views of one to the other. Senator William Knowland, although voting for most of Eisenhower's legislative program, made known on occasion that he did not regard it as his duty as Republican floor leader to be an apologist for the President's program. Senator Hugh Scott, who succeeded the late Everett Dirksen as minority floor leader, differed with President Nixon on several important matters and was joined by the Republican whip and conference chairman in voting against the President's nomination of Clement Haynsworth to the Supreme Court. Even though the average Senate Republican supported Mr. Nixon's position 66 percent of the time, Scott's percentage was 78 percent in support. The House Republican leader, Gerald Ford, went along with President Nixon 76 percent of the time compared with the House Republican average of 57 percent. However, there were many Republicans in both houses who scored higher in support of the President than did the floor leaders. This has not been unusual in congressional party leadership. Despite the numerous examples of conflict between floor leaders and their Presidents, it is fair to say that it is the floor leader's function to integrate the forces of the party and as much as possible to rally the latter behind the President's program.

David B. Truman has observed that the floor leaders tend to be near the voting center of their respective parties rather than toward the extreme right or left.[9] They are pivotal within the congressional party, and to the extent that the party has a focus, it is the floor leader. "His behavior seems to emphasize and to reflect the common ties of party, a kind of trusteeship for the party record and for the survival of that somewhat anomalous group."[10] A successful floor leader is sensitive to

[8] See "The Majority Leader in the Legislative Process," in Amry Vandenbosch (ed.), *The Process of Government*, Bureau of Government Research, University of Kentucky, Lexington, 1949, pp. 36ff.

[9] For his conceptualization and illustrations of the role of the floor leaders see Truman, *op. cit.*, chaps. 4 and 6.

[10] *Ibid.*, p. 144.

the forces building up behind legislation and his role (shared with others) is to mediate. He does not want to lose, and he knows that victory will likely depend on yielding in one thing but exercising power to win in another.

A system of whips is used for purposes of communication between the leadership and rank-and-file members. In the House, each party has a whip and a deputy whip. When they control the House, the Democrats have upwards of 18 assistant whips, each of whom is responsible for a zone. The deans of the delegations in each zone name the whips. Republicans have fewer assistant whips, and they are appointed by the whip. In the Senate there are seldom more than one or two whips. The whips and their assistants facilitate and expedite contacts with the entire congressional party within a short period of time. They serve as polltakers, canvasing the state delegations on various matters. Information such as the leadership's stand on an issue is sent quickly through the whips; they are also important in rounding up absent members and in trying to keep party members in line. Leadership methods and devices are different in each house, and it is appropriate that separate though brief consideration be given to each.

PARTY LEADERSHIP IN THE HOUSE

Speaker. The Speaker of the House is the top partisan officer of the majority. He keeps party interests in mind in making decisions on the floor, in his power of recognition, and in addressing the House. He appoints select committees, which are useful in satisfying diverse constituency groups and in focusing attention on special problems such as small business or foreign aid. As a parliamentarian, the Speaker can employ devices highly important in getting legislation passed or defeated or in quashing opposition party tactics designed to embarrass the majority. Every Speaker has his own style of leadership. Sam Rayburn, who served as Speaker all but four years between 1940 and 1961, was often instrumental in welding a majority by leaving the rostrum and going to the floor to debate and negotiate. He wanted no caucuses or policy committees that would interfere with his operation of the House or challenge his leadership. When he felt strongly enough on an issue, he went in person to the Democrats on the Ways and Means or other committees and prodded and stirred them to action and compromise. He was dedicated to keeping the Northern and Southern Democrats together and opposed caucuses because they might result in splitting the congressional party. Rayburn served as counselor and friend to freshmen congressmen and in return expected support from them. He sponsored and promoted many able young men who became known as "the Speaker's boys." It followed that the leadership was Rayburn and whoever else he wished to include. Floor leaders under this kind of strong speakership were definitely secondary and deputy in influence. Much of the secret of Rayburn's success was due to great personal influence built up over a long time, beginning with his election to the House in 1912. He therefore combined both formal and personal powers and made wise use of his powers.

Rules Committee. The Rules Committee of the House is one of the most powerful instruments of leadership, and even the powerful Rayburn was often unable to get his way with it. Briefly, the committee fixes the timetable of the House and determines when bills shall come up, the duration of debate, and the time and manner of voting on them. It can bring in open or closed rules for amending measures on the floor, give priority to those bills and amendments it favors, or obstruct those it opposes. It is far more than a traffic officer on the legislative highway because it interjects itself into the realm of policy by deciding what bills it will expedite, hinder, bury, or try to modify. Committee chairmen must plead before it in an effort to get measures on the floor. For a time, the Rules Committee bottled up Alaska and Hawaii statehood, grain shipments to India, and the wage and hour law, to mention but a very few. On many occasions, it has not reflected the majority party's position on certain priority matters. Appropriation bills in the House are, however, privileged business, and this committee is most powerful in its own area.

Originally the Rules Committee was regarded as an agent of the majority party, but since 1937 it has often functioned as a coalition of Southern Democrats and Northern Republicans inclined toward a conservative if not an obstructional approach. As such, it has been more an instrument of coalition rather than party control. Whenever the House leadership and the Rules Committee are in agreement, the latter is highly useful in accelerating legislative action; but its opposition to other programs of the majority has been a subject of controversy. Since the committee is composed on a seniority basis, its majority was often not in the broad center of the Republican or Democratic congressional parties. Beginning in 1961, the committee's membership underwent some change, with a few prominent liberals being added.[11] Although at times the Committee has aided party control in the Houses, it cannot be classified as a reliable mechanism to further the interests of the majority party.

[11] Robert L. Peabody, "The Enlarged Rules Committee," in Robert L. Peabody and Nelson W. Polsky (eds.), *New Perspectives on the House of Representatives,* Rand McNally & Company, Chicago, 1963, chap. 6. A general work is James A. Robinson, *The House Rules Committee,* The Bobbs-Merrill Company, Inc., Indianapolis, 1963.

THE PARTY IN LEGISLATURE AND JUDICIARY
235

Republican Policy Committee. As seen earlier in the national party organizations, the minority has greater need for a policy committee than the
majority party. It is difficult at best for minority party members of Congress to influence policy, and they seek concerted action to maximize
their effectiveness. A policy committee offers an instrument for pursuing
such objectives. With the White House as a policy-coordinating mechanism, there is less need for a policy committee when the same party
controls Congress. House Republicans since 1949 have had an unofficial
policy group with an ex officio membership varying between twenty-five
and forty members, which is broadly representative of the new and
older members.[12] Although the committee does not formulate a party
position on legislation, then impose this view on the members, it has
served a variety of useful purposes.

The Republican Policy Committee is a center of communication
useful for discovering consensus—or lack of it—on policy. Its staff does
research on alternative policy programs. The committee has been involved in power struggles and conflicts between leaders and followers
and serves as a means of avoiding surprise on the floor. The strengths
and weaknesses of the party and its leadership are made more apparent
to the membership. Policy committees also gain publicity for the party
as well as contributing to the development of unity within the party on
some matters. As Charles O. Jones has observed, a minority party may
affect the policy-making process. "If an issue divides the majority, policy
formulators may have to court minority party votes: the minority may be
developing alternative proposals which become attractive to those
affected by a policy problem and thus these proposals may be taken over
by the majority party."[13]

Democratic Study Group. The tripartite nature of the House of Representatives is shown in the establishment of the Democratic Study Group,
which was formed by liberal Democrats in 1959 to counter the strong
control exercised by the conservative Democrats, Rules Committee, and
Southern Democrats in general. In order to avoid having its activities
labeled as oppositional, it took the name Democratic Study Group and
set up an office with a small staff to conduct policy research and to
coordinate diverse interests.[14] The Democratic Study Group is limited
to Northern liberal Democrats (about 125 in number) and places

[12] For a full account of the development and activities of this body see Charles O. Jones,
Party and Policy-Making: The House Republican Policy Committee, Rutgers University Press, New Brunswick,
N.J., 1964.
[13] "The Minority Party and Policy-Making in the House of Representatives," *American
Political Science Review*, vol. 62, pp. 492–493, 1968.
[14] For the genesis of this group, see Kenneth Kofmehl, "The Institutionalization of a Voting
Bloc," *Western Political Quarterly*, vol. 17, pp. 256–272, 1964.

its allegiance in the national party platform. Most particularly, it is a spearhead for liberal legislation since it improved communications among liberal House Democrats and helped avoid their fragmentation into factions. The group is structured through elective officials, an executive and steering committee, and a whip system whereby members can be quickly brought to the floor. By proclaiming itself a regionally based organization designed to promote programs of mutual concern, rather than an ideological grouping, the Democratic Study Group is more acceptable and less embarrassing to the leadership.

SENATE PARTY LEADERSHIP

Personalized Style.   Senate leadership differs in many respects from that of the House. House procedure is more rigidly controlled, and the individual member is limited in debate. Senators may bring up bills on the floor and talk at length on any matter, but legislative scheduling is not left to chance. Practically speaking, the majority floor leader in consultation with his policy committee and the minority leader arranges most of the schedule. Leadership by both the elected and the seniority leaders is highly personal and highly complex. Numerous senators are subject-matter specialists and become prestigious because of their knowledge of a particular problem. Sometimes one man or a very few men become the key to legislative outcome.

The majority floor leader of the Senate plays a highly important role, particularly in determining the order in which bills will be considered. It may be said that all senators are equal, but some senators are more equal than others, and the floor leader is a particularly "unequal" man. His role varies materially from time to time and depends on whether his party controls the White House and whether the President is strong and aggressive or relatively passive in legislative leadership. His personal relationship with the minority leader and his skill in handling the members of his own party are also important in legislative success—or lack of it. Unlike the Speaker, the floor leader of the Senate does not possess formal powers; therefore, his strength must be built on personal skills and whatever he can mobilize from the conference and the policy committees. The majority leader is also at the center of a communications network in a complex institution. He is likely to possess more information than anyone else and has much power in making committee assignments for new members and dispensing individual favors. Each floor leader has his own style and effectiveness, as demonstrated by the differences between the operations of Lyndon B. Johnson, who served as Democratic leader beginning in 1953,[15] and those of Mike Mansfield, who succeeded him in 1961.

Leadership arrangements differ considerably between the two parties.[16] Republicans select separate persons for floor leader, conference chairman, steering committee chairmen, and policy committee chairman. Democrats place all these positions in the hands of the floor leader. Republican leadership tends to be more institutionalized and the Democratic leadership more personalized. This became especially marked after the death of Sen. Robert A. Taft in 1953, who as policy chairman and floor leader carried great prestige with Republican senators.

Senate Policy Committees. In recent years, each of the political parties in the Senate has utilized a party policy committee.[17] Congress appropriates funds for their use and has charged them with "the formulation of overall legislative policy of the respective parties." Each committee is given a staff "to assist in study, analysis, and research on problems involved in policy determinations." Both the composition and uses of committees have shown much variation between the parties in part because the Democrats have been in the majority a large portion of the time and because the Republicans have oriented their policy bodies in keeping with their minority status.

The Senate Republican Policy Committee has fluctuated considerably in size. At one time (1955) every Republican senator up for reelection in 1956 was placed on the policy body, involving a total of twenty-three; in 1957 in a radical change the membership was reduced to fifteen, including as ex officio members the secretary of the conference, the whip, the floor leader, and the chairmen of the campaign and personnel committees and of the committee on committees; other members are elected by the conference. In the Ninety-first Congress, the membership quite adequately reflected regional representation and the liberal, center, and conservative viewpoints of the Republican senatorial party. The Republican rule prohibits a senator from serving more than two years at a time and thus probably helps to keep the body from being

[15] One of the best analyses of Johnson's style is that by Ralph K. Huitt, "Democratic Party Leadership in the Senate," *American Political Science Review*, vol. 55, pp. 333–344, 1961. See also Rowland Evans and Robert Novak, *Lyndon B. Johnson: The Exercise of Power*, The New American Library, Inc., New York, 1966.

[16] Recommended works on Senate leadership: Donald R. Matthews, *U.S. Senators and Their World*, University of North Carolina Press, Chapel Hill, 1960; Lawrence K. Pettit and Edward Keynes (eds.), *The Legislative Process in the Senate*, Rand McNally & Company, Chicago, 1969.

[17] For a detailed account of these bodies from their creation in 1947 to 1958, see Hugh A. Bone, *Party Committees and National Politics*, University of Washington Press, Seattle (third printing, 1968), chap. 6.

in the hands of senior members. In 1970, the committee had one fresh-man senator and nearly half of its members had served in the Senate less than six years.

The Democratic Policy Committee membership differs consider-ably from that of its Republican counterpart. It seldom exceeds nine in number and contains persons of long seniority who are permitted to serve continuously. Turnover occurs when members drop out of the Senate or when there are changes in the three ex officio members (floor leader, whip, and conference secretary). The floor leader, who serves as chairman, generally picks the members and ratification by the conference is *pro forma*. Unlike the standing committee chairmanship, the Democratic Policy Committee is not dominated by the South—only two Southerners were on the committee in 1970.

The Republican Policy Committee has been institutionalized by the adoption of rules that define and limit its authority; the Democrats have not recorded the functions of their committee. The Republican staff produces a large number of publications and memos to provide their senators with materials on important legislation and assists them in drafting speeches. As a matter of policy, the staff work and publica-tions are related to party interests, to attacking the Democratic record, and to extolling Republican accomplishments. In contrast, the Demo-cratic committee issues virtually no publications. Both committees meet privately but a Republican *Memo* keeps its senators informed of decisions and actions. Decisions of the Democratic committee are made known by word of mouth and statements to the press by the chairman.

The Democratic Policy Committee has been what the floor leader has chosen to make it. Senator Alben Barkley, its first chairman, preferred to have younger, less well-established men on the committee because he felt that they would be easier to control and would work harder in order to make reputations. Although he began by having weekly meetings, he abandoned the practice and as an "old pro" resorted to personal informal leadership, using his committee members to help him out. His successors, Senators Scott Lucas and Ernest McFarland, were not so secure, experienced, or prestigious as Barkley and used the committees in a way to strengthen their positions. Lucas employed it to schedule bills for Senate consideration and to plan floor strategy. Lyndon Johnson used the committee to formulate issues to embarrass the opposition party. For example, he got it to endorse Eisenhower's proposals on foreign affairs, thus placing the Republicans on the de-fensive because they were often divided on such matters.

When Mike Mansfield became floor leader and chairman of the policy committee in 1961, a few senators proposed that Vice President

Johnson be kept as chairman of the committee, but this was turned down by Senate Democrats; Johnson, however, attended a number of policy committee luncheons. Mansfield at once employed the committee very differently than his predecessor. He drastically reduced the staff and used it much more operationally and less personally than Johnson. Mansfield also took the position that in policy he was one among equals and not the leader. Some difference in this perception of role was undoubtedly due to the fact that Johnson led a Senate majority party that did not control the White House. Mansfield, on the other hand, was expected to take his cue from Presidents Kennedy and Johnson on policy and to map strategy to gain Democratic and Senate support for it. Accordingly, he invited Senate Democrats to attend policy committee luncheons where he reported on his meetings with the President.

When Mr. Nixon became President, the chairmen of the respective policy committees found their situation changed again. As under Eisenhower, the Republican chairmen, Everett Dirksen and his successor, Hugh Scott, used the committee to report presidential views and attitudes. The Democratic chairman no longer had his party leader in the White House; but he was still the Senate majority leader, with responsibility for trying to bring about party unity and was concerned with maintaining a majority and helping his party win back the Presidency. This situation points up again the need for studying congressional party leadership strategies in the context of partisan control of Congress and the Presidency.[18] The role of the party in the legislative process is greatly affected by whether or not the same party controls the Presidency and both houses. If the President faces one or both houses in control of the opposing party, he obviously has great difficulty in securing enactment of his legislative program. In this century, about half of the Presidents have had periods in which they were forced to work with the Congress wholly or in part controlled by the opposition party.

In conclusion, it may be said of the policy committees that they are misnamed. They do not determine and proclaim a party position on very many pieces of legislation, and only a few senators have publicly advocated that they do so. The decentralization and fragmentation of power, the prerogatives of individual power and seniority, and the habits of independence are so well entrenched that few senators are willing to place authority in a policy body. A senator often wishes to obtain support, if not sponsorship, of important legislation from senators of the opposite party; this is difficult to achieve if either party declares a measure to be party policy. The environment of Congress is

[18]Although not referring specifically to the Senate policy committee, Ripley's *Majority Party Leadership in Congress* is recommended for its conceptual treatment of this problem.

not conducive to delegating the authority to lay down a yardstick for judging a lawmaker's vote to a party committee. If a party line is unknown or obscure, a senator has more latitude and less chance of embarrassment at election time.

At the same time, the Senate policy committees should not be written off as of negligible influence on the senatorial parties; in fact they are useful to the party leadership, and there has been sentiment for abandoning them. Many issues of importance are discussed in both committees, even when no attempt is made at policy agreement. The discussions help accommodate factionalism and etch, for the party leadership, the areas of agreement and disagreement. The committees review programs submitted by their party's President or someone else and decide whether they have partisan overtones and should be adopted as party policy; in a sense, the committees make decisions as to what is party and nonparty. The role is one of sifting, evaluating, and ratifying more than of originating and creating. In terms of Senate tradition, the role of reviewer is more dominant than that of drafter and formulator of public policy.

However intangible their effect, the policy committees (as well as all other party agents) exert psychological influences and pressures for party regularity. The label "party policy committee" gives some appearance of leadership. When the chairman of the committee makes a pronouncement on behalf of it, the act itself creates some impression of a party position. There are pressures for conformity, notwithstanding a senator's individualism, and emulation is a vital part of the totality of legislative behavior. When a respected member speaks as a policy committee member, others will not oppose him without important reasons. To the extent that policy committees are worked into the fabric of interpersonal relations in the Senate, they can achieve success. The committees are another symbol of the presence of party in legislative politics.

THE CONGRESSIONAL PARTY

The student of government is interested in understanding that complex institution known as the representative body. Our brief review has emphasized that understanding is a matter of knowledge, both about the individual legislator and about his constituency and institutional structures. Constituency pressures, norms, and informal as well as formal structures of the legislative body operate on his perspectives and goals. Out of a confused and very complicated picture, we can nonetheless generalize that party leadership groups mediate the various influences and constellation of forces that work on the elected representative. Parties are important even though constituency interests often appear to

THE PARTY IN LEGISLATURE AND JUDICIARY

outweigh the demands for party loyalty. Professor Truman's analysis of the congressional party in one Congress tended to show that when the floor leader and seniority leaders differed, the former seemed to speak for the party. Although the fortunes of members of Congress were not identical with those of the legislative party, they were not completely independent of it. It is a fair assumption that the same would hold for most Congresses. The political party label, despite the number of dissidents who are elected under its banner, is one of the forces for unification in Congress. But one of the greatest unifiers of a congressional party is the centripetal influence of a Presidential spokesman.

In Table 3-2, party divisions on important roll calls were recorded, and the extensive literature on roll-call behavior points to party label as an important influence. Most members follow the party leadership except on matters affecting their district or on which they have strong personal convictions contrary to party policy. It is true that on a great majority of roll calls there is not a party division in which a majority of one party votes in opposition to a majority of the other. In 1969, this kind of party unity prevailed in only 36 percent of the roll calls in the Senate and 31 percent of the roll calls in the House. However, these roll calls were very important; and on them, collectively, the average Democrat voted with his party 63 percent of the time and the average Republican had a 62 percent party unity vote. The party influence is also suggested by the fact that when two senators of the same state are from the same party, they have tended to vote the same on roll calls about 85 percent of the time; when they are of opposite parties, there is usually greater disagreement, running as high as 40 percent at times.

Intraparty friendships have stronger legislative consequences than interparty friendships. Whip organizations help both parties to obtain the maximum number of party votes on controversial bills. Party pressures and labels are psychological pressures, and most congressmen prefer to go along with a majority of their party when they can. When a congressman identifies the interest of his constituency with the party's program and when the party appears helpful in his reelection, party loyalty is usually high. As Ralph K. Huitt observes, ". . . the party usually has an emotional appeal for its members which is reinforced by the sharing of common hazards under its banner at election time. There are very practical, selfish reasons for maintaining the party tie, too; Congress is organized on party lines and in the hands of the leaders are many small and a few large resources for strengthening the hand of the loyal partisan."[19]

[19] "Congressional Organization and Operations in the Field of Money and Credit," in *Fiscal and Debt Management Policies*, Commission on Money and Credit, Prentice-Hall, Inc., Englewood Cliffs, N.J., 1963, p. 23.

PARTY ROLE IN STATE LEGISLATURES

The influence of party and the role of leadership in the fifty state legislatures vary so widely that fruitful comparisons are very difficult, and
generalizations are almost impossible. Scholars are proceeding, nonetheless, to make roll-call analyses and to study aspects of the party variable
in the state legislatures.[20] In a sense almost anything one says about
state legislative parties can be found somewhere. The role of parties in
state legislatures is different from that in Congress although in some
states the leadership and processes are quite similar to those of the
United States House of Representatives. Despite the infinite variations,
a few broadly applicable statements can be made.

A wide variation in the degree of party voting can be expected
when one considers a spectrum ranging from one-party to highly competitive two-party systems. (When nearly all members of a body are
Democrats, how can there be a "party" vote?) But party voting does not
vary proportionately with party competition in the state.[21] Colorado,
with a high degree of competition for control at all levels of government,
shows a relatively low degree of party voting. Connecticut, Massachusetts, New York, Pennsylvania, and Rhode Island have a higher index of
party cohesion than Congress. Party voting is more evident in the
larger, urban, industrial states, where alignments follow urban-rurual
lines. Yet California's legislative parties are not polarized along these
lines, and they are not very cohesive but are becoming more so. Democratic representation in urban states comes largely from the cities, and
Republican representation is strongest in rural areas, but there are many
exceptions. Each party commonly elects a number of representatives
from both types of areas. Popular assumption has it that party competition is greatest in urban areas, but this is not always true. In one-party
states, voting patterns may center around a governor and his program or
urban-rural or regional alignments.[22]

In competitive northern states, party lines are frequently visible
on liberal-conservative issues with Democrats giving much support to
labor, welfare, and liberalized disability benefits legislation and Republicans fostering the interests of the business community. As is often the

[20] There are an enormous number of articles and small monographs on party considerations
and voting in the states. In addition to the standard textbooks in the legislative process, two works
that have brought together findings on state legislative parties are Malcolm E. Jewell, *The State Legislature: Politics and Practice*, Random House, Inc., New York, 1969, and Wilder Crane, Jr., and Meredith
W. Watts, Jr., *State Legislative Systems*, Prentice-Hall, Inc., Englewood Cliffs, N.J., 1968. An old work
with many data on party and other mechanisms is Belle Zeller (ed.), *American State Legislatures*, Thomas
Y. Crowell Company, New York, 1954.

[21] Party roll calls in numerous states are found in Crane and Watts, *op. cit.*, pp. 93–95, and
in Jewell, *op. cit.*, pp. 109–117.

[22] See Samuel C. Patterson, "Dimensions of Voting Behavior in a One-Party Legislature,"
Public Opinion Quarterly, vol. 26, pp. 185–200, 1962.

case in Congress, legislators of the two parties frequently differ over tax structure and spending. A study by Richard Dawson and James Robinson casts some doubt on whether lively competition in itself results in more generous social welfare policies.[23] These programs are apparently more closely related to socioeconomic factors, particularly to per capita income. Yet evidence suggests that in many states high party conflict is likely on measures dealing with labor-management questions, taxes and finance, social welfare, and land use. On such direct party matters as reapportionment, election laws, primaries, conventions, registration, civil service (where patronage may be involved), and gubernatorial appointments, it is not surprising to see high if not unanimous party cohesion. The same is to be expected on legislative leadership questions, such as the selection of the speaker of the lower house, president pro tem of the upper house, and chairmen of committees.

Conversely, the influence of party in state legislative alignments is not likely to be very important in such issues as gambling, liquor, crime and penal systems, highways, local government, water resources, health, and education. These and many other propositions about party conflict and legislative policy outputs, however, are in need of further examination. For example, on certain minor issues such as dog licenses or a local project for a popular fellow member, legislators are willing to build up "points" by supporting their partisan colleagues.

Party voting is also affected by majority-minority status. Minority parties in the state legislatures seem to have somewhat greater unity and higher cohesion than do majority parties, but exceptions can readily be found. Majority leaders often find cohesion is improved when the margin of control is reduced. Large majorities give latitude to individual members since many of the dominant party are convinced that their votes are not crucial to producing a majority. Generally both majority and minority parties have interest factional conflicts.

Finally, partisan voting is influenced by the legislator's own personal perceptions, the party organizational arrangements, and the skills of the leaders. One finds party men who are loyal because they see the party program as important. Some legislators are consistently mavericks who deviate regularly from party positions because of independent thought or constituency considerations. There are those who are indifferent to the party label and do not feel it important. Legislators, therefore, respond in quite different ways to pleas for party loyalty. Support of the party position, except for the strongly oriented party man, is more likely if it can be linked with other factors such as class, religion, ethnic background, or ideology.

[23]"Inter-party Competition, Economic Variables, and Welfare Policies in the American States," *Journal of Politics*, vol. 25, pp. 265–289, 1963.

The leadership can utilize party as a reference group (a group to whose norms the legislator refers for his behavior) to get support.[24] The party label helps the legislator to maintain identity. Over time, one's views on issues may be shaped by party identification. In many state legislatures, unlike Congress, the party caucus meets regularly; and party positions are discussed. On numerous matters, a party position is established in the caucus; and members are expected to go along. Some of the "stronger" governors have appeared at the caucuses to plead for unity. Floor leaders and speakers urge members "not to embarrass the governor" by voting in opposition to him. Much of the party influence is dependent, in the final analysis, on the skills of the leaders, whose power is highly personal and who can use their knowledge and skills to persuade members to rally behind what they identify as the party's program.

PARTIES AND THE COURTS

Treatment of the role of political parties in government is incomplete without some reference to their impact on the judiciary. Judges are linked into the state political system and into the norms of state politics. Negroes have found, for example, that they have a better chance for favorable decisions in the Southern federal courts than in the state courts.[25] Even so, black claimants have been more successful in the courts than in other parts of the state political system. In about half of the states, all or most judges are chosen in partisan elections.[26] In many other states, the governor and/or the legislature appoints the judges. Where chosen on a nonpartisan ballot, the party identification of judicial candidates is often known. Overall, Republicans have had considerably greater advantage in obtaining positions on the state benches than have the Democrats.[27] Although partisan election of judges obtains in many states, the judiciary does not always reflect the strength of the two parties, because of long overlapping terms of judges. Other nations have not considered it wise to permit judges to be subject to the temptation of a popular election and made the judiciary appointive, often with appointments restricted to persons specifically trained for the bench.

[24] For an analysis of illustrative leadership techniques in Connecticut, see James D. Barber, "Leadership Strategies for Legislative Party Cohesion," *Journal of Politics*, vol. 28, pp. 347–367, 1966. See also his *The Lawmakers: Recruitment and Adaptation to Legislative Life*, Yale University Press, New Haven, Conn., 1965.

[25] Kenneth N. Vines, "Federal District Judges and Race Relations Cases in the South," *Journal of Politics*, vol. 26, pp. 337–357, 1964, and "Southern State Supreme Courts and Race Relations," *Western Political Quarterly*, vol. 28, pp. 5–18, 1965.

[26] Methods of selection of judges in the fifty states is found in *The Book of the States, 1968–69*, Table 3, pp. 110–111.

[27] See Herbert Jacob, "The Effect of Institutional Differences in the Recruitment Process: The Case of State Judges," *Journal of Public Law*, vol. 13, pp. 104–119, 1964, and S. Sidney Ulmer, "The Political Party Variable in the Michigan Supreme Court," *Journal of Public Law*, vol. 11, pp. 352–362, 1962.

Political Functions of Partisanly Elected Judges. State and local party organizations are likely to be interested in retaining partisan, popular
election of judges because of the patronage at the disposal of the bench.
Auctioneers, clerks, guardians, receivers, referees, and trusteeships are
distributed among political leaders and offer a source of manpower in
campaigns and of revenue in the form of campaign contributions. Probate and surrogate jobs are potentially lucrative to the party. Persons
wishing judgeships are looked over by the party organization, not only
in terms of their ability and vote-getting powers, but also for their willingness to turn over some or all patronage to it. A number of judges do
political work for the ticket during a campaign, in some cases openly,
but more often quietly.

In addition to patronage and campaign activity, members of the
bench can be useful in rendering personal service and legal advice to
members of the organization and in giving preferential treatment to
political favorites. When this is done today, it is done with care and
circumspection. In the past in boss-controlled cities there was at times
collusion between judges and the police administration, with guaranteed
protection to underworld friends of the machine, even against the
police. "Political" decisions could be rendered in civil service cases, and
there was some legal graft in decisions involving bankruptcies, fore-
closures, and estates. Today it is very rare to find judges serving machines
in these ways, but incidents do break into print from time to time. The
present-day judge is more likely to operate above board, but parties are
able to use his prestige, knowledge, and advice to advance the cause of
some of those in the party. In municipal elections, party chairmen may
use victories in judicial posts as morale builders for the party by citing
them as evidence of a trend, "a vote of confidence in the Nixon administration," a "repudiation" of a state administration, and so on. Local
party leaders appear at times to have made a reality, at least in their
own minds, of the "party-in-the-judiciary."

Judicial nominations serve a multitude of political functions.
They help attract to the party promising young lawyers who give it
years of service in the hope of social and economic security and freedom
from the drudgery of further political chores. In a number of counties
in states with strong party organization and a partisan judicial ballot,
few young lawyers can hope to become judges unless they perform many
years of service to a party. The party leaders say in effect, "You stay with
us, and some day you'll be a magistrate or a judge." The young lawyer
then becomes attached to a political club and, if he "works out all right,"
may obtain a clerkship in the judge's office, become a referee or a counsel for a legislative committee, and so on, until a vacancy occurs in one
of the smaller judgeships. By this time he has become fully educated in
party politics, has acquired an "appreciation" and "understanding" not

forgotten when occupying the bench. In New York the channels to judicial office are effectively controlled by the parties, and the inducement to seek them is, among other things, financial, with excellent chances for a lifetime job through fairly easy reelection once in fourteen years.

Like other elective positions, judicial offices are politically useful as consolations. A chain or catalyst reaction can be set off by the opening of a judgeship, which makes room for others to vacate positions and move on. Although likely to be publicly denied, certain officeholders are sometimes "kicked upstairs" to a court position for political reasons. A person may be moved from position of attorney general because he has alienated interests or because he must make way for someone else to take over his position. Judgeships then are potentially politically negotiable, like many administrative or elective posts, and may be used to pay political debts or to enhance the positions of certain leaders within a party.

Judicial conventions in New York are used to balance the party ticket ethnically and religiously, to reward certain suburbs, and to penalize others. One nomination to the State Supreme Court went to a Puerto Rican and was employed to generate enthusiasm for the entire ticket and to motivate Puerto Ricans to get themselves registered and to the polls. Officials of the Liberal party sometimes form coalitions with Republicans on judicial appointments to show that they do not invariably wear the Democratic party's collar and to obtain some patronage or other preferment.

These examples of party-judgeship relations may deem to deny the concept of an impartial, independent bench and to cast aspersions on the integrity of the decisions of judges, if not to accuse them of rank partisanship and favoritism in questions of law. Many states have excellent judiciaries, even though judges are popularly elected. However, it is clear that in matters of personnel the judge is loyal to his party and that the potential judge who possesses vote-getting ability stands a greater chance of elevation to the bench than one who does not have these qualities of availability. The parties offer a channel for nomination and election to judicial positions that might not be open to persons who would otherwise have to depend on an executive for appointment.

Federal Appointments. Although judges of the federal courts are appointed by the President and confirmed by the Senate, political considerations are paramount in judicial appointments to the lower federal courts. The federal bench offers some patronage opportunities and also a chance to reward loyal party men who can qualify for the office. The customs and traditions in nominating and confirming judges of the lower courts differ markedly from those connected with justices of the

Supreme Court.[28] Appointments to the district courts are essentially patronage, with United States senators or state party organizations in most cases virtually making the actual choice. Sponsoring senators often announce the appointment themselves. The President has a much freer hand in the selection of circuit court judges, whose districts cover several states, than of district judges, who serve within individual states. Party considerations are not so important as social philosophy in Supreme Court appointments, and for them senatorial courtesy is not an overriding consideration. In actions on Supreme Court nominees, the Senate is not unduly concerned about the views of the senators from the nominee's state and has frequently turned down nominations having their backing. A glance at the background of those appointed to the Supreme Court is illustrative of former Supreme Court Justice Felix Frankfurter's assertion that "the correlation between prior judicial experience and fitness for the functions of the Supreme Court is zero." Only a small number of justices had careers only of judicial experience before their appointments. Between 1900 and 1964, the largest single group of appointees were without such experience and came directly from elective public office or from a federal position. Of the last five Chief Justices, only Harlan F. Stone and Warren E. Burger had not held an elective office. Several persons whose principal activity was elective politics were appointed to the Court, and the smallest number were appointed directly from private practice or law faculties.

Sixteen justices either had previously served on federal or state courts or were promoted directly from them. Several of these were mixtures of jurists and politicians. William H. Moody, Fred M. Vinson, and Sherman Minton, for example, went from politics to the bench and were back in politics when appointed to the Supreme Court. Charles Evans Hughes went from Governor of New York to an associate justiceship, then resigned to run unsuccessfully as Republican candidate for President in 1916. He then returned to private law practice and was appointed Chief Justice in 1930. William R. Day, William Howard Taft, and Mahlon Pitney served in political office between their earlier judicial experience and their choice for the Supreme Court. Thus fewer than a dozen justices were limited only to judicial experience before their appointments.[29]

The appointments to federal courts in the South have taken on peculiar significance in recent years, and every prospective judge in the South is closely scrutinized for his views on racial issues. President Kennedy learned that his freedom of selection was severely restricted by the

[28] For political and other factors in appointments to the federal courts see Joseph P. Harris, *The Advice and Consent of the Senate*, University of California Press, Berkeley, 1953, chap. 17.
[29] Since the Court's establishment in 1789, however, about half the justices had had some judicial experience before being appointed to the Supreme Court.

TABLE 8-1   Partisan affiliation of federal judges at time of appointment

Appointing President	Democrat	Republican	Other or unknown	Total appointed
Taft	10	47	5	62
Wilson	71	1		72
Harding	2	49		51
Coolidge	4	77	3	84
Hoover	12	57		69
Roosevelt	217	8		225
Truman	118	13		131
Eisenhower	11	175		186
Kennedy	110	11	3	124
Johnson	159	9		168

Source: *Hearings before Subcommittee 5 of the House Judiciary Committee on Bills to Provide Appointment of Additional Circuit and District Judges*, 87th Cong., 1st Sess., Mar. 1 and 2, 1961, pp. 402-403, and *Congressional Quarterly*, Inc. for Kennedy and Johnson. Figures include only those confirmed by the Senate.

deep-seated tradition that Southern senators control judicial appointments by a President of their party. He had to work within the political lines of the South and found that several of his appointees rendered decisions at sharp variance with the positions argued by the Department of Justice in civil rights cases. Eisenhower appointees, on the other hand, were essentially beyond the control of the Southern senators and were free from segregation-oriented commitments. Several of them assumed leading roles in civil rights matters and were most helpful to the Kennedy administration.

Other factors that enter into the choice of justices are geography and religion, although there is no ironclad rule. There has been a tendency to scatter appointments among various sections of the country. In 1970, for example, the Chief Justice came from Minnesota and the eight associate justices were from Alabama, Colorado, Washington, Minnesota (two), New Jersey, New York, and Ohio—representative of every major section of the country. During the present century, at least one Catholic and one Jew have sat on the Court, but officially there is no Catholic or Jewish seat.

As shown in Table 8-1 most Presidents look to members of their own party for the great majority of positions on all levels of the federal courts. Senator Alexander Wiley, Republican from Wisconsin, in 1947 launched an attack on what he called the "New Deal, grossly lopsided Democratic leftist" character of the federal bench.[30] He said that he might approve some additional "conservative" Democrats but called the Roosevelt-Truman appointments an "indefensible overrepresentation of the Democratic Party." President Eisenhower swung appointments

[30] *The New York Times*, Jan. 6 and 10, 1947.

strongly in the direction of Republicans, and appointees of Presidents Kennedy and Johnson were almost all Democrats. Obviously, American Presidents tend to select judges from their own party, and exhortation to the contrary will scarcely bring about change. Despite the criticism of using judicial appointments as patronage, the custom has been in operation for at least three-quarters of a century. The American Bar Association reports[31] that from the first Cleveland administration to 1955 no President made less than 82 percent of his judicial appointments from his own party, and partisanship is somewhat greater in the selection of lower federal judges since it is customary to have at least one member of the opposition party on the Supreme Court.

The Supreme Court has from time to time been brought into national campaigns. Senator Goldwater in 1964 made it an important issue and President Johnson said it was not an appropriate subject for campaign oratory. Goldwater asserted that the Court was diminishing the freedom of state and local officials to handle their problems and especially condemned the Court's decisions on reapportionment of legislatures and for holding prayers in the public schools as unconstitutional. One study demonstrated a sizable correlation between attitudes toward the Court and support for Goldwater although it made no claim that the campaign was responsible for the correlation.[32] Although this study made no correlation between party identification and attitudes toward the Supreme Court or Goldwater, an analysis of polls conducted from 1937 to date suggests that the political party focusing on the President supplies a broad orientation to the Court as an institution. "Democrats are distinctly more favorable toward the Court than are Republicans, except when there is a Republican President; at those times Republicans and Democrats move closer together in their approval of the Court, and the party differential is eliminated, other factors emerging as the correlates of attitude."[33] In general the sharp polarization between Republicans and Democrats toward the Court in 1937 has remained to the present, although it was substantially reduced during the Eisenhower years.

Party Affiliation and Judicial Decisions. The extent to which one's party faith influences judicial behavior is moot. Do, for example, judges show the same value positions as their political parties? To answer this question affirmatively, we should have to assume first that a judge's party has a position and second that this position is visible to the judge and to

[31]*Annual Reports of the American Bar Association*, vol. 81, p. 439, 1956.
[32]Walter F. Murphy and Joseph Tanenhaus, "Public Opinion and the Supreme Court," *Public Opinion Quarterly*, vol. 32, pp. 31–50, 1968.
[33]Kenneth M. Dolbeare and Phillip E. Hammond, "The Political Party Basis of Attitudes toward the Supreme Court," *Public Opinion Quarterly*, vol. 32, pp. 16–30, 1968.

those studying his rulings. Studies on the party variable in judicial decisions are being conducted and in time will shed considerable light on its importance. Some analyses have been published, and they point toward the following conclusions: First, there is considerable evidence that party is a more important variable in the legislative process than in the judicial process. It is easier to establish criteria of party differences in the former, and it is possible to resort to countless roll calls to determine the degree and consistency of support of a party position.

Second, judges on the same court may have similar liberal or conservative viewpoints even though they are members of different political parties. Chief Justice Earl Warren, a Republican, shared opinion after opinion with his liberal colleagues who were Democrats, but he came, in the first instance, from the progressive wing of the party in California. A judge's tendency to have a liberal or conservative viewpoint will not necessarily mean that he is or was a member of the political party most closely corresponding to his social views. In this he is no different from legislators who stay with a party holding national views at variance with their own.

Third, in the face of the problems that make correlations difficult, there is evidence that, for whatever the reason, nonunanimous decisions tend to show some party differentials among judges. Ulmer's study of Michigan Supreme Court justices found that on numerous decisions dealing with workmen's compensation and unemployment insurance claims, the Democratic justices were more favorable toward claimants than the Republican judges. This could be testimony to the homogeneity of social attitudes among justices of similar party faith, but Ulmer asserts that "Democratic justice is more sensitive to the claims of the unemployed and injured than Republican justice."[34]

Stuart S. Nagel's broader studies of the decisions of some 300 state and federal judges in fifteen fields found more or less similar characteristics.[35] Democratic judges tended toward the liberal direction to a greater extent than Republican judges. Democrats, for example, were more prone than Republicans to favor the defense in criminal cases, the wife in a divorce settlement, the administrative agency in business regulation, the claimant in unemployment compensation, the government in tax cases, the debtor in credit-debtor cases, the injured party in motor vehicle cases, and the labor union in union-management matters. Nagel is not implying that some judges consciously vote for a party line but that it is more likely for them to "rely on their personal

[34] Ulmer, *op. cit.*, p. 362.
[35] Stuart S. Nagel, "Political Party Affiliation and Judges' Decisions," *American Political Science Review*, vol. 60, pp. 843–850, 1961. See also Stuart S. Nagel, "Political Parties and Judicial Review in American History," *Journal of Public Law*, vol. 11, pp. 328–340, 1962; and Wallace Mendelson, "Judicial Review and Party Politics," *Vanderbilt Law Review*, vol. 12, pp. 447–457, 1959.

standards of value in reaching a decision, and these same personal standards also frequently account for their party affiliation. That is to say that party affiliation and decisional propensity for the liberal or conservative position correlate with each other because they are frequently effects of the same cause."[36] A party affiliation may reinforce the judge's values.

Attributing a judicial decision to party influence demands caution. It is highly probable that a liberal-conservative syndrome is more influential than a Democratic-Republican one. What is important in the study of judicial decisions (as is true in legislative and executive ones as well) is the personal background of the judge. His socioeconomic status, his previous occupations, his associations, and his intensities of feeling are all part of his makeup and condition his outlook on the bench. There are institutional expectations of detachment and objectivity, which likewise have their influence on him and serve over time to neutralize certain experiences in his background. He is, in a way, expected to act differently, or at least less partisanly, on the bench than the legislator and executive in their public roles. But judicial behavior, as other types of political behavior, has its roots in one's experiences before accession to the bench, and these, as well as the factors operative on the judge while on the bench, afford a most interesting area of investigation. At this stage of our knowledge the social, economic, and political views of justices appear to be more important than their party preferences.

In concluding this section on the party-in-the-government, we may repeat that the political party is a significant tie, a thread running through all branches of government in the separation-of-powers system. Party influence can be seen to be greater at one time than at another but is apparent in bringing together in some common cause the popularly elected executive, certain administrators, and the legislators; its relationship to the judiciary remains vague and amorphous, but even here the party role is at least partially visible. Parties compete with other factors bidding for the ear of public men; they are but one of the variables affecting their official conduct. Some officials are more influenced by parties than others, for the thrust and intensity of party loyalty and feeling differs markedly from person to person. Despite this, parties promote political stability; they provide an instrument for cooperation among public officials themselves and with some of the general public in policy making. The party is an integrating institution; it is indispensable in drawing leadership from the inner and outer recesses of the community to the government. In Part Five we shall discuss how the decentralized, nonideological American major parties perform their function of selecting and electing men and women to public office.

[36] Nagel, "Political Party Affiliation and Judges' Decisions," p. 847.

FOR FURTHER READING

Burns, James M.: *The Deadlock of Democracy*, 1963.

Clapp, Charles L.: *The Congressman: His Work as He Sees It*, 1963.

Danelski, David J.: *A Supreme Court Justice Is Appointed*, 1964.

Francis, Wayne L.: *Legislative Issues in the Fifty States: A Comparative Analysis*, 1967.

Froman, Lewis A., Jr.: *Congressmen and Their Constituencies*, 1963.

Gross, Bertram M.: *The Legislative Struggle*, 1953.

Heard, Alexander (ed.): *State Legislatures in American Politics*, 1966.

Keefe, William J., and Morris S. Ogul: *The American Legislative Process: Congress and the States*, 1968.

Matthews, Donald R.: *U.S. Senators and Their World*, 1960.

Murphy, Walter F., and C. Herman Pritchett: *Courts, Judges and Politics*, 1961.

Patterson, Samuel C. (ed.): *Midwest Legislative Politics*, 1967.

Robinson, James A.: *Congress and Foreign Policy-making*, 1962.

Schubert, Glendon: *Judicial Policy-Making*, 1965.

_____: *The Judicial Mind: The Attitudes and Ideologies of Supreme Court Justices, 1946–1963*, 1965.

Thomas, Norman C., and Karl A. Lamb: *Congress: Politics and Practice*, 1964.

Wahlke, John C., et al.: *The Legislative System*, 1962.

Westerfield, H. B.: *Foreign Policy and Party Politics: Pearl Harbor to Korea*, 1955.

White, William S.: *Citadel: The Story of the U.S. Senate*, 1957.

PART FIVE NOMINATIONS AND ELECTIONS

> The right of popular government is incomplete
> unless it includes the right of the voters not merely
> to choose between candidates when they have
> been nominated but also the right to determine who
> these candidates shall be.
>
> THEODORE ROOSEVELT

CHAPTER 9 RECRUITMENT OF CANDIDATES

In nearly all modern nations, certain public offices are filled by popular election. But here the similarity disappears. In numerous totalitarian nations, the ruling party draws up a list of its nominees with little or no help from outside sources. The voter is then allowed to subscribe to or disapprove of the list. If he disapproves, he has no alternative nominee to support but must be content with merely voting no or, in a few instances, with writing in an opposing name. Since all parties are outlawed except the one in power, the end result is essentially the same as appointment of the palace guard by an absolute monarch.

The approach of democratic nations differs substantially in emphasizing a meaningful suffrage as one involving one group of persons running against another. In most democratic nations other than the United States, the crucial function of proposing candidates is performed by the electoral political party. In the United States, many aspects of the nominating process are not within the exclusive province of parties; nevertheless, the selection of candidates and conducting campaigns are major reasons for being. During the months from announcements of candidacies to the day of general election the parties are more visible than between elections. The greatest incentive to join parties comes during elections. Nominations and general elections which, taken together, constitute the electoral process, tie the electoral and government parties more closely together than at any other time with the common goal of capturing public office. The five chapters of this section will examine the party roles and other factors brought to bear on the electoral system. This affords a chance to look at parties in the context of the offices they seek rather than in an issue context, although issues are one of the resources used to attain office.

This chapter examines major factors in the process of recruitment, which involves screening those persons who have the personality characteristics, motivations, and requisites for elective office. Informal and formal mechanisms are used to select candidates and to build support for designation; and a great variety of social, political, personal, and institutional considerations enter the process.

BECOMING A CANDIDATE

Before sketching the development of the mechanisms, we shall consider the participants, conditions, and the system underlying the process of recruitment. With many if not most candidates there is some degree of self-recruitment. Comparatively few are genuinely drafted and few self-starters simply announce their candidacy without consultation with party and other leaders. Probably not many potential candidates indulge in thorough self-appraisal and evaluation of the institutional factors at work—and some later wish they had! The nomination process is essentially coalition building, and many fail to understand the realities of putting together a coalition that can first win the designation and then build incrementally to win the election.

Personal Considerations. It is well established that public men tend to have personality traits that motivate them to seek office. (These were observed in Chapter 5.) They have drives, needs, and values that predispose them to political activity. Also, they are likely to come from social positions that will provide resources helpful in seeking office—among them prestige, education, visibility, and the higher-status occupations. Further, various informal recruiting groups are aware that some attributes are more important than others for potential success at the polls. Anyone who considers becoming a candidate should carefully evaluate his own qualifications in terms of motivation, resources, and opportunity. Women, representatives of ethnic minorities, uneducated and low-income persons, who possess the internal drive, more often than not lack resources and may confront situational factors that weaken their chances for success.

In assessing a possible candidacy, an aspirant should consider whether he is seeking nomination for the first time or, as an incumbent officeholder, he is seeking nomination for a different office. When a person holds an office that is manifestly in line for the next office he seeks, he gains an advantage in the direct primary since he is known to some voters by reason of his present office. An incumbent seeking re-nomination for the same office is in a favored position in the primary because he likely has some influence if not control over the party organization in his bailiwick. In seeking office initially, one is particularly faced with personal questions of how badly he wants the office and for what purposes. What would be the personal sacrifices and costs to him, in terms of his family, occupation, and social relationships, in running a campaign and, if he wins, in holding office? Does he want the office badly enough to make the personal sacrifices whether he wins or loses? An evaluation of prospects for a general election as well as primary election victory are a part of this appraisal.

He should estimate what manpower, money, and other resources that he will need and will be available to him. A highly important element in probable success is name familiarity. In the American open society, many persons become well-known in some private endeavor, an important asset when seeking the nomination. Consideration of winners of primaries throughout the nation shows that many had achieved prominence and exposure that helped them to enter at a higher level than would ordinarily be expected. Before he became Governor of New Jersey, Woodrow Wilson achieved prominence as a college president and after-dinner speaker. Motion-picture actors George Murphy and Ronald Reagan were successful on first try for top California offices. George Romney was a well-known automobile executive in Michigan. Lesser offices have been captured by prominent athletes. A number of college professors have found ready-made supporters among their graduates.

One's relationships and contacts with private interest groups constitute a resource that might compensate at least in part for lack of a celebrated name. Lester G. Seligman's study of party recruitment in Oregon found that seeking the nomination was largely a "group enterprise" in which would-be nominees relied on their social relationships to fulfill their objectives.[1] Among the groups providing primary instigation of candidacy or secondary support were business, farm, labor,

[1] "Party Recruitment and Party Structure: A Case Study," *American Political Science Review*, vol. 55, pp. 77–86, 1961.

church, and local community groups. A medical professional organization was primarily responsible for advancing one of its lobbyists as a
candidate. Newspapers and trade associations afford examples of other
groups that are influential in candidates' entries into primaries.

As might be expected, party organizations varying from the
county executive to the Young Republicans or Women's Democratic
Club are found in the process of selection of candidates. Party chairmen,
factional leaders, and state and local officeholders are also among those
potentially helpful or capable of giving secondary support to prospective candidates. It is not unusual for leaders of the minority party to seek
and draft persons to run because of the failure of volunteers to enter a
race where defeat seems certain in the general election. Yet a party organization that wishes to field a full slate of candidates must persuade
someone to run for office even in the face of an almost certain defeat at
the hands of a popular incumbent or candidate of the opposition party.
Drafted candidates are often, but by no means invariably, drawn from
the ranks of party activists. Sometimes the leaders approach well-known
persons outside the party activists. Sometimes the leaders approach
well-known persons outside the party and promise them backing for a
"long-shot" attempt. Such a co-opted person may attract enough votes
from independents and the opposition party to win or, if losing, help the
prestige of the minority party.

Institutional-Situational Factors. The political environment of the moment enters into the strategies of those seeking nomination. One factor
is the number of other persons who want the nomination and the support for each. Another is whether an incumbent is being challenged.
Majority-minority party status and the presence or absence of an overriding issue are in the situational background. A candidate's relationship
to party officials such as precinct committeemen can also be a significant
asset (or weakness) in a party primary. Obviously, the nominating system
itself, that is, whether it is a closed or open primary or convention
imposes certain conditions on an aspirant.

Broadly, the opportunity rates for becoming an elective public
official vary a great deal and depend on the number of offices available,
the size of the electoral constituency, and the voting habits of the constituency. One reason—though perhaps not publicly acknowledged—
for retention of the long ballot is to give the minority party more opportunity to capture lesser offices and build up challenges for top posts such
as governor or United States senator.

Joseph A. Schlesinger studied the opportunity rates to achieve
a major political office during a twelve-year period in each state. He
found the greatest number of chances per 100,000 population to achieve
office in Nevada (15.62), Vermont (12.18), and Delaware (10.69), and

smallest number of chances in New York (1.81), California, and New Jersey (1.88 each).[2] Real chances for attaining an office vary some from the maximum chances because of turnover rates during the time period.

Turnover or transitory offices are a part of the political system. Where the state constitution limits terms of office, opportunities for attaining an office are increased, for such offices must be vacated at periodic intervals. In other cases, turnover is high because of competition and the difficulty of reelection. Governors, lieutenant governors and attorneys general usually fall in this class; and this turnover improves chances for nonincumbents to attain offices.

The United States senatorship emerges as a career office with average tenure of senators varying from eight years in Kentucky to as high as twenty-four years in some other states. United States representatives, too, especially the South, are often elected to serve many successive terms. In the absence of legal restraints, the same person has often been able to hold a position such as state auditor, treasurer, or secretary of state for several terms, with outsiders having little real chance for a successful challenge. The state legislatures vary enormously in opportunity rates; but turnover is usually high, with legislators leaving the position voluntarily to run for higher office or to return to their private pursuits. For this reason, many persons ambitious for office try initially for a state legislative position.

There is no certain route or ladder to higher office, but those aspiring to upward mobility find that the structure in opportunities is national in scope from the lowest local position to Congress and the Presidency. Table 9-1 shows penultimate offices held by winning and losing candidates for governor and United States senator before becoming candidates for state executive or the national office. (It does not show the numerous offices held by many candidates before the penultimate one). The table shows that very few were without any previous office-holding experience before becoming a candidate for either of the offices. Moreover, a slightly higher percentage of the losers were those who tried for the office without previous experience in public office. Obviously, if one wishes to become a successful candidate for governor the surer path is through the state legislature, another statewide position, or a law enforcement post — some 58 percent held such office at the time they ran. Elevation to the Senate runs much less directly from the state legislature or law enforcement and more heavily from the United States House of Representatives or statewide position — nearly half moved from one of these two offices to the Senate. Also, the higher the office, the more evidence of orderly advancement. Schlesinger found that

[2] Joseph A. Schlesinger, *Ambition and Politics: Political Careers in the United States*, Rand McNally & Company, Chicago, 1966, pp. 50–51. Chapters 2 and 3 are recommended for analyses of political opportunities in the states.

TABLE 9-1   Previous office careers of governors and United States senators

Penultimate previous office	Governor*		Senator†	
	Winner	Loser	Winner	Loser
State legislature	18.88%	19.77%	8.89%	13.70%
Law enforcement	19.34	20.91	12.67	17.78
Statewide elective	19.97	15.23	22.22	14.29
Congress	9.52	6.36	26.67	14.29
Administrative	13.26	13.64	14.44	21.57
Local elective	6.86	12.73	4.67	6.12
No previous office	8.11	9.32	8.22	11.37

Source: Adapted from Joseph A. Schlesinger, *Ambition and Politics: Political Careers in the United States,* Rand McNally & Company, 1966, pp. 91–96.
*1900 to 1958.
†1914 to 1958.

"men who come to the office of governor and senator through the important penultimate offices of lieutenant governor or United States
representative have more previous office experience than men who
come from the lesser office of state legislator. Very few of the governors
(11 percent) who become senators start as governors; only 18 percent
of the United States representatives who became senators start in
Congress."[3]

The realistic candidate also appraises movement among different
kinds of offices within the separation-of-powers system. Local judges
are likely to find ambition more readily satisfied in seeking a state judicial position than a state executive or federal legislative office. Congressmen infrequently seek the office of governor and not many local
elective officials have gone on directly to the governorship. State legislative floor leaders, on the other hand, frequently deal with governors
and can feature in their campaigns that they feel equipped to become
chief executive. An officer such as attorney general who has a statewide
electorate has the same constituency should he become a candidate for
governor; a mayor, county commissioner, or legislator is not so situated.
Popular mayors have often found in primaries that their drawing power
outside their city is not large enough to win. Few mayors of New York,
Chicago, and Los Angeles have succeeded in capturing nominations for
governor or United States senator and those with such ambitions are
often privately discouraged by party leaders from seeking the posts.

These general observations do not apply in every state since the
opportunities and patterns vary markedly from state to state. Yet, in the
larger picture, they demonstrate the importance of constitutional, legal,
and situational factors that face those who seek the designation of their
party for the first office or, if an incumbent, desire to move to another.

[3] *Ibid.,* p. 97.

DESIGNATION THROUGH CAUCUS AND CONVENTION

Nominating machinery in the United States has developed from the relatively simple to the complex, from a mere self-announcement to an elaborate system, first of caucuses, then of conventions, and now of direct primary election. In early America, persons in an area generally knew each other, and candidates for a local office presented themselves to the electorate on their own announcement. Sometimes town meetings were held, and the nomination was offered to a certain person. He accepted and agreed to run as an obligation. The more common practice now is for the man to seek the office.

The nominating caucus, as it is popularly understood today, is a preliminary and private meeting of certain self-appointed members of a political party for the purpose of selecting candidates.[4] In colonial Boston, even before the establishment of parties, the caucus was used for choosing candidates in small areas.

After the Revolution, the choice of statewide candidates posed a problem because of the difficulties of transportation and communication. Caucus members at one end of a state could not easily confer with those at the other. Soon, therefore, a convenient device known as the legislative caucus developed; the party members in the state legislature met while in the capital to decide upon and publicly announce the ticket for statewide offices. In the early days of its operation, the legislative caucus had much to recommend it. It was simple and inexpensive. It overcame the geographical barriers standing in the way of canvasing party leaders in the communities. The caucus also placed nominations in the hands of the party's representatives and provided the voters with some guidance in the selection of candidates. Nominations were made by men who were in the government and who had some knowledge of the talents and abilities required for public office. More than this, the caucus members were widely acquainted with men who possessed the requisites for public office.

In spite of its merits, the caucus was short-lived and was criticized on many grounds. The popularity of the legislative branch also began to decline, and it was natural for the public to express less confidence in the legislators' choices. A major objection to the legislative

[4]The term *caucus* is used in a number of different senses today. The nominating caucus is to be distinguished from the meetings or conferences of party members in a legislature for the purpose of deciding on committee assignments and on the party's position on public issues; the party caucuses are often referred to as the Senate Republican caucus, the House Democratic caucus, and the like. Before 1830, there were at least three types of nominating caucus—the informal type held by local party leaders, the legislative caucuses composed of party members of the legislature, and mongrel or mixed caucuses in which legislators and outside representatives united to select party candidates. In some New England states today, the caucus is a precinct meeting of all enrolled party members called for the purpose of nominating candidates; more properly, this resembles a primary, for it is an open rather than a secret meeting and includes all party members instead of a few.

caucus stemmed from its undemocratic character. The growing equalitarianism of the West viewed the caucus as lending itself to bargains and deals of the few, with the many left out of the choice of personnel. Thanks in part to Andrew Jackson and his supporters, the death knell was rung on the never thoroughly institutionalized congressional caucus in 1828, when no presidential nominees were placed in the field by it. With the congressional caucus discredited, the device could not hope to survive in the states.

As dissatisfaction with the caucus increased, younger men within the parties began to protest the arrogance of those who controlled it, and they counseled the people to demand a voice in the selection of the candidates. Even when the caucus was in widespread use, several Middle Atlantic states were using the delegate convention to make nominations for county offices. Capitalizing on democratic impulses that condemned the caucus as autocratic, Republican politicians in 1824 issued a call in several states for a state nominating convention to choose candidates for governor. The convention consisted of as many delegates as there were representatives in the state legislature. By the end of the decade the state convention became widely used.

In theory at least, the convention possessed outstanding merit. The stairway of conventions from local to state and eventually to the national level provided a hierarchy of deliberative bodies to consider candidates and issues. Here divisive interests within the counties and state could be compromised and ironed out. The convention offered a vehicle to reduce extreme factionalism and to promote unity. Compromise nominations would result in balanced tickets from all parts of the state or county. Nominations would more likely include able but not widely known men who remained in political oblivion under the caucus system. The delegate convention appeared to offer an excellent example of representative democracy. Supposedly, the people would choose the best and most outstanding men to represent them in the convention. The Constitution itself could be pointed to as the product of a convention of wise men. The men chosen to participate in the conventions, moreover, would have to answer to the voters of their party for the nominations made and the policies drafted.

Experience with the convention on state and local levels failed to bear out these merits. Most of the weaknesses of the convention system in the nineteenth century were due to their unrepresentative composition and undemocratic organization and procedure. The unit of representation and apportionment of delegates was left to the party committees so that when delegate districts were drawn up by the party there was a tendency to resort to gerrymandering in favor of the faction in power. The factional and machine leaders were well organized and successfully chose either themselves or their own men as delegates to attend the convention. All too frequently the "best" persons failed to participate in the selection of delegates. Underworld elements were in a position to influence the choice of nominees through their men in the convention. The buying and selling of places in the convention also was not unknown.

Although the convention offered a chance to democratize nominations, it failed to elicit widespread popular enthusiasm. Voters did not go to the polls in large numbers to choose delegates to the convention, and many considered it an uninteresting burden. Public-spirited members of the party too often shunned the opportunity to seek a place in the convention. Others who were delegates often found themselves hopelessly outnumbered and ineffective in the face of such a professional perversion of the convention. These abuses, leading to an ever-widening gap between voters and delegates, made it extremely difficult for the convention system to fulfill the expectations of honest popular control of nominations.

In Delaware and Indiana, the convention is still an important agency since it nominates the statewide candidates. New York replaced the statewide nomination convention in 1967 by giving the state committees power to designate their candidates; others who have a 25 percent committee vote or gather 10,000 petition signatures can challenge the committees' choices in a statewide primary. Connecticut and Massachusetts combine the convention with a challenge primary. Conventions nominate statewide candidates; and, if no other candidates challenges them, their names go on the general election ballot without an intervening primary. If a challenger amasses at least 20 percent of the convention vote he can take the choice into a primary.[5] The Republican party in the South often takes advantage of state laws permitting the use of conventions instead of primaries. A few states employ the convention for certain judicial and other offices. More than a quarter of the states have retained provision for the use of conventions either for some candidates or for some aspects of nomination. Conventions permit the party leaders to maintain more control over candidates and officeholders than is possible in the primaries, and some advocates of strong parties recommend their readoption.

Party conventions are rather widely used to select party officers and a majority of delegates to the national conventions are chosen by congressional district and state conventions. Many conventions are scenes of bitter struggles over party leadership.

[5] See Duane Lockhard, *Connecticut's Challenge Primary: A Study in Legislative Politics*, McGraw-Hill Book Company, New York, 1960.

NOMINATION BY PRIMARY ELECTION

Development. The origin of the direct primary elections remains somewhat obscure, but they seem to have been first used by the Democratic party in Crawford County, Pennsylvania, in 1842. This Crawford County System was voluntarily instituted by numerous local party organizations in parts of the South after the Civil War. It was characterized by many of the same abuses as the convention, with manipulation and fraudulent counting of ballots. By 1900, most of the present features of primaries had appeared, but still no state had enacted a mandatory law putting primaries on the same footing as the election. When Robert M. La Follette became Governor of Wisconsin, he succeeded in pushing through a mandatory statewide primary system in 1903. The party convention was relieved of all its nominating functions, which were assumed by the primaries. Mandatory direct primary laws were soon widely adopted in other states, but the movement was not completed until 1955, when Connecticut adopted it.[6]

The growth of primaries was not limited to any one section, but the Eastern seaboard states were slower to adopt it. It proceeded more rapidly where social and economic discontent was greater. Initial motivation stemmed from a desire to provide greater public participation in the selection of officials in places where the convention of one party in practice monopolized their designation. In the one-party Southern states, for example, the direct primary was widely adopted in order to give voters some voice in the selection of public officers. Strong democratic inclinations led Western states to substitute the primary for the convention, and the primaries became part of the gospel of the Progressive movement. The selection process was brought under considerable popular control, and the influence of party organization in nominating was minimized. The American political party began as a voluntary, extralegal institution without constitutional sanction and remained essentially an extralegal institution until after the Civil War when laws were enacted for protecting party caucuses and conventions against corrupt practices. Thereafter, legal regulations spread rapidly in all states and were increased in scope. The primaries required much regulation, and today a discussion of the regulation of parties is to a considerable extent a discussion of direct primary laws in most states. There are only a few statutes dealing with state and county conventions,

[6] There are many variations in application and detail. The student is urged to make a careful analysis of the legal structure and operation of the primaries in his own state. A compilation of primary laws was prepared by the League of Women Voters of New York and published by the National Municipal League in 1958 under the title *Compilation of the Forty-eight Direct Primary Systems.* For a brief history of primaries see V. O. Key, Jr., *American State Politics: An Introduction.* Alfred A. Knopf, Inc., New York, 1956. The biennial *Book of the States* summarizes the state-by-state methods of nominations.

such as those defining what constitutes a convention and setting the time for it. The regulations of the nominating process in the states indicate the importance with which this historic function of party is regarded.

Types of Partisan Primaries. The state legislatures, in addition to authorizing the holding of primaries at public expense and providing for certain technical details, must decide on the important policy question of what type of primary. Essentially this involves determining how and whom to qualify for participation in the primary election. The South and the great majority of the rest of the states use closed primaries, in which only those persons willing to submit to a test of party membership may cast their votes.

Tests of membership are imposed in one of two ways. The enrollment system simply requires the voter to state his party affiliation at the time of registration or when he appears to vote in the primary. On the day of the primary, he identifies himself to the polling officials and receives the ballot of his designated party. Under the challenge system the voter declares his party affiliation when he applies to vote in the primary. If challenged, the election officials ask him to assert that he belongs to the party, that he supported its candidates at the last election, or that he intends to vote for them at the coming election. Persons giving no affiliation may not vote. Persons can change parties at the next opportunity for registration or file a declaration with a clerk a certain period of time prior to the election.

Closed primaries are based on the principle that only voters who are willing to enroll in the party or publicly declare their affiliation with it should be permitted to have a voice in selecting the party's candidates. The party election is closed to independents and to adherents of the opposition who might "raid" the primary by voting for weak candidates.

Idaho, Michigan, Minnesota, Montana, North Dakota, Utah, and Wisconsin use the open primary, which permits all qualified voters to participate in the primary election without a membership test. The voter is given a single ballot with all parties listed, but he is permitted to vote in only one party column. If he votes for candidates of more than one party, his ballot is rejected. A variation in Wisconsin and Idaho gives the voter ballots of all parties of which he marks candidates for one party and returns the other ballots to a "blank ballot" box. Alaska and Washington provide a still wider open system, popularly called the blanket primary, which permits voters to vote for candidates of either party. The primary ballot contains the names of all candidates for party nominations, grouped by offices, as in the general election. The voter may support Democratic candidates for certain offices and Republicans for others. He is free to vote for the candidates of his choice irrespective of party affiliation. Unlike the closed primaries, the various styles of open primaries are not limited to a party electorate and all registered voters can participate in the nominating process without any evidence of party membership.

Nonpartisan Primaries. In the nonpartisan primary the candidates run irrespective of party affiliation, and the ballots carry no party labels. The persons receiving the first and second highest number of votes for the office become the candidates at the election, although frequently it is provided that any candidate who receives a majority of the votes in the primary is declared elected. In many cities only a single election is held; the candidate who receives the highest vote for each office is elected. The nonpartisan primary is predicated on the assumption that freedom from partisanship is desirable in the nominations for certain offices, mainly local and judicial public offices. Because these positions are essentially administrative, it is thought desirable to eliminate the influence of national and state party labels and to free the officials from the pressures that might be exerted by party heads.[7]

In theory, if not always in practice, the nonpartisan primary possesses considerable merit for local offices. The troublesome problem of party tests is avoided, and national party issues will not be infused into local elections. Municipal partisan primaries and elections are replete with illustrations of the interjection of the extraneous issues of national and state politics. In the choice of judges and school officials particularly, nonpartisanship is to be encouraged. Proponents believe that more efficient management of these offices may be obtained through the elimination of party politics. On the whole, advocates of the non-partisan primary believe that the system encourages both independent candidates and independent voting. In some jurisdictions, final elections are eliminated for those offices in which candidates in the primaries obtain a majority vote. Even if the primary fails to obviate the need for a final election, it at least reduces the number of names on the ballot in the general election. However, all types of primaries are a sifting and eliminating process and reduce the number of candidates in a final election.

Many party politicans oppose the nonpartisan primary because it takes away some control over patronage and nominations. In many cities, the nonpartisan primary has not seriously handicapped the party machines, and they have learned to live with it. Not infrequently the

---

[7]A great many cities use nonpartisan primaries for the selection of councilmen. Nonpartisan nomination of state and local judges, school officials, and various township and local offices is also fairly widespread.

parties actually enter nominees in the primary without benefit of label. Word is passed "down the line" that certain candidates are "ours." Open, official party endorsements, however, are usually avoided. There are still many independents in nonpartisan primaries and elections who run and win without any party's tacit endorsement and who remain truly nonpartisan. It is naïve, however, to assume that in the larger cities nomination and election can be won without an organization. Political interest groups, good-government leagues, and personal organizations give help of one kind or another.

From one point of view, a higher degree of political literacy is required of voters in nonpartisan primaries because they cannot rely on a party label unless a known partisan is on the ballot. Voters must expend some effort to learn which interests are behind a candidate. To date the nonpartisan primary's usefulness is limited essentially to local positions and to school superintendents and judges in some states. It has not been seriously advocated for governors or congressmen and is used only in Minnesota and Nebraska for selecting state legislators.

Party organizations as a rule remain unenthusiastic about non-partisan primaries, and their criticisms apply as well to nonpartisan elections. The system diminishes the role of the party organization in the nominating and campaigning process, although in many cases the party organization is present in the background. Incumbent nonpartisan city councilmen seem to have a better chance at political survival than councillors in partisan cities.[8] Nonpartisan incumbents do not usually face the organized criticism of an opposition party. In many communities, persons find they must choose between a career in partisan or non-partisan politics. As one becomes a success in a nonpartisan office, he may diminish his chances for becoming a candidate for a partisan office. Thus the nonpartisan system may reduce recruitment chances for the parties and also weaken the party organizations, for nonpartisan office-holders are often unavailable for party activity.

THE PARTISAN PRIMARY IN THEORY AND PRACTICE

The frequent and often heated arguments about types of primaries and about primaries in general highlight certain discrepancies in theory and practice, a situation making the various state nominating systems a most intriguing subject for study and speculation. Preference for the closed, open, or nonpartisan primary is not simply a matter of totaling the perceived assets and liabilities of each type. In the final analysis, the choice rests in a considerable measure on one's general outlook on the role of a

[8] See Charles Gilbert and Christopher Claque, "Electoral Competition and Electoral Systems in Large Cities," *Journal of Politics*, vol. 24, pp. 341–344, 1962.

party in state, county, and local elections. Is one system, in a normative sense, "better" than another? Does one method consistently produce demonstrably more capable nominees than another? Which system is the most "rational" from the standpoint of (1) the voter, (2) the candidate, (3) the party officialdom, and (4) party activists and adherents? Can any type of primary impose a high degree of responsibility on a party organization for the selection of candidates yet keep open the channels of recruitment to qualified persons? These questions are far more easily raised than satisfactorily answered. In the remainder of the chapter some suggestions and hypotheses will be advanced.[9] Further, the impact of primary systems on party organizations and their efforts to live with and to circumvent restrictions imposed by the primaries require attention.

Electorate and Primaries. Primaries of all types offer the electorate a chance to participate in the nominating process—an opportunity that presumably should be welcomed as "returning government to the people." Outside the South, where more persons may vote in the Democratic primary than in the general election, turnout in the primary has been disappointing to its more enthusiastic proponents. Voters are more likely to turn out in contested than in uncontested primaries, but even in the former, public participation is often disappointing. V. O. Key, Jr., found that in three out of four primaries in non-Southern states not more than 35 percent of the potential electorate voted in gubernatorial primaries. In contrast, well over half the electorate voted in general elections from 1926 to 1952.[10]

The hypothesis might be advanced that a blanket, aggregate primary fosters a large electorate participation because it is open to all registered voters without membership test. Figure 9-1 shows participation of registered voters in primaries and in general elections in Washington. In the absence of comparable figures in other non-Southern states, conclusions are not easily drawn.[11] Primary participation is seen

[9] The National Municipal League drafted a model primary law containing provisions for (1) a short ballot, (2) authorization for preprimary endorsements by political party organizations or conferences with appropriate designation of endorsed candidates on the ballot, (3) adequate provisions for individual filing, (4) mandatory use of the primary for all parties polling 10 percent or more of the vote at the preceding election, and (5) holding the primary in the autumn within two months of the general election. The type of primary would depend on "party traditions and history within the state." See *A Model Direct Primary System*, prepared by Joseph P. Harris, 1951.

[10] Key, *op. cit.*, pp. 134–135.

[11] On the Washington primary see the author's chapter on Washington in Frank H. Jonas (ed.), *Politics in the American West*, University of Utah Press, Salt Lake City, 1969; Daniel M. Ogden, Jr., "Washington's Popular Primary," *Research Studies of Washington State College*, vol. 19, pp. 139–161, 1951; and Hugh A. Bone and Daniel M. Ogden, Jr., *Washington Politics*, New York University Press, New York, 1960, pp. 37–41.

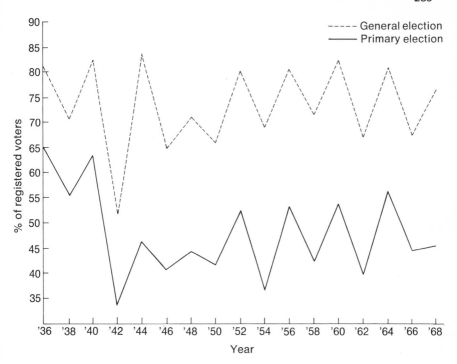

FIGURE 9-1   Percentage of registered voters participating in Washington primaries and general elections, 1936–1968.

to vary enormously between presidential years, when statewide candidates are nominated, and the midterm legislative and congressional primaries. Save for 1948 and 1968, with lows of 45 percent, the statewide primaries have attracted at least 55 percent of the registered voters, a creditable showing, compared with those of many other Northern states, but well below the 80 percent average turnout for the general elections. In both midterm and statewide primary years, voter participation in the primary election generally averages about 25 percent less than that in the general election. In Wisconsin, and most likely elsewhere, the primary voters generally are more interested and more active in politics than others in the entire electorate.[12] It is likely also that the more loyal and strongly identified partisans turn out to a larger extent than the

[12] See Austin Ranney and Leon D. Epstein, "The Two Electorates: Voters and Non-Voters," *Journal of Politics*, vol. 28, pp. 598–616, 1966. The Washington primary electorate has not been as fully studied as this general electorate. The author finds that, in general, the small towns and counties have a somewhat better turnout in primaries than is found in the larger metropolitan areas, where presumably party organizations would be more active in getting out the vote. See Hugh A. Bone, "The 1962 Election in Washington," *Western Political Quarterly*, vol. 16, pp. 472–473, 1963.

weaker partisans and, in the open primaries, than independents. Although Ranney and Epstein did not find primary voters to be ones assuming more extreme ideological positions in Wisconsin, primaries can be found where rightists or leftists turned out in large numbers to try to nominate a person nearer their views than a center candidate.

Persons with a strong party attachment and interest in party politics generally prefer a closed primary system, which keeps out independents and members of the opposition party. Loyal partisans argue that a more orthodox party man will receive the nomination and thus will strengthen party responsibility for program. Better discipline can be imposed if only enrolled party voters participate in the selection process. If the primary is opened to voters from disciplined groups outside the party, nomination may easily go to a person whose obligations to his party are weak. Moreover, one of the purposes of a primary is to settle intraparty differences over personalities without outside interference.

Independents and reformers incline toward the open primaries. They see the closed primary as putting party discipline above personal integrity. Open primaries assure a voter an opportunity to participate in the selection of candidates without at the same time forcing him to disclose his party affiliation. Many independents and weak partisans resent having to declare a party affiliation in order to vote in the important direct primary election. Some object on principle, and others fear social ostracism or economic reprisals and sanctions if they declare for a party that is not favored by the ruling group.

Private interest groups whose membership is predominantly of one party are likely to prefer a closed primary, for it permits them to exercise much influence over their party's nomination. At the same time, open primaries afford an opportunity for interest groups to defeat contenders unfriendly to their objectives. In open primaries, a group's leadership, seeing few contests in their own party's primary, may suggest crossing over to support the more acceptable of the opposition's candidates only to revert in the general election to support of their own party's nominee.

Party politicans and candidates complain about "raiding" or a crossover of voters aimed to nominate a weak opponent. Some voters may admit to a crossover but declare that it was for the purpose of getting the "best man," not the weakest, nominated. Many charges about raiding are difficult to prove. It is contended by politicians and by many academicians that the open and blanket primaries permit raiding, and the latter to a greater degree than the former. Although this is true, the contention that no raiding is possible in a closed primary may be seriously questioned. Even in closed primaries, voters insist on switching their parties; and both candidates and parties will encourage raiding if they can find ways to facilitate it.[13]

The Washington blanket primary has shown some paradox between postulate and practice. The state is one of the more competitive two-party ones; and the blanket primary has not served to blur the programmatic approaches of the party, either in its platform or in its deeds, when controlling the state government. Its Republican governors and legislators have been more conservative in approach than the Democrats. Precinct organizations leave much to be wished for but compares well with other states of similar size and complexion. Daniel M. Ogden, Jr., has made a more thorough study than anyone else of the Washington blanket primary and believes it to be a highly advantageous type of primary.[14] As to the most serious charge against it, that of raiding, his statistical studies show that, while theoretically possible, it very rarely occurs. The little crossing over that has taken place has been to support a good person on the other side rather than a weak candidate.

The greatest impact of the primary system on voters is to increase their burden. It is not a choice, as in a general election, between a Republican and a Democrat but may involve selection from a long list of candidates—a dozen gubernatorial hopefuls may appear on the ballot though this many is rare.[15] Southern Democratic primaries attempt to solve this problem of "plurality" nominations by scheduling a runoff between the two highest. Here the voter's choice is greatly simplified. As will be seen shortly, several states give the voter at least some cue by preprimary conventions that designate which candidate or candidates are favored by delegates at the convention.

Impact on Candidates. Direct primaries, irrespective of type, pose many problems for those aspiring to obtain the nomination. In the convention system, a potential nominee conducts a campaign to win delegate votes. In a primary he must appeal to a much broader electorate. If he is to obtain public office, he must wage two campaigns, one to convince certain voters to nominate him, the other to appeal to the whole electorate in the general election. The primary raises special organizational

[13] Clarence Berdahl notes that organized raiding in the closed primary in Illinois has occurred on many occasions. He believes, however, that a changeover from the "challenge" to the "enrollment" system in effect in about half of the states would effectively prevent raiding. See Assembly on Illinois Political Parties, *Illinois Political Parties*, published as a University of Illinois Bulletin, vol. 57, no. 54, pp. 27–28, 1960. Professor Berdahl has prepared a most comprehensive analysis of primary laws under the title "Party Membership in the United States," *American Political Science Review*, vol. 36, pp. 16–50, 241–262, 1942.

[14] See Ogden, "Washington's Popular Primary," *op. cit.*

[15] Fourteen candidates filed for governor in Alabama in 1958 and eight in Tennessee. See Richard M. Scammon, *Southern Primaries 58*, Governmental Affairs Institute, Washington, D.C., 1959.

and financial problems for him. In a contested primary, there is usually some degree of neutrality within the party organization, and an aspirant does not have full access to the manpower and financial resources. He must build his own organization and obtain his own funds without using the party's treasury. These obstacles are often so formidable that a person of modest means is kept from either entering or winning the primary. He may go to pressure groups for money and endorsements only to find that they will promise him help in the general election if he wins the primary. If on the other hand he receives too much help from a powerful group in the primary, his opponents may charge him with being a puppet of that group.

As to the type of primary preferred by various hopefuls, a hypothesis suggests that insurgents, mavericks, and those who come from outside the party or have been associated with it only in a marginal way would prefer the open and blanket primary arrangements. Conversely, persons active in a party and possessing the image of a "good Republican" or a "good Democrat" are likely to prefer a primary limited to registered partisans. Such persons would capitalize on their party loyalty and activity and could maximize their strength among party voters. In a sense also their electorate is smaller than in an open primary and can easily be less costly in terms of both organization and finances.

In the largest cities the primary ballot often becomes very long, carrying a hundred or more names. There is some evidence that when a voter is unfamiliar with the names of would-be nominees for a given office, he resolves the problem by checking a name at or near the top. In order to overcome the advantage to some candidates from this, many states require that the ballots be printed with names rotated.

The primary system appears to open the doors to persons ambitious to hold office and give opportunity to those who might have little chance of a convention designation. However, for a great many offices, there is no contest in primary elections; therefore, the voter has no choice. Over a period of time in Wisconsin more than half of the candidates for the state legislature (53.5 percent) were without competitors in primaries and two-thirds of the bids for nomination in the 1958 primaries in Pennsylvania went uncontested. This may be one instance where the type of primary system is an important factor in the number of contests. In Washington from 1948 through 1968, only about 9 percent of the seats in both houses of the legislature went uncontested in presidential years and 13 percent in off years. Challengers believe they can draw enough strength from the opposition's voters and from independents to capture the primary in a popularity contest. The fact that weak partisans and mavericks can often win in the primaries is a major reason why the Washington legislature, despite pleadings from party chairmen, will not adopt a closed primary.[16]

Democratic state legislative primaries in the South are likely to be much more contested irrespective of incumbency.[17] Some 94 percent of the primaries were contested in Louisiána and about 87 percent in Alabama. Percentages were markedly lower in Tennessee, Texas, and North Carolina. Great variations, of course, are shown; but, in general, there are fewer contested legislative primaries in the rural districts and in the more heavily black districts. The high competition in Louisiana is probably due to the bifactional nature of the state's politics and the use of legislative slates to contest nearly all positions.

Impact on Party Organizations. A large number of party leaders privately if not publicly prefer conventions, where the party hierarchy can control nominations and "balance" the ticket "rationally" with appropriate recognition of the major factions in the party. Though state chairmen and other officials generally proclaim a "hands-off" policy, they are usually omnipresent and at work in lining up delegates behind their choices. Failing this, the next choice of the leaders is a convention designation, providing only for a challenge in the primary as in Connecticut.[18]

The list of well-known objections of organization leaders to the primaries is lengthy. Primaries are seen as considerably more costly than holding a convention, and they siphon off funds to potential nominees making it more difficult to get money for the general election campaign. Primaries diminish the power of the organization to reward the faithful with nomination, thus assuring at least some control over the loyalties of officeholders. Primaries prevent denial of renomination to mavericks and may even result in nomination of persons opposed to the party's positions. Further, the primaries can result in the nomination of persons who are poorly qualified, likely losers, or embarrassing to the party. In terms of electability, the party leaders contend that the primary often results in an unbalanced ticket with less electoral strength than a ticket they could put together in a convention. Because one man may denounce another seeking the same office, the primaries are also seen as weakening tickets and fostering or adding to party splits.[19]

[16] State legislators have often told the author "without the blanket primary I could never have been nominated."

[17] Comprehensive data and analysis on the subject is provided by Malcolm E. Jewell, *Legislative Representation in the Contemporary South,* The Duke University Press, Durham, N.C., 1967, chap. 2.

[18] Joseph P. Lyford has an interesting account of the state chairman's activities in denying him the nomination for congressman-at-large in Connecticut. See *Candidate,* Holt, Rinehart and Winston, Inc., New York, 1959.

[19] This may be more fear than fact. See Andrew Hacker, "Does a 'Divisive' Primary Harm a Candidate's Election Chances?" *American Political Science Review,* vol. 69, pp. 105–110, 1965.

The party officialdom realizes that, notwithstanding what it considers an undesirable impact on the organization, primaries are here to stay. Generally, activists champion the closed primary as the best of the alternatives. Strong party adherents see a psychological and moral value in requiring persons to submit to tests of party faith before voting in a primary. They believe that a closed affair results in nominating stronger partisans and encouraging party responsibility and gives them greater opportunity to influence the outcome of nominations. A closed primary is more easily protected from raiding.

In conclusion, partisanship can be encouraged by election laws and ballot forms. Most Southern states have a closed party primary and a party-column, single-choice (one mark for a straight ticket) general election ballot.[20] This system promotes the interests of the Democratic party in the area. Outside the South, only fifteen states provide this strong impetus to party voting. The miscellany of requirements are probably symbolic of the ambivalence of viewpoints about party voting held by legislatures and electorate.

Party Influences on the Primaries. Influence and control by party officials over nominations failed to disappear with the spread of primaries. Many county chairmen remain officially neutral in primaries, but others do not. Participation in the primary is sometimes official but probably more often unofficial and behind the scenes. The role of party officials in contests in the primaries varies from complete hands-off policy to informal or nominal assistance to outright or acknowledged choice.

Local party leaders can and do have influence in primary contests, and informal slatemaking by party leaders is far more prevalent than most citizens realize. There is a strong desire on the part of the party leader to avoid fights in the primary that may weaken the party in the general election. The late Sen. Richard L. Neuberger, however, once remarked that he thought contests in the primary aided the party by stirring up voter interest in the candidates and issues. When an acceptable incumbent seeks renomination or where the leaders through private bargaining and agreement favor a nominee, challengers are discouraged. There are many subtle and not so subtle ways for leaders to show their displeasure of new entrants. Aspiring candidates are told that they should wait their turn; and they may be warned that, even if nominated, they will not receive party help in the general election. Protocol in many, if not most, areas dictates that a person desiring to enter a primary should first sound out the county chairman and other

[20]Additional discussion of this point together with reproductions of ballots is found in chap. 15.

party leaders before announcing his intentions. A cool reception may discourage him from filing. The views of candidates for other offices on the ticket may be made known to party leaders who in turn will try to dissuade potential competitors from seeking a nomination.

The influence of the party officialdom may be more negative than positive. Its views, privately expressed, can be a strong deterrent to one who lacks the popularity to offend or to buck the organization. Information on who kept whom from entering a primary would be difficult if not impossible to obtain. Often we read that certain persons suddenly decide to withdraw from the primary, and certainly in many cases the "word" from someone in the hierarchy was instrumental. As a result, many primary elections are uncontested.

The posture of the organization toward certain primary races is affected by the situation. When a popular incumbent seeks renomination and is unopposed, he generally receives public endorsement by the chairman and leaders. If an unknown opponent challenges an incumbent, a chairman may feel that he can give at least tacit support to the incumbent without incurring serious criticism.

In New York City, the county chairmen customarily draw up a slate for citywide offices in order to avoid primary fights. In 1953, a poll of Democratic party leaders showed opposition to the renomination of Mayor Vincent Impellitteri, and he failed to get endorsement. The mayor ran without endorsement in the party primary and was defeated by the candidate chosen by the party leaders, Robert Wagner. After due consideration, Impellitteri decided not to run in the general election as an independent, and Wagner won the election. Subsequently, however, Wagner ran for reelection in opposition to the organization candidate and won. Political machines in New York City regularly prepare a slate to be "ratified" by the county committees. Aspirants for municipal offices there and in other areas where such practices prevail, know that the organization's active and strong endorsement carries fair promise of success; they cannot take lightly, therefore, the prospects of running without organizational support.

In 75 percent of the primaries in Pennsylvania, the party organizations attempted intervention.[21] Party influences appear greater in the big cities but are by no means limited to them. In Oklahoma, more than half the county chairmen in both parties were found to be encouraging or actively seeking well-qualified candidates to run for the state legislature.[22] One study of a middle-sized Midwestern city found

[21] Frank J. Sorauf, *Party and Representation*, Atherton Press, Inc., New York, 1963, chap. 5.

[22] Samuel C. Patterson, "Characteristics of Party Leaders," *Western Political Quarterly*, vol. 16, pp. 347–349, 1963. Isolated studies find other county chairman doing likewise, but in many counties chairmen stay out of recruitment.

widespread activity by precinct captains in primary elections for minor city and county officials. The authors report

> . . . the strong impression we have that "party organization" often means *candidate* organization. In several of the campaigns we analyzed, the support of the precinct captains was divided almost equally among the candidates, and there are campaigns in which each of the candidates has just about equal worker strength. In short, some candidates seem to be able to split the official party organization and organize an effective campaign organization without the blessing of the top leaders. In fact, the top leadership waits until a day or so before the election before giving the "word" on which candidate to support.[23]

This study suggests the semantic difference between *official organization* and *official support.* An organization has a hierarchy of county chairmen, state committeemen, division leaders, and finally the precinct committeemen. Often, as in the above case, there will be a division within the organization itself, with the precinct officials freer from traditions of neutrality than those higher up. Organization in practice may be powerful mayors and officeholders rather than party committeemen. If party clubs and extralegal party groups are "official," then there is often vigorous participation on behalf of a particular slate in the primaries.

Preprimary Conventions. In several states, slatemaking by party organization has been at least partially formalized through conventions held before the primary. There have been several styles: sporadic endorsements by party conventions; endorsements by official conventions with legal sanction; designation by unofficial organizations; and formal designation of one candidate by the state committee (New York) or state convention (Connecticut and Massachusetts), with the option of a challenge in the primary by those failing to win the convention nomination. The last-mentioned category was covered earlier in the chapter. As in New York, state committees in Rhode Island make the nominations for statewide office. The candidate's name goes on the ballot first and is identified by an asterisk. The party management does not have to display its choices until the closing date for all nominations. No opportunity is given for scrutiny of the proposed party slate and mounting of a counterattack.

Local conventions, political clubs, and auxiliary groups take it upon themselves to recommend publicly the nomination of a particular person, often an incumbent, because of a situation at the moment. Such announcement may occur when a candidate for nomination has little or no opposition in the primary, and the action is used to promote unity

---

[23] Phillips Cutright and Peter H. Rossi, "Party Organization in Primary Elections," *American Journal of Sociology,* vol. 64, p. 269, 1958. The authors gathered many of their data through interviews with precinct captains of both parties. The city was kept anonymous.

behind him in the general election. It may be used to isolate an unpopular incumbent whom the convention would like to see replaced by a person more popular with the convention. In Minnesota, preprimary endorsement is optional, and the Democratic-Farmer-Labor party (DFL) has used it to try to build an effective party.[24] Tradition against the device was strong among Republicans before 1960, but since then the party's constitution permits endorsement by vote of 60 percent of the delegates. The DFL requires a two-thirds vote. State legislators are elected on a nonpartisan ballot, and the DFL uses endorsements to give weight to candidates of liberal persuasion. Endorsement is not made known on the ballot but the public's attention is called to it in the press and sometimes through sample ballots containing the names of endorsees. From 1944 to 1960, about four-fifths of the endorsed candidates won nomination.

Idaho, Colorado, and Utah have variations of legally sanctioned preprimary convention endorsement[25] and, unlike Connecticut and Massachusetts, permit endorsement of more than one candidate. In Idaho, all candidates receiving at least 20 percent of the ballots cast in the convention, when at least two receive more than 20 percent, are officially endorsed. Unendorsed candidates who receive at least 10 percent of the assembly vote may file a second declaration and run as unendorsed candidates. Utah requires each convention to designate the two candidates receiving the two highest number of votes with no maximum required. No one else can secure a position on the ballot, so voters are limited to the two choices presented by the convention. If a candidate gets 80 percent of the convention vote, his name and none other advances immediately to the final vote.

Colorado has used a system requiring formal preprimary party endorsement ("designation" according to the law) continuously since 1912.[26] All candidates polling more than 20 percent of a convention endorsement vote go on the ballot in the order of their vote percentage. The conventions, called assemblies, have in reality designated nearly all of the party's candidates either because only a single candidate was named or because of the great advantage resulting from being listed first on the ballot. Without broad support within the assembly, prospective candidates are eliminated. Competition is markedly reduced in the primaries and for the Colorado House fewer than one-fourth of the

[24]See G. T. Mitau, *Politics in Minnesota,* The University of Minnesota Press, Minneapolis, 1960. Minnesota gave legal sanction to preprimary endorsements only from 1921 to 1923.
[25]These states along with New Mexico, which abandoned the system in 1967, have had a long, interesting history with endorsements, including many changes. Their development will be found in respective chapters in Jonas, *op. cit.*
[26]The state has, therefore, had the most extensive experience with the endorsement of more than one candidate. A comprehensive work on the device is that of R. John Eyre and Curtis Martin, *The Colorado Preprimary System,* Bureau of Governmental Research and Service, University of Colorado, Boulder, 1967.

primaries have been contested. In effect, primary contests are pre-determined by assembly action, and primary elections serve a very limited purpose. In four primary elections for governor or United States senator, the average primary vote was only 20 percent.[27]

A final variation of endorsement, that by unofficial assemblies, finds illustration in California.[28] Regular committees are forbidden by law to designate candidates. In both parties, nominations are now largely made by these extralegal groups because most other aspirants are discouraged from entering the primaries without endorsement. Harris and Rowe note that the "success of the Republican party has been due in no small measure to the activities of the Assembly in bringing forward suitable candidates. By endorsing a single candidate for each office, the Republican Assembly has avoided primary contests between two or more Republican candidates and as a result the party has been able to control its own nominations."[29]

It is not easy to generalize the results of the diverse systems of preprimary designations either by official or extralegal bodies. Numerous party officials fear the pitfalls of public endorsement and have not advocated it. Nebraska discontinued the system after a few years because it appeared to contribute to party disunity. In California, the Republican Assembly fell under right-wing control in 1964 and many moderate Republicans became concerned that it did not reflect the prevailing Republican thinking. Conservative Democrats have sometimes bemoaned the "ultraliberal" character of the Democratic Council. It is not surprising that the preprimary endorsement system is under attack for restricting the access of some to elective office and diminishing the role of rank-and-file party voters.

Scholars reviewing the Colorado and California systems agree that they have strengthened and vitalized the parties. Designations are denied to nonentities, and candidates expecting to make a serious bid for nomination must solicit and obtain support from party activists.[30] Preprimary endorsements help to balance popular control and party control; and, in Colorado at least, have increased party competition because nearly every position on the ticket is filled most of the time. The convention links local committees with the state organizations and thereby probably reduces organizational atrophy.

[27] Comparative figures for votes in other states are found in a table in *ibid.*, p. 65.

[28] These organizations, known as the California Republican Assembly and California Democratic Council, have been in existence respectively since 1934 and 1953. See Joseph P. Harris, *California Politics*, Chandler Publishing Co., San Francisco, 1967, pp. 48–53, and Francis Carney, *The Rise of Democratic Clubs in California*, Holt, Rinehart and Winston, Inc., New York, 1958.

[29] Joseph P. Harris and Leonard Rowe, *California Politics*, Stanford University Press, Stanford, Calif., 1959, pp. 38–39.

[30] The concluding chapter of Eyre and Martin, *op. cit.*, is especially recommended on the results of the Colorado system.

Observers are inclined to agree that the system does not necessarily achieve party responsibility and cohesion in the legislature. As V. O. Key, Jr., pointed out some time ago, party unity is not manufactured and results "from a fundamental parallelism of interest among the constituencies represented . . . party unity in the legislature is not induced by extra-legislative forces."[31]

THE PRIMARY IN RETROSPECT

Half a century of experience with the direct primary method of nomination has resulted in a great variety of experience. One can point to at least one state's experimentation to prove or disprove almost any good or bad contention about the primary. The primaries were designed as a tool of popular control, yet the old-style political machines learned how to get their choices nominated, and party control in one degree or another is still possible if there is a party organization and if it wants to influence the primary. Party organizations, however, tend to prefer negotiation to a primary battle that might threaten harmony in the general election.

From a pragmatic point of view, the acid test of a nominating system rests on its success in encouraging and elevating thoroughly qualified citizens to run for public office against other persons who are also able, from the standpoint of technical and political know-how, to serve effectively in public office. Which system has consistently produced the "best" nominees: the Indiana convention, the New Jersey closed primary, the Minnesota open primary, the Washington blanket primary, or preprimary endorsement mechanisms? Only a rash person would care to argue that any one of them has proved itself demonstrably better over a period of time, although he might have his preference in terms of which is the most rational system. In each state, one can point to highly successful governors and senators and to unsuccessful ones. "Good" candidates and "poor" candidates have been put forth in every state of the Union. This suggests that the system alone is not the only problem in finding qualified persons to run for public office. At the same time, it is desirable to have a nominating process that does not shut the door to capable and dedicated persons who want to try for elective office.

Scholars for the most part agree that the primary has fulfilled neither the hopes of advocates nor the fears of antagonists. It has resulted neither in turning government over to the people nor in destroying party organization. There is some degree of popular control over nominations in most states, but it is far less extensive than original advocates envisaged. Further, the system is so complex as to be not well understood by a great many voters.

[31] *Op. cit.*, p. 277.

Party organizations still put up a fight to retain control over nominations. Party leaders themselves know that they may stand defeat in a final election and survive but that defeat in the primary is likely to mean that they will no longer retain control over the organization. They are faced, therefore, with either maintaining a strict neutrality with the hope of remaining in power irrespective of the winner or seeing that their intervention is successful. In broad terms, party organizations are to one degree or another (varying in each state) imprisoned by the direct primary system. Yet they have been able to circumvent legal restrictions and maintain, in many cases, considerable domination over the process of nomination by primaries. Because of the multiplicity of positions on a primary ballot, the party organization usually focuses attention on a few offices so that its involvement becomes selective rather than all-encompassing. The exception is the preprimary convention, which requires the delegates to be attentive to all offices and, if designation can go to more than one person, to rate the order of names on the ballot.

Several observations about the primary system are well documented. Primaries outside the South have failed to attract voter participation at any consistently high level. The primary election has served the peculiar needs of the Democratic-dominated South because the winner of that party's primary has generally been assured of election. Democratic primaries at times bring out as many or more voters than sharply contested general elections in two-party areas. In *United States v. Classic* the Supreme Court recognized that the primary in some states effectively controlled the choice of the person elected and that the primary was an integral part of the electoral process. The primary in the South and the runoff, when used, become, in effect, the real election, for the outcome of the general election is often a foregone conclusion. As Southern Republicans gain strength and become serious contenders, they probably will make greater use of their own primary, and the general election will become of greater importance.

The significance of the primary of the majority party, however, extends far beyond the South. Cortez A. M. Ewing's study of the elections to the House of Representatives from 1896 to 1946 found that about half the representatives elected were reasonably certain of election after receiving the nomination.[32] Incumbents of state and local offices are often unopposed in the party primary. Many incumbents tend to build up a "bipartisan" status after a period of time without serious opposition either in their own primary or in the general elections.

Voters in major-party primaries everywhere have singular responsibility and power. If one party is dominant, its primaries are

[32]"Primaries as Elections," *Southwestern Social Science Quarterly*, vol. 29, pp. 293–298, 1948–1949.

likely to be contested, but contests are exceptional in the minority that has little chance of winning. Certain factions and interests within a party realize the important stake they have in the outcome of the primary election and may coalesce around a well-known figure so that he can win a plurality. If there is no runoff primary, the action in effect results in control of the office. In other words, in states with a weak minority party, decisions about who will rule may, practically speaking, be transferred to the majority party's primary. In "safe" districts, the electoral decision is, in effect, transferred from the general election to the primary election. This may lead voters to register in the major party's primary in order to have a voice in the government and politics of the state. Laws regulating primaries in these states are likely to be determined by the majority party for its own benefit.

From one point of view, the primary seems to be a haphazard, unplanned method of nomination compared with the party process of selection elsewhere. Persons without previous service to a party or in public office may enter a primary for a state or big city office and win it. In the process, the primary electorate may pass over deserving experienced persons. There are undoubtedly many anomalies in the system. Yet the primary may help to recruit into the party new faces that the party executives may have overlooked. In the idealized model, the direct primary is one of the institutions that help to maintain the open political society. No one group or person controls access to the electorate eligible to vote in the primary. It has just been observed, however, that deviations from the model regularly occur and that party organizations in fact are usually not fully neutral.

Nomination is the first of the major formalized steps that are taken to seek control of government. If the party organization controls the nomination process, entry to public office is only through the party. A primary is seldom, if ever completely dominated by a group of party leaders and activists. The real significance of the primary is that it helps to keep open and flexible the channels of recruitment to public office. It provides a method or alternative means of gaining power other than winning the support of leaders in the party. The open primary does this somewhat better than the closed primary. The number of candidates in a primary as well as voter turnout in a general way often reflects the strength or weakness of a party organization — testimony to the fact that the party officialdom remains concerned with the nominating function and does not leave it to founder on the waves of so-called popular control.

Those who believe that primaries would democratize the nominating process overlook the fact that the political machine that dominated the caucus and convention can also dominate the primary and that leadership is quite as necessary in the nominating process as in elections. When leadership is out of harmony with membership, it becomes the latter's function to replace it, and the primary offers a channel for doing so. The primary, although often deserted both in challengers and in voters, is the proverbial "shotgun behind the door," a weapon that groups of the party electorate can use to challenge the organizations to bring about changes in personnel. The fact that the primary is so deserted should not obscure its potentiality.

In conclusion, the nominating process is best viewed as a process of recruitment, and it has a profound impact on the type of person entering public life. The system used is bound to affect recruitment, but the effect of the direct primary is by no means fully or carefully documented. Sometimes persons of distinction and honor are chosen, and sometimes they are not. A primary election, moreover, is only one of the mechanisms for bringing citizens into public positions. Much informal selection and grooming takes place before the filing date for the primary, and the primary often simply legitimizes the choice.

The contested primary opens the door to the person with name familiarity and/or money to conduct a campaign. To what extent it consistently works against those who possess neither can hardly be ascertained. On the other hand, under the caucus and convention arrangements, money and public reputation were often important in securing consideration in the selection of the party's nominees. In itself, the primary fulfills the objective of opportunity for persons of diverse backgrounds, means, and talents to seek public office. But the mechanisms of recruitment, as just observed, are not limited to the primary. The primary, therefore, must be set in the larger political context of the process of selection.

CONGRESSIONAL NOMINATIONS AND THE NATIONAL PARTIES

The overwhelming majority of candidates for Congress are nominated in primaries.[33] An added element not present in local nominations is the greater concern of national party leaders and deserves mention before discussing the problems of presidential nominations. There is a general

---

[33] Britain is often cited as the classic example of the alternative of selection of parliamentary candidates by the extraparliamentary constituency associations composed of rank-and-file party members. Although the associations are subject to certain formal controls by the national party committees, the latter tend to ratify the choice of a constituency group. With the rarest of exceptions, incumbents who wish to stand again are "readopted." The selection process is described and evaluated by Austin Ranney in *Pathways to Parliament: Candidate Selection in Britain,* The University of Wisconsin Press, Madison, 1965. A general reference work on recruitment and characteristics of leaders in various nations is Lewis J. Edinger (ed.), *Political Leadership in Industrialized Societies: Studies in Comparative Analysis,* John Wiley & Sons, Inc., New York, 1967.

tradition that Presidents and chairmen of national and congressional campaign committees remain neutral in congressional primaries. Nevertheless, there are circumstances under which they will intervene. If the party does not hold the seat, the national leaders may take a hand in encouraging those prospects who are wavering by assuring them of White House backing. The Eisenhower administration sought the entry of several prominent persons into Senate races and indicated White House aid would be forthcoming. One caused the administration embarrassment in Oregon, where it was publicly reported that Secretary of the Interior Douglas McKay was seeking the nomination with its blessing. McKay was challenged by a popular Republican but won. Both sides were unhappy — McKay because he thought he was the sole entrant, and his opponent because of "national interference." The Nixon Administration was active in 1969 and 1970 in seeking strong candidates for Congress in hope of overcoming Democratic majorities.

The author discussed the problem of "intervention" with former officials of the congressional campaign committees of both parties. These men admitted in a very diplomatic way that at times they had joined with local officials to evaluate the prospects of certain persons in terms of encouraging them to run in the primaries. Congressional campaign committees are interested in strong candidates in each district. Where there is no incumbent and presumably no consensus among the local officials, the fieldmen of the national committees feel free to discuss names of potential candidates. Such discussion of course is highly circumspect.[34] In strongly one-party areas, the out-party is faced with getting someone to run for purposes of building up the party and keeping some semblance of an organization intact. Under such circumstances, the national fieldmen may lend their encouragement to the person whom the local organizations are trying to get to enter the primary.

Incumbency poses different problems and practices. In 1954, the Republican Congressional Committee gave campaign funds to fifty-two Republican incumbent congressmen in April. Many of those receiving money were in districts where primary elections had not yet been held; however, in each instance the incumbent was not being contested in the primary. On occasion, Democratic practice has been similar. The view of the national campaign committees is that funds given incumbents are not to help them win the primary but to get their "organizational and educational work started early." As a general rule, however, the incumbent will not receive financial or other assistance until after the primary.

Very different practices obtain where an incumbent is being contested in the primary. Here tradition is strong that national officials

[34]On this point see Hugh A. Bone, *Party Committees and National Politics*, University of Washington Press, Seattle (third printing, 1968), pp. 142–143.

stay out. The ill-fated "purge" attempted by President Roosevelt in 1938 is often cited as violating political tradition. Roosevelt justified his endorsement of the liberal candidate by saying,

> . . . as the head of the Democratic party . . . charged with the responsibility of carrying out the definitely liberal declaration of principles set forth in the 1936 Democratic platform, I feel that I have every right to speak in those few instances where there may be a clear issue between candidates for a Democratic nomination involving principles or invoking a clear misuse of my own name.

His participation was effective when he endorsed incumbents who were supported by the state political organization but ineffective when he opposed incumbents who had the support of the party organization. The so-called purge stirred up a hornet's nest of opposition, both within the party and outside it, costing Roosevelt some prestige. He made no similar move in subsequent years, nor have his successors.

Although no one has made an intensive study of the thousands of primaries held over a period of time, it is nonetheless possible to draw a few additional generalizations. It costs money and requires an effective organization to unseat an incumbent. This is another reason why incumbents in areas of competitive two-party politics are usually successful in obtaining renomination even with a contest. In a given primary election, the great majority of incumbent congressmen and senators are renominated without a contest. There is an unwritten practice that if an incumbent is doing an effective job, particularly for his district and state, he shall go unchallenged for renomination and that he shall have tacit support of the organization. V. O. Key, Jr., has noted that Southern Democratic incumbents are likely to be contested for renomination since victory in the Democratic primary contains high assurance in the general election.[35] Conversely where vigorous two-party competition occurs and the electoral outcome is in doubt, there may be less inclination to challenge an incumbent.

In conclusion, congressional nominations provide another striking illustration of the familiar pattern of American party politics — decentralization. Nominations for the Presidency and vice presidency are made at a national conclave, while their congressional compatriots are designated by voters in hundreds of widely separate contests from Honolulu to Augusta and from Fairbanks to Miami. The national candidates and congressional committees are expected to remain aloof from these contests except when incumbents are not contested. Proposing the party's candidate is a purely local affair, and in many states the open primary will permit other than loyal party members to participate in the process. Parenthetically, there is little evidence that senators chosen in

[35] *Southern Politics*, Alfred A. Knopf, Inc., New York, 1949, chaps. 11–20.

open primaries have less voting cohesion on roll calls than their colleagues selected in closed primaries. Most senators from open primary states have party unity scores as good as or better than the average from closed primary states.

Recruitment processes are often inadequate and highly individualistic. Rarely is an incumbent denied renomination or seriously opposed in the non-Southern states. (Thomas Kuchel of California, Senate minority whip, was a recent example when he lost to a conservative Republican in the 1968 Republican primary.) Superannuation, unpopular actions, failure to continue to "bring home the bacon," and ideological differences may lead to challenge of an incumbent in the primary. Generally speaking, the decentralized, localistic process of nominating persons to Congress emphasizes parochial interest rather than efforts to strengthen the national party.

FOR FURTHER READING

Books and articles on nominations in specific states are numerous; because of the few general works and the great variation in state practices, most of the important materials are found in the several state studies.

Dallinger, F. W.: *Nominations for Elective Office in the United States*, 1903.
Ewing, Cortez A. M.: *Primary Elections in the South*, 1953.
Kingdon, John W.: *Candidates for Office: Beliefs and Strategies*, 1968.
Merriam, Charles E., and Louise Overacker: *Primary Elections*, 1928.
Sikorsky, Igor I., Jr.: *Convention at Large*, 1964.
Smith, Rhoten A., and Clarence J. Hein: *Republican Primary Fight: A Study in Factionalism*, 1958.

All is over. As you step out of the building you inhale with relief the gentle breeze which tempers the scorching heat of July; you come to yourself; you recover your sensibility, which has been blunted by the incessant uproar, and your faculty of judgment, which has been held in abeyance amid the pandemonium in which day after day has passed. You collect your impressions, and you realize what a colossal travesty of popular institutions you have just been witnessing. A greedy crowd of officeholders, or of office seekers, disguised as delegates of the people, on pretense of holding the grand council of the party, indulged in, or were victims of, intrigues and maneuvers, the object of which was the chief magistracy of the greatest republic of the two hemispheres – the succession to the Washingtons and Jeffersons . . . . Yet, when you carry your thoughts back from the scene which you have just witnessed and review the line of Presidents, you find that if they have not all been great men – far from it – they were all honorable men; and you cannot help repeating the American saying: "God takes care of drunkards, of little children, and of the United States."

M. OSTROGORSKI

CHAPTER 10 PRESIDENTIAL NOMINATIONS

The American national party convention has no counterpart anywhere in the world. Although in some nations some formulation of a party's program takes place at a national conference, the convention in the United States is unique in terms of nominating nationwide candidates for public office. The amazing spectacle is now carried to the world via radio, television, and film and is properly regarded as one of the greatest political shows on earth. To Americans, it seems a logical method for picking presidential and vice presidential nominees. In true pragmatic fashion, the United States voter would probably ask, "How else could you choose them?"

In the first two elections, no nominations were necessary, and the Electoral College chose George Washington. From 1796 to 1824, most candidates were named by congressional caucuses of the respective parties.[1] When only a few Federalists were elected to Congress, Federalist leaders met in secret to designate their choices. Parliamentary democracies tend to choose their prime ministers and opposition leaders in this way. Had this system continued to be used in the United States, the candidates in many elections would undoubtedly have been different. For example, Democratic lawmakers might well have selected Speaker Champ Clark over Woodrow Wilson and Speaker John Garner over Franklin D. Roosevelt. Republican congressmen doubtless would have chosen Robert Taft over Eisenhower and never would have selected Willkie.

The caucus system was abandoned because it appeared aristocratic and undemocratic and gave Congress too much control over presidential candidacies. It also centralized control over a highly decentralized political system. Opposition to the system came from local party leaders, who saw that it was out of harmony with the emerging democracy. The convention idea was growing even during the caucus era but took some time to become fully institutionalized. Secret meetings of Federalist leaders in 1808 and 1812 to name their candidates were a step toward a national nominating convention. Andrew Jackson could not get the nomination by caucus and campaigned against the congressional "King Caucus." In 1824, William H. Crawford became the last candidate to be nominated by caucus. State legislatures and local conventions named John Quincy Adams and Jackson. Credit for the first national convention generally goes to that of the Anti-Masonic party, held in 1831. President Jackson used the national convention in 1832 to back his choice for Vice President, Martin Van Buren. During the next few elections the Whigs and Democrats used the convention to ratify a preordained choice for President and to try to agree on a Vice President. By 1844 the conventions reached their full stature.[2]

---

[1] See C. S. Thompson, *The Rise and Fall of the Congressional Caucus*, Yale University Press, New Haven, Conn., 1902.

[2] Since 1954, a massive literature on national conventions has been forthcoming; before then, a number of works appeared about specific conventions. The reader is referred to the five-volume work of Paul T. David et al., *Presidential Nominating Politics in 1952*, The Johns Hopkins Press, Baltimore, 1954, for a state-by-state analysis of the selection of delegations that year. See also Paul David et al., *The Politics of National Party Conventions*, The Brookings Institution, Washington, D.C., 1960 (published in revised abridged paperback edition in 1964 by Vintage Books, Random House, Inc., New York); and Gerald Pomper, *Nominating the President: The Politics of Convention Choice*, Northwestern University Press, Evanston, Ill., 1963. These works, which contain extensive bibliographies, are recommended for their comprehensive treatment of all aspects of national conventions. Extensive historical data and special materials on the 1968 convention are found in Congressional Quarterly Service, *Convention Guide*, published as Part 1 of the June 7, 1968, *Congressional Quarterly Weekly Report*.

SELECTION OF DELEGATES

The national committees fix the time and place of the conventions and
· allot the number of delegates to each state in accordance with the rules
established by the preceding convention. Because a huge auditorium
and extensive hotel facilities are needed, conventions are held only in
very large cities. The amount of money a city will pay for the convention
is one of the important factors considered by the national committee.
Cities find that a convention brings large sums of money into the community; thus they are anxious to host the event.

Apportionment. In the first conventions, each state was accorded the
number of delegates and votes that it had in the Electoral College, but
later this number was doubled to permit larger delegations from each
state. Beginning in 1916, the Republican apportionment system underwent a series of changes because the South had a larger representation
in Republican conventions than seemed warranted by its Republican
voting strength in elections. Present Republican rules grant each state
four delegates-at-large, two additional delegates-at-large for each repre-
sentative-at-large, and six additional delegates-at-large from each state
casting its electoral vote for the Republican nominee for President or
for United States senator or for governor since the last Republican convention. Each congressional district casting 2,000 or more votes for a
Republican presidential elector or for the party's nominee for Congress
is entitled to a delegate; it receives an additional delegate if more than
10,000 votes were cast for the same offices in the last preceding election.
In addition, the District of Columbia, Puerto Rico, and the Virgin Is-
lands are given representation.

Democrats drew strength from nearly all the states, and their
original apportionment did not give great influence to sections where
their voting power was weak. Nonetheless, from 1944 through 1956
they added four bonus votes for each state casting its electoral vote for
the Democratic nominee at the previous presidential election. In 1960,
this was abandoned in favor of a new method of allocation which gave
each state 2½ convention votes for each member of Congress. If the
number thus computed resulted in a fraction, the state was given an
additional half vote to bring its total to a whole number. Each member
of the national committee was designated as delegate from his state or
territory with a half-vote each. No state was to have fewer convention
votes than it had at the previous convention, and a state was given the
option of electing either as many delegates as it had votes or twice as
many delegates with one-half vote each.

The Democrats changed their formula again in 1964 and retained essentially the same allocations in 1968, each time providing that

no state would have fewer full delegates than it had had in previous conventions.[3] The major purpose of the 1964 change was to yield to demands of the big states to allocate bonus votes in proportion to the popular vote cast for the presidential candidate at the last election. The 1968 schedule provided that (1) each state receive three convention votes for each electoral vote; (2) each state be given one bonus vote for every 100,000 popular votes cast for the Democratic candidate for President in 1964 (fractions over 50,000 were counted, but no state received less than one such bonus); (3) states that voted for Johnson in 1964 be given an extra "victory" bonus of ten votes, (4) each state be given one vote for each of its national committeemen, but no alternates were allowed for them. Because of Republican presidential victories in the Deep South in 1964, that area had slightly reduced strength overall in the 1968 Democratic convention.

The Democratic rules provided for total voting strength of 2,622 in the 1968 convention with 2,989 delegates permitted to attend. When 2,512 alternates were added, the total delegation consisted of 5,611 persons! In contrast, the Republicans had 2,666 delegates with a total voting strength of 1,333. The increase in the size of the convention is one of the greatest changes in party organizations in recent years; in 1948 by comparison, Republicans had a total voting strength of 1,094 and the Democrats 1,234. The large convention permits the reward of more party workers, allows more people to participate in demonstrations, and creates a greater spectacle for the television audience.

Choice of Delegates by State Committees and Conventions. Of the three methods used in the states to select delegates—party committees, party conventions, and party primaries—the fewest number are selected by committees. In Arizona, Arkansas, Georgia, and Louisiana, delegates are customarily chosen by the state committees, but details and procedures vary in these states. In Arkansas, for example, a presidential primary must be held if a presidential candidate requests one but the state committee still selects the delegates; and in Arizona the party's state committee is regarded as a convention. In New York and Pennsylvania, the at-large delegates are chosen by the state committees, and in Massachusetts the state chairman appoints the delegates-at-large but his selections can be challenged in the primary.

[3] Many useful data on allocations for both conventions and the methods used in each state to select delegates to the national conventions in 1968 were published by the U.S. Government Printing Office, Washington, D.C., in January, 1968, for the Secretary of the Senate under the title *Nomination and Election of the President and Vice President of the United States Including the Manner of Selecting Delegates to the National Political Conventions.*

More delegates are chosen by state conventions than by the party votes at presidential primaries. Great variation exists in the constitution and procedures of the district and state conventions. Certain groups may feel aggrieved with treatment accorded them and hold a rump convention to name their own slate of delegates with the result that the national convention must choose between rival delegations. In several states, partisans attend precinct caucuses to express presidential preferences and to select delegates to county conventions, and so on, up to the state convention, which chooses the delegates to the national convention. A common practice is for the congressional district conventions to choose district delegates and for the state convention to designate the at-large national convention delegates. In a few cases, all district and at-large delegates are named at the state party convention. Whatever the mechanism, in only a few states does the voter have a direct voice in the choice of delegates to the national convention. The best he can hope for is to choose the men who select the delegates, but often he chooses men who choose still other men to select the delegates.

The position of national delegate is eagerly sought, and there are never enough places for all the party officers, campaign contributors, and public officeholders who want them. A person wishing to become a delegate must build up prestige and friendship among those who will be delegates to the local and state conventions. Much maneuvering takes place, often months in advance of the local conventions. A would-be delegate has to decide whether it is better to commit himself to a certain presidential hopeful or faction within the party or to appear neutral and hope he will be a compromise choice. Often governors, congressmen, and powerful party leaders are given delegate positions and many serve as the chairman or as the state's representative on a major national convention committee. It is probable, although not fully documented, that more party officials and active partisans are selected as delegates in the convention process than in the direct primaries.

A major overall issue surrounding convention-selected delegates concerns mandating, or instructing, the delegates. Formal instructions may vary in intensity of commitment and in direction. Some conventions pass a resolution that is binding on the delegation to support a favorite son or a leading candidate for one or two ballots or until released. Other conventions may express a preference or recommendation without attempting to bind the delegates. An uninstructed delegation strengthens the bargaining position of the leaders of the state's delegation, provided they are able to control their delegates. Some party politicans, however, believe that firm commitments and a unit rule requiring that a state's vote be cast en bloc (determined by the majority) strengthen the delegation in the national convention.

Election in Primaries. The first presidential primary was used in Florida in 1904, and the device became an article of progressive Republican faith and quickly spread, reaching a peak in 1916 with use in twenty-two states. At one time or another, half of the states have used direct election of delegates or called for expression of voter preference for presidential nominees. The primary has declined in popularity—only about one-third of the states have used it in recent years—but as many as 40 percent of the delegates are elected in the primaries. In 1968, fourteen states held preferential presidential primaries (Maryland and the District of Columbia held such primaries in 1964 but neither did so in 1968).[4] In chronological order they were New Hampshire, Wisconsin, Pennyslvania, Massachusetts, Ohio, Indiana, West Virginia, Nebraska, Oregon, Florida, California, South Dakota, New Jersey, and Illinois. In West Virginia, which usually holds a primary, there were no entries. No candidates filed in Illinois so the preference poll was withdrawn, but there were some 16,000 write-in votes.

The varieties of presidential primaries are so many and differ in such detail that, when held, they usually leave the public confused and wondering what the results demonstrated. Indiana uses a presidential preference vote with a separate election of national convention delegates by the state convention. Delegates are bound to support the preference winners on the first ballot. In New Hampshire, delegates are elected in the primary and voters may express a preference as well, but the latter is advisory. Delegates may run as pledged or not pledged to a candidate. In another variation, South Dakota blends preference vote and delegation selection. One may mark his ballot for a slate favoring a certain presidential candidate; party organizations often prefer to enter an unpledged slate. California and Wisconsin used variations of this combined vote in 1968.

The preference vote is likely to assume the most significance in Oregon, since the names of all serious aspirants are generally on the ballot and write-ins are possible for those whose names were not filed on the seventieth day prior to the primary. The Oregon secretary of state is directed to place on the ballot all names of those whose "candidacy is generally recognized in the national news media throughout the United States." If a person does not wish his name on the ballot he must file an affidavit that he is not a candidate and does not intend to become

---

[4]The most up-to-date analytical work on the subject is James W. Davis, *Presidential Primaries: Road to the White House,* copyright Thomas Y. Crowell Company, New York, 1967. The volume is also a storehouse of information including statistics on the presidential primary votes from 1912 through 1964. Presidential primary laws undergo such rapid revision that no attempt is made here to outline the individual state laws, since they quickly become obsolete. Extensive data on the 1968 primaries are found in the *Congressional Quarterly Weekly Report,* vol. 26, pp. 463–468, March 8, 1968.

one. Delegates are permitted to identify their preferences but are committed to support the winner of the preference poll irrespective of their own preference. The Nebraska legislature adopted the essential features of the Oregon plan in 1968.

Presidential primaries are criticized on many grounds. Party chairmen see them in terms of raising money at the wrong time for the wrong reasons. When they go to persons for funds after the convention, the prospective donor may refuse on the ground that he gave money during the primaries to one of the presidential hopefuls. The same complaint, of course, can be made for the primary system of nomination for other offices. Some regard the primaries as too costly and as favoring the person who is wealthy or who can attract money from outside the state.[5] The importance of relative ability to purchase quantities of television time generates contentions that the nomination can be "bought" and that the system of checks and balances within the party organization in selecting nominees is neutralized or wiped out.

Critics see the primaries as meaningless popularity contests, exhausting the prospective nominees by requiring them to campaign for months before the convention. The degree to which the preference vote is binding varies and in many cases is not binding at all. Further, primaries are seldom a real test of the strength of all the leading contenders. Aspirants tend to avoid primaries in which they feel they might make a poor showing or where a favorite son preempts the delegation. It is customary not to challenge the favorite son in his primary, and delegates enjoy the flexibility they possess when released by him at the convention.

The 1968 Republican primaries were not very meaningful as they left the field largely to Richard Nixon. Governor Rockefeller did not permit his name to be entered in any primaries (though he did well in a few write-in campaigns). Governor Romney of Michigan withdrew before the New Hampshire primary but too late to have his name removed. Although Governor Reagan's name appeared on several ballots, he waged no active campaign for votes in those states.

In 1968, Sens. Robert Kennedy and Eugene McCarthy were pitted against each other only in the Indiana, Nebraska, Oregon, California, and South Dakota Democratic primaries. Hubert Humphrey entered the presidential contest in April, after the closing date for filing in nearly all primary states. It was possible, however, for his name to be

[5] Because no report on preconvention expenses either in primaries or state conventions is required, there is no way to check the accuracy of figures given out by aspirants and the press. Eisenhower forces were reported to have spent $2.5 million in 1952; Rockefeller, according to *The New York Times,* June 17, 1964, spent $5 million before withdrawing and, without entering the primaries, spent $7 million in 1968. Some $7 million was raised collectively by local and national Goldwater committees before the convention.

written in on ballots in seven states, but he waged no campaign to have this done.[6] His entry tightened the contest; and, even before the assassination of Senator Kennedy on the night of the California primary (June 5), it seemed certain he would be able to offer a serious challenge because he could not be knocked out in primaries.

Other difficulties diminish the effectiveness of presidential primaries as an accurate reflection of the desires of the party voters. They are held on different dates over a three-month period, often under such dissimilar conditions that meaningful comparisons are wanting. The separation of delegate selection from preference polls in several states may distract the attention of voters from the election of delegates — and it is the delegates who vote in conventions. Popular voting strength is not necessarily correlated with corresponding delegate voting strength. In Massachusetts the preference poll is binding for one ballot; Governor Rockefeller in 1968 won a write-in vote of 30 percent and captured the support of all delegates, although Nixon received about 26 percent and Governor Volpe as a favorite son polled 29.5 percent.

Primary Strength and Nomination. Primaries have killed off not only candidates of little popular strength before the convention but even candidates of stature. Wendell Willkie withdrew after being beaten by Gov. Thomas E. Dewey in the 1944 Wisconsin primaries; Hubert Humphrey withdrew after losing to John F. Kennedy in the 1960 Wisconsin and West Virginia primaries. Even though the losing candidate may not withdraw, defeats in the primary hurt his cause, as evidenced in the rather poor showing in 1952 by Sen. Robert A. Taft. Eisenhower supporters cited Taft's primary showings as "documentary evidence" that "Taft can't win."

Many prominent candidates have been helped by primary victories, which have put a stronger foundation under their contention; for example, Roosevelt in 1932, Dewey's victory over Stassen in Oregon in 1948, Stevenson's over Kefauver in 1956, and the victories of Eisenhower in 1952 and Kennedy in 1960. Goldwater's primary record was not particularly impressive; he lost in Massachusetts, New Hampshire, Oregon, and Pennsylvania. However, when he won the final and big one in California, his lead in delegates was too large for others to overcome. On the other hand, among those winning nomination without a plurality of primary votes (excluding incumbent Presidents) were Landon, Willkie, Dewey (1944 and 1948), Stevenson (1952), and Humphrey (1968). Victories in the primaries, therefore, offer no assurance of nomination, as evidenced by Democrats McAdoo in 1924, Kefauver in 1952,

[6] The 1968 primaries did not attract a high vote — about 3,560,000 in the Republican contests and 6,700,000 in the Democratic primaries.

and McCarthy in 1968 and Republicans Borah in 1936, Dewey in 1940, and MacArthur in 1944.

Preconvention Strategies. Although likely to be the most important single decision, entry or nonentry into the primaries is by no means the only stratagem to be decided. Conventions are now less easily controlled by old-style leaders and bosses, although certain state chairmen are sufficiently powerful and influential to control uncommitted and favor-ite-son votes.[7] Because candidates with 40 percent or more of the total vote on the first ballot usually go on to win the nomination, the aspirants make every effort to mount a huge vote at the onset; and the leading candidate or candidates urge delegates to get on the band wagon.[8] Supporters point out to the uncommitted the desirability of being for their man before the convention. Thinly disguised hints of patronage are dangled before delegates before their arrival in the convention city. These activities make it difficult to get a successful "stop movement" against the leading candidate. This was particularly true of Gov. Nelson Rockefeller both in 1964 and 1968; he found large numbers of local party leaders with rather strong and private commitments to Goldwater and to Nixon respectively, and only a few Republican governors would declare for him as they had for Eisenhower in 1952. In extensive campaigning throughout the country in 1968, Mr. Nixon often dropped the names of popular governors and senators as excellent potential vice presidential nominees. This tactic helped to keep delegations committed to Nixon or to prevent them from pledging themselves to Rockefeller or Reagan; the latter action might be inimical to the chances of their favored leaders to become Nixon's running mate.

Although it was widely believed that Senators McCarthy and Kennedy were breaking precedent in 1968 by challenging an incumbent President, history shows other such challenges. Theodore Roosevelt substantially outpolled President Taft in the 1912 primaries, a fact that encouraged the Roosevelt third-party effort. Senators Hiram Johnson and Robert La Follette challenged Calvin Coolidge in 1924, forcing Coolidge's managers to change strategy and to wage an aggressive presidential primary campaign for him. A former senator, Joseph

[7] On leadership of state delegations in 1960, see Paul Tillett (ed.), *Inside Politics: The National Conventions, 1960,* Oceana Publications, Inc., Dobbs Ferry, N.Y., 1962, parts IV and V. There is extensive popular literature on strategies in periodicals and books. F. Clifton White with William J. Gill published a most informative account in *Suite 3505: The Story of the Draft Goldwater Movement,* Arlington House, Inc., New Rochelle, N.Y., 1967; and Theodore H. White covered the record of presidential campaigns beginning in 1960 *The Making of the President, 1960, The Making of the President, 1964,* and *The Making of the President, 1968,* Atheneum Publishers, New York, 1961, 1965, and 1969.

[8] In only four of the last thirteen Democratic conventions has more than one ballot been necessary, and only three times have the Republicans needed more than one ballot.

France of Maryland, challenged Herbert Hoover in 1932 and, though entering fewer primaries than the President, substantially outpolled him. In the absence of a declaration by President Eisenhower that he would seek nomination in 1956, Sen. William Knowland permitted his name to be filed in several primaries. Even after Eisenhower announced his intention to run again on February 29, a few Knowland-pledged delegates let their names remain on the ballot but polled only a small vote. Governor George C. Wallace challenged President Johnson in several states and, although not winning in any of them, drew a creditable vote.

An important part of strategy is timing—when and where to announce. In a rare instance, such as with Adlai Stevenson in 1952, no official preconvention announcement was made; and he waited successfully for the convention to come to him with a "draft." Generally, hopefuls travel widely throughout the nation a year or two in advance of the convention then dramatically announce the "encouragement" that local leaders are giving them to enter the race. Official announcements too early lead to mobilization of the opposition; a front-runner may put himself in a precarious position by causing competitors to form a coalition against him. With few exceptions, announcements usually come between December and February, the latter date being necessary to fulfill filing requirements for the first presidential primary in New Hampshire in March.

Values of a Diversified Selection System. A hybrid system of choosing national convention delegates by both state conventions and primaries gives greater flexibility to candidates and to the nominating process itself. Aspirants are not forced to rely exclusively on party voters as would be required by a national presidential primary or mandatory state primaries or winning over hundreds of party activists in scores of congressional and state conventions. Candidates who might be sidetracked by party leaders can use the primaries to demonstrate their popular appeal, with options kept open for the presidential nomination. Contenders are forced today to campaign under all kinds of conditions and the general public has a chance to size up strengths and weaknesses of various hopefuls.

Of the electrifying surprises of spring 1968 (the challenge to President Johnson by Sens. Kennedy and McCarthy, the President's removal of himself, Romney's early entry and withdrawal from the New Hampshire before election day), none caused greater astonishment among newsmen than Gov. Nelson Rockefeller's announcement on March 24 before a nationwide television audience that he would not actively seek the Republican nomination, followed forty days later by his assertion that he would be a candidate. During the interval, his organization had been dismantled. His name appeared on no primary ballots but he did get 125,000 write-in votes, which included a first-ballot support in Massachusetts. His strategy was twofold: First, he would meet privately with delegates already selected, urging them to remain flexible and uncommitted and noting that in nationwide polls he was a stronger candidate against either Humphrey or McCarthy than was Nixon. Second, he would put on an intensive personal campaign and would purchase television time and expensive full-page ads in major newspapers to enhance his cause and to try to attract supporters left politically homeless by the death of Senator Kennedy. It was Rockefeller's belief that these tactics would raise his percentage on the opinion polls and would convince convention delegates that he was the more likely Republican winner in November.

The 1968 preconvention campaign also showed the viability of the open, hybrid system that permits aspirants blocked by one method to keep politically alive by another. Senator Eugene McCarthy of Minnesota generated little enthusiasm among the party leaders and could not hope to obtain sizable strength in states using conventions to choose delegates. By entering primaries and doing reasonably well, he became "the candidate who won't go away." His initial success in New Hampshire gave his cause a lift and showed that Lyndon Johnson was vulnerable. This revelation led a short time later to Sen. Robert Kennedy's entry; in absence of McCarthy's exposure of Johnson's weakness, Kennedy probably would not have entered unless Johnson officially withdrew. Vice President Humphrey's lateness of entry kept him from winning any significant number of delegates in the primaries but the alternate route of concentrating on convention-selected delegates was open to him. His many loyal supporters in local Democratic organizations concentrated on controlling credentials committees and otherwise influencing convention choices.

Richard Nixon has always been enormously popular among Republican party workers and the men and women who become delegates. His loss in 1960 to John F. Kennedy and his failure to win the California governorship in 1962 were believed to have ended his political career. But he remained active as a Republican fund raiser and speaker.[9] To show wide voter appeal and to overcome the "loser" image, he decided to enter all the major Republican primaries in 1968 as well as till the soil of state conventions. Governor Ronald Reagan's name was

[9] In 1966 alone, Nixon made campaign appearances for Republican candidates in thirty-five states; and he estimates that he traveled more than 200,000 miles from 1965 to 1968 helping to build party organizations and raise funds. See *U.S. News & World Report*, July 15, 1968, pp. 48–52 on Nixon record.

in every primary and garnered some support, but many observers declared as early as May that Nixon had the nomination "locked up." The mixed system of conventions and primaries opens up competition for the presidency and pressures candidates who might wish to blitz the national convention to campaign openly for the nomination. "Without the primaries," writes James W. Davis,

> The national convention delegates would be left to rely solely on public opinion polls, their own observations, and their own consciences in picking the presidential candidates. . . . The majority of the delegates are still free to make their choice of the candidate they feel best merits the nomination. The convention can still operate as a broker to reconcile differences and factions of the party as well as draft the platform and rally the party faithful.[10]

CONVENTION COMPOSITION AND LEADERSHIP

Characteristics of Delegates. Ostrogorski saw national conventions as composed of "a greedy crowd of officeholders, or of office seekers, disguised as delegates of the people." Other writers criticize conventions as unrepresentative and often lacking in reputability and competence. Adequate studies of delegates to conventions in the distant past are lacking, but surveys of the makeup of the institutions since 1948 tend to cast a different light on the men and women who become delegates.[11]

Briefly, the average age of delegates is around fifty. Women constitute only a little more than 10 percent and newsmen reported there were only 14 black delegates to the 1964 Republican convention. Blacks increased their representation in 1968 but still held only 26 delegate and 52 alternate positions in the 1968 Republican convention; respective numbers in the Democratic convention were 182 and 141. In terms of religious preference, Protestants greatly predominate, although Catholics fare much better in Democratic conventions. A considerable number of delegates have held public office, and from one-fourth to one-third of the delegates have attended past conventions.

The occupational and income distribution are shown in Tables 10-1 and 10-2. Because delegates were asked to indicate whether they were public, party, or union officials in addition to their principal occupations, percentages in Table 10-1 add up to more than 100 percent. A sizable majority are party officials and the 1964 study found that 83.4

[10]*Op. cit.,* p. 27.
[11]Summaries of the various studies are presented in David et al., *The Politics of National Party Conventions,* chap. 14. See also Kevin L. McKeough and John F. Bibby, *The Costs of Political Participation: A Study of National Convention Delegates,* Citizens' Research Foundation Study no. 14, Princeton, N.J., 1968. Most studies are based on representative samples because of the impossibility of compiling data on every one of the thousands of delegates. There are variations in each convention, but a general pattern is observable.

TABLE 10-1 Occupational distribution of national convention delegates, 1964

Occupations	Democrats	Republicans
Public officials	36.8%	20.8%
Party officials	54.6	60.6
Union members	4.1	1.8
Union officials	0.6	0.0
Lawyers and judges	29.3	21.0
Publishers, editors, broadcasters	1.7	1.4
Businessmen	26.2	32.3
Other professions	6.6	7.6
Farmers and ranchers	6.4	5.9
Homemakers	6.2	10.3
All others	6.8	9.1

Source: Kevin L. McKeough and John F. Bibby, *The Costs of Political Participation: A Study of National Convention Delegates,* Citizens' Research Foundation Study no. 14, Princeton, N.J., 1968, pp. 83–84.

TABLE 10-2 Income distribution of convention delegates, 1964

Reported annual income	Democratic	Republican
$50,000 or more	10.1%	14.0%
25,000–49,999	19.9	24.7
20,000–24,999	13.4	11.7
15,000–19,999	16.7	16.2
10,000–14,999	24.6	20.2
5,000– 9,999	11.9	11.5
3,500– 4,999	2.2	1.3
Under 3,500	0.6	0.4

Source: Kevin L. McKeough and John F. Bibby, *The Costs of Political Participation: A Study of National Convention Delegates,* Citizens' Research Foundation Study no. 14, Princeton, N.J., 1968, pp. 83–84.

percent of the Democratic and 88 percent of the Republican delegates claimed to be regular contributors to their state party organizations; median contributions in 1962 were, respectively, $239 and $231.[12] A big majority of the delegates admitted that they personally assumed their costs in campaigning for the job of delegate. At the national convention, Democratic delegates, on the average, spent $455 and Republicans, $647. Obviously delegates are differentiated from the mass electorate by their high incomes, and most assume a large share of their personal expenses in attending the convention. Money appears to be a determinant of who can participate in presidential nominating politics. The great majority of governors and United States senators are delegates or alternates, but only about 40 percent of the United States representatives attend the conventions as delegates.

[12] McKeough and Bibby, *op. cit.,* p. 87.

Succinctly, the composition of national conventions is no more a typical cross section than is that of Congress or state legislative bodies. Delegates tend to be party activists and college educated, to come from a business or a profession, and to have above-average incomes. Yet it should hardly be expected that conventions be a microcosm of the nation. One significant study also shows that the delegates are not ideologically a cross section of their own party's rank-and-file supporters.[13] In the Republican party particularly, leaders' views were quite different from those of followers, with the former more conservative on public questions. Republican followers disagreed more with their own leaders than with the leaders of the Democratic party. This is another illustration of the fact that rank-and-file voters are not very ideological and that Republican and Democratic leaders tend to have more pronounced positions than do their followers.

The difference in attitudes toward issues and government between convention delegates and partisans back home would be certain to lead to tension between the two if delegates invariably acted solely on their real views. In 1964, for example, delegates voted in a great majority for Goldwater and received much criticism for not reflecting the views of their own party's followers. Most of the time this disregard for rank-and-file views does not occur because convention leadership is in the hands of men long active in party politics who have attended previous conventions and are experienced in the ways of practical politics. Their operating beliefs are based upon electoral reality, which may call for accommodation with their real beliefs in the interests of unity and victory. For this reason, conventions have tended to choose an Eisenhower or a Nixon over a Rockefeller or a Taft.

Oratory and Organization. The national chairman calls the first session to order, and welcoming speeches follow. After the chairman has delivered his address, the gavel is turned over to the temporary chairman, who usually delivers the keynote address. This speech supposedly outlines the job of the convention. Like many of those to follow, the speech is often flamboyant and extravagant in phraseology and castigates the opposition. With ever-increasing crescendo, the minority-party keynote speaker charges his party to "save the nation" from the party in power; he concludes in eloquence, like Claude Bowers, the Democratic keynoter in 1928:

[13] The study was conducted in 1958. See Herbert McClosky, Paul J. Hoffman, and Rosemary O'Hara, "Issue Conflict and Consensus among Party Leaders and Followers," *American Political Science Review*, vol. 54, pp. 406–427, 1960. Characteristics of delegates who become convention leaders have been noted by Samuel J. Eldersveld and Dwaine Marvick, "National Convention Leadership: 1952 and 1956," *Western Political Quarterly*, vol. 14, pp. 176–194, 1961.

We shall win because our cause is just. The predatory forces before us seek a triumph for the sake of sacking. Their shock troops are the Black Horse Cavalry whose hoof beats have made hideous music on Pennsylvania Avenue during the last eight years. They are led by the money-mad cynics and scoffers and we go forth to battle for the cause of man. In the presence of such a foe "he who dallies is a dastard and he who doubts is damned." In this convention we close debate and grasp the sword. The time has come. The battle hour has struck. Then to your tents, O Israel.[14]

Senator Alben Barkley's ringing keynote address in 1948 resulted in a thunderous ovation and demonstration and helped him win the vice presidential nomination, even though up to that time President Truman had not placed his stamp of approval on the Kentucky Senator. Recent keynoters have failed to electrify the delegates to the same extent; the speech now appears directed toward the television public rather than toward the delegates.

Except for the oratory and entertainment, the first two or three days of the convention floor activities are somewhat dull for delegates anxious to nominate candidates. Routine matters, such as electing a permanent organization, seating delegates, providing for rules and order of business, and adopting a platform must be taken care of. The standing committees that handle these four functions usually consist of one person from each state and territory. The resolutions committee is the sole exception.

In some states in which delegates are chosen by state conventions, rival delegations may be selected, and the national convention is called upon to decide who are bona fide delegates from the state. Party rules require each delegate and alternate to file his credentials with the national committee a few weeks before the convention, and delegates are seated temporarily on the basis of this list. The convention's credentials committee must certify this list before delegates can be seated, and its report is presented before the convention adopts the platform or makes nominations. At most conventions this is a routine matter, but when numerous contests do arise, they can disrupt convention harmony.

In 1964, a floor fight involving the Alabama and Mississippi delegations was avoided when the Democratic convention, by a voice vote, adopted the rule that delegates would be seated if they signed a pledge to support the nominees of the convention. Some of each delegation did sign, others left the convention. The Freedom Democratic party delegation, which challenged the all-white regular Mississippi delegation, was given two seats with the regulars, provided that they signed the pledge. The compromise, urged by President Johnson in the interest of harmony, placated a large number of, but not all, the Southern delegates and had the virtue of heading off a ruinous walkout by

[14] *The New York Times,* June 27, 1928.

other Southern delegations. The rule further provided that in 1968 the state Democratic parties would not discriminate in color, creed, or national origin in the selection of their delegation and that electors would be "pledged formally and in good conscience" to the election of the nominees appearing under the Democratic party label. The rule adopted in 1968 by the Republicans that henceforth barred racial discrimination in state delegations may be a source of conflict in future Republican conventions.

An unprecedented number of credentials disputes characterized the 1968 Democratic convention.[15] These conflicts arose from alleged racial discrimination in state party affairs, especially in the South; other violations of state party rules; failure of regular delegations to satisfy requirements of national party loyalty; and "undemocratic" procedures in the selection of delegates.[16] Supporters of Sen. Eugene McCarthy in several states argued they had been denied proportional representation in the selection of delegates. In other cases, it was charged that the requirement that a delegate be a bona fide Democrat was not observed. Compromises worked out by the credentials committee seated both the regular and the challenging racially mixed group from Georgia, splitting the votes between them. Challengers from Mississippi were seated, as were the regulars from Alabama, but with the provision that the latter be required to take a loyalty oath as a precondition to seating at the convention. Many of the regulars later walked out. On the fifteen other challenges, the recommendations of the majority of the credentials committee were accepted, several by voice vote or roll call on the floor of the convention. The credentials fights were symptomatic of the divisions among delegates and their angry mood.

Loyalty raises the question of what a national political party can do and should do, within a framework that permits it to remain a viable political entity while allowing room for individual conscience. This has been a serious problem for Democratic conventions as evidenced particularly by the wrangling over a "loyalty oath" in 1952, when an effort was made to pledge all delegates to see that the convention's nominees appeared on the ballots in their states under the designation

[15]A comprehensive account of these is found in John R. Schmidt and Wayne W. Whalis, "Credentials Contests at the 1968—and 1972—Democratic National Conventions," *Harvard Law Review*, vol. 82, pp. 1438–1470, 1969. For a shorter summary of the contests, see *Congressional Quarterly*, Aug. 30, 1968, p. 2286. Depending on how one groups the challenges, there were eighteen different contests.

[16]"Undemocratic" procedures in the selection of delegates raised questions of the legitimacy of the convention itself and, if unresolved, may alienate rank-and-file members. The 1968 convention directed the national committee to establish a committee to evaluate delegate selection. In 1969, a Commission on Party Structure and Delegate Selection headed by Sen. George McGovern of South Dakota in 1969 held hearings throughout the country. There is a regular committee on rules and order of business for each party's convention but it does not function between conventions.

of the Democratic party. The purpose was to prevent "bolting" Southern delegations from mounting a third-party slate under the Democratic label, as had happened in 1948. Since 1956, the national convention has operated under a rule requiring that a state party, in certifying delegates to the national convention, undertakes to place the convention's nominees on their ballots "under the Democratic party."[17]

THE PLATFORM

Preparation. Although it takes second place to the excitement over nominations, the drafting of a platform is a major function of the convention. Platforms have evolved from almost exclusively negative documents into widely publicized statements of party faith.[18] The task of drafting the platform is assigned to the committee on resolutions, composed of two persons from each state or territorial delegation. Manifestly it would be difficult for a committee of this size to formulate a satisfactory set of resolutions within a few hours after the opening of the convention. In practice, therefore, a draft of a platform is prepared before the convention begins by a platform group appointed by the national committee.

The scope of this group is illustrated by a subcommittee appointed in January, 1952, by the Republican National Committee to collect, digest, and transmit platform suggestions to the resolutions committee. The subcommittee received 325 suggestions from state and local organizations. The research director of the national committee consolidated the suggestions and sent them to the resolutions committee. In 1960, the Democrats sent panels into various cities inviting views on what should go into the platform. In New York City alone, fifty-three witnesses appeared to give proposals.[19] Republican governors, eager to highlight emphasis on urban problems, held hearings in various cities in 1968 to invite suggestions especially for the urban planks.

[17] On the loyalty issue from 1948 through 1960, see Abraham Holtzman, *The Loyalty Pledge Controversy in the Democratic Party*, McGraw-Hill Book Company, New York, 1962. Discussions of the 1964 loyalty issues are found in *The New York Times*, Aug. 25 and 26, 1964.

[18] See Edward F. Cooke, "Drafting the 1952 Platforms," *Western Political Quarterly*, vol. 9, pp. 669–712, 1956, for a full account of the preparation of both parties' platforms. Charles A. H. Thomson and Frances M. Shattuck provide an interesting analysis of the 1956 platforms in *The 1956 Presidential Campaign*, The Brookings Institution, Washington, D.C., 1960, chaps. 4 and 6. The first fully developed platform was adopted by the Democrats in 1840. Copies of major- and minor-party platforms have been brought together by Kirk H. Porter and Donald B. Johnson in *National Party Platforms, 1840–1960*, The University of Illinois Press, Urbana, Ill., 1961.

[19] For an account of this meeting, see *The New York Times*, June 22, 1960. When the resolutions committee formally met in Los Angeles, it was presented with extensive data for the platform.

The platform committees customarily convene a week before the conventions to hold hearings, edit the preliminary platform, and put it into final form for submission to the convention. The hearings give publicity to prominent persons in the party who are running for lesser offices as well as to state and local aspirants. Spokesmen for the presidential contenders, and often the aspirants themselves, are given a chance to put forth their views; usually their appearances are televised for the nation.

Through the hearings, dozens of persons from pressure groups are brought into contact with the committee and, indirectly, with the party officialdom. The fact that platforms are usually ambiguous has not kept private groups from trying to influence them. Witnesses stress the need to profess the party's warm heart for veterans, labor, farmers, minorities, the American way, business (particularly small business), and so on. Testimony given before platform bodies may be newsworthy and gain free publicity. The same interest groups, and often the same persons, appear before both parties. The Chamber of Commerce, the National Association of Manufacturers, and the American Farm Bureau Federation are likely to find a more friendly reception at the Republican meeting than at the Democratic hearings, and the AFL-CIO and Farmers Union feel more at home with the Democrats. Invariably clear-cut proposals for policy planks are submitted by such hardy perennials as the National Association for the Advancement of Colored People, the American Legion, the National Education Association, Zionist groups, women's rights leagues, pensioners, and foreign policy societies.

The preconvention hearings serve an educational purpose for many members of the platform committee, for candidates, and for the general public. They show the antithetical positions of groups and factions and indicate areas of consensus. The regular platform committee realizes where compromises must be made and, with a few days remaining before presentation to the convention, can devote some of its energies to accommodation. If great divergencies appeared only a few hours before the resolutions were to go to the floor of the convention, there might well be insufficient time to reconcile differences. In general, however, the testimony has little effect on the platform, the major provisions of which have already been agreed upon.

If the incumbent is certain to be renominated or, as in the case of Vice President Nixon in 1960, the choice of candidate is a foregone conclusion, the President or apparent nominee takes a hand in shaping the platform. For an incumbent President, the platform must be an exclusive defense and general blueprint for the future. Raymond Moley asserts that President Roosevelt wrote the 1936 platform and that the resolutions committee made but the slightest alteration in it.[20] The Hoover administration is reported to have written the 1932 Republican platform. The influences of the Eisenhower administration were far more circumspect in 1956, but newsmen learned that certain of the executive department groups furnished recommendations and that most of the platform was in the hands of strongly pro-Eisenhower men. President Johnson determined the major lines of the 1964 platform and the Vietnam plank in 1968.

Party leaders and delegates for the most part wish to avoid floor fights. Once struggles over issues and policies become open, they reveal to the public divisions and lack of harmony. In every convention, strenuous effort is made to settle policy questions off the floor and away from television cameras. But even so, it is often difficult to keep either the delegates or the interested public from learning of intraparty clashes.

In 1960, Gov. Nelson Rockefeller of New York thought the preliminary draft, especially in civil rights and national defense, lacked a sense of urgency, and he seemed, by implication, ready to take the question to the floor of the convention. Rockefeller's enemies saw his stand as a form of political blackmail, but he would not retreat. To head off an open fight, Nixon made a secret visit to Rockefeller on the Saturday night before the opening of the convention and emerged with a statement, popularly called the Fourteen-point Compact of Fifth Avenue. The statement was considerably more liberal than that prepared by the platform committee. President Eisenhower was reported to be furious because the Nixon-Rockefeller draft seemed to some extent to reflect on his foresight in the national defense area. Southerners and Sen. Barry Goldwater felt that they had been betrayed, and the Senator called it "a Republican Munich." Several members of the platform committee said that a mockery had been made of its deliberations. Nixon met with key members of the platform committee and exerted pressure for the requested changes. He was convinced that Rockefeller had to be placated and a floor fight avoided. The Nixon-Rockefeller proposals, with some modifications, prevailed in the platform committee. Rockefeller withdrew threats of a floor fight on the platform and announced his support of Nixon.

The incident illustrates how an influential contender for the nomination can force changes in a platform by posing the possibility of a floor fight. It also is indicative of the fact that a sure nominee (Nixon) can dictate the contents of a platform and exercise power at a crucial point in order to preserve outward unity. It further demonstrates that

[20] Raymond Moley, *After Seven Years*, Harper & Row, Publishers, Incorporated, New York, 1939, pp. 346–347.

a party will go far to reconcile dissident factions and that a strong faction can, on some planks, dictate its terms. In 1968, Nixon and Rockefeller forces teamed up to force changes in the preliminary platform so as to try to hold the "doves" who wanted a strong Vietnam peace plank and the "hawks" who in the phrase of former President Eisenhower, would tolerate no "camouflaged surrender." The tactic employed was to incorporate language of all factions into a compromise plank but in such a manner as to place the Republican party on the side of achieving peace in Vietnam. Likewise, on domestic questions, moderates kept conservatives at bay by accepting some conservative statements on crime and foreign trade without altering the comparatively liberal thrust of the platform. In a display of harmony, no amendments were accepted from the floor.

Acceptance. The platform is presented to the delegates before the nominating speeches and balloting. Much more often than not, the platform is accepted with little or no real debate, even though there is generally at least one large issue over which the platform committee has battled. We have just seen that great effort is exerted to avoid a renewal of the struggle on the floor of the convention.

Two dramatic exceptions to acceptance without debate occurred in the 1948 and 1968 Democratic conventions. In 1948, Northern and Southern extremists were unwilling to accept the compromise statement on civil rights presented by the resolutions committee. Southern delegates placed before the convention a minority plank that would have largely nullified the committee's proposal. Some Northerners responded with a strong, specific counterplank, which was adopted by a vote of 651½ to 582½. Without waiting for the presidential nominations, half of the Alabama delegation and all the Mississippi delegation walked out of the convention; and the way was paved for the States' Rights party, which succeeded in taking four states away from President Truman in the election.

In 1968, a McCarthy-McGovern Vietnam plank was presented on the floor of the convention to challenge the majority report, which in general supported the administration's policies. After a landmark debate without parallel, the majority vote supported the administration by about 60 percent. The bitterness of the debate and a 40 percent dissent signaled the difficulty Hubert Humphrey would have in holding his party together in the general election. Although Sen. George McGovern supported Mr. Humphrey on the evening of the latter's acceptance, Senator McCarthy, largely because of the Vietnam policy, refused to have anything to do with the Humphrey-Muskie ticket; and several of his followers talked of a fourth-party ticket. McCarthy, however, gave no encouragement to this proposal. He endorsed Humphrey late in the campaign.

Role of Platform. Over the years, platforms have provoked much cynicism and skepticism. Most literature about them decries their ambiguity and their failure to pinpoint clear-cut differences between the parties. They avoid specific issues and, instead, monotonously "point with pride" and "view with alarm." Their purpose, Lord Bryce once observed, is "neither to define nor to convince, but rather to attract and confuse." They are criticized for making promises that the winning party has little hope or intention to keep. Before his nomination in 1964, Sen. Barry Goldwater said, "At best, political platforms are a packet of misinformation and lies." Finally, platforms are seen as "vote catchers," without binding the nominee chosen shortly after their adoption. Such doubts invite a careful look at the significance and role of the resolutions. The very fact that the drafting of platforms, state and national, has survived as a convention function attests to the belief by party leaders that the practice has some value. If platforms are of no consequence, why are there so often severe intraparty squabbles in their preparation and why is such widespread attention given to them by those outside the party?

In analyzing party platforms from 1944 to 1964, Gerald Pomper utilized a framework of "rationality" from a voter's and from a party's point of view.[21] Though he found them serving both purposes they "probably serve the cause of party-rationality better than that of voter-rationality." A platform serves a party when it contributes to electoral goals by fitting into the party's campaign strategy of the moment and by handling policy questions in a way to bring about victory. Past records of the party are presented favorably in comparison with the opposition. The party wishes to include policies known to be favored by a majority of voters and certain minorities but not opposed by any substantial minority. Where voter preferences are uncertain, the party position is kept vague. A party purpose is served by involving large numbers of party activists, supporters, and factional leaders in thinking about principles, issues and approaches to the solution of problems. Platforms afford a chance to make concessions and to bargain in the interest of enlarging the coalition for the November election. The platform may attract financial donors and care must be taken not to offend large contributors. A platform should try to avoid phrases and language which, taken out of context, would be embarrassing to the candidate.

[21] See "'If Elected, I Promise': American Party Platforms," *Midwest Journal of Political Science,* vol. 11, pp. 318–352, August, 1967. See also his *Elections in America,* Dodd, Mead & Company, Inc., New York, 1968, chap. 8.

From a voter's standpoint, a good platform states some general party policy commitments and intentions. It awakens at least some of the electorate to problems and points out some weaknesses of the opposition party. A meaningful platform indicates future positions of the party in areas of particular interest to the voter, with some consistency from one election to another. A platform gives the opposition a yardstick in succeeding years by which it could, with the voter looking on, call attention to discrepancies between promises and performance.

Overall, platforms during the past generation do show differences in the approaches of the two parties to many problems. Democrats have pledged larger federal participation in nearly every area from river-basin development to health care while Republicans have stressed to a larger extent local and private sector participation. Platforms provide some index of factionalism as well as agreement within the party and have shown who are the new men of power, such as Nixon and Rockefeller in 1960 and the Goldwater conservatives in 1964. As for "living up to the platform,"[22] nominees seldom repudiate positions indicated in platforms, but they do interpret and modify them in the ensuing campaign. In a rapidly changing world, slavish adherence to a platform written some time before, subject at best to wide interpretation, seems an unreasonable expectation.

THE PRESIDENTIAL NOMINATIONS

Nominating Speeches. With resolutions and routine matters out of the way, the great drama for which the delegates have waited begins. The secretary begins the roll call of the states from Alabama to the territories. As each state's name is called, it is entitled to put forth a name or to yield to another state to place a name in nomination. There is much maneuvering among heads of delegations to get states to yield for purposes of making nominations or seconding addresses.

Nominating speeches are something of a keynote speech in miniature. First the opposition is berated. Then the speaker extols "the man who" will do the job the country needs. He usually withholds the man's name until the last sentence. Governor Theodore R. McKeldin, placing Eisenhower in nomination in 1952, concluded his address: "Believing, as I do, that the hands of Providence have in the past guided the destiny of the Nation in times of peril I feel that we may indeed say to this man, 'Thou art come to the kingdom for such a time as this.' It is with pride that I place before this convention for President of the United States the name of Dwight David Eisenhower." As if an electric button

[22]John P. Bradley finds party platforms meaningful in the field of social security. See "Party Platforms and Party Performance Concerning Social Security," *Polity*, vol. 1, pp. 337–358, 1969.

has been pushed, mention of the candidate's name causes banners to appear throughout the convention floor; bands play, and supporters march up and down the aisle. Visitors in the galleries often shout, sing, and wave flags during the pandemonium. Many of the demonstrators are not delegates but "professionals" brought in from outside. The chairman lets the demonstration run for the length of time prescribed by the rules (10 to 20 minutes in recent conventions) and then tries to re-establish order. Demonstrators for the major aspirants try to outdo one another in boisterous noise, color, and length. A series of short seconding addresses are made by persons who show broad sectional and factional support for the nominee.

The exaggerations in speeches and the bedlam of the demonstrations horrify many viewers, who criticize the convention system as a circus beneath the dignity of the process of choosing a possible future President. Delegates themselves realize that the size, length, and noise of the demonstrations will probably change no votes but may show the nation and fellow delegates that there is some enthusiasm for their man. Television audiences probably enjoy—up to a point—these great shows on the floor, and it occupies the delegates while leaders are negotiating and planning strategy in hotel rooms miles away. Demonstrations also give some delegates a chance to give vent to their frustrations over the platform of certain defeat for their man.

"The People's Choice."   The balloting begins with an air of great tenseness after the nominating speeches. It is now that all the preconvention maneuvers are put to the test. At this point the aspirant's managers keep the pressure on the delegates. It is here that hopefuls try to collect their IOUs from delegates to make them stay in line or to win them over by negotiation. Some aspirants have counted on deadlock and have built their hopes on "in depth" second- and succeeding-ballot strength—they will now learn the depth of their strength. Money, skillful preconvention tactics, public appearances, preconvention opinion polls, and "breaks" are brought into play as the states one by one answer the roll call. But a happy combination of these factors alone will not assure nomination without those basic qualities of believed "electability" and "availability." The convention realizes (perhaps more than most idealists) that a man will not become President unless he can win. It is the prime job of the delegates to pick a winner. This accounts for the seemingly illogical behavior of the Republican convention in passing up Robert A. Taft, who was "Mr. Republican," for Dwight D. Eisenhower, who was reported never to have voted in a Republican primary.

Election potential is not easily measured but the preconvention poll has been one guideline. With the lone exception of 1964, the

Republican nominee (beginning in 1936) has been the one leading the poll of rank-and-file Republican voters. A week before the Republican convention opened in 1968, the Gallup poll showed Nixon the choice of 60 percent of the Republicans, with Rockefeller gaining only 23 percent and Reagan 7 percent. In a national cross-sectional sample, Gallup also found Nixon stronger against Democratic opponents than Rockefeller, but the Harris poll showed the reverse. Partisans of the two aspirants denounced the inconsistency of the polls. Gallup and Harris then issued a joint statement accounting for the discrepancy largely in terms that the polling was done by the two agencies one week apart. The fact that Rockefeller tied his hopes to a dramatic lead in the polls by convention time hurt his cause when the Gallup poll showed Nixon ahead.[23] Eisenhower's high popularity over Sen. Robert A. Taft in 1952 undoubtedly aided his nomination, and Kennedy and Nixon profited by strong showings in the polls. Humphrey's following among Democratic voters in 1968 was shown to be stronger than McCarthy's despite the articulate, enthusiastic support of the latter's followers.

Support by mass media, indicating "prominence," and reasonably good showings in the presidential primaries, also are influential in the convention choice. Attitudes of interest groups enter into the convention choice—often in a negative way. The influence of physicians against Harold Stassen in 1948, of labor leaders against Barkley and Taft in 1952, and against Johnson in 1960, of certain financial interests against Rockefeller in 1960, although not single determinative factors, nonetheless weakened their causes.[24] Both parties try to avoid alienating sections, particularly the South.

Some of the older, long-established traditions clustered around nominees, appear to be breaking down but are still evident in one degree or another. Such traditions established that a nominee should be a white, Protestant, family man from a large and pivotal state north of the Mason-Dixon line. Rocky Mountain and New England states seldom have provided serious contenders; Goldwater, however, cracked not only the tradition against Westerners (California excepted) but also that against small states. Television may well break down the sectional and small-state handicaps but has added another requisite—the ability to project an "effective image" into the voter's home. In addition, the nominee is expected to have had some experience in elective public office—Willkie and Eisenhower were conspicuous exceptions.

Both parties have tended to select nominees tending toward the political mean, or center. This centrist tendency has hurt the chances of

[23]Gallup-Harris statement and polls, together with Crossley poll, found in *The New York Times*, Aug. 2, 1968.

[24]Further consideration of interest-group influence in nominations is given in Chap. 20.

so-called liberal Republicans such as Earl Warren, Harold Stassen (in the 1940s and 1950s), and Nelson Rockefeller, as well as those of such conservatives as Gen. Douglas MacArthur, Robert A. Taft, and Ronald Reagan; it has worked in favor of Willkie, Dewey, Eisenhower, and Nixon. In the 1950s, Gov. Averill Harriman and Sen. Hubert Humphrey appeared as left-of-center aspirants, and Sens. Richard Russell and Lyndon Johnson suffered from both a Southern sectional handicap and a conservative image. Adlai Stevenson and John F. Kennedy were more acceptable to all factions.

Despite his 1960 defeat, compounded by a seemingly disastrous loss of the California governorship in 1962, Richard Nixon showed himself one of the most resilient and durable politicians of modern times. By his own admission, his 1968 nomination was made possible by a vacuum within the party leadership. Although there were several attractive governors and senators, the Republican governors and influential bodies were unable to coalesce around any one person, and Nixon had no serious opposition in the primaries. Rockefeller vacillated, and Reagan kept a favorite-son posture until after the convention opened. Romney, who led the polls in 1967, declined in the polls in 1968 and withdrew before the New Hampshire primary. Meanwhile, Nixon visited almost every state beginning with the 1964 campaign and spoke at hundreds of fund-raising dinners. He became "Mr. Republican" and highly popular with the activists who would become delegates to the convention. As one delegate phrased it, "Nixon's always been there when we needed him. Two years ago he came out to Idaho and gave us a tremendous shot in the arm. And we went 100 percent Republican. . . . He's always been straight for the party from top to bottom."[25]

The choice of Goldwater in 1964 appeared to violate nearly all the historic axioms of convention politics. He was a factional candidate of the right in his party, ran poorly on the polls among Republican voters, and did not have to make significant platform or other concessions. He won because conservatives after 1960 mounted a successful effort to capture control of the convention. As was Nixon in 1968, Goldwater was very strong with the Southern delegations; and the moderates and liberals both before and during the convention failed to unite around a single alternative who could get a majority of the delegates.[26]

[25] *The New York Times*, Aug. 5, 1968.
[26] As noted earlier, the Goldwater nomination may be cited as an example of party leaders in the convention acting in accordance with their real views rather than their operating ones. A comprehensive account of the winning Goldwater convention coalition is provided by John H. Kessel, *The Goldwater Coalition: Republican Stretegies in 1964*, The Bobbs-Merrill Company, Inc., Indianapolis, 1968. An account by Goldwater's political technician, F. Clifton White, with William J. Gill, is also informative: *Suite 3505: The Story of the Draft Goldwater Movement*, Arlington House. Inc., New Rochelle, N.Y., 1967.

Although the Nixon and Humphrey nominations were criticized by many of their fellow partisans, they were the preferred choices of their parties' county chairman, many of whom were delegates. Gallup's survey of Republican chairmen before the convention found Nixon preferred by 52 percent, with Reagan a poor second, and Rockefeller trailing with only 14 percent. Before Sen. Robert Kennedy's assassination in June, 1968, 70 percent of the Democratic county chairmen preferred Humphrey, 16 percent Kennedy, and only 5 percent McCarthy. With Kennedy removed, the county leaders preferred Humphrey over McCarthy 82 to 13 percent.[27]

VICE PRESIDENTIAL NOMINATIONS

After the presidential nomination, and usually with a half day or an overnight interval, the convention proceeds to choose its candidate for Vice President. Names are placed in nomination, and a ballot is taken in the same manner as for President. This is usually an anticlimax, for the delegates are emotionally spent and customarily are told who is to be the nominee. Often states come pledged to a favorite son and have a nominator with speech in hand. The nominator soon finds himself pressured to withdraw so that only one person will be nominated. Representative Charles Halleck of Indiana, permanent chairman of the 1960 Republican convention, once described the procedure for choosing the vice presidential nominee as follows: "You don't run for vice president. When a presidential nominee is named, he and other party leaders sit around in a room and select the vice presidential candidate. I've been in the room when that was done several times."

In 1956, Adlai Stevenson threw the selection of his running mate to an open convention, a rare procedure. This apparently delighted the delegates, and much of the press applauded the move. Predictions that this would set a precedent proved premature as Kennedy and Nixon, after consultation with party leaders, named their choices. Midwesterners were dismayed with Lodge, as were Northern urban liberals with Johnson, but they acceded to the requests. Custom has dictated that the vice presidential nominee be *persona grata* to the presidential candidate; compatibility is a seemingly reasonable requirement.

Of the three major functions performed by the conventions— drafting a platform, nominating a candidate for President, and nominating a candidate for Vice President—observers would probably say that, in the perspective of history, delegates have performed worst the last-mentioned job. The writers of the Constitution undoubtedly felt that the electoral college would select a highly competent person to

[27] See *Gallup Opinion Index*, Gallup International, Princeton, N.J., July, 1968.

serve as the backstop, "only one hearbeat from the Presidency." A look at many of those serving a second place on the ticket suggests that conventions have assumed that the President is immortal and that their "second man" would never become President. Although there have been excellent choices, the long-term record suggests that political qualifications rather than recognized presidential stature is the most important factor in selection.

Running mates are usually chosen with an eye to balancing the ticket geographically and ideologically, lending certain campaign strength, or providing some consolation to a defeated faction in order to achieve party unity. In many cases, for the Vice President to have succeeded to the Presidency would have meant a shift from a majority or dominant wing of the party to a minority faction. This happened when Andrew Johnson (a Democrat) succeeded Lincoln and when Theodore Roosevelt succeeded McKinley. Nixon was widely regarded as a conservative and was nominated because he was acceptable to the Taft wing. Many Eisenhower Republicans remained suspicious of him until 1956, when he seemed clearly to have moved into the moderate majority faction of the party. His renomination, therefore, was logical.

President Lyndon B. Johnson made a dramatic appearance before the Democratic National Convention in 1964 to endorse Sen. Hubert H. Humphrey of Minnesota as his running mate. The President particularly stressed Humphrey's qualifications for the Presidency should the occasion arise. Humphrey's selection added little to a balanced ticket in terms of section and religion. During his twenty years in elective public office, he had moved from a militant liberal position to one somewhat nearer the political center and had learned to get along with Senate conservatives, while Johnson had moved from the right to the center, so the two men were not far apart in terms of policy.

Richard Nixon caused great surprise and some dismay in designating Gov. Spiro T. Agnew of Maryland for vice presidential nominee in 1968. Agnew, who had been governor only two years, was not widely known nationally. Moreover, Mr. Nixon had taken a poll among party leaders to test sentiment for a running mate, and it was expected that he would choose one of many popular Northerners such as Sen. Mark Hatfield of Oregon and Charles Percy of Illinois and Mayor Lindsay of New York.[28] In protest, a minority supported Gov. George Romney of Michigan and forced a roll call on the floor, but Agnew easily won.

[28] Mr. Nixon also held the usual closed-door conferences at the convention on the vice presidency. According to *Congressional Quarterly*, governors from large urban states were underrepresented at these meetings. See report on the conferences in the issue of the *Weekly Report*, Sept. 18, 1968, pp. 24–25.

Objection to Agnew stemmed from the feeling that he would not add strength to the ticket and that Nixon was capitulating to Southern delegates who opposed virtually all prominent Northerners for the position. Nixon saw Agnew as a candidate who would not alienate the South yet would not offend the North either. The choice was consonant with Mr. Nixon's preoccupation with unity on all matters before the convention. In the spring, Mr. Nixon had announced that "law and order" was the basic issue in 1968, and Agnew had had experience in Baltimore and in the state of Maryland with urban problems and in handling public demonstrations. His Greek ancestry, moreover, might be useful in terms of ethnic votes.

Mr. Humphrey's selection of Sen. Edmund S. Muskie of Maine was generally expected and occasioned only a small dissenting vote on the floor. Muskie was somewhat better known than Agnew. In his native Maine, he had served several terms in the legislature and one term as Governor and had been in the United States Senate for ten years. His selection brought much public experience to the ticket and his Polish Catholic background might help to hold ethnic votes sensitive to the "white backlash" issue. It was believed also that he would be a good campaigner and would appeal to young people. In general, both Agnew and Muskie shared the policy views of the top of their tickets and had the virtue of being noncontroversial compared with such controversial options as Rockefeller and McCarthy.

The deaths of Presidents Roosevelt and Kennedy emphasized the need for choosing a vice presidential candidate capable of performing the enormous responsibilities of President, should the need arise. Observers of government, therefore, have emphasized the importance of extrapolitical qualities in the vice presidential candidate, such as demonstrated executive ability and thorough familiarity with foreign and domestic issues. Yet, the selection of running mates still indicates a strong dominance of political factors, and presidential nominees show no tendency to pick running mates who might overshadow them in campaigning or in public relations.

PERSPECTIVE ON THE CONVENTION

Criticisms. After all conventions, many Americans express agreement with Ostrogorski that they are "a colossal travesty of popular institutions." Criticism was especially sharp in 1968 when Republicans took more than seven hours of tedious nominating speeches and artificial demonstrations before they started to ballot for the presidential nomination. The Democrats were shown on television tearing their party

apart in fights over credentials and the Vietnam plank. Altercations between police and demonstrators in downtown Chicago while the convention was in session provoked angry, disrupting speeches on the floor—
though the convention system could hardly be blamed for events in
Chicago's Loop.

Conventions are condemned as antiquated and undemocratic
with charges against the chairman of steamroller and dictatorial rulings.
The sheer size of conventions and the methods of selecting delegates
make for control in many cases by professional party leaders rather than
for a grass-roots expression of party members. Much of the real work of
the convention goes on behind the scenes, and the floor activities are
merely results of agreements reached outside the convention itself. This
is true of almost all large conventions, and necessarily so. Delegates
themselves often owe their positions to the organization and are far
from being free agents. Although some work is done in secret, it does
not follow that the unseen activities are invariably sheer contrivance to
frustrate the popular will.

Some are unhappy with what appears as a decline in deliberation over candidates, with delegates in effect doing no more than ratifying obvious nominations. Gerald Pomper's analysis of nomination
trends identifies four categories: (1) no real choice available, ratification
only; (2) limited but significant choice; (3) choice among major candidates, eventual selection after first ballot; and (4) fullest freedom of
choice.[29] In about half the conventions, delegates were found to have
had no real influence over the nomination, and this type of nomination
or one of highly limited choice appears to be on the increase. This is
undoubtedly due to forces outside the convention including public
opinion polls, mass-media campaigning, presidential primaries, and the
practice in this century of renominating incumbent Presidents who
desire another term. Some modern critics fail to recall that in the old
days many national conventions were exercises in maneuvering state
delegations by powerful party leaders, practices which also provoked the
familiar cries of "undemocratic."

With only occasional exceptions, all conventions come under
sharp attack from those who disagree with the choice for presidential
nomination. This was especially true in 1968, when McCarthy and Rockefeller supporters decried a system that resulted in an unhappy choice,
in their point of view, between Humphrey and Nixon. Yet as noted
before, both men were shown on national public opinion polls taken
just before the conventions to be preferred by a majority of their own
party's voters. This rank-and-file preference did not hold for Goldwater

[29] Gerald Pomper, *Nominating the President: The Politics of Convention Choice*, Northwestern
University Press, Evanston, Ill., 1963, chap. 8.

in 1964, but it has been quite generally the case. Some critics see undue emphasis placed upon a man's "availability," determined by such factors as residence, family life, party loyalty, and capacity to work with organization politicians. It cannot be denied that since 1832 some mediocrities have been nominated and some have been elected and highly competent men have been passed over in favor of those less qualified.

The convention's role in determining party policy and program has always invited criticism. Resolutions are seen as a ritual, not a program; and shortcomings in a platform are easy to find. Yet, many persons are involved in the drafting process, and platforms do have a place in party life. Platforms written by a national committee or by congressional leaders would probably be less sensitive to the accommodation of diverse claims. Public officeholders do have a hand in formulating the resolutions but not an exclusive one. There is often inadequate consideration of public policy formulation between elections but this is hardly the fault of the convention, which meets quadrennially. A full-dress debate on Vietnam policy took place in the 1968 Democratic convention, and without the convention it would never have been held before a nationwide television audience.

Alternatives. Notwithstanding valid criticisms of the convention, alternatives appear less acceptable. Party activists are unlikely to favor a return to nomination by congressional caucus or to place responsibility in the hands of the national committee or a more representative national party council. A number of persons, including some members of Congress, have recommended the holding of a nationwide primary with all major candidates for each party listed on separate ballots. In terms of majority rule, the proposal looks attractive; and it would presumably do away with "unbossed" decisions and the demeaning "circus" spectacle. A national primary system would give to millions of party members direct and equal voice in choosing nominees; but it raises many problems in administration, and the various costs as well as benefits require appraisal.

First, who would be permitted to vote and how would eligibility be ascertained? Would an independent be permitted to select the primary ballot of either party or would independents be kept out of the primary unless they registered as partisans? In the several open primary states today where party registration is not required for primary elections, independents may and often do vote. In Wisconsin's presidential primary, Republicans can vote in the Democratic primary and vice versa, and raiding would be possible on a nationwide scale if each state permitted independents to participate in the selection process. If independents are to be kept out of this vital stage in the election process, the proposal could best be facilitated by a federal closed presidential primary law; but such a statute would have considerable impact on the diverse types of state primary systems and would invade a field traditionally left to the states.

Another thorny problem relates to whether a majority or a plurality would be sufficient to nominate. If a majority were needed, then runoff primaries would be required. If any plurality figure were acceptable, then a person receiving even less than 40 percent of the vote could be nominated. If, for example, anything below 40 or 45 percent would require a runoff, the two candidates of the extreme wings might get into the finals with a moderate contender who was everyone's second choice being eliminated from the election. Also, a genuine draft, such as the one for Adlai Stevenson in 1952, would be impossible under a direct primary. Related problems are the sustaining of voter interest for two if not three presidential ballots, the limitation of the number of contenders on a national primary ballot, and the probable escalation of both financial and personal-energy costs for aspirants. Presumably, the system would deal a death blow to favorite-son candidacies unless a long, cluttered ballot were permitted. (Republicans had seven favorite sons placed in nomination in 1968).

Another problem would be the selection of a vice presidential nominee. If the running mate were selected by a national primary ballot, the result might be an illogical ticket with the second place filled by a person considered undesirable by the presidential nominee. The present system of choice by the latter could be maintained by scheduling a national convention after the primary to ratify the vice presidential selection. The convention also could transact party business, write the platform, and serve as a forum for the acceptance speeches as it does now. But, this would necessitate the choosing of delegates and pave the way for struggles over credentials and resolutions as is presently the case. In other words, the arrangement would raise the same problems experienced with the present system, with the exception that certain groups of voters would assume responsibility for picking the presidential nominees.

Defense of the System. The strength of the convention method, not evident in the primary, is its potential for deliberation and compromise. The system works to assure the nomination of a candidate approaching the political mean within the party. It tends to sift through candidates and pass over the more extreme in favor of persons who, although maybe not the first choice, are acceptable. To select a person out of tune with the times or one who is anathema to certain factions in the party is to invite disaster. The successful candidate with very rare exceptions is one on whom the major party elements have secured a minimum of agreement. Then all groups in the party are expected to close ranks behind the new candidate to rise or to fall with him. Losers parade before the nationwide television audience and the convention, pledging support to the winner and urging their supporters to back him to the hilt. Such an impact or show of unity would be difficult to achieve in a national primary.

In selecting their nominees, conventions designate the kind of party leader they want and determine the kind of President the nation will have. These are long-run functions that are often not given full consideration because of the short-run objective of nominating the man most likely to win. Delegates may have some idea of a man's aptitude or his disposition toward a weak or strong executive and his ability to bargain and handle his own party leaders in the legislature, but this is not likely to be the determining factor in nomination. A man cannot exercise the authority of the Presidency unless he is elected. Moreover, men can grow in office and develop capacities for the exacting tasks of party and legislative leadership. Granted that conventions may not always pick the best man for President, one wonders whether the primary system would place more capable men in the White House. One value of a convention is that it includes numerous governors, mayors, and lawmakers who recognize the qualities needed in the successful operation of high elective office.

Variations in primaries require hopefuls to adjust to different sets of competitors in varying places under different conditions and popular attitudes. This exposure helps to indicate how those who would be nominated can handle themselves in the context of campaigning and bargaining. The exacting process also requires that a candidate show his skill in handling and negotiating with local party leaders, subleaders, and factions in those areas where delegates are chosen in conventions. Both skills, winning the public and persuading party leaders, are required in the Presidency; the preconvention system provides something of a testing ground for situations that confront the Chief Executive.

The convention system has kept open opportunities for the Presidency and Vice Presidency. Although the number of persons available at a given time is highly limited, the convention can settle on a person who meets the needs of the time. Although advancement is usually made through elective public office, the convention can and does go outside when its traditional formula fails to yield the "man of the hour." Herbert Hoover, Wendell Willkie, and Dwight Eisenhower were selected over men with experience in elective public office. Governors in both parties in 1960 and 1968 were not available or lacked large popular followings, and the conventions turned elsewhere. Governors appear to be less desirable as presidential candidates, because so many have to champion tax increases in their own states and find it difficult to identify themselves with foreign policy.

A national convention is not just one convention. It contains itself scores of conventions; it is the peak of a system. Its opening day is preceded by hundreds of state, congressional district, and county conventions concerned with electing delegates and sometimes with instructing them and proposing policies. As delegates assemble in the convention city, another constellation of conventions begins. Each state has caucuses, and the standing committees hold many meetings. Labor union delegates, farm-state delegates, black delegates, and others are likely to caucus individually. Delegates committed to a leading contender often meet with his strategists and leaders. Crucial decisions are made and compromises are hammered out in these lesser conventions. The great convention gives sanction to many of them and helps provide unity as delegates sit together to listen to speeches blistering the opposition and pridefully exalting their own party and its heroes.

A convention is more than nominations. It is a colorful conclave and is deeply embedded in the American tradition. Delegates return home with news, gossip, and a feeling that they have experienced a great act in party life. They bring enthusiasm and leadership to the ensuing campaign. Many help assuage the disappointed back home by explaining why a certain man was nominated and another was not. The delegate relates his visits to hotel rooms where he met the party's factotums and candidates. His faith has been affirmed and his spirits reinforced. Not every delegate comes home "pepped up," but it is fair to say that the great majority do and they are willing to close ranks and take on the "enemy." These psychological values must not be overlooked. Rightly or wrongly, the delegate believes that he comes home a better Republican or Democrat, much as the Legionnaire, Shriner, or Rotarian comes home from his convention with a greater feeling of loyalty.

Friends of the convention process are by no means satisfied with it and recognize the need for improvement. Effective reform will demand realistic attitudes toward democratic practice together with an understanding of where changes have been and can be made. From a practical standpoint, changes must be directed toward two facets: (1) the process of selecting delegates in the states and territories, and (2) the operation of the convention itself from the opening gavel to adjournment. The decisions of the convention are very largely determined by the selection of the delegates—a process that starts in many states more than six months in advance of the convention.

To illustrate, the 1968 Democratic National Convention exemplified what has frequently happened in past conventions of both parties. A militant minority—in this instance, it was largely opposed to the administration's foreign policy in Vietnam—were furious that they did not get their way in either the presidential nomination or in the platform plank on Vietnam; and many threatened to walk out or bolt the party in November. Some charged the convention was "rigged" and that they were silenced, revealing (and creating) a confusion over the right to be heard as against being heeded. The many roll calls on credentials and the debate over Vietnam afforded them ample opportunity to be heard and as *The New York Times* observed, "The fast-moving debate between the opposing sides on the Vietnam plank was the most spirited intellectual confrontation on that issue that has taken place, surpassing the usually one-sided campus teach-ins or discussions in the Senate. . . . It was a vital convention where the live issues were faced and fought out."[30] In every convention, ideally at least, all major viewpoints ought to be heard but no way has been devised whereby all viewpoints can be adopted.

Bitter cries about a "participatory democracy," tended to obscure the substantial changes that were taking place within the 1968 Democratic National Convention. The unit rule whereby state delegations could cast a unanimous ballot based on a majority vote of the delegation was abolished. Minority opinion has often been smothered by this rule, with dissenters in effect being forced to vote the majority line. The unit rule was further outlawed in precinct, county, and state proceedings for 1972. Several decisions of the credentials committee resulted in the seating of black delegates, leading the Georgia state chairman to say, "The white conservative vote in the South is not wanted by the present leaders of the Democratic party."[31] A black was placed in nomination for President and another for Vice President; and not only lily-white delegations from the South but also party organizations in the North were put on notice that failure to recruit blacks, Puerto Ricans, and Mexican-Americans into their ranks would invite the loss of seats at subsequent conventions.

Acting under a mandate of the Democratic National Committee, the party's national chairman in 1968 appointed a Commission on Party Structure and Delegate Selection to recommend changes and to assist

[30] Aug. 30, 1968.
[31] *The New York Times*, Aug. 28, 1968.

the state parties "to assure that all Democrats of the state will have meaningful and timely opportunities to participate fully in the election or selection" of convention delegates. Under the chairmanship of Sen. George McGovern, the commission recommended eighteen changes to be acted upon at the 1972 convention.[32] Among the recommendations are the use of proportional representation for the selection of at least some delegates, with attempts to bring more women, blacks, and young people as delegates or alternates; the abolition of proxy votes; opening of all meetings of the state parties to all members; and prohibition of delegate selection before January of the convention year. State apportionments should also better reflect the sizes of the states' presidential votes. The conventions of the seventies, therefore, will likely see numerous changes.

The effort to make the composition of a convention more representative has a long history, with many changes being made in the apportionment formulas. But these changes have tended to increase the size of the convention—now approaching inefficient if not ridiculous proportions. Television personnel complain that they cannot wade through aisles choked with delegates and delegates resent "security checks" and being "pushed around." Delegates report they often have no notion of what is taking place on the platform because of noise and confusion.

Each state might well appraise its system for selecting delegates. Some delegations are overcrowded with party officialdom and office-holders, and the practice in a few states of appointment of some delegates by a governor or party agency invites criticism. Many excellent representatives of the party do not become delegates because they cannot afford the financial expense incident to travel and participation in the national convention. Preference primary laws and rules governing local convention selection of delegates leave much to be wished in many states.

The tedium of conventions for television viewers is appreciated and efforts have been made to reduce the length of nominating speeches and demonstrations. Present-day conventions appear timed and staged largely for television audiences; they are now run as much for the public as for the party. But convention managers have trouble running a show for television and conducting the business of the meeting. Time-consuming activities on the floor are often stalling devices employed by contenders, and conventions have to take enough time to arrive at a consensus and work out compromises.

[32] Space forbids consideration here. A summary account is found in the *Congressional Quarterly*, Nov. 28, 1969, pp. 2418–2419.

Presidential nominating politics has not escaped the problem of nominating politics at lower levels, that of money. Unless one can profit by certain "breaks," the costs of preconvention campaigning run into millions of dollars. The financial factor is one over which the party organizations and the conventions have but small control. But in prescribing the manner of selecting delegates and in rules governing the convention proceedings, party officials can do much to keep open the channels to the nation's highest public office.

FOR FURTHER READING

Bain, Richard A.: *Convention Decisions and Voting Records*, 1960.

Ernst, Henry: *The Primary That Made a President: West Virginia, 1960,* 1962.

Johnson, Walter: *How We Drafted Adlai Stevenson*, 1955.

Knebel, Fletcher, and Charles W. Bailey: *Convention*, 1964. (A novel.)

Martin, Ralph G.: *Ballots to Band Wagons: The Exciting Events behind Five Major Political Conventions*, 1964.

Moos, Malcolm, and Stephen Hess: *Hats in the Ring*, 1960.

Ogden, Daniel M., Jr., and Arthur L. Peterson: *Electing the President, 1964*, 1964.

Pohl, Frederick, and Cyril M. Kornbluth: *Presidential Year*, 1956.

Polsby, Nelson W., and Aaron B. Wildavsky: *Presidential Elections: Strategies of American Electoral Politics*, 1968.

Roseboom, Eugene H.: *A History of Presidential Elections*, 1959.

Both parties customarily publish the proceedings of their national conventions.

Democracy's ceremonial, its feast,
its great function is the elections.
H. G. WELLS

CHAPTER 11 CAMPAIGN ORGANIZATION AND STRATEGY

Accession to power is necessary in every political society. Characteristically it takes place after vigorous contests, for those who exercise power are accorded deference and prestige and are able to reward those who aided them in various ways. Inheritance and rule through family line has been a common method for the selection of rulers throughout history and is still found in tribal societies and in the monarchies of some modern nations. Violent overthrow of the incumbents is the method by which many dictators come to power, even though they may have used some legalistic façade to allege legitimacy. In turn, there is little opportunity to upset them except by force.

Legislative positions in democratic societies, except in some upper houses, are filled by elections. There are some striking differences between American elections and those in the parliamentary democracies. In the latter, the prime minister and members of parliament hold their positions until the parliament is dissolved or until a stated period of time has passed, such as five years in Great Britain and Canada. The party in power can ordinarily select the date for the election. This is often highly advantageous. In the United States, the majority party has no control over the date but knows years in advance the day it must go to the electorate. When elections result from the dissolution of parliament, there is a ready-made campaign issue. When campaigns are required by the calendar, there may be no overriding issues, and they may have to be manufactured.

American elections are strikingly longer than those in most other nations. Presidential aspirants begin unofficial campaigns more than a year in advance of a national convention. Usually the candidate announces his candidacy by January of the election year, in time to campaign in the primaries, which begin as early as March. The national convention, which is held in July or August, is the first big hurdle. The election campaign begins soon after. A presidential campaign is unbelievably exhausting to the candidates and is an enormous and awesome spectacle of organization and showmanship. Candidates for state and local offices, with some exceptions noted previously, must wage one campaign to win nomination and, if successful, another to win in the general election. As a rule, the same appeals, slogans, publicity, and images of candidates are used in both campaigns, and hence the primary and general election campaigns must be regarded as two parts of the same contest.

Into every speech, rally, and campaign piece go careful thought and planning. The planning and execution of a political campaign involve (1) preparation of a master design or overall strategy, (2) selection of issues and the working out of detailed strategy, (3) activation of existing organization and the creation of new and subsidiary agencies, (4) counteroffensives, (5) campaign techniques, (6) campaign publicity, and (7) finance. The first four of these are considered in this chapter, the remainder in the two chapters to follow.

MASTER STRATEGY

Analyzing the Electorate.　The overall strategy of a presidential campaign is decided on as soon as possible after the national conventions. It may even be done before the conventions when a President's renomination is assured or when it seems reasonably certain that a particular person will receive the party designation. The decisions as well as the persons who make them are kept confidential and even years later may not be fully known. Undoubtedly the two Roosevelts, Kennedy, and Nixon had much to do with deciding on general strategy, whereas the McKinley,

Harding, and Eisenhower campaigns were in the hands of seasoned party leaders who dictated their general nature.

Irrespective of who determines the strategy, it must start with an understanding of the electorate to whom appeals will be directed. An electorate is not homogeneous. At the center of the voting public, whether it is a legislative district or a statewide or national constituency, is the inner core of party workers. These are the precinct, county, and other workers making up the party officialdom. Their support is personally solicited and will be virtually essential to carrying out the campaign. Campaign strategy must not weaken or alienate this core of activists but, if possible, must inspire a heady enthusiasm, high morale, and *esprit de corps* within it.

A second tier of members, larger numerically than the comparatively small nucleus just mentioned, is composed of strong, loyal partisans. These are consistent supporters of the party who pride themselves on their attachment to the party and admit to voting a straight ticket most of the time. This group gives the party a strong base with which to begin a campaign. Although not active in the party organization on a regular basis, these partisans can frequently be counted on, if required, to make campaign donations, attend rallies, and fulfill campaign duties.

A third group is composed of those citizens perhaps best designated as nominals, or party sympathizers. These persons acknowledge themselves as Republicans or Democrats and probably register as such. Their party ties are not unbreakable, and they can be shaken loose from their moorings to deviate in a given election for a particular office or maybe even for the entire opposition slate. The "weak" Democrats voted in droves for Dwight D. Eisenhower but remained generally loyal to Democratic candidates for Congress. Similarly "weak" Republicans may be enticed on a short-run basis to support popular Democrats. Since 1936, it appears that nominal Democrats rather markedly outnumber nominal Republicans.[1]

A fourth class of voters are either on the periphery or entirely outside the realm of party affiliation. These are the self-styled independents who refuse to enroll as party members and to participate in primaries except in states where open primaries admit them with no strings attached. Independents tend to insist that they ignore party labels and split their tickets in an effort to vote for the best candidate. Some analysts of voting behavior believe that this group is not so large as popularly believed, that many persons who call themselves independent do, in reality, have a party affiliation. They are more appropriately designated as independent Republicans or independent Democrats and

[1] For an elaboration of this point, see Chap. 16.

would approximate the viewpoints of the nominals. Independents, real or partial, must be appealed to, for they may well hold the balance of power in close elections. Some are potential members of a party and, if they can be won over, will strengthen the party in future elections.

In conclusion, two-party constituencies comprise nearly all the adult voting population. Even young persons not yet of voting age are potential activists in the party and may soon become voting members. The different categories of membership are built up and maintained by different kinds of rewards. Inner-core people may be induced by patronage, eventual opportunity to run for public office, and the exercise of power. Intellectuals and leaders of interest groups may become partisans because of policies. Nominal members may have their faith reinforced by appeals to tradition, images of the party, and by the quality of the party's candidates.

In addition to degrees of commitment to a party and different levels of interest and information among the electorate, there are marked degrees of participation. The highly interested and partisan voters turn out more regularly to vote than others. Core voters are likely to vote without having to be stimulated by campaign appeals. Peripheral and sporadic voters will be more likely to respond if something in the campaign arouses their interest. Much campaign strategy is therefore devoted to reaching potential supporters who might stay away from the polls because of lack of interest.

In summary, a theory of campaigns must comprehend the behavior of voters. One of the first steps in preparing the overall strategy of a campaign at any level is the completion of a constituency profile—a function now aided by research and depth polling. This intelligence effort aims at ascertaining such political characteristics as party makeup, recent history and political performance, the number and party affiliation of registered voters, and the degree of straight-ticket voting. The relationship of party units to nonparty organizations and to other party committees is useful political information. Included in the profile are socioeconomic characteristics such as nationality, race, religion, income, education, approximate numbers, and voting labels and behavior of members of labor unions, farmers, businessmen, professionals, white-collar workers, and other groups.

During the present era, Democratic and Republican core voters and loyal partisans in the national constituency appear almost to offset each other, but a substantial majority of the millions of others incline toward the Democratic party. Republican strategy has logically geared itself to winning nominal and weak Democrats while holding the Republican-inclined voters. Democratic presidential strategy has dictated that a candidate hold all strong Democrats and keep weakly oriented and nominal Democrats from defecting to the opposition. On the other hand the strategy of candidates for Congress and state offices might not be similar because of the different political composition of their constituencies. Party membership is not evenly distributed, and few legislative districts or even states are microcosms of the national constituency.

Evaluation of Political Resources. Only in the rarest of cases is a person without any resources elected to public office—and even though such accession was without money or organization, the candidate himself must be viewed as a resource. David A. Leuthold notes that for a candidate "an election campaign can be considered as the process of acquiring and using the political resources that can secure votes. The resources that a candidate is able to acquire and the uses that he makes of them will significantly determine the success of his campaign, and thus the competitiveness of the elector."[2] This concept of the mobilization of resources is a useful one to the scholar and has an intensely practical application for the candidate and his managers. Campaign organization and strategy are unlikely to be fully effective without a thorough inventory of resources and a careful allocation of them.

Financial backing and campaign workers are the two most obvious resources, and candidates seek both in abundance. There are, however, numerous other resources less easy to evaluate but nonetheless important. Support of one's own party is an asset presumably inherited upon receiving the nomination. But the significance of support is influenced by the effectiveness (or lack of it) of the party activists, their intensity of feeling and enthusiasm for the candidate, and the amount of money which the organization can and is willing to allocate to the particular nominee. The party resources are seldom available in any large amount to the candidate for a nonpartisan office.

A second type of support is found in nonparty organizations and influential personages. These include the more or less conventional widely known racial, ethnic, professional, religious, and occupational groups. A veteran may be able to tap his friends in the American Legion for help, and a professor venturing into politics might obtain assistance from alumni and students. A potential source of strength for state and local candidates is the press, including weekly newspapers. The candidate who can get friendly treatment in the local news media, radio reference to his campaign, and perhaps editorial endorsement possesses a resource useful in obtaining name familiarity and voter awareness of his existence. The candidate seeks to make news or to advocate a program that will catch the eye of a columnist. Although seldom seen by

[2] David A. Leuthold, *Electioneering in a Democracy: Campaigns for Congress,* John Wiley & Sons, Inc., New York, 1968, pp. 1–2.

the outsider, the nuances of relationships with the press and community leaders are prime considerations in any strategy for winning public office.

A third source of strength relates to issues. Modern polling techniques and the research agencies of colleges and some private organizations are useful in ascertaining voters' attitudes on public questions. This information can be used by candidates in selecting issues with the greatest popular appeal, which are emphasized in literature and speeches. Position papers, including analyses of and prescriptions for solving problems, are usually prepared in part on the basis of research.

Finally, one of the greatest if not the most important of resources is the candidate himself. Appraising the nominee is a complicated matter not easily reduced to measurement except possibly his personal wealth and the funds that he is prepared to put into his own campaign. Among the personal qualifications will be the candidate's experience, honesty, integrity, education, physical and intellectual vigor, and speaking ability. His ability to project an image of conviction, purpose, independence, sincerity, leadership, decisiveness, charisma, and a "nice personality" will be a most important asset. The reputation, awareness, and record of the candidate—or lack of it—are other factors entering into consideration of a master strategy. Illustrative of other types of resources possessed by the candidate would be his ability to command a personal entourage of skill and competence, access to advertising firms and equipment, and his own personal relations with party leaders and prospective financial donors.

Situational Factors. A final set of ingredients to be fitted into the campaign picture includes the political environment and the climate of the moment. These are the situational components over which a candidate has very little control or no control at all. His strategy must be formulated to maximize those things of advantage to him and to neutralize the influence of things working against him—an effort calling for a high degree of skill.

Incumbency is certain to have much effect on strategy. The officeholder seeking reelection must perforce defend his record and try to avoid being placed too much on the defensive. He must decide whether to ignore his opponent or directly confront him. At the same time, an incumbent has enormous advantages, including the fact that his name is widely known to his constituents. In addition, if he is a Congressman, he has a sizable staff at his disposal, which is ordinarily used primarily to serve his district and to conduct his campaign for reelection. Incumbents are usually able to raise adequate campaign funds. Challengers of an incumbent generally rely on attack while building a favorable personal image and a reputation of offering a good replacement. The strength and weaknesses of one's opponent and of one's self are situational factors difficult to view objectively, but they are of great importance. The character and popularity of others on the party ticket is to be considered in deciding whether to conduct a separate campaign or to run as member of a team. The wounds left by a divisive direct primary election will need to be healed if a close race is in prospect. Direct primary opponents as well as party leaders are potentially valuable resources to a candidate, and winning the election may be possible only with their actual support. Diplomacy is required in requesting their participation in the campaign or, as a minimum, public endorsement. Some direct primary campaigns are so bitter that neither the winning candidate nor his unsuccessful rivals and their supporters are left with room for postprimary maneuvering—a situation to be avoided.

As noted before, the voting habits of the constituency, the patterns of straight-ticket and split-ticket votings, and the degree of party competitiveness are beyond control of the candidate but must be woven into the campaign plan. The same holds true for issues. Candidates are not entirely free to manipulate issues or to dodge them. Like it or not, the context of the 1932 election forced President Hoover to deal with the issue of the Great Depression. In 1968, Vice President Humphrey had to discuss the Vietnam war over which the party was bitterly divided, but Richard Nixon was able to avoid this explosive issue. Throughout the nation in 1968, candidates for nearly all offices, irrespective of personal inclination, had to speak on the issue of "law and order" because it appeared to be the top domestic concern.

Party, Personality, and Platform. Campaign decision making at the outset concerns how to weave party, candidate, and issues into an overall plan. These three variables are not isolated from one or another and, ideally, would reinforce one another. Yet all are unlikely to merit equal emphasis and the relative costs and gambles of accentuating one over the others require careful analysis. In primary and nonpartisan elections, the personality of the candidates overshadows the issues, which is often true in final elections as well.

Appeals addressed to the party regulars, who are likely to be the core of an electoral coalition, are designed to reinforce their party loyalties and reactivate their interest. If one party enjoys a substantial advantage in party membership, the majority party will make strong appeals to party loyalty while the minority party will select appeals (and candidates) that are attractive to voters of both parties and to independents.

Modern campaigns are more and more designed to publicize the candidate, to build up a favorable image of him, and to give him characteristics that will appeal to large numbers of voters. Senator Edmund Muskie, as Democratic vice presidential nominee, stated candidly during his campaign that the most significant issue was not so much specific problems but "how people react to the candidates as men, as men they can have confidence in, in terms of their personal qualities, approach to problems, their character, just the presence they exude, and confidence they generate by their physical presence and the way they talk and respond to people."[3] Strategists must decide which aspects of the candidate's assets, including his family and background, are to be emphasized and how to focus attention on the opposition's weaknesses.

Issues are often secondary, but there must be a pretense of presenting them. It must be decided which issues are to receive extensive discussion, which are to be mentioned in passing, and which ignored or evaded. Decisions on these matters may be made in part after private polling of voters, personal contact and by mail.[4] Incumbent congressmen often enjoy an advantage here, as they can use mail to determine voter attitudes. Campaign arguments grow largely out of external events and may be determined even before the primaries and national conventions. Republicans won national congressional victories in 1946 by capitalizing on price controls and postwar reaction; and, in 1952, they made extensive use of the triple issues featured on their literature: "Crime, Korea, and Communism." Scandals and conflict-of-interest issues are always regarded by the out-party as appropriate appeals to show the ethical shortcomings of the party in power.

A great many practicioners and observers of campaigns counsel against being very specific on issues when a candidate is ahead or appears to stand a good chance of winning. Presumably by talking in generalities and avoiding taking stands on controversial issues, he hopes to avoid alienating a segment of voters. In contrast, a minor-party candidate hopes to win votes by taking definite stands on issues. By the same logic, a Republican candidate in an overwhelmingly Democratic district might feel he could take more risks in specific advocacy than the "sure winner." Because the electoral decision and mandate are so complex, equating issues with outcome must be approached with caution.

[3] See interview with Muskie reported in *The New York Times*, Sept. 28, 1968. For extensive elaboration of the same theme, see Gene Wykoff, *The Image Candidates: American Politics in the Age of Television*, The Macmillan Company, New York, 1968.

[4] There is not much scholarly material either on the candidate's search for information on the content of issues or on his own attempts to determine voter opinions. See Leuthold, *op. cit.*, Chap. 4.

Leuthold studied the role and presentation of issues in ten congressional districts in the San Francisco Bay Area and found that competitive candidates presented more information on more issues than noncompetitive candidates.[5] Among noncompetitive candidates, "the most extensive presentations of information were by the sure losers who were trying hard to be competitive." It is not unusual to find urban congressmen denouncing farm price supports but soft-pedaling attacks on labor union practices or saying little about them. Rural colleagues would likely do the reverse. Incumbents have been known to brush off controversy by simply asserting "my record speaks for itself." Managers in local races sometimes form "gentlemen's agreements" not to bring up certain issues.

Evasion and avoidance may be based on the assumption that people hear what they want to hear and see what they want to see. To some extent, evasion or dealing with an issue in a noncommittal way permits the candidate who is popular for reasons unassociated with policies to be all things to all men. If elected, he is free to deal with issues in a flexible manner because he had made no specific promises. Several of these and other axioms and strategies may be illustrated by brief reference to recent presidential contests.

Eisenhower-Stevenson: A Contrast. General Eisenhower's 1952 campaign was in most respects traditional and conventional. Even before the national convention, all polls showed him the likely winner over any Democrat nominated. (A number of Democrats had boomed him for nomination on their ticket in 1948.) Expediency dictated that Eisenhower's Republicanism be played down. In Texas, for example, he was billed simply as "Texas-born Ike"; and his party affiliation was soft-pedaled, especially in strongly Democratic areas. At the same time, his managers persuaded him to give blanket endorsement to all Republican candidates for Congress, a boost to local Republican organizations.

Like Dewey in 1948, General Eisenhower spoke in general terms and likened his campaign to "a fighting crusade for Americans who want again to hold their heads high, for Americans who want again to be proud of the men and women in their government." He repeatedly talked of the "mess" in Washington and denounced corruption. In speaking of the enormous crowds that turned out to greet him trainside, James Reston wrote, "They like the little moral lectures that evoke groans from the press car. They like his looks and his expressive ges-

<hr/>

[5] *Ibid.*, p. 121. Concerning the most important reason for a voter's decision, he found that in 1962 44 percent of the voters rated the candidate, 31 percent specified the party, 13 percent cited the issues, with the remainder giving such other influences as family or group (p. 14).

tures. They like his angry little outbursts against corruption, and his essays on America. And what may sound like dynamic platitudes to some ears on the train . . . nevertheless usually win the loudest applause on the station platform."[6]

For those wanting both a balanced budget and national security, Eisenhower promised "solvency and security." States' righters were pleased by his condemnation of the "idea of whole-hog federal government." He denounced the "stumble-fumble-bumble" foreign policy and promised, late in the campaign, to go to Korea if elected. The Korean conflict was unpopular with a large part of the population, yet it would have been unpolitic to attack it directly. The promise to go to Korea implied a promise to end a war that was wearying and seemed to be stalemated. The Korean proposal had an electrifying effect and caught the Democratic high command unawares. It was unable to combat successfully this appealing promise. This provides a good example of the importance of timing in campaigning. The Eisenhower campaign showed the marks of the tenets of public relations experts. They believe that issues should be handled with brevity and simplicity and be kept relatively uninvolved.

In many respects, Gov. Adlai Stevenson's campaign was an antithesis of Eisenhower's. He conducted what the *Christian Science Monitor* called one of the most unorthodox campaigns in history. As an unknown running against a popular hero, he felt that the only way he could win would be to reach and "talk sense to the American people on all issues." He relied heavily on national television to reach his audiences and drew around him excellent writers in order to prepare brilliant addresses. His speeches were interspersed with wit, anecdotes, and wisecracks far beyond what is usually found in campaigns. Stevenson also refused to give blanket endorsement to all Democratic candidates running for Congress.

The Governor often told the people what he thought they ought to hear rather than what they wanted to hear and frequently took the impolitic side. He chose an editors and publishers convention to talk on "the one-party press" and said some things not well received. He selected the South to present his unpopular stands on the highly controversial question of state ownership of the submerged coastal lands containing rich oil deposits and on civil rights legislation. Eisenhower soft-pedaled the latter and came out for state ownership of the tidelands. Stevenson told the American Legion at its convention that he would oppose demands of pressure groups and would "resist pressures from

[6] *The New York Times*, Sept. 17, 1952.

veterans, too, if I think their demands are excessive or in conflict with the public interest, which must always be the paramount interest."

Stevenson's speeches generally delighted the "eggheads," and a book of his speeches became a best seller—a fact without precedent in the annals of campaign oratory. Whether Stevenson's specific discussion of issues resulted in a net gain or loss of votes cannot be known. Undoubtedly many voters were won over by his freshness of approach and candor, and newspaper reporters were particularly impressed by the quality of his speeches. But many voters did not like his wit, sophistication, and frank talk.

Unlike that of 1948, the 1952 campaign emphasized personalities; one either was "madly for Adlai" or "liked Ike." Party labels received little emphasis. The Citizens for Eisenhower and Volunteers for Stevenson made great appeals to vote "for the man" and directed their campaigns to nominal Republicans and Democrats alike. The 1952 campaign emphasis was on issues and personalities.

The 1956 election was a rematch, and Stevenson was pounding for issues but could not find many over which he could get the people excited.[7] People "liked Ike" even more, and he was aided by a late October flare-up in the Middle East and economic indices indicating fair prosperity and a downward trend in unemployment. Democrats condemned the "failure" of the Eisenhower foreign policy in the Middle East, and observers wondered whether they could turn this to their advantage. Fearing that he might lose on the peace issue, the Republicans figured that Eisenhower could recoup by calling attention to his role as Commander in Chief. Vice President Nixon, after consulting with the President's top assistant, Sherman Adams, set the new official line by saying, "This is not the moment to replace the greatest Commander in Chief America has ever had in war or peace with a jittery, inexperienced novice who is eager to have the job but who is utterly unqualified to make the great decisions demanded by the times.[8]

The election was a referendum on Eisenhower the man, and he won handily. The majority of voters apparently were not convinced that Stevenson's call for "vigorous, full-time leadership" was necessary and were satisfied with Eisenhower's record on major problems. Walter Lippmann stated the view of most objective observers that the campaign was clean

[7]A summary of the manner in which President Eisenhower and Adlai Stevenson handled policy issues in 1956 is found in Stanley Kelley, *Political Campaigning*, The Brookings Institution, Washington, D.C., 1960, pp. 51–61. See also Charles A. H. Thomson and Frances M. Shattuck, *The 1956 Presidential Campaign*, The Brookings Institution, Washington, D.C., chaps. 10–12.

[8]*The New York Times*, Oct. 30, 1956. Nixon incidentally had a major role in the campaign. He traveled more than 35,000 miles, shoring up local Republican organizations, aiding his party's nominees, and making a large number of important speeches.

. . . but not enlightening or interesting. It takes two to bring on a debate, and the President refused to be provoked into debating anything. Since there was a great contented majority behind him, he did not have to admit that there was an issue to debate. . . . The correspondents, the commentators, and the pollsters have been essentially right in distinguishing between Eisenhower and his party. He has had an enormous vote of confidence. The Republican party has not had one.[9]

The Kennedy-Nixon Contest. In a great majority of elections in this century, an incumbent President was seeking reelection. Usually the President ran on his record, assumed the posture of a superior position, ignored the name of his opponent, and, with a few exceptions, did not himself campaign intensely. Opponents stumped the country and attacked the record of the incumbent. The Nixon-Kennedy contest presented a nonincumbent situation and shattered many precedents. It brought out a record vote of 68,832,670 and was the closest presidential race in seventy-six years. It saw the first nationally televised debates between presidential nominees, and both candidates broke all-time records for miles traveled during the campaign.

When two nonincumbents seek office, there is a tendency for the electorate to turn out in larger numbers than is generally the case when the election is a referendum on the man in office. There was a spectacular increase in the percentage of the vote in the elections of 1920, 1928, 1952, and 1960, when two new personalities were vying for the Presidency. The very fact that neither candidate is an incumbent stimulates large numbers to take an interest in an election and to want to help render a verdict. Strategy must of necessity be somewhat different from that used when one of the contenders is seeking to remain in office.

A candidate of the party holding the Presidency possesses both advantages and disadvantages. The presidential party has control over the great fact-finding agencies of the federal government, which are available to the potential heir. Many in the administration have hopes of continuing in office with their party's candidate and are willing to assist in the campaign in one way or another. If the outgoing President is as popular as Eisenhower was, his blessing and active intervention on behalf of his designated successor may be most helpful. Nixon failed to bring Eisenhower into the campaign, however, until near the close and hence did not effectively utilize his support, which may have cost him the election. The heir apparent is handicapped if the outgoing administration is unpopular. The candidate cannot completely repudiate his predecessor; on the contrary, he is obligated to some extent to defend his party. James Cox in 1920, Adlai Stevenson in 1952, and Hubert

[9]*The New York Herald Tribune,* Nov. 9, 1956.

Humphrey in 1968 were in the embarrassing position of following Presidents with whom millions had become disenchanted.

Nixon started the 1960 presidential campaign with many advantages of incumbency. The Republican National Committee began in 1959 and 1960 to speak of the "Eisenhower-Nixon administration." Nixon as an active Vice President enjoyed a constant and favorable press and was eager to become intimately associated with Eisenhower, whose administration was believed to be enormously popular with voters. Strategy dictated that he cling to the person of Eisenhower. In the closing days of the campaign, he increasingly identified himself with the President; he appeared publicly in the same automobile through miles of driving in New York City. Senator Kennedy was led to comment that Eisenhower was "leading the rescue squad. Mr. Eisenhower is not a candidate — Mr. Nixon is." In further use of the technique of linking himself with Eisenhower, Nixon often remarked, "I have had tutelage by one of the great men of our country," and, "I have often heard President Eisenhower discussing . . .," or, "Now, as far as President Eisenhower is concerned, I have often heard him discuss. . . ."

Kennedy's campaign style was strikingly different. Reporters observed that he seemed self-conscious about using his personality. Instead of waiting for applause after making a popular point, he went rapidly on to the next point. In short, the Kennedy emphasis seemed to be party, issués, and personality, in that order. Nixon's order of stress was on the man or personality, followed by issues, with little emphasis on the Republican label. Oddly enough, many commentators felt that even though personality was not given priority by Kennedy, he probably won more on that ground than on either issues or the party label. Most of his party's candidates ran many percentage points ahead of him. For all this, however, the party label could hardly have been a handicap.

Campaign strategists must be on the alert for "breaks" that can be turned to their advantage or to the disadvantage of the opposition. In late October, 1960, the Reverend Dr. Martin Luther King, Jr., was arrested for his part in a demonstration in Atlanta seeking to open lunch counters in department stores to blacks. A judge ruled that Dr. King, by his arrest, had violated his probation on a technical traffic charge (failure to have a driver's license in Georgia), and he was ordered to jail. Senator Kennedy telephoned Dr. King's wife in Atlanta to express his sympathy. His brother Robert phoned the judge to see whether King could be released on bail pending appeal, and King was eventually freed on bail. Mr. Nixon's aides said that he would have no comment on the case.

The Kennedy forces, however, publicized the phone calls and the contrasting no-comment position of Mr. Nixon. About 2 million pieces of literature featuring this matter were distributed during the last week of the campaign, and they were widely used. A quarter of a million handbills entitled, "No-comment Nixon versus a Candidate with a Heart, Senator Kennedy," were handed out among black voters in Chicago. Since Kennedy carried Illinois by a plurality of less than 9,000 votes, this eleventh-hour break may have made the difference in carrying the state. After the campaign, the Republican national chairman credited the large Negro vote with being the determining factor in the electoral outcome.

Perhaps the most critical strategem employed by Nixon was the creation of an image, a tactic which California public relations men emphasized during Nixon's political ascendancy. From his acceptance address until election eve, the Vice President sought in all his appearances to project the image of an experienced, wise, and capable statesman, an idealistic leader who was taking the high road and who would not trade brickbats with his opponent. The image was tinctured with humility. He referred to his modest background (a contrast with Kennedy's "silverspoon life"), such as "grinding hamburger in my father's little grocery store in Yerba Linda." In erecting a wholesome, constructive image, he made many references to his wife and daughters, and Mrs. Nixon was with him on many of his campaign swings. This tactic was also designed to overcome the negative image of Nixon as a ruthless man, lacking in principle, and bent on achieving his ends that the Democrats and critics of Nixon had built up over his career.

Before the campaign began, Nixon told newsmen that he would rely heavily on generalizations, and he avoided specifics and detail. By projecting a "nice guy" image, one puts an opponent in the position of attacking an ideal rather than a man. This may make the opponent, who is perhaps also a "nice guy," nonetheless something of a villain for deigning to attack. Eisenhower probably unconsciously enjoyed this type of image and during much of his Presidency was so remarkably immune from criticism that Democrats often privately muttered that he was "untouchable." This lesson was not lost on Nixon.

Mr. Kennedy's approach to the campaign was, perforce, quite different. Public polls put Nixon ahead in the race after the Republican convention in August. Congress met in late August to try to complete unfinished business and accomplished little. Republicans therefore charged that Kennedy and Johnson could not prevail with Congress, an obvious example of their inability to lead if they should be elected. Kennedy also appeared to be hampered by his Catholic faith, his youth, and his alleged inexperience. Senator Kennedy decided to meet the so-called "Catholic issue" head on. He mentioned it in his acceptance address and in many speeches. In a televised meeting with Protestant ministers in Houston, Texas, the Senator unequivocally declared his dedication to the doctrine of separation of church and state. He took questions from the floor and answered them with candor and courage. Even ministers opposed to him commended his poise and performance. Democratic tacticians filmed the meeting, and it was widely shown throughout the nation during the campaign. Democratic tacticians, aided by Kennedy's large number of personal appearances, put on a massive campaign effort in those states where the Catholic issue might well help rather than hurt, particularly in New York, New Jersey, Pennsylvania, Michigan, Illinois, Ohio, and California.

The television debates, especially the first one, gave Kennedy one of his greatest breaks, and he quickly made the most of it. It gave him the opportunity to answer the charge of immaturity and inexperience and placed him on an equal footing with his opponent. Mr. Nixon was known as an eloquent speaker and an outstanding debater, and several Kennedy supporters before the debates privately felt that he had made a serious mistake in accepting the offer of the networks. In the first debate, he quickly pointed out that he and Nixon both started out the same year in Congress and therefore had an equal number of years in elective public office. He showed a surprising ability to quote detailed facts and figures and was fast on his feet in argument. The consensus of the press was that he got the better of his adversary in the first encounter and that he showed a remarkable knowledge on a variety of problems. During the rest of the campaign he tended to be specific in contrast with the more general approach of Nixon. He also made promises for action in many domestic areas. In so doing, Kennedy tried to give the impression that Nixon was satisfied with things as they were and was leader of a party content to rest on the status quo.

Perhaps the greatest contrast in stratagems was between Nixon's accent on individuals and Kennedy's emphasis on parties. Kennedy stressed that vast collective thing known as the Democratic party. Since the Democrats outnumbered the Republicans and since many had defected to vote for Eisenhower, Kennedy's appeal was for them to "return home" under his leadership. All Kennedy needed in order to win was to get large numbers of Democrats to vote Democratic. He clung vigorously to the label and never let his audience forget that he was a Democrat and that his party "had done the most for the people."

Nixon emphasized personality. He stressed what he and Eisenhower, not the Republican party, had done in the past eight years. He said in effect, "Vote for me, I am the most experienced and best trained man." On many occasions he admonished listeners to ignore party labels and to vote on the basis of who was the best man and who had the best demonstrated program for peace, prosperity, and progress. As a member of the minority party, he knew that he could not be elected solely with Republican votes. He needed the votes of independents and weak Democrats and could hardly hope to win them by extolling Republicanism alone.

The Johnson-Goldwater Contest. The 1964 presidential campaign offered many contrasts to its predecessors.[10] The opposition was forced to run against an incumbent who had been President less than a year but who was highly successful in securing enactment of his legislative programs. Johnson lacked the personal magnetism of Kennedy and had to rely upon other resources to mobilize voter support. For the first time in the memory of most people, the majority of the nation's most widely distributed newspapers and newsmagazines endorsed the Democratic presidential candidate, and many Southern newspapers that had always supported Democrats urged their readers to back Goldwater. These and other crossovers of preference symbolized the sharp undercurrents in the campaign.

The Republicans emerged from their 1964 national convention badly divided and in need of working for internal unity if they were to stand any chance of winning the election. Goldwater forces made few concessions to the party's moderates at the convention, and the Senator himself after the convention showed little skill in or inclination toward bringing them into his coalition. He seemed to feel party loyalty alone would bring the prominent liberal Republican officeholders to his side, but many responded by giving only token support, or no support at all. That the Senator also ran far behind Johnson on public opinion polls was discouraging to some activists and local Republican candidates who were concerned about their own elections and Goldwater's effect on them. Senator Goldwater, moreover, was given to blunt talk and had written extensively as an apostle of conservatism. He had voted against the 1964 federal civil rights bill, which had been supported by about two-thirds of the Republicans in the Senate. Excerpts from his speeches and parts of his voting record made him vulnerable to attack, and Democrats were able during the course of the campaign to place him on the defensive, thus necessitating changes in his campaign strategy.

[10] The nomination of Barry Goldwater and the ensuing election have been extensively recorded, resulting in important theoretical and conceptual analysis. See especially John H. Kessel, *The Goldwater Coalition: Republican Strategies in 1964*, The Bobbs-Merrill Company, Inc., Indianapolis, 1968, and Karl A. Lamb and Paul A. Smith, *Campaign Decision-Making: The Presidential Election of 1964*, Wadsworth Publishing Company, Inc., Belmont, Calif., 1968. See also Milton Cummings, Jr., *The National Election of 1964*, The Brookings Institution, Washington, D.C., 1966; Theodore H. White, *The Making of the President, 1964*, Atheneum Publishers, New York, 1965; and Bernard Cosman and Robert J. Huckshorn (eds.), *Republican Politics: The 1964 Campaign and Its Aftermath for the Party*, Frederick A. Praeger, Inc., New York, 1968.

Goldwater's campaign was woven around several broad but interrelated approaches, which his strategists hoped would capture the votes of the South, rally the foreign policy hard-liners, and espouse a brand of conservatism that would give the voters "not an echo but a choice." As with all challengers of an incumbent, he appealed to the discontented and dissatisfied to join him. Senator Goldwater himself publicly acknowledged before his nomination that he had little chance of winning without carrying most of the South. Although Goldwater never took a segregationist stand, his statement that the nation's aim was "neither to establish a segregated society nor to establish an integrated society. It is to preserve a free society" was interpreted by Southerners as friendly to their own feelings. His support of state's rights and his voting record on civil rights were popular and offered the Southerner a sharp contrast to President Johnson's approach to racial questions. Repeated emphasis upon freedom from federal interference and attacks on lawlessness were viewed by many voters as aimed at demonstrations by blacks that had occurred in some cities during the summer of 1964. Although Goldwater personally did not make racist appeals or follow a "Southern strategy," some of his supporters did. He did not publicly write off the Negro vote but he exerted little effort to woo the blacks in Northern cities. Many observers felt, therefore, that he would benefit from a white backlash vote because some normally Democratic voters who were worried about Negro competition for jobs and houses would vote for him.

On foreign policy Senator Goldwater criticized the "giveaways," the United Nations, the tolerance of communism in Cuba, the "mess in Vietnam," and asserted that our defense weapons were lagging in development. The Johnson administration's "weak line" against communism was attacked and Goldwater felt that we must "recognize that Communism is our enemy . . . [we must] confront Communism with a firm policy of resistance." His campaign argument appealed to a longing for an earlier time, when the United States was perceived as omnipotent in terms of world power.

His appeals to conservative ideologues were in the main also shared by Southerners and those who wished a more militant anti-communist line. The Supreme Court was accused of exercising "raw and naked power." "Of all three branches of government," Goldwater asserted, "today's Supreme Court is least faithful to the constitutional tradition of limited government and to the principle of legitimacy in the exercise of power." The old standbys of conservative doctrine such as protests against high taxes and expansion of government were articulated as well as emphasis upon local initiative. His strategy was also buttressed by stress on middle-class morality, individual freedom, self-reliance, hard work, and frugality. On one occasion he remarked, "I want the Presidency to dilute power."

President Johnson's strategy differentiated itself sharply from that of his opponent but was more or less conventional for an incumbent. He was well ahead on the public opinion polls, and his tactics included taking positions on issues similar to those of Democratic nominees since Franklin Roosevelt. He therefore emphasized peace, prosperity, preparedness, and the federal "Great Society" programs benefiting regions and groups. Where Kennedy emphasized the Democratic label, Johnson laid considerably less stress on it. In contrast Goldwater stressed Republicanism more than Nixon, and at times came close to a blanket indictment of the follies of the Democratic party. His strong orientation toward party activists were shown in his selection of Republican National Chairman William Miller as his running mate and in building the Republican national quarters to a size double that of the Democrats. He also augmented its communication with the state and local organizations.

Johnson's political career had been one of "consensus politics," of winning wide group support and trying to expand the center, bringing as many liberals and conservatives as possible into his coalition. With Goldwater making strong appeal to the political right and not especially concerned with the left and center, Johnson's personal modus operandi was quickly adopted as a major strategy. He avoided the dichotomy of liberals versus conservatives and strove to have "moderate" and "responsible" Republicans join him. Democratic orators picked up the preconvention charge of liberal Republican Governors Rockefeller and Scranton that Goldwater was not in the mainstream of the party's thinking but much to the right of it. To counteract possible backlash appeal of his opponent to white workers, Johnson noted Goldwater's support of right-to-work laws and his allegedly antilabor voting record. Federal civil rights laws and welfare programs were useful issues to lay before blacks and certain ethnic groups, and the newly registered blacks were mobilized on behalf of Johnson and Humphrey.

Democratic strategy in the South consisted in emphasizing that Johnson was from Texas and that he had defended the South by trying to reduce antagonisms between it and Democratic groups. The President appeared in the South, and Mrs. Johnson conducted a whistle-stop tour through Southern states, an action without precedent. Conservation and federal works programs received special play in the West. Economic appeals and emphasis on benefits for various groups were useful in all sections and helpful in overcoming certain other antagonisms.

Although Goldwater and Johnson at the outset centered their campaigns around issues, the campaign became more and more a matter of personality. Goldwater in October said that the watchwords of the President and his "curious crew" were "drift, deception, and defeat." The President was depicted as a slick politician without principles. Implicitly, Goldwater was under a different but nonetheless personal attack, and persons seemed to be passionately for or against him. Democrats charged that he was impulsive and trigger-happy and could not be trusted with the direction of foreign affairs. Toward the end of the campaign, attention was directed more toward Goldwater than Johnson; "Goldwaterism" became the central issue. Kessel noted that a national sample of voters gave far more negative comments about Goldwater than about Johnson.[11] To a great extent, all presidential campaigns are centered around the perceived ability, competence, stability, and personality of the candidates—but the 1964 campaign more so than usual. The electorate was witnessing an attempt on Goldwater's part to build a new coalition (different from that of Eisenhower and Nixon) by offering a challenge to the basic direction that the nation had been traveling since the 1930s. He emphasized issues rather than *ad hominem* appeals to groups, with a strong bid to conservatism rather than to groups. He offered a challenge to liberalism and, to a considerable extent, to what was called in broad terms the middle-of-the-road national consensus.

Though not seemingly brooking large in initial strategy of either party, the war-and-peace issue became important in the large majority received by Johnson.[12] The opposition depicted Goldwater as reckless, capricious, and even belligerent, raising the question of whether he could work effectively for peace. The recurring theme that his hand would be on the nuclear trigger was apparently quite effective in leading many Republicans to forsake their party. Goldwater recognized the effectiveness of this theme against him and was placed on the defensive when trying to convince the voters that he was as trustworthy in handling international relations as his opponent. The 1964 pre-election period afforded many examples of the unforeseen developments that often materialize in campaigns and result in considerable change in the tone of political argument.

The Humphrey-Nixon Campaign. The 1968 presidential campaign was about as different from its 1964 predecessor as it could have been and had only two or three elements comparable with the Kennedy-Nixon

---

[11] *Op. cit.,* p. 273. This work provides many insights into both parties' strategies.

[12] Within a short period in October, unexpected foreign events dominated the headlines, including Khrushchev's ouster in the Soviet Union, the election of a Labour Government in Britain, and the explosion of a nuclear device in Communist China. Johnson immediately capitalized on these events, stressing the need for care in administering foreign policy.

contest, despite the presence of the same Republican candidate in each. As in 1948, neither candidate appeared to have much charisma and the two parties were threatened by a third party headed by a Southern Democrat. Both Truman and Humphrey as candidates of the majority party had to combat serious erosion of the Democratic coalition resulting from desertions of leftists disgruntled over foreign policy and of conservatives concerned about civil rights matters. The challenge to Humphrey, however, was much more serious; former Gov. George C. Wallace of Alabama was on the ballot in all fifty states, whereas J. Strom Thurmond's name was entered in only fifteen states, mostly Border and Southern. Henry Wallace's name in 1948, however, appeared on nearly all ballots.

Until March 31, 1968, it appeared that the election was certain to be a contest between President Johnson and Mr. Nixon. The President's withdrawal that day threw the party into chaos and was compounded by the assassination in June of Sen. Robert Kennedy, who had become a leading challenger for the nomination along with Senator McCarthy and Vice President Humphrey. Humphrey emerged from the Democratic convention with a bitterly divided party and without a huge, enthusiastic campaign organization or adequate finance. Even before the Democratic convention, Mr. Nixon forged ahead in the polls; and by September 22 the Gallup Poll had him leading by an incredible 43 to 28 percent over Humphrey, with Wallace getting 21 percent. As late as one month before the election, *The New York Times* gave Nixon 380 electoral votes (only 270 needed to win) with only 28 electoral votes and five states in Humphrey's column. From the beginning of the campaign to the day before the election, Humphrey was cast in the underdog role. In the final hours, the polls showed Nixon and Humphrey close to a tie, which indeed it turned out to be.

The Nixon strategy was apparent from the beginning and varied little throughout the campaign. With the polls showing him well ahead, his Electoral College victory was based upon holding as much of Goldwater's Southern strength as possible, then adding the Border States, the Midwest, and the Mountain and Western states. To be safe, he would need also to carry Illinois or Ohio. By accommodating with Sen. Strom Thurmond of South Carolina and selecting Gov. Spiro Agnew of Maryland, he maximized his strength in the Border-Southern area and neutralized Wallace enough to limit the latter to five states. The 67 electoral votes that Mr. Nixon won in Virginia, both the Carolinas, Florida, Tennessee, and Kentucky made up for his loss of New York and Pennsylvania. He made no special attempt to woo black voters and showed that he could win with negligible Negro support and while losing virtually all the big cities in the North and West. Although he was criticized for choosing Agnew and for using the "Southern strategy," he successfully competed with Wallace; and the two of them kept Humphrey to the lowest Democratic Southern and Border State electoral vote in history.

In contrast, the Humphrey forces began the campaign without any backlog of electoral votes from Southern and Border States, although they had a chance to carry Texas and traditionally Democratic Maryland and West Virginia. The electoral victory was to be forged by carrying the eastern tier from Maine to Virginia and adding such big-city states in the North as Illinois, Michigan, and Ohio, plus Humphrey's home state of Minnesota. California was rated a toss-up and worth working for but would not be needed if the others fell into place. In electoral-vote outcome, the strategies of the two principals worked out pretty much as predicted. However, Humphrey's loss of New Jersey, Missouri, and both Illinois and Ohio to Nixon held him far short of an electoral majority.

With this basic electoral configuration in mind, Nixon put together an organization and a strategy to maintain what he started with, namely, a well-unified party and the image of a plausible spokesman for a wide variety of protests. To keep the South from Humphrey and to pick up votes that seemed to be going to Wallace, Nixon avoided a head-on clash with Wallace. Instead of attacking the Governor's policies and capabilities personally he argued that a Wallace vote was a wasted vote and would only help Humphrey. Only Nixon, it was pointed out, could win and bring about the conservative changes in Washington that Southerners desired. Very late in the game, Nixon called Wallace "unfit" for the Presidency; but by and large he handled Wallace in a way to make it possible for the latter's supporters to vote Republican. In contrast, Humphrey was much more blunt in attacking Wallace because he needed to persuade Northern Democrats who were leaning to Wallace to desert the latter in order to avoid turning the country over to Nixon.

As in 1960, Nixon as the candidate of the minority party played down the Republican label. As one enjoying quite full Republican support, he did not need to remind his own partisans of his Republicanism. In seeking the votes of independents and nominal Democrats, Nixon emphasized that Humphrey was incapable of uniting his own party let alone the country and that he was a part of the Johnson-Humphrey team that had led the country into a "mess." His campaign managers portrayed him as the most experienced candidate who could pull the country together and who enjoyed the respect of the nation. Nixon avoided appearance on television programs where he would be questioned by members of the press until the very end of the campaign.

This tactic reduced possibilities that he might make statements that could be turned into liabilities. A rally in Boston, for example, was canceled when it appeared that hecklers and demonstrators might not be handled successfully. In contrast, hecklers gave Humphrey a rough time and he had many unhappy confrontations with them. Nixon also refused to be drawn into television debates, saying that he would meet Humphrey but would not give Wallace a build-up by being featured in a personal debate with both the major-party rivals. He later refused a Humphrey offer for a purchase of television time for a two-way debate. Succinctly, Nixon functioned from a superior position permitting him to appear as a statesman above the battle. It was not easy to place him on the defensive; and he had great maneuverability in his strategy of offense against incumbents, which was summarized in his oft-repeated sentence: "The American people know this country cannot afford four more years of Hubert Humphrey."

Humphrey's contrasting strategy called for rallying the old Democratic coalition of big-city voters, the poor, ethnic and religious minorities, and of course labor union families. The very high labor defection to Wallace shown in early polls called for frontal attack on the former Governor's allegedly bad labor record. The traditional appeals of Democratic candidates for continued support of the party's social and welfare programs were widely used, together with warnings that a Republican victory would endanger them. Humphrey repeatedly challenged Nixon to debate, and lashed out against his silence on issues, and called him Richard the Chicken Hearted. Concisely, the strategies of the two candidates were largely "textbook" and what might be expected respectively of the front-runner candidate of the minority party and the underdog nominee of the majority party on the defensive in the context of a political environment of protest.

One element rather different from most national campaigns was the issue made of the vice presidential nominees. With two weeks left in the campaign, the Harris Poll found that Senator Muskie was much more popular than Governor Agnew (41 to 24 percent) and that Gen. Curtis LeMay was less popular than Governor Wallace. These findings led the Democrats to feature Muskie and to depict the weakness, if not to question the competence, of Agnew as a potential President. Some correspondents saw Humphrey as "running on Muskie's coattails." LeMay was depicted as too military and too casual about the use of nuclear weapons.

Three basic concerns dominated the campaign debate. Democrats had split themselves over the nation's role in Vietnam; many were militantly opposed to the Johnson program and called for a bombing halt and disengagement. Vice President Humphrey perforce had to support administration policy in Vietnam but tried to establish his independence of Johnson by indicating he was prepared to seek new solutions upon election. A bombing halt ordered by the President five days before the election relieved Humphrey's burden somewhat by bringing more enthusiastic support from some of the "doves." Consistent with his "unity strategy," Nixon said he would not discuss Vietnam policy because he did not want to weaken the President's hand during the negotiations taking place with North Vietnam at that time. Wallace also supported the President and advocated a military solution if the other attempts at peace failed. In effect, all three candidates supported the current unpopular policy but Humphrey appeared to suffer most because he was a member of the Johnson administration.

Widespread demonstrations both on and off campuses, violence and burnings by civil rights protesters, and the increase of crimes made "law and order" a top issue. Earlier in the campaign, Nixon said this was a more important concern with the voters than Vietnam. George Wallace made "law and order" central to his campaign and forced the other two contenders to spend much time trying to take a hard line against public disorder. This emphasis on the presidential level caused candidates down to the local levels to vie with each other on this issue — often to the point of demagoguery. Humphrey started out wanting to campaign on a "politics of joy," optimism, and prosperity but found this very difficult to do with evidence of discontent manifesting itself along the campaign trail. Both Nixon and Wallace blamed the Supreme Court decisions for some of the crime; and, as did Goldwater in 1964, they brought the Court into the campaign. As is usually the case with an out-party candidate, Nixon scored the "drop in American prestige" abroad and brought cheers from his audiences with the repeated assertion that "the American flag must never be used as a doormat."

Nixon and Wallace catered to the politics of widespread protest and dissatisfaction over foreign policy, the progress of the civil rights revolution, urban living, black militants, law and order, the Supreme Court, public education, federal programs, left-wing revolutionaries, and such hardy perennials as high prices and high taxes. Wallace drew applause from his followers as he denounced Northern newspapers and the television media and asserted the public opinion polls were "rigged." Nixon's managers blistered the final Harris Poll showing Humphrey leading as "a gratuitous concoction" that would not "con the voters."

The fact that no candidate received more than 43 percent of the popular vote left the mandate in doubt. It seemed not centered on a candidate such as Roosevelt, Eisenhower, or Johnson in 1964; nor did it show great preference for one party over another. It probably can be said the election was more issue-dominated than candidate-dominated but hardly clear-cut on what people wanted in the way of solutions. The most notable aspect of strategy was that Nixon stuck to his plan and won the election without engaging in debates or visiting all fifty states as he did in 1960.

MANAGEMENT AND ORGANIZATION

American campaign decision making and its implementation are enormously complex. The scope of the problem increases considerably as the size of the constituency increases. Campaigns for minor offices, such as state representative, and those for major offices, such as for the United States Senate, mayor of a large city, governor, or President, differ greatly. Running a political campaign is different from running a labor union or a corporation. Campaign organizations must rely in part on amateurs and volunteers. They are temporary, ad hoc organizations that are usually put together quickly. Campaigns seldom afford much time to replace key men—paid or unpaid—when they fail or do not live up to expectations. Communications within a gubernatorial or presidential campaign organization are not as easily facilitated as in the corporation.

In a statewide or presidential organization (and often in those for lower offices as well) there are several separate and distinct parts, some of which exist only for publicity purposes. First, there is the regular party headquarters of chairmen, district leaders, precinct leaders, and staff. Several party auxiliaries such as youths', men's, and women's groups are often integrated into the party organization, but at times they operate quite apart. Second, there are diverse, independent political action committees directly or indirectly connected with occupational and social groups such as labor, business, agriculture, medicine, and veterans. Third, the broadly constituted citizens committee exemplified by the Nixon-Agnew Victory Committee and Citizens for Humphrey-Muskie. Finally, the candidate's personal entourage often remains in the center of the disparate, decentralized organization. As most likely closest to the candidate, it has immediate access to him and is vital in terms of advice, intelligence, and information that it can supply.

Campaign Decision Making.   For the endless number of decisions that must be made, is there to be an overall strategy and, if so, who is to make it? At the onset there must be the decision about who is to make the decisions! What information and research is needed? What are the logistical problems and who is best suited to handle them? How will money be raised? Who will write what speeches? How can the disparate campaign groups be coordinated if not integrated? The observer finds great difficulty in finding answers to these questions during a campaign because decisions in the main are made in private. After campaigns, some workers write memoirs and make public how and why certain decisions were made. During the campaign, however, the public sees mostly the outputs (decisions) rather than the inputs or the factors behind the strategies.

Lamb and Smith see two general models of campaign decision making—"comprehensive" and "incremental."[13] The comprehensive model calls for a centralized, hierarchal structure and a chain of command, with those of the top deciding the major policy questions and ranking the goals. In this case, most probably the candidate and his associates would develop a master plan and make all basic if not most decisions. Alternatives would be carefully canvased and evaluated on the basis of available information. Decisions then are communicated to specialists who execute them.

Undoubtedly many campaigns for lesser offices operate this way or attempt to do so. The candidate may have a small organization and a constituency of fairly predictable voting behavior, with a small chance of external events upsetting decisions made early in the campaign. When applied to the presidential level, it is less promising. Among the limitations of the plan is the inability of decision makers to obtain all the information needed to evaluate alternatives. There is also the question of capacity to determine which information is most relevant. Further, "leading decision-makers must be prepared to intervene in decisions of small scope as well as of large. There will be cases in which the scope of one set of questions is not demonstrably larger than that of another. Moreover, how does one 'prove' that the consequences of certain decisions are greater than the consequences of others?"[14] The distribution of power among the diverse campaign organizations and workers makes it difficult to impose a set of goals and policies from the top. There is also the danger of inflexibility if slavish adherence to an overall plan is expected and of a potential failure to react rapidly enough to unforeseen events that arise during the campaign.

An incremental approach to making decisions in campaigns lacks the coherence, discipline, and order of the comprehensive model. Decisions are made in piecemeal fashion at many points in the formal structure of authority. "Ends or goals are not left exclusively to leaders, while subordinates consider only means or techniques. Diverse goals,

[13] *Op. cit.* The authors were able to study this campaign from the vantage of being sufficiently "inside" and have applied this theoretical framework to it.
[14] *Ibid.*, p. 24. Lamb and Smith saw the Goldwater campaign as an example of attempted use of the comprehensive model and regarded it as *less* successful than the incremental system of the Johnson campaign.

strategies, and tactics can be inserted for consideration, and collective choices are ordinarily the product of reconstruction and revision of various decision-makers."[15] Although there is likely to be a general strategy, speeches are not prepared far in advance so that there is ample room for concentrating on immediate needs and adapting one's strategy to external events. There will be bargaining, compromise, and consultation among those making the decisions, with each trying to gain help or approval of others. When coordination or decisions cannot be reached at the lower level, the candidate or persons close to him may need to intervene, but they nonetheless remain sensitive to the views and interests of other leaders. The incremental model allows organizational decentralization and flexibility. However, confusion may arise, there may be lapses and gaps, which, in some form, would lead to working at cross-purposes or costly delays. But as Lamb and Smith note, "The policy values of geographic and functional interests are pulled through the activities of many incremental decision-makers. . . . Following an incremental strategy, they readily incorporate new issues into the party's position at their level."[16]

Regular Party Committees. At one time, the national chairman directed the presidential campaign, but his role in determining strategy and managing the campaign has diminished in recent years. Hopefuls such as Kennedy, Nixon, and Goldwater have huge organizations in operation before the national conventions; these organizations are retained after the nomination, when the national chairman finds himself more in the role of the coordinator and executor. However, his job remains an enormous one and is becoming increasingly important in midterm congressional campaigns. He must recruit a vastly increased headquarters staff, travel at times to meet with local leaders and reconcile, if possible, differences between local and national interests.

In the main, the national chairman has his hands full in putting together the huge headquarters operation in Washington, D.C. The staff is greatly augmented. Democrats increased their staff from 85 in 1967 to 317 in 1968, and in the same period Republicans increased theirs from 138 to 484.[17] It is not unusual for the party in power to use some of the staffs of executive agencies, and some are transferred from the federal payroll to the national committee during the campaign. Staff expansion requires rental of additional space in nearby buildings, raising new problems of communication between the units. Sometimes

[15] *Ibid.*, p. 31.
[16] *Ibid.*, p. 224.
[17] Nixon decided to set up a huge headquarters in New York City with 300 employees, and the staff at the Republican National Committee headquarters was increased by 184 for a collective total of 484.

suboffices are opened in Chicago and New York. There is a reshuffling of existing divisions and a creation of new units in the interest of focusing attention on special problems and permitting greater emphasis upon voting elements. Figure 11-1 shows the 1968 Republican campaign

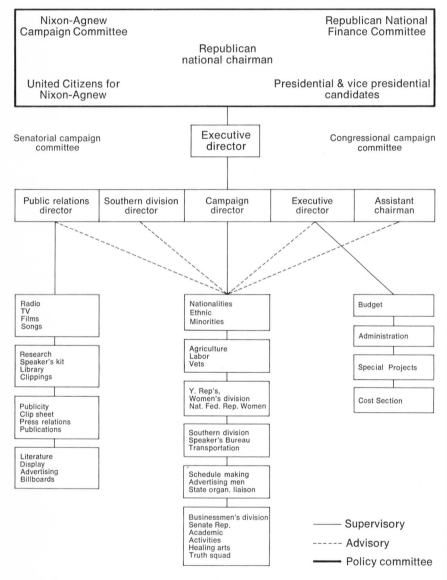

FIGURE 11-1 Republican national campaign organization. (Source: Unofficial chart prepared by author.)

arrangements. Persons in charge of the various groups are expected to carry on programs to enhance the standing of the party. The party program and its candidates are explained to the clientele of these groups, and in turn the attitudes of the groups toward the party are ascertained and communicated to the higher echelons of the party. The problem of selecting these key campaign assignments and assigning financial and other resources to the individual units calls for much skill.[18]

Campaign management, like the party system itself, is decentralized and is carried on locally through the channels of nonparty groups and the party county, municipal, ward, and election district organizations. In the larger states, the state central committees commonly rent a suite of rooms in a large hotel or office building for a campaign headquarters. Receptionists route local leaders and interested persons who come in for materials to the appropriate sections. The headquarters tries to create an atmosphere of optimism, enthusiasm, and expectation of victory.

Functions of a local chairman are similar to those of the national chairman; the local chairman must build an army of workers, mainly volunteers, who will ring doorbells, man the phones, do odd jobs around the headquarters, send out literature, and talk persuasively to visitors. He must find persons of various kinds of competence and influence. College professors and students are being increasingly used for research work and for compiling voter profiles. Journalists, public relations men, speech writers, radio and television professionals, and persons having expertise in certain policy areas are sought out. Posts concerned with registration, canvasing, absentee voter ballots and voting procedures must be manned. In addition to volunteers, paid secretarial assistance and workers for registration and election days must be recruited. In a Boston mayorality election, one campaign organization alone was estimated to have 1,500 workers either at the polls or driving cars on election day. The number of paid and unpaid workers used in many large cities reaches proportions amazing to the uninitiated in political campaigns.

Because campaigns are going on simultaneously for many different offices, even in midterm years, most problems of communication and coordination arise. For the student of elections, the great variations in organization and emphasis make it difficult to draw conclusions and to find recurring patterns in the role and functions of the regular party organizations in campaigns. Yet some general observations can be made and compared with practices in one's own community to see the extent to which they prevail.

[18] Kessel, *op. cit.*, chap. 5, gives an informative account of how the Republican national headquarters was reorganized and staffed for the 1964 campaign.

Very few candidates are content to leave the management and operation of the campaign to the regular party organization. Even state legislative candidates in the larger districts often open offices and bring together a staff distinct from that of the regular organization. Almost every candidate for a statewide office and for Congress in the more competitive districts has his own campaign manager, as well as space in a party office, if not headquarters. Decentralization enables the nominee to concentrate on local issues and to make exclusive use of his employees and personal friends who may be more enthusiastic about the candidate than his party or the rest of the ticket.

County and legislative district organizations, however, are expected to support all the party's ticket, though this is done with varying degrees of enthusiasm. In a number of areas, there are "courthouse rings," which are likely to be both a part of and apart from the county committee. They consist of local officeholders, some party functionaries, and various businessmen and attorneys who wish to dominate local politics for special reasons often remote from the election of statewide and federal officials. However, if the congressional district is composed of more than one county, the nominee tries to get the actual support of these quasi-party courthouse organizations. In parts of the South, the congressional Democratic primaries are scenes of intraparty contests between rival courthouse rings, and hopefuls regard it as important to get support from such groups. With the increase in numbers of Republican candidates for Congress in the South, stakes are raised in the struggle for control of and help from these county-oriented groups. Various auxiliary party committees and clubs frequently take over special fund raising and other campaign activities. Democratic youth clubs in many states did more on behalf of Adlai Stevenson than the regular organization.

A key figure in every election is the county chairman, who helps nominees for county and state legislative positions and plans itineraries for state and federal candidates as they come through the county. An important function of the regular party organization is to turn out large and enthusiastic crowds at political rallies, especially when candidates for major offices speak. The county chairman meets with advance men from the national office to arrange for parades, crowds, security, meetings, and so on. Chairmen see that presidential and even statewide candidates are adequately briefed on local problems before they make speeches in the county. Every effort is made to present the ticket as a team and to mobilize precinct leaders for campaign efforts on behalf of the entire ticket. When the presidential nominee is present for a rally, many state and local candidates are introduced and receive his blessing. "Coattail riding" is one of the oldest practices of politics. The ride is not invariably a one-way affair; presidential nominees often find it advantageous to be seen with popular local figures. One of the biggest problems of party chairmen and campaign managers involves deciding whose intervention is needed on behalf of whom and who is to be avoided. In such situations, the incremental model of decision making is likely to be more effective and realistic than the comprehensive model, in which decisions are made from the top.

Nonparty Committees. To an increasing degree, independent political action committees are assuming a vital part in campaigns. There is considerable diversity among these groups, some defying classification. Three types are reasonably easy to identify. First are those more or less permanently organized groups with a continuing interest in public policies. The best known of these is the AFL-CIO Committee for Political Education (COPE). Between campaigns, COPE prepares voting records of senators and representatives on bills of interest to labor. It makes endorsements and assists those recommended. COPE creates its own organization in some communities with block and precinct workers paralleling the party organization. No other occupational group is comparably organized for political campaigns, but chambers of commerce and other private groups often conduct registration and "get-out-the-vote" campaigns. The Americans for Democratic Action, the National Farmers Union, and the National Committee for an Effective Congress, to mention but three permanently organized groups, endorse candidates and provide some financial assistance. Generally speaking, permanently organized political interest groups are strongly oriented toward programs and issues, and campaign efforts are one of their most important methods of furthering their causes.

Though often publicly denied, certain business establishments, labor unions, and other organizations give what amounts to leave with pay to some of their staff and organizers to work for specific candidates or parties during campaigns. These men may give most of their time to campaign endeavors because the private group has such an important stake in the outcome of the election. Charges of "bought" campaigns, "slush funds," "fraud," "paid" organizers, and the like are made during and after campaigns, but it would be difficult to forbid by law such private interest assistance to campaigns. The practice does raise implications about the free democratic society and the problem of the candidate who has no such assistance.

A second category consists of a large number of ad hoc groups with some particular occupational, ethnic, or other base. These are groups usually formed after the primaries or national conventions to appeal to certain groups. They draw up an imposing roster of names and honorary chairmen and throw themselves into the drive for votes. Examples of these committees in presidential campaigns are Servicemen's Wives to Reelect Roosevelt, Veterans for Truman and Barkley, Lawyers for Nixon-Lodge, Farmers for Kennedy-Johnson, Brothers for Goldwater, Rival Americans for Humphrey-Muskie, and Older Citizens for Humphrey-Muskie. These committees usually never meet and evaporate rapidly after an election. Some are reconstructed at a subsequent election if they have a base in a private interest group. "Healing Arts" committees, for example, appear in nearly every campaign, often drawing their leadership from influential persons in the county medical societies who are concerned with public health insurance proposals.

Nonparty groups are especially prolific on local levels, both for candidates and for ballot propositions. Recreationists may form a Clean-Water Campaign Committee to elect candidates who will fight to prevent pulp mills from pouring effluents into streams, and educators and parents may create a Save Our Schools group to gain support for school levies or to endorse proeducation candidates. No list of these temporary political committees has been compiled, but they would number in the thousands in any general election.

A third type of nonparty group is more broadly constituted, cuts across ethnic and occupational lines, and purports to be a citizens group. Beginning with the highly developed Win with Willkie clubs in 1940, they have assumed much importance in national elections. The groups function under such titles as National Citizens for Eisenhower and Nixon,[19] Citizens for Kennedy-Johnson, Citizens for Humphrey-Muskie, and Victory Committee for Nixon-Agnew. These organizations welcome disaffected members of the opposition party as evidence of bipartisan ground swell for their candidate. Some state and local affiliates of these national citizens organizations are found; and, collectively, they pour huge sums of money into the national campaign to augment the resources of the regular party committees. Other groups are little more than dummy committees subsidized and staffed by party organizations to give the appearance of nonpartisan support for the candidates.

Rationale of Diversified Organization. The proliferation of campaign groups is the result of many forces and certain inherent characteristics of the American political system. The long ballot necessitates extensive organization in order to bring the multiplicity of candidates and issues before the electorate. A single unified organization would make difficult adequate emphasis from a central location on each of the offices to be filled in the divergent election districts. Candidates for the United

---

[19] On activities of Eisenhower and Stevenson clubs, see *Hearings before the Special Committee to Investigate Campaign Expenditures,* U.S. House of Representatives, 82d Cong. 2d Sess., 1952.

States House of Representatives report that they would get lost between the statewide and the local campaigns without their own organizations.

The costliness of campaigns together with restrictions on campaign expenditures also necessitate multiformity of organizations. Each committee working for the election of federal candidates is limited to expenditures of $3 million per year, and donors are restricted to a maximum contribution of $5,000 per committee. Additional citizens and various ad hoc committees are formed to circumvent these limits.

Further motivation for the dispersion of campaign management is found in the complexion of the electorate. As observed earlier, one finds strong and weak partisans, those highly interested and others entirely disinterested in the outcome, independents who are passionately oriented to issues, and partisans and nonpartisans who are uninterested in ideologies and program. Not all groups respond to the same stimulus, and they must be approached in diverse ways. Because of strong partisan attachment, some people can be moved to vote largely by a party label. Regular party organizations generally aim at this group and will probably have greater success in holding and reinforcing party voters than they will with voters having only casual party attachment. The regular party committees emphasize party loyalty and straight-ticket voting.

Other groups within the electorate may be strongly concerned with class, ethnic, or other programs. When they see a relationship between their interests and the campaign, they are likely to respond on election day. Thus specific groups with vocational bases, such as labor, medicine, farming, and education, and groups dedicated to the goals of veterans, blacks, and so on, may be more easily reached by members of a group purporting to represent them specifically. These associations direct appeals to like-minded persons and place more emphasis on issues per se than the regular organizations can.

The citizens and volunteers generally accentuate the personality and the "man." Perhaps more citizens committees than not consist of strong partisans who wish to give the appearance of nonpartisan support of the candidate. Campaign publicity sponsored by high-sounding, nonpartisan or bipartisan groups is believed to be more effective with the politically inexperienced voter than the same publicity sponsored by the party organization. Such titles as Youth for Jones, Veterans for Smith, Farmers for Anderson, and Citizens for Burke may in reality be fronts for regular party committees. The party managers may feel that this organizational circumspection will help to obscure the fact that the effort is a party one. Commonly, nationwide televised presidential programs are sponsored by a citizens committee, both for monetary reasons and to avoid the party label while calling attention to the virtues of the candidate.

TABLE 11-1   Relative emphasis of campaign organization

Type of organization	Variable emphasized		
	Party	Candidate	Issues
Regular party committee	□	△	△
Citizens committees	○	□	△
Private interest groups	○	△	□
Ad hoc socioeconomic groups	○	△	□
Major emphasis	□		
Secondary emphasis	△		
Peripheral emphasis	○		

A number of independent committees are essentially fictitious or paper bodies that never meet and have little existence except in the imagination of a publicity writer. They are simply devices of the candidate (and often paid for by him) to use prominent names as a basis of indicating broad support. The politically unsophisticated person is often baffled at the long list of independent and nonparty groups. He probably has little knowledge of the leadership or the goals of the maze of committees. Moreover, it is only with difficulty that he could learn which are bona fide and which are contrived.

Table 11-1 shows in broad terms the differentiation in emphasis and campaign appeal by type of organization. Few organizations attempt to give equal emphasis to the three elements of party, candidate, and issues. Regular party organizations may purport to do so, but they are more interested in appealing to the party-oriented and emphasize party more than the other three types of campaign organization. Party is likely to receive little or no emphasis in the campaign literature of citizens groups, and the various political action arms of private interest groups as well as the ad hoc socio-ethnic-economic groups regard the party emphasis as peripheral most of the time.

Implications and Problems.   The projection of both temporary and permanent nonparty groups into the political arena has heightened interest in campaigns. Each type of group has a different emphasis, and its rewards and motivations vary from those of the party associations. Big-city machines are still important in campaigns, but they are unable to reach all the electorate or command campaign talent. A nonparty committee is also an incremental way for supplying intelligence on the moods of smaller publics and for suggesting how to reach them. More manpower is likely to be available through the hosts of campaign committees because they attract persons without strong party orientation who might, for one reason or another, be reluctant to work through the regular Democratic or Republican organizations. The nonparty groups provide for a candidate individuality that might otherwise be lost in a larger campaign and also, as noted before, are an important financial resource.

Problems. Despite recognizable assets, the creation and operation of scores of local campaigns result in logistical, communication, and co-ordination problems. Occasional inconsistencies in both management and policy decisions are certain to occur. The independent nonparty committees cause problems in delineation and role and relationship with the regular party committees; and, as a result, party leaders are not invariably enthusiastic about them.

The 1940 Willkie clubs bypassed the Republican National Com-mittee and made important decisions of strategy that the latter felt were its prerogative and some bad feelings developed. In the 1944 and 1948 campaigns, the Dewey organizations subordinated the citizens groups. In order to avoid tensions in 1952, top officials of the Republican Na-tional Committee and of citizens for Eisenhower-Nixon engaged in three days of tense negotiation and, among other arrangements, chose a single person to serve as liaison between the two groups. The same year, the Democratic national chairman found the Stevenson volunteer groups "colliding in attempting to get a radio or television program, or radio and television time," and concluded that, financially at least, the national campaign should be centered in one agency.[20] But he recog-nized that to require direction by a single agency would not "be consistent with the liberty that should be for individuals to join together and cam-paign for a person of their choice."

For the first time in many years, the Republican campaign in 1964 was centralized in the national committee. Goldwater men were quickly moved into key positions in the national committee, and firm control over the revamped national office was established. "State chair-men were given veto power over the appointment of the Citizens' for Goldwater-Miller chairmen in their respective states. The official chan-nels of communication and command were designated as running from the R N C headquarters to the state headquarters and only thereafter to the Citizen's groups in each state. Furthermore, the Citizens' group was conceived as an adjunct to the logistics arm of the campaign structure."[21] Several regional directors, each responsible for the campaign efforts of a group of states, were appointed.

The relationship between party committees and nonparty com-mittees is unlikely to be committed to an organization chart, and ar-rangements are worked out in each election on the basis of expediency.

[20] *Ibid.,* pp. 148–149.
[21] Lamb and Smith, *op. cit.,* p. 106.

Willkie and Eisehnower lacked strong party identification and citizens groups were able to play a larger role than was the case with Dewey, Truman, Goldwater, and Johnson. Locally, where party organization is weak and ineffective, nonparty groups are often more important than the party committees. Whether the 1968 Nixon campaign organization will be used as a model in the future remains to be seen but it was widely touted as a massive, highly efficient machine.[22] It was a three-headed affair with national campaign management in the hands of John Mitchell, a partner in Nixon's law firm. The principal organization, the Nixon-Agnew Campaign Committee, operated from New York City with smaller branches elsewhere. National Chairman Ray Bliss headed the Republican National Committee with a staff only slightly augmented in size from the preceding year. The huge United Citizens for Nixon-Agnew with about 500 workers was, as the national committee, located in Washington, D.C. For good measure, the Republican Finance Committee was also located in New York City. A policy committee of senior advisors from all four groups plus a few others made major decisions and acted as coordinator (see Figure 11-1).

The values of the Nixon organization as well as the use of separate citizens campaign organizations result in reaching certain marginal voters helpful in building the election coalition. Incrementally, they add the potential of intelligence, information, manpower, and the highly important ingredient of money. At the same time, nonparty campaign personnel may not be an unmixed blessing for the regular party politicians. They may ask for patronage, which, if granted, may diminish the number of rewards available to the party faithful. Other preferments may be asked, such as licenses, legislation, and entrée—again placing them in competition with those directly affiliated with the party. Nonparty campaign committees reflect dispersion of power at a point of utmost influence—the ascent to political power.

In addition to the "natural" considerations, local party leaders are inclined to regard the citizens as amateurs who make unpolitic remarks and work at cross-purposes to the party organization. Organization leaders do not wish to give contact or strategy to the nonparty workers. Notwithstanding jealousies and jurisdictional disputes among the party and nonparty campaign groups, the help and resources pro-

[22] The *Congressional Quarterly* provided comprehensive factual material on Nixon and Humphrey campaign organization. See Oct. 18, 1968, pp. 2871–2875 (Nixon), and Nov. 1, 1968, pp. 3049–3055 (Humphrey). The organizations of the two national campaigns were vastly different, with the Democrats centering in the Democratic National Committee. National Committee Chairman Lawrence F. O'Brien gave ad hoc assignments to individuals to solve particular problems rather than the advance detailing of responsibilities that typified the Nixon-Agnew campaign effort. Republican national organization for the 1970 elections is found in the *Congressional Quarterly*, Jan. 23, 1970, pp. 223–227.

vided the the latter place party leaders in a position of not being able to look a gift horse in the mouth.

The role played by a candidate's personal organization varies so much that it defies generalization. Nixon and Kennedy in 1960 kept a tight grip on their own organizations in strategy and decision making; Eisenhower left management to others. In 1968, Nixon left many more decisions to his personal staff. Many personal organizations are composed of the candidate's personal friends, and few "old hands" and miscellaneous persons who enjoy his confidence. They usually have easy access to the candidate and are useful as a cohesive force and as quick decision makers as crises arise. The personal organization functions much of the time as a staff group, with party and nonparty more likely cast as line operations.

CAMPAIGN MANAGEMENT FIRMS

To the regular party and nonparty groups have been added the increasingly important campaign management organizations. The ancestry of modern public relations in political campaigns extends back into the late nineteenth century, and by the 1920s experienced newspaper men were found in campaign headquarters. The Whitaker-Baxter organization in California appeared in politics in the late 1930s; and, by 1950, because of phenomenal success, it had become a part of the permanent landscape in that state and something of a model elsewhere.[23] Running a campaign is not a full-time occupation for most firms, but they are much in demand by candidates for national office, statewide offices, and offices in the majority of large cities. Some state legislative and other lesser-office candidates employ firms to assist in if not to run their campaigns. Because party organizations are rarely available or involved, public relations organizations are being used increasingly by candidates for nonpartisan offices and to assist in campaigns for initiative and referendum propositions.

Professional public relations are brought into political campaigns for several reasons. Radio and television added a dimension that was costly but could reach masses of voters, and party leaders found it necessary to get expert advice on how best to handle them. The media brought into existence new opportunities for manipulation of candidates, issues, and voters. Since candidates seldom have unlimited funds and wish to get the most for their campaign dollar, they need experts to

[23] Periodical literature on public relations men is extensive. Two of the better-known accounts of modern-day activities by advertising and other firms are Stanley Kelley, *Professional Public Relations and Political Power*, The Johns Hopkins Press, Baltimore, 1956; and Stephen C. Shadagg, *How to Win and Election: The Art of Political Victory*, Taplinger Publishing Co., Inc., New York, 1964.

tell them how best to use the vast but expensive media. In populous urban states, political campaigning today is conducted largely by publicity groups designed to reach the mass of voters, and the political boss and machine have to a large extent been supplanted by the professional public relations organization, which is expert in using publicity techniques to reach the mass of voters.

Such techniques such as public opinion polling, sophisticated research techniques, compilation of constituency profiles, and use of electronic data processing equipment for banking data that can later be retrieved, call for expertise seldom possessed by the "old hands" in the party organization. A corps of specialists in these matters is now found in the entourage of presidential nominees and in those of many statewide candidates.

The introduction of the public relations element in campaign management has not been without controversy. Some see the public relation experts as amoral image makers who merchandize candidates as they would soap. Allegedly, they are personally unconcerned whether the candidate is good or bad; their job is to sell him, and their reward is money. An oft-attributed remark of one practitioner is that "Jello isn't very solid either, but they sell a hell of a lot of it." Political scientist Malcolm Moos, onetime speech writer for President Eisenhower, feels their role has been increased at the expense of the party leadership. "Befogged by the arguments put up by public-relations men about the effectiveness of one appeal rather than another," he writes. "The higher councils of political parties frequently give in completely. . . . Further, the transfer of power from the party professionals to the advertising orders brings threats from a new direction. For it promises to dry up much of the heady enthusiasm that flows from decision-making and other responsibilities long exercised by the politicians."[24] Other criticisms of the use of public relations men are that they may mislead voters by erecting and packaging an image that does not square with reality and that those unable to afford expensive agencies to run their campaigns are at a distinct disadvantage.

The adverse effects of public relations technicians on the democratic society and party system are easy to overstate, both because of lack of information and the variation of their roles in campaigns. Undoubtedly, many public relations specialists do advise the use of campaign appeals based on personality instead of issues, but seasoned politicians have often recommended the same tactic. The reverse has been true when the management firms have based some campaigns on certain big issues and advised on how best to present the issues before the public.

[24]Malcolm Moos, *The Republicans*, Random House, Inc., New York, 1956, p. 497.

In some capacities, the public relations man is basically a technician who executes rather than determines campaign strategy. In this capacity, he is valuable for advising clients on recruiting and organizing volunteer workers, raising funds, scheduling rallies, and best use of radio and television time. He can prepare spot announcements, coach the candidate on television appearances, and design campaign literature. Newspapermen handle press releases and arrange press conferences, seeking the maximum impact of a story on the public. With a core of specialists, the modern candidate can handle problems such as transportation; advance men; ferreting out various kinds of political intelligence; blueprinting certain strategies; identifying key groups to be readied, points of attack, and themes to be used as issues. Managing firms base their decisions to a considerable degree on political intelligence, which they often collect themselves.

Little misgiving exists about the use of public relations men in the capacity of intelligence technicians. More controversy arises when the "ad men" become the central strategists and major decision makers. Whitaker and Baxter in California virtually made all strategy decisions and assumed responsibility for campaign expenditures with little left in the way of policy decision to candidates and their organizations. One professional manager candidly told an investigating committee that he had started out simply as a public relations adviser to a candidate for the United States Senate, but because so many jobs had to be done, he soon wrote all speeches, handled all publicity, and determined the strategy. Party committees were largely used for doing research, managing travel throughout the state, and distributing literature.[25] To the extent that the campaign management firms make the decisions on issues and on how to portray the candidate, they have taken over functions formerly performed by the candidate and party leaders; and the party functionaries are left with the role of execution and administration. But public relations men feel themselves compelled to decide on strategy and in many cases feel this is a necessary adjunct to their role as technicians. Some committees utilize public relations experts on a year-round basis as consultants. Whether desirable or not, the public relations men are becoming an integral part of the party apparatus.

FOR FURTHER READING

See references at end of Chapter 12.

[25] See Henry Turner, *Politics in the United States*, McGraw-Hill Book Company, New York, pp. 361–375. See also Robert J. Pitchell, "The Influence of Professional Campaign Management Firms in Partisan Elections in California," *Western Political Quarterly*, vol. 9, pp. 278–300, 1955.

CHAPTER 12 CAMPAIGN TECHNIQUES

Considerable transformation has taken place in campaign techniques.
Andrew Jackson is credited (perhaps apocryphally) with fathering the
torchlight parade. The spread of the railroads after the Civil War gave
impetus to the whistle-stop and the campaign special train, and it quickly
became a major device for presidential nominees. People poured to the
depots from miles around to see the candidates appear on the back
platform. In larger towns the trains would wait while the candidate was
paraded to a ball park or fairgrounds for a giant rally. Local political
organizations were responsible for getting the crowds out. The campaign special was used with great success by President Truman in 1948,
but in the last generation much less reliance has been placed on it.

The advent of radio in the 1920s brought a marked change in
campaigning. It brought the voices of candidates into homes, making it
possible to reach each voter with several speeches instead of only the

one (if that) delivered at a local rally. In presidential elections, radio made speeches nationwide and required that candidates avoid demagogic appeals to local prejudices. Franklin D. Roosevelt's success with radio led to widespread emulation by his opponents and by candidates for lesser offices. Roosevelt also started a new technique of beginning the presidential campaign before the delegates left the convention hall. In 1932 he made a dramatic flight to Chicago to accept the nomination in person, and nominees since that time have made such appearances.

Television, which was not widely used until 1952, further revolutionized campaign methods and became especially useful for "building the image." It is now possible for every presidential candidate and his family to be seen on television screens in every state.[1]

The jet age further changed the tactics of stumping. Formerly the campaign special train took the candidate slowly through a state, stopping at each little hamlet. The candidate spent long hours, often a full day or more, in a given state. Then the train would proceed to the next state, and so on. Eisenhower made much use of this technique in 1952 but forsook it in 1956 for the most part and made great use of massive rallies at airports. Beginning in 1960, presidential candidates have rarely spent more than a few hours in a given state. Whereas the train made it possible for several thousand to see a candidate in person each day, the jet makes it possible, through stepped-up automated campaigns, for hundreds of thousands of persons to see him in a single day in places as far apart as 2,000 or more miles. With television and newspaper coverage in each place, exposure of the candidate reaches fantastically larger audiences in many more places than in the early 1950s. Right or wrong, managers see much greater news value in the shotgun method of hitting many widely scattered areas in a given day rather than two or three "single-shot" visits.

THE PSYCHOLOGY OF CAMPAIGNING

"There's only one way to hold a district," said Plunkitt of Tammany Hall, "you must study human nature and act accordin'. You can't study human nature in books. . . . To learn human nature you have to go among the people, see them and be seen. . . . I know what they like and what they don't like, what they are strong at and what they are weak in, and I reach them by approachin' at the right side."[2] A one-time league organizer gave the following instructions for seeking money

---

[1] In one of the best "how-to-do-it" political campaign books, Maurice McCaffrey argues that television has replaced the rally as our nation's political forum. See *Advertising Wins Elections*, Gilbert Publishing Co., Minneapolis, Minn., 1962.

[2] W. L. Riordan, *Plunkitt of Tammany Hall*, Alfred A. Knopf, Inc., New York, 1948, pp. 33–34.

or possibly votes: "Find out the damn fool's hobby and talk it. If he likes religion talk Jesus Christ; if he is against government damn the democrats; if he is afraid of whiskey preach prohibition; if he wants to talk hogs, talk hogs—talk anything he'll listen to, but talk, talk until you get his Goddamn John Hancock to a check for six dollars."[3]

The best interests of a healthy society are not served by pampering to prejudices, as suggested by Plunkitt, but the wise campaigner studies his district and the mood and temper of his voting public. Techniques that succeed in New Orleans do not necessarily win in Portland or Pittsburgh. Political and social environments vary from place to place and even from time to time in the same locality. A candidate is interested in knowing the frustrations, aspirations, insecurities, and desires of the voting public. Adequate political intelligence is necessary in order to decide between alternative techniques. For this reason parties and candidates are carrying on more and more research into voting behavior and into the demographical characteristics of a district including income, occupation, age, sex, ethnic background, education, degree of political participation, and so on. The voting behavior of various groups will be considered subsequently, but some general psychological considerations in campaigning require mention here.

Reference was made earlier to the composition of the electorate, including the hard-core following of the candidate or his party, the loyal partisans, the latent party voters, and the independents. One useful analysis notes that a campaign may or will produce one of three effects— activation, reinforcement, or conversion.[4] Some persons will not vote unless their latent predispositions are aroused. Campaigners try to activate this group, many of whom may be inclined to stay home on election day. Here the candidate and his party must find ways to get the voter so stirred and excited that he will be motivated to register and to vote on election day. What techniques can be used to activate him? Must the voter be made angry with the opposition? Must he be frightened that the success of the opposition would be harmful to his personal interest?

A campaign organization is also concerned with fighting erosion of its general adherents. Voters like to be told that they are right and to be given additional evidence for and rationalizations of their views. Techniques designed to reinforce their beliefs are therefore important to the campaign. A few voters are susceptible to conversion and often do not make up their minds until near election day.

[3] Quoted in Samuel Lubell, *The Future of American Politics*, Harper & Row, Publishers, Incorporated, New York, 1951, p. 138.

[4] Paul Lazarsfeld et al., *The People's Choice: How the Voter Makes Up His Mind*, Columbia University Press, New York, 1948.

Psychologically, as well as materially, campaign techniques are matters of selected emphasis. Most of the energy needs to be directed toward winning the votes of the party sympathizers and independents. Nominal adherents need to have their loyalties renewed, and an attempt must be made to drive a wedge between the nominees and lukewarm supporters of the opposition party. For persons with weak party ties or with no party faith, the symbols of party loyalty are not very effective. Although ear-splitting, rafter-shattering rallies, demogogic appeals to "Americanism," and damnation of "bureaucracy" may reinforce loyal partisans and hard-core followers and spur them to greater activity, they do not necessarily convert the waiverers. A pocketbook, bread-and-butter appeal for property owners and taxpayers, a school appeal for parents, a recreation program for the sportsman, and so on, may win parents, a recreation program for the sportsman, and so on, may win more votes in local elections than emotional appeals based on generalities.

Emphasis is also conditioned by geography. The greatest effort in presidential campaigns is in the large and the doubtful states. With Nixon and Kennedy both barnstorming in the South, this was somewhat less true in 1960. There is striking variation in the support that different congressional candidates secure on the same ticket at the same time. In congressional campaigns most financial and physical effort is expended in some 150 to 200 so-called marginal districts. These are districts where the winning candidate won no more than 55 percent of the popular vote and where, therefore, there appears a good chance of winning by a comparatively small shift of voters.

Part of the psychology of campaign appeals is based on the desire of a listener to have a frame of reference and a standard for judging issues and men. If the candidate can contribute to this desire, he has made some progress toward gaining a chance for a friendly hearing with the voter. A listener is more susceptible to suggestion when he has no adequate mental context on which he may base an interpretation of an event. In the many areas of foreign affairs, the hearer often has no knowledge and may therefore accept snap and superficial suggestions and remedies. A man with a rigidly structured mental context may be completely unsusceptible to ideas coming from an outgroup, while uncritically accepting those from his own group. Thus, the rabid partisan is generally quick to believe his own candidates and equally quick to accuse the opposition of barefaced lies. For this reason astute campaigners try to know their audiences and adapt their speeches accordingly.

Campaigns provide an especially good opportunity to make use of myths. The definition of this term varies, but the concise description by Robert MacIver is useful in this connection. MacIver sees a social myth as "a value-impregnated belief" that is "alogical" and not amenable to proof.[5] In a campaign, the candidate uses the myth to knit his followers, to explain and rationalize the world for his listeners, and to voice their aspirations for the good life. The myth often is based on emotion. It can be used to analyze what is happening and to predict what will happen to the myth if the opposition wins. "Americanism," "justice," "law and order," "freedom," "equality," and "individualism" are a part of the belief system and are freely spread throughout campaign oratory. Because of the widely held view of many managers that voters like to vote mad protest, words are likewise involved with exhortations to cast a ballot against "crime," "corruption," "communism," "labor bosses," and "bureaucrats."

A shrewd campaign strategist recognizes that people cannot get along without a belief system within which to fit to their lives and the world around them. This belief system becomes the "truth." Most people recognize that their political system has deficiencies and does not account for everything. But they want their beliefs reinforced and their doubts resolved. Because politics is very complex, the campaigner uses techniques and symbols to simplify it for the recipient; if the appeals are to be successful, they must be related and adapted to the needs of the citizens.

In the open society, with competitors possessing somewhat comparable resources, one side cannot fully distort reality and contradict that which is obvious to the person to whom appeals are directed. Counterappeals are quickly drafted. Further, a hungry, unemployed man will not believe a claim for universal prosperity and affluence and blacks in some communities have learned that, despite assurances of white politicians to the contrary, they do not enjoy full economic and political rights.

Campaigns give the observer of political life an unusual chance to study the use of myths and the manipulation of symbols and devices in the engineering of consent. These are a part of the techniques of the struggle for power and influence. Attention will now be given to these as evidenced in American elections.

DEVICES

Word and Symbol Manipulation.   Campaign appeals employ almost every artifice of the language. On the positive side, the candidate and party are associated with a long list of virtue words and goals. These include support for "social justice," "the common man," "the American way," "private enterprise," "progress," and "constitutional government." Conversely, the opposition has been associated with "Wall Street," "big

[5] *The Web of Government*, The Macmillan Company, New York, 1947, pp. 4ff.

business," "exploiters," "left-wingers," "racism," "reactionaries" and so on. Putting the two appeals in juxtaposition, President Eisenhower in support of congressional Republicans in 1954 asserted that the "critical choice is either to choose left-wing government or sensible, forward-looking government—spendthrift government or responsible government—overpowering federal government or government kept close to home—frustrated stymied government or efficient government."

The utilization of incomplete facts and figures and quotation out of context are common practices. The "ins" often claim a high level of employment while the "outs" emphasize that in some states the unemployment record is the highest in a decade. Paradoxically, both may be right. Also, one side may use numbers and the other percentages to "prove" an economic point to their own advantage—both may be correct but neither is presenting the full story. Cost of living is a perennial issue; and contestants bombard the electorate with statistics and counter-statistics containing discrepancies without either side explaining the real significance of the figures. Borrowing tactics from adversary proceedings, a typical campaigner often considers it part of the game to take an excerpt from an opponent's speech or writing and blow it up out of context in such a way as to make the opponent look dangerous, foolish, or incompetent.[6]

Support for the cause may be sought by employing testimonials and transfers. The Bill of Rights, the Constitution, Uncle Sam, the church, and the Declaration of Independence are associated with candidate or organization. A labor union publication called *The Bible and the Working Man* identifies union objectives with the Bible. In presenting the 1968 third-party candidate to a crowd, one introducer said "I believe Governor Wallace is the anointed of God. I believe he is the savior of this country." Opponents of public health insurance equated private medical practice with Christianity; health insurance was called a monster anti-Christ. Thousands of copies of Sir Luke Fildes' painting "The Doctor," showed a kindly, bearded physician of the 1840s sitting head in hand beside a bedridden child, were distributed in the American Medical Association's effort to defeat national health insurance. The poster reproductions were captioned "Keep Politics out of This Picture."

On the assumption that the masses have their heroes, whose prestige can rub off onto certain products, testimonials of popular actresses, athletes, and entertainers are used to huckster toothpaste,

---

[6] In earlier times, there was much tedious research into the writings and speeches of opponents. Thanks to modern technology, materials of this type can be banked in computers and retrieved as needed. A "recordat" in the Republican National Committee headquarters in 1968 had everything that President Johnson and Hubert Humphrey had said in recent years on many topics. Such easily obtained materials were highly useful in preparing counterattacks and for calling attention to inconsistencies between past and present statements.

cigarettes, and automobiles. This device is also used in political campaigns. In 1968, professional basketball and football players and actors appeared in spots with endorsements of Humphrey or Nixon. Newspaper ads for candidates from local judges to President feature imposing names from the legal, medical, and educational professions, clergymen, civic leaders, and writers as endorsers. Whether these testimonials really provide an effective cue or reference to the extent of influencing votes is not known, but public support of popular figures is assiduously sought.

Campaigns are matters of coalition building so devices are used to mobilize group support. With voters who have strong reference group attachments, testimonials emphasizing "our" candidate may be effective. Special appeals to that end are designed to capture the vote of veterans, blacks, farmers, Jews, and so on. Independents are asked to vote for the "good government" nominee who will win over the political machine (the opponent's organization). The appeal to belong and to follow "one's kind" is an attractive one. Voting behavior studies show a tendency in voters to be influenced by personal friends and to vote with their group.

The advent of mass newspapers and television has provided instruments for emphasizing the "plain folks," family-man emphasis. The Republican National Committee in 1960 put out a beautiful 32-page rotogravure magazine, "Meet Mr. Nixon." The Vice President was shown in a large number of poses with his parents, wife, and daughters, and the family cat and dog. One of his daughters, Julie, was shown cooking muffins "while her father has a pre-breakfast cup of coffee"; another showed him going through phonograph records with Tricia who "would rather listen to music than eat." Other pictures showed Mr. and Mrs. Nixon visiting the site of the former Warsaw ghetto, greeting President Eisenhower, handling hecklers in Peru, and meeting world leaders, labor leaders, and other heads of American groups. Several pages of pictures showed that the "Nixons were a plain family," reared in modest circumstances; they showed Mr. Nixon on the football field and in the Navy. His mother was quoted as saying, "He had to work so hard that he missed out on a lot of fun."

Senator Kennedy's managers could not portray their candidate's humble background but on their brochures managed to show him as a "man of the people"; he was photographed talking with "older citizens," farmers, workingmen in factories, and was shown as a hero in the Navy. Another page of pictures showed him as "a devoted husband and father coming from an American family in which public service has long been a tradition." Mrs. Kennedy and their daughter Caroline were also photographed in typical activities.

Innuendo is one of the cleverist devices. It is a process of imparting information so as to leave the impression that the election of the opposition will be a near calamity. If, at a later date, the charge is shown to be incorrect, the one making it may defend himself or fend off a libel suit by insisting that he was misunderstood. Insinuations have been made that opponents are "soft on communism" or "soft on integration." Governor Agnew said Humphrey was "squishy soft on communism" but later withdrew the remark after widespread citicism. Persons counseling moderation in race relations in parts of the South are sometimes subject to innuendo of being "nigger lovers."

Defamation and Invective. Belittling one's opponent as incompetent, inexperienced, or unprepared for the position sought is an acceptable tactic unless carried too far—and no one has successfully drawn a line of fairness. Democrats used it against Willkie; and a piece of anti-Kennedy literature read "Don't send a boy to do a man's job." Democrats made an issue of the lack of experience of the Republican vice presidential nominee, Spiro T. Agnew, and asked, "Spiro who?" One television spot featured an oscillograph, its lines moving up and down recording heart beats. The sound track carried loud, thumping noises of the human heart. The commercial ended when the faces of Agnew and Muskie, the Democratic vice presidential nominee, came on the screen, with the announcer asking, "Which of these men do you want—a heartbeat away from the Presidency?"

Campaign literature depicted Abraham Lincoln as a "vulgar, fourth-rate lawyer," William Jennings Bryan a "lunatic," Franklin Pierce a "coward and drunkard," and Gen. William H. Harrison a "clodpoll, a dunderpate, a ninnyhammer" too ignorant to know "a bee from a bull's foot." In lusty, gusty Chicago of the 1920s, Mayor "Big Bill" Thompson of Chicago remarked about an opponent, "The people have grown tired of this blubbering jungle hippopotamus defending his gangsters and crooked contractors by slobbering insults. . . . He calls me loony. Did you ever see a lurching, shambling imbecile with the flabby joints of a barnyard hog, whose diseased mind didn't defend its own lunacy by snarling at others."

There are not many comparable oratorical gems in modern campaigns, but in 1952 Nixon charged that Adlai Stevenson "holds a Ph.D. degree from Acheson's college of cowardly communist containment." Some of Nixon's opponents called him "Tricky Dick," and Humphrey criticized Nixon's choice of Agnew as "the most eccentric political appointment since the Roman emperor Caligula named his horse a consul." Humphrey was confronted by heckler signs that called him a "fascist pig," and a "murderer" because of his association with the

Vietnam policy. Goldwater was labeled by some opponents as "Barry the warmonger."

Candidates are often slandered by outright falsehoods regarding their loyalty and patriotism or their personal lives, and some attacks are maliciously designed to stir negative emotions. Guilt by association has been "established" by use of faked photographs or other devices.[7] Republican opponents of General Eisenhower in the New Hampshire primaries in 1952 attempted to represent him as friendly to communists by means of a photograph purporting to show him drinking with Russian Marshal Zhukov. The caption ran: "Zhukov, Communist General, Decorates Drinking Partner Eisenhower at Frankfort, Germany." A television spot in 1968 showed maimed, wounded soldiers, poverty, misery, and crime in the streets with Humphrey smilingly looking over the scene. Although it was mean to satirize his "politics of joy," it could be interpreted to mean his approval of war, want, and public disorder; protests led to its quick withdrawal.

The 1962 Brown-Nixon gubernatorial contest in California was particularly notable for its use of "communist smear" techniques and culminated in three court orders prohibiting further distribution of several of the campaign pieces. One leaflet alleged that Governor Edmund Brown was soft on communism and that the Democratic party had been captured by a left-wing group (the California Democratic Council) that favored the admission of Communist China to the United Nations. Another used cropped photographs showing Brown bowing with folded hands to Russian Premier Khrushchev, when in fact he was exchanging a greeting with a visiting Laotian, using the Laotian form of goodbye. Another photograph showed the Governor ostensibly cheering the Council for passing a resolution proposing UN admission for Red China, when in fact the complete picture showed him with others cheering a child with infantile paralysis in the opening of a financial drive. It was also found that one of these pamphlets appeared over the sponsorship of the "Committee for the Preservation of the Democratic Party in California" with an address of a leading San Francisco bank, but inquiry found the committee a fictitious one and the bank address unauthorized. These exposures and the doctored photographs helped to discredit the charge that Brown was soft on communism.

During the presidential campaigns of 1928 and 1960, the Catholic faith of one of the nominees provoked widespread discussion, even though the opponents decried it as an issue. Attitudes toward church-

---

[7]Over a period of time there are, unfortunately, many instances of "smear" tactics. A number are documented and evaluated in Bruce L. Felknor, *Dirty Politics*, W. W. Norton & Company, Inc., New York, 1966, and in Hugh A. Bone, *Smear Politics: An Analysis of 1940 Campaign Literature*, Public Affairs Press, Washington, D.C., 1941.

state relations seem legitimate items for campaign discussion, and
Senator Kennedy made his views known in detail. Nonetheless, whisper-
ing campaigns continued against him as they had against Gov. Alfred
E. Smith. Anonymous anti-Catholic literature that was widely circulated
indicating that Kennedy would break down American traditions on
church-state matters and that he would fill the federal service with
Catholic appointees and bring Church influence into the government
and nation. One church paper asserted that "if Kennedy is elected, the
Vatican will know more and more of our top secrets. The tremendous
'spy' network of the Roman Church already has many of them. As a
matter of fact, her espionage agents make the professionals in the
Kremlin's spy system look like grammar school kids playing cops and
robbers!"[8] No documentation of the alleged espionage was given.

In addition to published unethical attacks, the old-style whisper-
ing campaign persists. Unfounded rumors are often circulated about a
candidate's sex life, gambling and drinking habits, and financial manipu-
lations. The candidate's family may be attacked in a whisper campaign.
Incumbent legislators are sometimes falsely accused of taking junkets
and vacations at the taxpayer's expense.

Control of Smear Tactics. Although Congress and many states have enacted laws forbidding the distribution of anonymous campaign literature there continue to be instances of unidentified or falsely identified
sponsors of campaign publicity. Many are of the "hate" variety, appealing to anti-Semitism, anti-Catholicism, and animosities directed against
diverse other minority or political groups. They are usually issued by
party zealots who resort to desperate means in order to win or by nonparty groups who seize upon the laissez faire of a campaign to proselytize
their own causes. In most states, laws prohibit the issuance of scurrilous
materials, but they are not enforced. Nevertheless, they have some effect
by expressing society's disapproval of unethical appeals.

Laws requiring identification of the sponsor of campaign literature have been buttressed on occasion by congressional investigation of
charges of unethical appeals, as in the case of the Butler-Tydings campaign (1950). These investigations expose unethical and corrupt campaign practices but usually stop short of action against the offending
successful candidates.

On several occasions, victimized candidates have resorted to suits
charging opponents with slander. It is not easy for injured candidates
to win such suits because it is particularly difficult to prove that one's
reputation has been permanently damaged. The position of the court

[8] *The Sword of the Lord,* Sept. 16, 1960.

also has usually been that a candidate for public office must accept the risk of sharp personal attack. During the 1950s, two West Coast candidates for Congress were charged with Communist activity. Both plaintiffs won damages, and one defendant was forced to make a public retraction. Nevertheless, the two who used the tactics were not deprived of their offices and indeed were reelected. The suits appeared to have a salutary effect, for neither congressman resorted to such techniques in subsequent campaigns. Sometimes, as a political tactic, suits are filed during campaigns for the purpose of publicizing defamatory materials, only to be dropped after the election. On a meet-the-press program shortly before the 1968 election, Richard Nixon threatened to take legal steps against *The New York Times* for its editorial on the alleged "conflict-in-interest" activities of his running mate, Spiro Agnew. The *Times*, however, published no retraction; and the affair was quietly dropped after the election.

The most effective deterrent of the use of smear tactics in political campaigns is the disapproval of an informed public opinion. Candidates are reluctant to resort to mud slinging, demagoguery, and questionable tactics if they face a prospective unfavorable public reaction. Aroused voters, civil leaders, and newspapers can exact a higher standard than the law allows. Several civic groups publicly denounced anonymous anti-Catholic literature circulated in 1960. Antidefamation leagues and civic unity organizations keep track of appeals they feel promote hate and rancor and call the public's attention to them both during and between campaigns.

In 1954, the Fair Campaign Practices Committee was established as a nonpartisan, nonprofit corporation devoted to raising ethical standards in political campaigns.[9] The committee conducts state-by-state analyses of smear charges and attempts to document them. It invites each candidate to sign a pledge that he will observe the committee's "Code of Fair Campaign Practices." A candidate who feels that his opponent is violating the code can file a protest with the committee, which looks into the matter. The effectiveness of the committee's work is not easily evaluated, but the press has given laudatory publicity to its work and has probably increased public awareness of the problem.

The controlling of unfair appeals rests in restraints imposed by the candidate himself as well as the outside influences of law and public opinion. This self-restraint has not been fully researched, but an analysis of unfair tactics in a number of congressional campaigns in the San Francisco Bay Area found that the great majority of such unfair appeals were perpetrated by people inexperienced in politics, mostly

[9] Space is not available here to analyze and report on the many activities of this committee. Its bulletins and publications are obtainable from its office: 328 Pennsylvania Ave. S.E., Washington, D.C.

on behalf of nonincumbents.[10] Incumbents have learned that today's opponent might be tomorrow's ally and that one should not alienate potential allies by making vicious personal charges. A congressman's socialization and appreciation of congressional norms is likely to lead him to recognize that the rules of the game suggest the avoidance of abrasiveness with opponents. Also, if one comes from a safe district, he has nothing to gain by being unfair. On the other hand, competitive candidates with an office to gain and facing likely defeat notoriously resort to sharp attacks on their opponents.[11]

PUBLICIZING THE CANDIDATE

Literature. American ingenuity is nowhere better shown than in campaign designs, from calling cards to billboards; campaign literature shows amazing diversity, and there is seemingly no end to inventiveness in voter appeals. Few voters escape messages from their congressman carried to them through franked mail, or campaign appeals in the form of handbills, leaflets, dodgers, matchbooks, broadsides, windshield stickers, open letters, bumper strips, front yard placards, and even highway signs. A local candidate named Egg put out an egg cup inscribed "Vote for a Good Egg" and Candidate Hamburger distributed campaign publicity in the size and shape of the famous sandwich. A candidate whose name was Sugar distributed cube sugar carrying his appeal for votes. Brewers have carried political advertising on beer-bottle caps. Doorbell ringers present kiddies with free soldier hats and kites bearing their candidate's name. Small planes fly over football stadiums with streamers beseeching spectators to vote for "Green for Sheriff." Campaign buttons appear to be about as old as campaigns. Multipage booklets resembling *Life* or *Look* in format are widely used though very expensive. Great-great-grandfather saw the faces of candidates on wooden fences.

Billboards came into use in 1916 and have remained, despite expense, a favorite way to obtain name familiarity. Where not illegal, posters appear on telephone poles. "Traveling-billboards" on the sides of transit buses advertise names of candidates. A few communities permit signs inside buses—a practice sometimes bringing protest from riders. The billboard is a single-message medium that focuses on candidate identity and is one medium that continues to work on election day (much other political advertising is illegal on election day).

A study of the political advertising in several California congressional races found that more than half of the appeals were based on the

---

[10] See David A. Leuthold, *Electioneering in a Democracy: Campaigns for Congress,* John Wiley & Sons, Inc., New York, 1968, pp. 118–119.

[11] See *Ibid.,* p. 119.

qualities of the candidate and that much of it emphasized the name and picture of the candidate.[12] The next largest number of appeals were based on party affiliation, followed by issues and groups. The most common types of appeals based on groups were simply statements that the candidate had support from senior citizens, labor unions, and so forth. There was considerable variation in the uses of party label by Republicans and Democrats, appeals by incumbents and nonincumbents, and volume of appeals. All these suggest that advertising is based upon resources and how its designers see the situational factors. McCaffrey, a veteran in campaign advertising, believes that direct mail is a waste of money because it is not read.[13] He believes that printed material is the least effective campaign technique and that person-to-person distribution is the only way by which it can be made effective. Many candidates for local offices are convinced that literature handed out during house-to-house doorbelling yields good results. Comparisons of precincts doorbelled with those that were not have shown better turnout and support for the candidate in the former.[14]

There are no definitive answers on the relative success or value of the types of publicity, devices, and appeals. Undoubtedly much money is wasted on publicity, for voters become as hardened to political advertising as they do to commercial advertising. A few generalizations are evident. In strongly partisan neighborhoods, billboard and local newspaper advertising along "institutional" lines calling for citizens to "Vote Republican" or "Vote Democratic" may be profitable for the county committee. Rural voters can often be reached best through mailings. Below the top offices, candidates recognize the importance of name familiarity spread through attractive billboards, posters, and literature left when ringing a doorbell. Pamphlets emphasizing some issues may appeal to the more discriminating reader, while the sensational circular with cartoons and pictures may capture the fancy of the voter less interested in politics. The great decentralization of American campaigns, with its emphasis on personality, is taking focus away from general party advertising for the whole ticket. Each nominee tends to put out his own publicity and run his own advertising, which seldom carries the names of his colleagues on the ballot. Chances are, he considers some of them a "drag on the ticket" and desires not to be associated with them in the public mind. This atomism makes political advertising more expensive than institutional or team advertising. But in an era of split-

[12]*Ibid.*, chap. 9.

[13]*Op. cit.*, chap. 10. McCaffrey also argues that television has replaced the rally as the nation's political forum. Stephen C. Shadegg in his *How to Win an Election*, Taplinger Publishing Co., Inc., New York, 1964, chap. 12, gives specific suggestions for the most effective use of direct mail. Research is being employed to reduce the admittedly enormous wastage of resources in campaigns.

[14]Unpublished analysis of this type in Seattle by the author notes this is quite frequently but not invariably true.

ticket voting, the candidate wants to personalize his cause and to some extent to disassociate himself from the image of partnership.

Parades and Rallies. Notwithstanding the advent of television, modern managers do not advise "front-porch" campaigns, in which the candidate rarely ventures out into public. Public appearances bring out crowds, stir enthusiasm among party workers, and exhilarate the candidate—and often exhaust him as well. A large turnout does not occur spontaneously but requires careful planning and arduous efforts by the local party organization, which gets out the party regulars. The purpose of rallies is not so much to win voters, for those who turn out are largely strong partisans, but to secure favorable publicity and television coverage. While Eisenhower and Johnson as popular incumbents could probably have been reelected with highly restricted public appearances, they chose to subject themselves to the public. Problems of protecting the President during these appearances worry the Secret Service but the risks are nonetheless taken because it is believed highly important that they be seen. Nonincumbents, of course, follow an arduous course of travel and circuit riding. Demands for local appearances of popular presidential candidates come from candidates who are interested in possible coattail riding and aid to the ticket. If the top candidate is unpopular, the local nominees are less anxious to be seen and photographed with him and some have been known to absent themselves from such festivities. Several days before the visit of a presidential nominee, advance men from the national office come into the city to check travel routes, security precautions, and a myriad of other details. In 1968, the Nixon organization had eighty advance men with full authority to veto any aspects of arrangements they disliked. As alter-ego men of Nixon they knew his likes and dislikes and put themselves in his place as they evaluated plans and made changes accordingly. (The Nixon group had, in addition, thirty rally men whose function it was to make certain that the smallest details for the Nixon rallies were in order.) Advance men are regarded as very important parts of the campaign organization today, even though most people are largely unaware of their role and activities.

Motorcades with screaming-siren escorts and ticker tape attract attention and crowds. Where possible, these are scheduled during lunch hour while workers are likely to be out in the streets and can be used for augmenting the estimates of the size of the crowd.

Barnstorming by special trains, formerly used by presidential candidates, was used in 1968 for short-mileage trips; they are likely to be employed only on special occasions in the future. In 1964, President Johnson's Alabama-born wife departed from Virginia on the Lady Bird Special, which wended its way through eight Southern states. Southern governors and other officials climbed aboard the train with the purpose of invoking traditional Southern support for the party. In North Carolina, Mrs. Johnson said her reason for the trip "was to say to you that to this Democratic candidate and his wife, the South is a respected, valued, and beloved part of this country."[15] Special trains permit candidates and their families to be seen in person from rear platforms by thousands of rural and small-town residents who would likely never attend a big city rally. It permits brief reference by candidates to matters of local interest—provided the candidate is briefed before each stop. It gives newsmen and managers a chance to view responses of crowds, an opportunity not permitted by plane travel.

In the belief that voters love a good show, rallies still are held primarily because the parades and the meetings will be reported on television. Though it is no longer so easy to get massive crowds to pack the galleries as in former years, the shows still go on in flag-bedecked halls, emblazoned with banners and pictures of candidates. Music is an indispensible item in the campaign pantry and phonograph records or live bands are used to stir the emotions and ready the audience for orators to follow. Stars of theater and television are often pressed into service to appear at rallies to entertain crowds before the candidate's arrival. Athletes, ice skaters, comedians, gospel singers, and even opera stars have appeared to delight partisan audiences and to introduce various state and local candidates who seize the opportunity for exposure on the same platform with national candidates. Some rallies are used for passing the hat and collecting funds. The revivalist character of the Wallace meetings made them highly successful financial ventures.

Indoor rallies and street meetings run the risk of inviting heckling but may also be manipulated to the advantage of a candidate. One candidate for governor used a successful plant by having someone call out during his speech "Give 'em hell!" whereupon the candidate responded, "I don't want to give them hell, I want to give them leadership." The retort invariably brought favorable reaction. In 1968, George Wallace was heckled at nearly all of his appearances and, with only a few exceptions, used the disturbances to dramatize his crusade for "law and order." When young people tried to shout him down, he turned their actions into an asset by saying, "You go ahead and have your day now because after November 5 your day is going to end." To youths with long hair he said, "Hi there, Sweetie! . . . Oh, excuse me! You're a boy. I thought you were a girl." Interruptions often led him to remark that if a demonstrator should lie down in front of his car, it would be the "last time he would ever do so." His audiences roared with delight.

15 Cited in John H. Kessel, *The Goldwater Tradition: Republican Strategies in 1964*, The Bobbs-Merrill Company, Inc., Indianapolis, 1968, p. 233. Reprinted by permission of the publisher.

On the other hand, early in the campaign militant hecklers disrupted Humphrey meetings, who was unaccustomed to such tactics. Nixon's public appearances were carefully planned to handle such heckling, including an all-girl cheering section to shout down the hecklers. As vice presidential nominee, Sen. Edmund Muskie had some success with the tactic of inviting one spokesman for the hecklers to the platform, with the understanding that the crowd was to listen quietly to the heckler in return for permitting Muskie to speak without being interrupted.

ELECTRONIC MEDIA IN CAMPAIGNS

Advent of Radio and Television. Radio was first used extensively in the campaign of 1928, and managers soon learned that a speech had to be tailored to a microphone. Many of Gov. Alfred E. Smith's speeches were extemporaneous and were not well suited for radio. Although an effective campaigner in New York, his diction and Bowery accent made an unfavorable impression in national broadcasts. Thereafter, speeches were written with radio audiences in mind. Radio forced presidential candidates to be more restrained in expressing their positions on sectional problems. In the good old days, rabid partisans came to rallies to hear the nominee lambaste the opposition and to direct appeals to local prejudices. Radio put a damper on such oratory and helped to "nationalize" campaigns. Candidates, knowing that their voices were being carried hundreds or thousands of miles to nonpartisans as well as to partisans, had to exercise greater restraint, lest they offend the literary sensitivities of independents and nominal adherents of the opposition party.

Radio permitted candidates to address voters directly, so that they did not have to rely on summaries prepared by newspaper reporters, who might emphasize quotations out of context to the detriment of the nominee. The reverse, of course, was also true. No longer could the candidate falsely accuse a reporter of misquoting. The voter can hear the speaker verbatim and make up his own mind about what was actually said. Electronic media brought about a new dimension for availability—the ability to project by speech and inflection a good image, a radio or television personality. Franklin Roosevelt's effective radio personality undoubtedly did much to neutralize the opposition of most of the press to his candidacy and reelections.

Television offers the same opportunities as radio for change and expansion in campaign techniques and provides additional ones. Television has required and facilitated somewhat greater experimentation than radio. The Democrats in 1952 used television largely to bring to the nation the speeches of the comparatively unknown Adlai Stevenson.

While his speeches were refreshing, audiences appeared to tire of the straight half-hour speech in 1956. Thirty minutes seemed a long time for one person to sustain an audience with a speech. As a result, a good deal of experimentation has taken place. The spot announcement, of from one to five minutes, has become popular and has the advantage of not seriously disrupting the viewers' regular programs.

When an entire program is preempted for a political commercial, angry calls are made to the station; and party managers wish to avoid alienating viewers who are potential voters. Half-hour to one-hour programs in 1968 were relatively few in number, except for the traditional election-eve programs. Mr. Nixon has long used a marathon "telethon" on the day before election. The public is invited to phone in questions "collect" and he answers them on a national or regional network. Humphrey forces used this device effectively with television stars and motion picture actors shown taking the questions by phone, then relaying them to Mr. Humphrey or to Mr. Muskie who shared the program with him. Questions answered on television shows are usually screened to avoid those that the candidate does not want to answer.

A feature of the newer television election programs is the showing of external events such as war, poverty, and working conditions with commentary by the candidate or a supporter and concluding with the name or slogan dominating the screen such as "Nixon's the One!" This avoids overexposure of the candidate, while trying to associate him with issues and causes. Another Nixon commercial flashed the faces of President de Gaulle of France and Premier Fidel Castro of Cuba on the screen before the viewers were asked whom Americans wanted to speak for them around the world.

A documentary of Humphrey's life was well received, as was an half-hour televised informal conversation between Humphrey and Muskie. Beginning in the 1950s, Nixon employed carefully controlled televised panel programs, "Nixon Has the Answers," in which the public had opportunity to hear answers to questions in a relaxed setting. Radio was again used by both major parties in the 1968 presidential campaign. In the belief that thoughtful persons will listen and concentrate on a radio speech and to counter the charge that he was not discussing the issues, Nixon used the medium to present his views on certain issues; and he received good newspaper coverage. President Johnson used nationwide radio rather than television speeches to support Mr. Humphrey. Radio spot announcements are widely employed by candidates for local offices and those supporting or opposing ballot propositions. Radio is less costly than television, but campaign managers are faced with the problem of determining the timing of spots. Surveys show television audiences are larger in the evening. Also there are more radio than television stations in the cities so that the number of persons listening to a given radio station is likely to be less than the number of viewers watching programs on a given television channel. Radio and television announcements must be scattered throughout the day and evening, as people listen and watch at different times of day. The rule followed by modern advertising men for both media at all times, "Be brief," results in sloganeering rather than discussion of the issues and candidates.

The Great Debates. A significant development in the 1960 campaign was the series of four joint television appearances of candidates Kennedy and Nixon carried on all network during prime evening hours. Radio stations rebroadcast the meetings at different hours for those who might have missed the initial ones. As a result, nearly everyone in the nation was able to view or to hear one or more of what were popularly called "debates." The Kennedy-Nixon format consisted of questions by newsmen in the studio with each candidate given specific time for an answer and a rebuttal.

The debates were very popular and widely heralded as ushering in a new era in campaigning, mass appeals, and political education. The event was credited with having attracted the largest audience in television history. Frank Stanton, president of the Columbia Broadcasting System, testified that 101 million Americans saw one or more of the four debates, with more than half of the television families seeing three of the four debates and more than a quarter of them viewing all four encounters.[16] These figures are the more remarkable when compared to audiences viewing paid political broadcasts of only one political party, which attracted, during prime evening hours, less than one-third of the audience witnessing the average debate. The confrontations attracted a much larger audience than the programs they preempted, while the average paid political broadcast usually attracts much less audience than the program it replaces.

This innovation made it possible, for the first time, for partisans of both major parties to see and to hear both candidates on the same issues and subjects. This is in contrast with the usual political program, which is so often tuned off by the faithful of the other side. Only a negligible number tuned the debates off after the opening statements. Men in the industry were astounded when their minute-by-minute checks showed the audience remarkably stable throughout the hour-long broadcast. The television debates attracted far more people than

[16] See his report in Sidney Kraus (ed.), *The Great Debates: Background — Perspectives — Effects*, Indiana University Press, Bloomington, 1962, chap. 4. The work is recommended for its comprehensive treatment of the debates.

is usual for political broadcasts and covered both sides of more subjects than was formerly the case.

The debates inspired extensive research; some thirty-one independent studies were located. At least a chapter in itself would be required to summarize the findings.[17] The surveys did, however, indicate that only a small minority did not like the debates, mainly because they thought their man had been bettered. The debates made some issues more salient and helped some people learn where the candidates stood. A quarter of the respondents in one study mentioned that the debates helped them learn something about the issues, and many remembered some of the content of the debates. It seems probable that the debates increased the level of information as well as the interest of a number of citizens.

As might be expected, the debates were more effective in focusing attention on candidates than on issues. With only an exception or two, the various studies showed that Kennedy improved his image considerably more than Nixon and that more Democrats reported an improved opinion of Kennedy than Republicans reported improvement of their opinion of Nixon. After the first debate, Kennedy gained three percentage points in the Gallup Poll, while Nixon lost one. Before the debate, 46 percent of the respondents expressed their intention to vote for Kennedy, 47 percent were for Nixon, with the remainder undecided; the changes were to 49, 46, and 5 percent, respectively. There is little doubt that Democrats were strengthened in their image and in support of Kennedy, but most polling experts were cautious in claiming that the debates determined the final outcome of the election.

From the public's point of view, the face-to-face encounter helps to keep the candidates "honest." They are less likely to make extreme, unsupported statements when their opponent is present to challenge them. A careful reading of campaign remarks by Kennedy and Nixon while out on the hustings showed them to be less inhibited than when they met each other in the studio. Each man during the debate found himself having to modify or to explain what appeared to be some of his rather dogmatic utterances. The debate technique probably imposes some restraint and responsibility for campaign statements not imposed by appearances before partisan crowds of one's own predisposition.

The debates came in for sharp criticism, and there were expressions that "never again" should presidential nominees face each other in such debates because the winner is not necessarily the best man but the one most "glib" and "fluent" or with the best "personality."

[17] Fortunately this has been done by Elihu Katz and Jacob J. Feldman in *ibid.*, chap. 11.

Many Republicans privately felt that Nixon lost the election because his television technique was a little less effective than that of his opponent. Although admitting that they kindled interest, newsman Edward R. Murrow said of the debates, "They were a puny contribution, capsuled, homogenized, perhaps dangerous in its future implication." Others saw the debate as corrupting the public judgment and asserted that the qualities needed to "win" a debate were not likely to be those needed to make a good President.

Before his nomination in 1968, Mr. Nixon had expressed a willingness to engage in television debates irrespective of who his Democratic opponent might be. This appeared good strategy at the time, when he was running behind on the polls and felt he could avoid the mistakes of 1960. However, he refused to accept Governor Rockefeller's challenge to appear on television before the convention.[18] After his nomination, he emerged in a front-running position and it no longer looked like good strategy to meet Humphrey. Following the hallowed dictum that you should not "publicize an opponent," he avoided debate on the ground that George Wallace would have to be included and that this would only enhance the visibility of the third-party candidate. This argument points up the fact that strategic considerations of competition rather than principle are likely to dictate whether contenders will meet each other on television. There are, therefore, both a "voter interest" and a "candidate interest," with the latter almost certain to prevail. The strategy is optional for a candidate; and, despite pressure from the opposition, the decision to debate rests with him.

Notwithstanding the absence of presidential campaign debates since 1960, quite a number of such confrontations are used in state and local campaigns. In every instance, the results and the impact of such debates have been uncertain. With some reluctance, Sen. Wayne Morse of Oregon agreed in 1968 to one state-wide television debate with his Republican challenger, Robert Packwood. Newsmen were of the opinion that Packwood came out the better. Whether this was the difference in the razor-thin electoral victory of Packwood is moot. Incumbent Gov. Daniel J. Evans of Washington appeared in several television debates in 1968 with his challenger and went on to a sizable electoral victory.

Problems. Many problems, both for the candidate and for the democratic theorist, came in with the new electronic media.[19] Two of these

[18]Senators Eugene McCarthy and Robert Kennedy had one comparatively innocuous face-to-face discussion before the California primary in 1968. After Kennedy's assassination, Humphrey, like Nixon, chose not to indulge in a television debate with his opponent for the nomination.

[19]For an overall general discussion, see Bernard Rubins, *Political Television*, Wadsworth Publishing Company, Inc., Belmont, Calif., 1967.

are access and expense. While the treasuries of Republicans and Democrats may permit relatively comparable access, such is not the case with minor-party candidates. Congress faces the problem that the "equal-time" provisions of the law would allow free television to third-party candidates, irrespective of the fact that they may have little or no public support.

Major-party candidates for local and for congressional offices find telecasts desirable but perhaps quite wasteful because they reach audiences outside their districts. Yet when an opponent buys such time the candidate may feel compelled to do so, often at the risk of depleting scarce resources. Further, campaign managers realize that there is still much question about the actual impact of television appearances and the degree to which they are reinforcers or converters of opinion. If campaigns are to arouse civic interest, focus attention on some issues, and provide the public with information about the candidates and parties, there must be a fair degree of access by all parties to the channels of communication and no party or candidate should be able to control the lion's share. The ingenuity and ability of candidates to make the best use of the media is hardly less important than obtaining media time in the first place.

Those who decry the use of the public relations men in campaigns criticize the extensive use of television, which emphasizes the image of candidates instead of the discussion of issues. Viewers judge style rather than the substance of arguments presented by the candidates. Although the viewer is provided with clues to a candidate's character by his appearance, demeanor, and presentation, television does not necessarily enable the viewer to judge his qualities of public leadership. After a study of television in campaigns, Gene Wyckoff concludes that it "transfigures candidates into personal images or characterizations that can be quite unique to the medium. . . . It is necessary to have a term to describe this unique image, a term such as *image candidate.* . . . Most image techniques employed by political propagandists to enhance the appeal of their client seek to exploit television's inherent theatricality and viewers' tendencies to see the candidates as dramatic characters. By controlling the presentation or theatrical setting of candidates on paid political programs and commercials, propagandists can encourage viewers to perceive a favorable characterization of the client candidate.[20]

Unquestionably, television features "imagery," but the overall impact and results are by no means clear. Television has not yet replaced campaign materials found in magazines, newspapers, and literature.

[20]Gene Wyckoff, *The Image Candidates: American Politics in the Age of Television,* The Macmillan Company, New York, 1968, pp. 216, 230.

Nor have political rallies and canvases become a thing of the past. Television supplements these devices, and each of them provides different techniques and emphases. Unless a candidate has public appeal, no amount of "Madison Avenue techniques" is likely to elect him. The charges against the use of television would become more serious if it were the sole method of presenting parties, candidates, and issues; however, it is but one of many competitors for the voter's attention. Rarely are candidates endorsed by television stations and many problems would arise if they were. Meanwhile, newspapers often endorse with editorial comment and feature columnists who expose strengths and weaknesses of nominees—this also helps to counterbalance the impact of television, especially in state and local elections.

"Getting a good press" is an important art whether on radio and television or in the newspaper. The way stories are carried makes much difference. A confrontation between blacks and police in Miami during the 1968 Republican convention resulted in some fatalities. But to viewers, the incidents did not seem related to the convention, and Republicans escaped a "bad press." In contrast, the battle between Chicago police and peace demonstrators miles away from the Democratic convention was repeatedly shown on television and cognizance was taken of it on the floor of the convention. Many viewers held the Democrats responsible for the disorders and for alleged police brutality. It was television coverage, however, not the press accounts, that produced the results.

Focusing cameras on hecklers or on demeanor of crowds takes attention away from a candidate's speech and leaves an unfavorable impression. This practice angers the candidate but is often interesting to the viewer. Newspapers, of course, decide where and how to feature the candidates, his pronouncements, and his activities; and supporters may be as unhappy with such editorial decisions as with television. It is a basic rule of the game that candidates must make the most of their opportunities in all public appearances and use them to counteract unfavorable impressions from segments presented by the various type of media.

POLLING AND FEEDBACKS

Polls are used not only as sources of intelligence for strategy in campaigning but also, on occasion, to influence voters. The Gallup and Harris Polls in presidential contests make public the strength of candidates at intervals during the campaign and also the location of that strength geographically and demographically. Managers can see how a Hunphrey rates in the Northeast, a Wallace in the Border States, and a Nixon in the Great Plains. Further, information on how the candidate is faring with the young voters, the blue-collar workers, and racial minorities is helpful in deciding how and where to spend available resources.

The general public is much less aware of the extensive use of surveys in state and local contests. A number of party organizations employ confidential private polls covering a wide range of subjects, to determine the salience of issues. A candidate can tell how his views agree with those of the voters and can select those that receive the strongest public support and play down those that have the least public support. For example, if he is a strong civil rights man but a poll of his district shows a strong backlash, he may choose to soft-pedal civil rights and to concentrate on other issues. Hubert Humphrey found that many voters felt Nixon should debate him on television and increased his attacks on this point. Newsmen, in turn, noticed that audiences responded favorably to Humphrey's challenge in this area.

Polls also provide information on the candidate's image with the voters in such aspects as sincerity, experience, and leadership qualities, enabling "image builders" on his staff to revise their appeals.

When polls show that the candidate is ahead, the results may be "leaked" to reporters, to prospective financial donors, and to others, with a view toward improving the morale of campaign workers, obtaining money, redoubling efforts all down the line to create a psychology of likely victory. In short, the polls are publicized by the side that is ahead and may force the opposition to discount them publicly and fight possible erosion.

Polls are one of the ways of taking soundings of the progress and consequences of strategies. It is easy to be deceived by a "headquarters view" that things are in "good shape," when this is not the case. There is always fear that bad news will sap the vitality of the organization. Polls may show a great variation from the estimates by the candidate's managers. The question then is whether to believe the poll. Although polls are expensive, one can order a second one taken. Since a poll is only a picture at a given moment, the strength of the candidates can easily change between polls. There are always problems in interpreting the polls and in detecting bias in the questions.

Feedback may be obtained in other ways, such as audience response. Candidates soon learn which appeals bring cheers and which receive little or no applause. They must also decide whether the wit, barbs, and phrases that bring rafter-shattering applause result in votes. Harry Truman ran behind on the polls but predicted his own victory because of audience response—he remarked, "I'm going to win, I've seen it in their faces." Audience size and reaction, however, are most difficult to evaluate. A large crowd may be due to local organizational efforts or a curiosity to see the candidate rather than a sign of great popularity.

The mass media, particularly newspapers, are assiduously used to determine consequences and reactions. Staff members read the press accounts and monitor television and radio commentators. Here again there is the problem of the objectivity of reporters and of the staff members who evaluate the views of the newsmen. At the same time, the reactions of the more objective reporters may be useful in modifying campaign technique and strategies.

Other subjective evaluations are based on the calls people make to the party headquarters and volume of requests for campaign literature, buttons, and bumper strips. The number of those volunteering to do party work and mailing in contributions may indicate heightened or flagging interest. Precinct committeemen's reports can also be valuable in the feedback process.

PURPOSIVE CAMPAIGNING

A Theory of Techniques. Despite the many "tool kit" manuals telling how to win elections, there are no foolproof generalizations about successful techniques. Flexibility, opportunism, and adaptability are part of the game. However, analyses of campaigns over the years permit some conclusions, which may be put together in the form of empirical theory applicable to most contests.

At the outset, a campaign is a process of holding the coalition responsible for one's nomination and enlarging it by including voters of other groups. The campaign becomes a contest to win incremental votes. To win, a candidate does not need all the votes but simply a majority or a plurality. In areas where one party has a substantial majority of the registered voters, its candidates and campaign managers use appeals that reinforce latent party loyalties and motivate party members to go to the polls to vote for party candidates. The minority party must mobilize its party voters but must also seek the votes of those with weak party identification and voters of the majority party. The minority party must of necessity soft-pedal partisanship and the party label. Both, of course, seek the votes of the uncommitted independents. In the main, however, registration and campaign efforts are directed toward one's own supporters. As noted earlier in the chapter, campaigning is a process of activation, reinforcement, reassurance, and conversion.

For legislative positions, the odds strongly favor the selection of incumbents. Of incumbents in Congress who seek reelection, upwards of 90 percent of the representatives are successful and about 75 percent of the senators are reelected. Techniques and strategies for incumbents and nonincumbents differ. Incumbents conduct campaigns designed to reinforce past loyalties and to maintain their previously successful winning coalitions. Challengers must attack the incumbent and his record and undermine his coalition while building an opposing coalition.

Choice of techniques rests mainly on the perceptions of the candidates and their managers concerning the loyalty and attitudes of the electorate at the time of the campaign. Their evaluation leads them to sort out the methods that appear to hold the most promise for mobilizing the greatest number of voters. Even when there is agreement on the context of the election, the strategists may differ on the appeals and techniques to be used. Some will argue that face-to-face contact and interaction with voters is needed. Others will insist that voters will be more receptive to television or radio spot announcements and other publicity.

The level of office sought, as well as financial resources, influences techniques. Because of the high cost, state legislative candidates use television and radio much less than do candidates for higher office. They usually rely upon newspaper and billboard advertising, house-to-house canvasing, direct mailings, and small meetings of followers. These factors lead the candidate for local office to try to find canvasers to carry his cause door-to-door and to rely more heavily on interest-group support than perhaps is the case with congressional candidates. The state legislative candidate knows also the mass media are less likely to give attention to his actions.

Campaign managers agree that a candidate's opponent should not be publicized and that a few comparatively simple campaign themes are preferable to shotgun coverage of many. For this reason, advertising men usually urge that a piece of campaign literature not be cluttered with too much information. Common practice dictates that the candidate must try to put the opposition on the defensive but must be prepared to react to his campaign tactics. The type of campaign waged by the opponent is almost certain to influence the strategy, vigor, and methods used in the campaign.

Finally, all candidates and their campaign staffs seek the active support of group leaders through whom others will become interested and involved in the campaign, thereby widening the number of people involved and expanding the coalition. This involvement is especially important for the minority party, for a small turnout of voters usually favors incumbents. An incumbent needs to get his own supporters and party identifiers to the polls while the opposition needs to compensate by getting other factors to work for him. In national elections, at least, nonvoting is somewhat higher among nominal Democrats than among nominal Republicans. Regardless of the advantage of incumbency (where it pertains), it is to the Democrats' interest to increase the turnout in presidential elections and to conduct registration and voting drives, especially in lower-income areas.

A theory of techniques must embrace opportunism, because swiftly changing events make it difficult to formulate and stay with a blueprint. Strategy that is rational for a Democratic candidate for the United States Senate will necessarily differ from that suitable for a Democratic candidate for the United States House of Representatives in the same state because of the different characteristics of their constituencies. The candidate must rely upon his awareness and that of his advisers as to how voters will react to him, the party strength and weaknesses, and the issues that will be most effective in gaining votes. He must also estimate the cost of conducting a campaign to reach the voters, how the necessary funds can be raised, and what support he can enlist from the press and organized groups. These factors, together with the factor of incumbency, are the critical elements in planning campaign strategy for a partisan office. A campaign for a nonpartisan office would be put together somewhat differently, because the party variable is of much less importance.

Policy Discussion. Although issues are discussed in a campaign, an election is rarely a plebiscite on a particular policy. The decisions of some voters may be influenced by one issue, and those of other voters by other issues. Positions of major candidates on key issues are often quite similar, even though expressed differently. It is difficult, if not impossible, to interpret the election results as a mandate for a particular policy.

The element of issues points up the reconciling of general public interest with a candidate interest. In looking at the former, Stanley Kelley, Jr., argues that "campaign discussion should help voters to make rational voting decisions." Such decisions, he writes, "require full information about the alternatives to be voted upon, full knowledge of all effects that would attend the choice of each alternative, and a comprehensive and logically consistent system of preferences, within which values may be assigned to these effects."[21] This ideal is far from realization in most campaigns and victory does not appear to be predicated on the assumption that political man is a rational animal. Yet certain types of debates, policy and position papers, press conferences, and some publicity help to etch candidate positions on public policies. Locally sponsored forums of candidates for municipal and other offices,

---

[21] *Political Campaigning,* The Brookings Institution, Washington, D.C., 1960, pp. 10–11. This work covers the range of problems in improving campaigns.

though not often well-attended, tend to reveal candidates' approaches to matters of special concern to the community.

Although not necessarily antithetical to the public-interest concept, the candidate-party interest in the discussion of issues may be quite different. Nominees see issues as a device for getting votes. It may serve their interest to be vague, general, or noncommital on policies and to operate on the assumption that a candidate-centered rather than issue-centered campaign is a better road to victory. A shrewd candidate appreciates that a relevant issue differs from group to group and from person to person. If elected, the politician wants to be relatively uncommitted and free to handle problems in the most rational (and political) way after he assumes office. Hard-line commitment to a course of action during a campaign may hamper or embarrass the officeholder when confronted with the later responsibilities and realities of exercising power. He may find that the public interest requires a solution different from the one he proposed in the campaign. It is fortunate that specific public policies are decided, not in the hustings, but afterward, when there is greater opportunity for rational consideration and responsible decision. Except for the popular initiative process in some states, policy initiatives in the final analysis rest, not with the voter, but with the officeholder.

If one views campaigns as something of an adversary proceeding with the voters as the jury, the presentation of policies is seen in a different light. Each party is expected to emphasize the strongest aspects of its own case and to omit or play down weaknesses. Each party attacks what he sees as the vulnerable parts of his opponent's position. Neither party tries to present all aspects, including those that might weaken his own case. Therefore, in campaigning, one discusses those policies and in those terms that enable him to lead from strength and to avoid areas where he is weakest.

The temper of the times, the views of the district, the candidate's perception of the electoral setting, and the competitiveness of the contest have impelling effects on the explicitness of the victory. Candidates whose chances of winning are slight are not afraid of losing votes and often take militant stands in the hope that they might become more competitive. Sure winners from a safe district do not need to be very specific and ride into office with few promises. Leuthold notes that in several congressional campaigns the competitive candidates presented more information on more issues than did noncompetitive candidates.[22] Senator Barry Goldwater of Arizona has often taken a militant stand for right-to-work legislation; but, if he were seeking, with hope of success,

[22] *Op. cit.*, p. 121.

the senatorship in heavily unionized Michigan, it seems doubtful that he would take such a forthright position on that issue.

In a normative sense, a "good" campaign stimulates effective deliberation on some issues as well as on the qualities of the candidates. Voters are aware of certain of their particular interests, but few are interested in a broad range of issues. They like to feel that they understood at least some issues and that they cast their ballots in a way that might help to resolve some of the questions. The voters' interests are served by campaign discussion that helps them to perceive fairly accurately the areas of agreement and disagreement between the candidates' approaches to public policies.

A Wisconsin study found "the winners tend to believe more than the losers that the voters in their district decided how to cast their ballots not by blind party voting, but according to issues of the election and the man who was seeking the office. . . . On the other hand, the unsuccessful candidates blame the electorate for their loss by emphasizing the importance of the party label, and by downgrading the importance of issues and the candidates. They deprecate the electorate's decision because, after all, it was not a wise decision."[23] The same study found that "because he believes that voters and media are paying greater attention to his pronouncements . . . the candidate for Congress is more likely than the state legislative candidate to campaign on relatively specific issues of governmental policy and even to give a more ideological cast to his comments about politics."[24]

A complicating factor for candidates in policy discussion is that of salience. Most elections feature choices of candidates for more than one level of government so the voter is met with discussion of national, state, and local issues during the same campaign. He may say that the issues at all levels are or should be of equal importance to him, an ideal unlikely to be fulfilled. His attention will be drawn in all directions, but his interest is likely to be selective because of the difficulty of concentrating on all of them. Also, within each level of government, some matters will be of greater consequence to him than others. For this reason, candidates for office, even of the same party, are in competition with each other to discuss matters of concern to the voter. Ideally at least, candidates should confine their appeals to matters relating to the office they seek or issues on which they will pass if elected. Yet candidates often discuss issues unrelated to the office they seek, which is often little more than demagoguery. Each competitor, to some extent, must see what

[23]John W. Kingdon, "Politicians' Beliefs about Voters," *American Political Science Review*, vol. 66, pp. 139–140, 1967.
[24]John W. Kingdon, *Candidates for Office: Beliefs and Strategies*, Random House, Inc., New York, 1968, p. 141.

others on his ticket are discussing and where he can get the voters' attention for his office. Only in rare instances will the same issue appear to have salience from the top to the bottom of the ticket. The "law and order" and civil rights issues in 1968 afford one such example, with seemingly candidates for every office from county commissioner and state legislature to governor and President choosing to discuss it.

Uses of Campaigns. Frustration, cynicism, and even disdain about popular elections, as well as skepticism about the efficacy of campaigns and elections, are not uncommon. The mandate of the voters, if any, is seen as unclear. The discontent is partly due to the picture of the voter as an uninformed, disinterested fellow who responds in a vague way to his perceptions (which are often misperceptions) of party labels, candidate characteristics, and the issues presented to him (consideration of voting behavior is reserved for later chapters). There is also criticism of the system itself, including emphasis on the "image candidates," an outmoded Electoral College, excessive campaign expenditures, and the like. The problem is aggravated by the divergent ways in which theorists and observers evaluate elections. With different criteria and expectations of the purposes and uses of campaigns, it is not surprising to find a lack of agreement.[25] Arguments over elections bear great similarity to those about democracy. Our summary must be limited to the general functions of campaigns.

Except for initiatives and referenda, the electorate does not determine public policy through the act of voting. Rather the influence is indirect, as voters choose men who will exercise power and who must come up for reelection on the basis of what they have done. Elections are a way of influencing government by rendering a decision on who shall rule. The politician knows that in the next campaign the opposition will likely ask him questions in public and he must defend at least some of his policy positions. Elections, then, have an impact on politicians for they know judgment will be passed on them retrospectively.

In the next place, the electoral process has varying degrees of effect on voters. Many have their interest in public affairs at least temporarily kindled. Others become excited enough to make campaign donations, engage in electioneering, or perhaps join a campaign organization. Those becoming actively engaged undoubtedly enjoy some

[25] One of the most comprehensive treatments of both the philosophical and practical aspects is Gerald M. Pomper, *Elections in America: Control and Influence in Democratic Politics*, Dodd, Mead & Company, Inc., New York, 1968. Two volumes of essays also present extensive treatment of elections: M. Kent Jennings and L. Harmon Zeigler (eds.), *The Electoral Process*, Prentice-Hall, Inc., Englewood Cliffs, N.J., 1966; *The Electoral Process* in successive issues, Spring and Summer, 1962 of *Law and Contemporary Problems*.

thrill of taking part in a democratic process. Still others engage in discussion, listen to campaign argument, and read more about public affairs than previously. Campaigns make them more attentive to and aware of political problems. This awareness may create a discontent leading them to vote against an incumbent or party. Some believe that their vote will be helpful in ameliorating problems. The campaign and its outcome provide an audit of the party's stewardship and establish a confidence or nonconfidence in the ruling group. As a result of the ritual directed at him, the voter feels that there has been a useful discussion resulting in an acceptable collective judgment—even if his candidate lost. Some of his opinions and attitudes have been reinforced, and some even changed. He senses that campaigns are a method of giving consent and legitimacy to one of the competitors for office and, to a lesser extent, to some positions on issues and to a political party.

A campaign gives some focus to political parties and to the general record of the party in office. Kennedy, Johnson, and Humphrey followed their predecessors in emphasizing the overall record of the Democratic party and its approach to national and international problems. Eisenhower used the campaigns of 1956 and 1958 to articulate "Modern Republicanism" and its approach to public problems. Although the image of a party is made essentially on the basis of its record in office, campaigns reinforce that image.

Both primary and general elections are likely to determine the victorious and losing factions of the party and who shall control it between elections. General election campaigns are occasions for binding up wounds within a party. A party's greatest unity and widest loyalty usually come during a campaign. Without this unity, the party's candidates are likely to be defeated unless they represent a strongly dominant party that can afford substantial erosion and still win. The campaign brings all segments of the party together—its activists, officeholders, new nominees, youth, financial donors, and voters. Vague though the concept may be, the entity of "party" and its so-called "program" receives its most intensive play during the electoral process. Campaigns give parties a chance to locate new talent, to bring it into the organization, and, hopefully, to retain it after the election. The election gives party leaders a chance to locate new types of support and to study where support is being lost. Postmortems of the defeated party commonly lead to some changes believed necessary for "rebuilding" the organizations. Campaigns have the psychological values of renewing loyalties of activists and partisans. They afford an outlet for aggression and for the activists' desires. They alleviate some of the frustrations of politics for officeholders, challengers, and their supporters.

In sum, campaigns, in addition to performing an information function, are functional events for the public, the politicians, and the activists. American campaigns could be improved by shortening their length, which tends to exhaust candidates and their treasuries. Fewer speeches and less emotional oratory would be better than the long endurance contests that characterize presidential and many other campaigns. A vital requirement if campaigns are to be fully functional is honest and energetic competition between contenders, a process affording citizens both choice and protection.

FOR FURTHER READING

Anderson, Walt: *Campaigns: Cases in Political Conflict*, 1970.
Bans, Herbert M., and William B. Ross: *Politics Battle Plan*, 1968.
Blumer, Jay G., and Dennis McQuail: *Television in Politics*, 1968.
Campbell, Angus, et al.: *Elections and the Political Order*, 1966.
Cummings, Milton C. (ed.): *The National Election of 1964*, 1966.
David, Paul T. (ed.): *The Presidential Election and Transitions, 1960–1961*, 1961.
Farley, James A.: *Jim Farley's Story*, 1948.
Ferguson, L. C., and R. H. Smuckler: *Politics in the Press*, 1952.
Gosnell, Harold F.: *Champion Campaigner: Franklin D. Roosevelt*, 1952.
Kent, Frank R.: *Political Behavior*, 1928.
——: *The Great Game of Politics*, 1924.
Levin, Murray B.: *Kennedy Campaigning: The System and the Style as Practiced by Senator Edward Kennedy*, 1966.
Mazo, Earl (ed.): *The Great Debates*, 1962.
McGinnis, Joe: *The Selling of a President*, 1969.
Ogden, Daniel M., Jr., and Arthur L. Peterson: *Electing the President, 1968*, 1968.
Packard, Vance: *The Hidden Persuaders*, 1958.
Perry, James M.: *The New Politics: The Expanding Technology of Political Manipulation*, 1968.
Polsby, Nelson W., and Aaron B. Wildavsky: *Presidential Elections*, 1968.
Pool, Ithiel de Sola, et al.: *Candidates, Issues and Strategies*, 1964.
Rubin, Bernard: *Political Television*, 1964.
Schneider, J. G.: *The Golden Kazoo*, 1956. (A novel.)
Thomson, Charles A. H.: *Television and Presidential Politics*, 1956.
Wallace, David: *First Tuesday: A Study of Rationality in Voting*, 1964.
Weisbard, Marvin R.: *Campaigning for President: A New Look at the Road to the White House*, 1964.

Politics has got so expensive that it takes
a lot of money to get beat with.

WILL ROGERS

CHAPTER 13 FINANCING CAMPAIGNS AND PARTIES

THE HIGH COST OF CAMPAIGNS

Money has always been a factor in American elections, but large-scale finance is a development of the past seventy-five years. It is estimated that the Democratic National Committee spent $25,000 to elect Buchanan in 1856. Four years later, Republicans spent $100,000 to elect Abraham Lincoln — about the cost of half an hour on a nationwide television hookup in 1960. In many states, figures of $250,000 to $750,000 for a United States Senate seat or a governorship are expected. New York and California gubernatorial races now commonly run $2 million for each major-party candidate. Governor Nelson Rockefeller of New York spent more than $5 million to win reelection in 1966, probably the most expensive statewide campaign in American history. As Will Rogers observed, money to get beat with runs into a tidy figure. Alan Cranston of California spent about $1 million only to lose the Democratic primary

TABLE 13-1 Political spending 1960–1968: reported total national-level spending

Political group	1960	1964	1968
Republican	$10,587,000	$11,973,000	$29,563,000
Democratic	11,300,000	17,187,000	13,578,000
Labor and miscellaneous	3,127,000	5,628,000	12,502,000
American Independent (Wallace)	...	...	7,243,000
	$25,014,000	$34,788,000	$62,886,000

Source: Adapted from figures compiled by Herbert Alexander, *Financing the 1960 Election* and *Financing the 1964 Election*, Citizens' Research Foundation, Princeton, N.J., 1962 and 1966, and (for 1968) *Congressional Quarterly*, Dec. 5, 1969, p. 2435.

nomination for the Senate in 1964 and estimated the primary cost more than $2 million for all candidates.[1] Milton Shapp won the Democratic gubernatorial primary in Pennsylvania in 1966 but lost the general election with a collective expenditure of $2.5 million out of his own pocket! Senator Joseph Clark of Pennsylvania said his losing the 1968 bid for reelection cost about $5 million. Candidates for mayor of New York City expect to spend, win or lose, about $2 million on their campaigns.

Although these figures are startling, they understate the sums expended because so many expenditures go unreported. Reported national-level expenditures during presidential election years are shown in Table 13-1.[2] To get a fuller picture one must add the increasing and known-to-be-large expenditures by state and local groups on behalf of the national ticket. Heard and Alexander, therefore, estimate actual expenditures much higher than those reported. Their educated guesses indicate actual expenditures as follows: 1952, $140 million; 1956, $155 million; 1960, $175 million; 1964, $200 million; and 1968, $300 million. Of the $300 million total in 1968, one-third is attributed to the presidential contests alone, the balance for the congressional offices.

Except where state laws require it, moneys expended to get the presidential nomination are not reported. A spectacular increase in pre-

[1] *San Francisco Chronicle*, Nov. 18, 1964. For account of the costliness of primaries in this state, see John R. Owens, *Money and Politics in California: Democratic Senatorial Primary, 1964*, Citizens' Research Foundation, Princeton, N.J., 1966. The Foundation has published several state political finance studies including H. Gaylon Greenhill, *Labor Money in Politics, 1964* (1966); Donald G. Balmer, *Financing State Campaigns; Multnomah County, Oregon, 1964* (1966); *Money as a Campaign Resource: Tennessee Democratic Senatorial Primaries, 1948–1964* (1966); Elston Roady and Carl D. McMurray, *Republican Campaign Financing in Florida, 1963–1967* (1969).

[2] *The Congressional Quarterly* annually reports campaign expenditures, and House and Senate committees frequently make their own analyses and estimates. For the years before 1962, see the comprehensive work of Alexander Heard, *The Costs of Democracy*, The University of North Carolina Press, Chapel Hill, 1960, revised and updated in paperback edition in 1962. Herbert Alexander has the most authoritative data on presidential election spending. See his *Financing the 1960 Election* and *Financing the 1964 Election*, both published by the Citizens' Research Foundation, Princeton, N.J., 1962 and 1966, and his report "Financing Parties and Campaigns in 1968," prepared for the annual meeting of the American Political Science Association, September, 1969. Many of the data in this section are drawn from Alexander's studies.

convention cost took place in the 1960s. In 1964, Goldwater forces spent what was believed to be an unprecedented $5.5 million before the convention, followed by $3 million spent on behalf of Rockefeller, $827,000 for Scranton, $100,000 for Lodge, and about $70,000 each for Nixon and Stassen.[3] Some half a million dollars were spent on Nixon's nomination in 1960 and $10 million in 1968. Humphrey's respective costs were $250,000 and $4 million. The combination of Kennedy, McCarthy, Humphrey, Romney, and Rockefeller brought more left-of-center and moderate money onto the political scene than ever before. By piecing together bits of information Alexander estimated 1968 preconvention campaign costs as follows: Rockefeller $7 million, Reagan $800,000, Romney $1 million, Stassen $90,000, Johnson $500,000, Kennedy $9 million, McCarthy $9 million, and McGovern $100,000.

Off-year expenditures, while considerably less, still run high. Even in odd-numbered years, much money is necessary for *party* finance as distinguished from campaign finance. Figures ran $8,818,000 in 1963, $10,893,000 in 1965, and $10,478,000 in 1967. In the last-mentioned year, there was a big drop in Democratic expenditures, which was partially offset by an increase in Republican spending to get ready for the 1968 campaign.

Despite insufficiency of accurate data, a few generalizations can be made about campaign finance. The cost of campaigns is now increasing more rapidly than the voter population, general inflation, or the gross national product. Heard noted that from 1940 through 1956 costs of campaigning and cost of living prices remained closely in balance.[4] From 1956 to 1964, increase in campaigning expense outstripped increase in the price level 29 to 4.5 percent. The whopping 1968 figures showed increases of 40 to 50 percent. Besides the obvious factors of inflation (4 to 5 percent per year) and increased size of the electorate, other forces contribute to skyrocketing campaign costs. Many candidates now hire advertising firms to arrange their campaign, and these fees are added to the conventional travel, office space, and printing costs. More money is spent on public opinion polls than in earlier years. Rockefeller is believed to have spent $250,000 in polls alone in 1968 and the Nixon forces invested heavily both before and after the national conventions. The single most important increase is for radio and television. In times past, volunteer labor constituted a great resource. Today the shift to media campaigning requires much higher cash outlay and the percentage of noncash costs is declining.

[3]Alexander, *Financing the 1964 Election*, p. 30.

[4]*Op. cit.*, p. 375. Costs also appear to outstrip increase in voters and prices in some or all states. In Wisconsin the cost per voter rose from $0.94 in 1950 to $1.42 in 1958 and to $3.01 in 1966. David Adamany, *Financing Politics: Recent Wisconsin Elections*, University of Wisconsin Press, Madison, 1969, p. 55. This work is recommended for comprehensive treatment of factual and conceptual treatment of party finance.

In each election there is a *real* cost and a *committed* cost, often with considerable discrepancy between the two. This discrepancy has made calculation of expenditures difficult if not misleading. Many candidates finish a campaign in debt, with the debts sometimes settled for 33 cents on the dollar or some other figure. Free publicity or media time is also an actual cost of a campaign, although it may not show up in official accounts of expense or income.

Every election has a different set of variables and the need for and role of money changes from campaign to campaign. Money is but *one* of many variables and probably a dependent variable at that. Among the factors certain to influence financial outlays to one degree or another are (1) party identification, (2) name familiarity, (3) strength of the candidate's campaign organization and relationships to others on the ticket, (4) incumbency, (5) presence of a third-party candidate, (6) levels of competition for nomination within each party, and (7) ideological character of the campaign.

For the unknown candidate for Congress or for the state legislature, money can help buy visibility and name familiarity. For the popular incumbent without formidable opposition, it may not be necessary to raise sizable funds. But if a challenger threatens to make a real contest of it, the officeholder may feel that a big war chest is needed. The real expenditure may be in a primary; and, having won the nomination, a candidate in a one-party district may be reelected year after year with little or no expenditure. In many primaries, there is no adversary process. The existence and vitality of a party organization, its loyalty and willingness to work for a candidate, and the extent to which nonparty citizens groups are available to assist also determine the amount of funds required. Although its effect is not known, ideology appears an important motive for contributing to campaigns. Thus, the type and context of the election have important bearing on the money factor.

Republicans, with the notable exceptions of 1912, 1916, and 1964, have outspent Democrats in national elections. Very few third parties are able to muster funds comparable to the American Independent party of George Wallace in 1968.

Finally, campaign spending is up at all levels. An Ohio congressman testified before a congressional committee that his earlier campaigns for the office cost about $3,000 but rose to $86,000 in 1968; and he claimed his opponent's costs topped $150,000.[5]

THE ANATOMY OF SPENDING

Although the collection and disbursement of funds is at the heart of the campaign process, the researcher is greatly handicapped by the

[5] *Seattle Times*, Oct. 24, 1968.

TABLE 13-2 Democratic national campaign spending costs, 1968*

Type of expenditure	Amount
Advertising	$6,624,000
Travel	875,000
Personnel	759,000
Communications	722,000
Field expenses	779,000
Subventions to state and local committees	380,000
Polls and surveys	262,000
Miscellaneous	164,000

Source: Adaptation from Herbert Alexander, "Financing Parties and Campaigns in 1968," report prepared for 1969 annual meeting of the American Political Science Association, p. 65.
*In round numbers.

absence of reliable, uniform data on the sources and uses of political money. Because financial needs vary from election to election, the problem of drawing conclusions about campaign finance over a period of time becomes further complicated. At one time, the Republican National Committee regularly charted the allocation of its expenditures so that one could study changes between presidential years, off years, and odd years. The last one it published, 1960, is shown in Figure 13-1. Since that time, scholars have been unable to obtain comparable breakdowns. With a few exceptions, records of state campaign finance are meager, making it almost impossible to determine the pattern of income and expenditures over a continuum except to say that they show an upward trend. We shall attempt, nonetheless, to report what has been learned about major sources of income and about the items on which money has been spent in recent national elections.

Table 13-2 shows the categories of officially reported expenditures by the Democratic National Committee and fifty-five special committees that aided the 1968 ticket. Although the breakdown differs so radically from that of the Republicans shown in Figure 13-1 as to make comparisons quite meaningless, it gives a very rough picture of allocations. Since 1948, national committees have tended in presidential elections to spend about one-third of their budgets for radio and television, about 20 percent each for field services, and the remainder for miscellaneous items. Local and state campaign budgets would show quite different ratios, with heavier sums for campaign publicity and less for radio and television and with sizable allocations for such election-day activities as poll watchers and transportation and for campaign headquarters, which are usually opened before the primaries.

Table 13-3 shows the costs of broadcasting in presidential years. The increasing proportion of expenditures for television is particularly obvious. Generally, from 30 to 45 percent of the expenditure was for presidential and vice presidential candidates. In 1968, media expenditure of the Democratic National Committee on behalf of Humphrey included $1,043,000 for radio and television production, $3,525,000 for television time, $425,450 for radio time, and $428,642 for newspaper space.

The radical increase in broadcast costs in 1968 reflected in part the presence of a formidable third-party candidate. Total primary and

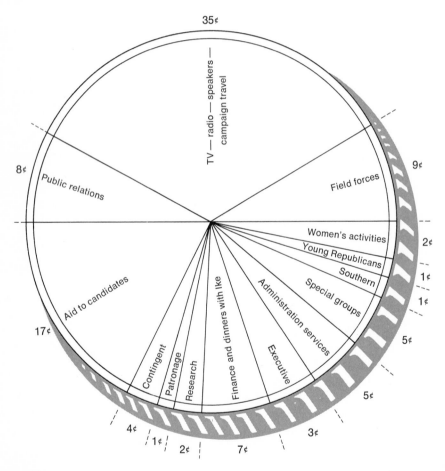

FIGURE 13-1 Allocation of combined funds of Republican national, senatorial, and congressional committees, 1960 (cents per dollar). (Source: Republican National Finance Committee.)

TABLE 13-3 Distribution of general-election broadcast costs, 1952–1968 (in millions)

	1956	1960	1964	1968
Total	$9.8	$14.2	$24.6	$40.4
Republicans	5.4	7.6	13.0	22.5
Democrats	4.1	6.2	11.0	15.4
Other	0.3	0.4	0.6	2.5
Television	6.6	10.0	17.5	27.0
Radio	3.2	4.2	7.1	13.4

Source: *Survey of Political Broadcasting: Primary and General Election Campaigns of 1968,* Federal Communications Commission, Washington, D.C., 1969.

general-election broadcast expenditures were in excess of $60 million, with large amounts spent by Kennedy and McCarthy before the Democratic National Convention. Throughout the nation, for all national and local candidates, Democratic primary expenditures exceeded Republicans expenditures $12.4 million to $5.4 million; but, as shown in Table 13-3, Republicans spent substantially more for general-election broadcasts than did the Democrats. National broadcast expenditures (network and non-network) for the presidential and vice presidential contests consumed 48.3 percent of the total; races for the United States Senate, 17.7 percent; gubernatorial elections, 10.5 percent; and all other races 23.5 percent.[6]

Since the 1950s, there has been a tendency to spend proportionately more on spot announcements on the assumption that viewers will not tune them out, as they might an announced half-hour program. Even the spots are costly. In 1968, a one-minute statement during prime time in Los Angeles ran as high as $2,300; in Boston, $1,700; and on a national network, $55,000, though prices were usually lower than these figures. A fantastic number of short announcements appear—the Federal Communications Commission (FCC) reported 5 million radio and television announcements in 1968, with only 9 percent of them charged as program time and 91 percent charged as spot announcements.

Among other tidbits found in diverse studies of expenditure items is an estimate that $5 million was spent at all levels in 1964 for public opinion polling.[7] In 1968 an advertising firm produced 20.5 million buttons for Nixon-Agnew at a cost of $300,000, 9 million

[6]A wealth of information and state-by-state figures for political broadcasts are found in *Survey of Political Broadcasting: Primary and General Election Campaigns of 1968,* Federal Communications Commission, Washington, D.C., 1969.

[7]Alexander, *Financing the 1964 Election,* p. 60.

bumper strips at the same price, and 12,000 paper dresses and jewelry for $90,000. Some 3.5 million printed speeches and position papers cost half a million dollars!

In analyzing the anatomy of spending, one observes the great proliferation of committees created to subvent the Hatch Act limitations of $3 million per committee per year. These may be established for a specific or general purpose, as illustrated by TV for Nixon-Agnew, which disbursed $620,000; Thurmond Speaks, which spent $131,000; and Victory '68, which put out $2,219,000. Democrats had many more committees, such as Architects for Humphrey-Muskie, Entertainers for Humphrey-Muskie, Librarians for Humphrey-Muskie, Pilots for Humphrey-Muskie, Rural Electric Americans for Humphrey-Muskie, and United Chiropracters for Humphrey-Muskie.[8] In 1964, there were twenty-six national-level labor political action committees, which disbursed $661,000 largely for Democrats. The American Medical Political Action Committee spent $402,000 in 1964, mostly for Republicans, and gave congressional candidates $682,000 in 1968.

Generally speaking, Republicans have been more successful in centralizing the collecting and disbursing of official party committee campaign funds; but they too have relied heavily on ad hoc campaign committees to supplement regular party efforts. In 1968, ninety-seven national-level committees reported spending for the Democratic cause and forty-six for Republicans. The decentralization of funds complicates the obtaining of factual information about financing and tends to obscure many of the real costs.

WHO GIVES

The student of party finance is baffled by the proliferation of fund-raising committees. Formerly, the national committees made subventions to the state and auxiliary committees. But the Hatch Acts reduced the tendency for the national committees to channel their funds to local committees. In fact, the national committees carefully husband their funds in order to keep within the statutory limitations. There is an increasing tendency to create "independent," "nonpartisan" committees to take over the major burden of collecting and distributing the campaign money. This may lead to duplication and multiple appeals to the same donor. At the same time, diverse groups help tap more sources and raise more funds than would be the case if only a single party committee made the appeal. Labor committees direct monetary requests to members of unions, healing arts committees to physicians, and bankers' groups to bankers. The citizens Nixon-Agnew Committee was undoubt-

[8]A listing of 1968 campaign committees together with their income and outgo is found in *Congressional Quarterly, Weekly Report,* Dec. 13, 1968, and Apr. 11, 1969.

edly able to get more money from independents and Democrats than would have been forthcoming in response to an appeal directly from the Republican National Committee.

Individual Contributions. Individuals comprise the major source of revenue for the major parties. Thousands of persons from all walks of life contribute from a few cents to thousands of dollars. In totals, the number of contributors varies considerably. Heard estimated donors at 8 million in 1950 and 10 million in 1960. The University of Michigan Survey Research Center's national sample in 1964 found about 11 percent who said they contributed; the Gallup sample was 12 percent. Republican donors generally outnumber Democratic contributors by 1 million to 2 million. Because small sums (under $100) donated to national candidates need not be reported, projections from national samples run much larger than the number officially recorded as donors.

Both the number of donors and variation in size of contributions undergo striking change from election to election. Incumbency, personal attractiveness, and ideology of the candidates are probably the main factors in this variation. In the 1950s, the Republicans obtained a much larger percentage of their total funds from contributions in excess of $500 than did the Democrats. In 1960, however, contributions of the "fat cats" was almost equally divided, 59 percent for the national Republican cause and 58 percent for the Democrats. In a radical turnabout in 1964, Republicans obtained only 28 percent of their funds from contributions greater than $500; the Democrats secured 69 percent in such amounts. Conservatives apparently rallied to the Goldwater cause, and the Senator was able to tap sources who had not contributed to the Eisenhower and Nixon campaigns.[9] In 1968, Wallace garnered the largest number of contributors of any candidate. His backers claimed 900,000 contributors but a more conservative estimate by one of his top managers placed the figure at 750,000. (Goldwater claimed 651,000 individual contributors in 1964.) A total of 551 persons gave $500 or more for about 7 percent of the total contributions. About 75 percent of the aggregate amount came from contributors of less than $100 each.

Although comparable figures are not available on Humphrey contributors, they numbered 93,000 after the convention, with 240 giving in amounts greater than $1,000. He drew more very large contributors than either Kennedy or Johnson. The total number of donors to Humphrey also was probably much smaller than for either Wallace or Nixon because of the huge number of contributions made to them before the national conventions. The preconvention uncertainty about

[9] For a comprehensive analysis of individual contributors to the 1964 campaign see Alexander, *Financing the 1964 Election,* chaps. 5 and 6. For the 1968 election see *Congressional Quarterly,* October 2, 1970, pp. 2417–2420.

the Humphrey nomination was a serious handicap to fund raising, and donations to his campaign were largely crowded into September and October. Because he seemed certain of nomination and appealed to conservatives, Goldwater attracted more than 300,000 contributors before his nomination, and these contributors were an excellent nucleus for a second tapping during the 1964 general election.

Large gifts from wealthy families constitute an important resource in both state and national elections. In the latter, the families give to many separate committees to get around the limitation of $5,000 for gifts by an individual to a single political committee. Eight individual contributors or family groups gave $50,000 or more to the 1968 Nixon postnomination campaign, and in 1960 his organization received $10,000 or more from ninety-five persons for a total of $1.5 million. The Lehman family contributed nearly $25,000 to the Kennedy campaign in 1960, while fifty-six persons in the du Pont family gave about $125,000 to Republicans. The Douglas Dillon and Henry Ford families contributed about $40,000 each to the Johnson campaign in 1964.

Family contributors to those seeking the presidential nomination are not subject to Hatch Act limitations. Governor Nelson Rockefeller's stepmother contributed $1.5 million to his efforts in 1968 and the Governor gave at least $350,000 to his own campaign and earlier had contributed $300,000 to Romney's campaign. Romney heavily contributed to his own campaign. Although the amounts are not specifically documented, the Kennedy family was known to have heavily subsidized the preconvention campaigns of John and Robert.

There is almost no end to devices and gimmicks of solicitation.[10] The Wallace party "passed the hat" at rallies; and, at times, results were quite productive. This technique, resembling an old-fashioned religious revival meeting, is often used by minor parties and occasionally by major parties. Mail solicitation is very common. Republicans sent 22 million solicitation letters in 1968 and received 450,000 gifts totaling $6.6 million. Newspapers and magazines are also used to carry appeals for money.

Republicans have long employed a sustaining fund from year to year to build a base for their campaigns; this fund permitted Nixon to begin his campaign with a surplus, though Goldwater started with a small deficit. In sharp contrast, the Democratic National Committee began the 1968 campaign (September 1) $420,000 in debt. Democrats had to borrow heavily, and by January, 1969, they were in debt by a huge $6.1 million. Short term corporate or other credit is frequently relied upon by both major parties. But the size of the 1968 debt was

---

[10] The previously cited monographs of Heard and Alexander provide a wealth of data on fund raising; our consideration is limited to mentioning the major devices.

unhealthy for the Democratic party and few would argue that such deficit spending is a desirable practice for the political system in general.

A considerable amount of individual giving comes through fund-raising dinners, gala events, cocktail parties, and clambakes.[11] These events feature such attractions as the candidates themselves or party luminaries, professional athletes, actors, and entertainers. Tickets may range from $1 to $1,000. One of the most successful fund-raising events was the closed-circuit television salute to Eisenhower in 1958, which netted over $4 million and provided the main financial base for the congressional campaign. Each national party in 1964 raised about $13 million by these kinds of events. Some of the fund-raising dinners are televised in order that financial appeals can go out to the viewing public. The dinners are a great bonanza for state and local candidates, with some able to raise virtually all they need from a single dinner. For the individual donor, the dinner has the added advantage of giving him something immediately tangible for his money, a chance to meet prominent persons in the party, and at least some feeling of involvement in the life of the party. Some of the Jackson and Lincoln Day dinners are little more than special assessments on persons holding public jobs; but many invitations go to others who are friends of the party or who may wish at some future time to do business with the party. It is not uncommon for businessmen to attend dinners of both parties; and there is a certain amount of split-ticket giving, for example, to the presidential candidate of one party and the senatorial nominee of another.

Occupational Giving. Numerous vocational groupings are formed during campaigns to solicit money from their members, for example, Nebraska Lawyers for Nixon-Agnew, Sport Stars for Humphrey-Muskie, and Jewelers for Humphrey-Muskie. Federal laws prohibit corporations and labor unions from making direct contributions from their treasuries; many states are not so restrictive. Leaders of corporations and unions do contribute as private citizens. Labor participates through separate political action arms such as the Committee on Political Education (COPE), which has its own treasury and has spent as much as $1 million in election years on registration alone. Labor contributions are very important to a great many candidates for state, local, and congressional offices. Much attention has been focused on labor's financial role in campaigns, yet surveys indicate that, among union members, about one person in eight gives to a political campaign as compared

[11] Political dinners appear to be about as old as the Democratic party, dating back at least to the 1830s. Dinners in earlier days, however, were designed not so much to raise money as to rally support. See Ronald F. Stinnett, *Democrats, Dinners, and Dollars: A History of the Democratic Party, Its Dinners, Its Ritual,* Iowa State University Press, Ames, 1968.

with about one in eleven from the rest of the electorate.[12] Labor at times has spent much money on ballot propositions, especially to defeat right-to-work initiatives. Although labor union leaders contribute individually to campaigns, the number of contributors and amounts contributed are much less than for management.

In 1964, a Business-Industry Political Action Committee (BIPAC) was organized to support congressional candidates, and it contributed $203,000 to help about 100 candidates in primaries and general elections. Though it helped some Democrats, it supported more Republicans. Democrats received large sums of money in the form of corporate advertising in their convention program book in 1964. Raising money from business in the form of advertising in party materials is a fairly common practice in both parties at all political levels. The Internal Revenue Service has stated that the purchase of advertising space in official party programs is a deductible business expense, but the amounts must be "reasonable." The term *reasonable* is particularly difficult of legal interpretation and has raised many problems.

Numerous analyses by the Gore Committee and Alexander Heard in the 1950s revealed substantial contributions from representatives of manufacturing firms, banking, life insurance, trade, and utilities. Of General Motors representatives, 66 percent contributed; Standard Oil, 36 percent; and U.S. Steel, 33 percent. More than half of the directors of these firms also made donations.[13]

Special mention should be made of contractors. One of the reasons contractors, unlike so many other businessmen, were heavy contributors to the Democrats from 1932 to 1944 was that the party was in power. In state and local politics, there is often an observable relationship between contributors and those seeking contracts or business with the state. Liquor wholesalers, where there are state-operated liquor stores, bond salesmen, road builders, suppliers of all kinds, holders of licenses, engineers, and even book salesmen frequently make campaign donations to incumbents or to those likely to win. Joseph Bernd came up with the significant discovery in Georgia that "figures on receipts by major candidates in recent years (1946-54) indicate that at least fifty percent of the money, handled by central headquarters and auxiliary groups, came from highway contractors and liquor dealers."[14]

Legislative investigations continue to show that gambling, liquor, slot machines, race tracks, and similar interests are frequently

---

[12] Detailed discussion of labor in campaigns in Heard, *op. cit.*, chap. 7 is updated in Alexander's reports for the 1960 and 1964 campaigns, *op. cit.* In 1964, thirty-one different national labor committees disbursed $3.7 million.

[13] See Heard, *op. cit.*, 1960 edition, pp. 112–120 for tables showing amounts and types of business giving.

[14] Joseph Bernd, *The Role of Campaign Funds in Georgia Primary Elections, 1936–1958*, The Georgia Journal, Inc., Macon, 1958, p. 3.

heavy contributors, although an effort is made to keep these contributions from becoming public knowledge because such publicity is likely to be harmful to the recipient. Business and labor interests are greatly involved in politics, and it is not surprising that their organizational leaders as well as the more interested constituents make contributions to parties and candidates. Business and labor leaders have increased efforts to get their colleagues and rank-and-file members interested in politics and have exhorted them to make financial contributions.

Much of the financial involvement of labor and, to a lesser extent, business is related to state and local politics. There is little congruity between election districts and the distribution of organized workers. There are far more union members in Michigan and Washington than in Florida and Mississippi. Business interests in Nevada are greatly different from those in Delaware, and involvement of the various types of business in each state stand in contrast. Labor prefers to donate directly to candidates rather than to the regular party committees, though, of course, others subsidize individual candidates.

Other Aspects. Scattered data and information from respondents surveyed by the Survey Research Center (SRC) of the University of Michigan suggest that farm operators are very infrequent donors and that there are more contributors from professional ranks (19 percent) than from any other group. Lawyers, physicians, and educators often contribute and are actively involved. A few officers of veterans organizations admit to making large donations; but there is little evidence of giving by Negro leaders and the poor lack the wherewithal.

The SCR's study of giving and religious preferences in 1952, 1956, and 1960 found that significantly more than 90 percent of gifts by Jews went to Democrats, compared with only 33 to 44 percent of the Protestant contributions. Of the Catholic donations, 46 percent went to Democrats in 1952, rising to 56 percent in 1956; and, with Kennedy, a fellow Catholic, at the top of the ticket in 1960, the percentage rose to 70 percent. There is evidence also that regular churchgoers are more sensitive to a candidate's religion than those who less frequently attend church. Whatever the economic, social, religious, or other interest, the Republican party has been able, with rare exceptions, to attract both more money and more givers. Also, the higher the family income, the higher the percentage giving to the Republican presidential candidate.

There is a high turnover among contributors—some have given in one election and not the next—suggesting wide differences in involvement, election by election. Repeat givers to national-level committees are relatively small in numbers. Among twenty-two donors of $500 or more to state committees in New York, Herbert E. Alexander found seven who had given regularly since 1946 and thirteen who had given off and on for about twenty years.[15] Disregarding size of contribution, half of all the persons who claimed to have made a contribution in 1956 said they did not do so in 1960, and half of those who said they gave in 1960 denied having done so in 1956.

We know less about those who make small donations except that there is a larger number of them than of large contributors. Party-faithful public employees are to be found in their ranks. Candidates usually put up some money for their own campaigns. Labor-union members give small contributions, as do those solicited from door to door and when the hat is passed at political rallies. Although contributions vary from state to state and election by election according to candidate and party, a small coterie at least can usually be depended on as habitual contributors, and these are likely to be known to state finance directors. Lester Milbrath's sample in North Carolina of regular donors to the party found that 80 percent gave at least once each two years.[16]

The percentage of donors, habitual and sporadic, is likely to bear some relationship to the effectiveness of solicitation procedures, for even the faithful need to be reminded and stimulated. Personal contact appears to be much more rewarding, especially for larger gifts, than appeals through mass media.

Motivations.   Despite the lack of information on many aspects of political contributions and the difficulty of understanding the true motivations of givers, surveys as well as reported contributions permit some generalizations. A wide variety of factors affect those making donations to parties and candidates. Traditional party loyalty may lead some to become regular contributors to a party. Their names are on the party headquarters list, and they may respond out of loyalty and feeling. Attachment to a particular candidate may motivate giving to him but not to his party when he is out of the running. Apparently college professors in unprecedented numbers dug down in their pockets and contributed small sums on behalf of Adlai Stevenson, while thousands of others, probably for the first time in their lives, gave to Stevenson's opponent because they "liked Ike."

Within a given electoral district the records and views of candidates and incumbents may be different enough to result in curious patterns of giving. Businessmen at odds, for example, with a Democratic state governor and Republican in their presidential leanings may

[15] "The Role of the Voluntary Fund Raiser: A Case Study in New York in 1952," Ph.D. dissertation, Yale University, New Haven, Conn., 1958.

[16] "The Motivations and Characteristics of Political Contributors: North Carolina General Election 1952," Ph.D. dissertation, University of North Carolina, Chapel Hill, N.C., 1956.

nonetheless contribute to a Democratic incumbent senator's campaign. This is caused by the fact that they have learned to deal satisfactorily with the senator, and he keeps federal projects coming to the state. An inexperienced Republican challenger would, if elected, be of less assistance to business groups and without the immediate channels of access that the incumbent had kept open. The nature of a major party at diverse levels of government within a state is often such that financial constituencies vary with positions.

Many interests give in order to gain access or entrée, or to have a "basis for talking" with public or party officials at some future time. Perhaps they are potential bidders for public contracts or wish to obtain loans or licenses, to receive key appointments, to obtain tariff favors, and so on. This may be one of the reasons some donors give to both parties. It probably helps explain why the victorious party suddenly finds itself the beneficiary of donations after the election. Both major parties rely to some extent on postelection contributions to wipe out debts contracted during the campaign. Victory dinners and gala inaugural affairs attract hundreds of ticket buyers who "forgot" to make campaign donations before the ballots were counted. In 1952 there were 271 postelection donations of more than $500 each to the Republican party.

To summarize, persons contribute to political parties for a wide variety of economic reasons. Business interests may be seeking favors, both legal and illegal, from the government. Labor and a host of others may hope to gain certain privileges, sympathetic enforcement (or non-enforcement) of laws and executive orders. Many contributors have a concern for legislation and public policy that could potentially benefit or harm them. Campaign gifts by public officeholders are understandable. They have a stake in the jobs they hold and the programs they espouse; a veiled threat of withheld endorsement or removal from office may be present as an "incentive" for donations. Some give because they want nomination or appointment to public office or because they aspire to a position of leadership in the party or in the community. The latter may see donation as a way of establishing goodwill. A large number of "fat cat" contributions come from wealthy persons who would like to be appointed to prestigious diplomatic posts abroad. The appointment of wealthy party members to diplomatic positions is an old custom.

Although it appears that much campaign giving rests upon a selfish motive, one would scarcely wish to argue that altruism or non-selfish incentives are always absent. The line between the two is indistinct, for almost any kind of giving is involved with some degree of satisfaction for the individual. Motives are complex, and a person may have more than one reason for giving. He may like both the party and the candidate and feel that he will benefit if his party's nominee emerges victorious. Many appeals for donations are based on the grounds of civic duty and contributing to the health of the Republic; a number undoubtedly respond without expectation of material reward or advantage. There are some who see political giving as a form of political participation, an involvement in politics a step beyond merely the casting of a vote. Some busy people look upon monetary giving as a substitute for giving their time to political activity. Ego satisfaction also provides motivation. Hence, an explanation of party finance purely in terms of *quid pro quo* motivations is a serious oversimplification.

The important thing is whether the recipient feels obliged to promote the interests of the contributor and what type of demands the latter makes on those elected to office. There is also the question of whether the large segments of the population who do not or cannot afford to hand money to candidates are disadvantaged. Many candidates refuse contributions for certain reasons, not the least of which is a fear that the generous donor may want something for his generosity in the form of special legislation or privilege. Candidates and political committees are often placed in the position of having to judge and evaluate the economic motivation of those willing to give.

ISSUES OF PUBLIC POLICY

In the literature on money in politics and especially in campaigns, lip service, if not dedication, has been given to certain principles. First, money alone should not be the deciding factor in who shall hold public office. That only the well-to-do should be able to run for office is a denial of the equalitarian tradition. Second, qualified, competent persons should be able to seek, with some chances of success, public office irrespective of their own personal finances. They should not be hampered by lack of money alone from competing on reasonably fair terms with their opponents. Third, persons elected to public office should be free agents in the sense that a special group cannot effectively demand that they pay off a political debt by pressing for a public policy not in the general interest. One of the nation's democratic values is that political parties, as well as candidates, should not be beholden to a small number of large contributors. Further, debt-ridden parties are not in the public interest and are a sign of inadequate financing of campaigns. Finally, the financing of campaigns should be conducted so as to retain public confidence in the electoral process and to keep that process free from cynical public suspicion that money has undue influence on the outcome of the election and on those currently in office.

Almost no one appears happy with existing party and campaign financial practices. Many observers and would-be candidates believe the principles summarized in the preceding paragraph go essentially unfulfilled. A director of a crime council in Massachusetts made the astounding estimate that organized crime contributes about 20 percent of the total campaign money in the United States.[17] Party officials and candidates do not like the debts and loans that must be paid off after the campaign. Public men have been accused of conflicts of interest growing out of campaign donations, and many feel obligated to some extent to donors.

Challengers find it more difficult to get money than incumbents. It is undoubtedly true that incumbents are less critical of present arrangements than nonincumbents, and this is a reason why laws are seldom changed. One state legislator who opposed regulation bluntly stated that he "did not want to make it easier for a future opponent to obtain campaign funds." Most present financial practices support the party in the government and make those holding office financially independent from the activists in the party organization. This situation irritates many organization people, for they have less control over public office. When the Republican Senatorial Campaign Committee sent Sen. Margaret Chase Smith a $2,500 campaign check in 1966, she returned it, according to the committee, "because she likes to finance herself."[18] Public men at all political levels believe that present diffused styles of raising money give them a desired independence from local party leaders. At the same time, the officeholder runs the risk of having to support the political objectives of his many contributors outside the party organization.

As noted in Chapter 12, money is only one campaign resource — but it is a highly important one. Personal charisma, volunteer workers, and name familiarity may reduce dependence on money, but very few candidates do not have some need for campaign money. As Adamany has noted, money is a desirable resource because it is convertible and transferable into other resources. "It can be used at locales distant from where it is raised. It thus permits greater maneuverability in the waging of a campaign than most other resources. . . . Manpower may be plentiful in one locale, but may not be needed there . . . yet it cannot be easily transferred."[19] Money can be transferred to purchase manpower, newspaper ads, and time on broadcast media in areas where it

[17]Associated Press dispatch, Sept. 1, 1969.

[18]*The New York Times*, Jan. 11, 1966. It may be noted in the same article that the committee channeled $22,623 to Sen. John G. Tower of Texas and $14,792 to Sen. Jack Miller of Iowa because they appeared to have the toughest races for reelection. The committee usually varies sums to candidates based upon their prospective chances and difficulties of election.

[19]*Op. cit.*, p. 11.

is most needed. Money is also important for party organizations between elections to exercise functions of vigil, to recruit workers and candidates, and to provide publicity. Public policy, therefore, must be concerned with finance on a continuing basis and not merely during a few weeks of campaigning.

ROLE OF GOVERNMENT IN POLITICAL FINANCE

Legislation. The enactment of public policy concerning the use of money in elections is a function of the state legislatures in the first instance. Thousands of state and local primary and general elections are under exclusive control of the states. Concurrently, the states and the national government legislate for congressional and presidential elections. Every state has some law on the subject, although in many cases it is rudimentary and does little more than outlaw barefaced corruption and purchase of votes. One may obtain a full picture of allowable financial practices of a given state, therefore, only by a study of its particular election laws. Generally speaking, the federal and state laws aim at four objectives: (1) publicity of sources of income and expenditures, (2) limitation on sources of income, (3) limitation on expenditures, and (4) prevention of bribery and pernicious political activity.

A few observations may be made about state laws.[20] Two-thirds of the states prohibit contributions from corporations, and about two-thirds of the fifty states place ceilings on the amount as well as limitations on the nature of campaign expenditures. Some states simply limit the amount that a nominee may spend in a primary and general election, and some hold a candidate's expenditure to a percentage of his salary. Another plan permits expenditures of a certain number of cents per vote cast in the preceding election. The great majority of states require at least some publicity of income and expenditures and outlaw bribery. The state laws have been experimental, and Congress in many instances based federal legislation on certain laws in the states.

Federal legislation began in 1871, when bribery and intimidation were prohibited. Then followed the Civil Service Reform Act of 1883 prohibiting United States government employees from soliciting or receiving contributions for political purposes. The act was intended to protect employees from demotion because of refusal to make a political contribution. In the first decade of the twentieth century, corporate contributions were forbidden, and the publicity feature was added. In 1925, limitations were made on the amount that candidates for the House and Senate might spend. In seeking the position of United States

[20] There is no recent monograph on state laws. *Congressional Quarterly*, Mar. 25, 1966, has considerable data on state regulation.

representative, one may spend $2,500 to $5,000, depending on the number of votes cast in the last election; senatorial figures vary from $10,000 to $25,000. Under the Hatch Acts of 1939 and 1940, individuals were prohibited from giving more than $5,000 to a political committee in any calendar year, and an interstate committee was limited to $3 million in receipts and expenditures during the same period.

The effects of state and national legislation have been generally disappointing in the face of American genius for finding loopholes in and getting around the law. The publicity feature is based on the presumably wholesome effects of making financial operations visible. Federal law requires the treasurer of a political committee to file statements quarterly with the clerk of the House. Included in these statements are the names and addresses of persons donating $100 or more within a calendar year, the total of all contributions and expenditures, and the names and addresses of all persons to whom an expenditure of at least $10 was made, together with the purpose of expenditures.

Publicity features provide some record of party finances and give inquiring reporters facts and figures otherwise unavailable. The public does get some information on sources of income and expenditures and may become somewhat cognizant of some of the problems of party finance.

At the same time, the publicity provisions have not fulfilled their promise.[21] Campaign statements are quite generally incomplete, and many items go unreported and are inaccurate. The statements are not audited, and the clerk of the House is indisposed to try to enforce the law against delinquents. Records are available for only a short period of time. Perhaps the greatest gap in publicity requirements at the federal level is the exclusion from mandatory filing of moneys spent in caucuses, conventions, state and presidential primaries, and preconvention campaigns. In the South, where the Democratic primaries are all-important, the filing of general election expenditures is not very meaningful.

As we have seen, laws attempting to place limitations on individual giving and on committee spending are easily circumvented by the establishment of independent political committees, each entitled to accept the maximum individual contribution and to spend the maximum amount allowed by law. Moreover, the term *political committee* is not clearly defined, and many self-styled educational organizations issue materials directly or indirectly related to the campaign but refuse to register on the ground that they are not political committees. The Hatch

[21] For an analysis of the inadequacies of the law and suggestions for obtaining effective disclosure, see Herbert E. Alexander, *Money, Politics, and Public Reporting*, Citizens Research Foundation, Princeton, N.J., 1960.

Act limitations tend to make the parties dependent on organizations other than the official party committees as agencies for raising money and conducting campaigns. This dispersal of fund raising and expending has undermined the publicity features of the law by making it difficult to locate all those responsible for financing.

Provisions prohibiting life insurance companies, business corporations, and labor unions from making contributions to political committees are also circumvented by individual contributions. There is nothing to prohibit a person from donating to a party out of his earnings and later being recipient of a bonus from his organizations. Private personnel can be, and rather frequently are, assigned to a campaign. The company may continue to pay the salary of the person while he works for a candidate. Parenthetically, the staffs of legislative committees also sometimes obtain leave of absence to work in campaigns; on occasions their salaries from the government continue during the few weeks that they are helping committee members or others with campaigning.

Business, labor, and other organizations contribute indirectly to campaigns through publicity in their journals and magazines that benefits a particular candidate or party. A person or organization for whom a candidate or party has done a favor may pay for an expense incurred in the campaign. A *New York Times* reporter found the New York law evaded this way: "The politician advises the business man to have a campaign printing job which may run into a thousand dollars done by a printer who does his firm's printing. The printer bills the business man, who lists it as a business expense for income tax purposes. The candidate gets his printing free and the report filed with the Board of Elections makes no mention of the contribution, although the law requires that the report list all contributions of money or 'other things of worth.'"[22] Free newspaper space and radio time may assist a candidate, yet their value in terms of dollars need not be reckoned or reported.

Revisions of the Law.   Public cynicism has resulted both from inadequate regulations and from the inability or unwillingness to enforce them. Greater public confidence would result from a willingness of lawmakers to tighten the laws deemed necessary and a careful execution of these provisions. Florida is one of the few states where the law appears to be effective in several respects. Although it places no limitations on expenditures, it imposes a limit of $1,000 on individual contributions and demands complete publicity of all expenditures and contributions, including services in lieu of cash contributions. Each person—the donor, the treasurer, and the candidate—is legally responsible for the accuracy

[22] *The New York Times*, Dec. 4, 1961.

of his reports. Persons holding dog- or horse-racing permits, operating a public utility subject to franchise, or holding a license for the sale of intoxicating beverages may not make contributions for either nomination or election of a candidate. Last-minute and postelection contributions as well as campaign indebtedness are prohibited. Although the law has been in effect only since 1952, Elston Roady finds it has diminished corrupting influences and has given Florida voters "an excellent profile of financial support of all candidates before the lever is pulled in the voting booth."[23] A few other states have laws which result in some control, but in most states large numbers of legislators are beneficiaries of the existing system and show little interest in legislating more effective controls.

Although publicity is one of the most persistent objectives in the American experiment, a number of other nations regard disclosures as unwise public policy. A legislative investigating committee in Sweden declared that free government would be placed in jeopardy by requiring publicity. A filing of names of contributors, the committee said, would "actually conflict with the principle of secrecy of the ballot." Norway likewise has frowned on laws governing contributions. Conservatives in Great Britain have opposed disclosure of party accounts on the ground that the financial strength of the Labour party would not be so fully revealed as that of their own.[24] Only parts of British campaign operations are reported. Americans seem unwilling to abandon the principle of financial reporting. A commission appointed by President Kennedy to study campaign finance upheld the practice of reporting but proposed several changes in the kinds of campaign reports. It recommended the creation of a Registry of Election Finance, which would report infractions of the law, buttressed by procedures by the Department of Justice to enforce statues.[25]

Most students of government advise revision of the law to include reporting of moneys involved in primary campaigns. Congressmen are much less enthusiastic about this than they are about embracing the principle of accountability in general elections. Yet the integral character of the nominating and electoral processes is such that the public would receive inadequate knowledge of money disbursed to gain public office if nominations were excluded from the picture.

[23] "Ten Years of Florida's 'Who Gave It—Who Got It' Law," *Law and Contemporary Problems*, vol. 27, part 2, p. 484, 1962.

[24] See R. T. McKenzie, *British Political Parties*, William Heinemann, Ltd., London, 1955, pp. 595–596. Jasper B. Shannon contrasts the United States experience with that in Norway in *Money and Politics*, Random House, Inc., New York, 1959. The last chapter is recommended for its discussion of "new directions" for resolving the problems of money in politics.

[25] Report of the President's Commission on Campaign Costs, *Financing Presidential Campaigns*, April, 1962, recommendations 3 and 4. Cited hereafter as the Commission's Report.

Direct Government Subsidization. Effective reporting of financial aspects of a campaign and limitation on contributions from individuals or groups do little in themselves to assure sufficient money to sustain political debate or to provide competitors with an opportunity to present themselves to the electorate. A positive approach calls for programs designed to see that adequate finance is provided through direct and indirect government subsidy as well as from private sources. Costa Rica, France, Mexico, Puerto Rico, and Uruguay, among others, have experimented with state assumption of some campaign costs. Political parties in Uruguay and Costa Rica are given sums by the government based on the number of votes received. In Puerto Rico, the principal parties draw a sum annually up to $75,000 a year and $150,000 in an election year.[26]

Although direct government subsidy has not become public policy in the United States, the proposal is not new. Colorado's statute that gave each party 25 cents per vote cast for governor at the last election was declared unconstitutional without a written opinion by the state supreme court in 1910. Presidents Theodore Roosevelt, Harry S. Truman, John F. Kennedy, and Lyndon B. Johnson endorsed public support in principle. Kennedy gave new impetus to discussion when he called for "some system by which the major burdens of presidential campaigns on both sides would be sustained by the national government." He referred with approval to proposals by the late Sen. Richard L. Neuberger for cash payments to the parties.

No great enthusiasm has been engendered for outright subsidization of political committees or candidates. Objections can be expected from some taxpayers with the feeling that "the politicians should pay their own way." Minor parties were concerned lest they would receive either no money or less money than the major parties. A number of persons, moreover, would object to any public help to third parties. A great many American donors prefer to give directly to candidates rather than to party organizations and would resist having their tax money go to political committees which would in turn determine allocations among candidates. Congress enacted a combined tax check-off and subsidy for the general election campaigns for President in 1966, but the bill was made inoperative a few months later pending approval of a substitute. No action had been taken by 1970, but at least the principle of subsidy was accepted by a congress even though it was not translated into viable law.

[26] For details on the Puerto Rican plan, see Heard, *op. cit.,* 1960 edition, pp. 432–434, and Henry Wells, *Government Financing of Political Parties in Puerto Rico,* Citizens' Research Foundation, Princeton, N.J., 1961. For a thoughtful analysis of subsidization by a proponent see Adamany, *op. cit.,* pp. 246–272.

Indirect Public Assistance. Indirect public financing is another matter. Direct primaries in most cases are paid for out of the public treasury; this saves the state and local parties the expense of nominating conventions. A number of states use candidate's pamphlets prepared and mailed to each registered voter by the election authorities. Each candidate is given a certain amount of space which permits him to put his case before the voters at a nominal cost. Oregon has used the voters' pamphlet successfully since 1908. The pamphlet has some potential as an instrument of political education but is not a significant means of defraying party expenditures. It adds only a little in terms of visibility for the candidate, as his message and picture constitute but a single page in what is often a large book of candidates. The parties and candidates are still required to resort to additional publicity that will focus attention on themselves.

The franking privilege for an incumbent congressman may be worth considerable money, for he can mail his speeches and newsletters to constituents both between and during campaigns. The very fact that an incumbent can use his office and secretaries, paid for by the government, is of indirect material assistance to him in his constituent relations and is a form of indirect public aid. Although it might seem logical and equitable to extend similar privileges to challengers, Congress is not disposed to that action. France provides state payment for election expenses including printing, postage, gasoline, and bill posting.

Another form of indirect help is the communications subsidy. A number of nations, including Great Britain, Canada, and Norway, provide equitable free time on the radio for political debate. In the United States, several publicly owned radio and television stations give free time to political parties during campaigns. Another proposal that would not cost the government anything would be to require television and radio stations to give some free time to candidates as a part of their public-service broadcasts. A problem with this suggestion, as with direct monetary aid, centers around the amount of time minor-party candidates should be given.

Measures have been introduced in Congress to require the television industry to lower rates or grant discounts for political broadcasts. The networks announced in 1969 that they planned to lower their rates to candidates substantially during the 1970s. Next to a certain amount of free time, this would be helpful to candidates who rely heavily on radio and television for their campaigns.

Tax Incentives. The commission's report recommended a tax incentive for political contributions in the form of either a credit against a tax due or a deduction from taxable income.[27] This suggestion was the culmination of much discussion of the idea dating from 1950 and followed the enactment of such laws by Minnesota, California, Missouri, Hawaii, and Arkansas. A major purpose of the tax credit is the encouragement of vast numbers of small gifts. Also, by giving a credit each year, the political parties might be the beneficiaries of a steadier income, which would help them solve their general problems of year-to-year financing, as opposed to contributions that come only during campaign months to be followed by "famine" between elections. The tax-incentive plan has the potential for a constructive approach to the problem of money in elections. However, in 1966 tax deductions for political contributions was taken only on 2 percent of all taxable returns.

PRIVATE RESPONSIBILITY FOR FINANCE

Broadening Financial Support. The only alternative to public support and subsidy is private giving, and those regarding the former as objectionable must find ways of stimulating private contributions. Political giving, moreover, is a form of political involvement, and there is evidence that contributors are more active in their party in all ways than noncontributors. This is not to argue that new donors will *ipso facto* become active in campaigns, but it is reasonable to assume that they may have greater interest—an old adage has it that where a man's gold is, there his heart is also. Widening the base of political giving offers the potential for broadening the base of involvement, a value of the democratic ethos. The Dollars for Democrats and Republican Neighbor-to-Neighbor drives are geared to small contributors. These are as much political and psychological devices as they are financial techniques (perhaps more so).

Broadening the base of financial support and resolving the great issues of campaign finance is one of the most frustrating problems in the American democracy. At the same time, there is no dearth of suggestions varying from private fund-raising efforts at bowling alleys to political party assessments from each primary election voter.[28] But problems of finance are enormously complex and center on (1) the public's attitude, (2) solicitation procedures and organizational arrangements, and (3) political party responsibility. To a considerable extent these are inter-related, and the success of one rests in part on the success of the others.

[27] For a discussion of alternative arrangements and their implications, see Herbert E. Alexander, *Tax Incentives for Political Contributions?* Citizens Research Foundation, Princeton, N.J., 1961.
[28] Many of these suggestions have been brought together by Herbert E. Alexander (ed.), *Money for Politics: A Miscellany of Ideas,* Citizens Research Foundation, Princeton, N.J., 1963.

The public's attitude has been far from understanding, with many citizens regarding contributions as a waste of money. They give huge sums to charities, spend freely on recreation and entertainment, and wager huge sums of money on the outcome of sports contests. But they do not consider that there is any return in donating to campaigns. It would be helpful to convince more of the citizenry that campaign expenses are necessary, a part of the proper functioning of the democratic society, and that contributing to parties is a form of participating in politics. The large number of contributions from "little people" to Goldwater and to Wallace suggests the hypothesis that the perceived leanings of a candidate can be used to attract campaign money.

One reason for the relatively small percentage of the population making contributions is the inadequacy of solicitation procedures. In 1960, there were more efforts to reach the masses for donations than ever before, with the American Heritage Foundation and other groups conducting a widespread campaign for gifts. Yet, a Gallup Poll conducted for the foundation that year found only 15 percent of the respondents or their immediate families who could recall having been asked to make political contributions; an even smaller percentage of union member respondents reported they had been canvased. Whether many more would give if asked is uncertain, but some public opinion polls have indicated that at least a third of those in the sample would give to their preferred party if asked.

Research undoubtedly would show where much money could be saved in campaign expenditures and which fund-raising procedures are most efficient. Party solicitors can also learn from the experience of private fund-raising organizations. Both parties rely heavily on successful businessmen who in turn write to fellow businessmen during every campaign. Experience points clearly to the fact that appeals through radio and newspaper advertising or general exhortation are much less effective than personal solicitation. In fact, direct solicitation is highly important and requires, for a major office, an army of fund raisers. One of the greatest problems is to differentiate between money for a *political party* and funds given directly to a *candidate*. With the strongly personalized politics in the United States, many more people prefer to give to a candidate rather than to a party. This raises the question of party responsibility.[29]

Party Responsibility. In many nations, the party itself assumes responsibility for financing campaigns, and the operation is usually centrally

[29] The role and problems of the party organization in finance are most complex and would require scores of pages for detailed treatment. Consideration here must of necessity be summary. A fuller account is found in Herbert E. Alexander, *Responsibility in Party Finance*, Citizens Research Foundation, Princeton, N.J., 1963. This work has a comprehensive bibliography on the subject, pp. 53–56.

organized. The basic situation in American politics, as has been seen over and over again, works against similar organizational arrangements. The dispersed centers of power and authority and the long ballot disrupt party responsibility in finance and encourage autonomy in money raising by candidates and numerous nonparty organizations. This results in inner contradictions if not self-defeating practices in the raising of money. Further, the need for money varies from election to election and from district to district. In some years there are bitter primary contests, with candidates siphoning off money that might go into general election contests. All these add up to the fact that there is vigorous competition among candidates of the same party for the campaign dollar. The potential donor is often solicited by more than one candidate and campaign committee. The John Birch Society and other right-wing groups obtain money that might go to Republican coffers, and left-wing dissidents sometimes compete with Democrats for money; all too often the goals of the parties do not meet a friendly response among sizable numbers of people.

The national-level party committees find it most difficult if not impossible to assume exclusive responsibility for financing the presidential and congressional campaigns. The national committees have been primarily dependent on large contributions, fund-raising dinners, and contributions in the form of quotas from state committees. National groups do not have the staff to conduct door-to-door personal solicitation campaigns or satisfactory means for reaching large numbers of donors. Reliance on the local party committees puts the national committee in the unhappy position of begging states to pay their quotas and of suffering whenever a local group's efforts are not effective. Local leaders, moreover, are under pressure to supply funds to their candidates for city office, the state legislature, and the courthouse positions, not to mention the statewide offices. Local politicians, as Alexander points out, ask themselves these questions: "Why take the trouble to raise excess funds for the state and national boys to spend? Can't we better spend our money electing mayors, state legislators, and other officials? Why stir the regulars who may resent the intrusion of outsiders? Why bring in people who are interested more in issues than in jobs, who think in national rather than local terms, who might challenge our control?"[30] National authorities must face these questions and show local party leaders the importance of national party needs.

Finance is a potential tool of party responsibility. One of the most common contentions of those advocating a more responsible national party system is that if the national committees could provide the

[30] *Ibid.*, p. 28.

major financial campaign resources for their candidates for Congress, the latter would have to rely less on local interests. In turn, elected congressmen would be more obligated to support national party positions. This would strengthen the national party in its programmatic objectives. At the same time the local interests, both party and private interest groups, are often unhappy about giving to the national-level bodies, who in turn would allocate money to congressional candidates. By giving directly to the latter, the local groups are in a position to maintain some degree of influence. Further, many congressmen do not wish to be bound to a national party program and would rather deal with constituency groups in fiscal matters than with the national party authorities. This by no means concludes the list of the unfavorable conditions incident to using finance as an implement to strengthen the national party but points up the political realities that have to be faced.

Despite these handicaps, party finance leaders have tried many approaches. They have used a separate hierarchy of finance committees and united drives, which attempt to raise money for all levels of the party's candidates in a single solicitation, thus avoiding multiple solicitation. The system calls for setting a quota for each state and placing responsibilities on the local finance leaders to see that it is met. Allocations are made, often after extensive negotiations, to operating party committees. Republicans initiated the plan, and Democrats also have attempted to put it into effect. In 1962, Republicans embarked on a National Sustaining Fund independent of the national quota system. The purpose of this plan, which local parties have tried from time to time, is to get thousands of people to contribute every year to provide steady, continued income. Republicans have had greater success with their sustaining-fund program and centralizing responsibility in the Republican National Finance Committee. Democrats meanwhile have somewhat counterbalanced this advantage with better mobilization of manpower. (This is another interesting variation between the political style of the parties. Democrats raise and spend money in rather different ways than Republicans just as they operate their headquarters and run campaigns in different fashions.) Both parties have learned that they must share control over solicitation with citizens, labor and, a host of ad hoc committees. The fact that the latter have become an accepted part of the political system indicates that they fill a vacuum left by the party organizations themselves.

Each party's congressional campaign committees are aware of the need to get money to incumbents who seek reelection long before the primaries, both for those opposed and those unopposed for renomination. Response to the need admittedly may involve the committees in primaries but they take the position that they are obligated to help incumbents and that such help is needed a year or more in advance. For example, the Democratic Senatorial Committee gave each of their incumbent senators up for reelection in 1970 some $10,000 in 1969. The House Democratic Committee likewise allowed each Democratic incumbent $1,000 in 1969 to be used for "political purposes."

Each party needs more permanent financing so as to assure adequate support for its nominees who are in need, and such financing would go far to provide fairly equal access to voters. However, successful party operations are of little help to persons seeking nomination in the direct primary. The Progressives brought in the device of the direct primary but did not foresee that a candidate might be forced to go to the "interests" for financial assistance unless he and his relatives and friends can afford subsidization on their own account. The hard fact of getting money to wage a primary election in effect prices an undetermined, but likely consequential, number of men and women out of the market of running for public office.

MONEY IN POLITICS: CHALLENGE TO RESEARCH

Political finance, as should be obvious from the foregoing discussion, raises a large number of tough normative questions not yet sufficiently answered. A handful of scholars and many public men are concerned with them. Politicians are giving attention to the intensely practical aspects of funding campaigns and party operations as well. A place to begin research and analysis is in one's own community. Along with several questions raised earlier in the chapter are many additional crucial ones exemplified by the following: Where does money fit in compared with other factors and variables in elections and party actions? What are the uses of money and what is the utility of funds to different types of parties? Do Republicans differ from Democrats in use of money and do third parties differ from the major parties? From a practical standpoint, what is the relationship of timing to financial need? Does the candidate or party get money at the right time, that is, in time for optimal use? Candidates often get money too late for it to be used advantageously. What is the relationship between cash and noncash contributions? Who makes decisions for the allocation of cash resources and what are the criteria?

A host of societal questions arise from the pecuniary aspects of politics. Among those not previously noted is whether the public is correspondingly informed in correlation to the increase in spending by candidates and parties. Are more and more expenditures really necessary in terms of the existing system? What are the links of money to power? What happens to losers in campaigns who emerge heavily in debt? How do interest groups decide to whom to contribute? For example, medical groups make many donations—is their purpose ideological, to gain access to those in public authority, or for more obscure reasons? Is it easier to raise funds for a politics of protest than for a politics of consensus? Finally, has any honest, thoroughly qualified person lost an election for lack of money?

In the extensive literature on political finance, few of these questions are systematically explored, and adequate political theory for this subdivision of politics is wanting.

FOR FURTHER READING

Many data on campaign finance are available in congressional hearings held during or shortly after campaigns. *Congressional Quarterly* also carries many data.

Alexander, Herbert, and Kevin L. McKeough: *Financing Campaigns for Governor: New Jersey, 1965,* 1969.
Hennessy, Bernard: *Dollars for Democrats, 1959,* 1960.
McNeill, Robert J.: *Democratic Campaign Financing in Indiana, 1964,* 1966.
National Municipal League: *Model State Campaign Contributions and Expenditures, Reporting Law,* 1961. (Mimeographed.)
Overacker, Louis: *Money in Elections,* 1932.
_____: *Presidential Campaign Funds,* 1946.
Press, O. C.: *Newspaper Advertising and Publicity Pamphlets,* 1955.
Roady, Elston, and Carl D. McMurray: *Republican Campaign Financing in Florida, 1963–1967,* 1969.
Rose, Richard: *Influencing Voters,* 1967.
White, John P., and John R. Owens: *Parties, Group Interests and Campaign Finance,* 1960.

PART SIX **POLITICAL SOCIALIZATION AND SUFFRAGE**

We look not at a given moment in the past but at a
sequence of time periods so as to be able to
appreciate the extent to which current behavior
or orientations are the outcome of a characteristic
pattern of development.

DAVID EASTON AND JACK DENNIS

A man is born into his political party just as he is
born into probable future membership in the church
of his parents.

J. WEST

CHAPTER 14 POLITICAL SOCIALIZATION

To this point, major attention has been focused on the development, growth, theory, and operation of political parties; and we have considered the functioning of parties in the government and the mobilization of the electorate to win public office. The remainder of the volume is concerned with the individual in politics—his politicization, voting behavior, and political participation. We shall also examine the bases that make up what we have called the party-in-the-electorate as distinct from the organizational activists and the party of the officeholders. We shall briefly examine in succession where the individual obtains his political values and education, the laws passed by the state to qualify him for voting and to assure that his vote is recorded, causal factors behind his vote, his opportunities for group participation, and finally his efforts to bring about changes in the political system.

The study of the individual in politics appropriately begins with his political socialization. The term is used to describe the process by which people become aware of politics and acquire values, interests, attitudes, and information about it.[1] The process may be conscious and deliberate, in that a person actively seeks political learning; or it may be unintentional, resulting from casual reference. Basically, studies of political socialization inquire into how a person's political loyalties, beliefs, and opinions originate and develop. What causes one to become a Republican or a Democrat? What is the basis of one's belief in public ownership, his attitude toward authority, and the political role that he decides to assume? To what extent are one's views reasoned responses or uncritical and nonrational? Because this is a learning process, psychologists as well as social scientists are interested in the subject and have been helpful in seeking understanding of it.

Early in life, the young citizen begins to acquire, primarily from members of his family, political attitudes and knowledge, religious beliefs, ethnic and class perceptions. In time, these become integrated (perhaps amorphously) into a system of values that shapes one's outlook. Later in life, his beliefs are influenced by values articulated by associates in an environment, such as a suburb into which he may have recently moved, a school, a club, peers, or by communications media. These various views and values with which he comes into contact inevitably affect his own, however slowly. His level of awareness also undergoes change. Learning and interest may lead to the assumption of a political role, which in turn fosters changes in his perceptions and brings new types of learning and politicalization.

It is not easy to isolate the sources of opinions and attitudes about politics. One cannot hope to evaluate precisely the relative importance and contributions of the home, church, school, media, locale, group, and other agents of socialization on which one's political behavior may be based. Attaining of political values, norms, motivations, and information is a sequential matter but the sequence is not the same for every person. A recognition of the factors that may or actually do lead to one's acquiring and formulating of political attitudes is important for gaining insight into the system itself.

THE FAMILY ENVIRONMENT

Although the home influence is not so great as it once was, it remains a basic educational unit in society. Political orientation is not something

[1] There is a substantial amount of periodical literature on socialization in general. On the political aspects, see especially Herbert H. Hyman, *Political Socialization: A Study in the Psychology of Political Behavior*, The Free Press, New York, 1959. His surveys include those of children in other nations as well as in the United States. See Also Roberta Sigel (ed.), "Political Socialization: Its Role in the Political Process," *Annals of the American Academy of Political and Social Science*, vol. 361, 1965, and the analytic work by Richard E. Dawson and Kenneth Prewitt, *Political Socialization*, Little, Brown and Company, Boston, 1969.

that begins abruptly in adult life. A child is usually taught conformity in the home, and he receives his parent's fundamental values and attitudes toward politicians in general, social classes, religions, races, and nationalities. Numerous studies establish an unmistakable family correspondence in views on matters of political orientation. Parents transmit politically relevant views to their children, and the offspring tend to accept them.[2] This, of course, does not happen in every family.

Party faith appears to be largely an acquisition from the parent. This inheritance is likely to persist in the first few votes if not through a lifetime. In a national sample of college graduates, Ernest Haveman and J. West found that 58 percent belonged to the same political party as their parents and only 15 percent had actually switched from the politics of their fathers.[3] Familial influence probably involves a separate contribution from each parent rather than a strictly unitary effort. When the two parents differ on party affiliation, both influences operate on the child, and the outcome is less but of determined effect. When husband and wife disagree or are in conflict, the wife is more likely to be "persuaded" than the husband.

Those moving away from the faith of their fathers are more likely to become independents than to switch to the opposite party. A child seems more likely to retain his parent's party affiliation than their ideology. It might be speculated that it is easier to change ideas than parties, but this has not been established by study.

A study of children in New Haven, Connecticut, found that party loyalties are acquired early.[4] More than 60 percent of the fourth-grade children were able to state a party preference, about the same percentage as is shown in the 21- to 24-year-old segment of national adult samples. Few children, however, can support their identification with information. By eighth grade, many of the children acquire some supportive knowledge for their party loyalty.

The family is likely to be the origin of first political awareness, the place where the youngster first hears of government and politics. One study of 2,500 university students found that 59 percent credited their families with their initial interest in politics, while 34 percent recalled their first awareness as coming from the schools.[5]

Family influence is not limited to party affiliation and orientation; there is evidence that it affects the strength of party membership

[2] A major work on the socialization of children is David Easton and Jack Dennis, *Children in the Political System: Origins of Political Legitimacy*, McGraw-Hill Book Company, New York, 1969.

[3] *They Went to College*, Harcourt, Brace & World, Inc., New York, 1952.

[4] Fred I. Greenstein, *Children and Politics*, Yale University Press, New Haven, Conn., 1965.

[5] Hugh Alvin Bone, Jr., "The Effect of College Training on Student Political Interests," unpublished Ph.D. dissertation, Northwestern University, Evanston, Ill., 1937, p. 67. It is, of course, more desirable to interview children directly rather than to rely upon adult retrospective recall.

and participation. Politically active parents with consistent party loyalties are more likely to produce strong party identifiers among their children.[6] Parents who are active in civic affairs are likely to promote the interest of their children in public affairs. Politically active persons are more likely to have had politically active fathers and siblings. Voting is often a household affair, with the family either staying at home or voting as a unit.[7] The family contribution to a child's political socialization, however, may not be large because of emphasis on nonpolitical concerns, such as lifework, careers, and entertainment. In career discussions in the home, there is little evidence that many parents encourage their children to consider politics as a career. If neither parent votes, there is a tendency for their children not to form any party attachment.

Greenstein found that the affective response of children to figures such as the President was positive, and that adult cynicism toward politics evidently develops at adolescence or later. Information about politics begins with awareness of the names of prominent figures, then gradually of their duties. "At each level of government, it is the *executive* who is understood before the legislative body and the individual legislators. Among the levels of government, the *federal* is the first at which there is awareness of both executive and legislature; the state level is the last about which learning takes place. . . . children seem first to become familiar with and adopt the orientations which are important in the behavior of adults; party rather than issue or candidate orientations . . . political orientations which are important to adults are first learned by children because these are the orientations adults are most likely to display before children and to be able to explain to children."[8]

Another study of children in grades two through eight found that they emerged from more or less "political primitive" through changes in their conception of government "that conforms to the requirements of a democratic political system."[9] A supportive image of government appears to be "widely and regularly reproduced for young new members" before they really know much about it and that it involves voting. Later experiences may disturb these earlier favorable images; but adult Americans are also generally supportive of their government, though not always of politicians.

The inculcation of the ideals of citizenship and democracy is a function of the family; the home is the primary social institution in all

[6] On this and related points see Angus Campbell, Philip E. Converse, Warren E. Miller, and Donald E. Stokes, *The American Voter*, John Wiley & Sons, Inc., New York, 1960, chap. 7.

[7] See William A. Glaser, "The Family and Voting Turnout," *Public Opinion Quarterly*, vol. 23. pp. 564–570, 1959.

[8] Greenstein, *op. cit.*, p. 155.

[9] See David Easton and Jack Dennis, "The Child's Image of Government," in Sigel, *op. cit.*, pp. 40–57.

countries and a prime agent in molding attitudes toward government, other races, public men, political parties, and various organizations. The family gives the child his role within the household and teaches him the adjustments he must make to it and to those outside the home. When public problems are ignored in family conversation and activity, any awareness the child receives in such matters must come from other sources, especially the schools, the communications media, and associates. After the formative years during which the influence of the family is paramount, the child expands his world to include others. As his contact grows, his friends and groups make demands on him; and he learns that, if he is to be acceptable, some of his views may have to be modified. Family values and opinions decline in their effect and no longer dominate his attitudes on public affairs, but ordinarily they remain an important influence.

FORMAL EDUCATION AND SOCIALIZATION

After the family, the school is probably the most important institution of the society for incubating and molding political attitudes. Parents start the socialization process, but the schools greatly enlarge it. What is especially important is that exposure to government is systematic— compared with the more casual, indirect influences of family and playmates. If a family has failed to kindle the child's political interests, the school may do so. It may teach views and facts at variance with those learned at home. In this instance, it may re-form rather than reinforce basic outlooks of students. The influence of formal education has been investigated, but little is known as to how it creates opinion. With larger numbers of students attending school and for a longer period of time, its potential for providing the citizen with the facts and insights essential for an active political role is on the increase. Further, the school is a community center and today brings programs of political interest to adults, in addition to its influence through instruction of the younger generation.

Educational institutions are recognized by society as organized transmitters of the culture, heritage, and group traditions of the community. The schools are constantly urged to broaden the curriculum by adding new courses. Legislators often try to get certain courses and emphases into the local school system. Pressure groups frequently have deep-seated anxieties over what is taught about labor-management relations, social security, the Bill of Rights, and war. School boards are under pressure from both sides over the teaching of controversial subjects, such as sex education. Around school administrators in many communities has swirled the question of "teaching communism." Much disagreement over emphasis given to these subjects and materials used in the schools is evident. Black-power spokesmen have taken great interest in school curricula and have requested the introduction of courses that will give students a better understanding of the role and problems of the black citizens. The movement could have considerable impact on the socialization of youth of all races.

The modern teacher tries to bring students into contact with newspapers, editorials, magazines, books, and radio and television programs, thus encouraging reading and viewing habits invaluable to political participation later in life. By using devices of involvement, opportunities are provided the student to learn techniques of political activity. Model or "mock" national party conventions, United Nations meetings, sessions of state legislatures and Congress are finding their way into colleges and into some high schools. "Straw" votes in elections and campaign debates are also widely used. Learning about the political process is also provided by student government. Twelve percent of the California State legislators credited school politics with contributing to their interest in political affairs.[10] This percentage may be smaller than expected, but it is far from negligible. Biographies of numerous men note that campus government and political debates were the beginning of their political careers.

Extracurricular activities are expected to impart the attributes of good citizenship. One study, however, found no direct relationship between participation in high school activities and attitude toward politics.[11] But it found that the teenager who participates feels more integrated into the informal high school status system. This feeling of integration is associated with social trust.

A minority of college students in recent years have undergone a highly politicized set of experiences through campus demonstrations. Black militants, objectors to the selective service system and foreign policy, and protestors against university practices have provided a threefold opportunity on the campus for students to engage in political activity. Tactics have varied from peaceful teach-ins to sit-ins in the offices of college authorities to the use of violence. Arrests and expulsion from school have been the fate of a few students. The impact of such political activities could be considerable if large numbers of students conclude that redress of grievances is impossible to achieve through established procedures. Some student leaders have asserted that results were not obtained until dramatic demonstrations, sit-ins, and even threat of force took place. The "establishment," it was avowed, will not make concessions until forced by students to do so.

[10] Heinz Eulau et al., *Legislative Behavior*, The Free Press, New York, 1959, p. 308.
[11] David Ziblett, "High School Extracurricular Activities and Political Socialization," in Sigel, *op. cit.*, pp. 20–31.

Socialization is a training in behavior as well as perception, and the campus ferment seems certain to have effect on faculty as well as students. Analysts believe a person's political behavior is influenced by the confidence he has in the system of which he is a part. As the student develops a feeling that political action can have an impact upon the political process, he believes it is worth while to perform civic duties. Education is related to a feeling of political efficacy, with those attending college ranking much higher on an efficacy scale than those attending only grade school.

Schools are institutions not only for awakening and developing political interests but also for reinforcing the mores, traditions, and biases of the community. Boards of educations are usually popularly elected, and educators must go to legislatures for school funds. This situation places education in the real world of politics. It tends to make teachers and school administrators sensitive to community values and wary of departing too far from the cherished views and myths of the community. Instructors are expected to be discreet in handling controversial questions. Hence, the effectiveness of the school in the process of the socialization and citizenship training is not exclusively dependent on the quality of the teachers, the materials, or the curriculum;[12] it rests in part on the latitude permitted by community attitudes.

THE CHURCH

The church is mentioned along with the family and school as a basic institutional influence on the citizen. It is a fair assumption, however, that the church is much less likely to contribute to a person's political orientations than the other two. Separation of state and church is taken for granted and, officially, churches prefer to be nonpartisan and aloof from the hurly-burly of political life in the United States. At the same time, American churches express themselves on most of the great issues requiring political action. They have often called for government action, particularly through lay auxiliary "social action" groups. Legislation affecting the taxation of church property, aid to parochial education, or a tenet of the church is understandably of direct concern.

Although literature on religion and politics is extensive, the role of the church as a political socializer of the individual has not been widely studied.[13]

[12] The influence of civics courses has not been established. One study found them unimportant in political socialization and orientation. See Kenneth P. Langton and M. Kent Jennings, "Political Socialization and the High School Curriculum in the United States," *American Political Science Review*, vol. 62, pp. 852–867, 1968.

[13] Two general works on the church and public affairs are Murray S. Stedman, Jr., *Religion and Politics in America*, Harcourt, Brace & World, Inc., New York, 1964, and Gerhard Lenski, *The Religious Factor; A Sociological Study of Religious Impact on Politics, Economics and Family Life*, Doubleday & Company, Inc., Garden City, N.Y., 1961.

The effect of church membership on a person's political attitudes is complicated by the fact that the saliency of church dogma and doctrine varies so much from person to person. Further, religious doctrine differs as between fundamental and modern Protestantism, Catholicism, and Jewry. Religious identification is related to party choices in some European countries but does not seem to be nearly so important in the United States. White Protestants are by far the strongest supporters of the Republican party, followed in turn by Catholics and Jews. In surveys, Jewish respondents are less likely to say they are Republicans and are more likely to call themselves independents than are either Catholics or Protestants. Lenski found that a Catholic education increased the probability of Catholics becoming Republicans. He found that "among Catholics with a Catholic education there was a shift of 16 percentage points toward the Republican camp, whereas among Catholics with a public education there was no shift either way."[14] His overall data lead him to suggest that "religious affiliation is an important factor influencing the party affiliation of present-day Americans."

Other students are less certain as to whether religion is a cause or a correlate. Socioeconomic group influences are important and one's party identification and political opinions may be the consequence of traditional group loyalties rather than a consequence of religious doctrine.[15] Jewish liberalism, for example, seems due to subcultural differences rather than to religious doctrine per se. A study of fundamental Protestantism, on the other hand, found that there were important doctrinal influences that significantly influenced political opinions and that the influence was in the direction of conservatism.[16] There are a number of general political positions taken by churches of which the member is most likely to be aware, as, for example, on civil rights and humanitarianism, exploitation and dishonesty, war and foreign policy, and conscientious objection. Lenski found the churches playing an important role in undergirding the principle of government of law not of men. Some Protestant sects take positions against use of intoxicating beverages and gambling. Christian Scientists oppose fluoridation. The Catholic hierarchy has opposed contraception, but the issue is being widely debated within the church. The Catholic church's militant stand against communism and Jewish support for Israel are other well-known positions.

Churches are probably in the best position of all groups to render opinions and to take public positions on the moral aspects of

[14] *Op. cit.,* p. 249.

[15] As noted in Chap. 17, religious identification and voting behavior of Protestants, Catholics, and Jews shows some constancies.

[16] Benton Johnson, "Ascetic Protestantism and Political Preference in the Deep South," *American Journal of Sociology,* vol. 69, pp. 359–366, 1964.

political issues. They publish journals read by large numbers of communicants; these publications deal in part with the church's responsibility in public affairs and the moral, if not doctrinal position, on some of the great questions of the times. Religious organizations stimulate interaction of communicants, increase mutual interests, help focus attention on the group's stake in political matters, and may even provide organs of political expression. Religious backers often try to exert an ameliorative effect on group struggles and to temper political debate. The fact that parties, candidates, and interest groups try to get the church "on their side" and to avoid alienating religious leaders indicates some recognition that the church is perceived to be influential with certain segments of the public.

GROUP INFLUENCES

Groups are of essential importance in the acquiring of political norms and party preferences, as well as exercising powerful influences on political behavior. Primary groups, which include one's family, personal friends in one's general age category and coworkers, provide a person with a political atmosphere of general mutual agreement and reinforcement of political ideas. A wide variety of secondary groups that influence the political ideas of their members include those that have as a base socioeconomic class, income, occupation, ethnic background, race, religion, educational level, and the like. Political orientation of the individual is likely to be stable when the attitudes and views of the primary groups reinforce each other; it is less stable when they are in conflict.

Association with social, fraternal, occupational, and ethnic or other groups reinforces some old motivations and aspirations, provides new ones, and gives the individual a means through which he may try to realize them. He finds himself with additional shared interests and goals; some of these may be political, others apolitical. Hyman notes that many middle-class young people are concerned about politics and that college increases their interest in political life. But when they become absorbed with business and professional matters "politics is unimportant and, if attended to, is dealt with as an agenda of the group into which [they have] moved."[17] The citizen acquires orientations toward social groupings and comes to identify himself politically in terms of these groupings.

The multitude of studies of groups have established several conclusions and hypotheses of importance to the subject of politicization. Identification with important social groups is acquired very early and at about the same time as political orientations are developed. The

[17] Hyman, *op. cit.*, p. 156.

secondary groups are not so much socializing agents as they are reinforcers and reference points.

The effectiveness of a group in giving or reinforcing an individual's political attitudes and behavior is conditioned by the political
relevance of the group for him and by the degree to which he identifies
himself with the group. A person joins a group in order to satisfy felt
needs. If the group fulfills these needs, he tends to accept the group's
values, political as well as otherwise. If he holds an office in the group instead of mere membership, he may accept its political values; at least
other leaders, if not the group itself, will expect him to do so. As a part of
the leadership and active minority he is likely to hear more discussion of
politically relevant issues and to see the necessity for becoming interested
in them. "Socially homogeneous groups," says Lane, "have a greater
political influence upon their members than do heterogeneous groups.
This is true because political loyalties tend to follow income, occupational, residential, and ethnic lines."[18]

Another potential influence of a group is the function of *reference*. Even if a person is not a formal member of an organization or
group, he may nonetheless identify himself with the goals and aspirations of those who are members and take some of his political cues from
them. In broad terms, a low-income person may regard himself as middle class and think in terms of its values. Many nonbusinessmen accept
the goals and beliefs of the American businessman, even though they
are not eligible to join the Chamber of Commerce. Business organizations are quite successful because so many people, including small
stockholders, regard themselves as capitalists or at least as having some
affinity with the business world. When a person identifies himself with a
group, whether he is a member or not, it becomes for him a reference
group. One's political opinions and behavior are likely to be affected by
his reference groups. Broad categories of reference groups as distinct
from specific organizations include race, religion, nationality and immi-
grant status, and socioeconomic status. Region or section and local place
of residence such as a city, a suburb, or a rural community are also used
as points of reference.

Persons perceiving a high degree of salience with their group
are more likely to think and behave in ways that distinguish members of
their group from nonmembers. Many persons belong to more than one
group. When these reference groups exert pressures in the same directions, they have a powerful reinforcing effect; but, when the individual
gets conflicting cross-pressures, he is forced into choices that may even
affect his standing in the group. (This raises a problem of group solidarity as well.) The results have not been fully studied, but it is certain that

[18] Robert E. Lane, *Political Life*, The Free Press, New York, 1959, p. 192.

the conflicts are not resolved in the same way by everyone. Some persons may retreat to noninvolvement and nonparticipation. Others minimize the conflict or fail to "see" the conflict. Still others moderate their viewpoint or become pragmatic and eclectic. When secondary-group and primary-group influences work in opposite directions, the latter will more likely, but not always, win out. What remains certain is that the degree of influence of a group on its members is a matter of considerable variation and offers an exciting subject for investigation, as it concerns psychological as well as many other factors.

COMMUNICATIONS MEDIA

Press. Other agents may strengthen and make more compelling the political and social values attained from primary influences, or they may serve as disturbing forces leading the individual to modify earlier notions, ideas, and views. Communications media are among the most important of the opinion-molding and opinion-reflecting agencies. Although the number of newspapers has been steadily declining since 1915, their circulation is on the increase. There are also a large number of weekly and foreign-language newspapers with impressive circulations. Taken together, the press, including the millions of copies of news magazines, reaches an overwhelming majority of Americans. How the press influences public opinion and politics and for what ends have been of perennial interest to observers of public affairs in all nations. A few of the relevant effects of the press on politics deserve mention here.

In contested national elections the press has batted about .500. The majority of the press from 1796 through 1968 endorsed the winning candidate 21 times and found itself on the losing side 20 times.[19] It is probable that in many communities where local candidates and issues are less well known, highly respected newspapers have greater influence on electoral outcome.

The effect of the press, however, is not to be judged solely in terms of winning elections. A major function of the press is to present and interpret political news. The more frequently an argument or issue appears in print, the more likely it is to be recognized and discussed by readers. If news of a labor strike is repeated in the columns more often than an antitrust suit, the strike is likely to become more familiar to readers. Repetition leads to recognition, causing the undecided reader more often than not to make up his mind in favor of a repeated argument. Consequently, the person with no strong convictions on an issue tends to accept his newspaper's position. Although the press is influential both in converting readers and in reinforcing their ideas, it most

[19] Frank Luther Mott compiled the figures for elections to 1944; see "Newspapers in Presidential Campaigns," *Public Opinion Quarterly*, vol. 8, pp. 348–367, 1944.

likely reinforces more than it converts. The influence of the press on readers is apt to be subtle. Much depends on where and when a news story appears in the paper, the wording of the headlines, whether it is carried in full or in edited excerpts, and of course whether the story is carried at all.

News items tell the reader who, what, and where, but seldom why. This is left to the editorials and to the columnists. The latter are one of the few remnants of the days of "personal" journalism when readers followed the views of their favorite editor with interest. The larger urban dailies carry half a dozen or more columnists with specialties ranging from local to international affairs. Columnists are more widely read than editorials. They render analytical and interpretive commentary on the news and provide the background necessary for an enlightened judgment. The syndicated political columnist provides the reader with information that the editor cannot obtain using his own resources and gives the reader viewpoints different from the editorials. Not every paper carries a balanced diet of columnists, and there may well be a great preponderance of columns of the same political faith. Columns, however, help to nationalize the information and opinions which a reader may obtain whether he lives in Georgia or Idaho.

The more reputable columnists probably have a good deal of influence on public men and on opinion leaders. Many of their analyses are inserted in the *Congressional Record* and are widely quoted elsewhere. There is a two-step flow of communication from the mass media, especially the press, to "opinion leaders," who then pass on what they read to everyday associates whom they influence.[20] It has become fashionable for business and professional people to subscribe to newsletters, which purport to forecast business conditions, foreign and domestic events, electoral outcomes, probable legislation, and so on. These are mailed to subscribers, willing to pay a sizable fee, to give them "advance," "confidential" information on what the government will do next. Partisan slants and wishful thinking often creep into the letters and many of them tell their clientele what they want to hear and ratify their existing predilections. Probably little more information is to be found in a newsletter than would be found in a good daily newspaper, but the letter is a great timesaver, and a subscription to it also becomes something of a status symbol.

To some extent the huge mass-circulation news magazines cater to the same needs as the newsletter. The magazines provide the busy reader with news and commentary in capsule form, embellished with

[20] Paul F. Lazarsfeld, *The People's Choice*, Columbia University Press, New York, 1948, p. 151. For a general work on communication, see Lucian Pye, *Communications and Political Development*, Princeton University Press, Princeton, N.J., 1963.

pictures, diagrams, and charts. These are more readable than a good many newspapers and also may give more background and interpretation. However, news magazines and newsletters are often partisan in reporting the news and fail to distinguish between news and views. The reader feels that by looking over the magazine each week he can keep abreast of major happenings. Many persons undoubtedly derive their impressions of politicians and their views on public policies from the news magazines.

During the 1870s, Thomas Nast chose the "Tammany Tiger" to depict the plunderings of the Tweed ring. The Boss was prompted to mutter that someone ought "to stop them damned pictures." But nobody did, and today practically all large metropolitan dailies have one or more cartoonists on the staff and carry syndicated cartoons as well. The political cartoon tells a story and is an editorial in itself. It conveys a point that is usually quickly understood by the reader. Treatment is usually strongly satirical, exaggerated, oversimplified, and often partisan. The effect of cartoons cannot be measured accurately, but they remain popular with publishers.

Raido and Television. As modes of political teaching and transmission, the effects of the press, radio, and television differ much from each other. The latter two are viewed as providers of entertainment and less as disseminators of information, though one can get an argument from television officials on this score. Social criticism of radio and television is not relevant to our immediate concerns, but their responsibilities and influences require passing mention.

Three major patterns are evident in developing, managing, and controlling broadcasting. Ruling cliques in the totalitarian countries seize all channels and, under strict monopoly of the government, employ them for ideological indoctrination, to stamp out opposition in their own country, to create unflattering images of other nations, and to control and manage political attitudes to perpetuate the party in power. (Newspapers, motion pictures, and the theater also come under state surveillance.) Concisely, the media are basic tools for manipulating mass public opinion and imposing a state-directed political socialization. With news and opinions largely controlled at the source, the mass attitudes can be oriented in directions desired by chiefs of state.

Most Western democracies also operate broadcasting under government monopolies, but keep it out of partisan contests by the in-party through strict rules. The costs of broadcasting are largely borne by license fees on sets. Public-affairs broadcasts aim at treating political minorities fairly. In several nations, limited private operation in competition with the government stations is permitted.

American radio and television were developed and have remained, except for a few publicly owned stations, in the hands of private
enterprise. The costliness of broadcast time may keep unpopular views
from being aired, as sponsors usually wish to avoid controversial public-
affairs programs for fear of alienating listeners. Less-affluent groups usually cannot hire commentators or sponsor broadcasts. The media rarely
endorse candidates or carry editorials of their own on controversial
public questions.

Television and, to a lesser extent, radio are widely used in political campaigns, including those for ballot propositions. This usage
in turn raises many questions of equal access and equal time to be
granted to contenders.[21] It seems clear that those most likely to seek
political information are already the best informed and that people who
follow election campaigns most closely on television are the same ones
who read about them in the newspapers and magazines. Forceful confrontations between police and peace protestors in Chicago during the
1968 Democratic National Convention were carried on television and
had much impact on delegates who witnessed them on sets in the convention hall. In general, the television coverage of the event had a
disrupting effect on the convention.

Communications Media and Political Socialization. There are several
types of communication content. One provides instruction and information, another contains cognitive content covering news from gossip to
public events. Some media contain normative content aiming at trans-
mitting and strengthening of norms, a form highly important in developing nations. Some media are more political or are seen as more
political than others. Columnists see their role in politics quite differently than do actors appearing in regular programs or writers of nonpolitical features. Political decision makers think all types of media
important. By giving or withholding publicity from candidates, parties,
and public causes, the media help an indeterminate number of people
to make up their minds. But because the media function within the social context, their specific roles as socializing agents are not clear.

The social milieu serves, perhaps innocently, to affirm traditional values. Arithmetic books whose problems are entirely phrased in
capitalistic and commercial terms deal with the real world as the accepted one. Black leaders today point to biases in history texts and
assert that treatment of the blacks in the press and motion pictures has
resulted in giving both whites and blacks stereotyped ideas. Television
and other media began in the 1960s to portray the black citizen in a

---

[21] The use of the media in campaigns is covered in Chap. 12.

different way than previously, with the aim of changing attitudes toward him and of meeting charges of racism.

Communications agencies are not likely to hit the citizen with a common thrust but have a cumulative effect on his interests and outlook. The press and news broadcasts through headlines and stories increase the citizen's awareness of public affairs. Exposure to the media increases political discussion, which in turn appears to increase exposure to the media.[22] Because of the enormous outpourings of the media, each citizen selects his own exposure. Persons like to read, see, and hear views that reaffirm their predispositions and attitudes. Individuals engage in selective exposure and selective perception; that is, they see and believe what they want. Even so, accumulated data show that those who are more exposed to media are more likely to be interested in politics and to be active participants.

The media probably have greater reinforcing than converting effect. But, like other institutions, the media may give the person without a particular context or viewpoint a frame of reference for judging local, national, and international events. He seeks out papers and commentators congenial to his beliefs to provide him with information and views on new events. Interest-group leaders who are aware of this may feature materials on political concerns with an eye to influencing the views of the membership. *The Journal of the American Medical Association* tells physicians of "dangers" of proposed health-related measures, as *The Machinist* warns its readers about proposals which the editors see as "antilabor."

In terms of encouraging such political participation as donating to campaigns, party activity, and voting, the communications media can have an important effect if they show some relevance between the activity and the individual's personal interests. Often the media fail to establish rapport with sections of the public, and the latter may even distrust them and be disinclined to believe them or follow their exhortations for political action. From another standpoint, reading and viewing may be dysfunctional in that citizens substitute them for political action. Some studies show that the failure of the media to establish ideological rapport with some of the public tends to discourage participation.

More material is presented on politics than is demanded by the public, suggesting that, instead of keeping politics from the people,

---

[22] Several of the findings of the major effects of the mass media are reviewed in Lane, *op. cit.*, chap. 19. Also useful for directing the reader toward the major studies and hypotheses on the mass media are Wilbur Schramm (ed.), *Mass Communications*, The University of Illinois Press, Urbana, Ill., 1949, and Lucian W. Pye (ed.), *Communications and Political Development*, Princeton University Press, Princeton, N.J., 1960.

the media often attempts to politicize a public that does not want to be politicized. The challenge to those who wish to increase the role of radio and television in political education is to combine solid educational material with entertainment. The apathetic may be attracted to an exciting television debate between principals because it combines drama and politics. Political novels may do the same. If politics can be related to one's own career or status, interest is likely to be heightened. The specialized magazines, if trusted as a reliable representative of one's own status, may stimulate the political interests of their patrons.

LOCALE AND SOCIALIZATION

Aristotle and other scholars who followed him pointed to the significance of geographic environment in the development of human institutions, in mankind's struggles, and in the behavior of men themselves. Many of the great religious, economic, ethnic, and political struggles were expressed in geographic symbols. Much of American politics before the present century was explained in terms of sectionalism.

Historians have looked to biographies and autobiographies of public men for their articulation of the deep-seated feelings and peculiarities of outlook of their status and areas. Their own political socialization led some public men to feel, perhaps intuitively, the grievances, needs, and aspirations indigenous to their surroundings. One can look at cultural traits, dialects, occupations, and demographic factors and attempt to relate them to political outlook. Populism, agrarian reform, urban radicalism, nativism, and various left- and right-wing causes in numerous instances were associated with locale and section.

National polls have noted sectional differences in responses to foreign and domestic policies and in party preferences. By analyzing voting results over a period of time, we can make rough estimates of the erosion of or change in party loyalties. On the assumption that state legislators and congressmen represent prevailing moods and impulses of their localities, roll-call votes and speeches by legislators of the "my district" variety are cited as evidence of sectional influences. Rightly or wrongly, politicians believe that their community or district has underlying biases, aspirations, and values, and that their duty is to discover and mirror them. Studies of state politics commonly begin by reference to political and social characteristics of various parts of the state.

There is little scholarly work on the section and political socialization and even whether locale should be regarded as an agent of socialization. Residence as a separate variable is very hard to evaluate, as one does not live in isolation but rather in contact with family, friends, and the communications media. These may be responsible for one's political outlook, with residence as a reinforcer rather than a molder or converter.[23] Socialization is a process of initial learning but may also be reinforcing and converting in effect. Viewed broadly, locale appears to have a political effect on the citizen but the degree of effect is unknown since it is in combination with other factors. A few well-known illustrations of common political attitudes of those sharing the same environment may be noted.

Sectionalism. Public policy affecting race relations and states' rights are deep-seated political values in the South. Even the growing economic diversity has not served to modify in a substantial way the general sectional attitudes on the questions. Confrontations between state and federal authorities have occurred since the decision of the United States Supreme Court in 1954 making segregation of the races in the public schools illegal. As Key pointed out, the backbone of Southern solidarity consists of whites of the "black belt" who set the general tone and of the others who follow.[24] The third-party candidacy of former Governor George C. Wallace of Alabama in 1968 served anew to reinforce and rekindle certain Southern attitudes and yielded him the electoral votes of five states.

No other section possesses so strong a tie as so-called Southern traditions but the East's melting-pot composition is very heterogeneous and its viewpoints on national civil rights legislation and ethnic politics often run counter to those of the South. Easterners are accustomed to "balanced tickets," rather strong party organization, and sharp labor-management views. At one time the East was much more "interventionist" in foreign policy than the "isolationist" Midwest, but such categorization is no longer very meaningful.

The Midwest is an amalgam of several large and many small cities together with great expanses of farm land. Its intrasectional differences are, therefore, greater than its differences as a section from other sections. There are large pockets of conservatism which emphasize individualism, self-reliance, and tendencies toward paternalism. Even so, farmers have been recipients of federal largess and one finds about as many "public works senators" as elsewhere, those who engage in senatorial activity that is devoted to obtaining federal contracts.

---

[23] Yet some studies indicate that community climates have a socializing impact on some individuals independent of socializing agents such as the family and peer groups. See, for example, Martin Levin, "Social Climates and Political Socialization," *Public Opinion Quarterly*, vol. 24, pp. 596–606, 1961.

[24] V. O. Key, Jr., *Southern Politics*, Alfred A. Knopf, Inc., New York, 1949.

The huge spaces from Colorado to the Pacific Ocean and from Canada to Mexico have made the Far West a region of almost unbelievable diversity and a region of mining, ranching, and farming. It is difficult to find deep-seated orientations on politics to which politicians can appeal, for the West is probably less closely knit than any other section. Migrants have poured into the Western states, and their traditions and voting patterns are less well established. The West has been the scene of experimentation with economic and political reform. Populism (which also reached into the South), free coinage of silver, and greenback currency were once rallying cries in areas west of Iowa. In the modern generation, pension politics has been a prominent issue.

The area west of the Mississippi River nurtured the recall of public officers, broadened manhood suffrage, fostered woman suffrage, and advanced the initiative and referendum. About half the states that provide for the initiative are in the West, and voters are accustomed to direct legislation and to making numerous vital policy decisions at the polls. The Far West is the only section boasting experience with all three direct primary systems—closed, open, and blanket. The scheme of pre-primary conventions for purposes of endorsing candidates has likewise seen the greatest amount of experimentation in the area. Voters have remained very suspicious of the old-style Eastern political machines and have used the various primary systems to try to head them off. The area has seen sharp shifts of opinion between the Republicans and Democrats. "Nonpartisanship" in municipal elections is particularly deeply rooted in the westernmost states.

Local Environment. The neighborhood one lives in is certain to possess political norms and attitudes, which influence both the long-time resident and the newcomer. We do know how the suburbs, the central cities, the small towns and rural areas have voted, but the influence of each environment on general political behavior, interests, and attitudes is not yet subject to generalization. It is true, for example, that newcomers often find the line of least resistance, acceptability, and respectability to be one of embracing the dominant political faith and attitudes of the place of their adoption? The suburbanite and the central-city resident seem to have differences in interest that cannot be explained exclusively in terms of race or class. Metropolitan-area government faces some problems different from those in the big city, the small town, and sparsely populated areas.

When one moves from one locale to another does some "political conversion" take place? The question needs to be divided into the effect on party identification and the effect on political attitudes and outlook. There are many pockets of staunch Republicanism and of monolithic Democratic preference but the degree of change undergone by in-migrants is uncertain because party loyalty is shown to be quite durable. Bernard C. Lazerwitz questions whether the movement of central-city Democrats into solid Republican suburbs results in a basic shift of party loyalties. His data suggest a growth in strength of suburban Democratic parties tending to create a two-party system where formerly one-party control was exercised.[25] G. E. Janosik noted a greater degree of independent voting in suburbia, especially where the population is sparcer. "Political workers of both parties in those sections assert that the electorate resents the slightest attempt to encourage a citizen to avail himself of the right to vote, much less induce him to support a particular party. This is true even of communities where the large majority of voters support the more powerful, that is, the Republican party."[26] Using presidential and congressional elections, Herbert Hirsch found that the suburban presidential vote follows national trends and, in the same areas, congressional vote did also but was somewhat more stable.[27] Reapportionment, therefore, did not result in significantly greater Republican strength.

Environmental conversion may, however, take place in areas other than avowed partisanship. Interracial living sets up conflict; and, when the proportion of minorities increases beyond a tolerance level, whites tend to move out. Overcrowding of dwellings and areas set up competition for housing and jobs and "law and order" attitudes undergo change as crime increases. The busing of school children and integration of schools undoubtedly have their effects on one's socialization, even though the effects cannot be adequately measured. The problems of urbanism have fashioned the great political issues of the times, with the very role of government itself a major issue. Urbanism increases the strains on the two parties, forcing them into a wider range of interests and policies than was formerly the case. These stresses may in time erode party loyalties and change organizational participation and political behavior. The degree of suburban nonpartisanship has been on the increase and upwards of 70 percent of the suburban governments are legally nonpartisan. At the local level, "no-party" leaders are taking over functions formerly performed by partisan leaders.

Size of city was found by V. O. Key, Jr., to show differences in the relationship between class and political attitudes. Blue-collar workers in large metropolitan areas differ more from their white-collar cohorts

[25] "Surburban Voting Trends: 1948–1956," *Social Forces*, vol. 39, pp. 29–36, 1960.

[26] "The New Surburbia," *Current History*, vol. 31, p. 95, 1956. Various aspects of city-suburb politics are covered in Philip B. Coulter (ed), *Politics of Metropolitan Areas: Selected Readings*, Thomas Y. Crowell Company, New York, 1967.

[27] "Suburban Voting and National Trends: A Research Note," *Western Political Quarterly*, vol. 21, pp. 508–514, 1968.

in their attitudes toward policy issues than they do in smaller cities.[28] In smaller cities, working-class attitudes were more like white-collar middle-class attitudes. Other studies found that in some small cities workers are less likely to vote Democratic than laborers in large cities. Again whether place of residence is the major factor in the difference or whether it is due to other variables is not known.

One study of Southern racial attitudes points to the significance of locale on questions of integration and segregation.[29] Larger proportions of strict segregationists are found among people in rural areas than in urban areas, among people who grew up in counties with a large concentration of blacks than in counties with fewer blacks, and in the states of the Deep South than in the peripheral Southern states such as Tennessee, Texas, North Carolina, and Virginia. Many Southerners who travel and are exposed to non-Southern customs modify their views as do veterans who serve outside the South. Of the veterans sampled, 55 percent favored strict segregation, as compared with 63 percent of all adult white males and 65 percent of all white females. Although it is true that the better-educated Southerners are more likely to travel, exposure to non-Southern customs is, nevertheless, found to have an independent effect. At every level of education, greater mobility brings a decrease of strict segregationist views, but only for those with high education does the "shift accrue primarily to the benefit of integrationist beliefs."

Within the confines of the great metropolitan areas where the great majority of Americans live are neighborhoods where matters of party-faith outlook on issues are strong and sharp. Political differences exist between the East Side and West Side, the river district and the "heights," the "skid row" and the "Park Avenue." Suburbs often differ radically from one another. In view of the disparateness in school training within families and churches and within geographic boundaries, it is hazardous to attribute beliefs and specific political socialization effects to whole sections, states, or communities. At the same time, it would be unwise to dismiss as inconsequential the effect of locale on millions of citizens in terms of nominal party faith, voting behavior, attitudes toward public affairs, customs of political participation, and what one accepts as his political belief system. The life styles of persons differ markedly among residents of rural areas, small towns, and large cities. It is a mistake to assume that all citizens in each area think alike or are

---

[28] *Public Opinion and American Democracy*, Alfred A. Knopf, Inc., New York, 1961, pp. 116–118.

[29] Donald R. Matthews and James W. Prothero, "Southern Racial Attitudes: Conflict, Awareness, and Political Change," *Annals of the American Academy of Political and Social Science*, vol. 344, pp. 108–121, 1962.

politicized in the same way. There are, in fact, great contrasts in the political attitudes and voting behavior of residents of different sections in the same country or city. The immediate milieu within which one lives is, nevertheless, likely to have some effect on his socialization.

POLITICAL DEVELOPMENT—AN ENDLESS PROCESS

The socialization concept is comparatively new in political inquiry and is used at both a "system" level and an "individual" level.[30] In the former case, political socialization is studied as a process of induction into the political system. The system becomes a dependent variable and one studies how socialization affects political stability, change, or disintegration. It is concerned with the end product of attitudes, values, and feelings of people toward the system. To perpetuate itself, a system must educate its young politically and transmit its heritage to the maturing members or construct a new heritage for them. This, then, is the function of political socialization.

The more extensive analysis has focused on the individual as the dependent variable and on how he has come to possess certain political orientations. It has studied the process by which political interest is acquired. The end product for the individual is a set of beliefs and orientations toward the system, how he sees it and his own role in it. It is a learning process and looks at the impact of environment on behavior but recognizes that the politicalization process has roots both in society and in personality. This approach tries to locate the genesis of political beliefs and interests and follow them through life. The individual and systems approaches are not antithetical but represent common concerns with divergent emphasis and permit broadening of the concept.

The process by which political interests, attitudes and values are acquired and developed is a continuous affair. It may take place during any phase of life. One's home, relatives, friends, school, and church are all relevant to acculturation in the American polity. The citizen's initial political interest is most likely to be acquired through them. They give him many of his political values and attitudes, his class and ethnic perception, and an undetermined but probably considerable amount of information and misinformation. If one agent fails to reach a person, then another probably will. If the child fails to acquire a definite political heritage from his family, the schools offer another environment for his political development. Throughout his life the family, the church, and the school (as an adult community center) may continue as reinforcing

[30]A discussion of the concept together with a useful summary of the findings of political socialization empirical research has been prepared by Richard E. Dawson in "Political Socialization," in *Political Science Annual 1966*, The Bobbs-Merrill Company, Inc., Indianapolis, 1966, pp. 1–84.

and persisting forces in his political viewpoints. The place where a person resides may also condition his outlook and modify influences of primary and secondary political forces.

In the American pluralist society the fraternal, social, economic, and political groups also have their impact on the political man. They may slowly erode the attitudes that he accepted from his home and school and provide him with at least some new political values and rationales. They give him instruments for articulating if not materializing important public and private goals. It is hardly surprising, therefore, that political parties and pressure groups have provided the subject matter for volumes and volumes.

No variables in the process of socialization operate in isolation. Instead, they react on each other, making the study of the force of each agent both difficult and fascinating. When many agents of socialization act on the individual at the same time, he becomes cross-pressured, and the influences of the primary groups on the individual are disturbed. Political conflicts between a person's reference groups may dilute rather than heighten his partisanship and lead him to withdraw from or decrease his political activity. Other effects may lead him to identify with only one of the reference groups, to moderate his viewpoints, or to fail to see that there is any serious conflict and hence to play down its importance. As a general matter, the role of one's group or groups is somewhat similar to that of the family. It identifies interests, defines goals and needs, and helps establish patterns of belief and behavior.

Political activities and roles are mainly adult preoccupations and there is likely to be a time gap between acquiring one's orientations and getting personally involved with voting and other forms of participation. This allows time for changes and alternatives to take place. One's occupation, socioeconomic status, and reference-group associations may be changed, expanded, or contracted. Inconsistencies may develop and the socialization process is more intense at one time than at another. There may be periods, therefore, of discontinuity. It is sometimes believed that disengagement comes from age. This is being questioned. On the contrary, some scholars find that, barring senility, political interest increases with age and that the trend is not reversed as one grows older.

We have advanced the hypothesis and supposition that the primary groups and one's associations are strongly influential in producing the "political personality." They are basic to the formation and conditioning of one's political character, attitudes, and perspectives. They provide the person with the knowledge and skills necessary for his participation in the political society. Further, they affect his motivation for voting and for membership in parties and political groups. Conversely, they may contribute to his being apolitical, disinterested, and essentially passive in the political process. At the same time, one's politicalization is unlikely to be determined by one single influence. As Sidney Verba has warned, "Political behavior is not determined solely by the predispositions that an individual brings into the political process from his experiences and training in primary groups. It is also affected by the way in which the political system interacts with these dispositions."[31]

FOR FURTHER READING

Almond, Gabriel, and Sidney Verba: *The Civic Culture*, 1963.
Banfield, Edward C: *Political Influence*, 1961.
Coleman, James S. (ed.): *Education and Political Culture*, 1965.
Fenton, John H.: *Politics in the Border States*, 1957.
Fuchs, Lawrence H.: *The Political Behavior of American Jews*, 1956.
Jacob, Phillip E.: *Changing Values in College: An Exploratory Study of the Impact of College Teaching*, 1957.
Jonas, Frank: *Politics in the American West*, 1969.
Katz, Elihu, and Paul Lazarsfeld: *Personal Influences: The Part Played by People in the Flow of Mass Communications*, 1964.
Klapper, Joseph T.: *The Effects of Mass Communication*, 1960.
Lipset, Seymour M.: *Political Man: The Social Basis of Politics*, 1963.
Lockhard, Duane: *New England State Politics*, 1959.
Matthews, Donald R., and James W. Prothero: *Negroes and the New Southern Politics*, 1966.
Milbrath, Lester: *Political Participation*, 1965.
Mitchell, William C.: *The American Polity*, 1962.
McGill, Ralph: *The South and the Southerner*, 1964.
Strong, Donald S.: *Urban Republicanism in the South*, 1960.
Turner, F. J.: *The Significance of Sections in American History*, 1932.

[31] *Small Groups and Political Behavior*, Princeton University Press, Princeton, N.J., 1961, p. 37.

CHAPTER 15 SUFFRAGE PROBLEMS

A key question in every political society is who shall participate in the control of government and on what basis. Who is to govern and who is to choose those who govern are of central importance. Elective public officeholders are not the only ones who make decisions affecting the public interest, but the fact that they are given responsibility for making some of the most vital ones justifies major concern with the rules for franchise and with those who exercise it or who fail to do so. Minimum participation has usually consisted of the right of all or some of the citizenry to vote for their rulers, a practice denied in some monarchies and dictatorships. Although the pages of history are filled with theories and claims that voting is a "natural" right, the franchise in reality is conferred or withheld by the state. In full-fledged autocracies, the ruler and his lieutenants, for all practical purposes, decide who should vote and when—and sometimes decree that no one shall. In the democracies, the legislature is the decision maker of the terms of the suffrage.

Throughout history, from the Greek democracies to the present, suffrage has been denied or permitted on the basis of age, sex, citizenship, religion, race, property ownership, criminal record, residence, payment of taxes, group affiliation, literacy, intelligence, and on many other bases. In general terms, suffrage requirements are methods, usually indirect, of allocating power among certain citizens and groups. It is to be expected, therefore, that suffrage has been demanded by those seeking political emancipation and a voice in the management of government.

Two characteristics dominated the suffrage decisions in the early history of the United States—state prerogative and property ownership. The latter has been abandoned and the former somewhat modified. There was some sentiment for nationalizing suffrage laws in 1787, but the matter was left to the states for several reasons. The framers of the Constitution were not interested in broad, universal suffrage. The wide diversity of voting qualifications existing in the thirteen states would have made consensus over the constitutional requirements difficult to achieve. In this century, after historic debate, federal amendments forbade the states to deny the ballot to a person because of sex or race. But some remained disenfranchised for other reasons. The voteless citizens of the District of Columbia in 1964 became beneficiaries of a constitutional amendment permitting them to vote for presidential electors. Another 1964 amendment prohibits the use of poll taxes as a voting requirement for federal offices. Congress has legislated on literacy tests and registration and discussed, but not acted upon, lowering age requirements for voting. With the historic issues of property qualifications, Negro suffrage, and woman suffrage resolved, current discussions in Congress and in the states center around lowering the voting age, residence requirements, literacy tests, and the enforcement of civil rights laws in certain Southern communities.[1]

ISSUES IN LEGAL QUALIFICATIONS

Age. Presidents Eisenhower, Kennedy, Johnson, and Nixon recommended conferring suffrage at age eighteen as did the President's Commission on Registration and Voting in 1963.[2] Georgia in 1943 and Kentucky in 1955 adopted the eighteen-year-old rule, and Alaska came into the Union with a nineteen-year-old provision and Hawaii with a

[1] *The Book of the States* carries summaries of state laws on qualifications for voting and related matters.

[2] The commission was appointed by President Kennedy and made some twenty-one recommendations on election and suffrage contained in a sixty-nine-page document entitled *Report on Registration and Voting Participation,* published by the U.S. Government Printing Office. The report is pertinent to the concerns of this chapter.

twenty-year-old requirement. A considerable number of nations set a minimum age of less than twenty-one for voting eligibility, and several other countries make age exceptions because of military or marital status. Mexico equates age of maturity with marriage. A married man of eighteen can vote, while an unmarried male has to wait until age twenty-one. Notwithstanding these developments, forty-six American states keep the twenty-one year age level for voting. Several state legislatures in the 1960s submitted lower voting age amendments to the electorate only to see them defeated. Under a cloud of constitutional questions Congress passed a law in 1970 lowering the voting age to eighteen.

The extension of franchise to younger people is arguable on the grounds that prolonged school attendance and increased college enrollments have enabled them to obtain background satisfactory enough to permit fair judgments. Many young men and women are married and parents by the age of twenty-one; they have a stake in the political society and therefore should have a voice in choosing public officials, determining school levies, and the like. Further, the franchise might serve to increase political interest among young people and to aid recruitment of youth into political parties and organizations.

The opposition believes youngsters are immature and emotionally unstable, and the traditions surrounding the age of twenty-one remain strong. Great lobbying organizations have failed to pressure the state legislatures for reduction of the voting age, and legislators have often viewed the matter in terms of whether a change would benefit or harm their own reelection and their party. Oddly, the thrust of the various student and youth rebellions has not generally included pressure for reduced voting age. As such the political climate was not conducive to change.

Residence. During the nineteenth century, each state worked out its own residence requirements for voting. By the end of the century, every state required relatively long residence in the state, with shorter periods spent in such local subdivisions as counties, towns, and precincts. Residence requirements underlined the importance of state citizenship in a federal system but applied to voting for national as well as state and local offices. Residence requirements are defended on the ground that new residents are not sufficiently informed about state and local candidates and issues to exercise the suffrage. It is said that these requirements also provide protection against election frauds by voting transients and floaters, but corrupt political machines have found ways to circumvent such requirements.

It is estimated that residence requirements keep over 5 million persons from becoming registered and are an important cause of non-voting.[3] A trend toward the reduction in length of residence for voting qualification is underway with requirements varying from three months to one year in the state. As of 1970, well over half of the states required one year's residence and nearly all imposed county or district residence requirements of shorter duration. Voters who change residence within the same county or city are usually permitted to transfer their registration to their new addresses (though many neglect to do so in time), and some states permit them to vote in their previous precinct at the next election. Residence requirements function as symbols of political independence of states in the federal union.[4] This may be part of the reason why longer residence requirements are found in the South. All tend to cling to the one-year provision and Mississippi requires a two-year domicile.

The theory of an "enlightened electorate" as a norm for voting in state-local elections has little validity where voting for President is concerned. A person who moves is likely to have opportunity to appraise presidential nominees, yet millions of them were found to lose their vote because of insufficiency of residence. Wisconsin took the lead in recognizing this inequity in 1954 and eliminated the state residence requirement as a condition to voting for President. Using diverse arrangements of a "bob-tail" ballot, a large number of states permitted newcomers to vote for President in the 1968 election.

In the 1970 Voting Rights Act Congress abolished all durational residency requirements for voting for President and Vice President. Henceforth qualified residents of a state may vote for President and Vice President if they apply for registration thirty days prior to presidential elections. Absentee ballots for presidential elections are also to be provided for upon application not later than seven days before the election. The seventies are seeing many state legislative debates on reducing residency requirements for voting in state and local elections.

Literacy Tests.   About one-third of the states use some form of literacy test with variations defying generalization. New York requires that all applicants who cannot prove a sixth-grade education must take a literacy test designed by the State Education Department and in 1968 3.8 percent failed to pass it. Some states require a person to read and write or

[3]On the effect of domicile provisions, see Morris S. Ogul, "Residence Requirements as Barriers to Voting in Presidential Elections," *Midwest Journal of Political Science*, vol. 3, pp. 254ff., 1959.

[4]On this point, see W. Ross Yates, "The Function of Residence Requirements," *Western Political Quarterly*, vol. 15, p. 471, 1962.

to interpret an article of the Constitution or other prose. Many states assume literacy if the applicant can read and accurately fill out a registration form. Literacy tests are supported on the ground that they weed out those lacking the equipment for comprehending political issues. Historically, a principal purpose was to minimize the electoral power of low-income groups.

A major problem where tests are used is one of appointing registrars free from politics and local pressures. For years, areas in the South arbitrarily administered the law to keep blacks and some whites from enfranchisement. In the 1965 Voting Rights Act, Congress suspended literacy tests and similar devices where less than 50 percent of the voting-age population voted in the 1964 Presidential election and gave the United States Attorney General the power to appoint federal examiners to supervise registration.[5] The ban applied largely to parts of the South and to one county each in Hawaii and Arizona. In 1969, the Nixon Administration suggested that the "regional legislation" not be extended and that literacy tests be banned everywhere. Congress responded by including in the 1970 omnibus Voting Rights law prohibitions against literacy tests, the use of "educational achievement," or "good moral character" as prerequisites to voting in any election.

All states deny the vote to aliens, to the mentally ill, and to inmates of penal institutions. "Bad character" and prostitution have been used in some places to deny registration. Only a few states recognize citizens living on federal reservations as citizens of the state for the purpose of voting. An indeterminate number of Americans living on such land over which the federal government has exclusive jurisdiction are without a vote.

All but two or three states require persons to register before they can vote, with registrars determining the claimant's qualification at the time. The problem for newcomers and first voters is to seek out the place of registration and take the time to go and register. Registration books are closed several days or weeks before election day and some persons forget until too late.

Registration procedures and voting requirements undoubtedly keep many millions of persons from exercising the franchise. The U.S. Census Bureau reported that, of those of voting age, 70.3 percent were registered to vote in 1966 and 75.4 percent in 1968. Nonwhite registration tends to lag more than 10 percent behind the whites. The substantial percentage of persons of voting age who are not registered is due to many causes, but failure to meet residence and other qualifica-

<hr>

[5] A comprehensive report on this act and state literacy laws is found in the *Congressional Quarterly*, Aug. 1, 1969.

tions and inconvenience or difficulty of registration are highly contributory factors.

NEGRO SUFFRAGE

Early History. Members of ethnic and racial minorities have experienced more difficulty registering and fulfilling voting qualifications than whites. Blacks, as the largest single racial minority, faced a particularly long and arduous struggle in securing the franchise after the enactment of the Fifteenth Amendment. Congress imposed Negro suffrage on ten Southern states through the Reconstruction Act of 1867. After the withdrawal of federal troops a decade later, white Southerners moved to exclude the blacks from the ballot box and political life, though in some places blacks continued to vote.

Many of the older techniques such as the grandfather clause, and white primaries eventually ran afoul of the courts.[6] Literacy tests until recently were quite effective in keeping blacks disfranchised. (The grandfather clause had permitted descendants of voters who were qualified before the Reconstruction to vote without passing the literacy test, thus enfranchising certain whites while discriminating against blacks.) As noted, the tests are now under attack and can be used much less successfully to discriminate by white Southern registrars than formerly.

After the barriers to Negro participation in direct primaries were removed, many obstacles to mass franchise still remained. Economically poor blacks could ill afford to pay poll taxes, which remained in some states until abolished by constitutional amendment in 1964. The "custom" of blacks to refrain from voting, often induced by social and economic pressures, is a barrier slowly overcome. Lack of interest and education or failure to recognize the importance of the franchise also resulted in a slow rate of increase in Negro registration. Intimidation, overt and subtle, was employed in many communities to keep blacks from attempting to register.

Even in the absence of intimidation and in the presence of active attempts by blacks to qualify for voting, success was unspectacular because the registration process remained almost exclusively in the hands of white registrars. Many made registration particularly difficult for blacks, who were often quizzed at greater length and more severely

[6]Considerations of space prohibit an account of the litigation here. Two general works are Henry L. Moon, *Balance of Power: The Negro Vote*, Doubleday & Company, Inc., Garden City, N.Y., 1948, and Margaret Price, *The Negro Ballot in the South*, Southern Regional Council, Atlanta, Ga., 1959. The two cases dealing with Negro exclusion from the primaries are especially instructive: *United States v. Classic*, 313 U.S. 299 (1941) and *Smith v. Allwright*, 321 U.S. 649 (1944).

than others—and those in working clothes more extensively than those whose appearance indicated that they were business or professional men. Blacks were given difficult passages to read or to interpret and were often told their answers to questions based on those passages, were "wrong." In some instances, evidence of "bad character," vagrancy, or altercations with police were used as grounds for refusing registration. Delay tactics were used such as keeping blacks waiting in line a long time, then turning them away with such comments as "The office is closed for the day" or "We are fresh out of application blanks." In some communities, blacks were told where to go to register; on arriving there, they found only a vacant lot of an empty building. With tensions rising as a result of the school desegregation cases and Negro agitation, some election officials became stricter in their application of suffrage requirements. Blacks, of course, could resort to suits against officials, but this was a long and costly process.

Negro qualification for voting varied drastically from state to state and even from county to county within the same state. Some outside the South failed to appreciate the differences and believed that disfranchisement was universal in the South—a most inaccurate picture. Further, Negro registration and voting throughout the nation have always been proportionately less than for whites but the difference was less than the overall percentage in the South.

Federal Intervention. In the late fifties and sixties, a massive attack from two directions resulted in a dramatic breakthrough for black voting rights in the South. One came from a series of federal laws resulting in federal intervention, the other in form of a civil rights movement designed to encourage blacks to try to vote and to help them to register. Students and lawyers from various parts of the country went into Southern communities to aid local black leaders in the process. This resulted in some places in beatings and even murders, which dramatized the cause throughout the nation and contributed to greater intervention by all three branches of the federal government. Congressional response came in the form of four civil rights acts (1957, 1960, 1964, and 1965), which were designed to combat discrimination against the potential black voter.

Briefly, the 1957 law provides for federal intervention in areas where white registrars arbitrarily discriminate against black applicants. This law, with the 1960 amendments, authorizes the United States Attorney General to file a civil suit against a state official who deprives a person of his voting rights. The individual denied registration may appeal to the Attorney General, who in turn may seek a court injunction to compel the officer to cease discrimination. If the officer disregards the court order, he may be tried for contempt of court. However, a jury trial is required, and congressional opponents of the provision felt that it weakened the law considerably. If the Department of Justice obtains a court finding that a "pattern" or "practice" of racial discrimination exists in any district, the federal court can designate voting referees to secure registration of black voters in the district. The law also set up a Civil Rights Commission to investigate discrimination and to study problems of "equal protection of the laws." The commission has issued reports designed to increase public awareness of the civil rights matters. Whereas formerly suits had to be financed by the National Association for the Advancement of Colored People and other groups, now the national authorities could also do so. The Justice Department could, moreover, initiate suits to require the registration of qualified persons, avoiding the long delays that had often characterized the private suits.

Notwithstanding the 1957 act, there was no spectacular increase in black voter registration for the 1958 election. The Southern Regional Council estimated a net gain of fewer than 30,000 in eleven Southern states and a grand total of 1,300,000. While some states showed perceptible increases, there were purges of lists in other states and required reregistration, resulting in fewer registrations. The greatest significance of the 1957 and 1960 acts, however, was the modification of private litigation as the major way of securing the enforcement of the right to vote. Henceforth the federal government could become an active participant in assisting blacks. In the first historic action of its kind, a federal judge in Louisiana in 1962 found a pattern of discrimination prevailing and ordered the registration of a few blacks. In 1965, the Supreme Court invalidated the Louisiana interpretation test on the grounds that its discriminatory enforcement made it clear that it was a device for keeping blacks from voting.[7]

After President Johnson's strong appeals for further congressional action, the 1964 and 1965 acts threw out literacy tests if the citizen had completed sixth grade and forbade oral literacy tests and denials based on minor omissions in application forms. Provision was made, under certain conditions, for direct participation by federal authorities to register voters and to see that they were allowed to vote and that their ballots were honestly counted. The United States Attorney General can, without court intervention, appoint civil service examiners to register blacks. Examiners may impound ballots and appoint poll watchers. Local officials are not displaced provided they can prove that

[7] *Louisiana v. United States*, 380 U.S. 145 (1965).

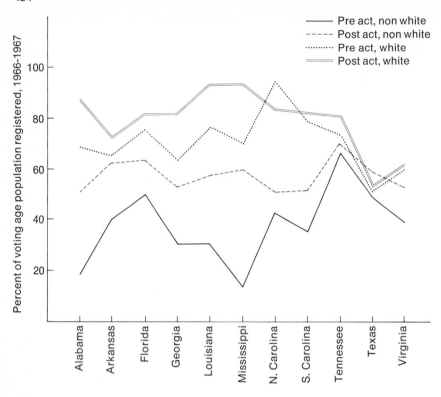

Figure 15-1 Voter registration by race before and after passage of the Voting Rights Act, 1965. *(Source: U.S. Commission on Civil Rights.)*

during the previous five years they have not kept blacks from voting because of race.

Current Status. The cumulative result of these laws, as is shown in Figure 15-1, has been a striking increase in the number of blacks registered.[8] Providing for equal opportunity with whites in registration also significantly increased the number of blacks voting, but they still remain considerably behind whites in actual voting. In 1965, Donald R. Matthews and James W. Prothero in a comprehensive study of Southern Negroes in politics reported that "86 percent of the voting-age whites

---

[8] Various reports of the U.S. Civil Rights Commission and the Southern Regional Council give many detailed data of black registration and voting. Percentages in Figure 15-1 are largely adopted from the commission's *Political Participation*, Washington, D.C., 1968, pp. 12–13. The Southern Regional Council estimated that 65 percent of blacks of voting age in eleven Southern states were registered as of the beginning of 1970. More than 80 percent of the whites were registered. Additional aspects of Negro voting behavior are noted in Chaps. 17 and 18.

in the South have voted in at least one election; only 41 percent of the adult Negroes have ever voted."[9] The U.S. Census Bureau estimate in 1968 ran higher than this, but still noted that only 51.4 percent of the nonwhite Southerners compared to 61.9 percent of the white Southerners voted in that election. The Matthews-Prothero study found further that blacks who vote do so less regularly than do Southern whites and tend to refrain from voting for lesser office such as municipal and school board officials more than do whites. Finally, as is true in registration, there are marked variations between whites and blacks in different counties. Strongest resistance to black suffrage is found in areas where a large black turnout could easily affect the outcome of an election.

Turnouts by blacks outside the South are greater but still generally fall short of those for whites. Even with ease of registration and well-publicized drives by the black leaders, Census Bureau estimates in the 1968 election placed non-South black voting more than 10 percent below that for whites. Adam Clayton Powell's Harlem district had an estimated 400,000 population in 1968, yet only 45,000 persons voted for a congressional candidate. Other heavily black congressional districts appear to have better turnouts, but voting often falls below that for somewhat comparable white districts. Apathy and nonvoting are factors that the black leaders are trying to overcome. As Roy Wilkins of the National Association for the Advancement of Colored People (NAACP) recognized, "Politicians count influence in terms of ballots in the box. If the ballots are not there, a city can have a million Negroes for all the clubhouse boys care."

As a rapidly increasing percentage of blacks register and vote in the South, the Commission on Civil Rights has noted the growth of new forms of discrimination.[10] In some communities, whites are quietly moving to abolish offices sought by black candidates. Where there are prospects of a large, perhaps even a majority, Negro vote, efforts may be made to change some offices from elective to appointive. Raising filing fees, keeping political information from potential black candidates, failure to certify nominating petitions, and extension of terms of incumbent white officials are techniques used in some communities to place obstacles in the way of Negro aspirants to public office. Negroes have learned that redistricting and gerrymandering are sometimes attempted to dilute the overall Negro vote. The courts' continuation of the one-man–one-vote doctrine may be used in the 1970s to fight gerrymandering against Negro areas.

[9]*Negroes and the New Southern Politics*, Harcourt, Brace & World, Inc., New York, 1966, p. 44. The work is recommended for its comprehensive covering of Southern Negro participation in the 1960s.

[10]See its *Political Participation*, part III, *op. cit.*

THE IMPACT OF SUFFRAGE

The vote is but one aspect of the blacks' struggle against discrimination. In general, it is helping them to pressure officials for better education, housing, welfare, and job opportunities to the extent that these are under direct control of the public sector. The vote can have little influence on the private sector where other methods must be employed. On the other hand, very substantial changes have taken place in the South since the 1965 Voting Rights law. Negro political participation has increased, and the more federal examiners the higher the rate of Negro political activity.[11] There are more black voters, candidates, and office-holders than before 1965.

William R. Keech's findings in studies of Negro suffrage in Durham, North Carolina, and Tuskegee, Alabama, undoubtedly have relevance for other communities.[12] In Tuskegee, black votes brought a radical change in the distribution of public services such as recreation and garbage collection. Blacks were hired for the first time for municipal service positions and were appointed to local boards. Their votes were instrumental in securing a very extensive turnover among those elected to public office. But these gains came abruptly only when the blacks became a *majority* of the electorate. "When Negroes were a minority of the electorate," Keech notes, "they were left out in the cold, even though they were a very substantial minority."[13] In Durham, with less than a majority, blacks made some gains and exercised influence over elections.

Since fair employment and integration in the private sector are rather removed from the vote, black successes tend to be in areas under control of the public sector. Further, government bodies eliminate discrimination in their agencies more readily than they pass and enforce laws integrating public accommodations and guaranteeing equal access to housing. Black votes secure incremental adjustments in existing policies more easily than they obtain totally new programs. Although not invariably the case, it is probable that the higher the black proportion of the electorate, the greater the payoffs of black voting. This is likely to be true on ballot propositions where the saliency of issues is more readily seen than in the case of candidates. At the same time, when vigorous efforts are made to mobilize the black voters behind a specific candidate or proposition, the anxieties and fears of whites are aroused, resulting in a turn out en masse to try to nullify the black vote.

[11] On this point, see Johnnie Daniel, "Negro Political Behavior and Community Political and Socioeconomic Structural Factors," *Social Forces*, vol. 47, pp. 274–280, 1969. See also Matthews and Prothero, *op. cit.*

[12] *The Impact of Negro Voting: The Role of the Vote in the Quest for Equality*, Rand McNally & Company, Chicago, 1968.

[13] *Ibid.*, p. 94.

SUFFRAGE AND OFFICEHOLDING

As certain classes and groups obtained the franchise, their leaders expressed hope that either they or their members could more easily be elected to party offices and to public office. One of the more important and immediate consequences of woman suffrage was equal representation on the national committees and on many, if not most, state and county committees of the parties. Women's auxiliaries took over an increasing share of the work of the parties at all levels, and campaign organizations have come to rely heavily on women for office duties in headquarters and for various types of campaign activity. Although women serve in equal numbers on some of the committees of the national conventions, they have had much less success in being selected as delegates to the national convention. Only rarely are more than 10 to 15 percent of the regular delegates women, although the percentage of alternates usually runs considerably higher.

Unlike woman suffrage, enfranchisement of Negroes did not automatically result in blacks securing positions on party committees in large numbers; almost everywhere they have not yet achieved full participation in party life. But changes are underway to eliminate discrimination against blacks in national convention delegations and in state party affairs. They cannot, of course, claim with women that they are entitled to half the representation on party groups or to vice-chairmenships. Nevertheless, an increasing number of blacks are attaining positions in the party officialdom. In predominantly black neighborhoods in the North, precinct and district leadership positions are more or less automatically filled by blacks.

Before 1960, blacks tended to be shut out of public officeholding in the South and won election to comparatively few positions in the North. A turning point was reached in 1962, with one black elected to the Georgia Senate, and by the end of the sixties several Negroes elsewhere obtained elective statewide positions and appointments to the bench, including the Supreme Court. At the beginning of the seventies, blacks held more than 1,100 of the elective offices (0.2 percent), including some in every Southern state. About half of the elected officeholders were in the Southern states and a majority of these were city officials. Blacks held no offices in nine Northern states where they comprised less than 1 percent of the population in each state. The four states with the largest number of black officials were, in order, Michigan, California, Ohio, and Alabama. There were twenty-nine black mayors heading municipal governments, including those of the sizable cities of Cleveland, Ohio, and Gary, Indiana; and a black ran a strong race for mayor of Los Angeles in 1969. A considerable number of blacks were elected to nonpartisan city council positions. Where party labels were used, successful Democrats outnumbered Republicans by 625 to 40 in the 1968 elections (figures supplied by the national committees). In several Southern states, however, not a single black person had been elected to the state legislatures by 1970, but there were fourteen black mayors of small towns and of Chapel Hill, North Carolina. The Southern Regional Council, formed in 1944, has set up several centers to help black candidates and officials; and an Institute for Black Officials was created in 1967.

That granting suffrage to a particular group does not result in corresponding capture of political offices is particularly shown in the case of women. Accurate figures on women officeholders are wanting, but the Republican National Committee estimated that 30,000 women were serving on city and county assemblies in 1963. At a given time, only 300 to 400 of the almost 8,000 state legislators are women and only a very few hold the office of state secretary of state or mayor. In 1961, nineteen women held seats in the two houses of Congress—the high point for women in Congress since ratification of the Nineteenth Amendment in 1920. This representation dropped to one United States Senator and ten House members in the Ninety-first Congress (1969–1971), almost exactly the same number of seats as held by blacks.[14]

To advert to the relationship of suffrage laws to democratic theory, the franchise is effective for popular control, but an undeterminate number, running into millions, of citizens are unable by reason of public laws or their administration to use this tool. Since elections allocate political power, the power (officeholders and their appointees) is controlled by those who can vote rather easily or who are willing to make the effort to overcome the restrictions of election laws. As a group, transients tend to have their power diluted compared with those who qualify to vote and remain in the vicinity. Whether this results in a somewhat different type of elected official than would be the case with an actual effective universal suffrage is moot. One might speculate that a more conservative candidate stands to benefit from restrictive suffrage laws. Suffrage laws are but one factor in voting behavior. Psychological and sociological variables are very important, and our attention is directed to them in the chapters immediately following. The case of women illustrates the lag between establishment of civic equality and acceptance of that equality in the customs of society. Suffrage did not bring anywhere near corresponding success in elective leadership opportunities. This is still true of Negro suffrage but may be less true in the

---

[14]Statistics and analysis of women in the state legislatures and in Congress are found in Emmy E. Werner, "Women in Congress: 1917–1964," *Western Political Quarterly*, vol. 19, pp. 16–36, 1966.

future. Cultural patterns, desire to play an active role in politics, and social and psychological variables are very important in voting behavior as well as who can seek public office with some hope of success.

ADMINISTRATION OF ELECTION LAWS

It is of little profit for an individual to be politically interested and knowledgeable if for one reason or another he is kept from registration or if his vote is falsely counted or not counted at all. Consequently, the administration of suffrage and voting laws, as well as adequate machinery, is of high importance. As in the case of nominations, the administration of elections has evolved from the simple to the complex. The checking of those who have fulfilled the voting qualifications and the supervision of actual balloting are essentially different operations and are often performed by different sets of persons. Registration and election administration, although separated, are designed to prevent fraud.

There has been a great decline in the uses of intimidation, impersonation at the polls on election day, and dishonest counts, thanks in part to voting machines, better officials, and improved procedures. Yet alleged election irregularities still occur in parts of the United States, and the Nixon forces were particularly incensed in 1960 at practices in Chicago. Many of the new democracies and semidemocracies are struggling with problems of fraud on election day. Efficient and honest administration of elections remains a problem and a challenge to those societies operating under free, periodic election with a guaranteed secret ballot.

In most of the European democracies, the government assumes the responsibility for preparing a complete register of voters; this is often done by a canvas. Frequent censuses may be used to add or strike out names. Voter records, therefore, are kept reasonably well up to date without requiring the voter to appear personally. Only a few communities in the United States use this nonpersonal system. In most parts of the country, the voter must assume the responsibility for his own registration and present himself personally before the registration officials.[15]

Election Machinery. Election administration is a governmental function calling for the identification of registered voters, the distribution of ballots (or the operation of voting machines), and the counting of ballots. Generally these functions are performed by a bipartisan precinct

[15]Current issues are covered in Joseph P. Harris, *Model Voter Registration System*, National Municipal League, New York, 1957. A few communities have arrangements for allowing voters whose names do not appear on the list to vote if they present satisfactory evidence at the time that they are fully qualified. North Dakota abolished registration in 1951.

election board. Where registration is done in the precincts, the same board may perform both functions. The local boards are appointed in diverse ways, including nomination by a city or county board of elections, a city or county council, or a county court judge, or by popular election. With a few exceptions, appointments are made on a patronage basis with the consent of a party chairman or district captain. Where there are three on the board, not more than two may belong to the same party, and clerkships to help the election judges are likewise distributed on a party basis. While this may provide security by providing for each party to watch the other, it does not necessarily give protection to independent or third-party candidates, nor does it necessarily mean that the election judges are trained or competent. In only a few communities are applicants required to take an examination to obtain the job. In some cases training is provided, and where voting machines are used, inspectors are often required to take instruction in the operation of the machines.

Many state laws recognize that some protection is needed for both major and minor candidates because election officials are personally interested in the outcome of the election. Therefore permission is frequently made for each party to have watchers at or near the guard rail at each precinct, with authority to challenge any voter and to inspect the records. Watchers may be allowed to examine ballot boxes or machines before the polls open and during the count. Watchers have not completely stopped chicanery but certainly have reduced the amount of it. Many candidates are unable to employ enough watchers to cover all polling places.

In a national election, it is estimated that about half the votes are cast by machines. Voting machines reduce opportunities for fraud and error and inaccurate or intentionally dishonest reports of precinct results, since the machine results are easily compared with those reported by the election officials. Machines speed up the entire voting process and make the results quickly available after the closing of the polls. Machines are expensive and must be stored and maintained between elections, and many local authorities have argued that the community cannot afford them. Voting machine companies contend that, with the amortization of purchase costs over many years plus savings in paper ballots and in the reduction in the number of election officials needed, election costs can actually be reduced by machines.

The years ahead will see pronounced changes, with the replacement of the older types of voting machines by electronic data-processing machines. The Coleman electronic vote tally system was first employed in a California county in 1962 and uses a paper ballot similar to the conventional one. The voter marks the ballot with a special stamp. Ballots are taken to the processing center and fed to a ballot reader which counts up to hundreds of ballots per minute. Precinct totals are punched and printed on cards.

Another type of device is the Harris votomatic recorder. A punch card fits into a vote recorder that contains a replica of the standard ballot (see Figure 15-2). The voter inserts the card and punches it with a stylus; if improperly inserted, it will not punch. Cards are dispatched to centrally located electronic computers and can be counted at a rate of 800 per minutes. The recorder weighs only 5 pounds and is stored in much less space than a voting machine.

Local authorities are often slow to make changes, and these new devices will probably be adopted gradually. In the meantime, millions of paper ballots will continue to be arduously counted by procedures often prescribed in minute detail.

Recounts. Provisions for a recount are usually afforded to losers as a right and when there is evidence of fraud. A number of states require the petitioner to finance the recount, a factor deterring a recount or limiting it to certain selected election districts. Recanvasing voting machine results is relatively inexpensive and a fast operation, but recounting paper ballots is more costly and time-consuming. It appears to be sound policy to have the public bear some, if not all, of the cost of

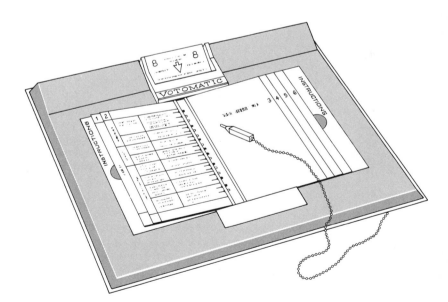

Figure 15-2 Harris votomatic recorder.

recounts as a protection of the sanctity of elections. Restrictions on recounts can be prescribed in order to deter frivolous and unnecessary
requests for a recanvas.

In a given year, a number of recounts will be of considerable
importance. It is not at all uncommon for one or more races for Congress
to hinge on a recount. One of the most celebrated recounts was the long
one following the 1962 election for governor of Minnesota. After nearly
five months, in which a number of disputed regular and absentee ballots were finally ruled on by the courts, Karl Rolvaag, who was on the
short end of the initial canvas by 142 votes, was declared the winner by
91 votes over incumbent Gov. Elmer L. Anderson. (About 1,240,000
votes were cast for the office.) Reversals are not at all uncommon.[16] The
fact that recounts produce reversals is not *ipso facto* evidence of fraud
in the initial counting. Honest mistakes due to fatigue, erroneous addition, borderline markings, or incorrect markings may be detected on
the basis of more careful and leisurely scrutiny.

Absentee Voting.   Party leaders in states and districts with highly competitive primaries and general elections are more aware than most of the
general public that absentee ballots may be of crucial importance. In
one state election, no less than six seats in the state legislature were
unsettled until the absentee ballots were counted, and numerous local
government races have been determined by absentees. The close Nixon-
Kennedy race in California in 1960 demonstrated the dramatic importance of these ballots in a statewide contest. The day after the election,
Kennedy's lead appeared safe, even though it had dwindled as the final
precinct reports came in. Then the state's 243,000 absentee ballots were
counted. Kennedy's lead vanished, and Nixon emerged with a final
plurality of about 36,000 votes.[17] What is significant is that Republicans constituted only 40 percent of the registered voters; but about 60
percent of those who applied for absentee ballots were Republicans and
about 61 percent of the absentees voted for Nixon. The Republican
candidate for governor of Rhode Island won in 1962 on the strength
of a large proportion of absentee ballots. Absentees rarely benefit the

[16] In 1960, the official tabulation sheets in Hawaii revealed a 141-vote majority for Nixon.
But errors in the vote totals were reported before official certification was made. A group of Democrats
filed a recount petition in the Honolulu circuit court, and the judge ordered a recount in a few precincts which resulted in a diminution of Nixon strength. Then a complete recheck reversed the first
count and gave Kennedy the state by a margin of 115. For an interesting account, see Daniel W.
Tuttle, Jr., "The 1960 Election in Hawaii," *Western Political Quarterly*, vol. 14, no. 1, part 2, pp. 337–
338, 1961. On recounts see Ronald F. Stinnett and Charles H. Backstrom, *Recount*, National Document
Publishers, Washington, D.C., 1964.

[17] For a summary of the absentee vote, see *Western Political Quarterly*, vol. 14, no. 1, part 2,
p. 317, 1961.

Democrats; where they do, it is likely to favor a well-known incumbent over a less well-known Republican challenger.

Laws on absentee voting are far from uniform, and details likewise show much variation.[18] But their general purpose is to give traveling Americans or persons unable to go to the polls because of age or illness a chance to record their choices; this at times is decisive on candidates and propositions. Military personnel are usually separated from civilian absentee voting. For diverse reasons, Congress was reluctant to enact a comprehensive soldier-vote law during World War II and provided a federal ballot only for residents of states failing to make adequate provision. Congress repealed the federal short ballot law in 1946, leaving the soldier-vote question in the hands of each state. Today Congress remains content with urging the states to enact servicemen's vote provisions and about three-fourths of the states have such arrangements.

Write-in Provisions. Most states permit voters to write in names if they do not wish to support any of the candidates listed on the ballot. For election officials, there is a problem of whether to insist on correct spelling and full names. In some 1952 presidential primaries, election boards had to decide whether to accept such designations as "Ike," "Isenhour," and "Izenhower." Whether or not to count a certain write-in is usually left to the discretion of election judges. Precinct leaders and local officials have sometimes been elected by a handful of write-ins. A shock occurred in 1954 when J. Strom Thurmond of South Carolina was elected to the United States Senate by a write-in vote of 143,000 to 83,000 for the candidate running as a Democrat. The incident pointed to the potentiality of this provision in election. A huge write-in vote for Henry Cabot Lodge won the 1964 New Hampshire preferential primary and brought him into serious contention for the presidential nomination.

Effect of Ballot Position. Politicians have usually felt, rightly or wrongly, that voters unfamiliar with any of the candidates will tend to vote for the first name on the list. The problem of "position effect" has only recently been under study, and to date there is still no comprehensive or definitive national or regional study of the phenomenon. Surveys by educational psychologists and social scientists indicate that when people are asked to select one or more items of a series, they tend to favor those appearing in certain positions, particularly first.

[18]A summary and analysis of absentee voting systems as of 1960 will be found in Constance E. Smith, *Voting and Election Laws*, Oceana Publications, New York, 1960, chap. 4; state-by-state provisions are found on pp. 89–99.

Henry M. Bain and Donald S. Hecock surveyed the literature regarding position on the ballot and conducted studies of their own in some primary and nonpartisan elections in Michigan.[19] They found "statistically significant evidence of position effect in primary and non-partisan elections in several Michigan cities." First position in a vertical list on paper ballots was preferred, and the top row was favored in most cases on voting machines, although there was some doubt about this conclusion. Position effect was greater for those offices in which the incumbent has less attention or visibility to the public. Ignorance of who the candidates are is probably the major reason for delaying one's choices until entering the polls. Why one selects the first name rather than others (if this is the case) remains an intriguing question. In the meantime, since there seems to be an advantage by reason of position on the ballots and on the voting machines, it becomes important that ways and means be worked out to distribute this advantage as equitably as possible. About half the states use a system which allocates positions on the ballot alphabetically, in order of filing, or by lot. Although these may appear fair on the surface, they are far more arbitrary than the rotation of names on the ballot, a practice followed by the other half of the states. Rotation complicates the work of the election officials and increases the cost of printing the ballot, but the effort seems worth while in terms of equality of opportunity. The very fact that names on the ballot should have to be rotated indicates that the voter lacks information and conviction about a candidate. Had he been certain of the name of the person for whom he wished to vote before he entered the polls, position on the ballot would be of little importance. Position effect is not basically a problem of election administration but of political education and results from a long ballot.

Short Ballot. The short ballot, or the reduction in the number of offices to be filled by popular election, has long been advocated as a necessary political reform. A few of the newer constitutions in states such as Alaska, Hawaii, Michigan, and New Jersey have reduced the number of elective state offices, thus reducing the burden of choices to be made by the voter. But most states are slow to adopt this type of constitutional reform. Another suggestion is to hold separate elections for different levels of government. This enables the electorate to concentrate on fewer officers with potentially greater opportunity to discriminate among positions and candidates. A great many municipal and school elections are now held separately. Since 1910, moreover, nearly every city has shortened its ballot, and new forms of city government place

[19] *Ballot Position and Voter's Choice,* Wayne State University Press, Detroit, Mich., 1957.

selection of personnel, formerly on the ballot, in the hands of the mayor or a city manager. But most states still hold national and state elections at the same time and many include county offices as well. The voter's burden remains essentially undiminished despite agitation to reduce it; blind voting is still encouraged by the "tablecloth ballot."[20] The long ballot and election machinery in general are not models of sound public administration, and both are still looked upon as the province of party organization.

EFFECTS OF BALLOT FORMS

Although all states use the Australian ballot there is much variation in form. Some states use a consolidated ballot listing candidates for all levels of office; others use separate ballots for national and local offices. Two major forms (with variations in each) are used for grouping names on the ballot—the Massachusetts office-block arrangement and the Indiana party-column ballot. The latter is used by about thirty states. (See Figures 15-3 and 15-4.)

Since the Massachusetts form, first adopted in 1888, groups names according to office sought, the voter must mark each office, thereby using some conscious effort in voting for each office. Party leaders did not like this system because it did not facilitate straight-party voting, and they devised the Indiana form, which listed all party candidates in a single column vertically or horizontally on voting machines. The name of the party is printed at the top of a column with a circle or square so that if the voter so chooses he can put a single mark to vote for every candidate in the column. In voting machines, one can pull a lever beside the party label and accomplish the same purpose. A few states put the names in a party column but omit the circle, requiring the voter to go down the column or across the machine checking each candidate. This system, as well as the office-block ballot, places a greater burden on the straight-ticket voter since he cannot support every candidate of one party by one operation. Twenty-seven states permit straight-ticket voting ("single-choice" ballot) in one form or another, and twenty-three states require the voter to cast a separate vote for each candidate on the ballot for whom he wishes his vote to be registered.[21]

Both primary and general election laws can be used to facilitate partisanship. Generally, party officials much prefer the closed primary

[20] It is hard to tell which state would win the prize for a long ballot, but one Indiana ballot a few years ago would surely be a runner-up. The ballot itself measured 2,414 square inches and contained 246 names for 58 offices! Apparently with a straight face the officials printed on the bottom of the ballot the warning "Each voter is allowed not more than one minute in which to vote."

[21] For a good summary of the arguments for and against the office-block and party-column ballot, see *Council Comments*, Citizens Research Council of Michigan, no. 757, Sept. 18, 1964.

SAMPLE BALLOT
GENERAL ELECTION
NOVEMBER 25, 1958

- J—CENTRAL AT-LARGE SENATORIAL DISTRICT
- M—FAIRBANKS-FORT YUKON SENATORIAL DISTRICT
- NO. 19—FAIRBANKS ELECTION DISTRICT

Mark "X" in the square at the left of name of each candidate
for whom you desire to vote.

**FOR GOVERNOR AND SECRETARY OF STATE
OF THE STATE OF ALASKA**
(Vote Only for Governor)

☐ BUTROVICH, JR., JOHN (GOVERNOR)	PHILLIPS, BRAD (SECRETARY OF STATE)	Republican
☐ DOLLINTER, MIKE (GOVERNOR)	HOLTON, DONALD W. (SECRETARY OF STATE)	Independent
☐ EGAN, WILLIAM A. (GOVERNOR)	WADE, HUGH J. (SECRETARY OF STATE)	Democrat
☐		

**FOR UNITED STATES SENATOR
FOR TERM A**
(Term To Be Determined by Authority of the United States)
(Vote for One)

☐ BARTLETT, E. L. (Bob)	Democrat
☐ CAPPER, KEITH	Independent
☐ ROBERTSON, R. E.	Republican
☐	

**FOR UNITED STATES SENATOR
FOR TERM B**
(Term To Be Determined by Authority of the United States)
(Vote for One)

☐ GRUENING, ERNEST	Democrat
☐ STEPOVICH, MIKE	Republican
☐	

**FOR UNITED STATES REPRESENTATIVE
FOR A TWO-YEAR TERM**
(Vote for One)

☐ BENSON, HENRY A.	Republican
☐ RIVERS, RALPH J.	Democrat
☐	

**FOR AT-LARGE DISTRICT J SENATOR
FOR A TWO-YEAR TERM**
(Vote for One)

☐ BINKLEY, CHARLES M. (Jim)	Republican
☐ BUTLER, STEWART P.	Independent
☐ McNEALY, R. J. (Bob)	Democrat
☐	

**FOR AT-LARGE DISTRICT J SENATOR
FOR A FOUR-YEAR TERM**
(Vote for One)

☐ JONES, RICHARD D. (Dick)	Republican
☐ McNABB, JR., GEORGE B.	Democrat
☐ NOYES, SHERMAN	Independent
☐ STUART, ALICE	Independent
☐	

**FOR DISTRICT M STATE SENATOR
FOR A FOUR-YEAR TERM**
(Vote for One)

☐ GILBERT, HUBERT A.	Democrat
☐ LONGWITH, B. C.	Alaska Party
☐ WIEN, ADA B. (Mrs. Noel)	Republican
☐	

**FOR STATE REPRESENTATIVES
FOR A TWO-YEAR TERM**
(Vote for Five)

☐ BOSWELL, J. C. (Jack)	Republican
☐ CHAPADOS, FRANK X.	Democrat
☐ COLLINS, E. B.	Republican
☐ GIERSDORF, ROBERT (Bob)	Democrat
☐ GREUEL, RICHARD J. (Dick)	Democrat
☐ JOY, LOUIS F. (Lou)	Republican
☐ MORING, AUBREY C.	Independent
☐ POLET, ALVIN (Al)	Republican
☐ PURVIS, CHARLES F.	Alaska Party
☐ RINGSTAD, KENNETH	Republican
☐ RYCZKOWSKI, ANTHONY	Independent
☐ SHELDON, R. E. (Bob)	Democrat
☐ TAYLOR, WARREN A.	Democrat
☐ WARBELOW, MARVIN E.	Independent
☐	
☐	
☐	
☐	
☐	

Figure 15-3 Alaska office-block ballot. No provision for straight-ticket voting by a single mark.

Figure 15-4 Indiana party-column ballot permitting straight-ticket voting by a single mark.

and party-column ballots, with the opportunity to vote a straight-ticket on the latter in one operation. These devices presumably develop partisan loyalties, both in voters and in would-be candidates. The effect of the party-column and office-block ballots is by no means fully known throughout the nation. Enough studies have been conducted, however, to establish the importance of ballot forms in determining the behavior of voters. One sample in the 1956 election confirmed the politicians' hunch that the Indiana party-column type aids straight-ticket voting, resulting in an increased number of voters doing so.[22] Conversely, the Massachusetts office-block type resulted in more split-ticket voting. What is equally significant, however, is that ballot form had little influence on strong partisans. About the same percentage of strong Republicans and strong Democrats voted straight tickets irrespective of which ballot they received. But the weak identifiers increased their straight-ticket voting under the party-column, single-choice system much more frequently, and the percentage increased even more pronouncedly among independents. Further, the office-block ballot increases split-ticket voting, but the best-informed and most interested voters appear least affected by the nature of the electoral machinery while the least-informed voters seem to be encouraged to split their tickets when the office block is used.

Ballot arrangements also seem to affect the extent of falloff or rolloff, that, is failure to vote for the less-advertised candidates and propositions. John P. White found a much larger rolloff in Michigan counties in which voting machines were used rather than traditional paper ballots.[23] Many voters seem to find machines confusing to operate and some fail to see the referenda on the face of the machine.

Ohio has been an on-again-off-again state in its use of party-column and office-block ballots; and, during the time it used the latter, there was more rolloff.[24] In a comparison of thirty-six states using the two types of ballots, the falloff between the vote for governor and that for United States representative from 1950 through 1962 was from 0.2 to 2.0 percent more on the office-block ballots.[25] Voter fatigue, moreover, was found to be greater among the poorly educated, peripherally involved voters. Evidence seems pretty clear that the more complex the ballot design, the more likely voters will neglect races at the bottom of the ticket. Candidates recognize this, and their campaign literature often features sample ballots with names circled to draw attention. Where the straight-ticket vote can benefit them, their publicity features both their names and the importance of voting a straight ticket.

[22]Angus Campbell and Warren E. Miller, "The Motivational Basis of Straight and Split Ticket Voting," *American Political Science Review*, vol. 61, pp. 293–312, 1957. See also Angus Campbell, Warren E. Miller, Philip E. Converse, and Donald E. Stokes, *The American Voter*, John Wiley & Sons, Inc., New York, 1960, chap. 11, for additional analysis of election laws and voting behaviors. Data used in these paragraphs are from these two sources.

[23]*Voting Machines and the 1958 Defeat of Constitutional Revision in Michigan*, Institute of Public Administration, University of Michigan, Ann Arbor, 1960. George B. Mathews found similar results in Iowa. See his *Effects of the Use of Voting Machines on Total Votes Cast: Iowa: 1920–1960*, Institute for Public Affairs, University of Iowa, Iowa City, 1964.

[24]An informative study of this matter is that of Jack L. Walker, "Ballot Forms and Voter Fatigue: An Analysis of the Office Block and Party Column Ballots," *Midwest Journal of Political Science*, vol. 10, pp. 448–463, 1966.

[25]*Ibid.*, p. 457.

TABLE 15-1 Average vote falloff for statewide offices, 1908–1956

Office	Ohio	South Dakota	Washington
President	0.37%	0.44%	0.11%
Governor	1.35	0.96	2.11
Lieutenant governor	6.30	4.46	7.19
Secretary of state	6.74	5.58	11.68
Auditor	6.87	6.57	12.67
Treasurer	7.29	6.58	9.81
Attorney general	7.43	7.36	10.07
Public lands commission		6.61	11.62
Insurance or utilities commissioner		7.28	12.09
Superintendent of public instruction		16.61	27.01

Note: Falloff represents the difference between the vote cast for a particular office and the total vote cast in the state. In the years when presidential electors' names appeared individually, the total vote cast for each party's winning elector was used. During these years there were two elections in Washington, three in Ohio, and four in South Dakota when the governor's race brought out more votes than that for President. Since all are averaged for the total period, falloff for governor is less than if elections where the governor led the ticket were omitted.

Generally speaking, the longer the ballot the greater the falloff in the vote for minor and local offices. Ohio, South Dakota, and Washington use the party-column ballot to elect a sizable number of state offices and provide an opportunity to view ballot fatigue or falloff from the top of the ticket. (Ohio abandoned the party-column ballot in 1956.) Voting participation for these offices in the three states is shown in Table 15-1 and provides another example of variations in state voting behavior. In all these states, a significant dropoff takes place with the office of lieutenant governor and proceeds rather rapidly thereafter (less so in Ohio than in South Dakota and Washington). In the two states electing the superintendent of public instruction, the vote falloff is more than double that for the lowest of the other state offices. The greater overall falloff in Washington might be attributed in part to the fact that the other two states permit straight party voting by means of a single cross or pull of the lever. However, this system was permitted in Washington until 1948, and in that election and in the two that followed there was only perceptible increase in dropout rate. The voting arrangement for a straight ticket, therefore, had little effect.

In conclusion, suffrage laws and ballot forms have considerable impact on voting turnout and in encouraging or discouraging partisanship. As the franchise is extended, party organizations must reach more voters and therefore will need more workers and more money.

Republicans have learned that they stand to profit by liberal provisions for absentee ballots, and they expend much effort in trying to inform and aid their potential voters in the use of them. Democrats are also active in this area, but many of their leaders believe that Democratic voters travel less and that it is more profitable to check working-class neighborhoods to see that everyone is registered and then brought to the polls on election day. They have learned that narrow margins for their candidates at the polls are often erased by the absentee-ballot count for Republicans.

Data point to the hypothesis that election laws favoring or restricting both partisanship and participation have their greatest impact on the less involved and less politically motivated citizens. Highly motivated persons will likely make every effort to vote, irrespective of the degree of restriction of suffrage laws. Highly motivated partisans are likely to vote a straight ticket regardless of ballot form or the ease of casting a straight ballot. The less motivated may vote less regularly in the face of restrictive laws and may show a greater tendency to split their tickets if partisanship is not facilitated. It is interesting to speculate whether some party politicians have felt this to be true and have, over the years, designed election laws to keep the less motivated from voting in primaries or in general elections. Restrictive laws and registration procedures in the South were designed to reduce voting by blacks—and sometimes voting by certain whites as well. These persons, moreover, were not strongly motivated and were easily discouraged from voting by the mores of the community. In this case, the election laws reinforced the environmental factors. Outside the South today examples would be less easy to find.

Political party organizations are not necessarily victims and prisoners of election laws, although sometimes they are. A case in point is the Washington blanket primary, which was adopted by popular initiative and survived a challenge in the courts by a party organization. But many election laws result from the initiative of the parties. Legislators, acting with the support of their parties, have made changes in the registration system, in the absentee and write-in provisions, and in the primaries and have proposed constitutional amendments dealing with residence, age, dates of elections, and the timing of gubernatorial elections to coincide (or not) with presidential elections. The out-party has often tried to stir sentiment for changes that might place it in a better position. A historian who observed election laws concluded that many of them "were intended for no other purpose than to insure the supremacy of the temporarily dominant party."[26] With election laws, as with so many other aspects of the American political system, the familiar refrain reappears—election laws have an impact on parties, but parties likewise greatly influence election laws.

[26]R. P. McCormick, *The History of Voting in New Jersey*, Rutgers University Press, New Brunswick, N.J., 1953, p. 163.

FOR FURTHER READING

Albright, Spencer D.: *The American Ballot,* 1942.

Eldersveld, Samuel J., and A. A. Applegate: *Michigan's Recounts for Governor, 1950 and 1952: A Systematic Analysis of Election Error,* 1954.

Halloway, Harry: *The Politics of the Southern Negro: From Exclusion to Big City Organization,* 1969.

Harper, Ita H.: *The History of Woman Suffrage,* 1922.

Johnson, J. B.: *Registration for Voting in the United States,* 1946.

Lang, Kurt, and Gladys Lang: *Voting and Nonvoting: Implications of Broadcasting Returns Before Polls Are Closed,* 1968.

McGovney, Dudley O.: *The American Suffrage Medley,* 1949.

Pollock, James K.: *Absentee Voting and Registration,* 1942.

Porter, Kirk H.: *A History of Suffrage in the United States,* 1918.

PART SEVEN VOTING BEHAVIOR AND PARTICIPATION

Men are urged to certain ends but the political scene
in which they act is perceived and given meaning.
Some cognitive map accompanies their movement
toward these ends.

HERBERT HYMAN

CHAPTER 16 PSYCHOLOGICAL INFLUENCES ON VOTING

Public officials are concerned with discovering opinions of all kinds, preponderant and minority, clear-cut and confused. But politicians find themselves saying with James Bryce, "Such is the din of voices that it is hard to say which cry prevails, which is swelled by the many, which only by a few throats." Once opinion is ascertained, the conscientious public servant is faced with evaluating it.

The public man is not alone in wanting to know what people think and feel. Businessmen are concerned with public attitudes toward their products. They employ market analysts to find out who is buying what and why. Box tops and coupons mailed in supposedly show where the market is—and is not. Telephones ring to find out which radio station the housewife is listening to or what she is watching on television. Many private groups such as business, labor, and farmers poll their memberships' views and sometimes even those of the general public for reasons less obviously commercial but directed toward strengthening their groups.

In addition to the unobscured motivations of politicians and commercialists, scholars and journalists have an insatiable appetite for analyzing the political man. They have not been content to look at figures recording how many votes a candidate received in what county. They want to study the voter before he goes to the polls and after he has gone. How, why, and when did he make up his mind? In addition to knowing the demography of voters, social scientists seek to learn their intensity of feeling and their perceptions of parties, issues, and candidates, as well as the interrelationships among them.

Perhaps the most significant development within the American political science profession since the end of World War II has been the application of increasingly more sophisticated techniques for studying, not only voting behavior, but also motivations and behavior of party and private group leaders and adherents, legislators, public administrators, popularly elected executives and judges. Numerous political scientists have joined their colleagues in psychology and the various social sciences in trying to obtain a better understanding of political behavior. This enterprise has resulted in a phenomenal number of books and titles on methodology as well as on substantive findings. In this chapter and in Chapters 17 and 18, we can allude to only a fraction of the analyses pertinent to voting and nonvoting. Our major interest is in developing generalizations about voting and the relationship of voting to the democratic process and the party system.

On election eve the press and commentators are replete with statements: "Watch Bucks County, it is always on the winning side." "The upstate returns are predominantly Republican, and it is simply a question of whether they will be large enough to wipe out the traditional Democratic pluralities downstate." "The farmers in the north central part of the state are Democratic." Careful voting studies may sustain these impressions, but they are teaching us that electoral decisions are an infinitely complex process. Social scientists remain wary of accepting any one factor as determinant in a person's voting decision. What is found in a microanalysis of one situation is not necessarily sustained by microanalysis in another. Recent research into voting preferences has attempted both to isolate the factors and to study their interrelationship and effect on one another. One group of scholars sees great importance in social determinants—the influence of one's social group, religion, occupation, economic status, and the like. The staff of the University of Michigan Survey Research Center (SRC) continues to analyze both demographic and party factors, but it still leans heavily on the importance of the voter's psychological conception of his own party identifications and how he sees candidates and issues. We shall look at these forthwith.[1]

Survey field research has yielded a vast accumulation of data on diverse factors impinging on the voters' choices. Some of the findings reinforce each other enough to support valid generalizations; others are contradictory. The student must expect to find discrepancies in data and interpretation and may be fortunate enough to participate in a survey pitting his own findings against those of others. In the pages to follow, the reader should recognize that the problem of perceptual distortion by respondents is present, as is the possible perceptual distortion of the respondent's view by the interviewer. Persons interviewed, with few exceptions, do not purposely distort their remarks, but there may be a good deal of unconscious, selective perception at work. One may select his candidate on the basis of some small or extended personal contact and then bring the issues and other attitudes into the picture to fit the candidate and the respondent's own views.

Time and events are of great significance in politics and electoral behavior. An inherent weakness of a survey of one election is that it is a snapshot in time and therefore limited. In order to obtain historical perspective on long-term changes (which are most important in political and voting behavior), repeated interviews between elections are necessary. To conduct surveys that are longitudinal is expensive and difficult but nonetheless valuable if we are to get an accurate view of change and stability in voting patterns. Explanatory theory of voting behavior can be useful to the extent that empirical evidence is gathered both widely and over a period of time and gathered with methods and questions affording a basis for comparison.

THEORIES OF VOTING

A person would find it comforting to approach the mass of statistics and data on voting from a simply formulated, all-embracing theory. The theory would explain why an individual votes as he does and would support the explanation with convincing data. It would also show the relation of the electoral process to the social system and the party system. Unhappily, no simple model has yet appeared that is acceptable to

[1] A pilot study made on the basis of 662 cases in 1948 was published in 1952 as *The People Elect a President* by the Michigan Survey Research Center (frequently cited hereinafter as the Center or SRC). The subsequent landmark study of the 1952 election, conducted by Angus Campbell, Gerald Garin and Warren E. Miller, was published as *The Voter Decides*, Harper & Row, Publishers, Incorporated, New York, 1954. Campbell and Miller were joined by Philip E. Converse and Donald E. Stokes in writing a massive work that included the 1956 election under the title *The American Voter*, John Wiley & Sons, Inc., New York, 1960. The work is social-psychological and theoretical and takes cognizance of the many social and psychological variables surrounding the data gathered 1948 through 1956. Donald Stokes joined Campbell, Converse, and Miller in an additional work in 1966, *Elections and the Social Order*, also published by Wiley.

all, and every theory has come under criticism, usually on the grounds of inadequacy.

The older general classical theory is becoming increasingly difficult to reconcile with modern surveys. Political man was seen as acting rationally in his political choices. He was viewed as interested in politics, eager to discuss public affairs, and possessed of some urge to participate. Further, the citizen was believed to vote on the basis of enlightened self-interest, values and principles. The authors of *Voting* challenged this view of the individual, and theirs and other data are likely to be convincing in this respect. Nonetheless, they argue that "the system of democracy does meet certain requirements for a going political organization. The individual members may not meet all the standards, but the whole nevertheless survives and grows. What are undervalued are certain collective properties that reside in the electorate as a whole and in the political and social system in which it functions."[2]

Another general theory places the voter in the center of a very complex environment with pressure coming at him from all directions. Family, friends, occupation, religion, ethnic background, income, socioeconomic status, and education influence him, perhaps unconsciously, in his voting habits. His social class, place of residence, and so on, give him a general political overview or orientation. These sociological variables do not all act in the same direction, so the person may be cross-pressured; when these influences are strong enough, they are likely to result in indecision, vacillation, splitting of tickets, and perhaps even nonvoting. Consideration of the relationship of these social and group variables is reserved for Chapter 17.

Another theory proceeds from an analysis of the attitudinal factors, with more emphasis on psychology and the individual's basic makeup. Party identification and perception of issues and candidates are seen as highly important in motivating the individual's voting behavior, and the authors of *The Voter Decides* give particular attention to these. These psychological factors and attitudes toward parties, issues, and men all receive attention in the balance of this chapter.

A further model would link together the sociostructural and the sociopsychological variables. In *The American Voter*, voting is regarded as an act following a sequence of events, using the "funnel of causality" as a metaphor.[3] As one moves from the "mouth" down to the "stem," one moves from prior, remote events to the more proximate ones and

[2] Bernard R. Berelson, Paul F. Lazarsfeld, and William N. McPhee, *Voting*, The University of Chicago Press, Chicago, 1954, p. 312.

[3] This analysis appears in a relevant chapter devoted to "theoretical orientation" in Campbell et al., *The American Voter*, chap. 2.

to the immediate voting act. An effort is made to separate the irrelevant from the relevant factors in the voting decision. If this could be done successfully, some prediction of voting behavior would be possible. Personal factors, of which the person is aware, and external conditions, of which he is not aware, are in the funnel and must be carefully studied and related along with relevant political and nonpolitical conditions. This constitutes both a complex and an enormous framework but challenges the student to see whether he can fit the variables into the funnel to offer a satisfactory explanation. The subject of voting behavior has produced many volumes and promises many more. Our attention must be limited to what the major variables are, what the data show about them, and what their implications are for the party system.

PSYCHOLOGICAL FACTORS

Statements about the individual's part in politics may seem unnecessarily obvious, not to say platitudinous, yet the significance of the individual is easily overlooked in the vast literature on mass behavior. The mass approach sees politics in terms of sets of interests, large and small, clashing with each other. It is "labor" or "business" who lobby; it is the "legislature" that makes laws, and the "newspaper" that influences public opinion. Yet individuals are not exclusively puppets in the hands of these interests. An individual is a member of many interest groups and of a so-called voting bloc. Individuals do not each have the same share in an interest group; some are more active in promoting its goals than others, just as some persons have a greater intensity of feeling for a political party, candidate, or policy than others. Some individuals' voting preferences remain reasonably constant, others are more easily upset. Shifts in preference may take place as a result both of long-run and short-run factors.

One of the most widely used, if not overworked, words in American politics and business is *image*. Advertising firms spend millions to develop favorable images for their companies and products. Public relations men and politicians worry about counteracting a bad image and getting or keeping a good image for their man. The Eisenhower "magic" in politics was supposedly based on a remarkably favorable image, while Mr. Nixon's image was not nearly so favorable, and he was regarded as controversial. Writing in 1922, Walter Lippmann attempted to explain public opinion by "pictures" inside our heads; he said:

> Those features of the world outside which have to do with the behavior of other human beings, insofar as that behavior crosses ours, is dependent upon us, or is interesting to us, we call roughly public affairs. The picture inside the heads of these human

beings, the pictures of themselves, of others, of their needs, purposes, and relationships, are their public opinions. Those pictures which are acted upon by groups of
people, or by individuals acting in the name of groups, are Public Opinion with capital
letters.[4]

Every person carries in his mind a picture or an image of the
world around him. Politically his "cognitive map" includes his perceptions of parties, candidates, issues, and groups. He probably feels that
certain things are going to happen and may relate his perceptions to
them. Many of these things carry favorable or unfavorable connotations.
He likes prosperity and dislikes "hard times." Taxes are irritating; a
buildup of Soviet military strength is alarming; appeasing the Soviets is
a mistake and potentially dangerous—but he does not want war. Political bosses, socialism, Richard M. Nixon, "socialized" medicine, and civil
rights legislation conjure different feelings in different persons. The
Supreme Court and integration in the public schools give rise to emotion-
charged and varying viewpoints in Chicago and in Oxford, Mississippi.

Modern psychology tells us that a person's mental picture of the
world rarely corresponds with the real world. Moreover, people perceive what they want to perceive. If we like a candidate, we tend to think
that he thinks as we do. We may borrow an illustration far removed from
politics. The highly successful Russian film director V. I. Pudovkin
experimented with using the same static, expressionless close-up of the
well-known Russian actor Mosjukin in combination with three other
bits of film. The first combination was the close-up following immediately by a shot of a plate of soup on a table; the second joined Mosjukin
with a coffin in which a dead woman lay; and the third showed a little
girl playing with a toy bear. "When we showed the three combinations to
an audience which had not been let into the secret," wrote Pudovkin,
"the result was terrific. The public raved about the acting of the artist.
They pointed out the heavy pensiveness of his mood over the forgotten
soup, were touched and moved by the deep sorrow with which he looked
on the dead woman, and admired the light, happy smile with which he
surveyed the girl at play. But we knew in all cases that the face was
exactly the same."[5]

During a political campaign, each person is bombarded with appeals to vote Democratic or Republican, to vote for Brown instead of
Smith, to support the American way of life, or to endorse a specific
policy position. The individual does not pay equal attention to all these
pleas. He welcomes some of them, turns others aside immediately, and
pays only a little attention to still others. He wishes to avoid conflict and

[4] Walter Lippmann, *Public Opinion*, p. 29, copyright 1922. By permission of The Macmillan
Company, publishers.
[5] *Film Technique and Film Acting*, Lund, Humphries & Co. Ltd., London, 1954, p. 140.

having to face up to inconsistent, disturbing facts running counter to his perceptions and images. He may reconcile the questions simply by looking the other way or attaching different degrees of importance to the individual items in conflict.

A senior citizen Southern Democrat who was a segregationist faced a conflict in 1968. He found himself as a Southern Democrat inclined toward Johnson and Humphrey as Democrats and liked their medical program for the aged. But their emphasis on a federal civil rights program was disturbing. George Wallace was a fellow Democrat and a critic of the civil rights program but with little chance of success under a third-party label. Nixon was a Republican and ambivalent on civil rights and some aspects of social security. How does such a voter conceptualize this situation and arrive at a voting decision, given the alternatives of 1968? Northern anti-Vietnam liberals liked Humphrey's social orientation but bitterly opposed his war position. How to resolve this dilemma?

Perceptual and cognitive developments start in childhood. The person develops sets of beliefs over the years and a method of screening incoming stimuli. Party influences, candidate appeals, and issue conflicts come at him in efforts to get him to record a judgment in a particular way. In the interests of analytic convenience these three influences are examined individually but the voting decision most likely involves all three of them and more too.[6]

THE SIGNIFICANCE OF PARTY IDENTIFICATION

Concept. There are many concepts of party affiliation. One is party registration for voting in the direct primary. This criterion is not applicable in a dozen states that have open primary systems. Furthermore, millions of voters do not vote in the primary or take the trouble to declare their preference in order to participate in the primary. Another criterion is to observe voting behavior. But split-ticket voting poses serious problems, and a number of voters may frequently support the national candidates of one party and the local candidates of the other. The degree of voting consistency from election to election constitutes still another criterion. Self-perception or self-classification is used by many survey agencies and may be combined with voting behavior in more than one election.

In order to ascertain self-image partisanship, respondents are asked questions something like this: "Do you generally regard yourself

[6] A few relevant works treating aspects of psychological factors in politics are Leroy N. Rieselback and George J. Balch, *Psychology and Politics: An Introductory Reader*, Holt, Rinehart and Winston, Inc., New York, 1969; Robert E. Lane, *Political Life*, The Free Press, New York, 1959; Lester Milbrath, *Political Participation*, Rand, McNally & Company, Chicago, 1965.

as a Democrat, Republican, independent, or what?" Those thinking of themselves as Democrats or Republicans are then asked, "Would you call yourself a strong or not very strong Democrat or Republican?" Those classifying themselves as independents are asked whether they think of themselves as closer to the Democratic or the Republican party. The last question helps to ascertain whether the so-called independent has leanings either way and may assist in discovering whether the respondent has a covert partisanship. Independents may style themselves as such in order to conceal their commitment to a party. The independent may also be checked by examining his voting behavior over a period of time, assuming of course that he will reveal how he voted in past elections. In short, the contradiction between voting behavior on the one hand and party registration or self-description on the other shows that no one index is infallible. Through self-classification and voting behavior over a period of time, a more reliable estimate of one's party identification is possible.

Perhaps the most significant aspect of party identification is that it takes on the characteristics of a psychological concept, and its function may be best understood in such terms. Millions of people attach or tie themselves to a political party ("I am a Democrat" or "I am a Republican") without ever registering as one, rarely voting in party primaries, or without making a financial contribution. Further, the identification does not necessarily denote a voting record. Earlier we saw many examples of persons registering one way and voting another, and split-ticket voting is quite common. There are also psychological degrees of membership, such as strong, fairly strong, weak, or leaning. In a word, an individual has, or may develop, an identification with a degree of intensity and feeling, and this intensity is found to have a marked influence on voting behavior.

A political party identification also functions as a supplier of attitudes and opinions and as a symbol for most of its adherents. Unlike a labor union or a medical society, a party is exclusively a political group concerned with winning power. Although people look to it for guidance, it is not a reference group in quite the same way as a union, a family, or a church. A reference group in the latter sense is one to whom people refer when confronted with something new. The person is aware that the group is reacting in a certain way, and he will also tend to react the same way even though he is not necessarily a formal member of the group.

Consistency. The Survey Research Center, using a national sample made a self-classification estimate of degrees of partisanship from the period 1952 to 1968. The results, as shown in Table 16-1, are remarkable in several respects. First, there is a very high degree of consistency

TABLE 16-1 Distribution of party identification, 1952–1968

Identification	1952	1954	1956	1958	1960	1962	1964	1966	1968
Strong Democrat	22%	22%	21%	23%	21%	23%	24%	18%	20%
Weak Democrat	25	25	23	24	25	23	22	28	25
Independent Dem.	10	9	7	7	8	7	7	9	10
Independent	5	7	9	8	8	8	10	12	11
Independ. Republican	7	6	8	4	7	6	5	7	9
Weak Republican	14	14	14	16	13	16	17	15	14
Strong Republican	13	13	15	13	14	12	11	10	10
Apolitical	4	4	3	5	4	5	4	1	1
Total	100%	100%	100%	100%	100%	100%	100%	100%	100%

Source: Supplied to author by the Survey Research Center, University of Michigan.

in party identification over the period. Categories of Republicans rarely varied more than 2 to 3 percent. The same was true with Democratic identifiers until 1966 when weak Democrats increased somewhat, presumably at the expense of the stronger Democrats. Second, the overwhelming majority of respondents were willing to identify themselves in some degree as a Democrat or Republican. At no time have so-called independents and apoliticals collectively exceeded 14 percent. Third, Democrats (independent, weak, strong) outnumbered Republicans on the average in a ratio of about 54 percent to 34 percent. The great preponderance of Democratic over Republican affiliation was shown in the June, 1968, Gallup Poll, which used a different question and a different sample from those of the Center: 46 percent of the respondents favored the Democrats; 27 percent, the Republicans; and 27 percent regarded themselves as independents. Gallup found a growth of independents between 1960 and 1968 largely due to disenchanted Southern Democrats who chose this independent rather than Republican classification.[7] (The Survey Research Center found a smaller growth of independents in the 1960s.) Gallup found the two parties nearly equal in numerical strength in 1940 followed by a slow Republican decline, which leveled off after 1960 to 25 to 30 percent.

There is a strong tendency for an individual's preferences to survive changes in residence, even when one's migration carries him to strongholds of the opposition.[8] Most persons do not change their party affiliations upon moving into an area dominated by persons of the opposite party. Further, the more strongly one identifies his partisanship, the more likely he is to support that party from election to election. In the Center's cross section of 1956 presidential voters, 82 percent of the strong party identifiers replied they always voted for the same party; this

[7]"Independent" voting is considered in Chap. 17.
[8]Summaries in this paragraph rely heavily upon data in Campbell et. al., *The American Voter*, chaps. 6 and 16.

diminished to 60 percent for weak partisans and 36 percent for independents leaning toward a party.

As one repeatedly votes for a party's candidates his psychological identification is increased. Voters of the older generation become more fixed in their party loyalty than younger ones. This may account for the fact that the younger voters gave George Wallace considerably more support in 1968 than the older persons to whom his policy positions, such as "law and order," might seem most attractive. Older people outside the South did not see Wallace as a legitimate Democrat and therefore considered him less a conventional candidate. Younger voters' ties are less well established, and the drag of party identification is less strong.

Other Characteristics. It is reasonably well established that the most partisan people are the most interested in election campaigns and have the highest rate of voting support for their own party's presidential candidate. The 1968 election had the disturbing factors of Vietnam, internal party dissension especially among Democrats, and a formidable third-party candidacy. Yet, as shown in Tables 16-2 and 16-5, party loyalty manifested itself. The idealized conception of the independent voter as one of high interest and low partisanship is not borne out by the figures in Table 16-3. The same general pattern of high partisanship and high concern over election outcome is shown in Table 16-4. There was, however, a small degree of alienation shown in 1968 compared to 1964. (Note that there are differences in percentages of those who declare themselves *interested* as contrasted with *concerned* to one degree or another.)

The importance of partisanship is shown also by the fact that the stronger the partisan, the greater the tendency to accept the party's attitudes toward domestic issues and toward the presidential candidates.[9] In other words, the stronger the Republican identification, the stronger the tendency of the individual Republican to approve its perceived attitudes on partisan attitudes and its presidential candidate. As soon as a person is nominated for President, the partisans identify with him, and the opposition's adherents take a less favorable view of him. As observed below, partisans tend to perceive their candidate's stands on issues as similar to their own and his opponent's positions as dissimilar. If a person has attitudes inconsistent with his party faith, the party may modify the contrary opinions. Or, if the attitudes are strong, one may change his party identification. Only rarely in American history has a large block of the electorate changed its party identification so as to bring about a realignment capable of affecting the course of elections for years to come.

[9] An elaboration of this point is found in Campbell et al., *The American Voter*, pp. 128ff.

TABLE 16-2 Sources of voting support by party identification, 1964 and 1968

Party identification	Johnson	Humphrey	Goldwater	Nixon	Wallace
Strong Democrat	41%	45%	4%	4%	15%
Moderate Democrat	29	33	13	13	31
Weak Democrat	11	12	3	6	14
Independent	6	5	4	10	16
Weak Republican	2	1	14	17	12
Moderate Republican	9	4	26	27	11
Strong Republican	2	1	36	23	2
Total	100%	101%*	100%	100%	101%*

Source: Basic data for Tables 16-2, 16-3, and 16-4 were provided to the author by the staff of the Inter-University Consortium on Political Research, University of Michigan. Their data were generated from the samples and data originally collected at the University of Michigan Survey Research Center. In several tables in this chapter and in Chapters 17 and 18, comparable special data were also supplied and are especially acknowledged as coming from the Consortium. Where the Center only is the sole acknowledged source, the data were not provided by the Consortium but came from the Center itself or other published sources of the Center's tabulations. Percentages and arrangements are by the author who also assumes sole responsibility for analytic interpretations. The author acknowledges the assistance of Philip Ogden, graduate student at the University of Washington, in preparing some of the tables using Consortium data.
*Total 101% because of rounding figures.

TABLE 16-3 Party identification and interest in 1968 campaign

	Strong party identifiers	Weak party identifiers	Independents
Very much interested	51%	47%	27%
Somewhat interested	36	37	43
Not much interested	13	16	30
Total	100%	100%	100%

Source: See Table 16-2.

TABLE 16-4 Party identification and concern over campaign outcome, 1964 and 1968

	Strong party identifiers		Weak party identifiers		Independents	
	1964	1968	1964	1968	1964	1968
Care very much	47%	41%	27%	27%	13%	16%
Care pretty much	39	41	36	34	25	30
Care a little	9	12	15	22	29	36
Don't care at all	5	6	22	17	33	18
Total	100%	100%	100%	100%	100%	100%

Source: See Table 16-2.

In sum, party identification colors one's attitudes toward issues and candidates and is always important. When short-term forces such as an overriding issue or exciting, charismatic candidates enter an election, party-label response is less important. Parties are relevant reference groups in voting and seem to be more important for older persons and for those more secure in their own status. Also, the more education a voter has and the less clear his status, the weaker are his loyalties to a party.

ISSUE AND CANDIDATE INFLUENCES

Issue Orientation. Public opinion polls show a relatively low level of public information and sophistication about issues on the part of a large segment of citizenry. The Survey Research Center assigned its 1956 respondents to various levels of conceptualization based on their responses in evaluating the good and bad in the two parties and presidential candidates.[10] The largest group was oriented toward "group benefits"; a second category conceived politics largely in terms of the goodness and badness of the times. Some mentioned no issues, and others conceptualized politics in more or less ideological terms. Using these criteria, the authors concluded that fewer than a fifth viewed politics in terms of liberal, conservative, or center ideologies. Yet journalists and politicians are wont to explain electoral outcome as "a victory for the right," "a trend toward the left," or a "return to the middle of the road." Without necessarily accepting the results as characteristic of a presidential election (and the authors make no such claim), the Center's analysis is nonetheless helpful in demonstrating degrees and kinds of visualization of issues.

Typical comments of the 45 percent who located a party or candidate in terms of a relationship toward a group were that the Republicans "are more for big business. . . . The little man gets crowded out. They cater to the big men." "Democrats have always helped the farmers. . . . They are more for the working class of people." Closely related to the group-benefit category but more sophisticated in perceiving both general and specific issues are the "ideologues" and "near ideologues." Answers of persons in these categories included, "Well, the Democratic party tends to favor socialized medicine — and I'm influenced in that because I come from a doctor's family." Of Republicans, one person said, "Well, I think they're more middle-of-the-road — more conservative."

Twenty-three percent were placed in the category of perceiving "good" and "bad" times but did not associate them with a series of policies or an ideological frame of reference. For example, an elderly person was appreciative of social security checks and associated them

[10] Results reported at length in *ibid.,* chap. 10.

with the Democrats but, under probing, had no further knowledge of politics. Others viewed the economic state of the family, a general recession, and war and peace in simple terms and did not connect them with ideology or a coherent body of doctrine or with a group interest.

In the lowest level of conceptualization were 17 percent who failed to comment on any issues in response to unstructured questions. Some pointed to mudslinging and chicanery as, "I hate the darned backbiting." Others took refuge in simply commenting that they had been raised as Democrats and would always be Democrats or that "parties don't make any difference." About two-fifths of this group retreated into a simple candidate orientation with "I vote for who I think is the best man." A characteristic of this fourth category is a relatively low turnout on election day, yet their members exceed those voters who appeared to have conceptions of issues.

John H. Kessel made a comprehensive study of the data gathered by the University of Michigan Survey Research Center in 1964 and found reinforcement for the general impression that the great Democratic advantages lie in the voters' perceptions of their domestic policies, "and in being regarded as the party more helpful to population groupings such as farmers, labor, minorities and so forth. A lesser, but still significant, Democratic advantage continues to be found in the electorate's perception of their philosophy and conduct of government, and in foreign policy. Both parties tend to be weak in areas where their opponents are strong."[11]

An analysis of voter perceptions of party differences over federal involvement with programs during President Johnson's term indicated (1966) that more than half see the Democrats as much more likely to support a larger federal role (Figure 16-1). At the national level at least the Democrats as a party enjoyed much advantage in the image they had of supporting programs in the field of jobs, health, education, civil rights, and foreign aid.[12] Findings of the Louis Harris Poll also clearly differentiated the supporters of the different candidates in 1964 and 1968. The rank order of opinions went consistently from right to left, from Wallace to Goldwater to Nixon to Johnson to Humphrey. Responses to the question "Which groups are responsible for trouble

---

[11] John H. Kessel, *The Goldwater Coalition: Republican Strategies in 1964.* The Bobbs-Merrill Company, Inc., Indianapolis, 1968, p. 258, reprinted by permission of the publisher. The SRC uses a sequence of questions to ascertain voter attitudes such as "Is there anything in particular that you like (don't like) about the Republican (Democratic) party? Is there anything in particular about Johnson (Goldwater) that might make you want to vote *for (against)* him? What do you think about the government's health program? Open-ended questions of this type permit interviewers to learn what views a person has on issues and how they are related to parties and candidates.

[12] It should be noted that this survey was taken at a time of high Johnson and Democratic popularity. Surveys at other times when Republicans were in control brought favorable reactions for that party. Republicans have often enjoyed higher approval for their ability to control inflation than do Democrats.

Which party do you think is more likely to want
the federal government to:

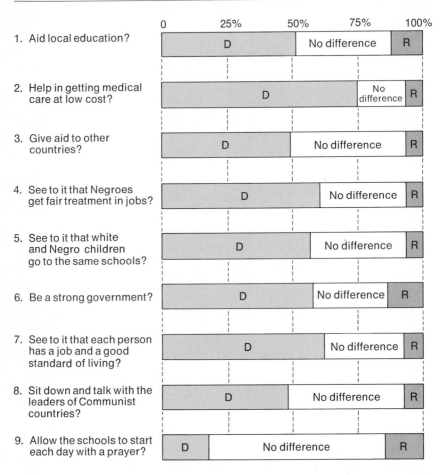

Figure 16-1   Voter perceptions of party differences over the role of the federal government, 1966.
The left-handed shaded portion of the graph represents Democratic percentages. *(Source: Data
supplied by Inter-University Consortium for Political Research.)*

in the country?" indicated that Wallace supporters were most strongly
right-wing. Communists, the federal government, Negroes, and ministers and priests were mentioned more frequently by Wallace voters than
by those who voted for Nixon and Humphrey.[13]

[13] See analysis and tables by Seymour M. Lipset and Earl Raab, "The Wallace Whitelash,"
Transaction, vol. 7, pp. 23–35, December 1969.

At the same time, a majority of state governorships were held by Republicans. After the 1969 elections, they had improved this advantage and held thirty-two of the executive positions.[14] Whatever else this may show, it seems clear that the voters of a great many states are less influenced by the party label in their gubernatorial preferences.

Candidate Attachment. American politics is commonly spoken of as a politics of personality, and it is a badge of status with some to proclaim that they pay little attention to party labels and "vote for the man." When the voter attempts to isolate the man from the party and issues, he presumably is looking toward personal qualities. A voter may be attracted to a candidate because he foresees him acting in certain ways. A nominee for prosecuting attorney or mayor may be seen as sure to "go after crooks" or "clean up the mess." A voter might believe that Nixon would balance the budget or that Humphrey would aid labor unions. Actually, there is often an issue lurking behind the orientation toward a candidate. The issue may be very unclear or perhaps specific, but the voter sees the person as having the qualities to act in a way desired by the voter.

Sometimes the tendency to identify with the candidate is so strong that one incorrectly perceives where the candidate stands on an issue. Politicians believe it an asset to be, in effect, all things to all men, to be able to run with the hares and hunt with the hounds. A blurred image may enable one to do this, for the voter likes to have his candidate think as he does. The Elmira, New York, study found that a partisan tended to see his candidate's stand as similar to his own and his opponent's position as dissimilar.[15] Conversely, a partisan tends not to perceive differences with his own candidate or similarities to the opposition. Further, the more strongly a voter feels about his choice, the more likely he is to see the candidate's stands on issues as similar to his own. Also, party preference does not seem to have a marked effect on the voter's perception of where candidates stand on policies. However, the "don't knows" are more frequent among partisans who take a different position from their own candidate. "Selective inattention" may also permit one to gloss over inconsistencies among the leaders of a party with which one identifies and to overlook the fact that one's own view of the leader's position is actually not the true position.

Persons may also be strongly drawn toward a candidate for personal reasons that are unrelated to expected actions or stands on issues.

---

[14] In the 1968 election, Republicans raised their total governorships to thirty-one but lost one seat when Gov. Spiro Agnew of Maryland resigned to become Vice President and was replaced by a Democrat. In 1969, Republicans captured the state executive positions from Democrats in New Jersey and Virginia.

[15] Berelson et al., *op. cit.*, chap. 10.

They like the "family men" or persons particularly believed to have integrity, sincerity, and good morals. Eisenhower's image as a kindly, nonpartisan, family man was found to be most important in his election; "I like Ike" was a widely held view. Even in 1956, after nearly four years in office, voter association of Eisenhower with domestic issues was surprisingly slight.[16] Personal attributes continued to dominate. Mr. Stevenson was widely traveled, gave much attention to foreign policies in his campaign speeches, yet made no significant impression on the electorate with relation to foreign affairs. Very few flaws in the Eisenhower image developed between 1952 and 1956. Personal qualities, including integrity, patriotism, religiosity, and sincerity, were more frequently mentioned in 1956; only age and health were significant unfavorable responses. His record as President and administrator received comparatively few references, leading to the conclusion "that in 1956 Eisenhower was honored not so much for his importance as President as for the quality of his person."[17] In contrast, the Stevenson image was found to have undergone a perceptible change for the worse between his two bids for the Presidency.

Returning to Kessels' study, Johnson in 1964 enjoyed a highly favorable image for his experience and ability, though in personal attractiveness he and Goldwater were rated[18] about the same. Judged by the number of comments from those interviewed, the personal candidacies appeared more salient for respondents than issues or party affiliation. Goldwater received many negative comments not only for his positions on domestic policies but also for his character and background, especially intelligence and impulsiveness. In contrast there was a favorable attitude toward Johnson as Kennedy's successor who could "carry out" the late President's policies. Attitudes also followed party identification. Of the Democrats, 90 percent made positive comments about Johnson's ability; this lowered to 84 percent from independents and to 67 percent from Republicans. Although 71 percent of the Republican respondents commented favorably on Goldwater's ability, this declined to 42 and 28 percent respectively among independents and Democrats. Again, the force of party identification shows through these figures.

INTERRELATIONSHIP OF INFLUENCES

Interaction of Variables. It is implied in these brief observations of psychological influences that a person's vote is determined in a complex

[16]Summaries in this paragraph are drawn from the interviews conducted by the Survey Research Center in 1952 and 1956. Results and tables are found in Campbell et al., *The American Voter*, chap. 3.

[17]*Ibid.*, p. 56.

[18]Data in this paragraph are taken from Kessel, *op. cit.*, chap. 9.

way, depending on how he totals up his feelings about parties, issues, and candidates. We considered each factor and illustrated some of the perceptions that respondents had toward each; yet it is obvious that there is an interaction between issue perception and personality, between party and candidate, and between issue position and party identification. The variables sometimes reinforce each other, other times set up opposition to each other. When voters were asked what they liked or disliked about Kennedy, Goldwater, or Humphrey, a number of them replied they liked or disliked the candidate's party. Party preferences tend to be acquired early in life, and remain the same for most of people's lives. An individual's vote will likely depend on how the more or less constant party preference squares with his short-run feelings about issues and his images of candidates.

When all three influences — party, issues, and personalities — are reasonably well harmonized, the majority party is likely to maintain or reinstate itself in power, as evidenced in 1936 through 1948 and in 1960. Stirring issues, exciting candidates, and strong dislikes may operate on the stabilizing factor of party identification on a short-run basis, resulting in deviations to Eisenhower in 1952 and 1956 and to Nixon or Wallace in 1968.

Although post-World War II voting studies are virtually unanimous in their conclusions that party identification is more closely related to the actual vote than any other single variable, we cannot always be certian of the sequence of the influences, and there is something of the chicken and egg dilemma. A person without strong party feelings may become violently disturbed over an issue. Then he can support a candidate and a party, the latter being the one toward which he had a parental or latent disposition. On the other hand, his feelings may be so intense and his party and candidate so much in opposition to his views that he will be drawn to the other party. Such conflicts undoubtedly led many voters to switch from Republican to Democratic in 1932 and to remain with their adopted party. Journalists are speculating that some upheaval is now in progress in the South, moving voters from Democratic to Republican because of the Kennedy and Johnson activities on behalf of civil rights. Party loyalty helps an identifier formulate his attitudes toward new issues and policies. Some people, particularly new voters, may be drawn into a party by the personality of one of its leaders, such as Franklin D. Roosevelt. But many young voters who were drawn to Eisenhower because of his symbolic qualities and personal attributes failed to become Republicans. This was probably due to the failure to associate Eisenhower with authentic Republicanism and because of the attractiveness of Kennedy in 1960, especially among the young.

In order for an issue to affect a partisan choice at the polls, a person must be aware of it, have some feeling about it, and identify it with a candidate and/or a party. A voter cannot vote directly for or against a policy except on measures submitted to popular vote, so he has to see the connection between a candidate and a party and his policy preference. It is highly probable that large numbers of voters fail to have a clear-cut understanding of issues and the party-candidate positions on them. For example, Sen. Eugene McCarthy, a sharp critic of the Johnson administration's Vietnam policy, entered the New Hampshire presidential primary in 1968. He offered the only alternative to Johnson at the time and polled a creditable vote not only from those opposed to Johnson's policy, but from some critics of the President who felt he did not pursue a hard enough line against Hanoi! Many in "hawkish" moods appeared to support McCarthy without having a perception of where he stood on the matter. A few other aspects of the 1968 campaign further illustrate the cross-current and interrelationships of man, issue, and party.

Case in Point: 1968: The 1968 electoral outcome reflected one of the most massive shifts from a party in American history. President Johnson received 61 percent of the popular vote, but Humphrey got slightly less than 43 percent. While Humphrey's net loss from the Johnson total was nearly 12 million votes, Nixon gained only 4.5 million over Goldwater and more than 2 million less than he had drawn against Kennedy in 1960. Among whites who voted in both elections, a full third switched party. Tables 16-2 and 16-5 show the defections and strengths of the candidates with degrees of party identifiers in 1968 compared to 1964 (SRC sample). About one Goldwater voter of every five turned either to Humphrey or to Wallace. But 40 percent of Nixon's votes came from citizens who had supported Johnson in 1964. The Johnson-Nixon switchers greatly outweighed the flow away from Goldwater to Humphrey and Wallace.[19]

With Goldwater as candidate, Johnson was able to carry 43 percent of the moderate Republicans while Goldwater carried only 18 percent of the moderate Democrats, with a large share of these from the South. Internal dissension within the Democratic party and the Humphrey candidacy dissipated this advantage and Nixon enjoyed a net gain in every category. A considerable portion of Nixon's strength, however, came from Republicans who were returning home after deserting Goldwater.

In 1968, as in 1952, a considerable majority of the electorate classified itself as Democratic, but the grievances with the incumbent's

---

[19] Estimates of switchers are based on the SRC sample. For a more complete analysis, see Philip E. Converse, Warren E. Miller, Jerrold G. Rusk, and Arthur C. Wolfe, "Continuity and Change in American Politics: Parties and Issues in the 1968 Election," *American Political Science Review*, vol. 68, pp. 1083–1105, 1969

TABLE 16-5 Percentages of various party identifiers shifting from the Democrats in 1964 to the Republicans in 1968

Party identification	Democratic vote		Republican vote		Net change
	1964	1968	1964	1968	(Gain GOP 1968)
Strong Democrat	95%	92%	5%	8%	3%
Moderate Democrat	82	68	18	32	14
Weak Democrat	90	64	10	36	26
Independent	77	30	23	70	47
Weak Republican	25	5	75	95	20
Moderate Republican	43	11	57	89	32
Strong Republican	10	3	90	97	7

Source: Inter-University Consortium on Political Research (see Table 16-2).
Note: Data aggregated to reflect only the Democratic-Republican contest; third parties are ignored.

record led to much desertion of the party—a case of short-run forces overrunning the stability of party identification. Interviews with SRC respondents showed that Humphrey was linked with and highly assimilated to the Johnson image. On public opinion polls, Humphrey showed strength with those for whom the Johnson administration enjoyed popularity or at least not too much disaffection. During the campaign, the Johnson popularity was at low ebb with scarcely 40 percent feeling the President was doing a good job.

The three overriding issues of Vietnam, racial confrontations, and "law and order" hurt the Democrats because many voters were critical of Johnson's performance in these areas. Many of the peace advocates who disliked the Vietnam policy faulted the President for not dealing more vigorously with peace demonstrators! Reactions showed that the public was beginning to feel the Republicans could do a better job in managing the Vietnam war. Backlash whites were crying for sterner suppression of black riots and bemoaned the breakdown of authority and discipline. Humphrey did not enjoy an image of being sufficiently different from or independent of Johnson in meeting these problems.

There were defections from both parties to Wallace, but he captured about 60 percent of his votes from persons who classified themselves as some degree of Democrat and only 25 percent of his votes came from the Republicans (Table 16-2).

The George Wallace candidacy was issue oriented. Half of the reasons volunteered by respondents of the SRC sample for favorable feelings toward him had to do with positions he took on current issues; only a little more than a quarter of the reactions favorable to Humphrey and Nixon were of this mold. Among whites voting for Wallace, 40 percent said they wanted segregation, but only 10 percent supporting the two major party candidates took this position. Of the white voters for the two major party candidates, 36 percent wanted a "tougher stand" in Vietnam even if it meant invasion; 67 percent of the Wallace voters took this position. Concisely, party label was important for Nixon and Humphrey, but issues were salient for Wallace. Interestingly, Wallace's voters were more favorable to the "liberal" label than were Nixon voters. This was probably due to his populism and support of much social legislation. In contrast, the Goldwater voters were more ideological in focus in terms of conservatism.[20]

In summary, the pull of the party label was not strong enough to combat the disadvantages Humphrey faced because of an association, in the minds of millions of switchers, with the Johnson administration, whose ability to cope with the great issues was causing deep-seated anxiety. Voters could not easily connect Nixon with these since he had not been in public office for eight years. Even though 1968 was a "deviating election," the fact remains that Humphrey still polled very heavily among his fellow Democrats with 90 percent of his votes coming from those seeing themselves as Democrats. While Nixon made much greater inroads into the Democratic vote than did Humphrey with Republicans, 67 percent of his vote came from self-classified Republicans.

One of the most striking aspects of the electoral outcome was the continued strength of congressional Democrats in the face of serious erosion at the presidential level. It is estimated that roughly 54 percent of the electorate split their ballots. Republicans added only four seats in the House and five in the Senate, leaving them still a minority party.[21] Democratic candidates for the House outpolled Republicans by well over a million votes and, through losing ground, their senatorial candidates bested Republicans by more than 300,000 votes.

In state elections, the factors hurting the Humphrey candidacy did not carry much weight. In forty-three state legislative races, the total Democratic vote was 57.5 percent or only 0.2 percent less than in 1966. As noted earlier, Republicans did well in state executive races, netting five seats to raise their control to thirty-one governorships.

Considerable split-ticket voting in state elections results in divided government of one kind or another in about a fifth of the states. It may be hypothesized that party identification is less influential in state and county elections than in presidential ones, but this has not yet been established by extensive research. In view of the fairly large number of modified one-party states, however, it seems obvious that party identification is a cue for voters in such elections as well.

[20] Further, the Goldwater vote was more urban than that of Wallace, who had appeal in small towns and rural areas. Wallace also received a larger share of the young and of those with only a grade-school education than Goldwater and had labor-union support, which was largely denied to Goldwater.

[21] The Wallace party did not field a national slate of congressional candidates, and it is not easy to predict the outcome had they chosen to do so. The few candidates running under the Wallace banner polled only 177,000 votes for the House and 171,000 for the Senate.

SIGNIFICANCE OF VOTER SURVEYS FOR PARTIES

One of the most important findings of survey research and of aggregate data used in this chapter is the great tenacity and durability of party identification, which in turn goes far toward explaining the tenacity and durability of the two-party system. General distaste for third parties exists except on very rare occasions. Both of the major parties begin each national campaign with a huge block of dependable identifiers whose commitment varies from strong to weak. The more zealous of these are inclined to be the most interested in the outcome of elections, to expose themselves to political information, to go to the polls in larger numbers, and to vote a straighter ticket. It is probable that the stronger the partisan, the more he sees party differences in policy position and the more strongly he supports his party's attitudes on issues.

It becomes essential for campaign activists to hold the ardent partisans and pursue the weaker ones on the opposite side as well as those in their own party. Identification with a party is to be distinguished from membership in it. A person may not belong to a party but may regularly support its nominees because he likes what the party appears to stand for and associates himself with its candidates. Party is a symbol in the minds of citizens, a psychological matter, not simply an institutional leadership device of the party or the government. Our increasing knowledge of the voter's perceptions necessitates some change in the function of party organization. In addition to administrative duties, such as registration and election work, local activists need to try to explain what the party stands for; to strengthen it with the faithful; and to win adherents, especially among new voters. This effort is especially necessary with the nominal and wavering voters. The massive split-ticket voting shows that a party identification does not mean *ipso facto* that candidates of the voter's own faith will receive his vote. Beliefs are important in choosing a party, and beliefs about how a party stands on issues are important considerations underlying a person's party identification.

A party enjoying a substantial majority of identifiers is likely to stay in power over long periods. Upheavals such as those occurring in 1860 and 1932 are rare and were not carefully studied at the time in order to discover the diverse reasons for the radical change in party affiliation. But the outcome of successive elections thereafter attested to the strength of a new dominant party majority. That voters are not strongly oriented toward ideology or passionately interested in public affairs has contributed toward low-tension politics and stability. The voter appears to have a general image that Republicans are more conservative than Democrats, even though he is often not aware of a party's or its candidate's stand on a specific issue. From the standpoint of political survival, it is probably true, as the authors of *Voting* assert, that if the voter "knows the big thing about the parties, he does not need to know all the little things. The basic role a party plays as an institution in American life is more important to his voting than a particular stand on a particular issue."[22] As has been said throughout this volume, moreover, competition for public office (nonpartisan elections excepted) takes place within the basic division of the electoral strength of the two parties, a fact in itself contributive to stability.

GAPS IN OUR KNOWLEDGE

The theories growing out of voter perception studies have mainly applied to national parties, issues, and candidates. These assumptions, influences, and explanations will be refined through a continuity of studies in the years ahead. Political scientists who relate their empirical evidence to psychological theory will be called on to review their assumptions and hypotheses as psychologists bring in new findings. Causal factors in voting will continue to offer a rich field for research and the application of rigorous empirical testing of the theories advanced by political sociologists.

Local and Nonpartisan Elections. A particular challenge to the student of voting behavior is afforded at the level of local parties, issues, and candidates. Membership in a party means little in terms of local elections in many American communities, and numerous voters register in the dominant party but vote in the opposite one. Further, elements present in national elections are not necessarily present to the same degree in local elections. Nonpartisan elections, now used in 60 percent of the municipalities with more than 5,000 population, offer a case in point. Party labels are missing on the ballots and for the most part in campaign literature and publicity. With the party factor diluted if not removed, what are the major guideposts for the voter? Issues and candidates remain in the forefront, and, if we believe the findings noted above, there is a relatively low level of awareness and perception of issues. How does the voter make up his mind? Can we be certain that the image of the candidate is likely to be the major factor in the voter's decision? What other elements or signals can the voter call up to help him choose from among the contenders? While awaiting extensive examinations of local elections, we can perhaps afford the luxury of speculation.

First, it is a fair assumption that voters view various offices in quite different lights and that, community by community, some offices are regarded as more competitive than others. The mayor's office may be seen quite differently from that of city controller, city clerk, and

[22] Berelson et al., *op. cit.*, p. 321.

library trustee; a judgeship may be placed in an entirely separate category in the voter's mind. There is little question in many cities using the nonpartisan ballot for municipal offices that the partisan affiliation of the candidates is well known. This is the likely case with mayoralty candidates, perhaps less so with the remainder. In these instances, the party may be a cue-giving device, even though the partisan affiliation of the candidates is played down and goes unmentioned officially. Party affiliation is, however, usually minimized by the candidates, who spend their time stressing their personal qualifications and plans for civic improvement. Only rarely does a nonpartisan mayoralty candidate appeal for votes on the basis of party loyalty; voters, moreover, would probably resent it.[23]

Second, candidates for the city council and many lesser offices as well as judges commonly enjoy long incumbency. Even though they were of known partisanship before their election, they become very nonpartisan in the public eye. Republican clubs in Seattle, for example, endorse city council incumbents for reelection who were, and presumably still are, Democrats. Parenthetically, as observed earlier, some state and local officers chosen on partisan ballots develop a similar aura of nonpartisanship and remain in office long after their party loses the governorship and other offices. There are other cases in which the partisan identity of councilmen and other officials has never been known. In nonpartisan elections, voters appear to be influenced largely by name familiarity and by the image projected by the candidate himself. Persons with reputations in business, civic and community affairs, or athletics successfully seek office as a result of name familiarity.

Third, the absence of party labels to guide them and without personal knowledge of the candidates, voters usually follow endorsement by the press, municipal leagues, and fraternal, occupational, and social groups. In judicial elections, endorsement by the bar association or by prominent attorneys may sway voters who have little background with which to make a judgment. Failing all else, the voter must rely on the most vague perception of what the office requires and what little he knows of a candidate's background. Religion, nationality, divorce, occupations, group identifications of the candidate may influence the voter even though none of these has relevance to the office sought.

In the very few studies of voting in nonpartisan elections, it is obvious that there are striking differences in the political cultures of the various locales. In Atlanta's mayoralty contests, for example, blacks are well organized by the Negro Voters' League and unity, if

[23] In their study of nonpartisan elections in Des Moines, Robert H. Salisbury and Gordon Black found that "traditional party affiliation makes a somewhat small contribution to the vote in nonpartisan elections than in partisan elections." See "Class and Party in Partisan and Non-partisan Elections: The Case of Des Moines," *American Political Science Review*, vol. 57, p. 588, 1963.

not enthusiasm, is mustered behind the most satisfactory candidate. This leads to a considerable amount of black voting.[24] In other cities, labor-conservative, business-labor and region within the city have supplied bases for voting when party affiliations are obscured.

Elections for nonpartisan school officials raise perhaps slightly different problems for the voter than elections for mayor and council, for the intervention of party is very often negligible. Some school board campaigns are waged almost exclusively around issues and satisfaction or dissatisfaction with the costs and curriculum of public education. During the bitter Nixon-Brown gubernatorial battle in California in 1962, a sharp contest was waged for the nonpartisan post of state superintendent. Two nonincumbent educators, vying for the post, debated face to face throughout the state. Although one was known to be a Republican and the other a Democrat, the two presented the electorate with clear-cut educational alternatives unrelated to party lines. One, the winner, campaigned as a forthright critic of John Dewey's progressive education theories; the other took a much more liberal approach. Both had fair images as candidates, so issues probably had much to do with the voter's decision.

Voting on Propositions. Public perceptions of ballot propositions have been subjected to little analysis by depth interview techniques. By looking at the outcome of propositions in a given community over a period of time, one could find evidence to prove almost anything he wished. In some elections, voters appear to exercise a rather high degree of understanding of the proposals and wise judgments in picking and choosing among a fairly long list of measures. In another election, the electoral decisions on some measures look totally irrational, with voters presumably failing to recognize and support their own self-interests. Parties sometimes take positions on measures, particularly if they are noncontroversial. Where parties remain aloof, presumably awareness and perception of the issue is the voter's sole guide. Perhaps this accounts for the drop-off in vote for propositions. But another element very often enters the picture—the position taken by interest groups. If the voter has a meaningful identification with one of the organizations endorsing or opposing a proposition and is aware of its support or opposition, he has a signpost if he wishes to use it. Here the nonparty reference group may play a determinative role in the voter's electoral decision. The outcome is often, if not usually, determined by the success of interested groups in arousing and getting their own members and sympathetic nonmembers to the polls. But on numerous technical and enormously

[24] M. Kent Jennings and Harmon Zeigler, "Class, Party, and Race in Four Types of Elections: The Case of Atlanta," *Journal of Politics*, vol. 66, pp. 391–407, 1966.

complex issues and amendments on which the electorate is asked to render a verdict, it is hard to formulate a theory explaining voting behavior.

Williams and Adrian in their study of voting on referendums in four northern middle-sized industrial cities found great variations in voter's responses to issues placed on the ballot.[25] Major support for council-sponsored referendums involving innovations and increased financial burdens came from the higher socioeconomic sectors in the cities. Opposition was greater in the working-class districts.[26]

A sample of Seattle voters in three different elections were asked where they obtained information on ballot propositions; with two out of three respondents, the voters' pamphlet received more mentions than any other single source.[27] The pamphlet is mailed to the homes of all registered voters and contains arguments for and against each proposition. On some propositions no negative arguments are carried; and, where this is the case, there has consistently been a small negative vote. The absence of negative argument generally indicates negligible party and pressure-group opposition. With such cues missing one might speculate that many voters refer to the pamphlet for affirmative argument and follow the recommendations by affirmative votes. Legislative-sponsored referenda and coalition-sponsored initiatives that provoke no significant opposition are quite generally accepted by the voters.

Because ballot propositions are largely episodic, the operative patterns of voting are much less likely than when candidates, partisan or nonpartisan, structure the alternatives. In many cities, however, certain coalitions line up against each other in support of measures that involve spending, educational policy, control of liquor, and racial relations. Jennings and Zeigler found racial overtones in Atlanta voting that on certain bond issues all strata gave support but the great affirmative vote in Negro precincts was not matched by that of any other group.[28]

Many propositions as well as a host of state and local offices would be better removed from the ballot. Until such time as this takes place—and the short-ballot movement proceeds at a snail's pace—voter

[25] Oliver Williams and Charles Adrian, *Four Cities: A Study in Comparative Policy-Making,* University of Pennsylvania Press, Philadelphia, 1963. The cities remained anonymous, being designated as Alpha, Beta, Delta, and Gamma. The study also found that nonpartisanship strengthened the influence of those persons traditionally voting Republican and whose values were those held by the upper end of the socioeconomic continuum.

[26] Other illuminating data on this point are found in Edward C. Banfield, "Public-Regardingness as a Value Premise in Voting Behavior," *American Political Science Review,* vol. 58, pp. 876–887, 1964.

[27] Newspapers were second in mention. Data have not been published.

[28] *Op. cit.,* p. 400. A comprehensive analysis of factors influencing votes on bond issues in De Kalb County, Georgia, is provided by Zeigler and coauthor Alvin Baskoff, *Voting Patterns in a Local Election,* J. B. Lippincott Company, Philadelphia, 1964.

perceptions of these matters are a challenge to the researcher. When strong party orientations are not applicable, what does an individual use for a frame of reference and standard of judgment? If we assume that a person is more susceptible to suggestion when he has no adequate mental context on which he can base an interpretation of a campaign statement, what kind of suggestion or signals is he most likely to receive? Campaign managers as well as students would like to know the answer to this one. What, if anything, can be done with voters whose mental context is so rigidly structured that they are insusceptible to ideas coming from an outgroup while they uncritically accept those from their own group? These do not exhaust the list of frontiers for which we need more adequate theories, but they give the scholar and practitioners of politics enough to ponder at the outset.

A considerable portion of this chapter has analyzed what some have called the "intervening variables" in voting behavior. These are the attitudes toward parties, issues, and candidates which most immediately insert themselves between more general and distant forces and the voter's decision. But feelings about issues, candidates, and parties are not the only dimensions and determinants of voting behavior. Behind these are many influences that affect these feelings and attitudes, such as family, religion, race, socioeconomic status, and the cross-pressures generated by them. They form the substance of the following chapter.

FOR FURTHER READING

Dahl, Robert A.: *Modern Political Analysis*, 1963.
Davies, James C.: *Human Nature in Politics*, 1963.
Eulau, Heinz: *The Behavioral Persuasion in Politics*, 1963.
Free, Lloyd A.: *The Political Beliefs of Americans: A Study of Public Opinion*, 1967.
Hyman, Herbert H.: *Political Socialization*, 1959.
Lane, Robert E.: *Political Ideology*, 1962.
Lasswell, Harold D.: *Psychopathology and Politics*, 1930.
Ranney, Austin: *Essays on the Behavioral Study of Politics*, 1962.
Smith, M. Brewster, Jerome S. Bruner, and Robert W. White: *Opinions and Personality*, 1956.
Storing, Herbert J. (ed.): *Essays on the Scientific Study of Politics*, 1961.
Stouffer, Samuel A.: *Communism, Conformity and Civil Liberties*, 1955.
Wallas, Graham: *Human Nature in Politics*, 1921.

Political demands are made in behalf of the egos with
which a given age identifies, and are justified by
reference to the resulting "we." Politics begins when
egos are emotionally bound together in relation to such
demands in the name of the identified groups.

HAROLD LASSWELL and ABRAHAM KAPLAN

CHAPTER 17 SOCIAL DIFFERENTIATION AND VOTING PREFERENCES

Man is born free, remarked Rousseau, but everywhere is in chains. The
young American may not be in chains, but he soon discovers that everywhere he is thrown in contact with people—first his family and relatives,
then his friends, and finally, his adult associates. Since very few choose
the life of a recluse or hermit, it is not surprising that a whole science,
with a steadily increasing amount of already vast literature, has developed to analyze man in relation to other human beings. Much of the
study is centered in the social forces which shape the lives and attitudes
of persons. Although it cannot be measured precisely, we know that
groups influence a person's political attitudes, interests, and actions.

The sociologist's conception of voting behavior tends to proceed
from the importance of occupation and from diverse demographic
characteristics such as socioeconomic status, religion, race, age, and sex.

There is undoubtedly a nexus between psychological factors and sociological ones. Without demeaning the efforts of the writers of *The American Voter*, among others, there is still to be formulated a full understanding and explanation of the relationship between these two influences. There are theoretical frontiers both here and in the strictly psychological explanations of why people vote as they do. A problem confronting the theorist of group influences on voting is the difficulty of isolating the impact of one group from that of another.

Data on voting behavior by social groups are available from many different sources, and in succeeding pages several of these are used, such as the U.S. Census Bureau, the Gallup and Harris Polls, and the University of Michigan Survey Research Center (SRC). The Republican National Committee has also compiled many useful data. Each uses different sets and numbers of respondents. For this reason variations in percentages are usually found, but perhaps more remarkable and reassuring is the fact that, in terms of overall patterns, the various sets of data point in the same direction and tend to reinforce each other.[1]

TYPES OF GROUPS

Primary Groups. At the outset, reaching one early in life, are primary groups consisting of people with whom one has frequent and regular face-to-face contacts. These include initially one's parents and those living in the household, then friends, and later, husbands and wives and coworkers. They exercise powerful effects on voting behavior. Studies point out that husband-wife pairs are probably the most politically homogeneous of all groups. Only one pair in twenty-two disagreed in the Erie County, Ohio, panel of husbands and wives, all of whom had decided to vote. There are three possible explanations of this high level of agreement. First, it is usually true that at the time of marriage the man and woman shared a similar political viewpoint if not the same party affiliation. Second, there is the influence, particularly, of the husband on the wife. In the national sample of *The Voter Decides*, 27 percent of the married women said that their husbands' opinions helped them decide on their choices, as contrasted with only 6 percent of the married men who admitted being influenced by their spouses.[2]

---

[1] Survey Research Center materials are extensively used in more comprehensive accounts than here by Angus Campbell et al., *The American Voter* (1960) and *Elections and the Political Order* (1966) published by John Wiley & Sons, Inc., New York, and William H. Flanigan, *Political Behavior of the American Electorate*, Allyn and Bacon, Inc., Boston, 1968. An account especially designed for the general reader and relying heavily on Census Bureau data and commercial polls is that by Jerry W. Friedheim, *Where Are the Voters?* Washington National Press, Inc., Washington, D.C., 1968.

[2] Angus Campbell, Gerald Gurin, and Warren E. Miller, *The Voter Decides*, Harper & Row, Publishers, Incorporated, New York, 1954, p. 206.

(Perhaps few men like to admit being influenced by their wives.) Third, members of a primary group are socially, economically, and ethnically alike and the same general influences are at work on them.

In the chapter on political socialization, a significant effect of parental party preference on offspring was observed. In the Survey Research Center's national sample in 1958, it was found that where both parents were Democrats and one or both were politically active, 50 percent of the offspring were "strong Democrats" and 29 percent identified themselves as "weak Democrats"; only 2 percent became "strong Republicans." Where parents had no consistent partisanship or were inactive politically, many fewer of the offspring were strong Republicans or Democrats, and more than twice as many classified themselves as independent. Family influence also appears operative on whether one votes at all. About three-fourths of the Center's 1952 panel of unmarried people whose families did not vote failed to vote.

People seek like-minded persons for their friends, and it is therefore not surprising that groups of friends very often show a high degree of political agreement, including party affiliation. In some cases, this homogeneity is almost as great as within families. The Elmira and Center panels have corroborated the close relationship of one's own vote to that of friends and coworkers.[3] The former indicates that voters who belong to politically mixed groups feel less strongly about their voting intentions than those whose friendship groups are all in the agreement. Ninety percent of the Center's 1952 respondents who did not vote had friends who were also nonvoters.

The immediate personal environment dominated by primary groups lends stability to the voter. These groups provide him with an atmosphere of political agreement and reinforce his views. The family transmits, indoctrinates, and sustains the political loyalties of its members. A person's political attachments are affected also by his family's life style, such as occupation, income, and religion.[4] When one is no longer under parents' influence, one's spouse, friends, and coworkers are around to bolster one's faith. Seldom do they challenge one's political faith, but rather support and bolster it. When they do challenge it, the voter is placed in a conflict situation and is cross-pressured. How

---

[3] The generalizations selected for mention in this and the following chapter are ones which have been corroborated by two or more national and regional studies. The reader will find a list of some 200 generalizations and findings growing out of the Elmira study and compared with the Center's and several other studies in Bernard R. Berelson, Paul F. Lazarsfeld, and William N. McPhee, *Voting*, The University of Chicago Press, Chicago, 1954, pp. 331-347. These in turn are compared with findings in Colorado, Iowa, Minnesota, and Washington, in William N. McPhee and William A. Glaser (eds.), *Public Opinion and Congressional Elections*, The Free Press, New York, 1962, pp. 259-272.

[4] On this point see Herbert McClosky and Harold E. Dahlgren, "Primary Group Influence on Party Loyalty," *The American Political Science Review*, vol. 53, pp. 757-776, 1959.

TABLE 17-1 Distinctiveness of presidential vote among certain groups, 1956

Group	Percentages
Union members	+20.4%
Negroes	
Non-South	+11.6
South	+15.4
Catholics	+ 2.9
Jews	+45.4

Source: Adapted from Angus Campbell, Warren E. Miller, Philip E. Converse, and Donald E. Stokes, *The American Voter*, John Wiley & Sons, Inc., New York, 1960, p. 300.
Note: The figure +20.4, for example, indicates the percentage by which members of unions deviated from nonunion voters of comparable life situations in voting for the Democratic candidate for President.

reconciliation is effected will be noted later after we have considered the influences of other types of groups.

Secondary Groups. The psychological determinants in the causal background of voting behavior as well as the influence of primary groups are apparent, even if not satisfactorily measured. From the tables appearing later in this chapter, it is clear that secondary groups are additional elements in the voting picture, but the problems of influence and conceptualization are very difficult. One study by the Center established the fact of group influence by means of a control group and a test group. Persons in both were selected on the basis of generally comparable life situations, such as the generations a participant's family had spent in the United States, age, income, education, and occupation. The major difference was that the control-group respondents were not members of the group (unions, Catholics). Table 17-1 shows the deviation in 1956 in percentage voting Democratic in the two-party vote. The Catholic–non-Catholic sample from the same general life situation showed only a small distinctiveness on the one hand, and the Jews a high distinctiveness on the other, with labor union members and Negroes in between.

Such analyses are not available for the large number of other groups, but this study indicates that some groups appear to have considerably stronger influence on the voting behavior than others. Further, in the case of these same categories, the persons who were more highly identified with their respective groups were, without exception, more inclined to vote Democratic, but not to the same extent. In other words, while there is a tendency for members of each of these groups to vote Democratic, those more highly identified with their group were more Democratic than those weakly identified with it.

This evidence of the influence of a group on its members invites further speculation and theorizing on the causal relation between group membership and one's vote. Nonprimary groups affect the individual, provided he realizes that he has a common affinity with them. Negroes and Japanese-Americans share an identification with other Negroes and Japanese-Americans. College professors may join the American Association of University Professors, but even if they do not, they are conscious of an identity with other professors; public school teachers join with others to conquer problems of adequate financial support, public goodwill, improved curriculum, and academic freedom. Jews, Catholics, farmers, seamen, municipal officials, truck drivers, and persons in scores of other social and occupational categories may meet only a relatively few of their fellows yet are conscious of common problems and outlook. There are other people, such as teen-agers, the elderly, and women, who have some common characteristics but who are less conscious of their identifications. Nonetheless, they may act or vote in a way that suggests a slight difference from others. Many of these shared interests become important enough for those interested to form an association to advance the group's interests.

Groups become points of reference for the individual. The degree of influence exercised by a group on the political views of one of its members is the object of much speculation.[5] In Chapter 16, it was observed that psychological attachment and feeling about a political party differ much in intensity from indifference to strong emotional involvement. This is likewise true of a nonparty group. Some persons feel keenly about their union or their veterans organization, while others have only a nominal membership and care little for it. It is a fair inference that the nominal members are more likely to deviate from the views of the group under the pressure of nongroup forces than those strongly identified with it. Generally, but not invariably, the longer one belongs to a group, the more one tends to strengthen his identification with it. Further, as groups are successful in maintaining their cohesiveness and a high degree of loyalty, they may have more success in wielding influence over their members.

A crucial factor in the relationship between a group and its members in political affairs and especially in voting is the extent to which

[5] For an explanation of some of the hypotheses involved, see Howard E. Freeman and Morris Showel, "The Political Influence of Voluntary Associations," *The Public Opinion Quarterly*, vol. 15, pp. 703–714, 1951–1952.

the group projects itself into the political level. A church laymen's organization, for example, may profess neutrality in presidential elections and indeed may rarely concern itself with political affairs. The AFL-CIO and its local affiliates as well as Americans for Constitutional Action make endorsements of candidates for public office and intervene, as it were, at the voting level. The church group is essentially not politically oriented in terms of ideology; the other two groups have a professed ideological position and want to direct the vote of their members toward the perceived group goals.

It is not enough that a group have professed political voting positions. Unless the members are aware of (1) the positions taken and (2) the revelance of the social characteristics of the group to political behavior, the group's influence may be ineffectual. Perceived political relevance and saliency, then, are vital to political influence. To be highly persuasive, group leaders will need to have the members look to them for leadership in the political sphere. If nonmembers look to them for hints, the leaders may also have some influence on them. This also works in reverse. When a nonmember perceives the position of a group he does not like, he may be impelled to vote the opposite way — the familiar "kiss-of-death" reaction to which politicians are very sensitive.

Finally, and one of the most serious problems for scholars of causal relationships, is the matter of direct and indirect influence. In the former, the member takes a cue from his group as a result of overt or subtle activity by the group. His political behavior is along the lines that his group expects of him; in other words, it is group-determined and quite consciously so. He tends to see, to one degree or another, the group position and is content, for one reason or another, to follow it. On many occasions, it would be difficult to prove that his outlook or vote was exclusively or mainly caused by the group's orientation, yet the two tend to coincide.[6] In this case, the person encounters stimuli that act independently upon him as well as on other members of his group and may bring similar responses. The group is not directly responsible for either the stimuli or the responses, but the group behavior nonetheless becomes distinctive. Blacks, for example, have felt discrimination in employment opportunities, education, housing, and compensation. Even without the National Urban League, the National Association for the Advancement of Colored People (NAACP) and appeals to them as a group, blacks might be expected to have distinctive characteristics in terms of their reaction to proposed legislation and candidates. The so-called Negro vote then is not necessarily due to the NAACP, to which only a fraction of Negroes belong, but is a reaction to status and prob-

---

[6]See Angus Campbell and Homer C. Cooper, *Group Differences in Attitudes and Votes*, Survey Research Center, The University of Michigan, Ann Arbor, Mich., 1956.

lems peculiar to many of their race in society. With these warnings about the exaggeration of the importance of this or that organization on the political behavior of members, we turn to some of the possible influences of social groups in relation to their political preferences.

SOCIAL CHARACTERISTICS AND PARTY PREFERENCES

Two major methods are used in ascertaining party preference and voting. One is to analyze the actual results of an election in precincts that are notable for having residents with an overwhelming characteristic or trait. One precinct has in it persons of very high income, another is 90 percent Jewish, another consists almost exclusively of farmers. Analyses of returns of such precincts are valuable in that they rest upon *actual* vote in contrast to stated party *preference* and *intention* to vote. But the data are not likely to show correlation between variables such as high- and low-income Jews and well-educated and less well-educated Catholics or Protestants. Aggregate data, moreover, rest on the assumption that the voters in a Jewish ward are all Jews—an unlikely situation. Further, many persons of distinctive characteristics, such as young people, women, and doctors, are not confined to any one precinct but are scattered throughout a community.

The panel survey based on a sample can take cognizance of an almost limitless number of variables. It requires careful drawing of the sample, adequate rapport between interviewer and respondent, and reliable memory of the latter in answering certain questions, such as, "Did you vote for a Republican or a Democratic congressman in 1970?" Also, since voter intention stated in October may not be voter action in November, postelection surveys on actual behavior become necessary if the most accurate picture is to be derived. Also there may be, and has been, a difference between reported party preference and actual voting when the candidate or events upset the long-term preference. Table 17-2 shows overall presidential party preferences as found by interviewers for the Gallup Poll immediately before and after each election in order to obtain the most reliable figure for actual voting.

Some percentage changes in party preference for House candidates took place in the midterm elections 1958 to 1966 (Table 17-3) but the overall group patterns persisted in the face of expected gains by the out-party (Republicans) in 1962 and 1966. There was an overall erosion in popular vote for congressional Democrats from the preceding election, with the biggest change away from the party on the part of the college educated, white-collar workers, union families, the young, whites, Catholics, and Jews. Blacks moved toward the party's congressional candidates.

Table 17-2 Vote by groups in presidential elections, 1952–1968

Demographic group	1952 Dem.	1956 Dem.	1960 Dem.	1964 Dem.	1968 Dem.	1968 Rep.	1968 Wallace
National	44.6%	42.4%	50.1%	61.3%	43.0%	43.4%	13.6%
Sex							
Men	47	45	52	60	41	43	16
Women	42	39	49	62	45	43	12
Race							
White	43	41	49	59	38	47	15
Nonwhite	79	61	68	94	85	12	3
Education							
College	34	31	39	52	37	54	9
High school	45	42	52	62	42	43	15
Grade school	52	50	55	66	52	33	15
Occupation							
Professional and business	36	32	42	54	34	56	10
White-collar workers	40	37	48	57	41	47	12
Manual workers	55	50	60	71	50	35	15
Farmers	33	46	48	53	29	51	20
Age							
Under 30 years	51	43	54	64	47	38	15
30-49 years	47	45	54	63	44	41	15
50 years and older	39	39	46	59	41	47	12
Religion							
Protestants	37	37	38	55	35	49	16
Catholics	56	51	78	76	59	33	8
Jews	77	75	81	78	80*	7*	3*

Source: Gallup Poll.
*Gallup had no breakdown for Jewish respondents; Michigan Survey Center sample substituted here.

Perhaps of more significance is the greater stability of support for Democratic congressmen over that for President. The vote for congressmen in midterm elections is also slightly more stable than in presidential years. The Southern votes for Democratic House candidates remained fairly constant even in the face of the pull of Goldwater, Nixon, and Wallace. In the north, however, Republican congressional percentages rose markedly in 1968 over 1964, even though their net gain of seats was not large. Another example of midterm Democratic congressional stability is seen in total popular vote margins over Republicans of 2,535,000 in 1962 and 1,304,000 in 1966. In contrast, Democratic congressional margins in the Kennedy victory were 6,095,000; under Johnson, 9 million, and 1,133,000 in the Nixon election. The pull of party label and effect of group identification appear stronger in the absence of a presidential personality.

Age and Sex. The popular contention that one grows more conservative with age has not yet been proved conclusively, but there is some evidence in that direction. Party attachment does show differences, with younger

TABLE 17-3 Vote for Democratic candidates for United States House of Representatives, 1958, 1962, and 1966

Demographic group	1958	1962	1966
Sex			
Men	59%	52%	52%
Women	54	52	55
Education			
Grade school education	66	59	61
High school education	57	54	53
College education	46	35	41
Occupation			
Professional and executive	48	41	42
White-collar workers	57	49	48
Manual workers	65	63	62
Farmers	53	50	50
Union families	72	69	65
Age			
21–29 years of age			
30–49 years of age			
Over 50 years of age	50	49	51
Race			
Whites	57	51	50
Blacks	69	74	81
Religion			
Protestants	49	41	45
Catholics	77	73	65
Jews	84	72	75

Source: Gallup Poll.

voters more Democratic and persons over fifty more Republican than the national average. If "conservative" means Republican, then the surveys give evidence of such change with age. One Center panel found that 49 percent of those from twenty-five to thirty years old were strong or weak Democrats, while 42 percent over seventy-five were so designated. Republicanism was embraced by 42 percent of senior citizens but by only 25 percent of the young people. What is more important is the tendency for people as they grow older to become more interested and more active in politics. This is not surprising as one's stake in society becomes greater with age; one becomes more aware of taxes and of public policies affecting one's status.

Young people are less tied to the current party system, and their voting appears to be more bound up with candidates and party leaders than with parties as such. The figures in Table 17-2 show that the twenty-one to twenty-nine age group radically shifted from Eisenhower to Kennedy to Johnson then slightly away from Humphrey. Also it is particularly evident that the strength of party identification grows with the years. The Center combined seven national samples between 1952 and

1957 and found an unmistakable trend toward strong Republican and strong Democratic identification with age. Only 24 percent in the twenty-one to twenty-four age level were strong identifiers. This rose to 31 percent for those from thirty to thirty-nine, then to 41 percent in the fifty to fifty-four bracket. At age seventy this reached 53 percent.[7]

Although women outnumber men in the United States, fewer women have voted, so that the electorate is about evenly divided between the sexes.[8] Although percentage differences appear in national samples, the range is not as wide as between ages and many social groups. Politicians who speak of a "women's vote," however, may not be completely dreaming so far as some national elections are concerned. Eisenhower seems to have done considerably better among women voters than Stevenson; Humphrey polled a larger female than male vote; a larger proportion of men than women preferred Wallace.

Students of school elections and propositions, on the strength of sampling, sometimes find quite substantial deviations between the male and female vote. Comprehensive research on this is still wanting.

Occupation and Education. Since the advent of the New Deal, polls consistently show that in the broad categories of occupations there is marked difference in party choices. Business, professional, technical, and managerial groups tend to prefer and to vote for Republican candidates for President. The self-index has risen and declined; but its margin has remained pronouncedly Republican, except for a sharp deviation in 1964 when voters all across the spectrum shifted to Johnson. Gallup's samples show lawyers, doctors, and many teachers as well as proprietors favoring the Republican party as the one best serving "the interest of business and professional people." White-collar workers have been only a little less oriented toward the Republicans.

College students will be quick to note a discrepancy between the Democratic leaning of their professors and other professionals who appear to be more Republican. Analysis of professors' party inclinations show that classifying them as professionals obscures wide variations in attitudes that they have from other professionals such as attorneys, engineers, and medical doctors as well as sharp differences within the professors' subgroups. Results of a mail survey of about 2,400 college professors are shown in Table 17-4.[9]

[7] See Campbell et al., *The American Voter*, p. 162.

[8] The Census Bureau, however, has noted a steady growth in the women's vote and estimated in absolute numbers in 1964 that nearly 2 million more women voted than men. See Friedheim, *op. cit.*, p. 41.

[9] For full report and analysis, see Henry G. Turner and Charles B. Spalding, "Political Attitudes and Behavior of Selected Academically Affiliated Professional Groups," *Polity*, vol. 1, pp. 309–336, 1969. A more specialized article on political scientists by the same authors is found in the *Western Political Quarterly*, vol. 16, pp. 650–665, 1963.

TABLE 17-4 Party preference of academics and parents

Discipline	Dem.	Rep.	Ind. and other	Both parents Democratic	Both parents Republican
Philosophy	79%	14%	8%	30%	38%
Sociology	78	10	12	36	36
Political science	74	16	10	30	36
History	74	20	7	33	41
Psychology	70	20	9	39	36
Botany	50	40	10	27	46
Geology	35	52	13	26	48
Mathematics	29	56	15	28	44
Engineering	27	62	11	25	45

Source: Henry G. Turner and Charles B. Spalding, "Political Attitudes and Behavior of Selected Academically Affiliated Professional Groups," *Polity*, vol. 1, p. 316, 1969.
Note: Because of rounding, figures do not always total 100.

The data show that college professors devoted to the study of social and political problems are oriented predominantly toward the Democrats and those in fields directed toward the application of knowledge for business endeavors lean Republican. Academics differ from most other groups in that adult socialization is more important than childhood socialization. Parental affiliations have much less influence on partisanship of offspring, and level of age and income, which are important in the general population, seem to be of only modest effect. Information gained in their professions and communication with colleagues in their own academic departments strongly influence political orientations. Again differing from the general electorate, for professors political ideology appears an important variable in selection of a party. "Policies of the party" was considered the single most important factor by the largest number of Republicans and Democrats in choosing the party. The results of this analysis of professional party preferences serve warning of the need for studying the behavior of subgroups within a broader category and indicate that the influence of variables differs within a single classification.

Skilled and semiskilled workers provide the crossing-over point to Democratic sympathizers. Families of trade-union members are more oriented toward the Democratic party than are nonunion families. Eisenhower and George Wallace made some inroads into the union and nonunion workers, but a majority still voted for Stevenson and Humphrey. (Occupational defections from the Democrats are shown in Figure 17-1.)

Agrarian voting behavior shows less consistency than that of labor or management. Under Roosevelt, farmers shifted in and out of support for him, then went strongly for Truman, then to Eisenhower. Farmers were nearly equally divided between Kennedy and Nixon; and, although Johnson received a majority on the Gallup sample (53 percent), the farmers moved less in his direction than did any other occupational group. Their shifts to Wallace and, to a lesser extent, to Nixon were spectacular. The variability of the agrarian voter is also shown in congressional voting and by the fact that he is more likely to split his ticket than either urban dwellers or nonfarmers who live in sparsely settled

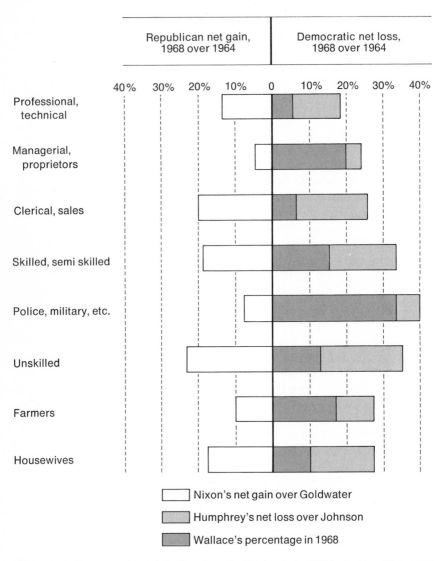

Figure 17-1 Net occupational defections from the Democrats in 1964 to the Republicans and A.I.P. in 1968.

areas. Historically, farmers have experimented with third parties, suggesting economic protest to be a motivation of some consequence.

The fluid character of the agrarian vote is not easily explained. Short-term economic forces lead farmers to react to prices and other conditions from election to election. They generally have a remoteness from national politics and a lower level of political involvement. Authors of *The American Voter* see the peculiarity as residing "in a state of mind, a total posture toward the ongoing political process that survives changes in external aspects of his life situation."[10] But what underlies that state of mind is not readily apparent.

Using data from the Survey Research Center's samples and a somewhat different occupational category from that of Gallup, Figure 17-1 shows shifts in voting behavior that may be due to short-term forces of the Goldwater candidacy in 1964 and the "law and order" and Vietnam issues in 1968. Whether this is a harbinger of an important realignment of some occupational groups cannot be known till after the 1972 and 1976 elections. Nixon was the beneficiary of considerable movement to him from the clerical, skilled, and unskilled workers and housewives; Wallace made very deep inroads into Democratic strength in the security forces, skilled and unskilled workers, and managers and proprietors. Wallace also got the much bigger share of the farmers who had supported Johnson in 1964 than did Nixon. It may be noticed that of the educational and occupational groupings the college educated defected the least from Johnson and only 9 percent of them in the Gallup sample supported Wallace in contrast to 15 percent for grade and high school educated (Table 17-2). Although college students and professors incline toward the Democrats, the older graduates have remained predominantly Republican.

Socioeconomic Factors.   Formal education is one criterion of status, although analysts regard it as secondary to occupation as a measure of status and of partisan differences. Whether education in itself causes the status—and for some it does—people of higher education generally come from higher-status backgrounds in the first place. Persons with higher education go into the higher-status occupations; thus on the surface at least a question might be raised whether one causes the other or whether they simply strengthen each other. The variable nonetheless is quite constant; persons with only grade school education who enter the lower-status occupations vote heavily Democratic, while college graduates who enter higher-status occupations are strongly Republican. High school graduates fall in between.

[10] Campbell et al., *The American Voter*, p. 408.

Party leaders and professional students of political behavior have long observed that, even in the absence of so-called class parties in the United States, there appears to be a significant relationship between economic and social status and one's party preference and voting habits. The fact that this relationship is observed, however, has not meant that it is easily explained.[11] In rather unsophisticated fashion, it is sometimes asserted that occupation is the greatest single determinant of one's vote or that the lower class votes Democratic and the high-income people are Republicans. Politicians speak of the "pocket-book appeal" or "belly radicalism." Statements like these often contain a kernel of truth, but they do not conceptualize the influence of one's psychological relationship to his occupation or grouping. They do not tell the extent to which a farmer votes psychologically as a farmer. The problem is made complex because the terms *class* and *socioeconomic status* are broad. Occupation is not necessarily congruent with high or low status, although many times it is so regarded. Socioeconomic status embraces a number of factors both subjective and objective — amount and kind of higher education, occupation, prestige, income, power, and even one's place of residence.

On the psychological side, class and status are what one sees oneself as being. There has been a good deal of misidentification of one's social class, and the growing popularity of the middle class has made it so socially respectable that people want to locate themselves in the middle range instead of at the extremes.

Of the respondents in national surveys, 80 to 90 percent see themselves as middle class, with the remaining either lower or upper class. But if respondents are given the alternative of belonging to a working-class or to a middle-class category, the results are very different and a majority see themselves as members of the working class. Three different scholars correlated the self-perception of respondents of their class and party identification during the last years of the Roosevelt, Truman, and Eisenhower administrations (see Table 17-5). Although class awareness is not a constant factor and varies considerably from one election to the next, these and other studies give evidence of considerable stability between class and party from 1936 to the present.[12]

Irrespective of what classifications one uses and with or without the "income" factor, the working class identifies more strongly with the Democrats, and as one moves up in status, income, and class, the identification with the Republican party becomes stronger. However, the Democratic identification of the working class does not mean that they vote

[11] See *ibid.*, chaps. 13 and 14.
[12] About 39 percent of the Center's 1962 sample refused to "class" themselves.

TABLE 17-5 Party preference of middle and working classes, 1944, 1952, and 1960

Party choice	Middle class			Working class		
	1944	1952	1960	1944	1952	1960
Democratic	49%	30%	35.9%	71%	54%	52.2%
Republican	49	69	60.4	29	43	43.1
Other, refusal	2	1	3.7	0	3	4.7

Source: 1944 data from Richard Centers, *The Psychology of Social Classes*, Princeton University Press, Princeton, N.J., 1949, p. 124; 1952 data from Heinz Eulau, "Perceptions of Class and Party in Voting Behavior: 1952," *American Political Science Review*, vol. 49, p. 364, 1955; 1960 data from Survey Research Center.

that party in every election, evidence being the considerable worker support for Eisenhower and for Nixon and Wallace in 1968;[13] and the class-party affinity does not obscure the many high-income persons who are Democratic and the many low-income Republicans. This has consequences, as we have seen, for the party system in terms of financial support and program.

ETHNORACIAL INFLUENCES
The melting-pot character of the American society is a significant shaping force both in terms of historical development and in contemporary politics. It affects the policies and programs of the two parties as well as their selection of candidates and campaign strategies. There is substantial evidence of the existence of ethnic identification, a propensity to use racial, religious, or national affiliation to relate to others. Ethnic and social politics are found almost anywhere in the United States but are more pronounced in cities and in some states.[14]

Nationalities. With the exception of the blacks few national surveys have attempted to analyze the voting preferences of ethnic groups over a period of time, but there are many studies of local ethnic voting and

[13] Interestingly, it was found in England that as workers' income increased and living standards improved, political orientations and party sympathies did not change. Workers remained staunch supporters of the Labour party. Work place and trade unionism helped to counter middle-class influences. The structure of group attachment, not extent of income and possessions, determines party preferences. See John H. Goldthorpe et al., *The Affluent Worker: Political Attitudes and Behavior*, Cambridge University Press, London, 1968. This seems generally true in the United States but to a lesser extent. A poll taken by the AFL-CIO in 1967 found 58 percent classifying themselves as Democrats, 17 percent independents, 16 percent Republicans with 9 percent undecided.

[14] Literature on cultural and political ethnicity is vast. Two major works are Peter J. Rose, *They and We: Racial and Ethnic Relations in the United States*, Random House, Inc., New York, 1964, and Harry A. Bailey, Jr., and Ellis Katz, *Ethnic Group Politics*, Charles E. Merrill Books, Inc., Columbus, Ohio, 1969. The latter includes many data on voting habits of ethnics up to 1960. However, some recent changes that seem to be taking place in voting behavior among certain ethnics are not reflected in this work.

involvement. Suffice it here to note that most of the first- and second-generation national groups are located in urban areas, although Scandinavians and Germans have scattered much more widely.[15] Since 1932, the big-cities' nationalities have favored the Democratic party. Germans and Scandinavians in smaller towns and rural areas often provide pockets of Republican strength. Yet old-style Republican city bosses and their Democratic counterparts befriended immigrants on their arrival and obtained their loyalties because the party of the boss provided a channel for climbing the social and economic ladder. But, like others in the electorate, they have had their party attachments shaken by events and candidates. A few illustrations of the force of ethnicity are instructive of this.

A study of Franco-Americans in Maine (a group numbering about one-sixth of the population) shows elements of stability and change. Before 1928, their presidential voting closely paralleled the general electorate with the ethnoreligious factor "the most important single conditioner of their electoral behavior during the initial phase of their political evolution."[16] After 1928, economic and religious considerations apart from ethnic ones became more prominent conditioners of partisanship; and they became staunchly Democratic, giving Truman 89 percent of their votes in 1948. Then followed a massive shift to Eisenhower, largely based on his personal and nonpartisan appeal. The shift was most notable among the middle- and upper-class Franco-Americans. In 1960, there was a fantastic shift to Kennedy, and the Senator duplicated the Truman vote of 89 percent; only 3 percent failed to vote, suggesting the high stimulation of the campaign. The upper and middle classes, as well as the lower class, moved to Kennedy because of their great enthusiasm for him personally, "not to mention his beautiful wife of partially French extraction," and his religion. They were particularly disturbed by anti-Catholic activities, and it apparently seemed no violation of status politics to vote for a patrician coreligionist when his opponent received support from those who sought to keep religion as a barrier to the highest office in the land.

When a candidate of one party is of the same extraction as an ethnic group, is the tie alone strong enough to pull a majority of its votes? Political leaders, seeing these prospects, often try to hedge by balanced tickets or offsetting factors. The largest single ethnic strain in Hawaii is the Japanese, who account for 37 percent of the population.

[15] Although 1952 was a "deviating" election, Survey Research Center's respondents divided in their support for Eisenhower as follows: German and Scandinavian, about 58 percent; English-Scottish, 55 percent, Irish-Catholic and Italian, 38 percent each; and Polish, 42 percent. See Campbell et al., *The Voter Decides*, pp. 76–79.

[16] David B. Walker, *Politics and Ethnocentrism: The Case of the Franco-Americans*, Bureau for Research in Municipal Government, Brunswick, Me., 1961, p. 29.

TABLE 17-6 Ethnic division of presidential preferences

Nationality	1952 Stevenson	1960 Kennedy	1964 Johnson
Scottish-English	31%	41%	59%
Irish	59	60	66
Italian	56	67	74
Polish	49	78	77
German	26	47	60

Source: Based on national samples—Figures for 1952 adapted from Angus Campbell, Gerald Gurin, and Warren E. Miller, *The Voter Decides*, Harper & Row, Publishers, Inc., New York, 1954, pp. 70ff; Harris survey figures used for 1960 and 1964.

One study found that voters of all minorities in Hawaii are sensitive to the ethnic origins of the candidates, but the relative importance of this sensitivity is difficult to determine.[17] It was discovered that voters were chiefly motivated by allegiance to party. However, secondary to party allegiance "was an apparent consideration of the ethnic extractions of the candidates." A close third was the weighing of the individual qualifications of the candidates themselves. In Hawaii's first four elections, en bloc voting by the Japanese, feared by some, did not materialize.'

In choices for President (Table 17-6), Irish and Italians remained most steadily Democratic from 1952 to 1964 and Scottish-English and Germans moved strikingly from strong support for Eisenhower to less for Nixon and then to Johnson. The Goldwater candidacy disturbed all the ethnic groups, but the Poles supported Kennedy and Johnson in about equal numbers. Why this was the case is open to speculation, but the figures suggest that a Republican presidential nominee appears to have a rock bottom of at least a quarter of the Polish vote.

A study of voting in the Newark, New Jersey, nonpartisan municipal elections and partisan elections of the state legislators affords a significant example of the effect of ethnicity.[18] In the mayor-council elections, there was no evidence of an influence of party affiliations or of policy coherence. Voters supported candidates of their own ethnic background. Most of the high positive correlations came from pairs of similar ethnic appeal but of opposed policies. "The negative correlations [showed[a disproportionate number of candidate pairs agreed on policy but of contrasting ethnic appeals." Candidates eschewed advertising in citywide newspapers in favor of publicity in neighborhood publications and sought major support through Italian and Negro groups.

[17]John M. Digman and Daniel W. Tuttle, "An Interpretation of an Election by Means of Obverse Factor Analysis," *The Journal of Social Psychology*, vol. 53, pp. 183–194, 1961.
[18]See Gerald Pomper, "Ethnic and Group Voting in Nonpartisan Municipal Elections," *Public Opinion Quarterly*, vol. 30, pp. 79–97, 1966. About a third of Newark's population at the time (1962) was of foreign birth or the children of immigrants and more than a third was Negro so that ethnic identifications are of great significance.

While ethnicity appeared to substitute ethnic pressures for those of party in nonpartisan elections, the reverse was true for the partisan state assembly contests. Here each party presented a "balanced ticket" including all ethnic groups (one each of Irish ancestry, an Italian, a Jew, and a black). Party was more important than ethnic background as shown by negative correlations of votes for candidates of the same ethnic group but of different parties.

The Newark story suggests that parties are a way, through balanced tickets, of bridging ethnic differences and achieving unified support for their candidates. Campaigning is a "slate" affair proposed by parties. When parties are removed, as in nonpartisan elections, group kinship apparently becomes more important than policy considerations.

A broad generalization is that ethnic groups that are most aware of their lower status and are unhappy with discrimination against them have shown a Democratic preference; the more assimilated tend to divide more evenly between the parties. In partisan elections, ethnic background is probably not a determinative referent, for it is usually modified or reinforced by such factors as socioeconomic status, religion, years removed from immigration, place of residence, and party label. For example, the Center's sample found 37 percent of the Irish Catholics voting for Eisenhower and 52 percent for Kennedy. But non-Irish Catholics voted 39 percent for Eisenhower and only 42 percent for Kennedy, suggesting the Irish Catholics were more effected by the Kennedy candidacy than were non-Irish Catholics.[19]

Overall, Democrats gained in the ethnic vote cast in 1960, but Republicans claimed gains among Slavic and Italian voters in 1964 while among voters of Latin-American heritage President Johnson received 90 percent support.[20]

Negroes and the Democratic Vote. Negroes were once firmly attached to the Republicans as the descendants of the Great Emancipator. Their strong adherence to the Democratic party today is one of the most significant reversals in political orientation in the history of the nation. The shift began in the 1930s and, unlike patterns of some other voting groups, the attachment was valid across the socioeconomic spectrum. The 1960 postelection Gallup Poll found 49 percent of its white respondents classifying themselves as Democrats to 68 percent of the black respondents, a percentage that continued to rise throughout the 1960s.

Speculation remains as to whether more non-Southern blacks think of themselves as Democrats than do those in the South. As shown

[19]Campbell et al., *Elections and the Political Order,* p. 105. Ethnic groups (excluding Nisei) tend also to be heavily Catholic groups so there is much interaction and reinforcement between ethnic and religious ties.

[20]Friedheim, *op. cit.,* p. 207.

TABLE 17-7 Party preferences of Southerners by race, 1961 and 1964

	White		Black	
	1961	1964	1961	1964
Strong Democrat	29%	35%	28%	53.0%
Weak Democrat	32	29	23	23.0
Independent Democrat	7	6	8	2.0
Independent	7	8	5	9.0
Independent Republican	5	6	4	1.5
Weak Republican	6	7	7	1.5
Strong Republican	8	7	3	1.0
Apolitical, don't know	6	1	22	9.0
	100%	99%*	100%	100.0%

Source: Donald R. Matthews and James W. Prothero, *Negroes and the New Southern Politics*, Harcourt, Brace & World, Inc., New York, 1966, p. 373.
*Does not add to 100% because of rounding.

in Table 17-7, Southern whites identifying themselves as Democrats rose slightly between 1961 and 1964 from 68 percent to 70 percent; but a spectacular rise took place in blacks classifying themselves as strong Democrats, with an overall Democratic increase from 59 to 78 percent, due in part to the change in many blacks from apolitical to Democratic. A corresponding erosion took place among blacks who considered themselves Republicans in 1961.

Consistency is shown not only in stated Negro preference but also in actual voting for Democratic candidates for Congress and for President. The Center's sample found that 64 percent of the blacks voted for Stevenson in 1956; in each subsequent presidential election, the percentage increased — 70 percent for Kennedy, higher for Johnson, and almost 97 percent for Humphrey! (The Gallup sample under the broad category "nonwhite" showed somewhat less increase, with Nixon doing better than Goldwater.) This strong preference of nonwhites for the Democratic candidate and the fact that Humphrey received only 35 percent of the white vote, indicate that the 1968 election was probably the most racially polarized in history. The white and black differential of 62 percent in candidate preference, moreover, is substantially larger than any other social differentiation or class change even in Western Europe. Although there is a striking dropoff in midterm voting, blacks also give heavy support to Democratic congressional candidates. Democratic strength, however, is kept below its potential because of considerable nonvoting among Negroes.

A marked difference occurs in the South between whites and blacks in that while both are overwhelmingly Democratic by preferred belief (an amazing consensus in itself) — in 1964 and 1968 whites voted in large numbers for Goldwater and Nixon while Negroes both thought

Democratic and voted for the party's presidential candidates. Further, proportionately more Southern blacks voted both for Kennedy and Johnson than did Southern whites. Northern whites voted for Johnson in substantially larger numbers than Southern whites.[21]

At subnational levels generally, blacks are Democratic by self-identification and in voting, but there are some exceptions. In Richmond, Virginia, a large majority voted for a Republican candidate for governor in 1961. Many blacks are registered Republicans in Baltimore, and local Republican candidates have often done well in Negro precincts. But the preponderance of black voting behavior remains Democratic at all levels. In 1967 in Philadelphia, when two prominent Republicans were put on the ticket and two other blacks ran for mayor as independents, the white Democratic mayoralty candidate rolled up in Negro wards a margin four times as large as his city-wide margin. Despite a sizable black registration in Youngstown, Ohio, a black mayoralty candidate running as a Republican was overwhelmingly defeated. Blacks, however, supported Republican Edward Brooke of Massachusetts, a black, for state attorney general and for United States senator. In Gary, Indiana, and Cleveland, Ohio, the reinforcing ties of race and Democratic party resulted in the election of black mayors in the face of a comparatively small white votes for them. The distinctiveness of the Negro Democratic vote is certainly due in part to the fact that blacks generally have lower socioeconomic status, which tends to be associated with Democratic affiliation, and to the long record of the party in support of federal civil rights legislation.

In nonpartisan local elections, an interesting situation is posed by the prospects of racial bloc voting when a Negro and a white candidate face each other. In a 1959 Memphis city election, both races showed themselves capable of competitive racial bloc voting.[22] Blacks gave the strongest backing ever to one of their race, but he lost the election because of an even more effective bloc vote on the part of white Memphians. In precincts that were 90 to 100 percent Negro, the black candidate received 94 percent of the vote with 6 percent scattered for white candidates. Conversely, comparable all-white precincts gave but 2 percent to the black candidate. In this instance, race was obviously divorced from all other variables and was virtually the only factor in the outcome. As noted above, quite similar racial ties were also found in Newark's nonpartisan elections. In nonpartisan elections in Durham, North Carolina,

[21] A comprehensive account of Southern white and black voting behavior is found in Donald R. Matthews and James W. Prothero, *Negroes and the New Southern Politics*, Harcourt, Brace & World, Inc., New York, 1966, chap. 13.

[22] W. Eugene Wright, *Memphis Politics: A Study in Racial Bloc Voting*, Eagleton Institute Cases in Practical Politics, case 27, McGraw-Hill Book Company, New York, 1962.

endorsement by a Negro voting league was also found to be productive of Negro voting cohesion.

Jews.[23]   In concluding this section on ethnic groups, the questions might be posed:. Is there a Jewish vote? Will Jews vote for a Jew? The broad, but perhaps unsatisfactory, answers are similar to those in reply to comparable questions about Irish, Czechs, or Poles. If by such a vote is meant, "Do all American Jews react the same way to parties, candidates, and issues?" the answer is no. But being Jewish (or Negro or Italian) does mean at times the adoption of certain political attitudes and even of distinctive voting behavior. Sometimes Jews vote for Jews, and sometimes they do not. Politicians are often quick to credit the prime importance of name voting in certain areas. With a heavy concentration of Jews in New York City, Jewish candidates do not invariably carry Jewish precincts. Herbert Lehman and Jacob Javits carried New York City handsomely, but Jews running on Republican tickets for mayor or other city offices have gone down to defeat, and Nelson Rockefeller did far better against Robert Morgenthau in the city in 1962 than against Averell Harriman in 1958. Clearly party or other voting factors have been more important in many Jewish communities than ethnicity.

Lawrence H. Fuchs believes that two basic values underpin Jewish political behavior and make it different in several respects from that of most other minorities. One is the embracing of an internationalist world view tending to attract support to candidates oriented toward internationalism. The other grows out of hostile pressures, insecurities, and discrimination, making for an orientation toward liberalism, welfare, and civil rights. From 1900 to the mid-1920s, more Jews voted for Republicans than for Democrats, and there were a considerable number of Republican Jewish officeholders. Woodrow Wilson made substantial inroads into the Jewish vote in 1912 and 1916; but Jews, like the rest of the country, returned to the Republican party in 1920. Alfred E. Smith cut heavily into the Jewish vote, and Franklin D. Roosevelt had spectacular success in bringing it into his coalition.

The National Opinion Research Center reported that in its 1940 and 1944 samples about 90 of every 100 Jews voted for Roosevelt. The Gallup Poll noted a drop to 77 percent for Stevenson in 1952, and

[23] In the literature, Jewish political behavior is sometimes treated under the "religious" category and at other times under the "ethnic" category. Treatment here is under the latter, not to be argumentative, but for the sake of convenience. Ethnics are usually regarded as those possessing continuity though biological descent and sharing a distinctive historical, social, and cultural tradition. Lawrence H. Fuchs, who has made the most comprehensive historical study of Jews in American politics, classifies Jews as an "ethnoreligious" group. See his *The Political Behavior of American Jews*, The Free Press, New York, 1955.

rising to 81 percent for Kennedy in 1960. What is particularly striking is that the Jewish vote for Stevenson was much greater than for any other demographic group studied, far exceeding both trade-union members and blacks. Eisenhower failed to make substantial inroads despite the fact that he was a professed internationalist and was associated as a successful military hero against the Nazis and a benefactor of the Jews. Stevenson won more votes, not only because he was a Democrat, but because of his image as liberal, intellectual, and internationalist. A further paradox and evidence of the constancy of Jewish support for Democratic candidates for the Presidency is that their well-to-do and older people do not vote Republican, as do comparable segments of most other groups. Although Jews consistently support United States Senator Jacob Javits, a Republican, they follow the Democratic label in congressional voting. The fact that Barry Goldwater was of Jewish stock had little if any effect on Jewish voters. In an SRC sample, 42 percent of the Jews classified themselves as independents, 50 percent Democrat, and 8 percent Republican. Despite the large claim of independency, it is obvious from voting statistics that in most national elections a very large majority vote Democratic.

Jews have shown strong third-party tendencies in New York City. They have constituted much of the leadership, drive, and voting strength (though this has not been measured) of the Liberal party in New York and the now-defunct American Labor party; and in earlier times, the Jewish ghettos were Socialist strongholds.[24] It would be difficult to explain the willingness of a significant number of Jews in New York City to support third-party candidates in terms other than ideology, issues, and to some extent intellectualism. Jews were often in the vanguard of third-party reform movements in municipal elections. In the heavily Jewish Bronx second assembly district, minor-party candidates for mayor received 57, 45, 55, and 44 percent of the vote in 1945, 1949, 1950, and 1953, respectively. In other states where the third-party alternative is unavailable, ticket splitting affords the Jewish voter a chance to maintain a consistency in voting for his approach to politics.

RELIGIOUS AFFILIATION AND THE VOTE

Modern literature on religion in politics is vast, and the 1960 campaign and election heightened the outpourings.[25] From the point of view of

[24] On the Socialist traditions and Jews, see *ibid.*, chap. 8.

[25] In addition to the several survey studies used in the last two chapters, among the works of particular relevance to the voting behavior of religious groups in 1960 are Philip E. Converse, Angus Campbell, Warren E. Miller, and Donald E. Stokes, "Stability and Change in 1960: A Reinstating Election," *American Political Science Review*, vol. 55, pp. 269–280, 1961; V. O. Key, Jr., in Paul T. David

TABLE 17-8   Non-South partisanship by religious and occupation groupings 1964.

Affiliation	Jewish 1964	Catholic 1964 White-collar	Catholic 1964 Blue-collar	Protestant 1964 White-collar	Protestant 1964 Blue-collar
Strong Democrat	28%	18%	31%	15%	16%
Weak Democrat	22	30	27	15	25
Independent	42	28	21	20	21
Weak Republican	8	8	7	22	17
Strong Republican	0	12	4	21	9
Apolitical or other	0	4	10	6	13

Source: Michigan Survey Research Center. No data available on white or blue-collar groupings for Jews.

long-term party affiliation of religious groups, some often overlooked, deep-seated factors enter the picture. National surveys indicate a Protestant preference for the Republican party and a Catholic preference for the Democratic. But these figures do not tell the socioeconomic composition of the religious group, which might help to explain party predilections. Samplings in Elmira, New York, and in Philadelphia corroborate the fact that upper-strata Catholics tend to vote Republican more than blue-collar Catholics although somewhat less than upper-strata Protestants. Low-income Protestants were much less Republican than middle- and high-income Protestants. The SRC national sample shows the generally similar tendencies (Table 17-8).[26]

In a study of metropolitan St. Louis, Greer found that a strong tie existed between the Democratic party and the Catholic electorate and further that there was very little difference in party preference between city and suburban Catholics. Those with Northern and Western European backgrounds who were third-generation and college educated tended to be more Republican (and to live in the suburbs) but still were far less Republican than comparable non-Catholics.[27] He concluded that religion has an "independent discriminating power." Another illustration of the ethnic-religious factor is the relatively strong Republican attachments of Hispanic Catholics in parts of the Southwest. The welter

(ed.), *The Presidential Election and Transition, 1960–1961*, The Brookings Institution, Washington, D.C., 1961, chap. 6; and Scott Greer, "Catholic Voters and the Democratic Party," *Public Opinion Quarterly*, vol. 25, pp. 611–625, 1961. Peter H. Odegard brought together four studies and a bibliography on Catholicism as a factor in elections in *Religion and Politics*, Oceana Publications, Inc., New York, 1960, chap. 5, published for the Eagleton Institute of Politics, Rutgers University, 1960. For Catholic voting on issues as well as candidates see John F. Fenton, *The Catholic Vote*, The Hauser Press, New Orleans, 1960, and Gerhard Lenski, *The Religious Factor*, Doubleday & Company, Inc., Garden City, N.Y., 1961, chap. 4.

[26] Additional data on voting differentials in North and South by race and religion are found in Table 18-8.

[27] Greer, *op. cit.*, p. 623.

of studies of religious electorates in certain metropolitan communities and regions and those based on a national sample reveal the necessity for caution in interpretations of the influence of religion in isolation from other variables, particularly ethnicity, number of generations in the United States, and socioeconomic status.

The Kennedy-Nixon contest brought much contradictory interpretation and superficial evaluation of the influence of religion on the vote. Some journalists heralded the outcome as evidence that religious affiliation of a presidential nominee was not of importance. Many reporters were of the opinion that, on balance, Kennedy's religion helped more than hindered him; others asserted the opposite and claimed that his popular majority, instead of being uncomfortably close, would have been by a margin of several millions had he been a Protestant. Careful studies by the staff of the Center as well as those by other scholars, however, do give substantiation to a number of aspects of the 1960 election.

Two aspects are apparent at the outset. First, religious differences unquestionably play an unusual part in shaping voting patterns. Interviewers of the Center's panel found the "silent issue" very much on the minds of respondents, and the latter brought it up even though it was not mentioned in the questions directed to them. The more thoroughly the election has been studied, the more evident has been the deep-seated character of the religious issue. Second, and hardly surprising, was the fact that this short-term force brought great cross-pressures for Republican Catholics and Democratic Protestants. The fact that some clergy and churches took public stands placed even more tensions on some voters. Broad-minded Protestants of diverse degrees of Republican or Democratic loyalty were troubled over the question of whether one's religion should be a barrier to holding the highest office in the land. The "great debates" on television set up further conflict, for they brought in the element of candidate, and Kennedy made a highly favorable impression. Less conflict, but not to be overlooked, was induced by the popularity of Eisenhower and his energetic activity on behalf of Nixon in the late stages of the campaign. Lyndon B. Johnson meanwhile placed Southerners under pressure to return to or to keep their Democratic faith. Senator Kennedy made very strong appeals to Democratic voters, which added the feature of party pull against a more orthodox Republican than Eisenhower. It was hardly surprising, therefore, that contending loyalties, vigorous campaigning, and televised debates brought a huge turnout, exceeding the 1956 election by more than 6 million. But size of turnout in itself is always a complicating factor for political scientists who would explain the electoral verdict!

Catholic preference for the Democratic party was strengthened by Governor Smith's candidacy in 1928 and by the impact of the New

TABLE 17-9 Church attendance percentage of Protestant Democrats and independents voting for Nixon

	Attendance			
	Regular	Often	Seldom	Never
Democrats (non-South)	36%	28%	11%	6%
Democrats (Southern)	40	36	18	*
Independents	83	72	61	*

Source: Survey Research Center (see Table 16-2).
*Sample too small to be of significance.

Deal. The Center's samples, beginning in 1952, showed that less than 20 percent of the Catholics identified themselves with the Republican party, with a considerable number calling themselves independents, and a majority Democratic. Of those identifying with the two parties in the 1950s, the ratio was about 5 to 2 Democratic. But Catholics defected in their vote to about a 50–50 split in the two Eisenhower contests. In 1958, the Catholic vote for Democratic candidates for Congress was well over 70 percent, and in 1960 it went still further to an 80 percent vote for Kennedy.[28]

One of the most interesting aspects of voting patterns among the Center's respondents was the marked relationship between church attendance and the presidential choices of Democratic and independent Protestants. Although the sample was small, the results in Table 17-9 show that the more frequent churchgoers defected substantially more to Nixon. Comparable statistics are not available, but there seemed to be a tendency for stronger Catholics to shift their votes to the Democratic column than the weaker Catholics. In a word, devoutness was more likely to cause a shift. Regularity of church attendance is by no means the only standard for identity with one's religion or the depth of feeling for it. If one's personal friends are also fellow religionists, there is the likelihood that the potential primary group will influence and reinforce political attitudes and voting. The 1968 election provided differentials within Protestant sects according to fundamentalism and other aspects of belief. Wallace pulled his heaviest vote both North and South from the Baptists and did poorest among the Lutherans and Episcopalians. Nixon's highest popularity was with Presbyterians and Methodists, Humphrey's with Lutherans and Episcopalians.[29]

[28] This affords a striking lesson in the significance of the choice of a base line from which to analyze voting shifts. The Catholic shift to Kennedy would seem much more substantial if the 1956 figures were used. Conversely, the Gallup estimate of the Democratic Protestant vote was 51 percent in 1958, 37 percent in 1956, and 38 percent in 1960.

[29] A breakdown of the 1968 vote by religious sects is found in Seymour M. Lipset and Earl Raab, "The Wallace Whitelash," *Transaction*, vol. 7, p. 28, December, 1969.

When one removes the influence of a presidential personality from elections, marked differences in party choices by religious affiliation is evident. As observed in Table 17-3 covering three midterm elections, Protestant vote for Democratic congressional candidates fluctuated from 41 to 49 percent; Catholic, 65 to 77 percent; and Jewish, 72 to 84 percent. Even with fluctuations, Protestants divide more evenly between the two major parties, with Republicans having an edge; the Democrats have a decided advantage with Catholics and overwhelming sympathy from Jews.

RESIDENCE AND PARTISANSHIP

Before leaving consideration of party choices and voting characteristics by demographic groups, it should be stated again that aggregate national data alone may not present an accurate picture of the importance of a particular demographic variable. In 1960, for example, Protestant areas showed substantial deviations within themselves from the vote given to Kennedy nationally. In the same election, voting habits of Italians in Boston and Providence were noticeably different as were those of other ethnoreligious groups in different cities.[30] Several tables in this chapter show South–Non-South differences. Social and ethnic groupings are too often looked upon as homogeneous voting categories; this view overlooks the effect of local conditions on the outcome of an election.

The regional differences are not as great as they once were, but it is obvious from Tables 17-10 and 17-11 that regional differences have varied 9 percent or more for a particular presidential candidate in every election since 1952 except in 1960 when the Kennedy vote varied only 5 percent.

There was considerable variation in congressional votes by region (Table 17-12); Republicans fared better in the West and Democrats in the South. (The comparatively heavy minor-party vote in the East (12 percent) is accounted for mainly by some 715,000 votes for those running under Conservative or Liberal party labels in New York.) Of 66 million votes cast for House candidates, the Wallace party garnered only 171,000. For some time, Democratic candidates for Congress have polled considerably better in the larger cities and Republicans in smaller cities and in rural areas. The 1968 election brought no basic changes in this pattern.

In conclusion, the tables on voting by demographic groupings over a period of time point out that changes are *unidirectional*. With the popularity of an Eisenhower or an unpopularity of a Goldwater or Johnson and Humphrey in 1968, there is movement along the whole political

[30] On this point, see Lucy S. Davidowicz and Leon J. Goldstein, *Politics in a Pluralist Democracy: Studies of Voting in the 1960 Election*, Institute of Human Relations Press, New York, 1963.

TABLE 17-10 Republican presidential percentage by regions, 1952–1964

Region	1952	1956	1960	1964
East	55%	60%	47%	32%
Midwest	58	59	52	39
South	49	51	49	48
West	58	57	51	40

Source: Gallup Poll.

TABLE 17-11 Presidential vote by regions, 1968

Region	Nixon	Humphrey	Wallace
East	42.7%	50.4%	6.9%
South	35.6	31.4	33.0
Midwest	46.8	43.8	9.4
West	48.9	44.0	7.1

Source: Data supplied by *Congressional Quarterly.*

TABLE 17-12 Republican congressional vote by regions, 1968

Region	Total vote percentage (all parties)	Two-party vote percentage
New England	49.3	50.1
Middle Atlantic	48.1	49.6
East North Central	54.6	54.6
West North Central	52.7	52.8
South	33.3	34.0
Border	45.7	45.9
Mountain	52.4	53.0
Pacific	52.2	52.9

Source: Republican National Committee, *The 1968 Elections* (1969).

spectrum in one direction. In other words, it is seldom that in the face of these events one group shifts one way, and others another. Blacks have generally been moving Democratic, providing an exception to this.[31]

THE POLITICAL INDEPENDENT AND THE SPLIT-TICKET VOTER
Complexity of Independence.   The number of self-identified independents has shown rather marked variation, due perhaps to the very fact of reliance on self-identification as well as on a time element. In the early 1960s, the Gallup Poll found 21 to 23 percent designating themselves as

[31] Gallup found some Negro movement to Nixon in 1968, but the Center's respondents gave a larger Negro percentage to Humphrey than to Johnson. Blacks were the only category that showed virtually no defection to Wallace. This is one of the few instances in which a demographic grouping held in the face of a strong short-term force pulling others in the opposite direction.

TABLES 17-13 Proportion of self-identified independent voters by demographic classification, 1968

National	27%	Religion	
Sex		Protestant	27%
Men	28	Catholic	27
Women	26	Jewish	24
Races		Section	
Northern whites	27	East	25
Southern whites	32	Midwest	28
Nonwhite	18	South	31
Education		West	25
College	34	Residents of cities	
High School	28	1,000,000 and over	24
Grade School	21	500,000–1,000,000	30
Occupation		50,000–500,000	30
Professional and business	32	25,000–50,000	24
Clerical-sales workers	29	Under 25,000	27
Farmers	21	Income levels	
Manual workers	29	$10,000 and over	30
Labor union	32	$ 7,000–$10,000	31
Nonunion	27	$ 5,000–$ 7,000	29
Age		$ 3,000–$ 5,000	25
21–29 years	40	Under $3,000	20
30–49 years	28		
50 and over	21		

Source: Gallup Poll, July, 1968.

independents; figures ran 20 percent in 1940, 29 percent in 1948, and 27 percent in 1968 (Table 17-13). The Survey Research Center found independents comprising 30 percent of its sample in 1968. The Center's figure (see Table 16-1 in the preceding chapter) embraces three classifications—the self-styled independent Republican and independent Democrat and those persons who give no inkling of inclining toward either party. If one takes only the last mentioned, the variation from 1952 to 1962 has been from 5 to 12 percent. Samuel Eldersveld believes that there are more independents than the self-identification indices of political analysts show.[32]

Independents are found in all classes and strata but there are observable variations by demographic classifications and regions as shown in Table 17-13. A larger number of voters who are young and college educated, who have high income and high-status occupations describe themselves as independent than do their opposites. Southerners profess greater independence than non-Southerners. This is attributable in part to Southerners opting from the Democratic party

[32]Samuel J. Eldersveld, "The Independent Voter," *American Political Science Review,* vol. 46, pp. 732–753, 1952. Gallup and Eldersveld employ different definitions of *independent,* accounting for a considerable amount of the difference in their figures on the number of independents.

toward the political right. A great many classifications vary from each other no more than 2 to 4 percent, which could be attributable to sampling errors. The greatest discrepancy between polls is found in Jewish respondents—SRC in 1964 found 42 percent in that category while only 24 percent of Gallup's Jewish interviewees so designated themselves.

The number of persons describing themselves as independents is not very meaningful and the concept itself suffers from the lack of a common standard of what constitutes an independent. Presumably an independent is one who sees himself as having no loyalty to one political party. Are the thousands of persons registered as Democrats but who frequently vote for Republicans independent? Of the Center's respondents in 1956 over thirty-five years of age who classified themselves as independents, 11 percent reported that they always, or nearly always, voted for the same party, yet the classical concept of an independent implies oscillation. Nonetheless, the independents' reported behavior was different from that of the strong identifiers, 80 percent of whom admitted supporting the same party. Conversely, 89 percent of the independents admitted casting ballots for different parties. Studies of independent voting in individual communities and states, which usually has meant split-ticket voting, go back to the turn of the century and are generally limited to one election. Taken separately through use of different measurements and indices, the data provide a hodgepodge picture and, if nothing else, show the complexity of the task of discovering the extent and types of independency. The aggregation of data based on a national survey, using comparable criteria over a long period of time, may in due course lead to adequate conceptualization. The Center is making some progress in this direction. A few incautious comments about political independency may be made.

Comparatively few respondents fit the ideal concept of an independent. Motivations for independency are likely to flow from reasons other than careful consideration and weighing of issues, candidates, and parties. A number of those poorly educated and with low incomes appear to have no great interest in issues or parties and often not in candidates either. It may well be that they have lesser feelings of political antagonism. Some independents are in the process of shifting allegiance from one major party to another or are new voters coming from parents who are of mixed affiliation or who are either not strongly partisan or perhaps independents themselves. It makes sense for young voters and even others who do not know where to go or who are uncertain to spend some time as independents before deciding on their allegiances. Some of those motivated toward independence are undoubtedly disillusioned about the ambivalence of parties on issues which have been particularly important to them. They may then have little attachment to either party and seek refuge in a third-party movement or a nonparty movement that is strongly oriented toward issues. There is evidence that many independents are cross-pressured and resolve their confusions by voting largely on the basis of candidates, voting a split ticket, or not voting at all. Some analysts believe that independents are more cross-pressured than either Democrats or Republicans. Like all other categories, there are degrees of independence and psychological attachments, and our research and hypotheses have not caught up with the unbelievable complexity of the motivations of those whose party loyalties are not strong. The long ballot itself invites independence and helps the cross-pressured voter to resolve inner conflicts by giving him many opportunities to split his ticket.

After analysis of political survey research on independents, William H. Flanigan concludes that they are not much interested in politics, especially of the partisan variety, and are not

> . . . emotionally involved in party clashes. On the other hand independents appear to have the information and the perspective on political affairs necessary for an evaluation of issues and candidates as competent as could be expected of partisans. Independents are no wiser or more virtuous than partisans; nor are they less so. It is not clear whether their lack of involvement means that independents are not easily aroused by political problems demanding their attention or whether their lack of involvement simply means independents are less biased by partisan dispositions. This uncertainty is troublesome because independents may not be sufficiently motivated to play the role of intelligently mediating disputes between Democrats and Republicans. On the other hand the self-perception of playing this mediating role may motivate independents effectively.[33]

Split-Ticket Voting. Independence in voting is characterized by (1) deserting from a major party to a third party, (2) long wavering on a decision, perhaps even leading to nonvoting or to marking the ballot only for some offices, (3) transferring allegiance from one major party to another, (4) lacking loyalty to any party, or (5) voting a split ticket. The last mentioned can be quantitatively ascertained up to a point by analyzing election statistics but such analysis sheds no light on the subjective reasons for voting across party lines. As used here, *split-ticket voting* refers to the practice of a voter discriminating among candidates on the same party ticket in any one election.

Party leaders are under the impression that since World War II split-ticket voting has been on the increase, and this may well be the case. In 1968, 54 percent of the Gallup Poll respondents reported that they split their votes between parties, 43 percent replied they voted a straight ticket, and 3 percent could not recall. "Democratic" Arkansas went for George Wallace, a Republican governor, and a Democratic United States

[33] *Political Behavior of the American Electorate,* pp. 43–44.

senator. Many other states could point to cross-voting resulting in various anomalies in partisan gubernatorial, state legislative, and congressional results. SRC samples found 38.3 percent who admitted voting a straight ticket in 1968 (Table 17-15).

The extensive split-ticket voting in 1968 was not exclusively the result of overriding events and a formidable third-party bid, as is evidenced by split-ticket voting in more tranquil times. In 1962, the Gallup Poll found 44 percent of the Democrats splitting their tickets (compared to 47 percent in 1968); Republican splits respectively were 42 and 45 percent. In both elections, 75 percent of the self-classified independents voted for candidates of different parties. In 1956, seventeen states split their president-governor-senator choices between the parties and sixteen did so in 1960.

Before 1932, there appears to have been less splitting for national-level offices in presidential election years. One such index was noted Chapter 2 (Figure 2-1); Republican percentages for the presidency and percentages of seats won by House Republicans approximated each other much more closely before than after the realignment that took place with the 1932 election. Thereafter, the Republican congressional party fell behind, indicating that a considerable number of voters who supported its presidential nominees transferred their votes to Democrats for Congress.[34]

Split-ticket voting takes many different forms. Some persons regularly split their tickets; others are inclined to vote straight tickets in most elections but from time to time are motivated to support the opposition candidates for one or more offices. Different kinds of voting behavior have consequences for campaign managers. Strategy is to be determined by which ones invite more splits over the years and in a particular election. Suppose that there are eight positions to be filled — President, United States senator and representative, governor, lieutenant governor, secretary of state, attorney general, and a member of the lower house of the state legislature. Here a voter might vote for a man like Eisenhower and a straight Democratic ticket for all remaining offices. Hundreds of thousands of Southern voters did just that, and Texas "Eisenhower Democrats" told loyal partisans that in reality they were not splitting their tickets when they voted for "Texas-born Ike." Nixon was also the beneficiary of this kind of split, although for different reasons. This kind of voting is not of serious consequence for Democratic candidates for Congress or for the state positions except that, if it persists over a period of time, Republicans for the lesser offices might also entice further splits for themselves. In other words, once a voter splits the top

[34] The strong "solid South" support for Democratic congressional candidates accounts for part of this discrepancy but by no means all of it.

of his ticket, he may tend to give individual consideration to each lower office. In 1962, Republicans for state and local offices made sizable inroads, causing some forebodings among Democrats who had felt they were safe because the defections occurred only at the presidential level. Enough of this kind of voting outside the South made the anomalous situation of a divided federal government from 1955 through 1960 and again in 1968.

Another type of split involves support for all of one party's candidates for federal office and for all of another party's candidates for state positions. Voting straight tickets at each level might be regarded as "rational" because one wished the Democrats, for example, to control the federal government and the Republicans the state government. The voter might tell himself that this avoids divided government at either level and assures, according to his light, "good" government at both. In a given election, it is doubtful that large numbers of voters deliberately choose this kind of federal-state split, although there are some states where the end result—conscious or not—is the same. This kind of split-ticket voting is more likely to be sporadic and unusual rather than customary.

The largest amount of split-ticket voting appears to involve crossing over for offices at both levels or particularly at the state level where from three to a dozen or more positions are to be filled. In this situation, we can speculate that many of the lesser offices are regarded not in strongly partisan terms but in personal terms, particularly in attitudes toward incumbents. Once in a while, an issue of a scandal may be associated with the office, leading to "throwing a rascal out" but permitting this party brethren to continue in office. Offices dealing with lands, utilities, or welfare may have group overtones leading to sharp cleavages across party lines.

Table 17-14 shows how SRC respondents split their tickets during the 1966 midterm election, in which all congressmen and most state legislatures were elected, almost three-fourth of the governors, and one-third of the United States senators. More than half the splits were not extensive, that is, the voter stayed with the same party for the governor and for Congress but split in support races for other state and/or local offices. In the second most common split (about 20 percent), the voter supported one party for the governorship but on the local level voted for the opposite (and quite likely his preferred) party. Split-ticket data for the 1968 election are presented separately in Table 17-15 because with only one-fourth of the governors elected plus a President, data are not analogous and valid comparison between the two elections cannot be made. There was less straight-ticket voting in the 1968 than in the 1966, though it will be noticed that less than 3 percent of the voters split

TABLE 17-14 Split-ticket patterns, national sample, 1966

Pattern	Percent
Straight ticket	46.2
Almost straight ticket. Vote one party for congressman, governor, senator but other party or parties for state/local offices	29.6
Governor and local split	10.6
Senator and local split	3.5
Congressman, only split	1.9
Split senator only	1.0 or less
Split governor only	1.0 or less
Split both senator and governor	1.0 or less
Other split patterns	6.2

Source: Data furnished by Inter-University Consortium for Political Research (see Table 16-2).

TABLE 17-15 Split-ticket patterns, national sample, 1968

Pattern	Percent
Straight ticket	38.3
State-local split only	15.8
Split on President only	2.7
Vote for same party for national offices, split for gubernatorial and state-local	2.1
Split on congressmen only	1.7
Split on senate only	1.0 or less
Split on governor only	1.0 or less
Other split patterns	34.4

Source: Data furnished by Inter-University Consortium for Political Research.

only for the Presidency. There was a wide variety of splits probably illustrative of the social ferment incident to "law and order" and peace issues which affected attitudes toward governors, senators, state legislators, and local candidates.

Split-ticket voting also shows considerable variation from state to state and even within a state. In 1950 midterm elections in which two or more state officials were also on the ballot, postelection interviews elicited information that only 29 percent split their tickets in Iowa while 49 percent did so in Minnesota. In the Western states, and most especially on the Pacific Coast, split-ticket voting has become more or less the norm, with straight-party sweeps the exception.[35] Comparison of raw percentages between states may not accurately depict split-ticket voting patterns because they do not take cognizance of the lengths of the ballots. New Jersey has only one and Alaska only two elective statewide officials,

[35] Frank Jonas (ed.), *Politics in the American West*, University of Utah Press, Salt Lake City, 1969. On ticket-splitting elsewhere, see Eldersveld, "The Independent Voter."

TABLE 17-16 Proportions voting straight ticket by demographic groups, 1968

Below 36%	37–42%	43–47%	48% and over
College education	30–49 years of age	Manual workers	Grade school education
High school education	Midwest	Farmers	50 years of age and over
White-collar workers	West	Protestant	Republican
Business and professional	$5,000 and over income	Catholic	Democratic
21–29 years of age	Under 50,000 population	East	Under $5,000 income
Independent		South 50,000 to 500,000 population	Over 500,000 population

Source: Gallup Poll.
Note: National average of those reporting they voted a straight ticket was 43 percent.

while most states have many more opportunities for "scratching" the ballot. The use of a ballot facilitating a straight-party vote by one mark on the ballot or a single pull of one lever can also be expected to encourage more straight-ticket voting.

Straight-ticket voting in national elections differs rather markedly by demographic classes as shown in Table 17-16. In 1968, extremes were represented by a reported 61 percent straight-ticket vote by those of grade school education and that of independents, of whom only 25 percent admitted straight party voting. Self-classified Republicans and Democrats respectively voted 53 and 49 percent "straight."[36] Generally the younger, better-educated, higher-income, business and professional voters split their tickets much more than their counterparts. Western voters also do so more than those in the East and the South. Little difference is shown in this respect as between men and women, suggesting that family patterns hold in the area of split-ticket voting as they do in partisan voting. A great majority of self-designated indpendents, moreover, reported that they vote in accordance with the tendencies of their fathers.

Although not fully established, it seems quite certain that the constancy of party identifiers in national elections is not equally valid in explaining the voting behavior for county and state offices. Eldersveld found that blacks in Detroit split their tickets more than voters of Canadian and English origin.[37]

[36] In 1964, with the absence of any popular third-party presidential candidate, SRC's respondents showed considerable split-ticket voting, which varied especially by strength of party identification. Percentages voting a straight ticket were strong Democrats, 49.9; weak Democrats, 23.1; Independent, 17.8; weak Republican, 23.1; strong Republican, 47.8.
[37] "The Independent Voter," p. 752.

Extensive split-ticket voting discourages coattail riding and shows that there are strong pulls against straight party voting. Television is probably an aid to younger, vigorous, and articulate candidates. Many voters judge on the basis of the "whole" man and not on appeals to party loyalty alone.

FOR FURTHER READING

See references at the end of Chapter 18.

It is evident that the only government which can
fully satisfy all the exigencies of the social state
is one in which the whole people participate; that
any participation, even in the smallest public
function, is useful; that the participation should
everywhere be as great as the general degree of
improvement of the community will allow; and
that nothing less can be ultimately desirable
than the admission of all to a share in the
sovereign power of the state.

JOHN STUART MILL

CHAPTER 18 POLITICAL PARTICIPATION AND ALIENATION

From the ancient political philosophers to the present, the degree and kind of participation in community affairs has received much discussion and speculation. Taking a cue from John Stuart Mill's credo as stated in the headnote, the modern social scientist is hard at work analyzing who is giving campaign money to whom, who is active in party organizations and conventions, and who is voting for whom. We have recorded some of these findings and observed their implications. It remains to consider who fails to vote in American elections and their reasons for nonparticipation. Consideration is also given in the next section to political participation through private interest groups.

Scholars use diverse methods for measuring the nature and extent of electoral participation. One is the correlation between census estimates of persons of voting age in a particular electoral subdivision and those actually casting ballots. Resulting figures are low because no account is taken of persons who, for one reason or another, are unable to qualify for voting. A second approach correlates the number of persons registered with those who actually vote. The figures will, of course, give quite a different picture. For example, under the first standard of "potential vote," only 51.3 percent of the residents of the new state of Hawaii voted in 1960, but of the registered voters 93.1 percent cast ballots; respective figures in California were 67.4 and 88.1 percent. Neither tells us the general percentages of persons by demographic group who voted or stayed away from the polls. Further, election and registration figures do not tell us why certain people failed to register or why those registered did not vote in a given election. Self-reports of a sample of respondents assist in ascertaining some psychological and demographic factors associated with participation. They can, of course, be subject to error, particularly if nonvoters do not wish to admit their dereliction. The U.S. Census Bureau finds that about 7 percent more people report having voted than is actually the case.[1]

While looking at specific facets of voter participation it is well to keep in mind the broad statistical profile of nonvoting. Of the total resident population of 120,000,000 eligible to vote in 1968, 73,160,000 actually cast ballots for President. Survey results of the U.S. Census Bureau found 74 percent of the nation's voting-age population were reported as registered and of those registered 91 percent voted.[2] From its sample, the Gallup Poll estimates that 15 million persons were registered but did not vote and another 10 million could have registered but did not. About 5 million could not meet residence requirements; 7 million were ill or disabled; and some 4 million either did not or could not obtain absentee ballots.

VOTING BY ELECTORAL LEVELS

National Elections. Presidential elections commonly bring out the greatest number of voters, but, as is seen in Table 18-1, there is marked fluctuation from election to election. The 1948 voter turnout was the lowest, for peacetime, in many years. But four years later, more than 13 million more voters turned out, an increase of more than 20 percent. The expanded turnout also resulted in a change of the party in power, although

[1] The Bureau biennially publishes a summary of voter participation by racial background. It includes data on those who reported voting and estimates of numbers actually voting. Robert E. Lane, *Political Life*, The Free Press, New York, 1959, gives an excellent summary of the findings and hypotheses relating to political participation; Seymour M. Lipset, *Political Man: The Social Bases of Politics*, Doubleday & Company, Inc., Garden City, N.Y., 1960, gives extensive attention to voting in the Western democracies.

[2] See "Voter Participation in November, 1968," U.S. Census Series P-20, no. 177, Dec. 27, 1968, and *Gallup Opinion Index*, December, 1968, pp. 6–7, Gallup International, Princeton, N.J.

TABLE 18-1 Estimated percentages of voting-age persons going to the polls

Year	Percent
1920	49.3
1922	32.4
1924	49.1
1926	30.1
1928	57.4
1930	34.1
1932	57.8
1934	41.8
1936	55.6
1938	44.5
1940	53.4
1942	32.7
1944	52.7
1946	37.6
1948	51.6
1950	41.6
1952	62.0
1954	42.5
1956	60.4
1958	43.4
1960	63.8
1962	46.5
1964	62.1
1966	48.3
1968	61.0

Source: For presidential years, U.S. Census; for mid-term elections, *Congressional Quarterly*, "Politics in America 1945–1964," p. 78, 1965.

there was not a shift of voter party preference. In other words, the surge to Eisenhower was not accompanied by corresponding increase in Republican party identification. In every election, there appears to be a basic, hard-core party vote. Except for the Republican split in 1912, the Landon vote in 1936 represented the rock bottom of core Republican strength. Even in that year, Landon polled 16,675,000 votes, or 37 percent of the two-party vote.

Angus Campbell speaks of the 1952 electoral outcome as a "surge election."[3] In the first place, millions of persons who failed to vote in 1948 were stimulated to vote. Of the Center's 1,600 respondents

[3]Angus Campbell, "Surge and Decline: A Study of Electoral Change," *Public Opinion Quarterly*, vol. 24, pp. 397–418, 1960, table 1, p. 405.

who failed to vote in 1948, 14 percent came to the polls and divided 4 to 3 for Eisenhower. There was also a dramatic shift of partisanship that was almost unidirectional; that is, 11 percent who voted Democratic in 1948 shifted to the Republican candidate, and only 1 percent of the Dewey voters went to Stevenson. Beyond party loyalty, there were no countervailing forces that the Democrats could muster against Eisenhower and such issues as Korea. In 1960, another high-stimulus election brought out 7 million more voters than in 1956. Of these, Nixon ran 1.5 million less than Eisenhower, but Kennedy was the beneficiary of about 8.5 million more votes than Stevenson received in 1956. There was less of a surge but till a remarkable shift.

A decrease in the percentage voting for President occurred in 1964 and an additional decline took place in 1968 despite a three-way contest for the Presidency and much social unrest. An interesting aspect of the 1968 election was the 3.6 percent decline of voters, both white and nonwhite, in the North and West but an increase in the South of 3.4 percent. The results of efforts to activate blacks was especially evident in the South, with 7.4 percent more reported voting than in 1964 while white percentages rose 2.7 percent. The saliency of civil rights and the Wallace candidacy undoubtedly brought a larger surge of voters in the South. Elsewhere there was some alienation on the part of militant citizens opposed to the Vietnam war and a lack of enthusiasm for the presidential nominees.

Variations in turnout in presidential voting are probably not due to a single factor. The low percentage of potential voters who voted in 1920 and 1924 was certainly attributable in part to the fact that women had not previously voted in most states, and many of them failed to take advantage of the opportunity. Similarly, problems of facilitating the soldier vote and other wartime factors held down percentages in 1944. It would be harder to find a similar explanation for the low participation in 1948, or in 1932 when the country was in a severe depression.

One of the most pronounced fluctuations in turnout is evidenced in midterm elections (see Table 18-1), with a falloff as high as 20 percent from the preceding presidential election.[4] The pull of a presidential candidate is missing, and many of the peripheral voters who did vote for President remain away from the polls in the following congressional elections. At midterm elections, the party controlling the Presidency almost always has suffered a loss of seats in Congress usually in both houses (see Table 18-2). Table 18-3, prepared by Campbell[5] and

---

[4] For an analytic account based on data drawn from several states in the 1950 election, see William N. McPhee and William A. Glaser (eds.), *Public Opinion and Congressional Elections*, The Free Press, New York, 1962, chap. 1.

[5] Campbell, *op. cit.*, p. 411.

TABLE 18-2 Midterm changes in majority party in Congress, seats gained or lost

Year	President	Senate	House
1906	Roosevelt	+ 3	−28
1910	Taft	−10	−56
1914	Wilson	+ 5	−66
1918	Wilson	− 6	−21
1922	Coolidge	− 6	−75
1926	Coolidge	− 7	−12
1930	Hoover	− 8	−51
1934	Roosevelt	+10	+ 9
1938	Roosevelt	− 6	−80
1942	Roosevelt	−10	−47
1946	Truman	−13	−56
1950	Truman	− 5	−28
1954	Eisenhower	− 1	−18
1958	Eisenhower	−13	−47
1962	Kennedy	+ 4	− 4
1966	Johnson	− 3	−47

TABLE 18-3 Partisanship of vote in 1956 and 1958

Vote for President, 1956	Vote for congressman, 1958	Percent
Democratic	Democratic	22
Republican	Republican	22
Democratic	Republican	2
Republican	Democratic	11
Democratic	Did not vote	6
Republican	Did not vote	12
Did not vote	Democratic	3
Did not vote	Republican	1
Did not vote	Did not vote	21

based on the Center's sample, shows where the Eisenhower voters went in 1958, a year of serious Republican setbacks in Congress. It is remarkable that while there was a 14 percent net dropoff in the total vote (SRC sample), the percentage of those remaining loyal to the Democrats and the Republicans and those not voting remained roughly equivalent. Turnout, therefore, was influential in the result. But turnout alone does not account for all electoral changes. Some voters undergo change between elections and reflect it in the next election.

State and Local Elections. Generally, the longer the ballot the greater the falloff in the vote cast for minor and local offices. The type of ballot doubtless affects voting participation for lesser state and local offices. In some states, the presidential vote is separated from the rest of the ballot. Where candidates are grouped by office on the ballot, the voter is required to register a choice for each office, which may reduce the number of votes for the lesser offices. Without the opportunity to vote a straight ticket in a single operation, weak identifiers and those with a low level of interest might be inclined to refrain from expressing a judgment for the minor offices.[6] Candidates recognize this and their campaign literature often features sample ballots specially marked to draw attention to their names. Conversely, where straight-ticket voting is a benefit to them, publicity will feature both their names and a suggestion to vote straight Republican (Democratic).

Apathy is far more prevalent in county and municipal elections than in state and national elections. Over two decades in Los Angeles city elections, turnout ranged from 10 to 61 percent, averaging around 41 percent. Among the local subdivisions of a single state, there may be sharp contrasts in voter participation for a particular office. In one Maryland gubernatorial election, there was a variation among counties from 28.8 to 56.5 percent turnout of registered voters. Three different types of elections in New Orleans in a single year illustrate the variety of attraction to voters. Among registered voters, 82 percent voted in the mayorality primary; the number then declined to 34 percent in the general election; and a school board election brought out 29 percent.[7]

Despite some contradictory findings in studies of cities in specific states, the most comprehensive study, which utilized comparative turnout figures from 282 cities, permits some cautious generalizations[8] (see Table 18-4). The study used three categories of factors—political and social structures and community continuity. Form of city government is found to have a more significant relationship to turnout than form of election. Turnout runs higher in mayor-council cities than in council-manager cities. Further, voting participation tends to run less in cities using nonpartisan ballots than in those using partisan ones (Table 18-4). In "reformed" cities with managers and nonpartisan ballots the political party as a mechanism for aggregating interests and getting out the vote is more removed and distant than in mayor-council and partisan elections.

A more surprising finding is that cities with more highly ethnic or less well-educated populations generally have higher levels of voting turnout, regardless of form of government and elections. This is despite the well-established fact that better-educated individuals vote more frequently than those with less education. Better-educated persons have channels other than merely voting through which to affect policy, but

[6]The subject of ballot forms and falloff was covered in Chap. 15. See also Table 15-4.
[7]See Leonard Reissman et al., *The New Orleans Voter*, Tulane University Studies in Political Science, New Orleans, 1955.
[8]Robert R. Alford and Eugene A. Lee "Voting Turnout in American Cities," *American Political Science Review*, vol. 62, pp. 796–813, 1968. See also Eugene A. Lee, *The Politics of Nonpartisanship*, University of California Press, Berkeley, 1960, chaps. 9 and 11.

TABLE 18-4 Mean percent of city registrants voting, by social and political structure

Characteristics of city	Partisan ballot		Nonpartisan ballot	
	Nonmanager	Manager	Nonmanager	Manager
Ethnicity				
High	65%	45%	58%	42%
Low	62	49	48	40
Education				
High	59	45	53	39
Low	66	50	57	44
Mobility				
High	60	40	52	39
Low	65	58	56	44
Age of city				
Old	66	47	57	43
New	60	45	51	38
All cities	64	47	55	40

Source: Adapted from Robert R. Alford and Eugene A. Lee, "Voting Turnout in American Cities," *American Political Science Review*, vol. 62, p. 808, 1968.

this factor in itself is not a full explanation. Clearly, much more research on the relationship of education and ethnicity to voting in city elections is needed. As Alford and Lee point out, "It may well be true—and we suspect—that in *all* cities, the better educated are more likely to vote than the less well-educated, despite the higher overall levels of voting turnout in less well-educated cities."[9]

Finally, and of less surprise, cities with more stable populations have higher voting turnout. There is likely more integration into the community where there is less mobility. The mean of adults voting in Eastern cities was 49 percent compared to 37 percent in the Midwest, 30 percent in the West and 23 percent in the South, with older cities having higher turnout than the younger ones. In conclusion, local-election levels of voting are the result of many combined influences, such as the vigor of sustained effort by party organizations, voluntary "good government" and other associations, and traditional behavior by groups that emphasize the importance (or lack of it) of turnout.

It is a safe guess that the electorate voting on local matters is more sporadic than and is different from the one voting in gubernatorial and national elections.[10] Further, with exceptions of Southern Democratic contests, electorate participation in primaries is usually consistently lower than in general elections; it is also somewhat different. In Wisconsin, the direct-primary voters of the two major parties differed some from each other but in general they were more interested and

[9]Alford and Lee, *op. cit.*, p. 811.
[10]For participation in local politics by class, see Robert A. Dahl, *Who Governs?* Yale University Press, New Haven, Conn., 1961, pp. 276–301.

more active in politics than the general electorate. At the same time, contrary to conventional wisdom, they did not hold more extreme ideological positions.[11] The basic differences other than size of the electorate in the various types of local elections are yet to undergo comprehensive analysis. But it is probable that local elections are viewed differently from those of other levels, making it rational for a voter to incline toward Republicanism in most national elections but to support Democrats locally, or vice versa. Many cities are controlled or strongly influenced over long periods of time by what is loosely viewed as the "establishment," with strong bipartisan composition. Aided by broadly composed municipal leagues and citizens associations, its supporters can be depended on to turn out and to have much to do with the attention or lack of attention focused on the city election. This effort affects both the turnout and the types of voters going to the polls.

A graph of voting on issues in a given state over a period of time would likely be saw-toothed. On such matters as liquor, gambling, right-to-work legislation, tax increases, veterans' bonuses, and racial questions, there is often a remarkably high level of interest, and more people may vote on such issues than for a number of the lesser statewide offices.

Participation is usually much less on technical questions and constitutional amendments than on questions about which powerful groups conduct spirited campaigns; this suggests an important relationship between awareness, interest, involvement, and voting response. In many local referendums on school issues, bonds, and charter amendments, propositions are defeated because a requisite number of voters, even if only 10 to 20 percent, could not be drawn to the polls; in such situations, the nonvoters in effect actually determine the election outcome. Initiatives may bring a larger turnout than referendums because the former would probably not be on the ballot unless a reasonably well-organized and well-financed interest group conducted campaigns for them.

DEMOGRAPHIC CHARACTERISTICS OF VOTER PARTICIPATION

Residence.   Mobility, as noted above, keeps many persons from fulfilling registration requirements; but it is not solely responsible for rather surprising differences in voting participation, both throughout the nation and within a given state and even within a city. At one extreme in 1968 were ten states whose turnout of the potential (as opposed to the registered) vote was 70 percent or better (see Table 18-5).[12] In contrast,

---

[11]Austin Ranney and Leon D. Epstein, "The Two Electorates: Voters and Non-Voters in a Wisconsin Primary," *Journal of Politics*, vol. 28, pp. 598–616, 1966.

[12]The U.S. Census found 74.3 percent of voting population *registered*, with 67.3 percent *reporting* they voted for President but, according to the Census estimates, only 61.0 percent actually voted. For state-by-state details and racial participation, see the U.S. Census Bureau's "Voter Participation in November 1968."

TABLE 18-5 Percentages by states of persons of voting age actually voting for President, 1968

70 percent and over	63–69 percent	56–62 percent	55 percent and under
Delaware	Colorado	California	Alabama
Idaho	Connecticut	Florida	Alaska
Illinois	Kansas	Hawaii	Arizona
Indiana	Maine	Missouri	Arkansas
Iowa	Massachusetts	Maryland	District of Columbia
Minnesota	Michigan	Nebraska	Georgia
New Hampshire	Montana	New Mexico	Kentucky
South Dakota	New Jersey	New York	Louisiana
Utah	North Dakota	Oklahoma	Mississippi
Washington	Ohio		Nevada
	Oregon		North Carolina
	Pennsylvania		South Carolina
	Rhode Island		Tennessee
	Vermont		Texas
	Wisconsin		Virginia
	Wyoming		

Source: U.S. Census estimate.
Note: Alphabetical rather than percentile arrangement. National average = 61 percent.

fifteen states had turnouts of 55 percent or less. The national average was 61 percent. The high-participation states, although all non-Southern, are scattered throughout the nation but follow no regional pattern. With the exception of Illinois, none of the states have huge big-city minorities, who often compose a larger-than-average percentage of nonvoters. Voter turnout is on the increase in the South but only Florida had moved above the 55 percent mark in 1968. Adjacent states sometimes show striking differentials, as evidenced by a very much higher turnout in Utah than in Nevada and in Delaware than in Maryland. Obviously one must look beyond geographical location to cultural makeup and traditions and to election laws to account for the rather striking variation of nonvoting.

Although some polls show a higher sense of political efficacy and civic duty among urban citizens than those in the open country, it has not been established that nonvoting is higher in the latter. V. O. Key, Jr., failed to find greater urban participation in Southern primaries.[13] Incomplete studies in Indiana and Washington indicate that urban areas often trail rural areas in voter turnout. The picture is confused by the fact that there seems to be greater variability in rural turnout and greater fluctuation in partisan vote division in rural areas than are found in metropolitan communities. Because of considerable rural nonvoting in the South, moreover, a national sample biases the picture for rural-urban percentages in a given Northern or Western community. Canada

[13] *Southern Politics*, Alfred A. Knopf, Inc., New York, 1949, pp. 510–513.

offers a fascinating comparison with the United States, in that turnouts in provincial elections often exceed those for federal elections; and, in the major provinces, rural-area participation surpasses that in the metropolitan areas.[14]

In greater Detroit, migration was found associated with a low frequency in voting.[15] The longer the residence in the community, the greater was the likelihood of voting; migrants were less motivated and less likely to vote than natives. As one becomes adjusted to the community, one tends to vote; and the influence of migration diminishes. Immigrants, after becoming citizens, often vote as frequently as nonimmigrants, suggesting that assimilation into the community improves electoral participation. Length of residence helps one to move ahead in status and in association with groups who vote. Mobility from community to community acts to decrease involvement because of reduction of one's chances to engage in community activity. But there are many exceptions to this, with some newcomers getting into politics quickly and easily.

Turnout by Groups.   Among the several surveys of voting and nonvoting, the U.S. Census Bureau's interviews with 65,000 persons from all states constitute the largest sample (Table 18-6). The surveys are conducted immediately following elections, and percentages are those of eligible voters who *reported* that they voted (or did not vote). Table 18-7, which uses somewhat different categories, shows nonvoting in 1964 and 1968. Although a few percentage-point differences are found from other smaller-sample surveys, all agree essentially on the broad categories of higher and lower participation.[16]

Among the deductions of electoral action or inaction that can be drawn from the data are that more eligible men than women vote, and more whites than nonwhites.[17] Education and income appear as probably the most important variables fostering greater voter turnout.

[14] See Harry A. Scarrow, "Patterns of Voter Turnout in Canada," *Midwest Journal of Political Science,* vol. 5, pp. 351–364, 1961.

[15] Harry Sharp, "Migration and Voting Behavior in a Metropolitan Community," *Public Opinion Quarterly,* vol. 19, pp. 206–209, 1955.

[16] Somewhat different classifications were used in a 1952 survey reported in Angus Campbell and Homer C. Cooper, *Group Differences in Attitudes and Votes,* Michigan Survey Research Center, Ann Arbor, Mich., 1956, chap. 3. It is similar to other studies; overall results are alike but there were a few striking variations in percentages.

[17] At this writing the most comprehensive data on voting participation by demographic classifications and residence are found in U.S. Bureau of the Census, *Current Population Reports,* Series P-20, no. 174, "Voting and Registration in the Election of November, 1966," U.S. Government Printing Office, Washington, D.C., 1968. The much shorter preliminary work on the 1968 elections, "Voting Participation in November 1968," was issued Dec. 27, 1968. Much useful historical data and voting trends are given in W. D. Burnham, "The Changing Shape of the American Political Universe," *American Political Science Review,* vol. 59, pp. 7–28, 1965.

TABLE 18-6 Percentage of persons reporting they voted by groups, 1964 and 1966

Group	Persons who voted	
	1964	1966
National	69.3%	55.4%
Sex		
Men	71.9	58.2
Women	67.0	53.0
Race		
White	70.7	57.1
Nonwhite	57.5	41.1
Negro	58.5	41.8
Age		
21–24 years	50.9	31.2
25–34 years	64.7	45.9
35–44 years	72.8	59.7
45–64 years	75.9	64.5
65 years and over	66.3	56.1
Occupation		
White-collar workers	82.0	67.2
Manual workers	65.6	49.8
Service workers	65.8	49.0
Farm workers	63.7	59.4
Section		
North and West	74.6	60.9
South	56.7	43.0
Residence		
Metropolitan	70.8	56.3
In central cities	69.5	54.1
Outside central cities	72.2	58.3
Nonmetropolitan	66.5	53.8
Education		
Elementary school (8 years)	67.0	53.4
High school (4 years)	76.1	60.1
College (4 years or more)	87.5	70.5
Annual family income		
Under $3,000	53.3	43.2
$3,000 to $4,999	62.7	47.2
$5,000 to $7,499	72.4	55.0
$7,500 to $9,999	78.3	62.6
$10,000 and over	84.9	69.5

Source: U.S. Census Bureau.

Higher participation is found among executive-professional and white-collar workers than among farmers and manual workers. It seems logical that exposure to political material increases with income, occupation, and education and that being better informed and more interested fosters a more active political role. Notwithstanding college student involvement in protests during the past decade, older persons have a con-

TABLE 18-7 Percentage of nonvoters by selected categories, 1964 and 1968

Group	1964 percent	1968 percent
Income		
Under $3,000	36%	39%
Over $10,000	13	12
Age		
Under 25 years	41	44
25–34 years	29	28
35–44 years	16	22
45–54 years	18	14
Occupation		
Professional, technical	11	11
Managers, proprietors	14	16
Clerical, sales	13	16
Skilled, semiskilled	23	30
Unskilled	38	39
Farmers and farm managers	21	12
Housewives	25	26
Social class		
Working	28	30
Middle	14	17

Source: Data supplied by Inter-University Consortium on Political Research (see Table 16-2).

siderably better voter participation than those in their twenties. This is probably due in part to the reinforcement of higher incomes, high-status occupations, and membership in more groups, with a greater possibility of group influence as one grows older.[18] Group membership is a cue but by no means definitive. Trade-union members on the whole, despite appeals of their leaders, nearly as often stay away from the polls as do workers not belonging to unions. However, there is a much higher nonvoting rate among the unemployed than the employed.

A number of young voters pass up their first or second opportunities to vote because of military service, new jobs, absence at college or because they have postponed becoming politically involved. Differing from older voters, young women seem as likely to vote as men in the same age bracket.

Jews, followed by Catholics and Protestants in that order, have the best voting record. In the Inter-University Consortium sample

[18] The disengagement hypothesis that, in transition from middle age to senescence, there is a progressive noninvolvement with other members in society does not seem to diminish to any great degree voting rates of the elderly whose health *permits* them to vote. Age perhaps has fewer distractions and less mobility, with a consequence of more available time for public affairs. For one pertinent study, see Norval D. Glenn and Michael Grimes, "Aging, Voting, and Political Interests," *American Sociological Review*, vol. 33, pp. 563–575, 1968.

TABLE 18-8 Voting and nonvoting by region, race, and religious preference, 1968

| Candidate | Non-South White | | | | Negro | |
	Protestant	Catholic	Jewish	Other	Protestant	Catholic
Humphrey	22	46	80	35	70	75
Nixon	53	32	7	19	2	0
Wallace	6	4	3*	8	0	0
Nonvoter	19	18	3	38	28	25

| Candidate | South White | | | Negro | |
	Protestant	Catholic	Other	Protestant	Catholic
Humphrey	16	33	22	56	86
Nixon	32.5	13	11	2	0
Wallace	19	25	0	0	0
Nonvoter	32.5	29	67	42	14

Source: Data supplied by Inter-University Consortium on Political Research (see Table 16-2).
*An additional 7 percent voted for other minor-party candidates. No Southern Jewish respondents were in the sample; the number of Negroes with no religious preference was so small as to be without significance, and they are not included in the table.

(Table 18-8) it will be noticed that in both the North and South nonvoting is higher among those who do not express a religious affiliation. Again one must look beyond religious membership to residence (such as the Protestant South), income, education, and occupation for explanatory theories of these variations, for there is nothing inherent in religious dogma to account for different rates of voter action. Mormonism, however, may influence turnout, as Utah is rather consistently in the top two or three states with the best percentage turnout in the nation. Church leaders emphasize voting and this in turn stirs non-Mormons to come to the polls.

As a general practice, the big-city ethnic groupings and nonwhites have a higher rate of nonvoting than Anglo-Saxon whites. In the Census Bureau's national sample in 1964 and 1968, whites ran about 13 percent greater in voter participation than did nonwhites. In the hotly contested New York City mayoralty election in 1969, although Puerto Ricans constituted more than 10 percent of the population, only 30 percent of them were even registered to vote. Turnout of blacks in congressional elections in Adam Clayton Powell's Harlem district has usually run very small. This is far from a complete picture, however. An increasing number of blacks are running for mayor; and, when there is such saliency for blacks, turnout is usually high. When Carl B. Stokes, a black, ran for mayor in Cleveland in 1967, it was estimated that a larger percentage of blacks voted than whites and Stokes received nearly all of the Negro vote. The white vote was polarized, with only about 10 percent supporting Stokes. He slightly improved his standing with white voters in his reelection bid and narrowly won by less than 4,000 votes.

Family and primary groups undoubtedly influence not only *how* but *if* one votes. Generally, married persons show a more active interest in politics than the unmarried, and those separated or divorced show less interest than those who are single.

MOTIVATION, INTEREST, AND TURNOUT

If one eliminates the young voters who pass up their first voting opportunity, there is probably not a large percentage of persons who have never voted, though it has been estimated as high as 15 percent.[19] Most Americans vote occasionally so that when one speaks of nonvoters it might be more accurate to refer to them as sporadic or occasional voters. However—and most important—the social composition of the stay-at-homes does not appear to change significantly from one election to the next, and the preceding pages have noted some of the groups that are more constant and those that are less constant in voting participation. It is obvious from the numbers of persons who do vote in presidential, midterm, and state and local elections that a sizable percentage vote in one election and not in another, and this expansion and contraction of the electorate is strongly related to interest. What is more, it often has great influence on the electoral outcome.

Stimulation leads to involvement and participation, but it is not easy to measure intensity of interest in a given election.[20] Stimulation can come from interest and involvement with a candidate. For this reason, lesser candidates wish to have a highly popular person at the top of the ticket, feeling that they may also capture the votes of his supporters. The less-motivated voters are sensitive to personal influences and personality and certain candidates may be able to stir them enough to get them to the polls. If an issue has great saliency, it may bring out persons who are not attracted either by party label or candidate. In one state, a right-to-work initiative polled more votes than were cast for the highest statewide candidate, a popular United States senator. Being exposed to mass media, attending a rally, and engaging in political conversation can also add to one's awareness of candidates, issues, and parties. Campaign activity, such as canvasing, stimulates voters and usually increases the

[19] William H. Flanigan cites this figure but includes those under thirty. He estimates that about half of the habitual nonvoters live in the South, with more than two-thirds of them women and one-fourth Negro. They come for the most part from very poor homes. See his *Political Behavior of the American Electorate*, Allyn and Bacon, Inc., Boston, 1968, pp. 20–35.

[20] Panel studies are more or less unanimous in their findings that as interest increases and as concern such as "caring a great deal who wins" heightens, turnout also increases, although not in precisely the same percentages.

number of potential voters who actually vote. The apathetic are slow to respond, but as various stimuli are increased, the turnout differences between the strongly and weakly motivated decrease.

Strong partisans usually have a higher level of interest and involvement and therefore a higher rate of participation (see figure 18-1). On the other hand, independents and weak identifiers have a poorer record of turnout. (Independent is sometimes a self-styled category to cover up one's lack of interest in and knowledge of public affairs.) The Center has noted that "intensity of preference affects not only whether the individual votes; it affects how 'strongly' he votes as well." Its 1956 panel study found also that the "person who thinks the outcome of the election is a foregone conclusion is not more likely to vote if his preference is strong. But the person who thinks the outcome is in doubt is more likely to vote if the intensity of his partisan preference is high."[21]

Other related psychological factors are the senses of civic duty and of political efficacy that one possesses. The Center's studies over more than one election have found that the strength of one's sense of obligation to perform his civic duties affects his participation.[22] The stronger the person's sense of citizen duty, the greater is the likelihood that he will vote. Where the feeling of obligation is not strong, voting is considerably more rare. A closely related factor is that of expectation. Some groups, especially those of upper status, are expected to be more politically involved. In the days after the adoption of woman suffrage, women did not foresee their role in politics as equal with men. It was "traditional" in parts of the South for blacks to refrain from voting until recently; they were "not expected to."

THE VOTING DECISION: RECAPITULATION

The great majority of the electorate view a campaign through what Gerald Pomper calls the "lens of partisanship."[23] In this context an individual looks at the election from a setting of party affiliation, family influences, life style, and group identifications. When these forces act in one direction and reinforce each other, the voter often reaches his decision early in a campaign and may incline to vote nearly a straight ticket. A person from a Republican family, who is in an upper-status occupation with a good income and is a Protestant, would be predisposed to stay

[21] Angus Campbell, Philip E. Converse, Warren E. Miller, and Donald E. Stokes, *The American Voter*, John Wiley & Sons, Inc., New York, 1960, p. 99.

[22] Scales and measurements of this factor are found in Angus Campbell, Gerald Gurin, and Warren E. Miller, *The Voter Decides*, Harper & Row, Publishers, Incorporated, New York, 1954, pp. 194–199.

[23] A thoughtful summary treatment of voting is found in his *Elections in America: Control and Influence in Democratic Politics*, Dodd, Mead & Company, Inc., New York, 1968, chaps. 4 and 5.

with Republican candidates. A young Catholic who is a manual worker has forces working on him in the direction of the Democrats.

On the other hand, in some elections forces appear that upset this stability. There are other people who are more or less under constant cross-pressure. Academic analysts have been aware of the cross-pressure phenomenon since the beginning of the century, but only recently have such effects been studied. It is most difficult to isolate each pressure and, by holding other variables constant, determine its extent. Irish-Catholic manufacturers are likely to be pulled both in a Republican and in a Democratic direction. Many individuals fall into more than one category; and other persons undergo changes in income, occupation, residence, or marital status. Belonging to different categories places one under cross-pressure. A group may have little or no influence on a person's vote unless he identifies in a strong and subjective way with it and there is a perceived group choice. Voting studies show that, with very rare exceptions, a minority in every classification opposes the voting

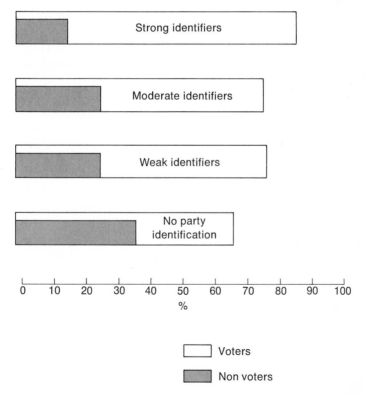

Figure 18-1 Ratio of voters to nonvoters within various party identification categories, 1968. *(Source: Data supplied by Inter-University Consortium for Political Research.)*

tendency of the majority. Many manual workers and Catholics vote for Republicans. Democratic presidential candidates get money and votes from the rich and Republicans obtain votes from the poor.

The relevance of group membership to a voting decision varies from election to election. In 1960, Kennedy's religion had great impact on voters. He drew a large number of Catholic manual workers who either supported Eisenhower or did not vote in 1956, but lost some of the Protestant workers who had supported Stevenson. The 1964 and 1968 races had high salience for blacks and for Southern whites, which had not been true in 1956 or 1960. The charisma (or lack of it) of candidates also stirs conflict and disturbs the forces of stability.

Cross-pressures differ in degree and in effect. The voter under strong crosscurrents is likely to be confused and to resolve the conflict by not voting for a particular candidate or proposition on the ballot. This caution of "when in doubt, leave it out" may be commendable and it leaves the outcome to those less in doubt. Nonvoting is a form of decision in the face of the cross-pulling of forces.

Another effect of cross-pressures for many is delay in making a decision. In 1948 neither Dewey nor Truman appeared to have much charisma. Further there was the pull of two minor-party candidates (Henry A. Wallace and J. Strom Thurmond). As the public opinion polls found to their dismay, there were many undecided voters late in the campaign with more than a predicted share of them finally voting for President Truman. Again in 1968, neither Humphrey nor Nixon had the personal popularity of an Eisenhower and many voters were pulled and hauled in different directions. There were a substantial number of late deciders and many last-minute switchers to Humphrey.[24] In contrast, the voting decisions were made much earlier in 1940, 1952, and 1956.

The 1969 New York mayoralty election affords an example of sharp cross-pressures that upset usually stable influences. Republican incumbent John Lindsay lost renomination in the Republican primary and ran at the head of two minor parties, Liberal and Independent. His Republican and Democratic opponents were less impressive as candidates, and party lines could not hold. Prominent leaders and officeholders of both major parties endorsed Lindsay, and he was able to win with a popular plurality of 42 percent. Lindsay polled heavily among the poor and the wealthy and not well with those of middle income. Samples showed Italians stayed with the two major-party candidates, Mario A. Procaccino and John J. Marchi, giving Lindsay only 15 percent; similarly, the Irish constituted only about one-fourth of the latter's

---

[24] The Gallup Poll reported that two weeks before election day one voter in every four had not yet made up his mind how he would vote for President.

support. But by capturing more than 40 percent of the Jewish vote and a huge bloc of the Negroes and Puerto Ricans, a victorious plurality coalition was put together.[25] As further indication of split-ticket voting and the ineffectiveness of local borough organizations to hold some of their traditional voters, the Democratic candidate for controller and the Republican candidate for city council president were elected.

The tenacity of party identification must not obscure the fact that the American electorate is flexible. Not only do the disinterested, the independents, and uninformed switch votes, but the interested and informed do also. Strong partisans show changes but in lesser proportions than the weaker identifiers and the nonaffiliated. The same forces that caused Catholics to move to Eisenhower caused white-collar and blue-collar workers, old and young to do so but not in the same percentages. The same was true in the move to Johnson in 1964. The authors of *The American Voter* found about 44 percent of the voters have at some time supported an opposition candidate for president in at least one election.[26] In view of the great switches in 1968 the figure today is likely well over 50 percent. In a given election, perhaps 30 percent of the voters either switched their party choice or were nonvoters in the preceding election.

V. O. Key, Jr., studied voter shifts in presidential elections from 1940 to 1960, using Gallup Poll data for classifying the electorate into "standpatters," who cast ballots for the same party's candidates in two successive elections, "switchers," who moved from one party to another in their vote, and "new voters," who were too young to vote previously or had been nonvoters.[27] In the 1960 election, he found 67 percent standpatters, 19 percent switchers, and 14 percent new voters. Nixon benefited by a greater standpatter vote; however, the advantage was more than offset by shifters moving to Kennedy.

Key's analysis of the switchers, however, is of significance. He found a parallelism between policy preferences and the direction of the vote. In other words, the switchers moved toward the party whose views on visible campaign issues were the same as their own. Standpatters, who stayed with the party, agreed with the orthodox position of the party. "From our analyses," Key writes, "the voter emerges as a person who appraises the actions of government, who has policy preferences, and who relates his vote to those appraisals."[28] This suggests that the switchers may well be more policy oriented than the standpatters. Some scholars are reluctant to accept this on the basis of evidence to date. The data

[25] *The New York Times*, Nov. 6, 1969.
[26] Campbell et al., *op. cit.*, p. 148.
[27] V. O. Key, Jr., with the assistance of Milton C. Cummings, Jr., *The Responsible Electorate: Rationality in Presidential Voting, 1936–1968*, Harvard University Press, Cambridge, Mass., 1966.
[28] *Ibid.*, pp. 58–59. By permission of Belknap Press Of Harvard University Press.

from Key plus the tables in our section nevertheless do show that voting decisions for millions of people are not exclusively matters of party label but that candidates and issues are often very significant short-term forces that must be reckoned with.

Broadly, the "floater" and sporadic voters are the ones who bring about change and determine the relative strength of the parties. Floaters are defined as those who do not make the same party choice in two successive elections and who are likely to change the most between elections.[29] By shifting, only a small percentage of the electorate can overturn the party in power. Many of the floaters are cross-pressured and vacillate in their voting decisions. Waiverers and shifters come in and out of the electorate as they are stirred by events, candidates, or exhortations of their group. They may, in fact, be more responsive to a situation than the regular steady voters. To the extent that they are kept within the control of the major parties, their participation does not disrupt the stability of the two-party system; but, if they turn to third parties or extremist candidates in the major parties, they can cause instability. The behavior, then, of floaters, independents, weak partisans, and inconsistent voters brings about the degree of party change.

PARTY ORGANIZATIONS AND VOTING BEHAVIOR

To be successful at the polls, party organizations use each of the three variables — party label, candidate, and issues — to strengthen their position. Because party identification is an enduring, long-run factor in a voter's choice, the party's prime objective becomes one of fortifying its image where favorable and of winning new adherents, particularly among young people whose party attachments are not as strong or hardened as those who are older.

Because secondary (though not necessarily politicized) groups may influence the votes of their members, it is advantageous for a party to try to exploit the leadership of secondary groups capable of bringing persons to or pushing them toward a party. Groups are useful in reinforcing those party identifications that are dominant within the group and may help weaken the attachments of those members who incline toward the opposite party. Further, the stronger the group identification, the greater the pressure on the member to follow its political viewpoints.

These facts are important to party leaders because each major party has as its clientele groups whose members, by varying majorities, prefer one party over another. Neither party psychologically attracts all

[29] See H. Daudt, *Floating Voters and the Floating Vote*, H. E. Stenfett Kroese, Leiden, 1961. Daudt is critical of many of the findings on these voters and does not agree that floaters are mainly poorly informed.

the members of the large secondary groups, but one party often commands a majority of a particular group. The role of the party, then, is to energize its relationship with its major clientele groups and to attempt as well to build bridges to as many other secondary groups as possible. A group's influence on the voting behavior of its own members is likely to be more effective when a contact is established between the leadership of the group and the leadership of the party. The nexus must be such as to show the salience and meaningfulness of the party for the individual member of the group. This is not a momentary devotion to a party's candidate—although this is helpful—but to the party as an enduring entity. If, as the data suggest, the more strongly attached the member is to a group, the more likely its influence, then it is logical for party leaders to cultivate the more committed secondary group members and to increase their number.

Data on political participation are of special value to party leaders since they show who votes and who does not and the relationship of high self-confidence and motivation to turnout. The patterns of participation can and should influence what the party organizations do. It is obvious that campaign organizations need to activate and reinforce the highly interested and motivated voters and make the less interested and low-motivated voters aware of the election. This calls for combining the functions of both interesting and informing the citizen. Party activists fail in many cases to heighten interest in local elections, and despite so-called educational efforts during campaigns, large numbers of citizens remain uninformed, have misconceptions of candidates and issues, and, under cross-pressures, do not vote.

At the same time, there is some evidence that party organizations are not helpless victims but are capable of expanding participation, even though this problem has not yet been widely or comparatively researched. Two examples will suffice to suggest the efficacy of activity. Using a body of interim data of the Center's 1952 sample, Morris Janowitz and Dwaine Marvick linked voting to mass media exposure.[30] Those exposed to mass media were much more likely to be regular party voters (Table 18-9). Nonvoting was much less among television and press users than among those not paying much attention to them; the differential was less with radio. All in all, the use of mass media by the candidates and parties increased turnout; that is, high involvement with the media led to increase in voting.

Turning to a second activity, canvasing (attempted persuasion by persons acting as spokesmen for the major parties), evidence also links this activity with reduction in nonvoting. The same study found

---

[30]Morris Janowitz and Dwaine Marvick, *Competitive Pressure and Democratic Consent*, Bureau of Government, Institute of Public Administration, The University of Michigan, Ann Arbor, 1956, chap. 5.

TABLE 18-9 Mass-media exposure and voting patterns, 1945–1952

	Mass-media audience			
	Television	Press	Radio	**Nonusers**
Regular party voters	57.2%	54.7%	45.7%	11.8%
Voting changers	31.8	32.4	28.4	30.1
Persistent nonvoters	11.0	12.9	25.9	58.1

Source: Adapted from Morris Janowitz and Dwaine Marvick, *Competitive Pressure and Democratic Consent*, Bureau of Government, Institute of Public Administration, The University of Michigan, Ann Arbor, 1956, p. 68.
Note: The figures are percentages, and mean, for example, that 58.1 percent of nonusers of mass media were persistent nonvoters, while 11.0 percent who were television viewers, 12.9 percent who were readers of the press, and 25.9 percent who were radio listeners were persistent nonvoters.

that of the 12 percent of the electorate canvased by one or both parties, a substantial number who might otherwise have failed to vote were activated to vote. "Among those not canvased 27.9 percent were non-voters in 1952; among canvased persons, only 12.7 percent did not vote."[31] A study in Detroit found that if the minority party strengthens its precinct work, it may increase votes by 5 percent over expectations, which means a 10 percent effect since the other side loses 5 percent.[32] Further, the party as a reference group was found to be second in importance only to a member of one's family, with opinions of political leaders considered important to about a fifth of the respondents. Without being able to state a comparative or specific figure, it seems clear that party canvasing definitely increases voting and is a worthwile activity. Canvasing, however, does not invariably result in a vote for the canvaser's party, but may activate some to vote for the opposition. Activists usually are aware of this, and many do not canvas in neighborhoods where voters are predominantly identified with the opposition party.

Party leaders do not always have detailed knowledge of the local community and often waste their efforts. The 1952 study found that the Republican canvas was inefficient in that it did not concentrate on groups likely to be influenced by doorbell ringing.[33] Both parties did canvas in competitive areas and did less work in the South, but both slighted the lower-lower class and devoted disproportionate effort among ethnic-religious minorities. The value of research, including familiarity with the findings of social scientists, should be apparent to party organizations. Parties are circumscribed by the "deficiencies" of political man in his perception, knowledge, and group influences. But

[31] *Ibid.*, p. 79.
[32] Daniel Katz and Samuel J. Eldersveld, "The Impact of Local Party Activity upon the Electorate," *Public Opinion Quarterly*, vol. 25, pp. 1–24, 1961. For the influence in Gary, Indiana, see Peter H. Rossi and Phillips H. Cutright, "The Impact of Party Organization in an Industrial Setting," in Morris Janowitz (ed.), *Community Political Systems*, The Free Press, New York, 1961, pp. 81–116.
[33] Janowitz and Marvick, *op. cit.*, chap. 6.

parties, armed with facts and intimate knowledge of voting behavior, can work with primary and secondary groups, utilize the mass media, and develop their internal organization and activity in order to increase their advantage in pursuing their prime objective—the winning of elections.

Campaigns followed by the act of voting link the three units of the party together—officeholders or would-be officeholders, the organization activists, and the party voters—in the common cause of seeking victory. Voters do not directly control policy by choosing a candidate but they influence it indirectly. Voters are aware of particular interests, although few are concerned with the broad range of policies. Relevant issues differ from person to person and from group to group, and when incumbents seek reelection, the voter is guided to some extent by retrospective appraisal of the record. A majority is made up of minorities, with each minority having somewhat different interests.

The public officeholder is influenced by anticipation of public reaction and the knowledge that periodically he must go back to the electors if he wishes to continue his stewardship. Politicians think policies important for survival—and are subtly or otherwise the subject of electoral threats. The threats may not materialize, but the incumbent must take cognizance of them. Politicians in a general sort of way must do what is consistent with their understanding of the desires of the majority-vote coalition.

These realities affect the outlook and behavior of the third section of the party—the party functionaries. As pointed out before, the activists tend to be more ideological than the party voters.[34] Policy divergencies between the party leaders do crop out in campaign publicity, and the party's public officials are made aware of the activist's positions—in fact, this often sets up tension between the two. The voter's more moderate attitudes toward issues in turn may lead the activists to act more moderately in the interests of election victory. Party leaders cannot afford to alienate potential voters for their own candidates, and they try to anticipate voter reaction to campaign positions and to personalities. The activists link the electorate to the public officeholder and their knowledge of *who* voted and *why* can be particularly important to policy makers.

NATURE OF POLITICAL PARTICIPATION

The functions and values of participation have received emphasis far back in history. Pericles felt participation should be encouraged on the

[34]A most pertinent article on this is Herbert McClosky, Paul J. Hoffman, and Rosemary O'Hara, "Issue Conflict and Consensus among Party Leaders and Followers," *American Political Science Review*, vol. 54, pp. 406–427, 1960.

grounds of ethical self-fulfillment. An individual derives self-satisfaction from performing civic duties. It gives one a sense of purpose, strengthens one's ego, and may therefore be of therapeutic and psychological value; it gives one recognition in his group. Activity may also be useful as a cathartic. More tangibly, political activity may bring personal or group benefits. Without the vote or political leverage, one cannot bargain as effectively for benefits from the government. Blacks have improved their opportunities for better housing, schools, public health services, recreational facilities, and many other services as they became politically active in their communities. Women found that the vote helped them overcome discrimination of various types. Political activity through trade unions has improved the lot of many who, although possessing the vote, were unable to obtain programs beneficial to them. Campaign donors may find that their contributions gain them access to policy makers. From the standpoint of the state, lay participation in law enforcement and the sanction of public opinion and legitimacy to hold office are needed if the state is to survive and function properly.

Voting is but one form of participation and quantitatively involves a larger number of citizens than any other activity. It is episodic and, for the overwhelming majority of persons, is almost the sole act because political activity is secondary in claims upon their time. The political society could not function if everyone limited himself exclusively to voting. We have examined numerous types of activists and their activities throughout this volume. It is appropriate before leaving the subject of voting behavior to summarize the broad range of opportunities and problems associated with participation other than the act of voting.

Levels of Activity Although democratic theory assumes that everyone has the opportunity if not the obligation for contributing to the operation of the political society, it is not an active responsibility for all in the sense that everyone operates on the same level. At one extreme, one finds apoliticals who do nothing in politics; at the other pole are public officeholders and leaders of political groups who earn their living in whole or in part from public affairs. In between are a variety of ways by which people relate themselves to their political system. Figure 18-2 suggests a clustering of types of political involvement proceeding from little or no activity to top leadership positions.[35] Many persons are engaged in more than one activity at a time.

[35] Literature on political participation is especially extensive. Two highly recommended works that bring together the results of studies of involvement and place them in a conceptual framework are Robert E. Lane, *Political Life*, The Free Press, New York, 1959, and Lester W. Milbrath, *Political Participation: How and Why Do People Get Involved In Politics?* Rand McNally & Company, Chicago, 1965. The author acknowledges the use of Milbrath's phraseology of the patterns "gladiatorial, transitional, and spectator" activities shown in Figure 18-2.

Figure 18-2 Levels of Political Involvement

GLADIATORIAL ACTIVITIES

Holding a public office
Holding a party office
Candidacy for public office
Raising political funds
Attendance at political party meetings, party membership
Active political campaigning (doorbelling, etc.)
Lobbying, political demonstrations*

TRANSITIONAL ACTIVITIES

Contributing money to a party or candidate
Visiting a campaign rally or party headquarters
Communication with a political leader

SPECTATOR ACTIVITIES

Wearing a campaign button
Initiating or engaging in political discussion
Voting
Watching or hearing political broadcasts
Reading political news and campaign materials

INACTION, APATHETIC, APOLITICAL

---

*These subjects are covered in subsequent chapters. Demonstrations that resort to violence or intent to disrupt public operations are not regarded as legitimate within a democratic framework.

A general characteristic of participation is that as one goes up the hierarchy shown in Figure 18-2, more time and energy, and usually more personal commitment, are required. Also, in a very general way, the higher levels involve persons who have higher education and/or are in the higher-income brackets and higher-status occupations.[36] As with certain voters, persons are in and out of different levels of participation. One may be a precinct captain and most active in politics for a time, only to withdraw from such gladiatorial preoccupations and become a spectator, content to read, discuss, and vote. Some persons participate largely at the community level, in such activities as parent teachers associations and educational politics; others become active in partisan politics for state and national offices or for national or statewide causes.

We cannot know at a given moment how many persons are engaged in each of the diverse types of activities, but through survey research a broad picture has been obtained. Perhaps a third of the American adult population at a particular moment are passive, paying

[36] This point is developed by Milbrath, *op. cit.*, chap. 5.

no attention to public affairs and not voting in any elections. The number is reduced somewhat in presidential election years when more turn out to vote but do nothing else.

Milbrath places 60 percent as largely in spectator roles. Because gladiators are also major contributors, it is almost impossible to estimate how many are engaged in "transitional" activities. Earlier, we noted that some 10 to 15 percent make financial contributions to parties or candidates but only a tiny number actively solicit contributions.

It is a guess that 1 to 2 percent are activists or in the gladiatorial class. The percentage is raised somewhat if one includes the volunteer sporadic workers whose interest is tied to a short-term goal of working for a particular candidate or a ballot proposition. At the same time, about a fourth of the electorate see themselves as "opinion leaders," who are not activists as such but who feel that other persons come to them for information and who talk to people in favor of issues, parties, or candidates.

The Politically Alienated. American politics is characterized by attitudes of cynicism and skepticism on the part of an undetermined, but far from negligible, percentage of voters. Lincoln Steffens paraphrased the muckraker's cynical belief in a "government of the people, by the rascals, for the rich." Murray B. Levin reports that results of interviews in Massachusetts in the 1960s suggest that a high proportion of voters still share a low sense of political efficacy and a suspicion of public officials.[37] Many believe that campaign donors expect a *quid pro quo* of political favors and that a ruling elite controls the community and governs in its own interest. Alienated voters feel themselves manipulated by forces that they cannot overthrow and feel that they are therefore excluded from any effective influence on government. They feel that they have insufficient information with which to cast a ballot and that it will make little difference for whom they vote anyway. They see candidates as dodging issues and engaging in deception for purposes of attaining political power. There is a disenchantment with politicians and the political process and a feeling that political reality and democratic values are poles apart. A number of voters develop hostility because corrupt politicians are unmasked from time to time or because they have an unfavorable impression of certain public officials.

Alienation and sense of efficacy are matters of degree and may be based on misunderstanding and lack of sophistication—but may also

---

[37] See *The Alienated Voter*, Holt, Rinehart and Winston, Inc., New York, 1960, and *The Compleat Politician*, The Bobbs-Merrill Company, Inc., Indianapolis, 1962. Cynical attitudes were also found in Philadelphia; see James Reichley, *The Art of Government: Reform and Organization Politics in Philadelphia*, The Fund for the Republic, New York, 1959.

rest on actuality. Attitudes of this kind lead the voter to feel that he is a hapless outsider, helpless and impotent where bringing about changes or exerting influence is concerned. This may lead to a refusal to participate in nominations and elections as a worker or financial contributor. It may result in nonvoting or, if a vote is cast, in the belief that both candidates are poorly qualified but that one is the lesser evil. The result may be a halfhearted interest in the outcome. The political process is lacking in meaning for the disenchanted and alienated, and this attitude may result in the failure to bring persons of talent and integrity into political life. At the extreme, it may lead to the perpetuation of mediocre, special-interest, if not corrupt, government and may delay the strengthening of the minority party or factions within the majority party capable of bringing improved government.

The relation of political cynicism to participation in politics is by no means clear. Certainly a number of, but by no means all, nonvoters believe that it is useless to vote and that politics will benefit certain classes or the dishonest. A study in Oregon found that the "politically cynical among the highly educated are almost completely inactive whereas the politically trusting among the highly educated are the most active participant of any category."[38] Cynicism may keep some people from voting but may motivate others to get into political activity, presumably to bring about some improvement. Irrespective of our full understanding of the politically alienated and cynical, few would argue that disdain for politics and politicians is desirable or would deny that one of the goals of a society is to develop and maintain respect and confidence in its political institutions, processes, and leaders.

The Conditions of Participation. Extensive nonparticipation is a characteristic of American culture.[39] It is not due only to political alienation, as some of those who are alienated are vigorous in their political protest activity. Rather there are a range of factors that lead individuals to stay out of politics or to devote time to it.[40] These include (1) personal, (2) economic, (3) social, and (4) political considerations. On the personal side there is mental laziness, an unwillingness to give serious thought to complicated political questions. One runs the risk of revealing factual

[38] Robert E. Agger, Marshall N. Goldstein, and Stanley A. Pearl, "Political Cynicism: Measurement and Meaning," *Journal of Politics*, vol. 23, p. 496, 1961. The article poses a number of alternative explanations of the variables associated with cynicism.

[39] Apathetic ranks are also large in many other countries. See Gabriel Almond and Sidney Verba, *The Civic Culture*, Princeton University Press, Princeton, N.J., 1963.

[40] Recommended reading for causes of nonparticipation are two articles by Morris Rosenberg: "Some Determinists of Political Apathy," *Public Opinion Quarterly*, vol. 18, pp. 249–366, 1954–1955 and "Self-Esteem and Concern with Public Affairs," in the same journal, vol. 21, pp. 201–211, 1962.

ignorance if not humiliation among friends and acquaintances. He may decide to hide his vulnerable ego in this respect by imposing limitations on his own discussion of candidates and issues or activities and limit himself to the privacy of casting a ballot. Even where this is not the case, family responsibilities, long working hours, and other presumably more important priorities discourage political involvement.

A sense of personal inadequacy and futility in a mass society leads one to regard his own political activity as an empty exercise that will not bring hoped-for results. One's vote or one's involvements are perceived as making little difference in relation to strong opposing forces. This may lead to an alienation wherein one sees elected representatives unresponsive, political machines in control, and the overpowering influence of the "establishment" whose locus of power is hardly known. Government is too "impersonal" and will not respond to him. Many of the disillusioned young of the 1960s saw the gap between the ideals of professed democracy and the realities of those in power as unbridgeable and chose to "drop out." Conversely, persons high in political efficacy and self-esteem are more likely to be trusting of politics and politicians and wish to be a cog in participatory democracy. Moreover, generally, the more sophisticated a person's knowledge and beliefs about politics, the greater the likelihood of his getting into it.

Politics involves controversy, which may have real or fancied consequences to one's social standing or occupation. Blacks in some Southern communities find that insistance on registration or participating is to invite ostracism if not violence. Membership in civil rights organizations is a liability for both whites and blacks in some communities. Being active in a political party, especially if it is a minority party in a one-party community, is sometimes not well received by the general public. Teachers have been reprimanded and some even dismissed for "indiscreet" participation in politics. Numerous businessmen assert that "politics is bad for business" and find it expedient to restrict their activity to voting. Married women have confessed to interviewers that their husbands, for diverse reasons, would disapprove of certain types of political participation; and they have refrained from them in the interests of marital harmony.

To the fear of consequences of activity in an unfriendly social and economic setting may be added the limitations imposed directly by the political system. The Hatch Acts restrict certain activities of federal employees. Closed primary laws keep one from voting in a direct primary unless he is willing to register and, in effect, make public his party choice. Other suffrage laws, such as residence requirements, were observed earlier. Some political organizations are tightly controlled and do not welcome newcomers. The time of American elections is arbitrarily fixed in advance in constitutions or charters. This may not fit the mood of the citizen who may have to wait quite some time for the next election to try to redress his grievances; he sees little opportunity to try to bring about change by activity here and now.

Nonparticipants and the infrequently involved are not distributed evenly through classes and geographical areas in the nation. The uneducated and lower-status citizens are handicapped, often through lack of time, difficulty of access, or a niche from which to work into the political system. Consequently, there is a question as to whether they receive fair representation, have opportunities to be politically effective, and receive a share of the benefits of government and the political society. It is not enough to know that one demographic group has a larger percentage of voters, activists, and opinion leaders. It is necessary to know why this is the case. Do those in the less-privileged strata have a chance to supply leaders, to vote, and to become informed? Do they have reason to have a sense of political efficacy, faith in public responsiveness and promise of an open political society? Negative answers to these questions provide a fertile ground for sharp protests and, as witnessed in the 1960s, for violence.

REQUISITES OF PARTICIPATION

The image of the ideal individual citizen is of one who is highly motivated politically and will act rationally and in the public interest in voting and in other activities. In order for him to function this way, he must be free to communicate, must have access to the information he needs, and must be given meaningful alternatives between policies and candidates. This volume is replete with data which suggest that this picture of the political man doesn't fit reality. The great majority of citizens are not greatly interested in political affairs and are relatively uninformed on many public issues and policies that affect their daily lives. They are, accordingly, unable to make public policies wisely and responsibly, but must select leaders who will act on their behalf and whom they will hold responsible when they go to the polls. Democracy does not require every man to decide on the thousands of policies and issues that require governmental decision or even to be greatly concerned about public affairs. It does need an intelligent, effective public opinion that guides its governors and holds them responsible for their acts. A healthy democracy requires some participation, such as voting, by the great majority of citizens, for the exercise of a wise franchise exerts a steadying force and brings about change. An effectively functioning political democracy also needs active participation by a minority of political activists and persons greatly concerned about particular government policies and programs, who act as leaders of public opinion.

Suffrage is of recent vintage in the history of man. Universal manhood suffrage in the United States is but a century old, and women have had the right for only half a century. It is hardly surprising, then, that voters have not fulfilled their ideal role. Critics have accused them of failing to transcend their own interest to vote in the public interest and have argued that many voters are unable to perceive their own best interests. The prescribed role in itself is unrealistic; we have expected too much of the so-called average citizen. In overall results — and perhaps with luck thrown in — the American voter has met his tests fairly well, at least in pragmatic terms. That political man has not behaved as the liberal democratic theorists hoped he would is not to argue that there can be no improvement in either quantity or quality of participation.

Improvement of political participation would begin by removing the obstacles to it where those restrictions have for their purpose the maintenance of inequality of political opportunity. Overhauling both of election laws encumbered by difficulty or inconvenience of registration and of voting restrictions that appear to have little philosophical justification is a prelude to bringing more persons into the active electorate. But these in themselves would not necessarily combat traditions in areas that discourage certain people from voting or which assert subtly or otherwise that political action is not a proper role for certain citizens.

If the average man is capable of responding to "wise and noble things," as John Stuart Mill asserted, it is not enough simply to remove such restrictions on his participation; the exercise of effective citizenship rests on positive grounds as well. Political life is an expression of values and goals of the citizenry, and the task is one of getting the people to relate themselves to them. Some of the public perceive a discrepancy between democratic ideals and values and the methods and practices used by politicians and organizations and perhaps the legislative product itself. A sense of efficacy and confidence on the one hand and participation on the other are very much a function of education. Broadening and diffusing educational opportunities help reduce the differences in participation that seem to come from socioeconomic status. A large vote could be obtained by a system of compulsory voting with fines for failure to vote, but this would fail in itself to generate either a feeling of high confidence in the political system or a knowledgeable electorate.

Logically, a citizen's awareness and interest should first be aroused in order that he be receptive to information. With adequate information, he is prepared for participation. Participation can be best improved by tying together the interest-information-action factors. A citizen needs to understand the activity (voting, opinion leading, organization contributing) itself and the kinds of knowledge necessary for fruitful functioning in it. Knowledge and education themselves are a part of the activity. Politics is not likely to be substantially improved unless all of these activities are interrelated. It seems a worthy objective to try to find out what knowledge is needed for what political activity and to provide education appropriate to the activity. For example, it can be demonstrated that participation and influence are enhanced by the skillful use of political resources. Voting power, campaign donations, and electioneering can very probably be maximized by group effort. Public opinion interviewers report that considerable numbers of persons say they have never been solicited for financial donations or personal activity and would respond if asked.

It seems desirable to relate activity to policy interests and knowledge, rather than simply voting or working for the sake of voting or working. "Get out the vote" campaigns may reverse the process by getting action first and then trying to relate it to policy or philosophy afterwards. Understanding something of political behavior as well as knowing something of candidates, issues, and party positions gives participation a substantive basis. Striking differences in opportunities to influence government exist, and the knowledge of the reasons for and extent of these inequalities in one's own community is a basic step toward equalization. There can be no guarantee that participation will invariably be responsible, but by integrating a democratic ideology with knowledge the chances of responsible participation will be greater.

Voluntary citizen involvement in politics is a major way of mobilizing political resources. If large numbers remain outside the realm of intelligent political action, oligarchy may take over—and the oligarchy may fail to represent the highest public interest. The ballot is not the only method of gaining political influence, but it is an important one if it is used with knowledge and understanding to assure competitive elections for public office. Citizens, as we have seen, can also join and become active in political parties with some opportunity to influence the party's program and candidates. Finally, groups who may be disadvantaged by limited power at the polls may organize a group or coalition of groups and by skillful action maximize their political resources. The next section of this book will analyze politicking through the channels of nonparty organizations.

FOR FURTHER READING

Barber, James A., Jr.: *Social Mobility and Voting*, 1970.
Bone, Hugh A., and Austin Ranney: *Politics and Voters*, 1971.
Bowen, Don R.: *Political Behavior and the American Public*, 1968.
Davies, James A.: *Human Nature in Politics*, 1963.

Fuchs, Lawrence H. (ed.): *American Ethnic Politics*, 1968.

Katz, Elihu, and Paul F. Lazarsfeld: *Political Influence*, 1955.

Ladd, Everett: *Negro Political Leadership in the South*, 1969.

Lang, Kurt: *Voting and Nonvoting: Implications of Broadcasting Returns Before Polls are Closed*, 1968.

Larson, Calvin J., and P. C. Washburn: *Power, Participation and Ideology*, 1969.

Litt, Edgar: *Beyond Pluralism: Ethnic Politics in America*, 1970.

McPherson, Thomas: *Political Obligation*, 1967.

Merriam, Charles E., and Harold Gosnell: *Non-voting*, 1924.

Pranger, Robert J.: *Action, Symbolism and Order: The Existential Dimensions of Politics and Citizenship*, 1968.

Roelofs, H. M.: *The Tension of Citizenship*, 1957.

Vincent, William S.: *Roles of the Citizen*, 1959.

PART EIGHT THE INTEREST-GROUP SOCIETY

CHAPTER 19 THE AMERICAN PLURALIST SOCIETY

In *The American Commonwealth,* Lord Bryce perceived that political parties were "the great moving forces" of politics. Many theories of parties place them in the center of the political stage; others suggest that although they do not occupy a central place, they should do so. Even though the role, position, and status of political parties show variation from nation to nation, the Western pluralistic societies tend to place certain types of other groups at the center of power in political decision making. There is little doubt that to a constantly increasing extent, American politics is the politics of organized groups. Careful comparative studies of the political role of groups in other Western democracies point to a similar conclusion.

Although interest or pressure groups, as they are commonly called, have attracted wide attention in recent decades, such groups existed prior to the adoption of the Constitution. In the widely quoted *Federalist* paper No. 10, James Madison pointed out that in civilized nations, "a landed interest, a manufacturing interest, a mercantile interest, with many lesser interests" are bound to grow up and to "divide themselves into many classes, actuated by different sentiments and views." A half century later Alexis de Tocqueville expressed his amazement at the American penchant for constantly forming associations not only to further economic interests but of "a thousand other kinds, religious, moral, serious, futile, general or restricted, enormous or diminutive." Journalists and muckrakers began their exposures of the behavior of powerful economic groups later in the century, and the Jacksonians had inveighed against the banking interests in particular before the Civil War. In wartime as in peacetime, there has been no moratorium on pressure politics.

Arthur F. Bentley presented the first systematic discussion of interest-group politics in *The Process of Government*, published in 1908. He saw certain groups as "collectives of action taking on enough form so as to be describable and valued in terms of their activities." The balance of the group pressures, he wrote, "*is* the existing state of society." It was not until the 1920s, however, that scholars began producing detailed studies of organized groups whose objectives required political action. A huge monographic and periodical literature has subsequently appeared, making available empirical materials from which writers have attempted to theorize and to speculate on the character and significance of these groups. There is by no means unanimity among social scientists, as to either the nature or the role of groups. We shall have to select from a literature of encyclopedic proportions some of the aspects of the group society that are relevant to the party system, public opinion, and the government.

THE SOCIOLOGY OF GROUPS

What Is a Pressure Group?   In the literature of politics, the terms *interest group* and *pressure group* are frequently used interchangeably. Some scholars attempt to make a distinction. The *Encyclopedia of the Social Sciences* distinguishes *interest* according to objectives and *pressure* according to techniques used. Because *pressure* has a questionable connotation, some writers shy away from its use. In perhaps the most comprehensive treatise on American political groups, David B. Truman characterizes an interest group as a "shared attitude group that makes certain claims upon other groups in the society," and "when it makes its claims through or upon any of the institutions of government, it becomes a political interest group."[1] Every group is an interest group or a group with an

[1] David B. Truman, *The Governmental Process*, Alfred A. Knopf, Inc., New York, 1951, p. 37. A more recent group-theory work and extensive bibliography on groups is Harmon Zeigler, *Interest Groups in American Society*, Prentice-Hall, Inc., Englewood Cliffs, N.J., 1964.

interest, but not every group attempts to influence public policy. Here we shall use the terms *pressure group* or *political interest group* to refer to groups that endeavor to influence public policy.

But some further refinement is necessary. A distinction is necessary between private groups such as the American Medical Association and public groups such as the Nebraska unicameral legislature or the Veterans Administration. All try to influence public policy. The legislature decides whether to sanction certain proposals by making them public law. The Veterans Administration carries a public program to both the President and Congress and at times works with groups outside the governmental structure who are interested in similar ends. The American Medical Association, on the other hand, is a private and unofficial group that functions outside the government establishment, trying to influence the latter to adopt or reject certain programs. The term *pressure groups* is ordinarily used to designate private, nongovernmental associations, although it should be noted that governmental agencies also exert pressures on policy makers.

We need to distinguish further between pressure groups and political parties, which also attempt to influence policy. In the foregoing sections of the book, political parties were regarded as more or less permanent, semipublic organizations of persons who attempt to capture the control of government by proposing and electing candidates to public office. Pressure groups ordinarily do not nominate candidates. Some of them, however, may endorse candidates and work for their election. A political party's reason for being is to capture elective public offices and remain in power; this is not so with pressure groups. Minor parties are at times so minor that they fail in a given election to run any of their adherents for office. The Socialist and Communist parties have been in and out of the party system in this sense, yet continue to speak of their group as a party. Minor parties therefore raise peculiar problems of definition, as do those amorphous nonparty groups, such as "Citizens Committee for Finnegan." The latter is not a party in the sense of fielding a slate of candidates, nor is it necessarily (and usually it is not) concerned with lobbying for a public policy or influencing the administrative branch of the government.

What one comes down to then is that there are many politically oriented groupings—official governmental bodies, semiofficial political parties, nonparty groups electorally oriented, and private interest groups. This last component of the political process occupies our attention in this section.

Motivation for Organization. People join organized groups for a wide variety of reasons. Perhaps the most visible and obvious reason is the furtherance of economic interests, a practice dating to antiquity. In modern times, there is a tendency for persons to form associations along producer lines rather than along consumer lines. People join groups to advance social interests closely associated with their well-being, and these may be served by the same organization, such as a labor union. Many people, while not overly enthusiastic about doing so, join associations of economic interest under pressure or when they realize that groups have resources not available to them as individuals. Membership seems essential to obtaining a job or to holding or advancing in it. A person may become convinced that he can accomplish less by remaining outside the organization and enter it reluctantly. When one set of privately organized economic interests enjoys success in obtaining public programs or influence in the community, those outside may see this as a threat and form countergroups, a case of pressure groups begetting pressure groups.

But people join groups for reasons not directly related to the promotion of their own immediate economic interests. For example, people may become members of an organization to abolish capital punishment, even though they are not incarcerated for a crime imposing the death penalty. One may wear false teeth yet belong to a group working for fluoridated drinking water. Similarly one may work for or against the United Nations, unicameralism, extension of the civil service, or a metro government plan for his own community yet not be directly involved. People are in groups to work for diverse ideological causes and to fight against the ideological causes advocated by others. Some of these causes are very short-lived, such as fighting for or against a ballot proposition; others, such as a foreign policy or a conservation program, may occupy years and years of group effort. Undoubtedly many people join causes and groups in order to satisfy their own psychological needs or for such reasons as prestige, fraternization, sociability, and personal contacts—not necessarily to further the purpose of the group itself.

Membership.   The number and variety of organized groups that seek to influence public policies are great. It is often asserted that there are more groups per thousand population in the United States than in any other country in the world. This may well be true since the number of interest groups might logically bear a relationship to the diversity and sentiments of the population. The heterogeneity of the American economy and population invites organization of expression. Because of the large number of groups, it is widely asserted that Americans are great "joiners" and that almost everyone belongs to one organization and more likely to a great many. Public men are known to have many organizational memberships, and it is assumed that they reflect a penchant of their constituents in this respect. This contention has little basis in fact. The actual fact of the matter points in the opposite direction, namely, that large numbers of persons remain outside organized groups, particularly if one excludes church associations.

There is a striking variation in the extent of membership in an organized group. At one extreme, the overwhelming majority of musicians belong to the American Federation of Musicians; at the other, a tiny number of consumers belong to a consumers league, and a very small percentage of blacks belong to the National Association for the Advancement of Colored People (NAACP) or a comparable organization. A large percentage of physicians belong to the American Medical Association, but analogous memberships in the American Bar Association and National Education Association are much smaller. Labor unions attract only about one-fourth of the working force, and scarcely one-third of the farmers are members of any farm organization. Even fewer farm laborers are affiliated. Urban dwellers appear to belong to more organizations than rural dwellers. The great majority of war veterans are not members of veterans associations.

Community-wide studies, as opposed to estimates of percentages of memberships of a specific populational group, point in the same direction. G. W. Blackwell and Scott Greer, for example, found that, excluding church groups, most urban individuals belong to only one organization or to none, and it seems unusual for more than half of the urban adults to belong to even one group.[2] A Philadelphia sample found 85 percent belonging to no civic or charitable organization and only 26 percent belonging to an occupational or professional association. A study of a panel of adults in Nebraska over a four-year period found a larger percentage of persons with memberships in groups. About 80 percent belonged to one or more associations but an individual's membership profile varied considerably even in a short period of time. Men and women were equally represented in civic-political groups, but membership was most characteristic in middle age with few respondents continuing their memberships beyond the age of 60. Membership turnover was high in these groups fluctuating with political groups designed to elect a candidate or working on behalf of a ballot proposition. A considerably smaller percentage were members of political groups than of church-related and many other groups. "Thirty per cent of the panel 40 through 59, and 24 per cent of those under 40 were active at one time or another in civic-political groups."[3] Persons in larger communities were more inclined to join political organizations than those in smaller communities.

[2] See their chapters in Roland Young (ed.), *Approaches to the Study of Politics*, Northwestern University Press, Evanston, Ill., 1958.
[3] Nicholas Babchuck and Alan Barth, "Voluntary Association Membership: A Longitudinal Analysis," *American Sociological Review*, vol. 34, p. 40, 1969. The article is also useful for summarizing many studies of group memberships.

Despite contrasting results from the various studies, certain tendencies appear in nearly all of them. In the aggregate of all types of groups, long-time residents are more likely to belong than recent migrants. Married persons are more likely to have group memberships than single persons, and more men belong to associations than women. Until recently, large numbers of youth and racial minorities belonged to no groups concerned with politics and political participation.

Of greater significance than simply the numbers of persons on group rolls is that every analysis of membership shows a social and economic bias. Those on the lower SES (social and economic status) levels are less likely to belong to any organization, and those in the upper classes are more likely to participate in rural organizations than wealthier ones, and the same tendency applies throughout other segments of the population. This same tendency is shown in other nations.[4] Although more people in cities than in rural areas appear involved in group activity, urbanization is unlikely the major or very important variable. In a five-nation study, little relationship was found between urban residence and disposition to be politically active.[5] Rather, social class and other involvement in social groups led to political activity. Persons active in community affairs are more likely to be active in political groups. Urbanization is somewhat associated with social class.

Studies of group memberships and participation led Schattschneider to comment:

> The flaw in the pluralist haven is that the heavenly chorus sings with a strong upper-class accent. Probably about 90 percent of the people cannot get into the pressure system. . . .
> The notion that a pressure system is automatically representative of the whole community is a myth fostered by the universalizing tendency of modern group theorists. *Pressure politics is a selective process* ill-designed to serve diffuse interests. The system is skewed, loaded, and unbalanced in favor of a fraction of a minority.[6]

At the same time, numbers of upper-class citizens remain aloof from organized groups. Very large numbers of others neither participate through political interest groups with any degree of regularity nor are represented directly by them.

The estimation of group membership is a tricky business, for leaders often exaggerate the number of adherents. At a given time,

[4] See Gabriel Almond and Sidney Verba, *The Civic Culture,* Princeton University Press, Princeton, N.J., 1963.

[5] Norman H. Nie, G. Bingham Powell, and Kenneth Prewitt, "Social Structure and Political Participation: Developmental Relationships, Part I," *American Political Science Review,* vol. 63, pp. 361–378, 1969.

[6] E. E. Schattschneider, *The Semi-Sovereign People,* Holt, Rinehart and Winston, Inc., New York, 1960, p. 33. For a summary of data on status and political participation, see Robert Lane, *Political Life,* The Free Press, New York, 1959, chap. 16, and Lester Milbrath, *Political Participation,* Rand, McNally & Company, Chicago, 1965.

many may be in arrears in their dues but carried on the rolls. Non-members may use an organization as a reference or guide for their own political attitudes and activities, and the group may possess resources beyond its own immediate members. Size of the organization is but one element—often not very important—in the influence and effectiveness of the interests it purports to represent. In the American pressure system, however, resources are unequally distributed both between and within groups.

Degrees of Participation. It is generally assumed that group members tend to have numerous values, attitudes, goals, and beliefs in common. But because the reasons for joining groups are so varied, there are bound to be differences in intensities of interests of the members in the group. Larger groups will likely be more heterogeneous than small ones, with both a greater range and intensity of attachment. A member has only so much time and energy for private pursuits and must allocate it accordingly. High interest in the group may cause him to assign considerable time to it, low interest may cause him to allocate a low priority to its demands on his time. Only a few persons are likely to devote all their resources to one activity. If some persons are willing to devote a vast portion of their time to the organization, others are generally willing to let them do so. All these factors add up to the fact that there are marked differences in membership attachments and activities.

Some organizations formally structure into their constitutions and bylaws categories of membership, designating members as associate or participating and perhaps noting that their privileges and benefits are different. Size of membership and location of it geographically will make for natural divisions. In national groupings, there will be many who are little more than "mail" members and whose only contact will be through written communication. The local parent-teacher association, on the other hand, is on a face-to-face basis. Despite the infinite variations of groups, three major types of membership participation are usually discernible, with various subdivisions within each classification. These are the active minority, the activist rank and file, and the passive members.

Leadership positions are held by the active minority who are willing to devote much energy to the group's affairs. Generally, the leaders take the most interest in the group's activities and feel the most strongly about its interests and goals. Often, although not invariably, the leaders are more issue oriented than the general membership. Leaders of the larger groups are usually remunerated and enjoy some material advantages from their positions. This may encourage leaders to be pragmatic and opportunistic about issues but may also lead them to be less flexible in their attitudes toward outgroups since they wish to appear to be fighting the good fight for their constitutents. They would be slow to modify the group's goals if such action appeared to weaken their own position with the membership. As expected, studies show leaders to be more knowledgeable about the issues and problems facing the group than the general membership. They are in a position to speak with considerable authority for it. The active minority may exaggerate the dangers from outside in order to secure their own position and preserve the internal cohesion of the group.

Leadership positions may be acquired and legitimatized in a formal way or may be exercised informally. Rules of some organizations place authority in the hands of a certain few, such as a board of directors, executive committee, or house of delegates. Conventions may be the sovereign authority, but the delegates of course cannot function as the day-to-day leadership. Even the elected presidents or chairmen of some groups do not, in practice, function as the real leaders. In large, complex organizations the paid officials, secretaries, and staffs have the skills and knowledge necessary for evolving programs and making decisions, which are given legitimacy through ratification by delegates to the convention. Those with greatest financial control may sometimes function as the key leaders or as an inner circle making major decisions. On the other hand, some leaders, such as George Meany and A. Philip Randolph of the labor unions and Roy Wilkins of the NAACP, hold the leadership for long periods of time and are the real leaders and spokesmen for the group. In smaller, less formal groups, leadership often falls to those having the leisure and personal security to labor for the organization with little or no remuneration.

Below the leaders one finds a tier of moderate activists, members who, except on rare occasions, never become or hope to become leaders. As interested followers of the group and its leaders, they take an interest in the programs, causes, and work of the association. Many of them regularly attend meetings and serve on committees. They tend to have reasonably strong identification with the group, but the degree of attachment and involvement varies considerably within this broad group and ebbs and flows over a period of time. The same level of interest cannot be sustained from year to year, but these active followers generally remain loyal and keep up with the major developments within the organization.

A third category of membership includes what are often a fairly large number of passive members. Some of these have no interest in the organization and may well have joined out of necessity or on appeal from friends. Others were once interested but lost their enthusiasm and give little attention to the group's affairs. Both of these subgroups as well as other passives may at critical times be rallied to take a momentary interest in affairs, vote in a group election, write to their congressmen, or attend a meeting, only to quickly lapse back into a state of indifference. The fact that they can be rallied, however, may be important to the survival of the group. One thing that nearly all the disinterested followers possess in common is a weak identification with the group.

In summary, the decisions and affairs of an organized group are in the hands of a small number, and the larger the group, the smaller the percentage of the activists and leaders. Attendance at small-group meetings is usually poor if one regards the democratic model as one of large participation and interest. The leadership elite become the opinion leaders and spokesmen for the group and are differentiated from the general membership by a higher rate of participation. This is likely to be relative and a matter of degree as the activist group undergoes change and as members in the lower echelons move up to leadership positions. It is well established that leadership is a relationship between the leader and the led and that the former hold their position, if the organization is democratic, only if they continue to maintain a successful relationship with their followers. A problem for the rank-and-file membership is to have the means to remove those leaders whom they perceive as no longer fulfilling the aspirations and challenges of the group and to replace them with new blood who appear better able to forward the group's goals. It has become axiomatic, moreover, for a group to cultivate the public image of being democratic.

Classification of Pressure Groups. Literature attempting to establish types of groups has proliferated the use of such terms as *struggle group, demand group, veto group, peak association, primary-secondary,* and *defensive-offensive.* These are used to help social scientists conceptualize the nature and role of different types of groups. The concept of public and special-interest groups has some utility but tells little of their specific goals and objectives. The internal structure of organizations (federated or unitary, for example) offers another basis of categorization, as does the geographical scope of operation, that is, neighborhood, state, regional, national, or international. Attempts have also been made to distinguish according to aims, techniques, or the responses that groups seek to elicit. None of these categories is without limitation. Here we may use a broadly functional classification of organized interests which seek, at least at times, to have an impact on government.

Multipurpose service groups unite people who share a common occupational, professional, ethnic, or religious background. For these groups, such as labor unions, chambers of commerce, farm associations, and professional societies, pressure politics is incidental and not the reason for being. Yet they become enmeshed in politics as they see existing or contemplated public programs affecting their membership.

Closely related to, if not an outgrowth or projection of, the multiple-purpose organization is the political action group whose specific purpose is to influence public policy and campaigns. Political arms of labor unions such as COPE (Committee on Political Education), and also AMPAC (American Medical Political Action Committee), BIPAC (Business-Industry Political Action Committee), and the political auxiliaries of churches have smaller membership than the creating organizations but are often powerful because of greater unity over objectives. Although they may appear to speak for the political concerns of the larger group, the latter need not assume responsibility for them.

Certain political action groups are unrelated to a major occupational or social interest but draw from many occupations and interests to promote a particular goal, such as an initiative, referendum, or a cause that is resolved when some public authority takes action. Some goal groups are organized on a permanent basis, such as the Women's Christian Temperance Union, the National Association for the Advancement of Colored People, the National Urban League, and foreign policy associations. Numerous associations promoting right-wing and left-wing causes spring up periodically, and a few, such as the Americans for Constitutional Action and the Americans for Democratic Action, become more or less permanent.

ECONOMIC INTERESTS AND PUBLIC POLICY

All the large economic interests have developed huge service organizations to serve their memberships in diverse ways and to enhance the general position of the interest and its constituents. These groups find that they must be able to deal with government and politicians, sometimes for economic survival. At the same time, they want to be free from government interference in their internal affairs. As the importance of the public sector increases relative to the private sector, pressure groups step up activity to defend what they have won, and, if possible, to obtain further gains through public policy. This calls for a high order of strategy, for a careful assessment of one's own needs and resources, and for an understanding of the resources of one's real or imagined adversaries. The balance of this chapter sketches the anatomy of organizations of major interests concerned with public policy and briefly notes their objectives, strengths, and resources.

Business. From the earliest days of the nation, the voice of businessmen has remained influential in the councils of government. Leaders in commerce and industry are the largest owners of property and wealth, which automatically makes them critically interested in public policies.

TABLE 19-1 Employment in the American economy, 1970

Category	Employees, in thousands
Mining	628
Manufacturing	20,122
Transportation—utilities	4,448
Wholesale and retail trade	14,644
Finance and real estate	3,559
Construction	3,411
Services	11,103
Government	12,227
Agriculture	3,422

Source: Monthly Labor Review, vol. 93, no. 5, May, 1970.

The growth and influence of business was aided somewhat with the decline in the relative importance of agriculture. A hundred years ago, less than a third of the population were employed in commerce, manufacturing, and mining; today well over half are gainfully employed in these pursuits (see Table 19-1). The economy is characterized by a high degree of concentration in business ownership, with a resulting condition of oligopoly (fewness of sellers) and monopolistic pricing behavior in many lines of manufacturing and trade. These give certain businesses great stakes in society, stakes which can be harmed, maintained, or advanced by tax and other programs of government.

The term *businessman* does not admit to so easy a definition on careful analysis as it does at first glance. Owners and owner-managers of business establishments are so recognized. Many who manage and direct corporations exercise control with little or no stock ownership in the companies they manage; this group, called management, is now considered to constitute entrepreneurship. Supervisory employees, agents, salesmen, and even certain professionals, such as pharmacists and architects, who may derive their income from commissions or a fixed salary are often regarded as being "in business." In many respects, these as well as many other persons in the American society have become businessmen in their own eyes as well as in the eyes of others because their psychology and outlook are identified with the entrepreneur. Millions of Americans who do not own businesses nonetheless take business as their reference group and follow the lead of those who profess to be the spokesmen for management or business.

Positions on many public issues engender at least a surface unity among those perceiving themselves as business oriented. Among these are opposition to governmental competition with private enterprise, public ownership, extension of the "welfare state," a balanced budget, and "excessive taxes." But because of dissimilarities of interest—some businesses are mainly concerned with distribution and others with re-distribution, while still others engage in regulatory functions—business is unable to speak with a single voice on even general issues and is not as monolithic as some of its adversaries believe. In the sharp congressional battle over extension of the surtax in 1969, the National Association of Manufacturers spoke in opposition, and the Chamber of Commerce of the United States was publicly in favor. Similar conflict of values within the business community are easily found.

Although general positions of business provide rallying cries, they often obscure the fact that the ranks of business are far from unified. In fact, there are many dissimilarities of interest that keep management from being united on many policies. Small businessmen often go to government to obtain protection from big business; and small businessmen have had their quarrels with bankers. There is a struggle between cooperative enterprises and other businesses and between those for fair-trade legislation and those against it. Small-business groups have trouble in building an organization capable of speaking for a common interest.[7] Although all businessmen agree with the slogan "What's good for business is good for the country," there is no single authoritative spokesman for finance, commerce, manufacturing, and trade. Each has its own organization, which speaks out when its estate seems threatened. For example, the American Banker's Association may register a sharp viewpoint on foreign and domestic loans, while the National Retail Dry Goods Association may remain silent.

The largest category of organizations through which business managers work to further political objectives is comprised of the trade associations. There are close to 14,000 of these groups, 1,700 of which are national.[8] A trade association is defined by the U.S. Department of Commerce as a nonprofit, cooperative, voluntary organization of business competitors designed to assist the industry in its problems, such as research and promotion, and in its relations with government and the public. Among the earliest was the American Brewers' Association (1862), which worked, among other things, for the reduction of the federal tax on beer. Trade associations arose in response to many different needs, and government at times has actually encouraged their formation. They have sought services from the government and its aid in protection from rivals. Although trade associations may not admit it publicly, they engage in political activities on every level from local

---

[7] The National Federation of Independent Business, Inc., appears to be the largest of the small-business pressure groups. For an analysis of large-business as well as small-business groups and an extensive bibliography of business organizations, see John H. Bunzel, *The American Small Businessman*, Alfred A. Knopf, Inc., New York, 1962. The U.S. House of Representatives had published voluminous materials on small business; these are listed in Bunzel, pp. 302ff.

[8] See U.S. Department of Commerce, *Directory of Trade Associations*, 1956.

to national and are often at the core of the politics of business. They are a major means by which business management takes its case to the government and are a source of information for legislative committees and for administrators.

Best-known of business groups are the two huge federations, the National Association of Manufacturers (NAM) and the Chamber of Commerce of the United States. The former rose out of the dislocations of the panic of 1893 and was designed to promote trade expansion. With the increase in the membership of the American Federation of Labor, formed a few years earlier, the NAM became involved in labor questions and adopted an aggressive open-shop policy. Its locals opposed the closed shop and campaigned against the "dangers of unionism." To the present day, the NAM's publications continue to be critical of labor unions, and some local associations have endorsed right-to-work proposals. Active membership in the NAM is limited to individuals, firms, and corporations engaged in manufacturing and approved by the board of directors.

Although having much in common, the Chamber of Commerce of the United States differs from the NAM in a number of ways. Since its creation in 1912, it has sought to integrate the opinions of the thousands of local chambers in order to speak authoritatively for American business. To achieve this purpose, it uses an unusual "referendum" system. A committee prepares a pro and con report on a question to go out to the membership. Each member (organization—not person) has a vote according to its size, and the policies adopted by majority vote become known as the official position of the national chamber on the subject. Since its membership is drawn from all types of business, the chamber is usually less specific and hard-hitting in its policy positions than the NAM. Policies favored by one segment of business may be opposed by other business groups. The chamber accordingly must confine its pronouncements to areas of general agreement by all business groups.

One additional group presenting the views of some of the business community is the Committee for Economic Development (CED) formed during World War II. CED conducts research and puts out policy statements for the general public and the press. It professes not to be a lobby but will present its views to Congress on request. The organization represents no one group of businessmen but generally speaks for the more progressive businessman.

A recent development within some of the business community is emphasis on getting the individual businessman into direct participation in politics. This is being fostered through individual courses and seminars in practical politics. It is inspired in part by the activities of political action committees of labor unions, which encourage rank-and-file campaigning. Many firms, led by the Ford Motor Company, sponsor courses in politics and give them to their executives on company time. In addition, a number of companies encourage their employees to make financial contributions to parties and candidates and to run for city council, state legislature, or other offices with full guarantee of job security while serving. Some business executives, however, are highly critical of this type of "businessman in politics" on the grounds that such activity simply confirms the suspicions of some, including Communists, that American society is dominated by big money. For example, Arnold H. Maremont, a Chicago industrialist, argued that business ought to "stay out of politics, period." He expressed the view that the "present campaign to inject business into politics is ill-conceived, extremely dangerous, a violation of our sound democratic system. It is when corporations begin running political classes, conducting political schools, and urging their executives to enter the political arena to expound the corporation viewpoint that I become deeply fearful of the consequences."[9]

Agriculture. When the late Sen. Henrik Shipstead of Minnesota first arrived in Washington, D.C., he is reputed to have said, "I am here to lead the farmers of Minnesota up to the public trough." Despite the farmer's pride in individualism, he is the recipient of many benefits at the hands of government; whether he has received more than other occupational groups from the "public trough" is arguable. Farming by its very nature is heavily dependent on public programs. There is need for adequate roads, communications, and protection and insurance from natural disasters such as animal diseases, blights, pests, drought, and floods. The farmer seeks public assistance in marketing, loans and audits, price supports, control over speculation in farm produce, and production controls. In the last generation the farmer has looked to government for assistance in farm welfare and betterment; he has secured much public help to make life more livable.

American agriculture has undergone radical changes as has the American economy in general. Once 90 percent of Americans lived on farms; now fewer than 10 percent do so. The farm economy has within it seeds of discontent and the potential for protest organization. The structure of agriculture shows numerous small-farm operators carrying on a second occupation during the course of the year. The agrarian interest is no longer one of the small dirt farmer. There is a difference between the commercial and the family farmer; the former is a businessman at home in the chamber of commerce and with those who keep

[9] From the column "The Easy Chair," *Harper's Magazine*, December, 1959, pp. 14ff.

accounts and meet payrolls. Smaller farms are decreasing in numbers, and the acreage of larger farms is increasing. More than 80 percent of national farm income is earned by only a third of the farms. The number of farm operators and farm owners is on the decline (see Table 19-1). In general, farm income per family is below that of the urban dweller, and Negro farm families present a special problem in rural poverty, with average incomes well below those for whites. Although tenant farming is on the decrease, a considerable number of farms are still tenant-operated.

These characteristics of the American agricultural economy make for deep-seated cleavages and conflicts among different types of farmers and for many voices purporting to speak for agriculture. Because farming interests, like those of industry and labor, are beset by internal cleavages, their organizations, objectives, and movements are likewise complex and interdependent. The term *farmer* embraces cotton or grain growers, livestock breeders, wool producers, dairy interests, rice producers, and truck gardeners. These interests have formed commodity associations resembling trade associations, such as the American Dairy Association, the California Walnut Growers Association, and the Texas and Southwestern Cattle Raisers Association. Each arose in response to particular conditions, and many today have become powerful lobbyists at various levels of government. Public officials who feel their pressure sometimes refer to them as the potato bloc, the beet lobby, the cotton bloc, the beekeepers' lobby, and in one state even the raspberry bloc.

The tobacco grower in South Carolina, the grape raiser in California, and the citrus grower in Florida appear not to have much in common, and this has helped to promote strength in the commodity association. But farmers found that commodity groups could not adequately represent common interests in agriculture and speak effectively for it to Congress or to the Secretary of Agriculture. Further, there was need for broader organizations to promote unity, to develop legislative programs, and to represent the farmers in numerous peripheral matters. Three national associations arose in response to these needs, the National Grange (1867), the Farmers' Educational and Cooperative Union, popularly called the Farmers' Union (1902), and the American Farm Bureau Federation (1920).[10]

The Grange is a fraternal organization devoted to enhancing the social and intellectual life of the farmer and is operative in three-fourths of the states. It operates on a hierarchy from county granges up

---

[10]For a study of the interaction of these groups and an extensive bibliography on the politics of agriculture see Christiana M. Campbell, *The Farm Bureau and the New Deal*, The University of Illinois Press, Urbana, Ill., 1962.

through the state to the national level. A large portion of the membership is centered in the North and East. Although it professes to be nonpolitical, it has always taken positions on important public issues of indirect as well as direct interest to the farmer. It is a stalwart champion of the dairy interests and a vehicle for protests against monopoly, corporate abuses, and graft in government. In its attitude toward organized labor, federal intervention and welfare programs, taxes and farm programs, the Grange usually finds itself representing the political middle or center. Local granges, however, may vary considerably from quite liberal to well right of center.

The center of gravity of the Farmers' Union is with the lower-income and marginal farmers. Its major strength is found in the Great Plains south from the Dakotas, an area with a rainfall deficiency. It has become a vehicle for the expression of left-wing agrarian politics. The union has achieved national prominence (despite its much smaller membership than the Grange or the Federation) for cooperation with labor unions and for the championship of policies at variance with other farm groups. It calls for high price support, family farms of "economic" size, aid to tenant farmers, and extension of welfare programs. The Farmers' Union is internationalist and not narrowly farm-centered, although its lobbying is usually only on farm interests. Much of its leadership is drawn from and its emphasis is on small, middle-class, but not necessarily impoverished, farmers. It is perhaps anomalous that the union is a liberal organization that actively functions in nominally Republican states among a farm population which probably sees itself as conservative.

Although among the newest national farm groups, the American Farm Bureau Federation (AFBF) is much the largest and functions in practically every state.[11] It is sometimes referred to as a corn-hog-cotton coalition with more than half of its membership coming from the Midwest, Alabama, and Mississippi. In its general position on political questions and farm programs, the AFBF moved from a more or less New Deal and centrist-oriented posture to the right and has become a spokesman for many of the larger, affluent farm owners. It opposes high price supports, denounces the larger federal role in terms that are delightful to ultraconservative business groups, and more and more follows policies paralleling those of organized business.

Not only are agrarian interests expressed through private associations, but powerful voices are raised in their behalf by various public

[11] See O. M. Kile, *The Farm Bureau through Three Decades*, Waverly Press, Baltimore, Md., 1948; and "The Farm Bureau," *Fortune*, June, 1944. For a keen analysis of this and other farm groups see Grant McConnell, *The Decline of Agrarian Democracy*, University of California Press, Berkeley, 1953.

agencies, particularly the U.S. Department of Agriculture. The Extension Service and the American Farm Bureau Federation have become common-law partners, and both are for decentralized administration. The Soil Conservation Service works through soil-conservation districts and with professional conservationists, bypassing the state colleges of agriculture and operating directly from Washington to the farmer. The Farmers Home Administration (FHA) has concentrated on loans to farmers unable to secure credit elsewhere. However, neither the FHA nor important private groups have been particularly concerned with speaking for farm labor and migratory workers. Entrenched agricultural interests continue to act on theoretical premises long outmoded. No agricultural public policy, due to the great diversity of farming, has been able to satisfy the needs of all farmers, and it is difficult to find compromises that will help all without hurting some.

Labor.   In the United States nearly everyone belongs (or believes he belongs) to the middle class. Most workers see themselves as members of the middle class, although some see themselves as members of a working class as distinct from the middle class. The absence of a feudal-aristocratic class at the other extreme has likewise contributed to the absence of an American class struggle on Old World lines. This has worked against a strong class-conscious labor movement and toward a tendency of the United States worker to regard his status as temporary. These factors, among others, made the growth of trade unionism slow until the passage of the Wagner Act in 1935. After a radical jump in union membership there has been a leveling-off tendency since the end of World War II, with 14 million to 17 million members (or about one-third of the employees in nonfarm establishments). Beginning in the 1950s, an actual decline in membership in some unions took place, despite an overall increase in the labor force. Laborsaving devices and automation are probable contributors to the fact that union growth is not keeping pace with the rise in the working forces of the nation.

Although labor's organizations have always had programs to serve the individual welfare of the members, often called strictly trade-union objectives, the unions' officials are in politics, and the political role of labor unions has increased and intensified in the past generation. The politics of labor is channeled into (1) intraunion politics and interunion jurisdictional disputes, (2) lobbying, (3) election activities, (4) public relations, and (5) labor political parties. At one time, some of the members and leaders wished to use unions to bring about socialism, to further the class struggle, and, before 1945, to aid the Communist party. Bitter quarrels ensued because the majority of members were not interested in furthering Marxian objectives. Labor had to fight off charges of radicalism, socialism, and un-Americanism.

Changes in the occupational structure of workers has made it difficult for labor to remain unified. The American Federation of Labor (AFL), created in 1886, originally spoke largely for craft workers. A split-off of industrial workers and the mine workers led to organization of the Congress for Industrial Organizations (CIO) in 1935 with the latter emphasizing more than the AFL the need for government legislation to supplement the achievements of collective bargaining. The CIO also tended to be less satisfied with the structure of society.

Labor has always been beset with schisms in the ranks, and the divisions permitted what many of their leaders thought had brought enactment of hostile legislation such as the Taft Hartley law (1947) and unfavorable access to the Eisenhower administration. This led to the AFL-CIO merger in 1955. Such strong national unions as the miners and teamsters were often in then out of the greater federations. The merger never fully healed dissension but mitigated rivalries somewhat. Each group's political action committees were put together in the Committee for Political Education (COPE), which helped to centralize responsibility for registration and electoral activities. But many unions still conduct their political activities outside COPE. With some local exceptions, labor has had greater access to the Democratic party, and its candidates have helped to tie unions together in common causes during campaigns.

Although collective bargaining remains central to the tactics of labor, unions tend to agree on support for legislation that extends social security, combats poverty, aids education, and expands general welfare programs. Some differences remain over emphasis and tactics. With the exception of the Liberal party in New York, which gets much support from the International Ladies Garment Workers, labor does not attempt to run a political party of its own but rather limits itself to endorsements and campaign support.

Despite the increase in population, labor-union membership has stabilized, and its ranks are slow to develop youthful, imaginative leadership. Its leaders are troubled about how to assimilate the growing numbers of white-collar workers, women, and blacks and how to meet the problems of the rapidly industrializing South. They must tread lightly on these problems, which are related to the stated national goal of equality. Automation is also causing problems. In the history of labor organization are found illustrations of practically every principle and facet of group life—examples of success and failure because of adherence to principle or to expediency, of protest and defection, of changes wrought by the upset of economic and political equilibrium, of changes made necessary by interaction with business and other groups. Labor's tactics have had to be adaptive and flexible, and failure commonly resulted when they were not.

The Professions.   If one has difficulty in defining with some precision the terms *businessman* and *farmer,* his problem will perhaps be even greater in identifying a professional. Law, medicine, engineering, and teaching have always been regarded as a large part of the professions. But the concept is broadening, and state law is being used to recognize as professional those engaged as beauticians, barbers, morticians, and professional athletes, to mention but a few. The United States census places under the rubric of the professions such diverse occupations as airplane pilots, dietitians, and surveyors. It is not easy, therefore, to identify a "professional" interest in public policy, even compared to a broad category such as the agrarian interest. For years, leaders of professional associations emphasized that their organizations were interested only in "elevating the profession" and had little concern with political objectives. Professional societies were—and to a considerable extent still are—distinguished from the general-purpose groups representing business, labor, and agriculture in having somewhat narrower political and legislative objectives. Many professional groups show reluctance to take positions on peripheral matters not related to the purpose of the societies themselves, and many of them avoid any semblance of becoming a political interest group. At the same time, one of the more important developments in American politics in the present era is the great increase in the political interests and activities of those who make their living in the professions.

A majority of the professional societies are concerned with one basic public policy objective, which usually emanates from the associations themselves. This is the use of public law to police the occupation by setting up certain work rules and details of the division of professional labor. By implication this may tend to restrict and control new entrants or to establish minimum regulations for preparation and practice. Statutes call for licenses, certificates (as in the case of public school teachers), or examinations. Presumably this protects the profession from quacks and imcompetents. State law is used to stake out jurisdictional boundaries and lines of autonomy and authority both within and between professions. Certain conformities as well as privileges are imposed on members.

Each profession has additional reasons for getting into politics when the comparative peace and equilibrium of the group are disturbed. For many years there has been a "politics of health" raging around proposals at both the state and national levels for various types of public health insurance and medical care programs. The American Medical Association (AMA) raises huge sums of money for lobbying and public relations programs in opposition to nearly all such proposals. It rallies pharmacists, owners of drugstores, hospital managers, nurses, dentists, and allied groups into "healing arts committees." Some of these are analogous to labor's political action committees in that they endorse candidates, raise money for them, register voters, and even facilitate voting by patients in hospitals. Dentists have projected themselves into vigorous campaigns in some communities in support of the addition of fluorine to water for purposes of combating tooth decay.

Although it is argued by some that politics can and should be kept out of education, the realities of public education make it inherently enmeshed with public policy. School officials are forced to seek adequate financial support at a time when other services such as welfare and highways are providing stiff competition for the tax dollar. Today, various groups are seeking equality of education opportunity within a given state and between states and some public support for parochial schools, such as purchase of equipment and transportation of pupils. Community-school relationships are sometimes strained by groups critical of curriculum and materials used in the schools. Finally, postwar inflation developed a critical salary problem for teachers, and school boards were (and still are) faced with keeping talented and promising men and women in the teaching profession. The National Education Association is aiding the cause by lobbying for increased federal aid to education. Local educational groups are rallying parent-teacher associations, and on infrequent occasions a strike or threat of it is used to dramatize school issues.

In short, medical and school associations find themselves in opposite stances toward public law once removed beyond matters of immediate licensing and certification. The medical societies fight to maintain the status quo and generally oppose the extension of public medical care programs. In contrast, the school forces must go to the government seeking appropriations and new authorizations and try to build alliances that will help them get aid from the government. The bar associations are in still a different position. They are more represented in government than any other group. Lawyers in large numbers sit in the legislative chambers and are in a position to see that their profession is adequately protected by statutory measures on admission to the bar. In more than half the states, the law requires one to be a member of the state bar association in order to be admitted to the bar. This provides an assured membership for the association. One does not become a member of the American Bar Association (ABA) by reason of affiliation with his state group, however, and fewer than half of the lawyers are ABA members. In contrast, more than two-thirds of the nation's physicians are members of the American Medical Association. Because it is so frequently in the headlines, the AMA is much more visible and more widely known than the ABA.

Although bar associations are mainly concerned with legislation relating to their profession and with judicial procedures, they are also interested in the development of public policy and in uniform state laws. Unlike laborers and farmers, as well as many other professionals, the lawyer usually finds it convenient to link his work with steady political participation and involvement, which may, in turn, bring new clients and increase his visibility should he seek elective public office. Lawyers, contrary to an opinion of some, do not vote in a conservative bloc in the state legislatures. The American Bar Association, frequently labeled "conservative," has publicly called for reform of the Electoral College.

Professional groups now perform more than guild functions of limiting their activities to matters immediately related to their profession. The "ivory tower" is being left more and more for the forum and legislative corridors. Political scientists are asked to advise Congress on how to reform itself and on changes in electoral laws. Scientists without solicitation give their views on political uses of nuclear energy and space explorations. College professors from various disciplines speak individually and sometimes through formal resolutions of their associations on foreign policy, the draft, political violence, and urban blight. Clergymen speak out on civil rights, desegregation, and crime. Writers' guilds voice views on matters ranging from congressional investigations to censorship. Peripheral matters aside, the professional, like members of other economic groups, finds that some knowledge of *Realpolitick* and power politics is becoming necessary for survival in the professions.

One of the most striking characteristics of professional societies is their great proliferation and the resultant new pluralism within each profession. Two general forces work to multiply groups. As the main or parent association brings in more and more members, the old leaders and elites are not quite so dominant, and some of them form separate associations of their own while maintaining their ties with the main body of the profession. Rank-and-file members who are specialists representing a new division of labor or who become somewhat unhappy with the dominant group split off and form their own professional units while' also maintaining their membership with the parent organization. Blacks who found they were unwelcome in medical societies or in bar associations formed their own groups. Religion, sex, age, region, and ideology offer five other bases for suborganization. Each association tends to develop its own governmental structure, an independent program, and often lobbyists. In many if not most cases, these groups are not subordinate to the parent group but develop on an equal or horizontal plane to it. This makes for greater complexity as well as specialization in the prelegislative lawmaking process, and provides for more precise and specialized representation for the professional.

OTHER INTEREST GROUPS

When one turns from the four broadly composed economic-vocational interest groups, he finds an endless number of persons organized on other bases and inviting or perhaps defying classification. Some of the nonoccupational multipurpose groups possess fairly strong political orientations. Others are basically oriented toward political action in the first instance and often with quite specific policy objectives. Still other groups are ideologically oriented and are sometimes referred to as the radical right and radical left. Veterans' organizations afford an example of the first group. They are designed to obtain benefits and protection for their members from government. Veterans of course are drawn from all occupational, social, and ethnic-religious groups but are tied together by memories of their military service and programs involving bonuses, civil service, veterans preferences, treatment of service-connected injuries, and vocational rehabilitation.

The American Legion is the largest and best-known veterans' organization. More books and monographs appear to have been written about it than about any other single group. Although avowedly "absolutely nonpolitical" according to its constitution, the Legion has been involved with politics since its creation in 1919. It became an uncompromising foe of the League of Nations and the World Court. Its Americanization program has led it to conduct investigations of school textbooks and materials and allegedly pacifist teachers. It has zealously gone after Communists and so-called Communist sympathizers, and it fought the Eighteenth Amendment and "radicalism." Its leadership has often had an economically conservative ideology. Some local legionnaire groups have fought the American Civil Liberties Union and have joined with right-wing groups in certain causes. Despite its worthy philanthropic and fraternal enterprises, the Legion has been a storm center in the politics of a number of communities. Although the Legion claimed membership of 3 million in 1969, there are many other groups such as the Disabled American Veterans, Veterans of Foreign Wars, and several smaller organizations formed by World War II veterans. Veterans' groups learn that servicemen soon settle back into their social and economic backgrounds and that a veterans' vote or sharp policy position are not established.

Although less politically oriented, church organizations are multipurpose with interest in some public policies. The churches, as Ebersole notes, have moved far beyond mere opposition to "liquor, war and sin."[12] Foreign policy, civil rights, fluoridation, abortion, birth control, integration, and health programs are only a few of the issues on which denominations have taken positions—and frequently on opposite sides. Where churches operate businesses and own property for investment purposes they become interested in tax-exemption policies and zoning ordinances. Churches often operate through the church itself. There is sharp dissent within the membership over the appropriateness of engaging in politics and over the policies espoused.

The citizen finds innumerable organizations, some fleeting, some long-lived, basically motivated by political education and activity. The League of Women Voters and local municipal leagues keep watch over local public affairs and speak for civic improvement. Some so-called good government associations, however, are fronts for special interests or classes of taxpayers. The American Association for the United Nations, National Council for the Prevention of War, Women's Christian Temperance Union, Firearms Lobby of America, American Cancer Society, National Reclamation Society, Society for Animal Protective Legislation, Trustees for Conservation illustrate but a few of the essentially single-cause associations registered as lobbyists or known to spend money for their political objectives.[13]

A characteristic of current American politics is the rash of organizations working on behalf of civil rights in general and the black community in particular. To some extent the Negro organizations divide themselves into the older organizations and those created in the 1950s and 1960s. The newer groups are constantly regrouping and are characterized by turnover in leadership and changes in tactics. No one person or group speaks authoritatively for the blacks and there are many bitter struggles among the black community leaders.[14] After the assassination of the Reverend Martin Luther King in 1968 and the passage of the several national civil rights laws, many of the Negro struggles shifted from the national to the local arenas.

One of the oldest and largest (450,000 in 1970) is the National Association for the Advancement of Colored People (NAACP), formed in 1909. It has concentrated on public policy and on winning victories

[12] Luke E. Ebersole, *Church Lobbying in the Nation's Capital*, The Macmillan Company, New York, 1951.

[13] The *Congressional Quarterly* regularly carries accounts of those groups that register as lobbyists before Congress. A great many miscellaneous political interest groups are identified and discussed by Zeigler, *op. cit.*

[14] The leadership and operation of a number of national and local Negro associations are covered by Stokely Carmichael and Charles V. Hamilton, *Black Power: The Politics of Liberation*, Vintage Books, Random House, Inc., New York, 1967.

in the courts for Negroes, thus immeasurably improving the legal status of blacks in such diverse areas as voting, housing, transportation, education, and service on juries. In general practice, the NAACP has sought advancement for the blacks within the framework of existing society through the use of peaceful methods. The National Urban League, through dozens of local affiliations, concentrates on working with employers to provide equal employment opportunity. It works behind the scenes with less emphasis upon litigation and legislation. Both organizations welcome white members, some of whom have held leadership positions.

The NAACP was too militant to suit certain whites in the South, and White Citizens Councils were formed to minimize its influence if not drive it out of existence. The councils are, in effect, a "control" group trying to preserve the status quo but leaving its value objectives undefined or unclear so as to bring the widest possible support from whites.

Many young blacks today are surprised to learn that the NAACP, at least in the South, was considered radical and militant. They see the organization as too moderate, lacking in militancy, and controlled by upper-class Negroes who have made it in the white man's society. The NAACP and its local branches are frequently scenes of sharp controversy over tactics if not goals. The NAACP largely avoids mass protest while the newer groups such as the Southern Christian Leadership Conference (SCLC), the Committee on Racial Equality (CORE), and the Student Nonviolent Coordinating Committee (SNCC) foster sit-ins, marches, demonstrations, and other dramatic forms of protest such as freedom rides. Much of the local black leadership has undergone a shift from accommodation to a protest orientation. A shift in the basis of leadership is also resulting in shifting goals in black organizations. The SCLC, after the assassination of its leader, Dr. King, continued its emphasis upon peaceful demonstrations; but many within CORE and SNCC advocate stronger forms of protest, which might call at times for a show of violence. These organizations have offered serious competition to both the Urban League and the NAACP.

Negro political activity and leadership is further fragmented over the issue of segregation and integration. "Black nationalism" was advocated after World War I and taken up by the Black Muslims of today who seek, by their own words, separation not integration or acceptance of partnership of the blacks in American life.

Depending on how one sees "black power," the concept, which has growing appeal among the militants, stands between separatism and integrations. As defined by Carmichael and Hamilton, black power means group solidarity in order to gain an effective bargaining position in a pluralistic society. Black people must lead and run their own organizations, control their own schools, and fully participate in the decision-making processes affecting the lives of black people.[15] It means participation of blacks in the operation of power. Black power is a tactic and does not necessarily assert either separation or integration of Negroes. As such it is often accepted as sound strategy by both groups.

Black student unions and the Black Panthers among others appeal to Negro youth to employ black power to achieve changes in college admissions, curricula, and in administrative practices to bring increasing numbers of blacks into college and to foster identity and pride in black culture and accomplishments. The Black Panthers function off as well as on campus on behalf of local causes and emphasize protection of the black man in his relation to police. The militant Revolutionary Action Movement functions largely off campus but is led by youth.

Black power is a term that is not well understood by some whites and that means different things to persons within the Negro community, yet it dominates the politics of many cities today. Public officials, both black and white, find it difficult to locate Negro leaders who have wide acceptance in the black population and are able to speak with authority for it.[16] The growing militancy of blacks and fragmented leadership is perhaps characteristic of a group whose position has been improving since the *Brown v. Board of Education* decision in 1954 calling for desegregation in public education.

POLITICS OF THE RIGHT AND THE LEFT

For more than a century, special-purpose groups have existed to advance one or more ideologies of the political left and the political right. These tend to be cyclical in character; only a few survive for long periods of time. In the 1950s and early 1960s, there was a resurgence of various types of articulate political conservatism variously denoted as the radical right, extreme right, and reactionary radical to distinguish them from moderate conservatives. It is easy to overgeneralize the composition and motivations of people associated with the movement because it is lacking in a coherent ideology or expression through one all-embracing minor party or organization.[17] The radical right contains both Republicans and Democrats and has attempted, with occasional local success,

---

[15] *Op. cit.*, chap. 11.

[16] In Cleveland in the mid-sixties, for example, some fifty different civil rights groups were in existence, and the effort to build a United Freedom Movement was only slightly successful. See Louis H. Masotti and Jerome R. Corsi, *Shoot-Out in Cleveland*, Bantam Books, Inc., New York, 1969, p. 6.

[17] There is an enormous body of periodical literature and newspaper articles on the new political right. In addition to Mark Sherwin, *The Extremists*, St. Martin's Press, Inc., New York, 1963, see Daniel Bell, *The End of Ideology*, Collier Books, New York, 1961; "Conservatism, Liberalism and National Issues," *The Annals of the American Academy of Political and Social Science*, vol. 344, November, 1962. Additional references are given at the end of this chapter.

to infiltrate Republican organizations. Prominent liberal and moderate Republicans have fought the extreme right because they believe that it will lead to fragmentation of the party. Senator Barry Goldwater, although expressing sympathy for some of the right's causes, has refused to lead a third party or to become its spokesman. The extreme right does not spend much time or money on conventional lobbying but more on arousing the public and attempting to get its followers to support ultraconservative candidates for public office. New York is one of the few places where some local strongly conservative candidates have polled a creditable vote. In an earlier chapter, cognizance was taken of the candidacy of former Gov. George Wallace's third-party effort in 1968. After the election, however, Wallace was disinclined to lead a united right-wing movement.

To a considerable extent, the new extreme rightists share a mood and a rebellion against the forces and changes brought about in the world and in the nation since the 1930s. Radical rightism thrives on anxiety and frustration over the turn of world affairs and is strongly nationalistic. Foreign aid and the United Nations are opposed, as expressed in the simplistic slogan, "Get the United Nations out of the United States and the United States out of the United Nations." Each frustration of American foreign policy adds further fuel to the agitation.

A theme that ties many right-wingers together is a conspiratorial theory of history. Beliefs of this kind have often cropped up in the nation's history. During the days of Andrew Jackson, an anti-Catholic book appeared under the title *Foreign Conspiracy against the Liberties of the United States,* which played upon fears of the spread of papal influence in the United States. The Know-Nothing party of the 1840s and Wall Street provided later groups with conspiratorial explanations. Isolationist leaders saw American entry into World War II as contrived by bankers, Jews, New Dealers, Roosevelt, and the Communists.

After World War II, the "communist influence" tactic was used by many groups in attacking such diverse programs as fluoridation of drinking water, metro government, sex education in the schools, the welfare state, and bans on nuclear testing. In the 1960s, some whites applied the conspiracy theory to Negro sit-ins and attempts to get the vote or to secure open housing. Some asserted that the widespread student revolts on the campuses could be traced to communism. All recent Presidents, former Chief Justice Earl Warren, and numerous other public men were accused by some of the extreme rightists as "soft on communism."

Ultraconservatism of this type is not limited to any one group or geographic section. Much of it is not racist or religious as was characteristic of many earlier hate groups. Such analyses as have been made of the modern right-wing groups observe *nouveau riche* among financial supporters. Numerous retired military men, former Communists, and elderly persons find the rightist explanations appealing. Fundamentalist Protestant sects and Catholic sectors appear more drawn to the doctrines than the less fundamentalist Protestants, liberal Catholics, and Jews. Many rightists are on the frustrated fringes of the middle class and have fears of big labor and big business; they seem to be more concerned about status politics and rationalizations than with material interests.

The organizational expression of rightist causes is not easily expressed. It tends to be monolithic, with formal control by top leaders. Many local groups have blossomed all over the United States.

The new American left differs in numerous respects from the older left in tactics and causes. For years the far left was predominantly socialist and Marxist and expressed itself through minor parties. In the 1950s, rightists, even without a charismatic leader, enjoyed much strength because there was not a militant left to fight it on its own grounds. A liberal non-Communist organization, the Americans for Democratic Action, was formed in 1947 and provided a haven for intellectuals and others pressing for a variety of liberal causes. It works closely at times with the Democratic party but parted company over the Vietnam war in the latter part of the sixties.

The left-wing causes blossomed during the 1960s.[18] Most persons attracted to the new left were not socialists; however, interest in Marxism, especially among the young and students, increased, and some of the old familiar war cries against the capitalist system were raised. Much of the movement, however, is protest rather than ideological prescription and, like the right, is highly diversified in leadership and objectives. The thrust is in three major directions.

The first developed from a growing militancy for civil rights, especially among blacks. Younger blacks became impatient with the slowness of legislation in combatting white racism and poverty. "Demands" were submitted to churches, business, colleges, and governors. Some, as observed in the preceding section, called for abandoning the goals of integration espoused by the liberal white "establishment" and older Negroes. Radical tactics and strategies are advocated to speed up the aspirations of blacks and to foster "black identity." Violence broke out in many American cities when militant blacks confronted public authority.

A second movement was centered around peace in Vietnam. But it soon was greatly broadened to attack the selective service system,

[18] Periodical literature likewise burgeoned. A few major books include Priscilla Long (ed.), *The New Left*, Porter Sargent, Publisher, New York, 1969; Kenneth Keniston, *Young Radicals*, Harcourt, Brace & World, Inc., New York, 1968; Carl Oglesby, *The New Left Reader*, Grove Press, Inc., New York, 1969. Additional references at end of chapter.

huge armaments, and the "industrial-military complex," which was seen as an alliance between defense contractors, the Pentagon, and a certain military mentality in Congress and elsewhere. The cause was dramatized by draft-card burning, sit-ins in army recruitment offices, peace parades, and the heckling of presidential nominees in 1968.

There are literally hundreds of peace groups representing approaches from pacifist to nonpacifist. The older groups, such as the American Friends Service Committee and National Council for the Prevention of War, continue to function, along with newer groups such as the Committee for a Sane Nuclear Policy (SANE), Women's Strike for Peace, and Turn Toward Peace. Many of the newer groups are more electorally oriented and concentrate some effort and money on electing "peace" candidates, one such group being the National Committee of 1,000 to Elect Peace Candidates.

Despite the widespread interest in peace and sporadic help from church groups, there is not yet a real mass movement for peace in terms of central leadership and organization. Many citizens concerned about armaments and huge defense budgets do not wish to be characterized as part of the new left and do not approve of draft-card burning or some of the activities of young militants. For this reason, probably only the latter can be appropriately associated with the current radicalism of the left. Among the new left militant peace groups are scores of local "peace in Vietnam" associations some of which are loosely connected with the Women's Strike for Peace and the Mobilization Committee to End the War in Vietnam. The Youth International Party (yippies) was formed in 1967 to mobilize young people and peace groups.

Civil rights and draft protests are not without precedent in American history. The third aspect of the new left, the student section, represents a much more novel aspect. American students have never been particularly active in politics nor have they been expected to participate actively in noncampus societal problems while in school. Political activity was regarded (and still is in many quarters) in negative terms. Debating, forums, discussion clubs, and Young Democrats and Young Republicans appealed to a small minority of students and were not generally looked upon with askance by faculty, administrators, and students themselves. The new campus radicalism, however, is a sharp break with norms and traditions. By 1970, very few college campuses had escaped confrontations between students and educational administrators and in some cases rebellions occurred in high schools.

Protests come from many directions but can be broadly classified into purely campus matters and national policies. Many student leaders tried to tie the two together and to involve students in off-campus as well as campus politics. Not all student protests were purely political in objectives; some were cultural and involved the sexual revolution, coeducational dormitories, modes of dress, freedom of speech in student newspapers, and numerous other matters. Demands were made for student participation in curriculum revision and school administration; student representation on boards of education; and the abolition of ROTC courses and armed services and business recruitment on the campus. Noncollege objectives included anti-war demonstrations, boycott of grapes, and civil rights.

The Students for a Democratic Society (SDS), although faction ridden itself, has been successful in politicizing enough of the students to bring about confrontations with campus authorities all over the country.[19] It sought and received support from the black student groups on many campuses; but, on some campuses, black students stood aloof from the SDS, believing the better tactic was to keep its objectives separate from those of the SDS. The SDS serves as a vehicle of protest against nearly everything both on and off campus. For this reason, many students who agree with some of the causes will not join them because they are not in agreement on all issues and on tactics. Several SDS leaders are avowedly pro-Mao and pro-Castro and tend to alienate students who were not Marxist in ideology. Some conservative student groups such as Young Americans for Freedom and Young Republicans, although requesting changes in university practices, can not accept the more militant causes and techniques of the SDS, and some of the civil rights groups, such as the Black Panthers, have engaged in counter-moves when the former conducted demonstrations on the campuses.

By 1970, full-fledged campus radicalism was embraced by only a minority of the student body; but increasingly larger numbers of students expressed dissatisfaction with teaching methods, examinations, the research emphasis for professorial promotion, the curriculum, academic requirements (which allegedly lack "relevancy" to life as it is), and various priorities established by university administrators. A Gallup study in May, 1969, found that 81 percent of the students believed they should have "greater say in the running of colleges"—only 25 percent of the general public was of this opinion.[20] At the same time, only 28 percent had actually participated in a demonstration. (Considering past conduct of students, however, this is a strikingly high figure.) Graduate

[19] Campus groups show a constant overturn and regrouping; many are short-lived. In addition to the Students for a Democratic Society, formed in 1962, other militant groups in 1970 were the Black Liberation Front, Students Afro-American Society, Young Socialist Alliance, and the two Communist youth groups, the Progressive Labor Party and W. E. B. Du Bois Club.

[20] For an extensive summary of this study see *U.S. News & World Report*, June 2, 1969, pp. 34ff.

students, Democrats, liberals, easterners, men, and persons whose parent's income exceeded $15,000 were demonstrators to a larger extent than were their counterparts.

The old left was usually class oriented and economic in approach. It was strongest in times of economic distress and attacked the system that permitted the people to be exploited. The new left youth leadership is often from the ranks of affluent youth and ranges much beyond economic emphasis. The newer reactionary right also does not stake out its claim within an economic framework, and its voices of protest have not acted as a counterbalancing force against the sections of the left that are mainly economic. Both the right and the left protest against the "quality of American life," the powerlessness of the individual, and the loss of individualism. They find that the great multipurpose organizations and political parties afford inadequate vehicles for expressing their dissent. They resort, therefore, to creating associations of their own; these serve the interests of some citizens in the pluralistic society but the tendency of some leaders to resort to terror, intimidation, and violence has strained the traditional civil liberties system and has given their opponents a "law and order" issue on which to attack them. This problem will be considered further in a later chapter.

FUNCTIONS OF ORGANIZED GROUPS

Citizens possess ultimate power in the United States by being able to vote the operators of their government into or out of office. But even the fullest knowledge of voting behavior leaves a most incomplete picture of how political power is organized, controlled, and expressed. Actual exercise of influence over government depends to a considerable extent on the outcome of the competition of "private governments" or powerful interests bent on shaping public policy. However, policy is not exclusively the result of combat between groups. Nevertheless, the individual comes more and more to have power and influence as the organization to which he belongs has power and influence.

Groups may be for something, against something, or a combination of both. With rare exceptions, most of them wish to endure long enough to accomplish their goals. Goals in turn are unlikely to remain constant and undergo modification. Most groups wish to endure and in order to do so develop and maintain an ideology and an organizational framework. With individual variations, organizational patterns begin with a small nucleus formulating a set of purposes, followed by efforts to widen membership. Organization is developed by drafting bylaws or a constitution providing for rules of governance, periodic conventions and meetings, and the general manner by which the group formulates its policies. A folklore, built around its objectives, becomes the gospel and myth by which it lives. Purposes are high sounding and public-spirited in tone, although the gap between *alleged* and *real* purposes may be wide. Stated ends and slogans follow patriotic symbols: the NAM promotes "The American System"; the American Legion fosters "Americanism." The American Medical Association labors for "private practice" and "freedom of choice of physician." The investor's lobby fights for "widows and orphans"; the publishers maintain "free speech and a free press"; and patriotic societies "save the Constitution." No one advocates "America second." Some may call their opponents socialists, reactionaries, "soft on communism," bosses, and so on, while professing themselves to be promoting the public interest.

Services to Membership. To reemphasize, only a small fraction of organized groups have aims that are 100 percent oriented toward public policy. Political objectives and activities change over a period of time. In a sense, a number of groups are like the occasional voter—they are in and out of the political process depending on how involved their interests are and whether their problems are seen to be capable of solution in whole or in part by government. The great majority of groups lack full-fledged politicalization. Activities and resources of the organization must be allocated between pressure-group functions and out-group relationships and services to the membership.

Groups combine and aggregate the goals of individuals. These objectives are expressed to the public and to government officials. Probably the function of defining the interests of its own partisans is of top importance for the group. The leadership creates images for the membership of other groups and public agencies. The image may not be a perfect one and often attributes a monolithic character to groups considered rivals or opponents. Information gathered by the staff and leadership is transmitted to the membership to help each member to formulate ideas about public affairs. Through journals such as *The Nations' Farmer* or *The Teamster*, the leadership communicates and molds sentiments of the members. Conventions and meetings are also useful for this purpose. A great portion of group activity involves interaction with people in one's own organization and on the same side of the public questions.

The individual, occupied with matters of livelihood, seldom approaches his representatives directly and regularly on economic matters. This function is performed for him by his organization. His needs and desires are likely to be more clearly and persuasively presented by a skilled spokesman for his group. The individual in this case maximizes his strength by collective action.

Further, a person may have little conception that certain of his needs can be advanced by government, but it is the business of the experts in his organization to know where to go and the best techniques to use for presenting these needs. In a sense, a group agent is performing a service for his fellow member, just as a physician or auto mechanic performs other services for him. Interest-group interaction is two-way; it takes the members' problems to government, and it brings back from government a service, advice, an interpretation, or perhaps the news that nothing can be done under existing law or practice. Organization leaders are also helpful in identifying actual and potential political friends and allies.

Services to Government.   Most state legislators candidly acknowledge that lobbyists are indispensable to lawmaking. Other public officials recognize the contributions that knowledgeable interest-group spokesmen render. The increasing complexity of the economic order makes it difficult, if not impossible, for lawmakers to understand the intricacies of the problems facing business, foreign trade, labor, and transportation, not to mention hundreds of other issues. Hours spent performing "errand boy" services and ceremonial functions leave the legislators insufficient time for study and reflection concerning issues. Most state legislatures have meager staff services, and lobbyists are a major source of information.

The services of interest groups extend far beyond the providing of data. Of prime importance to the public official are the probable effects of proposed policies on certain groups. Here the spokesmen for the groups can provide the policy maker with useful opinions, however biased. Very frequently the persons directly affected can render a useful judgment on practical application, especially on details.

Often escaping notice is the fact that interest groups may possess strength in their claim to specialized knowledge. Research and the mobilization of facts are often tools of power, for they are useful in convincing legislators (on the state more than on the national level) in the making of public decisions. Complicated charts and statistics urbanely presented by lobbyists and spokesmen for organized groups may be especially effective in the absence of intimate knowledge of a problem by a legislator or a staff member.

Some private groups are initiators of remedies and proposals calling for the passage of a specific bill, an administrative action, or a court order. Proposals stimulate debate and act as a catalyst, setting other forces in motion. Different groups at one time or another called for separate federal departments of health, education, and welfare. The ultimate response was the creation of a Cabinet office including all three.

Though this did not assauge each zealous separatist demand, it elevated each interest to Cabinet status. This creative function, both actual and potential, is most important and gives zest to the political process.

The lobby is a maligned institution, and there is a popular assumption that it operates nefariously as the "invisible government." The "third house" is actually a form of group representation. Legislators are chosen on a geographic basis, but technology and economics have changed the importance of geography. A person's basic interest lies less with his legislative district and state than with his social, fraternal, and occupational relationships. Yet the constitutional structure and election laws are not geared to bring about the election of representatives of organized minorities (proportional representation excepted). In a society of diverse pursuits and of a high degree of social differentiation, it is inevitable that special interests will want to be represented before, if not in, government. Through the basically extralegal channels of pressure politics then, the interest groups strive to compensate for the absence of formal recognition (except in a few instances observed in Chapter 18) in the structure of our government. Pressure politics is America's answer to the problem of occupational representation.

In summary, we may speak of the legitimate functions of interest groups as including (1) the formulation and integration of group policies and goals, (2) the presentation of the group's public policies to government officials, (3) the provision of specialized information to members, the general public, lawmakers, and administrations, and (4) the exercise of surveillance over public policies and administration to provide protective and "watchdog" services for their constituencies. Pressure groups help focus attention on the dereliction of public authorities and compel action. These activities have, on the whole, a salutary impact on the government.

Although recognizing the prime and useful roles of interest groups, cognizance must be taken that they may be dysfunctional and that their power cannot go unrestrained. After an examination of group tactics and strategies in the next chapter, we shall return to a consideration of the criticisms of group activities, group theory, and methods of accommodating demands and activities of the "interest-group society."

FOR FURTHER READING

Bailey, Harry A., Jr., and Ellis Katz (eds.): *Ethnic Group Politics*, 1969.
Bell, Daniel (ed.): *The Radical Right*, 1963.
Broyles, J. Allen: *The John Birch Society: Anatomy of Protest*, 1964.
Burrow, James G.: *AMA: Voice of Organized Medicine*, 1963.
Cohen, Mitchell, and Dennis Hale: *The New Student Left*, 1966.

Dahl, Robert A.: *Pluralist Democracy in the United States: Conflict and Consent,* 1967.

Epstein, Edwin M.: *The Corporation in American Politics,* 1970.

Hacker, Andrew: *Politics and the Corporation,* 1958.

Hofstadter, Richard: *The Paranoid Style in American Politics,* 1963.

Jacobs, Paul, and Saul Landau: *The New Radicals: A Report with Documents,* 1966.

Jacobson, Julius (ed.): *The Negro and the American Labor Movement,* 1968.

Kaufman, Arnold S.: *The Radical Liberal: New Man in American Politics,* 1968.

Latham, Earl: *The Group Basis of Politics: A Study in Basing Point Legislation,* 1952.

Machood, H. R.: *Pressure Groups in American Politics,* 1967.

McConnell, Grant: *Private Power and American Democracy,* 1966.

McKean, Dayton D.: *The Integrated Bar,* 1964.

Monsen, R. Joseph, Jr., and Mark W. Cannon: *The Makers of Public Policy: American Power Groups and Their Ideologies,* 1965.

Morgan, Richard E.: *The Politics of Religious Conflict: Church and State in America,* 1968.

Redekop, John H.: *The American Far Right,* 1968.

Rose, Arnold M.: *The Power Structure: Political Process in American Society,* 1967.

Schoenberger, Robert A.: *The American Right Wing: Readings in Political Behavior,* 1969.

Zisk, Betty H.: *American Political Interest Groups: Readings in Theory and Research,* 1969.

CHAPTER 20 **THE TACTICS OF INTEREST GROUPS**

Nearly every political interest group, and the large ones in particular, is concerned with four arenas of internal and external politics. First, there is the ever-present internal factional politics, which, if unbridled, will weaken it in functioning effectively in the other three battlegrounds. Second, the group wants to create and maintain a favorable public image without necessarily referring to any immediate objectives. Third, the organization must negotiate with other private organizations and political parties on a wide variety of matters, working with some as allies, attempting to neutralize potential opponents, and exerting defensive efforts against those adversaries with which it has not worked out mutual accommodation. Finally, it must carry on relationships with those institutions of government that make public-policy decisions. Struggles are likely to ensue on all four scenes nearly all the time.

Since many persons belong to more than one group, their overlapping membership (a term employed by David B. Truman) may lead to erosion of loyalty to one or more of their affiliations. Factionalism often results in bitter struggles for power within the organization. Internal frictions may disturb the stability and equilibrium of the organization and sap its strength, thus keeping it from presenting an image of unity to the outside world and to government. Outsiders may be uncertain about who speaks for the group and whether it will live up to its alliances and commitments. This raises the whole problem of democratic governance within the organization itself. Responsible governance of interest groups is one of the most important problems facing the pluralist society. The subject is, however, peripheral to this volume, and receives only passing mention.[1]

A few organizations employ devices that, on the surface at least, give the sanction of the membership to the positions of the leaders. Secret votes are sometimes taken by government authorities to determine whether members of labor unions wish to strike or to accept certain proposals by management. A few unions accept this voluntarily. The Chamber of Commerce has an elaborate referendum whereby questions are submitted to local chambers all over the nation together with a statement presenting each side of the question. The International Typographical Union (ITU) offers a deviation from the "iron law of oligarchy," which permits leaders of large groups to perpetuate themselves in power rather easily. Under such one-party government, it is difficult for a faction to organize regularly and effectively. The ITU, however, has established a two-party system; in nearly every election, there are at least two rival slates.[2]

Internal cohesion is maintained in many ways. As in most democratic institutions, the leadership must make compromises and concessions and try to head off cliques and factionalism that threaten the tenure of the leaders and the organization itself. Unity may be reinforced by focusing attention on an outside "enemy" and observing that dissension threatens all, including the dissenters. The emphasis on "we" in opposition to "they" is carried to members through internal propaganda in the house organs that are mailed to the homes of the members. Pressure-group journals are not known for their objectivity, and the leaders use them to warn the members of dangers from the outside. The raising of special funds to fight the enemy, "socialized medicine," has been an important technique of the American Medical Association in preserving internal unity.

[1] For an excellent treatment of internal politics and cohesion, see David B. Truman, *The Governmental Process*, Alfred A. Knopf, Inc., New York, 1951, chaps. 6 and 7, and Abraham Holtzman, *Interest Groups and Lobbying*, The Macmillan Company, New York, 1966, chap. 2.

[2] See Seymour M. Lipset, *Democracy in Private Government: A Case of the International Typographical Union*, Institute of Industrial Relations, University of California, Berkeley, 1952.

THE TACTICS OF INTEREST GROUPS
605

In its relationships with the outside world, an interest group has many tactics from which to choose. However, these are conditioned by the resources and size of the group and by the nature of the organizations with whom it is dealing. Some expend great effort in lobbying, others on public relations, taking cases to court or dealing with administrators or maintaining close liaison with civic and political party leaders. Tactics also vary as between immediate and long-range goals. The focus at one moment may be on a government agency and on public relations at another time.

PUBLIC RELATIONS

Publicity Objectives. Although public relations activities have not superseded attempts to influence public officials directly, a large corps of specialists is available to assist groups in what Edward L. Bernays calls "the engineering of consent." Most of the larger, multipurpose service groups maintain a publicity division, with public relations experts to prepare scripts, slogans, news releases, copy for trade journals, speeches for officials, and so on. Interest groups differ much in their reliance on public relations techniques. In some cases, a group's cause may be aided by avoiding publicity and utilizing the advantage of surprise. Military agencies worked in secret to draft legislation for control over atomic energy in order to avoid arousing atomic scientists who favored civilian control. When military control legislation was introduced, the opponents had to work fast to try to overcome the lack of access to information about the Army's activities.[3]

A considerable portion of propaganda or education is directed to the membership of the organization itself, even though it goes out to the public as well. Its purpose is to establish in high-sounding phrases a party line and to promote loyalty to the cause. Publicity is used to bolster sagging morale and to reinforce the myths of the group. It is the duty of the staff to explain complex issues to the membership and to the general public in simple, understandable terms. (This may also convince the rank and file that "headquarters" is doing its job and fighting "the good fight.") In a word, public relations is designed, not only to win over the general public, but also to promote internal solidarity and to prepare materials for public officials. The latter function is often shared with a research division.

In briefest terms, the public relations activities of an organization are carried on to (1) curry favor with the general public so that it will have a sympathetic attitude toward the organization and favor its general goals, (2) rationalize the group's goals in terms of the public interest, (3) neutralize criticisms of the opposition by answering attacks, (4) attract

[3] See Byron S. Miller, "A Law Is Passed—The Atomic Energy Act of 1946," *University of Chicago Law Review*, vol. 15, p. 804, 1948.

support (and perhaps even membership) from other groups who might share its objectives, and (5) mobilize the rank-and-file membership behind the organization's leadership.

Types of Public Relations. Business organizations were the first to employ extensive public relations. Corporations possess the financial resources to advertise and are the major clients for radio, newspapers, and television. In the selling of products, there is opportunity for getting customers, by subtle means, to support the general positions of business. Friendly newspaper columnists build up much goodwill for commerce and industry. Generalizations of business about its goals usually receive approbation from white-collar and professional groups and emphasize middle-class values, which all believe they share. It is a tribute to the public relations programs of business that many non-business people take it as their reference group and believe that what is good for General Motors (or most any other big business) is good for the country.[4]

Labor unions were very slow to resort to public relations and often suffered a bad public image. In recent years, organized labor has greatly stepped up its public relations programs. Publicity departments of labor unions and all other groups are constantly preparing stories that will have enough news value to be carried free in the press or broadcast as news.

Business groups were also among the very first to direct materials and propaganda to special groups of opinion leaders and influencers. Huge sums of money are spent to develop friendly relations with students, school administrators, college professors, churchmen, civic leaders, club presidents, and many others. Many colleges are beneficiaries of research funds provided by business. Numerous professors are invited to attend summer seminars or to accept internships in industrial concerns and have profited by learning the problems facing large corporations. Graduate scholarships for students are a part of the program. Labor unions have gradually moved into similar activities, although they have not invested nearly so much money in public relations. The United Steelworkers has an ambitious political education program for its leaders, designed to inform them on current issues.

Medical doctors numerically constitute one of the nation's smallest groups, yet they have profited from a superb public relations program. The reproduction of Sir Luke Fildes's painting of the doctor

---

[4] The public relations industry today is a billion dollar one. Although the book is mainly concerned with political campaigns, much valuable information on the role and implications of the public relations man is found in Stanley Kelley, *Professional Public Relations and Political Power,* The Johns Hopkins Press, Baltimore, 1956.

at the bedside of a sick child has inestimable sentimental value to the profession. In fighting public health insurance, the picture has been reproduced in quantities with accompanying text such as, "Would you change this picture? Compulsory health insurance is political medicine. It would bring a third party—a politician—between you and your doctor." Movies and television shows likewise have reinforced the image of the "men in white" and have been helpful in maintaining public support for the legislative objective of the medical societies.

A 1950 public relations program for the American Medical Association, directed by the California public relations firm of Whitaker and Baxter, was a colossal and apparently successful affair. It was designed to rally public opposition against President Truman's national health program, which featured health insurance. The program was entitled "Message of Freedom" and included more than half a million dollars for full-page newspaper advertisements and for advertising in national magazines and for spot announcements on most of the nation's radio stations. Tie-in advertising support was obtained from dry goods associations, railroads, power companies, drugstores, and hospitals. An advertising kit with posters was sent to 25,000 firms telling why they should participate in displaying the anti-health-insurance materials.[5]

Another part of the program, and a technique still used, was to get physicians to discuss the "unsound" character of health insurance with their patients. Numerous doctors enclosed anti-health-insurance literature with bills sent to patients. Reception-room literature may carry political messages. One pamphlet available in quantities carried the title *Can Politics Cure Appendicitis?* Medical groups are essentially in the position of trade associations. They lack the mass vote, so they utilize their financial resources to win the goodwill of the public for their political objectives.

Another example of public relations expenditures to defeat a proposal developed immediately after the Supreme Court ruled that producers of natural gas were subject to regulation. The oil and gas industry formed a nationwide committee to hire an advertising firm to carry their case against federal regulation of natural gas to the public and to Congress through mass communication. In 1956 alone, some $1,753,000 was spent on this "educational campaign."[6] Social scientists remain skeptical as to whether huge public relations expenditures and success in attaining positive or negative results in public policy demonstrate cause and effect. But interest-group leadership appears quite sold

[5] One religionist, Dan Gilbert, in a letter to all Protestant ministers, warmed up to the occasion by urging them to preach "against this monster of anti-Christ political medicine" and pleaded with "Christian believers everywhere to work and pray that our beloved land may be delivered from the blight of this monstrosity of Bolshevik bureaucracy."

[6] See *The New York Times*, June 15 and 16, 1956.

on the propaganda function of mobilizing, reinforcing, and channeling preexisting and latent attitudes in their favor.

Concisely, public relations is one of the avenues of political influence used by those who seek to mold public opinion both as a long-range and short-range strategy. Not long ago, public relations was not greatly important as a method of attaining political goals. Now the public appears as much the object of lobbying as the public decision makers. Private groups may bypass powerful party leaders and public officials by going directly to the public for mass support and attempting to "merchandise" their goals as the general welfare.

In the politics of public relations, certain groups are advantaged, and others are disadvantaged. No one profession has a large voting bloc, but law, medicine, and education enjoy "respectability" and find public relations a useful device for exploiting their prestige and for molding generally favorable attitudes toward their practitioners. Less financially affluent groups, such as migratory workers, are unable to afford expensive television time or the cost of printing slick magazines. Public relations resources, therefore, are unequal, and those who cannot afford them must find compensating devices or be handicapped.

It is debatable whether the use of slogans, attention catchers, and capsulized and oversimplified statements add materially to the public understanding of issues, but it has undoubtedly made the public more aware of them. When management buys a full-page advertisement to explain its side of a labor dispute and labor can afford a rejoinder (which has not always been true in the past), it may become a battle of presentations, with the citizen's obtaining little real understanding of the dispute. Public relations may help standardize and nationalize opinions, but it has not necessarily improved the public's ability to judge contentions or to engage in critical analysis of the values and policies espoused.

Mass Demonstrations.   Another device for obtaining public support for one's cause is the staging of a dramatic, overt demonstration. Women suffragettes put on massive parades and rallies. Labor unions picket a plant. Numbers of groups march in front of the White House carrying placards advertising their grievances. The National Association for the Advancement of Colored People (NAACP) devised the 1963 demonstrations in Birmingham, Alabama, against segregation in business establishments. School children were used in the demonstrations, which erupted in violence and resulted in the jailing of thousands of blacks and some whites. Pictures showing police using hoses and dogs against the demonstrators appeared in American newspapers everywhere and even in some foreign countries. The action undoubtedly brought further sympathy for the cause, at least outside Birmingham. Sit-ins in stores, freedom rides, marches through states, and the like, attracted persons outside the South; and some joined the demonstrations. These activities also gained much national publicity, won some converts, and resulted in editorial comment in every state. In the late 1960s, there were demonstrations in nearly all cities protesting the Vietnam war and the selective service system. Campus demonstrations on behalf of these causes and against college policies were also commonplace.

Demonstrations serve several purposes. Some, such as marching on the capital and picketing the White House or governors' mansions, are a form of lobbying since they are aimed in the first instance at public authorities. The union picket, the parade for peace, and the Negro demonstration, however, are often not aimed initially at the government. Rather, they are often directed at a specific private party or parties. They symbolize discontent, and participants hope that they will generate a positive attitude on the part of the indifferent or near-indifferent public and opinion leaders. Union pickets are designed to encourage sympathy from members of other unions not immediately involved, just as Negro demonstrations are meant to rally blacks or other potential sympathizers.

The use of the marching technique involves risks. A peaceful march may erupt into violence when someone heaves a rock. (Violence as a political technique is considered in Chapter 21.) The demonstration is often an open invitation for extremists and those emotionally involved to resort to violence or intimidation. Innocent bystanders may be hurt or become victims of terrorist strategy. The merits of the cause may be lost in personal recriminations and obscured by the tactic. Potential sympathizers find their attention focused on the tactic to the exclusion of the objective. A feeling of public indignation may harm the general purposes for which the demonstration is held. The public demonstration requires great skill and control by the leaders and also at times by the law-enforcement authorities who are charged with maintaining the public peace and safety. At the same time, a group may obtain far more free publicity and television coverage for its aims by a militant mass display than through such public relations efforts as distributing leaflets and obtaining conventional reporting of its activities in the press. Demonstrations and confrontations between labor and management and college students and administrations have at times led to public intervention with the issues lost in the overriding interest of "law and order."

PRESSURE GROUPS AND POLITICAL PARTIES

There is some difference of opinion among scholars about the distinction between interest groups and parties, though there is agreement that the latter is differentiated by seeking to have its membership elected to positions in the government, as pressure groups do not. There is also a difference of opinion on the degree to which the two major parties have lost their functions to nonparty groups and the extent to which they mediate group claims; some of this is undoubtedly due to time and locale. The two parties are far more influential in some communities than in others. In some places functional politics (labor, business, resources, education) dwarf party politics. Where traditions of nonpartisan elections are strong, the interest groups exercise much influence. In each community, therefore, one finds variations in styles of relationships between pressure groups and parties.

Briefly, political parties and pressure groups are dependent on each other. Both share political power and influence in running American politics. Interest groups find the parties a channel for gaining access to those in public authority. Parties in turn need group support to elect and maintain themselves in power. The loose party structure fosters a chain of party-private-group relationships between and during elections. Overlapping memberships help the parties educate and inform members of groups about the interests and problems of parties, and vice versa. This provides cross-fertilization of ideas and some material manpower assistance. Major opportunities for contacts between the two political groups are afforded through infiltration of each other's organization, nominations, campaigns, campaign finance, and party programs.[7]

Infiltration. Undoubtedly thousands of persons in the United States holding memberships in interest groups are also active in political party organizations, but we have nothing approximating an estimate of the number. Much of this overlapping membership is casual and unplanned. When members of either parties or interest groups are exhorted to join the other, we may speak of it as infiltration. The infiltration of interest groups by active partisans is less well publicized and less obvious than the reverse situation but is by no means unknown. One party chairman made it a studied policy to encourage his precinct committeemen to join pressure groups and to become active as well in cultural societies. The chairman believed that such a program would broaden opportunities to bring the party's cause to nonparty groups and build a favorable party image among persons unresponsive to partisan publicity. Moreover, some of the workers were would-be candidates, and activity in nonparty groups helped build support for a future campaign effort.

[7]A fuller account has been prepared by Hugh A. Bone, "Political Parties and Pressure Group Politics," *The Annals of the American Academy of Political and Social Science,* vol. 319, pp. 73–83, 1958.

The ward organizations of the Negro machine in Chicago have at times projected themselves into leadership fights within the local chapter of the NAACP. In one ward, the machine took out memberships in the NAACP for its precinct captains and jobholders and was able to place around 400 votes at the disposal of the candidate it favored for president—enough to elect him.[8]

Both national party offices, as seen earlier, have farm, veterans, ethnic, and many other divisions for the special purpose of getting the votes of these groups and of attracting talent from them to the party organization. Active partisans who serve in private groups are also useful in engineering invitations to party candidates and officials to speak to the group and in locating prospective donors. The partisans also serve as sources of intelligence on a host of matters, such as group views and attitudes about candidates and issues and matters of importance to the group, such as anniversaries.

With very few exceptions, it is easy for members of interest groups to infiltrate party clubs, the regular party organization, and its auxiliaries. Eager newcomers soon find that they have opportunities to hold coleadership posts, precinct positions, or offices in clubs. In turn this opens the way for them to attend party conventions, serve on committees, draft resolutions, campaign, and in time perhaps runs for public office. From these positions they can work for their pressure group's goals. But party activity may have an ameliorative effect in that participants learn the realities of party politics. Parties demand a loyalty from them that may in time be as great as or greater than their group affiliation. They may find themselves as mediators and interpreters between the two organizations.

On rare occasions, the infiltration, by unintentional accretion of influence or by design, results in the pressure group's becoming dominant in the party. The Non-Partisan League in North Dakota in 1918 took over the Republican party platform and finally the state government. It was able to accomplish this by placing nominees in the primaries and getting many of them elected and by taking over the organization. The John Birch Society and members of other right-wing groups have had some successes in infiltrating local Republican organizations. They elected enough district delegates in 1964 to select many pro-Goldwater delegates to the national convention.

In Rockford, Illinois, the CIO-PAC organized to elect precinct captains to swing the election of the Democratic chairman for Winnebago County. In Michigan, the labor unions have controlled up to one-third of the precinct positions in the Democratic party and often

[8] James Q. Wilson, *Negro Politics: The Search for Leadership*, The Free Press, New York, 1960, pp. 63–64.

govern the selection of party officers. The CIO captured control of the Michigan State Central Committee of the Democratic party by training and electing precinct captains and taking control of the party conventions. It also built a coalition with certain ethnic, liberal, and other labor groups and had noticeable influence on both primary and convention nominations.

Influencing Platforms.   Pressure groups are understandably concerned with all party activity directed toward public policy. For group members who are also party activists, there is opportunity to participate in policy discussions at club meetings and perhaps to serve on resolutions committees and study groups. The CIO coalition in Michigan brought new emphasis to the Democratic state platform and oriented it toward specific, liberal programs.

Pressure-group officials who are outside the party organization and convention regard it as a part of their job to try to influence the composition of the planks in party platforms and statements. They do this by talking with members of the platform committees both before and during a convention. The officials are usually present at conventions and are "on call" to talk formally or informally with delegates, especially members of the resolutions committees. In a number of states, pressure-group members actually sit on party platform committees and can present the position of their group firsthand. This is less easily accomplished in the resolutions committees of the national conventions. Here there are only two members from each state and little opportunity for achieving a balance among groups. Interest-group spokesmen must be content with filing statements with the platform committees, appearing in person during the hearings and buttonholing individual committee members. In our earlier consideration of drafting national platforms (Chapter 10), reference was made to the literally scores of spokesmen for interest groups who submit briefs and oral agreements before the opening of the conventions.[9]

The fact that platforms are usually ambiguous and general has not kept private groups from trying to influence them. The platform at all levels has become a method by which a political party can build a coalition of supporting interest groups, and these groups in turn can remind officeholders of platform pledges. Moreover, testimony given before platform bodies may be newsworthy and gain the organization free publicity. It is not unusual for the press to record a state or county platform as "strongly prolabor," a "bid for the minorities' vote," or a "victory for conservatives," thus suggesting the influence of domi-

---

[9]Edward F. Cooke, for example, noted seventy different spokesmen who presented arguments before the resolutions committee of the 1952 Republican National Convention. See "Drafting the 1952 Platform," *Western Political Quarterly*, vol. 9, pp. 669–712, 1966.

nant factors and interests. In the final platform it is not difficult to find planks on resources, housing, social security, and other subjects phrased in almost the same language as presented by an interest-group spokesman.

Nominations. There are no definitive studies on the role of pressure groups in the nominating process. Yet it is assumed—with logic and some evidence—that many nonparty groups are keenly interested in who will be nominated. Nominations reduce the number of contenders for public office. If an interest group cannot get two rivals favorable to its interest to contend in the general election, then it will hope to get one or at least to see the nomination of persons who are not hostile to it. Our knowledge of the presidential nominating process and the relation of groups to it is considerably more complete than for state and local nominations. In order to influence the presidential nomination, interest groups must first try to get some of their own members chosen as delegates or to influence or commit delegates selected in the states to favor or oppose the cause of certain aspirants. But it becomes necessary to make contacts with key delegation chairmen and others in the convention city.

Since the great majority of national convention delegates are party activists, private groups are unlikely to elect significant numbers of their members as delegates unless those persons were also active in the party. As seen in Chapter 10, large numbers of the delegates come from the college-educated, business, and professional classes rather than from organized labor, the farm population, or from minority ethnic or racial stock. Moreover, they are interested in picking a winner and are not likely to choose a person of their own group who might jeopardize victory because of his organizational connections.

Much pressure-group activity, therefore, takes place off the convention floor and is directed toward nonmembers of the group who are serving as delegates. In 1948, a group of physicians were especially active in defeating Harold Stassen's bid for the Republican nomination. Governor Adlai Stevenson's opposition to state ownership of submerged offshore lands was of concern to oil and gas interests, especially in the South, and delegates were made aware of his "liability." Telegrams on behalf of Wendell Willkie "rained" on the delegates in 1940; many of these were later discovered to be inspired by business groups rather than the spontaneous outpourings of grass-roots sentiments. The late Sen. Alben Barkley records in his memoirs that he was confident of the backing of organized labor, but on the eve of the convention of 1952 a group of labor men purporting to speak for these groups "but acting, so far as anyone has been able to learn, with no mandate from their respective organizations, gave out announcement that 'organized labor' could not support me because of my age."[10] The action he believed was the "kiss of death" for his candidacy. On the other hand, the vigorous activity on behalf of Sen. Eugene McCarthy before and during the Democratic National Convention in 1968 was unsuccessful.

Because decentralization is more apparent in the nominating process than in almost any other aspect of American parties, interest groups have many chances to influence the selection of candidates. The parts played by representatives of interest groups in state and local nominations would undoubtedly constitute a long string of fascinating narratives with much variation from community to community, from state to state, and from one election to the next. The record of the incumbent determines whether a group need be concerned with the nomination of a potential rival. For example, a prosecutor or a mayor might have been following a reasonably tolerant policy toward pinball machines and gaming devices. Meanwhile in the opposite party a rumor is spread that an aspirant, believed to be strict, intends to enter its primary. The gaming groups would suddenly become vitally concerned with defeating such a rival in the primary. In the next election, it might be that the pinball interests would see no threat in either party and refrain from substantial activity in either party's primary. Comparable situations could be cited for any number of local interest groups. The decision whether to support or oppose one or more candidates or remain neutral in a primary is likely to also be conditioned by the perception of an aspirant's chances for winning the nomination and, after that, the general election.

Potential candidates, as a rule, consult privately with party leaders and others prominent in civic and private groups, hoping to win their support. Relatively few successful candidates enter the primaries without first securing the backing of such party and group leaders. Would-be candidates who understand the realities of political life in the community approach members of their own group and out-groups to sound out potential support or nonsupport. A broker, for example, might confer with certain union heads to find out whether labor could be depended on to support him or at least to remain neutral; a union member might approach the school forces and small businessmen. Smart hopefuls always recognize the importance of consulting party chairmen. This behind-the-scenes effort will also help an interest group decide whether to promote one of its own aspirants through a faction within the party or to try to nominate him irrespective of factional support.

The kind of nominating system makes considerable difference in a group's opportunities to influence selection. In a few instances,

[10] *That Reminds Me*, Doubleday & Company, Inc., Garden City, N.Y., 1954, p. 230.

such as statewide offices in New York and Connecticut, nomination is made by convention, and interested groups attempt to build up strength with various delegations much in the style of the national conventions.[11] Where the closed primary with relatively tight slatemaking is handled by the party's executive committee, as in New York City, the interest groups, in theory at least, have less opportunity to affect selections directly than in an open primary arrangement. But the party leaders wish to avoid a challenge in the primary and will be cognizant that if they do not "balance the ticket" and recognize the importance of labor and ethnic groups, they may force a primary fight. As a result, even in a comparatively closed system, party slatemakers must reckon with the wishes of groups that might be in a position to challenge the organization slate. On occasion, leaders of the minority party have decided to go outside the ranks of the party and co-opt an entrant with group identifications in order to attract the support of his groups and perhaps enhance the prestige of the party. An open primary system affords outside groups somewhat greater opportunity and flexibility of operation than a closed primary. In open primaries, a group can maximize its strength by concentrating on primary contests in one party. Irrespective of what primary system is used, the prime factor is the informal negotiation taking place weeks and months before the filing date for the primary — and these are seldom matters of record either for the scholar or for the general public.

A number of risks are involved in group participation in nominations and must be carefully calculated. If the group puts forth one of its own members as an aspirant, the person will immediately be labeled and perhaps be handicapped among out-groups. Also this action or the open endorsement of the most acceptable of the contestants invites cleavage and discontent within one's own group and some political isolation from other groups in the community. Defeat of candidates receiving open support is also a blow at the prestige of the endorsers. In view of the potential risks of overt support, private-group leaders are more likely to regard quiet, concealed effort the better tactic. It may be the better part of discretion to wait and see who is nominated and then assess the group's position vis-à-vis the two candidates running in the general election.

Electoral Activity.   A strategic consideration for an interest group is whether to concern itself with both nominations and elections. We have just noted that there are many reasons for a group to become involved

---

[11] In Connecticut, opponents of candidates picked by the convention can "challenge" the selection in a primary. See Duane Lockard, *Connecticut's Challenge Primary: A Study in Legislative Politics,* Eagleton Institute Cases in Practical Politics, case 7, McGraw-Hill Book Company, New York, 1962.

with nominations. However, because of certain liabilities and limited resources, major activities are more consistently performed at the general-election phase. Getting one's own members registered to participate in both primary and general elections is an important and "respectable" activity consistent with the obligations and opportunities of the democratic ethos. In practice, groups concentrate in precincts where their potential is greater. Registration becomes a selective operation and is maximized if an organization's staff has carefully studied registration and voting figures of preceding elections.

Whether an interest group should get into politics beyond exhorting members to vote and facilitating their registration raises questions that bring internal disagreement at times. First is the degree of agreement over whether campaigning in the broadest sense is a legitimate function of group. Second is the weighing of the risks of political isolation against those of possibly participating on the losing side. Victory for the group's candidate may add to internal cohesion, but defeat may lead to dissension and loss of face for leaders who pressed for political action. Next, should the group assume a bipartisan posture and make endorsements in both parties, as, for example, a Republican for governor and a Democrat for congressman; or should the group support only candidates of one party? The former is a form of political insurance and electoral bet hedging. The latter may be good strategy if a group is cohesive and has a mass membership such as a labor union.[12] Even in the absence of mass membership a group may be cohesive enough to restrict its campaign activities to candidates of one party— the medical political action group support of almost exclusively Republican offers a case in point.

Once a group decides to enter the electoral arena, it has several action alternatives ranging from carrying political information in its journals, with little or no effort to state a specific position, to vigorous "getting out the vote." It has some four options for endorsement-financial support: (1) the group may conduct its financial activity openly, with public endorsement;[13] (2) raise funds and render services to a preferred candidate in a quiet, unadvertised manner; (3) make public endorsement without financial support; and (4) make its fund-raising lists and other valuable information available to its preferred candidates.

If a group decides on actual campaign activity, it has three choices of organizational arrangements. First, it may develop its own campaign organizations and may remain essentially independent of

[12] A work on this strategy is Fay Calkins, *The CIO and the Democratic Party*, The University of Chicago Press, Chicago, 1952.

[13] Group contributions to political campaigns are noted in Chap. 13 and need not be reviewed here.

the party organization although paralleling it to some extent. Some labor unions do this, and mention was made earlier of ad hoc nonparty organizations. These groups organize their own doorbell-ringing activities, take voters to the polls, telephone voting reminders, and even provide babysitters while mothers cast their ballots. Party leaders welcome the election-day assistance but are not enthusiastic about a separate nonparty campaign organization because it may work at cross purposes in strategy, and it may dilute or make less effective use of manpower resources. Victory may lead the group to demand patronage, with consequent loss of that patronage to the party regulars.

Second, a group may cooperate very closely with the party organization but permit the latter to maintain control over campaign direction. Under this arrangement, the group furnishes personnel to party headquarters, provides doorbell ringers, and distributes campaign literature. It may supply speakers, aid in sponsoring rallies, and mobilize the energies and finally the votes of its own members. Party chairmen and personal managers of candidates' campaigns prefer this arrangement for obvious reasons.

Third, combination of these two often develops, with both interest groups and parties retaining considerable autonomy. Pressure groups are generally less interested in the entire ticket and prefer to concentrate their energies on a few candidates. What actually takes place is an interest-group-candidate relationship rather than an interest-group-party relationship. Nominal and sporadic support may be given to others on the ticket, but special group attention is given one or two candidates, and there may be extensive independent action on his behalf.

Which pattern of nonparty-party relationships is adopted depends on local conditions, expediency, the party and group leadership, and the preference of the candidate. If the local group is a part of a federation, it may have to modify its tactics in order to harmonize with the position of its state and national leadership. For this and other reasons, much so-called group effort in campaigns is carried on by specially created ad hoc committees which absolve the permanent group from responsibility. A Veterans Committee for Thompson, led by the local commander of the American Legion, can influence fellow Legionnaires and still keep the Legion itself from being charged with sponsoring Thompson. Citizens committees and nonparty campaign committees permit private-group members to promote the group's campaign goals outside the formal, established organization and to maintain the facade of officially "keeping out of politics."

Endorsement can be handled in many different ways. Some organizations state outright endorsement in their membership journals. Others give a more concealed endorsement by printing voting records,

pledges, and qualifications in a manner leaving the reader little doubt
of preferred candidates; there are few objective ratings in interest-group
publications. Another common tactic is to have individual professional
or businessmen sponsor newspaper advertisements on behalf of a candidate. A Labor union may carry public endorsements over the official
name of the organization and paid for from the treasury of its political
action committee. Public endorsements run some risks; they may spur
rivals into compiling lists of their own or engaging in other effort. In
some cases, endorsement is a liability, especially if the group has a bad
image or active adversary.[14]

Labor-union endorsement is sometimes regarded as a liability
but the practice continues. Union leaders believe that endorsements
in midterm elections are especially necessary in the absence of a presidential contest, which brings out the vote. In 1958, 254 House members
who received official backing of labor or other groups were elected,
but in 1962 only 189 of the 330 endorsed candidates won election.[15]
In 1964, organized labor was openly involved with endorsements and
other activities in 350 House races and boasted 234 victories or 67 percent, an unusually high percentage of success. However, 173 of the
284 victories involved endorsement of incumbents. While interest-group
support may be important, it is not necessarily determinative because
both incumbents and nonincumbents win or lose elections for a variety
of reasons. However, when a candidate wins with a group's support,
its leaders feel that they have a channel of access that can be tapped.

The National Committee for an Effective Congress (NCEC),
formed in 1948, affords a most interesting example of an electoral
interest group based on an ideology.[16] Unlike the big multipurpose
groups, its sole reason for being is the election of preferred candidates. To 1965, the NCEC had participated in more than 300 elections
and had aided more than 40 percent of the Senate membership. It
had received more than 35,000 contributions.[17] Members are bound together not by occupation or economic interest but by ideological beliefs — support of moderate and liberal candidates and incumbents. Its

[14] Nicholas A. Masters notes that the CIO Political Action Committee "attempts to endorse
the candidate who most nearly meets the claims of the group and who commands the greatest prestige,
but it will endorse the mediocre or weak candidate if he is opposed by a candidate who is closely
identified with business groups." See "The Politics of Union Endorsement of Candidates in the Detroit
Area," *Midwest Journal of Political Science*, vol. 1, pp. 136–150, 1957.

[15] For an analysis of AFL-CIO endorsement as well as of other campaign activities of labor,
see Harry M. Scoble, "Organized Labor in Electoral Politics: Some Questions for the Discipline,"
Western Political Quarterly, vol. 16, pp. 666–685, 1963.

[16] A recommended work on this group as well as on interest-group politics in the electoral
arena in general is Harry M. Scoble, *Ideology and Electoral Action: A Comparative Case Study of the National
Committee for an Effective Congress*. Chandler Publishing Co., San Francisco, 1967.

[17] *Ibid.*, p. 9.

original major activities were fund raising and fund disbursement in marginal general-election contests for the United States Senate. Over the years, NCEC shifted emphasis from primarily defensive efforts of supporting incumbent senators to assisting in House races (it aided 74 candidates in 1964) and Southern Democratic primaries; it has also experimented with block grants-in-aid to such groups as the Democratic Study Group's electoral arm, the Democrats for Sound Government. It works with the Committee to Support Moderate Republicans for numerous candidates.

Through 1964, NCEC gave direct support to 296 congressional candidates, 78 percent of whom were Democrats. The overall rate of electoral success averaged 73 percent; 89 percent for Republicans and 69 percent for Democrats. The level of financial support also increased over the years, reaching $420,000 in 1964.

The correspondence between electoral power and legislative power for any single group is most difficult if not impossible to estimate. Scoble employed an index to try to ascertain the electoral impact of NCEC and concluded there was "a small not positive impact." More importantly, he concludes that "the acquisition of electoral power is *not* immediately followed by acquisition of legislative power, but the loss of electoral power *is* immediately followed by loss of legislative power." [18]

Campaigns are the arenas of contenders for power, and economic interests hoping to preserve or to change the status quo in public policy are certain to be potential donors. Because corporations and unions are forbidden by law, to contribute directly, separate action groups are created to raise and expend campaign money. Individuals are solicited to give money to "preserve the healthy business climate" or to "better the lot of the little man" by electing his friends. But donation is a complicated process, with money going through several hands and obscuring the original source. Money from individuals may in reality be emanating from groups that hope to gain access to the nominee if he is elected.

INITIATIVE AND REFERENDUM CAMPAIGNS

Ballot propositions give interest groups unable to secure adoption of their measures through state and local legislatures a chance to obtain some of their objectives or to overcome a defeat at the hands of the legislature, county commission, or town council. Less than half of the states (and most of them west of the Mississippi River) have adopted the initiative and referendum under which a certain percentage of the voters

[18] *Ibid.*, p. 244.

can place a measure on the ballot or require that a bill passed by the legislative body be referred to the voters before it goes into effect. About one-fourth of the states permit constitutional amendments to be proposed by initiative petition. In nearly all states, changes in the state constitution or the adoption of a new one requires the sanction of the electorate, and in most jurisdictions the public authorities are required to submit certain levy and bond propositions to the voters. In these cases, the representative bodies decide what to refer to the people, but interest groups have the opportunity to wage campaigns for and against such proposals.

Most initiatives are proposed after the legislature has rejected the proposal or failed to enact legislation acceptable to the group. A referendum, on the other hand, is a final check on the legislature and has the objective of maintaining the status quo, or keeping a law from going into effect. Conservatives therefore might use it as a tool against a liberal legislature, or liberals might use it to nullify a specific act of a conservative legislature. The groups sponsoring a referendum are generally those who fought a measure while it was being passed by the legislature. As a general matter, more persons are likely to vote on initiative and referendum measures than on constitutional amendments submitted by the legislature. The former are often less technical and frequently more controversial, inspiring publicity and campaigning.

Unlike constitutional amendments, initiatives and referendums (demanded by some of the voters) require organization to get them on the ballot. Thousands of signatures are needed, and the process of gathering them requires great effort. In California, which makes extensive use of the initiative and referendum, petitions to put measures on the ballot are usually circulated by commercial firms for a fee. It costs $100,000 or more to put a measure on the ballot, for several hundred thousand valid signatures are required. These are collected by petition "pushers," who are paid for each signature secured.

Once the proposition appears on the ballot, the campaign must be conducted in its behalf. Again, an organization will have to decide whether it has the resources to plan the strategy, design the publicity, provide the speakers for radio and television, and make the necessary telephone calls or whether it should hire a public relations firm to plan and conduct the campaign. Labor unions are often able to employ their regular election machinery, and local groups and farm bureaus frequently do the lion's share of the work for or against propositions. In these instances, campaigns are run from the organization's own offices and employ its own staff. But a great many campaigns are handled by public relations concerns hired by the interest groups. Business organizations may be small in numbers but affluent enough to afford advertisers to manage the bulk of the campaign.

A number of states do not require the reporting of income and disbursements for ballot propositions. Still others have such provisions, but, as with political campaigns, much of the financing goes unreported and is hidden in such names as "Committee for Clean Waters" or "Taxpayers Unlimited." As a result, information on the costs of direct-legislation campaigns is fragmentary. According to California records, the most expensive campaign was in 1956, when rival combinations of oil interests spent, officially, close to $5 million on an oil and gas conservation proposal. A right-to-work measure saw an expenditure of $3.5 million. Other million-dollar campaigns included a chain store and private school tax and a retirement proposal. Less money is likely to be spent on measures referred by a legislature than when a referendum is demanded by a group. In the former case, the legislature itself does not spend money on behalf of its own law. Although one finds many exceptions, it is most probably true that more often than not, the side spending the most money wins.[19]

Sometimes interest groups try to draw candidates into the campaign for propositions in the hope that they may use the campaign resources of the political parties to aid their causes. Literature for or against the propositions is given out at party headquarters and by precinct workers. Measures of special interest to labor unions often receive support in Democratic headquarters. There is some risk, however, in making a measure a "party" issue since many propositions do not fit neatly into a Democratic-Republican mold. A major appeal, of course, is through the journals of the organization, in which attempts are made to rally the membership to realize the importance of the initiative or referendum.

Only groups with substantial resources are able to circulate petitions requesting a referendum within the two or three months after legislative adjournment. Signatures for an initiative usually can be gathered over a much longer period of time. In general more initiatives lose than win; voters appear to vote no more readily than yes.[20] A group is therefore likely to undertake an initiative campaign only if it feels some chance of winning or if the matter is so important that a campaign will help to win over public opinion and result in victory in the long run.

[19] Winston W. Crouch believes this holds true in California. See *The Initiative and Referendum in California*, The Haynes Foundation, Los Angeles, 1950.

[20] The three Pacific Coast states freely employ the initiative process. Over the years, about half of the proposals in Washington were adopted; but, in California and Oregon, voters have approved only about one-third. The use of direct legislation devices in the respective Western states is covered in Frank Jonas (ed.), *Politics in the American West*, University of Utah Press, Salt Lake City, 1969.

A large vote for a defeated measure may be used as a talking point for some action in the legislature. The campaign may serve a group purpose by directing both the public's and the legislature's attention to evils in need of correction.

Voter response to propositions varies markedly with the type of proposition. It is not surprising that technical propositions and matters dealing with government organization often fail to attract much interest. But moral questions dealing with liquor, gambling, Sunday closing, racing, and sports are likely to bring a huge turnout. Propositions dealing with questions perceived to be related to the welfare of a particular group also stir the emotions and bring response; these are exemplified by right-to-work laws, pensions, public regulation, daylight saving time, and special taxes. Health matters such as vaccination, fluoridation of water, and licensing chiropractors also prod rival groups to action and often result in bitter campaigns and high participation. Sometimes groups try to keep down controversy and have their measure adopted as a "sleeper." But the present-day political interest group is alert to such matters, and it is rare that a group can put over a controversial measure without a rival campaign against it.

In summary, the cost of securing signatures, conducting a campaign, and educating the electorate about ballot propositions discourages all but fairly well-financed organizations from making use of direct legislation. Unless it can substitute manpower for money, a group may find this channel a futile one for accomplishing a legislative objective. Looking at the sponsorship of successful measures one finds educational forces, organized labor, employers, churches, farmers, public employees, sportsmen, commercial fishermen, liquor interests, organized "drys," pensioners, and specific industries like oil. Over the years, most of these interests have won some significant victories or staved off serious threats to some of their goals by waging campaigns. Sharecroppers, migrant laborers, blacks, and small, individual businesses have made little or no use of direct legislation since they are often not in a strategic or material position to do so.

Decision making by initiative and referendum is a definitive action, with a simple majority deciding yes or no. Legislative bodies usually cannot repeal or amend the action within a specific period of time, and executive approval is not needed. But it is a "single-shot" affair with no opportunity to bargain, as with a legislative decision. Logrolling and minimal vote trading, which might bring wider benefits to more groups through compromise, cannot be done by direct legislation. Also the costliness of the process to a group may lead it to feel that lobbying is a better investment. But if the legislative door is shut, with no opportunity to force it open, direct legislation is the "stick behind the door." To some extent, use of the initiative process is an index of influence within the legislature. If a group is successful, it need not resort to direct legislation; but, if its goals are unattainable in the legislature, it may use the initiative to mobilize the public on its behalf.

GROUP INTERESTS AND NONPARTISAN ELECTIONS

More than half of the municipalities of over 5,000 population use the nonpartisan ballot.[21] Nonpartisan election campaigns are often nonpartisan in form rather than in fact. Partisan group activity in local nonpartisan elections usually camouflages its partisanship by various devices. Seldom do party organizations openly and officially participate in nonpartisan campaigns. Candidates accordingly must seek other support. This gives the interest groups a chance to assist without being attacked for carrying on partisan activities. If the party organizations do not enter the campaign, the nonpartisan nominee must build his own organization, often without much patronage, and his group contacts and memberships may be helpful in this connection.

Evidence on the amount and extent of interest-group activity in nonpartisan elections is incomplete and often contradictory. This is not surprising in view of the fact that there are marked degrees of partisanship and differences in traditions and in the offices sought. For example, the campaign for one nonpartisan state superintendent of public education was, practically speaking, directed from the office of a state educational association whose membership was largely composed of teachers, school directors, and persons vitally concerned with curriculum and financial support of schools. The association also provided a sizable share of the candidate's campaign funds. Local bar associations or subgroups within them frequently make endorsements for judicial positions and buy newspaper space to state their position on the qualifications of candidates. At the same time, the educational and legal groups would rarely take such an active part in the election of a city councilman or a park commissioner. A group will therefore be more likely to participate openly when the office has particular salience and relevance to it.

Eugene Lee's study of more than 200 cities in California found certain groups and interests more active and influential than others in nonpartisan elections. In order of their mention of importance in city council races (where the nonpartisan ballot is used) were the local newspaper, merchants, service clubs, women's organizations, and veterans and lay church groups, with city employees and labor unions running

[21]See Charles R. Adrian, "A Typology for Nonpartisan Elections," *The Western Political Quarterly*, vol. 12, pp. 449–458, 1959. *Nonpartisan elections* as used here refers to those in which the ballots carry no party designations.

well behind the others.[22] The listing suggests that the somewhat more affluent and Republican-oriented are advantaged in the system. On the other hand, Charles E. Gilbert's study of large cities did not find that the Republican party was necessarily advantaged in nonpartisan politics.[23]

It is a reasonable assumption that political interest-group activity in nonpartisan campaigns is spasmodic. In 60 percent of the smaller California cities, no permanent group activity in local election politics was found, but in cities over 25,000, sustained activity was observed in about 80 percent of the cities. Merchants and business groups are much concerned with the outcome of races for nonpartisan municipal offices because of the likely effect on property taxes, licenses, enforcement of closing and zoning laws, municipal reform, and so on.

In nonpartisan elections, municipal and good-government leagues have a prime opportunity to influence the election through endorsements. Voter participation is lower in local elections, and a league's endorsements are generally avidly sought by candidates because they are read by persons who vote regularly. It is common for newspapers to carry the endorsements, and a much larger group of potential voters is thus reached. Citizens associations are largely composed of middle- and upper-class persons; thus they tend to reinforce the "Main Street" bias and influence. In North Carolina the Durham Committee on Negro Affairs, composed largely of Negro businessmen and professionals, has had much influence on the turnout of black voters in the city's municipal elections, and when it makes an endorsement of one of two white candidates, the endorsee has been significantly advantaged.[24]

The abolition of party designations leaves the lower-status groups without a reference-group label for judging candidates and uncertain which candidates would best serve their interests. At the same time, nonpartisan politics is strongly personal, and a candidate makes his own alliances among groups ranging from improvement and neighborhood clubs to the power elite in the community. In kind, group participation is not greatly different from that of partisan elections. There are groups that may actively recruit a candidate, publicly endorse him, and aid his campaign but remain aloof from the next campaign. Marvin A. Harder believes that an interest group is likely to recruit a candidate when "its members are unhappy with the *status quo*. Groups reasonably satisfied are not groups motivated to pick a candidate, finance his campaign, and do the necessary work to get him elected. As a conse-

[22] *The Politics of Nonpartisanship*, University of California Press, Berkeley, 1960.
[23] "Some Aspects of Nonpartisan Elections in Large Cities," *Midwest Journal of Political Science*, vol. 6, pp. 345–362, 1962.
[24] See Douglas S. Catlin, *A Case Study of a Negro Voters' League: The Durham Committee on Negro Affairs in Municipal Elections*, Department of Political Science, University of North Carolina, Chapel Hill, 1960. (Mimeographed.)

quence, the political arena is usually occupied only by protest groups and candidates running without group support."[25]

It is often asserted that in removing party labels and developing a nonparty approach to municipal problems, there is a desirable reduction of potential conflict, that is, of party struggle. Further, the managers of the government and power elite behind them wish to keep issues from becoming public and to resolve conflicts behind the scenes. This is better done by reducing the participation between rival groups in arriving at decisions. A good deal more evidence is needed before this thesis can be established as fact. There is not the same degree of group involvement in local-level campaigns, and those who are active in influencing the community decisions believe that this is a happy state of low-tension politics.

It is easy to find persons who believe that nonpartisan elections are conducive to issueless politics and that this is a desirable arrangement in the local community. Parenthetically, there is a contradiction on the question of interest in issues since the League of Women Voters and often several other groups commonly submit questionnaires to candidates to elicit their views on policies. These often have the effect of forcing nominees to take a position on public questions. Critics of the nonpartisan system argue that politics divorced from issues invites overemphasis on personality, if not demagoguery. Voters are unable to learn what groups are behind a given candidate, what his views on public affairs are, or what his qualifications are. Be that as it may, there is no significant tendency for municipalities to change from a nonpartisan to a partisan ballot, and interest groups will have to be content to operate within the system—and many appear to like it. The rather low level of voter interest in local elections poses both an opportunity and a handicap. Without vigorous active competitors and high voter interest, a group able to mobilize its own voter resources and newspaper support may be successful in electing its endorsees. At the same time, the lack of voter interest will tax a group's efforts and ingenuity to get out enough of its potential supporters to vote for its selections.

INFLUENCING GOVERNMENT

The tactics and strategies of group attempts to influence public authorities are also determined by many nonconstitutional factors mainly (1) the size and cohesion of its membership, (2) the distribution of its membership, (3) its prestige with the public and with government officials, (4) its ability to mobilize other groups on behalf of its goals,

[25] *Nonpartisan Election: A Political Illusion?* Holt, Rinehart and Winston, Inc., New York, 1958, p. 15. The work is recommended as a case study of organizing and waging a nonpartisan campaign for city commissioner in Wichita, Kan.

(5) the strength or weakness of political parties in the local legislature, and (6) its resources. The last mentioned is especially important as applied to its financial condition and the knowledge and skill of its own leaders and lobbyists. The direction of a group's energies undergoes modification with changed conditions and with changes in its resources. At one time, expediency dictates direct contact with a department head, at another, with a committee chairman, the chief executive, or legislative floor leader. Here we shall present a few illustrations of the nature and direction of pressure activities, suggest a few generalizations, and draw some inferences.[26]

Lobbying the Legislature. Because the legislative process is most complex, the techniques of access, both between groups and by the same group, may vary over a period of time and from bill to bill. Bicameral legislatures offer many critical stages, from bill introduction to signing by the executive, at which to defeat or emasculate a proposal; therefore, proponents must wage a continual battle. The cards are stacked more in favor of opponents than advocates. The citizen is usually unaware of the amount of defensive lobbying done by a whole group of interests whose theme in the legislative corridors is "leave us alone." Much effort is expended to keep bills from passing and may even include the putting forth of a rival bill to confuse or divert attention away from a particularly obnoxious measure.

After a group's leadership has ascertained that either defensive-negative or offensive-positive action is needed, it usually mobilizes the membership on behalf of an "official" statement. This permits the officials or the lobbyists they hire to speak with "authority" for the group and provides the rank and file with legislative goals and presumably interest in the legislative session. From this, the group agents utilize (1) personal contacts with legislators and their friends, (2) grass-roots communications to legislators, (3) alliances with out-groups also pursuing legislative objectives, and (4) formal contacts with legislative committees and activity at critical points of the process such as the rules-committee stage, voting, and conference committee.[27]

[26] The volume of literature on the subject is enormous and our treatment is necessarily brief. Major general works that include extensive bibliographic citations are *op cit.*, chaps. 11–16; brief. Major general works that include extensive bibliographic citations are Truman, *op cit.*, chaps. 11–16; Donald C. Blaisdell, *American Democracy Under Pressure*, The Ronald Press Company, New York, 1957, chaps. 4–8, 11–15; Harmon Zeigler, *Interest Groups in American Society*, Prentice-Hall, Inc., Englewood Cliffs, N.J., 1964, chaps. 9–11; Holtzman, *op. cit.;* and the issue "Unofficial Government" of *The Annals of the American Academy of Political and Social Science*, vol. 319, 1958.

[27] In the absence of a pattern of lobbying, for all measures, strategies, and techniques the case method is especially useful. A wealth of excellent literature on selected bills is, fortunately, available and worthy of reading. An older and newer volume respectively are Stephen K. Bailey and Howard D. Samuel, *Congress at Work*, Holt, Rinehart and Winston, Inc., New York, 1952, and John Bibby, *On Capitol Hill: Studies in the Legislative Process*, Holt, Rinehart and Winston, Inc., New York,

Personal Contacts. In state legislatures, but also in Congress, the single most important technique for a group is to have its agents and spokesmen build up a personal acquaintance, if not friendship, with very large numbers of legislators. This form of lobbying begins long before the opening of the session and even before the election. A group may have made a campaign donation or rendered other assistance to the lawmaker's election. This gives it access and contact. Immediately after the election, lobbyists make it a point to become acquainted with newcomers and to size up their abilities and positions on public questions as soon as possible. One highly successful lobbyist reported that between state legislative sessions he visited every state legislator at home, often making the acquaintance of the man's wife and children as well. Between the November election and the opening of the session in January, he made it a point to call on all freshmen. By the time the session opened, he prided himself with being on a first-name basis with almost every legislator. "My most important lobbying," he told the author, "is before the session opens. I've made friends with all of the legislators and if it becomes necessary they will talk to me during the session."

During the session, personal friendships are made and maintained by social or "plush-horse" lobbying. Washington and the various state capitals are highly social places, and dinners, stag affairs, cocktail parties, and other forms of social entertainment provide the opportunity for lawmaker (and wife) and agent (and wife) to meet. In the state capitals, some lobbyists have permanent hotel suites where legislators can "drop by" any time and enjoy a largess of food and liquor. Legislators usually find that there are "pigeons" who will take them out to lunch, that breweries will deliver a free case of beer on call, and that motion picture and race track operators will give the legislator and his family a "free pass." Golf matches, bridge parties, and free trips afford other chances for personal contacts. At one time, the motion picture industry provided a special railroad car for United States senators to travel to the Kentucky Derby, all expenses paid.

It remains a moot point whether a line can be drawn between social activity for its own sake and entertainment designed to influence the lawmaker's opinion. Social lobbying is used less than formerly, but it has by no means disappeared. Most congressmen could attend a cocktail or dinner party every evening if they wished. But parties are much less frequently attended than in the past, and many Washington hostesses

---

1967. A few single volumes are Daniel M. Berman, *A Bill Becomes a Law: The Civil Rights Act of 1960*, The Macmillan Company, New York, 1966; Frank J. Munger and Richard F. Fenno, Jr., *National Politics and Federal Aid to Education*, Syracuse University Press, Syracuse, 1960; and Eugene Feingold, *Medicare: Policy and Politics*, Chandler Publishing Co., San Francisco, 1966, which give extensive coverage to lobbying. A comprehensive work on tactics is Donald R. Hall, *Cooperative Lobbying—The Power of Pressure*, The University of Arizona Press, Tucson, 1969.

and lobbyists complain that legislators shun these social affairs. Congressmen are very busy, and some are wary. The long months in session make parties less glamorous than is likely the case with state legislators. It is easy to fictionalize that a solon's vote can be "bought" by a free drink or meal. Lobbyists are contemptuous of persons whose vote might be controlled this way, for it is easily lost to another who will dole out greater largess. The significant functions of the social affair are to strengthen personal friendship and respect, which can be tapped in the future, and to facilitate access. This is not to say that "legislative business" is never discussed during social occasions—for it often is—but its prime purpose is to build goodwill and foster friendly attitudes.

When legislators are members of groups, lobbyists can tap them as friends with a common association. At the time legislation was being considered to control guns, the National Rifleman's Association (NRA) could boast many members in Congress including the Senate President Pro Tem, a floor leader, and a whip, affording an effective potential "inside" lobby.

In interviews conducted by Lester Milbrath with more than 100 Washington lobbyists, he found that two-thirds of them perceived the personal presentation of their case as the most effective of all tactics. Closely rated to this was the arrangement with intermediaries who were constituents or close personal friends of the congressmen to plead group's point of view.[28]

Grass-Roots Communications. In some contrast, another study found that while congressmen regarded direct personal contacts effective, they put a high premium on *indirect* methods such as letters, petitions, telegrams and telephone calls.[29] The pushing of buttons back home to bring forth an avalanche of communications is a time-honored technique, provided large numbers of persons can be persuaded to participate. The National Rifleman's Association, with some 850,000 members, has employed this device and claims it can produce more than half a million letters, postcards, and telegrams within 72 hours.[30] Their letters are huge in volume and often well coordinated. Several senators reported more letters on gun control in 1969 than on any other single bill. The NRA letters repeated the slogan "Guns don't kill people; people kill people," and many equated proposed gun legislation with

[28]Lester Milbrath, "Lobbying as a Communications Process," *Public Opinion Quarterly*, vol. 24, pp. 32–53. See also his larger work, *The Washington Lobbyists*, Rand McNally & Company, Chicago, 1963, for extensive coverage of how lobbyists and legislators view each other.

[29]Andrew M. Scott and Margaret A. Hunt, *Congress and Lobbies: Image and Reality*, University of North Carolina Press, Chapel Hill, 1966.

[30]For a highly interesting account of the lobbying and public relations activities of this group, see Richard Harris, "If You Love Your Guns," *The New Yorker*, Apr. 20, 1968. The journal has reprinted this widely distributed lengthy article.

the "Red conspiracy." One Western senator told a reporter, "I'd rather be a deer in hunting season than a politician who has run afoul of the NRA crowd. Most of us are scared to death of them. They range from bus drivers to bank presidents, from Minutemen to four-star generals, and from morons to geniuses, but they have one thing in common: they don't want *anyone* to tell them *anything* about what to do with their guns, and they *mean* it."[31]

Grass-roots influence can also be exerted through persons back in the district upon whom congressmen depend for financial or other support and for information. Lobbyists may sell these people on the worthiness of their cause, which in turn is communicated to the representative. Some enterprising legislative agents have compiled lists of influential constituents along with useful information about legislators such as their organizational and fraternal connections, which may, at times, be useful for contacts.

Alliances and Combinations. A pressure group seldom has the field to itself. It is in competition with other groups who are trying to get the congressman's vote. For this reason, it is alert for potential allies who will support its objectives and help neutralize the power of the interest-group combinations in opposition. High-tariff forces have worked with each other to put over general tariff bills. Some thirty groups were welded together into a "baby bloc" to secure passage of the federal maternal health program. The Employment Act of 1948 grew out of a broad alliance of Democratic liberals, the labor unions, the NAACP, the American Veterans Committee, the Farmer's Union, and the Lawyers Guild.[32] Another form of alliance is the process of working together for river and harbor improvements. Here congressmen and their friends support requests for appropriations for projects in each other's areas, a practice termed logrolling.

Sometimes groups and firms, though in competition with each other for the consumer's dollar, put together a united-front committee to place their mutual-interest cause before the Congress and the administration. The General Gas Committee planned and coordinated the oil and gas lobbying behind the Natural Gas Bill. It was an ad hoc group of 667 members representing oil, gas and related industries that resolved internal differences in the interests of limiting the powers of the Federal Power Commission.[33] The Lumberman's Economic Survival Committee coordinates the mutual concerns of the softwood companies.

[31] *Ibid.*, reprint, pp. 4–5.
[32] See Stephen K. Bailey, *Congress Makes a Law*, Columbia University Press, New York, 1950. On a "catalyst" alliance to stimulate repeal of Chinese exclusion, see Fred W. Riggs, *Pressures on Congress*, Crown Publishers, Inc., New York, 1950.
[33] See Edith T. Carper, *Lobbying and the Natural Gas Bill*, Inter-University Case Studies, no. 72, The Bobbs-Merrill Company, Inc., Indianapolis, 1962. This program has produced many other case studies of lobbying.

The huge defense budget has produced some fascinating combinations of rivalries of one community against another and of one set of communities against another group. Lockheed, General Dynamics, and Boeing, for example, are recipients of huge contracts, and a given contract may result in high employment levels in several communities since the work is not likely to be done in one city. Thus labor, business, defense contractors, and other groups in a given city are vitally concerned with securing contracts in order to keep up employment levels and the economic well-being of the community. Added to this local community "bread-and-butter" interest are the military lobbies exemplified by the civilian service organizations backing the Army, the Navy, and the Air Force. These organizations get into arguments on behalf of certain defense concepts such as carriers versus bombers, small-war versus big-war capability, and the significance of placing weapons in a particular locality. Further, captains of defense industries are sometimes former military leaders. Thus a huge alliance can be built of defense contractors, certain civilian service groups, and members of a community strongly dependent on Army installations, shipbuilding contracts, or a special industry such as aerospace.

One of the techniques of alliances of this type is the exertion of pressures on the general public through advertisements. One concern advertised that certain cities were "sitting ducks" for the destruction by submarine-borne enemy missiles and that its own product is designed to deal with such enemy efforts. President Eisenhower at a news conference noted that advertisements were making other loose claims, such as the assertion that certain weapons were "in production" or would be ready long before schedule. Since weapon building is mainly in the hands of private enterprise, the defense effort requires intimate communication between policy makers and weapons manufacturers and has brought about a new "military-industrial complex" and intense lobbying for a share of the federal defense budget.

The billboard lobbies in the states have woven together trade associations, sign painters' unions, and often brewers and oil companies. Dummy highway-property organizations and bogus farmers' and workers' leagues often appear out of nowhere to flood legislators with communications. Billboard alliances, like most others, are fluid and flexible. A group combines with one group at one time and with another on the next occasion. The highway lobby in the states is often successful in mobilizing local constituencies and rank-and-file truckers and small businessmen.[34] Because of the need for forming new alliances at all

[34] Illustration is provided by Andrew Hacker, "Pressure Politics in Pennsylvania: The Truckers vs. the Railroads," in Alan F. Westin (ed.), *The Uses of Power: 7 Cases in American Politics*, Harcourt, Brace & World, Inc., New York, 1962, pp. 323–376. The volume also includes case studies in federal aid to education and foreign aid.

times there is often a camaraderie between legislative agents. They can help pinpoint for each other the trouble spots in the legislature and the loci of power and influence.

A group may make a political alliance with party leaders and with persons in the administrative agencies to reinforce each other and mobilize influence in the legislative body. Lobbyists like to be free to negotiate alliances and bargains but may not invariably do so because they are encumbered by rigid preferences and goals of the group's membership. A homogeneous group with highly specific objectives may impose limitations on the kinds of compromises that its spokesmen can negotiate.

Legislative Activities. The pressure points for influence during the legislative stages of bills are many and must be evaluated by interest-group spokesmen. In the state legislature, much effort is given to trying to influence the choice of speaker of the house, floor leaders, committee chairmanships, and the composition of the committees. In Congress, committee assignments are determined by seniority, and pressure groups are unlikely to have an effective control over them or the leadership. Some of the most seasoned lobbyists in the states maintain that most committee hearings are "window dressing" and hardly worth the time but that there are some important exceptions. In Congress, the lobby's energy is put into preparing statements to be presented at the hearings and into engineering invitations to present testimony.[35] Hearings have news value and serve the purpose of getting groups on record. Groups are usually concerned also with the reference of bills to committees since some committees are hostile or would like to bury a bill, while others would be sympathetic, report it favorably, and press for its adoption.

Both in Congress and in the state assemblies, the committee stage is crucial. Outside the committee-room hearings, lobbyists are using their personal contacts to the hilt trying to get an audience with the chairman, who holds great power over a bill, and with other members of the committee. Facts and figures are presented on how the bill will affect the parties, the need for amendment, and so on. Lobbyists in Congress often work with the committee staffs, supplying them with information and hoping through a staff member to get important considerations before the legislators themselves. In most legislative bodies, the recommendation of the standing committee is likely to represent the final action of that particular house. Therefore if the bill is reported

[35] For a comprehensive account of group activities at successive stages of the legislative process in Congress, see Bertram M. Gross, *The Legislative Struggle*, McGraw-Hill Book Company, New York, 1953. This volume is one of the best expositions of group theory as applied to the legislative process.

favorably, the advocates of a measure will have won a victory, and if the bill receives an unfavorable recommendation or a decision to pigeonhole, the opponents are entitled to be happy.

At least three other stages call for concentration of energy — the rules committee, floor action, and the conference committee. In many state legislatures as in the United States House, the rules committee is responsible for clearing bills for floor action. Unless one can get a friend in court to plead his case in the rules committee, which meets in secret, the legislature may never have a chance to act on it. Rules committee members often protect each other by refusing to disclose votes and positions taken during committee deliberations. Unless a group has sympathizers on the committee, it may never get its bill before the lower house and, what is more, may never know who was responsible for sidetracking it. Rules bodies are frequently used, therefore, to take pressures off members who would have to support a bill if it ever came up for a vote on the house floor.

If a bill emanating from a committee is not suitable to a group, its next chance is to fight for amendment on the floor or to get it recommitted. When the vote comes around, lobbyists count heads, try to ascertain who are uncommitted, and make an effort to persuade them. Groups often try to get their friends on the floor to schedule a roll call vote to put each legislator on record. Sometimes when a voice vote or standing vote is used, legislators will be asked by group spokesmen to record after the fact how they voted.

With rare exception, conference committees meet in executive sessions, and outside organizations have no access to them except as they may have their sympathizers appointed as conferees. Usually the chairmen and some of the standing committee members are on the conference committee, and the group knows their positions and to what extent they can be reached and influenced. The conferees must use a good deal of discretion, and lobbyists will try to reach them individually if possible. In terms of tactics, the rules committee and conference committee are comparable, for to be effective one must reach a member before he enters "the smoke-filled room" where the decisions are to be made.

Influence. The influence of private groups in legislative matters remains a moot point. One can hardly prove that a bill passed or was defeated because this or that organization put on pressure. Leaders of associations are wont to exaggerate claims of victory to impress the membership. In its recruitment program, the American Legion stresses how it secured the Veterans Administration and the bonus, and the National Association of Manufacturers pridefully points to its role in putting the Taft-Hartley Act on the books. A Farm Bureau Federation pamphlet gives a very long list of its "legislative accomplishments." The American Medical Association was reported to have been largely responsible for side-tracking Senate confirmation of an assistant secretary of Health, Education and Welfare requested by President Nixon. Conversely, instances are found in which, despite great effort, interest groups failed to attain their objectives. On foreign trade legislation, one study found great ineptitude in lobbying operations.[36]

It is not unusual for leaders of an organization to play upon the fears of their own membership by claiming the "great power" of an adversary. The tactic may strengthen their own position in the organization and promote internal cohesion through exaggerating the power of the opposition. Despite the many factors blurring the picture, a few characteristics of the influence of lobbyists do seem reasonably well established.

Legislators vary much in their orientations toward and responses to lobbyists.[37] Many legislators use the private-group agents for their own purposes and find them useful in facilitating their own legislative objectives. Such legislators on the whole regard lobbying favorably. Some others react neutrally or even hastily to lobbyists and do not have extensive contacts with them. Legislative advocates have been found to possess low visibility among numerous state legislators.

On the basis of interviews with congressmen, Scott and Hunt found that the lawmakers were jealous of their own prerogatives and felt, in terms of policy decision making, the influence of lobbyists to be overrated.[38] Those congressmen with the most seniority believed them less influential than newcomers. Further, congressmen are contacted more frequently in areas of their major working interests than in peripheral areas. Congressmen see the major role of interest groups as providing information and also support for the former's legislative interests. At the state level, adequate staff services are wanting, and lobbyists are especially useful in providing legislators with technical information and intelligence. Group representatives possessing experience, ability, and integrity appear to be listened to by lawmakers with more sympathy than those given to distortion of facts.

As spokesmen for a private group champion programs peripheral to their organization's interests, their influence is likely to decline.

[36] See Raymond A. Bauer et al., *American Business and Public Policy,* Atherton Press, Inc., New York, 1963. The study found that "the lobbyist becomes in effect a service bureau for those congressmen already agreeing with him, rather than an agent of direct persuasion" (pp. 252–253).
[37] A few of the works dealing with influence and with perceptions of legislators and lobbyists are Milbrath, *The Washington Lobbyists;* Zeigler, *Interest Groups in American Society;* J. C. Wahlke et al., *The Legislative System,* John Wiley & Sons, Inc., New York, 1962; Kenneth Janda et al., *Legislative Politics in Indiana,* Indiana University Press, Bloomington, 1961; and Wilder Crane, Jr., "A Test of Effectiveness of Interest-Group Pressures on Legislators," *Southwestern Social Science Quarterly,* vol. 41, pp. 335–340, 1960.
[38] *Congress and Lobbies: Image and Reality.*

Their views carry greater weight as they are restricted to the concerns of an organization. At the same time, a legislator can be expected to be more impressed by the number, variety, and character of groups supporting a measure than by the pleadings of a single group. Professional organizations and the League of Women Voters, for example, may work together with a great occupational federation on one bill but join with a different federation in opposition to another bill. The integrity of each is preserved, and the League escapes the charge of being consistently prounion or probusiness.

Legislators are not necessarily neutral persons, weighing the merits of bills before them; many representatives are actively identified with lobby groups that appear before the legislature. Private groups that have their own members and friends serving in the legislative body are greatly aided thereby. Even though these members are "marked" men in the awareness of their colleagues, they can operate from within committees and on the floor. Lawyers, farmers, and businessmen of diverse types are usually well represented in state legislatures, whereas labor unions and educational bodies have few representatives. Legislators who are actively associated with private groups may find their lot an unhappy one. Their membership expects them to be leaders for the group and accomplishers of deeds. They soon find that legislation is infinitely complicated and that the overall public interest is not necessarily precisely what the group stands for and wants. If they can moderate and compromise the group goals with the larger interest without being called traitors, they may have served both the private and the public interest.

To conclude, gaining access to the legislature requires careful analysis of one's own resources since no two groups are equal in the assets that they can tap. One group can mobilize a march on the capital and have the legislative corridors teeming with supporters—others cannot. Some interests are well represented because their own members sit in the legislature, while others may compensate through representation by skilled lobbyists. Prestige, alliances, and money are also resources. The extent to which there is a correlation between the amount spent for influence and the results is indeterminable. The amounts spent, as reported to the Clerk of the United States House, are of little use in assaying influence. Some 266 organizations reported spending $4.2 million in 1968. Business, labor, and citizens groups were, in order, the biggest spenders. The largest single spender was the United Federation of Postal Clerks ($170,000) but the American Medical Association, National Education Association, American Hospital Association, and the American Farm Bureau Federation also listed large sums.[39]

[39] Figures reported are likely to be very incomplete. They appear periodically in the *Congressional Quarterly;* and 1968 figures were taken from the issue of June 27, 1969, pp. 1128ff.

PRIVATE GROUPS AND ADMINISTRATION

Nature of Administration.   Administration can be regarded as a continuation and projection of the legislative process. Legislatures formulate compromises in the demands of the interests and in so doing may make laws imprecise, if not contradictory. This often leaves policy questions to be decided and clarified by the administrative agencies. Stated another way, administrators are engaged in the process of making decisions because legislatures lay down broad policies and programs, leaving to administrators the function of interpreting and implementing them.

Administrative agencies differ much in their function and in control by the popularly elected executive. There are boards and independent regulatory agencies that are not directly under the President or the governor. The federal independent regulatory agencies are involved with a broad complex of interests extending beyond the normal course of individual relationships with executive agencies.

Earliest of the regulated agencies to be created was the Interstate Commerce Commission (ICC). It deals with perhaps the most intricately organized area of the interest-group spectrum and finds itself in the political struggle between the railroad and trucking interests. To the Federal Communications Commission (FCC) is given the job of seeing that the broadcasting industry is operated in the public interest. The FCC has had to make decisions unpopular with certain powerful interests and minorities; these decisions concern such matters as lotteries, allocation of time for campaign speeches, liquor advertisements, religious programs, and access of Communists to the air waves. The FCC frequently submits proposed rules from the television industry to an all-industry advisory committee in the hope that the competing firms will provide the FCC with countervailing influences helpful to the public interest.

Generally, the independent regulatory commissions deal with policies affecting a broader skein of interests than the other executive agencies, but organized private groups are much concerned with the latter as well. In fact, there are few, if any, departments and bureaus in which some group is not interested. There are two types of administrative actions — coercive and noncoercive. The former involves the use of compulsory powers such as imposing restrictions and requiring licenses, and the affected interests try to influence the use and degree of coercion. Locally, the authority to grant permission for certain activities, such as fire burning, outdoor wiring, and small building, may be vitiated by pressures for nonenforcement. Similarly, groups may try to dilute enforcement of zoning and Sunday closing laws and laws regulating the discharge of effluents into rivers and lakes.

Noncoercive and service functions have vastly increased in scope. Public education, veterans' services, street repair and highway maintenance, conservation and public recreation facilities, fire protection, flood control, and social security services, to mention only a few, affect millions of persons, organized and unorganized. Pressures by citizens associations and improvement societies result in increased appropriations for parks, streets, and policy protection, and in changed bus schedules. Resort businesses, airlines, and farmers seek adequate staffing for the Weather Bureau. Automobile manufacturers, truckers, tourist clubs, oil companies, and many others join in promoting better highways and watch the Bureau of Public Roads' reviews and inspections of highways receiving federal support. The Bureau of Foreign and Domestic Commerce and the Reclamation Bureau have their "clients," and the Department of Agriculture probably wins the prize for its volume of appropriations and services for a single sector of the population. The State Department, on the other hand, has no built-in allies in the form of strong, natural clientele groups devoted to supporting the Department's foreign aid and other policies.[40]

Relationships. During the prelegislative stage, interest groups assist administrators in drafting legislation. Many bills of course are drafted by administrators with no help from outside groups, but in many cases there is collaboration. Such bills may be new programs, but more are amendments that administrators believe will improve existing programs and result in better benefits. Administrators also want the support of groups that may help them to get measures through the legislature.

After a law is passed, a chain of close relationships develops between the administering agency and interest groups. Contacts with the government are more frequently maintained with administrative officers than with members of the legislature. A congressman, for example, is only sporadically interested in the problems of public health, but the Public Health Service is concerned with them daily. Administrative handling of problems relieves Congress from some harassment by important and influential groups. As private associations become more satisfactorily represented in an administration, many of their demands are met, resulting in less pressure on Congress. Further, interest groups find it more advantageous to deal with one or a few administrators and agencies than to deal with individual congressmen and committees. If existing remedies are unavailable, then the interest group and administrators may be able to agree on some form of legislation that can be taken to Congress. The agency staff may perceive an

[40]Among the many works on administration, those especially relevant to our consideration are J. Leiper Freeman, *The Political Process: Executive Bureau—Legislative Committee Relations*, Random House, Inc., New York, 1955; William W. Boyer, *Bureaucracy on Trial*, The Bobbs-Merrill Company, Inc., Indianapolis, 1964; E. Pendleton Herring, *Public Administration and the Public Interest*, McGraw-Hill Book Company, New York, 1936; Avery Leiserson, *Administrative Regulation: A Study in Representation of Interests*, The University of Chicago Press, Chicago, 1942.

administrative remedy, making unnecessary the securing of objectives through the path of legislative lobbying and pressure politics.

The channels of access to administration vary from highly informal ones to those carrying legal sanction. Major methods by which organized interest spokesmen participate in the administrative process are (1) conferences and meetings, (2) advisory committees, (3) furnishing of administrative personnel, (4) delegation and devolution of authority to interest groups, and (5) lay participation in law enforcement.[41] Humane societies often do much of the enforcing of leash and related laws, and many groups have programs whereby their leaders and the membership participate in carrying out laws and in reporting laxities and problems.

Hundreds of conferences are held annually or more often between representatives of private groups and government officials. Cabinet secretaries and bureau heads are usually invited to the annual conventions of organizations. Administrators in the lower echelons commonly maintain memberships in these professional groups and regularly attend their meetings. Public officials become familiar with the desires and goals of groups, and the latter become aware of the thinking of administrators. Conferences afford an opportunity to appraise alternatives and to focus attention on differences and on the possibilities of compromise.

A more formal method of gaining face-to-face access is through advisory committees. Numerous agencies at all levels of government initiate provisions for such committees, and in some cases they are established by the law itself. Committees are composed of spokesmen or representatives from the various parties-in-interest immediately concerned with the problems of a government unit. City planning commissions frequently have attached to them advisory committees composed of realty interests and racial minorities, and the Forest Service consults with advisory boards representing farm, lumber, and livestock associations.

The advisory-committee arrangement involves implications and problems that are too complicated for extended treatment here. It may be observed in passing that for groups not having a representative on a committee, a channel of access is denied. This raises questions of fair play and of who is entitled to representation. There may be a question of keeping the committee truly advisory. It may try to impose its views on or control the administrators. For administrators, advisory committees provide a means of obtaining certain technical knowledge and viewpoints. In this sense they serve a purpose comparable to a legislative

---

[41] The series of Inter-University Case Studies, published by The Bobbs-Merrill Company, Inc., Indianapolis, provide interesting examples of the roles played by groups in the administrative process.

hearing and help identify forces favorable and opposed to a proposed administrative decision. Favorable groups are a potential resource in winning over the public and the legislature. Committee discussion may result in obligating some groups to support policies and in neutralizing others that might be in opposition had they not been privy to deliberations. Administrators use committees and meetings to alert individuals and groups to important issues and stakes.

As interest groups attempt to influence the selection of personnel for legislative committees and staffs, so they also attempt to influence appointments to executive agencies. It is not unusual for groups to push persons from within their own ranks for positions in certain agencies. Farm groups, for example, have tried with some success to get their people positions on farm committees and as county agents. In state administration, there are many boards and commissions composed in part of representatives of private groups.

Perhaps the most formalized recognition of group interests is where by law or by administrative discretion, responsibility for administering or carrying out a function of government is devolved upon or delegated to a group. Occupational licensing boards in the states receive legal sanction to operate what is more or less a guild system. In substance, this means that a compulsory licensing statute is administered by an independent board composed of officials nominated by various associations. State medical licensing boards are almost wholly composed of medical doctors who are in good standing in their medical societies. Where licensing is not performed by representatives of the profession itself, the association may attempt to influence the governor in his appointments to the board, and in some instances the association's nominees must be appointed.

The tendency has been for each department to develop its own autonomous structure of power relationships with clientele groups. When a group has consolidated its influence and representation with its agency, it may oppose executive reorganization. The Army Corps of Engineers and the Bureau of Reclamation have built up allies in Congress, resulting in formidable resistance to reorganization and to an integrated Columbia River Valley Authority. The Corps of Engineers has been so successful in building political support in Congress that it can even ward off the President and make its own arrangements with Congress on flood-control policies.[42]

In summary, interest groups seek access and attempt to influence the administrative process through (1) seeking appointment of friendly personnel in executive agencies, (2) obtaining favored treatment by the executive, (3) demanding informal or formal consultation on proposed policies and administrative techniques. Although not al-

---

[42] See Bailey and Samuel, *Congress at Work*, chap. 7.

ways true in fact, interest groups potentially can foster citizen participation in and control over the bureaucracy. They may help to modify a professionalism that has become insensitive or unresponsive to certain citizen viewpoints and needs. At the same time the executive is in some respects more vulnerable to pressures than the legislator. The former wishes to avoid adverse publicity and maintain and extend the goodwill of legislators and the general clientele of his agency. Also he does not want to become vulnerable within the executive establishment. Interest groups can play upon this general environment within which an administrator operates.

Of great importance, but perhaps not as fully appreciated, is the use made by the political executive and administrators of private groups in the attainment of their agency's and their personal goals. The executive uses private groups as a pipeline of information and ideas, and they may furnish him with special staff services that he does not possess. They provide him further with a feedback on the results of the agency's work.

Because administrative agencies must obtain sanction, appropriations, and authority from the legislature, they need allies in dealing with it. Here the administrators can use the professional associations of their own staffs to mobilize support.[43] Social welfare workers assist their colleagues in government and commissioners of welfare on certain mutual concerns in the legislature. President Lyndon B. Johnson and his Commissioner of Education, buttressed by high-powered legislative liaison officers, built a coalition successful in overcoming the opposition to federal aid to education. Interest groups are also highly useful in aiding the President and governors in upgrading their programs in the legislature and rallying the membership to communicate "their support of the executive" to the legislature.

Private groups are also useful to support the aims of one agency against another in intraexecutive department disputes. This is especially true in proposed reorganization. Railroads, for example, have been instrumental in defeating proposals that the functions of the ICC be assigned to an administrator directly responsible to the President.

INTEREST GROUPS AND THE COURTS

For political interest groups, trying to influence government is a never-ending process. Those wishing to defeat a proposal try to get it buried,

[43] This was tersely stated by a career official in these words: "The smart executive must be active in organizations outside government in order to mobilize their support when he needs it. If he can organize counter pressure, he can maintain the integrity of his program despite the pressures seeking to influence his behavior," In Marver H. Bernstein, *The Job of the Federal Executive*, The Brookings Institution, Washington, D.C., 1958, p. 133.

defeated, or drastically amended in one house. Failing this, they move to the other house for a second try. If this is unavailing, then efforts are concentrated on the executive for a veto, and forces are mobilized to see that the legislature sustains it. If the measure becomes law, their next recourse is to the administrative level, hoping for enforcement that will take at least some cognizance of their views. In the meantime, the leadership will analyze the possibilities for a judicial remedy. Oil interests wanting state control over the tidelands were defeated by an adverse court ruling that upheld federal title. They won in Congress only to be thwarted by a Presidential veto. But the election of a new President, Dwight D. Eisenhower, and a sympathetic Congress resulted in the passage of the legislation they sought. Often a group attempts to influence the executive and legislature at the same time and may have litigation pending as well.

Like the other coordinate branches of the government, the judiciary has the power to make decisions that profoundly affect the distribution of power of private groups. This comes from the power of judicial review, the interpretation of statutes, executive orders, treaties, and the Constitution. In addition, judges exercise considerable discretion in the issuing of injunctions, in the awarding of money damages, and in property settlements. The relationship of a group to the judiciary differs in several particulars from its contacts with the other branches of the government.[44]

In the first place, there is no self-starting mechanism in the courts comparable to the initiation of bills and administrative programs. Cases emanate from outside the courts, and there are limitations on lawsuits. Federal courts have limited jurisdiction and handle cases that are justiciable and not political in nature. There is a question as to what is political, and some critics of the Supreme Court hold that it is uninhibited and unrestrained in hearing political cases. A sizable share of the issues are brought before the courts by organized interest groups.

Recourse to the courts is often used after defeat or dissatisfaction at the hands of the other two branches. Litigation is usually a long and expensive process and is likely to be employed as a last resort. Because it is costly, the resource is not open to the less affluent and favors an organization with the means to carry through the effort. An exception to this occurs when lawyers are willing to donate their time or when a case involves a pauper and public assistance is available. Business has often fared well with the courts because it can afford to have its cases skillfully prepared and urbanely presented.

[44]On interest groups and the courts, see the pertinent chapters in Blaisdell, *op. cit.*; Zeigler, *op. cit.*; and Truman, *op. cit.*; and Clement Vose, "Litigation as a Form of Pressure Group Activity," *The Annals of the American Academy of Political and Social Science*, vol. 319, pp. 20–31, 1958.

Influencing Personnel. As a general rule, interest groups have less influence on the selection of personnel in the judicial branch and are less effective at the federal than at the state level in this respect. At the state and local level today, the bar associations very often make recommendations and in some cases engage in active campaigning. (About three-fourths of the states follow the elective principle for most or all of their judges.) Under the "Missouri plan," a nonpartisan commission of the bar submits names from which the governor appoints appellate court judges. In addition, about a dozen states provide for recall of judges—a procedure very rarely used but a potential threat. It stands to reason that the elected judge is likely to be more sensitive to public opinion and to the opinions of organized interest groups. Where he runs under a party label, party factions must be kept in mind as well, for there is always the problem of renomination and reelection.

Where judges are appointed and serve with tenure, as in the federal judiciary (depending only on good behavior), they have more independence from direct claims by organized groups. But executives choose judges carefully and are mindful of public opinion. The organized bar at all levels has sought influence and responsibility in the process of selecting judges; it has assumed that it has a duty to participate in the selection of judges. Beginning in 1945, the American Bar Association (ABA) has worked closely with the Department of Justice and the Senate Judiciary Committee in passing on the qualifications of prospective federal judges. The Justice Department compiles a list of qualified nominees, and a committee of the ABA investigates their professional qualifications—rating them as qualified, well-qualified, exceptionally well-qualified, or unqualified.[45] This evaluation is then sent to the Senate Judiciary Committee to help it to review the nominees proposed by the President. The ABA's committee works closely with the Senate committee.

Interest groups recognize the importance of bringing a case before the *right* judge. They study the backgrounds of judges and to what extent if any they may exploit their own prestige or social status in bringing the case.[46] A labor union is likely to prefer a judge with liberal

---

[45] The ABA's group, known as the Committee on the Federal Judiciary, is given power by the association to promote the nomination and confirmation of judges and has become an integral part of the selection process. See Joel B. Grossman, *The Role of the Bar Association in the Selection of Judges,* unpublished doctoral dissertation, University of Wisconsin, Madison, Wis., 1963. In this case, as with administrative personnel, a theoretical problem arises when a committee or the leadership of an interest group is given virtual veto power or partial control over the selection of public officials. Do officials in such cases feel responsible ultimately to an organized group or to the public? This question will continue to be debated.

[46] For one study of the relationship of background factors and adherence to precedent and to dissent, see John R. Schmidhauser, "*Stare Decisis,* Dissent, and the Background of the Justices of the Supreme Court of the United States," *University of Toronto Law Journal,* vol. 14, pp. 196–212, 1962.

sympathies, and a business organization is happier with one who was a corporation lawyer before being elevated to the bench.

Bringing Suit. A great deal of thought goes into the strategy of a suit involving a major policy. An organized interest must find a good plaintiff with a strong case. There is an advantage in sponsoring a suit from one's own membership, but it is not always easy to recruit someone from the ranks of the membership. An alternative is to help someone from outside who is contemplating or is already involved in litigation. Support of such a suit must be carefully appraised in terms of the group's interest since some of the membership may object on personal grounds or because the plaintiff is a stranger.

Another alternative is the use of *amici curiae*, or "friends of the court." This consists in permitting an individual or group to appear or file a brief in a case to which it is not a party. A long list of *amici curiae* appeared in connection with such diverse measures as the Federal Maternity and Infancy Act (involving the grant-in-aid principle), the first Agricultural Adjustment Act, and a railroad versus the ICC case in 1910, in which seventeen organizations participated in a single brief. Because *amici curiae* was regarded as being excessively utilized, the "rule of consent" was invoked in 1949. Thereafter consent had to be obtained by the party, and the number filing supporting briefs was reduced.[47] When the Solicitor General (since the United States government is a party in large numbers of cases) refuses consent, the Supreme Court can permit it. In the steel seizure case, for example, the CIO was permitted to file an *amicus curiae* brief, whereas the American Legion was not.

Several purposes are fulfilled by the filing of briefs or the presentation of oral argument as *amici.* A third party representing the government and/or other private groups may be brought into the proceedings. This can be done for the purpose of endorsing and strengthening the case of the litigant and adding to the list of allies. It results in the representation of an interest not otherwise represented. The procedure may serve a supplemental strategy and bring to the court's attention points and arguments absent from the main litigant's contentions as well as introduce subtle variations of the principal contentions. In civil rights cases, the American Civil Liberties Union and the American Jewish Congress have been active filers of *amici curiae* briefs; these have represented a broad minority-rights interest. Krislov sees the institution of the *amicus* brief as having moved by "neutrality to partisanship, from friendship to advocacy." It has been a means, he says, "of fostering partisan third party involvement through encouragement of group

---

[47] For an account of trends from 1949 to 1961 together with a table on written briefs and oral arguments of *amici curiae*, see Samuel Krislov, "The *Amicus Curiae* Brief: From Friendship to Advocacy," *The Yale Law Journal*, vol. 72, pp. 694–721, 1963.

representation by a self-conscious bench. The judges have sought to gain information from political groups as well as to give them a feeling of participation in the process of decision. Access to the legal process on the part of such organizations is a logical extension of realistic awareness of law as a process of social choice and policy making."[48]

A group may use a procedural advice known as a class action to save the time of the courts as well as time and money for large numbers of persons with the same interest. This permits one or more persons to sue not only in their own behalf but on behalf "of all others similarly situated." A black can institute a class action against state officials in a voting or desegregation case and try to prove that other black citizens are being similarly discriminated against. A court injunction can be issued, enjoining the officials from discriminating against the plaintiff and all others.

Another channel available for seeking judicial intervention is to persuade an executive department to begin a criminal prosecution or a civil suit—an important device in civil rights cases. Negro groups attempt to get the Justice Department to institute suits against state officials who are allegedly interfering with voting rights or engaging in discriminatory practices. The Nixon administration in its first year turned to the courts rather than relying exclusively on action by the Department of Health, Education, and Welfare to enforce desegregation in the public schools.

The human and material resources of organized interests are unequal and must be employed as economically and artfully as possible. In conluding this section on judicial access, it is to be noted that judges are insulated from outside pressures to a greater extent than legislators and administrators; but, because they are significant decision makers, certain groups utilize litigation to attain their ends. By carefully selecting test cases, the NAACP, through a special defense unit, has won some spectacular victories in the courts, when the group could not obtain redress from the executive and legislature on restrictive covenants, segregation, and discrimination. But highly trained lawyers are needed if judicial remedies are to be successful. A problem for the American democracy is the protection and representation of those interests that cannot afford to buy the resources to present skilled presentations before all branches of government.

FOR FURTHER READING

Bibby, John, and Roger Davidson: *On Capitol Hill: Studies in the Legislative Process*, 1967.
Dahl, Robert A.: *Who Governs?* 1962.

[48] *Ibid.*, p. 721.

Deakin, James: *The Lobbyists*, 1966.

Downs, Anthony: *Inside Bureaucracy*, 1967.

Eidenberg, Eugene, and Roy D. Morey: *An Act of Congress: The Legislative Process and the Making of Public Policy*, 1968.

de Grazia, Alfred: *Public and Republic: Political Representation in America*, 1951.

Ely, Lynn W., and Thomas W. Casstevens (eds.): *The Politics of Fair-Housing Legislation*, 1968.

Lane, Edgar: *Lobbying and the Law*, 1964.

Milbrath, Lester: *The Washington Lobbyists*, 1963.

Pitkin, Hanna F.: *The Concept of Representation*, 1967.

Rose, Arnold M.: *The Power Structure: Political Process in the American Society*, 1967.

Vose, Clement: *Caucasians Only*, 1959.

Zeigler, Harmon, and Michael A. Barr: *Lobbying: Interaction and Influence in American State Legislatures*, 1969.

To say that private men have nothing to do with
government is to say that private men have nothing
to do with their own happiness or misery;
that people ought not to concern themselves
whether they be naked or clothed, fed or starved,
deceived or instructed, protected or destroyed.

CATO

CHAPTER 21 THE CHALLENGE OF PROTEST POLITICS

A constantly reiterated theme of observers of government is that the process by which public policy is developed in the United States is highly diffused. In Chapter 20, notice was taken of efforts by organized interest groups to rally public opinion behind their objectives by the use of public relations and propaganda, mass communications, and active participation in primaries, conventions, and general elections. Political interest groups, political parties, legislators, administrators, independent commissioners, and often judges participate in formulating public programs, making for a complicated, confused, and messy picture; but this fragmentation gives organized interests highly diverse opportunities to influence policy. Moreover, the decentralized and atomized manner by which public policy is developed and administered and the comparatively weak party organization in Congress and in the state legislatures account in part for the influence of private interest groups on government. But even in the presence of a strong centralized party system as in Great Britain, pressure groups are highly influential in the policy process.

After a brief restatement of the theory and criticism of American pluralist (interest-group) politics, this final chapter looks at some of the challenges and threats to the system. One comes from those who maintain that certain goals cannot be achieved by the traditionally accepted tactics noted in Chapter 20. Some who hold this view justify recourse to various degrees of force and violence to bring changes in the system. So widespread as a tactic was the use of force or threat of it in the 1960s that it has become highly relevant to the study of American politics. Other challenges arise from the diverse highly articulated dissatisfactions with the structures, operation, and results of the system in terms of present-day realities. Following a review of diverse protests and tactics, this chapter concludes with an examination of alternative responses to them.

THE CASE FOR INTEREST-GROUP POLITICS

Defense of the System. The pluralist and interest-group society has been widely accepted by politicians, scholars, and much of the knowledgeable public, though it means somewhat different things to different people. Seen at its best, groups supplement the electoral process by giving the citizen additional ways of securing information and influence. Electoral mandates are ambiguous in terms of policy but groups step in and present policy preferences to public officials who in turn work out accommodating compromises. Representative government is strengthened and made more reflective of citizen demands than is the case of electoral politics, which selects lawmakers from a geographic district. Groups define and articulate the interests of their members; indeed this is their major function.

Groups compete with each other for favor with the government. Neither deadlock nor coercion are desirable, so negotiation follows. Hopefully, out of negotiation come solutions that, while not perfect, are in the general interest. The constant bargaining that takes place in adjusting demands and claims helps to bring about correctives, allocating, in at least some measure, the good things in life to all.

A virtue of the system, as seen by its proponents, is that it works for consensus (and usually obtains it), fosters stability, and reduces the scope and intensity of conflict. The process operates under established rules, with the outcome or result enjoying legitimacy. The pluralists are particularly concerned with the processes and means and the rules of the game, which, if followed, render a fair share of public satisfaction to each group. An important strength of the system is that it usually results in the peaceful management of conflict. Leaders, moreover, settle conflicts by informal means as well as by formal devices, and when the former is used there is a reduction of conflict among private leaders and formal officeholders.

Interest-group theory leaves room for intervention by government as the arbiter of the interests and the final allocator of values. Government interacts with the private power groups in ways noted in the preceding chapters. When all is said and done, writes Earl Latham, "the legislature referees the group struggle, ratifies the victories of the successful coalitions, and records the terms of surrenders, compromises and conquests in the form of statutes," but in this process, he notes, "the legislature does not play the inert part of the cash register, ringing up additions and withdrawals of strength, a mindless balance pointing and marking the weight and distribution of power among the contending groups."[1] Bureaucracies as well as legislatures are believed to be more or less faithful reflectors of group interests. The pluralists see room for positive government, but the more realistic of them do not necessarily argue that the legislative outcome is invariably the public interest or public good, because of the personal interests and motivations of the individual officeholders.

Only the most idealistic or naïve would argue that the interplay of interest groups suffices to make everyone happy and that, in and of itself, it supplies all needed self-correctives. But pluralists see these as being provided in various ways. One is to use political parties as an instrument for accommodating overpowerful private organizations. Strong parties in the state legislatures are believed capable of ameliorating the demands of lobbyist spokesmen, as are the centralized parties in parliamentary systems.

Another modifier of undue private influence is countervailing power. Pressure groups, so it is said, beget pressure groups. Big labor builds up to counterbalance big business. Left-wing groups help to ameliorate the power of right-wing organizations. Private utilities at times have fought public utilities to a stand-off. David B. Truman regards overlapping membership among organized groups as "the principal balancing force in the politics of a multigroup society such as the United States."[2] By belonging to several different organizations, a citizen has conflicting loyalties that tend to have a moderating effect on each other. A property-owning parent is interested in keeping down

---

[1] *The Group Basis of Politics*, Cornell University Press, Ithaca, N.Y., 1952, pp. 35, 37. Used by permission of Cornell University Press.

[2] *The Governmental Process*, Alfred A. Knopf, Inc., New York, 1951, p. 520. One of the best statements of the pluralist process is Charles E. Lindblom, *The Intelligence of Democracy*, The Free Press, New York, 1965.

taxes on real estate, but simultaneously wishes adequate appropriations for education.

But countervailing forces and the mitigating effects of overlapping memberships fall short of their potential for balance and equilibrium. Demands arise from disadvantaged sources for government intervention. Taxes and appropriations become instruments for a better division of resources. Power of weak groups may be built up by favorable legislation varying from improving job opportunities and limitations on campaign donations to subsidies. Regulatory legislation can be used to control the power of specific groups and to establish fairer rules of the game for the participants. Lobbying laws presumably help identify interest-group spokesmen and outlaw certain types of persuasion such as bribery.

Critique of Interest-Group Politics. Without necessarily objecting to the pluralist society, a number of scholars have attacked the interest-group or pluralist theory as it operates in modern America. Three statements illustrate the types of criticism of the claim that a group serves as a surrogate for the individual by building up a collective intelligence and converting it into political power. Joseph A. Schumpeter enters dissent because he sees a group's leadership as "able to fashion and, within very wide limits, even to create the will of the people. What we are confronted with in the analysis of political processes is largely not a genuine but a manufactured will."[3]

Professor W. Theodore Lowi charges that

> . . . liberalism has become a doctrine whose means are its ends, whose combatants are its clientele, whose standards are not even those of the mob but worse, are those the bargainers can fashion to fit the bargain. Delegation of power has become alienation of the public domain — the gift of sovereignty to private satrapies. The political barriers to withdrawal of delegation are high enough. But liberalism reinforces these through the rhetoric of justification and often of legal reinforcements. Public corporations — justified, oddly, as efficient planning instruments — permanently alienate rights of central coordination to the directors who own corporation bonds.[4]

Further, the liberal pluralists who justify the present system give insufficient attention to the ends and consequences of government. They seek pluralist government, "in which there is no formal specification of means or ends. In pluralistic government there is therefore no substance. Neither is there procedure. There is only process."[5]

[3] Joseph A. Schumpeter, *Capitalism, Socialism and Democracy*, Harper Torchbooks, Harper & Row, Publishers, Incorporated, New York, 1962, p. 263. See also E. E. Schattschneider, *The Semisovereign People*, Holt, Rinehart and Winston, Inc., New York, 1960.

[4] *The End of Liberalism: Ideology, Policy and the Crisis of Public Authority*, W. W. Norton & Company, Inc., New York, 1969, pp. 288–289.

[5] *Ibid.*, p. 97.

One final scholarly reproach comes from Allen Schick, who believes allocative decisions cannot be completely entrusted to the competitive market in terms of costs and benefits. He writes:

> The polluter does not pay for the social cost he engenders. . . . One of the aims of an interest group is to get others to pay for your benefits or to avoid paying your share of the costs. . . .
>
> Thus we hear proposals to award tax credits to air polluters in order to motivate them to cease their harmful activity. Where there are external benefits, powerful beneficiaries may refuse to tax themselves for their gain.
>
> Why doesn't the unseen hand of group competition keep everyone honest, making the polluter pay for the costs he imposes and society for the benefits it receives? The obvious answer is that not all interests are equally powerful. Polluters probably have better lobbies than city residents who breathe the air. And they use their political power to ratify, not to countermand, the edict of the market.[6]

Concisely, a general criticism of the processes of decision making is that it gives inadequate attention to the results of "giving in" to one group on the whole community. Pollution, for example, was an unforeseen effect of granting privileges to certain groups. A broader ecological look at the possible effects of a proposed policy on the total environment is difficult under the pressure of certain powerful interests. As a result of growing public awareness and pressure, public authorities at all levels have begun to take a much broader look at the policies and practices permitting extensive deterioration of air, water, and natural resources.

FORCE AND VIOLENCE AS POLITICAL TECHNIQUES

The contention that social and economic reforms can be best achieved by utilizing the traditional tactics of peaceful negotiation was challenged from many quarters in the 1960s. There were wide-scale violence and the threat of violence, symbolized by massive street demonstrations; confrontations between police and civil authorities on the one hand and protesters on the other; riots and burnings leading to colossal property losses and some lives; bombings, political assassinations, the building of paramilitary brigades, and various types of guerilla warfare. H. Rap Brown, civil rights leader, commented that, "Violence is as American as cherry pie!" Due in part to television, radio, and front-page newspaper features, more Americans were undoubtedly made aware of violence than ever before. They saw Molotov cocktails being thrown, policemen wielding clubs, arrests, burnings and looting, and the screaming and displaying of epithets. The legitimacy of political authority was put to severe tests, and reputable columnists saw a huge malaise over the land.

[6]Allen Schick, *Systems Politics and Budgeting*, The Brookings Institution, Washington, D.C., 1969, pp. 145, 146. Copyright by *Public Administration Review*.

Response to the outbreaks of violence and near violence resulted in a mushrooming of literature, panel discussions of violence at learned societies and on television, hurriedly created organizations to "improve communication" with the leaders of revolts, new courses on violence in the colleges, governmental studies of the outbreaks, and much else. Police in some communities reacted with vigorous if not repressive tactics. From some of these activities, Americans undoubtedly gained perspective on force as a political technique even though the nation remains divided on response to it.

Definition and Universality. *Force* and *violence* are frequently used interchangeably, and what may be violence to one person is not to another because there are degrees of each. One writer finds it useful to distinguish among capability, threat, and demonstration. *Force* is seen as capability and threat of action; *violence* is a "demonstration of force tending toward counterdemonstration and escalation or toward containment and settlement."[7] Political violence consists of acts of force that acquire political significance by changing the behavior of those in a bargaining situation.

The general expectation in a stable society is that a private person will utilize force or violence only for a defensive purpose. Its widespread use by individuals, organized and unorganized, during the 1960s, therefore, led to anxiety on the part of those who did not use violence; and it was viewed as a threat to stability and to duly constituted authority. But an analysis of violence must begin by pointing out that it is quite universal as a political technique and not uniquely "as American as cherry pie."[8]

Riots, violent tactics, and terrorism have been frequent in the history of the United States and have not been limited to any one group.

[7] H. L. Nieburg, *Political Violence: The Behavioral Process,* St. Martin's Press, Inc., New York, 1969, p. 13. The work contains an extensive bibliography. Our concern here is with the use of violence by private parties and not with the force employed by recognized public authorities to perpetuate their political position or to provide internal and external security by forcing compliance with an order.

[8] An extensive literature has been prepared by psychologists, sociologists, political scientists, newsmen, and governmental authorities. In the last mentioned are numerous congressional hearings, studies for the National Advisory Commission on Civil Disorders published by the U.S. Government Printing Office, and the Walker Report on violence during the Democratic National Convention of 1968, published by Bantam Books, New York, 1968, under the title *Rights in Conflict.* A few recent titles from social scientists include Henry Bienen, *Violence and Social Change,* The University of Chicago Press, Chicago, 1968; Carl Leiden and Karl M. Schmitt (eds.), *The Politics of Violence: Revolution in the Modern World,* Appleton-Century-Crofts, New York, 1968; Morris Janowitz, *Social Control of Escalated Riots,* University of Chicago Center for Policy Study, Chicago, 1968; Louis Masotti, and J. R. Corsi, *Shoot-Out in Cleveland,* Bantam Books, New York, 1969; and Louis Masotti and Dan R. Bowen (eds.), *Riots and Rebellion,* Sage Publications, Inc., Beverly Hills, Calif., 1968. See also the voluminous report prepared by Jerome Skolnick for National Commission on the Causes and Prevention of Violence under the title, *The Politics of Protest,* Simon and Schuster, Inc., New York, 1969. The work contains an extensive bibliography.

These tactics have been employed at times by such diverse sectors of the population as depressed farmers, black slaves, modern civil rights workers, antiwar demonstrators, labor-union pickets and reacting strike-breakers from management, self-appointed vigilantes, and the Ku Klux Klan. For the most part, riots and terrorism have been severely dis-approved by the public. Public intervention has usually been quick, the riot short-lived, and the tactic discredited if not the cause itself.

Whether it is true that Americans are more violent than other people is debatable; bloody political encounters take place in other democratic nations, though more frequently in some countries than others. Violence and war have characterized international relations from time immemorial. Dictatorships in Europe, Latin America, and Asia have not been spared from massive challenges on the part of citi-zens that have resulted in forceful public intervention to crush the revolts. Insurrection and rebellion are employed to challenge legitimacy. Revolutionaries are convinced that only violence can topple the regime, and they use weapons and even political assassination to accomplish their ends.

Force is utilized not only against constituted government au-thority but also quite frequently by one private party against another private party—labor against management, students against the uni-versity administration, one faction against another faction in the same organization, gangland warfare, the poor or dispossessed against the owners, and so on. A number of burnings and lootings during riots are directed against the owners of establishments who are seen as exploiters. More likely, however, they are by-products of violence and are genuinely disapproved of by the leaders of the revolt.

Uses and Functions. The Civil War illustrates the use of force to bring about secession followed by forceful reaction by the federal government in an attempt to restrain political separatism. A government uses show of force to reinforce, when confronted, its legitimacy.

Ideally, and usually in practice, threat of force and/or violence is used when the more conventional and peaceful means of redressing grievances result in failure or where resort to such techniques is per-cevied in advance to be ineffective. What its leaders hope to accomplish is to induce rapid and effective response to their demands. A modest protest, for example, may start out very peaceably to call the attention of the general public to grievances. If this does not succeed, a show of force such as a sit-in or a massive march will be attempted to put on additional pressure. By attaining dramatic visibility for their cause, if not concern that those in power would suffer consequential losses if they refuse to make changes, the users of force hope to get into a better bargaining position. In effect, the bargainers become more equal in power so that the more powerful side must give in on something.

Violence is sometimes used by those who cannot easily employ legitimate access to attain ends or better their status. Blacks in some Southern communities found they were denied opportunity to register in city halls for voting; they marched to call attention to their cause. Violence during the Selma, Alabama, march (1965) resulted in hastening a national civil rights voting law.

Participation in violence also offers the downtrodden a chance for affirming identity with others in common cause and is an act of commitment to it. A number of juveniles are undoubtedly drawn into acts of force for psychological reasons.[9] Juvenile delinquents aside, as Lewis A. Coser observes, "One can make the more general assertion that in all those situations in which both legitimate and illegitimate socio-economic achievement seems blocked, recourse to aggressive and violent behavior may be perceived as a significant area of 'achievement.' . . . Men tend to feel that only prowess in interpersonal violence and in aggressive sexual encounters allows the achievement of personal identity and permits gaining otherwise unavailable deference."[10]

Force is a symbol of discontent; and it is generally regarded as indicative of deep grievances which, if not placated, will lead to disruption of a function or service with serious economic or other consequences. Undoubtedly, this technique was efficacious in a great many situations in the 1960s. Student groups and blacks obtained many concessions and changes by it. Over the years, labor unions have won many victories by establishing unbreakable picket lines and by strong-arm tactics when necessary. The bitter peace confrontations, on the other hand, did not result in an immediate change in foreign policy; but they did dramatize the unpopularity of the Vietnam war and they did keep the pressure on the Johnson and Nixon administrations to attempt negotiations, to reduce bombing, and to work for disengagement. They also stiffened the backs of congressional critics of the war and of those who demanded a better draft system. Threat of violence, however, is more likely to bring about change in domestic than in foreign policies.

Dysfunctional Aspects of Force. What may be a genuine cause for protest may be lost in the focus of attention on the dramatic aspect of the tactic. Protesters stand to lose sympathizers for their cause because of public

[9] See, for example, Richard A. Cloward and Lloyd E. Ohlin, *Delinquency and Opportunity*, The Free Press, New York, 1960.
[10] "Some Social Functions of Violence," *The Annals of the American Academy and Political and Social Science*, vol. 364, p. 11, 1966.

disgust with the technique. When employers of force manipulate other groups to join them in the tactic, the latter may suffer some loss of sympathy for its cause. On some occasions, black militants, Vietnam protesters, student and other leaders have manipulated each other into using force, and they have succeeded only in alienating community attitudes toward all.

When a group accomplishes one objective by the demonstration of force, its leaders may rely upon it for the attainment of new goals. Others see the success of force elsewhere and conclude that they too need not rely on the traditional methods to achieve change. The use of forceful methods becomes contagious, and leaders try it first as a short-cut rather than resorting to it only after all nonviolent means have been exhausted.

Violence frequently has a catalytic effect and leads to polarization and counterescalation. Some of the riots unified the black community and students at Berkeley and elsewhere. Participants became even more united when police appeared, used tear gas, and made some arrests. In turn, other citizens became polarized against both the blacks and students. Violence runs the risk of alienating potential recruits and of failing to win over the previously indifferent.

Modern riots and threats of force have led to the stocking of arsenals and to the buildup of security forces. Black Panthers and the Black Liberation Front became paramilitary in some communities; in reaction, whites purchased weapons for defense. (Conversely, the blacks said that their weapons were necessary to protect themselves against armed whites.) This is one of the reasons for the difficulty in enacting gun-control legislation. Adversaries believe they must have their own arsenals in case a conflagration arises. The "establishment" becomes terrified and encourages strong reaction against the protesters. Calls for "law and order," tough police tactics, and abridgment of the liberties of the protesters are commonplace responses to extremist political tactics. An atmosphere of high anxiety and incipient terror is not conducive to equitable, social adjustment.

When some extremists have resorted to sniping and guerilla tactics, police have had difficulty in reacting against them in an isolated way without involving all the rest of the community. Blacks feel they must react en masse to support the acts of their own extremists and this reaction gives the few a power they ordinarily would not have; the same has occurred on some campuses. Escalation and counterescalation easily build to a situation in which tensions are aggravated and there is potential of mass confrontation resulting from an isolated and minor incident. The private stockpiling of guns, which aggravates the potential of guerilla warfare, not only is likely to lead to escalation but also may set the stage for future outbursts by encouraging some of the extremists to rely, perhaps unconsciously, on violence or threat of it rather than on orderly peaceful politics to bring change. At the same time, the private person who uses force does not necessarily thereby realize his demands and through the tactic may jeopardize the economic context on which he and others rely for their livelihood.

In summary, the scores of violent political outbreaks of the 1960s showed no pattern in the incidents which caused the confrontation.[11] Trouble breaks out in unexpected places. Outbreaks in the middle 1960s in Los Angeles, Newark, Detroit, and Cleveland indicated a ghetto syndrome of big cities. But confrontation politics has mushroomed in small industrial cities and on campuses, bringing to the surface deep-seated hostilities to diverse situations in all kinds of communities. The potential for violence existed but different kinds of incidents triggered it. Concisely, the important lesson for the observer of political societies is that there is always a latent potentiality for the use of force or threat of it. In addition to many outbreaks, there have been hundreds of "near misses," in which violence was averted because of quick reaction of authorities or leaders of private groups, who were able to stop it at the last moment.

Conflict is a characteristic of society and must be recognized as a part of the social process. Extreme or violent political behavior co-exists with peaceful behavior as a method of resolving conflict. It has both functional and dysfunctional tendencies. Ideally, if those legitimately in authority have the will and the mechanisms for settling conflict by persuasion, legislation, and discussion, private citizens need not resort to force. However, lack of communication and lack of appreciation of the depth or real nature of grievances sometimes contribute to failure to bring about peaceful accommodation. It is also true that on some issues those in authority do understand but, for one reason or another, will make few concessions because they regard the demands either as invalid or too costly to grant in view of their own status. White-initiated intimidation, threats, and in some cases assassination took place because of fear of what would happen if the blacks (and, in earlier times, poor whites) exercised the franchise.

Finally, the line between orderly "legitimate" tactics and the disruptive "illegitimate" ones is often confused. When a group stages a sit-in and stops the orderly operation of an office, it may, from its view-

[11] Space forbids treatment of the causes of violence in this volume. Sufficient here to note that recent explosions are traceable to frustrations over the Vietnam war and its attendant inflation, military costs, the draft, the magnitude of social change, increases in and movement of population, and the black revolution, which has been successful in achieving some Negro demands through diverse forceful tactics. But the incidents igniting eruptions often have no apparent direct relation to these deep-seated causes.

point, be using passive resistance and a nonviolent method. If it presents its demands and leaves when ordered out, it may see itself as engaged in peaceful protest. If the group refuses to leave, it is guilty of an illegal act of trespassing. But managers or administrative officials, on the other hand, may see any united sit-in, with or without physical clashes, as trespassing and an act of force. Physical presence in itself or a march of blacks through an all-white neighborhood, though legally permissable, are interpreted by some but not by others as an "intimidating" act. Movement in itself generally gives the dispossessed and aggrieved a feeling that they are doing something to bring about a political solution. Many of the demonstrations have been therapeutic for black and white, for students and college administrators. Perhaps the case may be made that a "little force or threat of it is functional and efficacious"; but the brutal use of force by authority or protesters is dangerous and dysfunctional, for it leads to polarization, hardening of attitudes, and unwillingness to negotiate. (But one can get a debate on this!)

Stated another way, the aggressive political behavior in the 1960s placed before the democratic theorist and the citizens who live in the system the question of where to draw the line between *legitimate* and *illegitimate* dissent. Voting, discussion, campaigning, letter writing, party and pressure-group activities are regarded as appropriate methods. Bombings, arson, lynchings, guerilla warfare, sniping and the hurling of missiles, and political assassination are regarded as illegitimate. But there is a gray area between the two, often centered in the types of activities that creep into some demonstrations, that is, the use of obscenities and subtle duress, and the nature of marches and sit-ins and public reaction to them.

Perhaps most important is the relationship between the tactics and the admissibility of urgency. The moral urgency of the cause and the depth of grievance will affect the selection of tactics. Preferably, those in public authority should evaluate which needs are most pressing and should establish priorities for handling them. When the aggrieved feel that this is not being done or is being done inadequately, the groundwork is laid for forceful protest. A great responsibility, therefore, rests upon government to act wisely to prevent situations that lead the unhappy to employ forceful measures to obtain redress of grievances. The courts are placed in the crucial position of recognizing the degree of urgency of the complaint and of drawing the lines of permissible tactics. (This was particularly true concerning forms of draft resistance and protest against the selective service system.)

The thrust of conscience and tolerance of tactics varies from person to person and from community to community and even from court to court. (In some communities, white violence has been more readily tolerated than black violence.) The nation not only must resolve the demands but must decide how it will respond to the tactics of those making demands. Its response to tactic and to substance call for adaptability and adjustment, or its troubles are certain to be compounded in both areas.

The massive rebellions exemplified by Newark, Washington, D.C., and Detroit may not repeat themselves in the 1970s because local leadership of the discontented believe they are less effective than small encounters. Despite a comparative quiet in the early 1970s in terms of large outbreaks, the number of small skirmishes remains large and stands as testimony to the existence of an extensive resort to confrontation politics by growing numbers politicized to use force or threat of it. They constitute a serious challenge to the system and must be coped with in ways different from those used for massive riots. The leaders of the political left working with public authorities could make a special contribution by showing alienated blacks and whites that social adjustments are attainable through nonviolent political methods.

NATURE OF PROTEST

In the late 1960s, the functioning of the American democracy, with its "new public philosophy" and "interest-group liberalism," came under massive verbal attack, which posed challenges that will occupy the nation in the 1970s. Some labeled it a crisis in values or a crisis of authority. The criticisms were not restricted to any one group. They came from youth, students, the poor, blacks and other minorities, from the left, right, and moderates, from laymen and from scholars. The challenges were stated in different terms and on different bases — they were political, social, economic, and moral.

Protest politics has been omnipresent in the American polity and has run from peaceful vocal protests and letter writing to the strike, mass demonstrations, and violence against both property and the person of those in authority. The populist revolt and the Progressive movement from 1890 to 1920, the bitter economic protests of the 1930s and resultant New Deal possessed some of the same characteristics of the revolt that became especially pronounced during the term of President Lyndon B. Johnson. But new groups became highly involved in the modern challenge, most notably youth and the blacks. Moreover, the demonstrations were less centered in economic discontent and were directed more at the political and moral aspects of the social system than was the case with the Populists and the unemployed in the 1930s. A "take to the streets" tactic was widely utilized. Few large cities escaped outbreaks, and most universities witnessed confrontations between administrators and students. Older forms of peaceful discussion were supplemented if not supplanted by sit-ins, demonstrations, and new tactics. (Sit-ins are not new, having been used in earlier generations, but they were employed much more extensively in the 1960s.)

Any classification of types of protests is certain to be unsatisfactory and an oversimplification. Moreover, the categories are likely to overlap. For convenience, our consideration may be covered under the headings of protests directed at (1) the social system and its concomitant culture and (2) the processes and results of political decision making. Some criticisms are directed at only one organization such as political parties, others at a broad range of institutions such as government, pressure groups, churches, and universities.

Protests Against the Social System   Despite extensive affluence as compared with earlier times, protest against the quality of life and living is widespread, expecially against urban blight, including inadequate housing, poverty, polluted air and water, and traffic problems. The well-known columnist of the *New Republic*, TRB, voiced what is said in millions of homes: "When I was a boy we didn't lock the house when we went out. Now we lock it, and women will not walk alone in the streets at night. This has been a degrading, a shocking change in everyday life. We have allowed a quiet fear to settle on America. We are afraid of each other."[12] The great rise in armed robberies and bodily assaults attests to the use of violence and illegal measures to attain ends.

Young people are especially critical of the middle-class values of their elders and charge them with hypocrisy and duplicity in economic and social relationships. They see the individual demeaned in an effort to make a living. As the price of belonging or acceptance, the individual too often finds that he must accept the values, biases, attitudes, and prejudices of his group's leadership. Little room is left for individual eccentricities and privacy. In an effort to protest these restrictive and materialistic values, some youths in the 1960s started hippie colonies and resorted to unconventional dress and speech.[13] Alienation shows itself in some cases in resort to drugs and sexual promiscuity. Younger idealists, as in the past, also decry the materialism of their elders and assert that economic legislation alone does not result in happiness. In general, the youth protest is social-moral not economic.

Black leaders, young and old, also denounce the existing societal values, in whose context racial minorities are discriminated against in

[12] Quoted in *Seattle Post Intelligencer*, Aug. 17, 1969.

[13] Irving Kristol advances the interesting thesis that the hippie sects are the only true radical sects in the American society today because "they are dropouts from the revolution of rising expectations and reject the materialistic ethos that is the basis of the modern social order." "The Old Politics, the New Politics, the *New* New Politics," *The New York Times Magazine*, Nov. 24, 1968.

nearly every aspect of living. Unlike protests of the better-off whites, the Negro protest is also strongly economic because a lack of economic affluence condemns blacks to ghetto living and to undesirable segregation outside the ghetto. (As seen earlier, some of the more militant blacks denounce the generally proclaimed goal of integration and urge blacks to set up their own culture outside that of whites.) Concisely, an increasing number of blacks are questioning the ability of the established political system to provide the Negro with a fair share of the benefits of a highly productive society.

Many persons who accept the general structure of society and see no crisis of values, nonetheless are highly critical of the way that the values are being realized and are mindful that some of them must undergo change and modification. This is true of millions of whites who, before 1954 when the Supreme Court handed down the first major desegregation decision, had more or less unconsciously accepted the separate-but-equal-accommodation concept for blacks but who thereafter changed to embrace integration as morally right. Many of them, however, have found that integration as a modus vivendi for day-to-day living is easier to accept intellectually than emotionally.

For many other whites, integration with all it connotes is not acceptable if pushed too fast. Some blame blacks for riots and crime, and "law and order" has become a code term used by those who want to slow down the process of black integration into the white man's society. The fact that Gov. George Wallace (the chief "law and order" candidate) could poll nearly 10 million votes in 1968 indicated that many citizens were alienated and unhappy with the turn of events in the sixties. For such persons, the Wallace movement dramatized the yearning to restore older values and to change the direction in which the country had been moving. Blacks and anti-Wallace whites tended to respond that "law and order" was too often law *without* justice and that it must be replaced by an emphasis upon law *with* justice.

The Vietnam war led to widespread disaffection. Draft resistance was dramatized, the "unfairness" of the selective service system, and the huge defense budget as well as the "military-industrial complex" came in for the sharpest of criticism.

Attack on Decisional Processes and Policy Outcomes.   Criticism of the pluralistic processes of bargaining and negotiation and of policy outcomes much antedates the 1970s but the weaknesses of the system were particularly glaring in that decade in terms of results. Its outputs were unable to keep widespread violent conflict from breaking out or to provide satisfactory response to many of the protests just observed. Dissatisfaction was manifest with (1) the major political parties, (2) unresponsiveness and unrepresentative character of political institutions, (3) the foreign policy–military aspects of national policy, and (4) priorities and outcomes brought forth in politics of the sixties.

Political parties and the electoral process were singled out for special criticism in 1968 for the way in which delegates to the national convention were chosen, for temporizing on the Vietnam plank, and for the selection by the conventions of Humphrey and Nixon and Agnew (in general, the choice of Muskie met with approval). The process of decision making in the two major parties and the failure to come to grips in a constructive way with contemporary problems led to condemnation of or to alienation from the party system. A lower turnout in the 1968 presidential election than in 1960 and 1964 was cited as evidence of dissatisfaction with the nomination choices. In 1968, 10,280,000 voters preferred a minor-party presidential candidate. There appeared also to be more widespread discontent with the Electoral College system than in many years. Criticisms of the national convention and the Electoral College have a long history, so such complaints were incremental rather than novel.

Further evidence of the dissatisfaction with partisan politics in the late 1960s was shown by phenomenal split-ticket voting and the increase in the numbers of self-classified independents, especially in the twenty-one to thirty age bracket. Although independents were originally found to be largely persons of low political awareness and involvement, many of the newer independents are college-educated and in the upper-status occupations. A great deal of protest, moreover, is outside the channel of party politics — "politics without parties." Concisely, instead of seeing parties as active intermediaries between people and their rulers, new structures are being sought to link the governed with the governors. Parties are not seen as effective channels for building countervailing power against the disliked "establishment."

A whole range of broadsides are directed against the processes of pluralist politics with allegations that they are lacking in participatory democracy. Too many persons are kept outside the system, with the result that political institutions are unresponsive to demands for change. Competition between groups is seen as unacceptably imperfect with all interests far from equitable or equivalent to each other. Many interests go unarticulated by an effective group and are left out of any meaningful participation in the decision-making process. Blacks could point to little representation, if any at all, on important policy-making boards or to being left out of private-group leadership positions. Senator Edmund Muskie observed that in 1969 throughout the entire nation slightly more than 1 percent of the local selective service board members were black and that more than one-fifth of the members were

70 years of age or more. He found that such boards were "not representative" and often operated unfairly and unjustly. "A draftee," he said, "seldom knows what his options are, or who to turn to for help and counsel." It is easy to find other boards in American communities inadequately reflecting important social and economic interests.

Attack on the "industrial-military complex" came from many quarters, including Congress. The concept originally came from President Eisenhower in an address delivered January 17, 1961, as he was leaving the Presidency. He said, in part,

> We must guard against the acquisition of unwarranted influence, whether sought or unsought by the military-industrial complex. The potential for the disastrous rise of misplaced power exists and will persist.
> We must never let the weight of this combination endanger our liberties or democratic processes. . . . Only an alert and knowledgeable citizenry can compel the proper meshing of the huge industrial and military machinery of defense with our peaceful methods and goals, so that security and liberty may prosper together.

Those who are disoriented and disaffected view the complex as fostering an aggressive American militarism, making the professional military men extremely effective in the councils of government, which consequently failed to negotiate energetically for the end of the Vietnam war. Huge defense expenditures take money from needed domestic programs. Some express fear that government has become the instrumentality of the "military-industrial complex." The military emphasis leads local communities to be preoccupied with procuring defense contracts. College students claim that especially in the 1960s this same military interest tended to subvert the research interests of faculty to the "war machine" and therefore is demoralizing to education. Because of the technical character of armament and the alleged need for internal security, the complex is also regarded as too secretive and therefore out of control.

Dissatisfaction with the methods and structures for arriving at decisions naturally gives rise to the charge that they fail to produce optimal outcomes. The mechanisms are seen as producing incremental results with little systematic canvas of alternatives and choices. Instead of genuine reform, the system turns to patchwork solutions and has shown itself incapable of innovative planning; or, as some would state it, the "establishment" is not interested in change or innovation because of threats to its own domain.

In briefest compass, the system is regarded as having fallen down on a rational allocation of resources and establishment of sensible priorities to meet the pressing problems of today. The poor, the disadvantaged blacks and whites, the transient workers, and residents in huge cities see too much allocated to national defense and perhaps space exploration with insufficient appropriation and programming for the myriad problems of the cities and for environmental concerns and for health. Policy outcomes resulting from these are at best highly unsatisfactory, say the critics. Some individual farmers received more than a million dollars to control crops or to not produce; tax policies favor oil and other interests while many families live below the poverty level. President Nixon, early in his administration, called the nation's welfare program a failure and recommended a new approach. This statement was regarded as particularly significant, coming as it did from a moderately conservative Republican President.

HOW MEET THE CHALLENGES?

The forcefulness and broad scope of the criticisms of the political system during the 1960s shocked many Americans out of their complacency. Tranquility in the fifties, unprecedented affluence, and high employment levels led many of the older generation at the outset to question what the protesters had to protest about. Blacks appeared better off than ever before, the percentage of poor appeared less (and the poor have "always been with us" anyway), more young people could afford college and trips to Europe, and so on. But what many of the satisfied citizens had not appreciated was that change for the better had been too long in coming and that responses to grievances had been inadequate. Further, some of the older values were being challenged as well as the political processes. Notwithstanding affluence, urban decay proceeded rapidly; great population increases and mobility also contributed to the decline of decent environment—fresh air and water, space, and safety—for millions of citizens.

 A small minority are content to meet the criticisms of modern America by a vigorous defense of all or most aspects of the system. Some scholars insist that changes in the party system would be very unwise and defend the contemporary interplay of interest groups as the best possible of political worlds in terms of processes, outputs, and stability. Some lawmakers and the business community scoff at the "military-industrial complex" as a figment of the imagination. But the majority of Americans apparently agree with many if not most of the criticisms of the system and have called for changes and reforms. Further, many of the criticisms are not new, and there is a recognition that the omnipresence of conflict in itself forces change. What kinds of responses, depth of changes, and in what directions are at the painful crux of the matter, which involves determination of the moral rightness, legitimacy, and urgency of the claims of the discontented. Because the current challenges differ so much, appropriate responses are complicated, and they too must differ. No pattern of reaction suits all situations. Three broad approaches are currently available and each has its adherents — the radical, the incremental, and the new politics. Because few approve the radical solutions and the incremental changes are the traditional well-known ones, greater attention will be given to the proposals of the new politics.

The Radical Approach. A revolutionary posture toward the present society calls for uprooting a great many institutions and replacing them with entirely new ones. Several nations of the world have followed this course since World War II, and newer developing nations have substituted new structures and constitutions for the old colonial arrangements. The United States seems unlikely to follow so radical an approach because the revolutionaries are few in number and have not yet convinced a majority that a drastic operation is necessary. In one area, revolutionary change is being undertaken — replacing the de jure segregation of blacks with integration into all aspects of the white man's society. The new fulfillment is probably the nation's most severe problem because de facto integration is not easily accomplished simply by passing laws. The problem of integration in the fullest sense is not soluble in the short run, though great strides have been taken. Such steps as have been taken have not satisfied some black militants, who now call for abandoning integration, at least as an immediate goal, and for a new separation based on black control of all activities affecting blacks. Polls, however, show that a majority of Negroes do not favor a separate black society.

Incremental Changes. A second approach would retain the present party and pressure-group system essentially as is. Change would be brought about by small increments in existing arrangements. More liberalized voting laws, some efforts to democratize parties and interest groups, some constitutional reform, and better staffing of state legislatures illustrate the efforts underway or proposed. Changes in budget processes and planning are seen as helpful in better determination of priorities and tax reforms to reduce inequities. Wage and social security laws would be expanded to embrace more citizens of all statuses, thereby improving their well being. The improvement of established institutions and processes by incrementalism is traditional and is generally approved by conservatives; in fact, it is going on all the time. Arguments concern rate of change and timing and the effects of one change on other parts of the system. If a state goes over to an annual legislative session, for example, will it better handle urban problems and what effect will it have on the kinds of persons who now are attracted as part-time amateurs to serve in short biennial sessions?

New Politics Approach. A third position stands somewhere between the radicals and the moderate incrementalists and attracts a growing number of blacks, young people, and liberals. While they acknowledge that certain useful improvements have resulted from small increments, the process has not been fast enough nor have changes moved in necessary new directions. Too often it seems to be a tokenism, form without real substance, and insensitive to the depth of urgency for bold actions. There is too much time lag between social change and government policies. Here we shall refer to this approach as the new politics or new progressives.

Although the broad outlines of the present system would be kept and even some patchwork solutions embraced, this approach calls for the search for new structures, additional mechanisms, new choices and alternatives, and different planning emphasis. In some respects, there is more than a resemblance between the progressives of the early twentieth century and the new progressives of the 1970s. Greater participatory democracy and much greater personal involvement of the individual in the political system characterize the approach. More people are to be given more power and new alternatives to better fulfill the American dream of developing human dignity and individual potentiality. Hopefully, this will encourage the disoriented to be reoriented, the drop-outs to be brought back in, and those who feel left out of the political society to find a place in it with the power to compel attention to their needs. Further, this would meet the criticism of many youth that in today's world the individual is powerless.

Two generations ago, many changes were incorporated into the political system to realize goals of this kind. A remarkable number of new devices were created — direct primaries, recall, initiative and referendum, proportional representation in city councils, and establishment of a host of new civic groups such as municipal leagues and the National Association for the Advancement of Colored People. Women's suffrage, popular election of senators, civil service reform, the Budget and Accounting Act of 1921, and corrupt practices laws were also added, with a view to correcting massive evils and improving the character of politics. These withstood the reaction of the twenties and most of them have become permanent parts of the system as we know it today.

The economic protests of the thirties resulted in the creation of few new political devices. Innovation was largely in the economic area. New power groups arose, and labor became especially active in politics. But the New Deal–Fair Deal mechanisms, as well as the old progressive devices, seem to the new progressives not well geared to meet the ecological and other problems of the seventies. However, few in the ranks of the new politics recommend repeal of the partisan or nonpartisan primaries, direct legislation, or the other old progressive reforms. Yet the older reforms seem not to be fully relevant to current needs. Presidential primaries are not being adopted in any substantial numbers, and fewer states use them than in 1920. Proportional representation used in a number of cities for the election of city councilmen was repealed in nearly all of them after World War II.

On the other hand, the movement for direct election of the President has gained momentum and the House of Representatives proposed a constitutional amendment for this purpose in 1969. A committee appointed by the Democratic National Committee has proposed a bold set of changes to reduce discrimination against the black persons in the choice of national convention delegations (see Chapter 10) and to democratize both the convention and party structures to give better articulation for a wider range of interests. Republicans are likewise considering ways of attracting more blacks and youth into the party organizations. Several local committees of both parties permit eighteen-year-olds to vote and to be elected delegates to conventions.

The new politics, with some success, has forced private-group organizations to be more representative by admitting blacks and young people and giving them an opportunity to attain positions of influence. As this is done, presumably the groups will become more sensitive to their aspirations, more innovative, and develop new alternatives and choices that can be carried to national and local decision makers.

A much-demanded change by youth, Indian, Chicano, and black leaders is for membership on decision-making boards. Student protesters have sought—and in many places gained—membership on college boards of regents, departmental committees, and faculty agencies. Blacks insist on membership from their own race on boards of education, welfare agencies, and a long list of organizations that make policies affecting the black community. In a great many communities, white leaders have taken account of the black demand for direct representation on such agencies and have taken steps in that direction. They have also tried to provide mechanisms by which blacks can exercise power over their own destinies within the accepted political channels.

For many in the new political movement, co-optation of dissidents for membership on existing boards is helpful but falls far short of providing responsive government. They wish in addition to create new mechanisms that will deal with the relevant problems of the day. These new mechanisms are easier to demand than to achieve because of a lack of clarity about what the new structures would do, how they would be constituted and appointed, the boundaries of their authority, and how they would relate themselves to established agencies. One purpose of new groups is to expand communications between the races, between blacks and other blacks, between the poor and those in authority, between students and faculty and college administrators, among many diverse other combinations that need to but cannot adequately communicate with each other. Throughout the country, hundreds of new committees and agencies have recently been created in response to complaints in two areas — racial relations and the campuses. Many more are being developed, with a view to giving blacks and students more opportunities to be heard and to be consulted in decisions directly affecting them.

Communication among dissidents is carried out by mobilization committees and by what has been called the underground press. Originally, this classification embraced a number of small presses at several universities and in several of the hippie colonies, exemplified by *The Berkeley Barb*, *The Village Voice*, *The East Village Other*, *Los Angeles Free Press*, and *The Guardian*. Now, however, there are more than a hundred magazines and journals bearing the rubric, and they have combined into an international Underground Press Syndicate (UPS). They all belong to the Liberation News Service (LNS), which they see as an alternative counterpart to the Associated Press and United Press International. Nor is the underground press confined to the United States — it has outlets in Britain, West Germany, Argentina, Colombia, Canada, Belgium, Switzerland, Sweden, Denmark, the Netherlands, Italy, Finland, and Australia.[14] Circulation in the United States was estimated at 300,000 in 1968 and 4.6 million throughout the world. The papers deal not only with news but also with strategies and approaches for exerting pressures on public authorities.

It is one thing to be consulted but another to bring the discontented into decision making in an authoritative way. The more militant blacks have insisted on full control of the black community, including its schools, its teachers, and its neighborhood functions. This demand causes increased racial tensions in some big cities. The concept of decentralization, with local areas making their own decisions, is attractive in principle to local leaders who are without power and is often embraced by them as the new politics. Decentralization in practice raises many questions and results in clashes between scholars and between administrators as to whether it is a workable, wise method. If organizational arrangements can be worked out that give balance to both communitywide and neighborhood interests, then a real contribution to politics can be made. But decentralization as visualized by subcommunity leaders is controversial and often exacerbates rather than ameliorates conflict. Pollution, housing, transportation, employment, and other problems are not exclusively neighborhood in nature; and

[14]See Peter Fryer, "A Map of the Underground," *Encounter*, October, 1967, pp. 6–20, and "Underground Press," *Times Literary Supplement*, Jan. 22, 1970, p. 84.

new local committees in themselves, though participatory in concept, are unlikely to provide the necessary machinery for responding to grievances.

Some of the aggrieved citizens advocate—and have adopted in some places—an ombudsman, citizen review boards of police actions, citizen planning boards, and specialized organizations to study and recommend solutions to specific problems or to generate discussion and thought on community priorities.

The revitalization of political parties and more ideological parties, as in the past, is called for by many of the new progressives. A number of them have infiltrated the parties or formed ideological factions and clubs to bring their parties up-to-date and get them to adopt forthright proposals for meeting the severe tests of modern America. A few of them obtain nomination and election to legislative bodies. But, as frequently shown in this volume, parties are a part of the subsystem of the polity. The political system has not accorded the prime responsibility to parties for formulating and enacting solutions to the great pressing issues. Polls still show the majority of Americans do not want ideological parties and that they wish their legislator to listen to many other voices— and most legislators want it this way.

The group of new radicals who, in effect, wish politics without parties pose a serious challenge to those who feel that parties should do more than simply nominate candidates and assist public relations firms in the conduct of campaigns.[15] Despite their shortcomings, parties are the major device for generating power on behalf of individuals who are powerless against others who are organizationally powerful and in control of government. For this reason, the revitalization of the party system rather than its obsolescence should be high on the agenda of the new politics.

Because there is some decline in the popularity of parties and because of extensive nonpartisanship in local government, two courses of action are needed; they are not, moreover, antithetical. One is to use nonparty structures to better articulate and aggregate interests on behalf of local programs. It involves more participation in and better representation on existing public and semipublic agencies and the creation of new ones where the established ones are insufficient.

Second, there is the necessity for building new alliances by establishing identity among the aspirations and interests of various groups whose ties are weak or nonexistent. For example, in recent years church leaders have teamed up with black leaders and blacks with peace leaders. Some new environmental councils have brought together traditional conservationists and recreationists with civic leaders concerned

---

[15] For a thoughtful article on this point, see William Dean Burnham, "The End of American Party Politics," *Transaction*, vol. 7, pp. 12–22, December, 1969.

with pollution. Alliances may be forged at a price, but the costs may be worth it if the combination results in getting responses from public authorities on mutual objectives. Imaginative new alliances are a potentially fruitful way to get political executives and legislatures to reevaluate priorities. They offer a method for bringing the disadvantaged and fringe groups into the mainstream of pluralist decision making. On national and state issues, these new alliances could work with the major parties and in so doing bring about some realignment of advantage to political parties.

It should go without saying that public authorities are faced with the necessity for focusing even more attention on the outcomes of government policies. With the demands for committing a huge block of national resources for defense in an insecure, nuclear world and the pressures to explore space while trying to improve the day-to-day quality of living, political leadership faces its severest test. Existing methods for establishing priorities and reviewing programs are not keeping pace with requirements. Procrastination, tokenism, a consensus politics, and balancing off of powerful pressure forces do not satisfy many in the polity, and theirs are the voices of rage. It is a first requirement that the system have available effective devices for all to be heard so that they feel they can employ legitimate means without use of force. The more militant protesters must appreciate that *while everyone should be heard not everyone can or should be heeded.* It falls to authorities to decide what shall be done. A confrontation politics that assumes that all demands of the confronters must be met on their terms else force will be used, invites anarchy and rule by those who can muster the greatest political muscle and techniques of intimidation. Justice in human affairs is always imperfect, but the goal is to work for the greatest possible equity.

The Social Scientist and the Challenge. The skilled social scientist has contributions to make to the new politics of the 1970s. Through the employment of modern technology and simulation, he has learned much about political processes, organizational theory and practice, motivations and role perceptions of public men, the causes of violence, the demography of leaders and voters, public attitudes and prejudices, and the sociology of the pressure system. Through the development of empirical theory, he has helped us better to understand organization and processes. He has provided decision makers with valuable information of all kinds. Textbooks in psychology, sociology, economics, communications, governmental processes, and comparative political experiences show a much greater sophistication than those of a generation ago. Citizens of all ages should be, and probably are, much better educated on public affairs and the roots of human behavior than ever before. Despite this (or maybe in part because of it) widespread discontent and tension characterize the time.

The social scientist can continue to show why the system works as it does even though the alienated may see him as a devil's advocate for the establishment. As one illustration, he can point out that institutionalization is a characteristic of modern society that tends to focus on internal processes at the expense of external demands and may block satisfactory linkages between by citizens and public authorities.[16] Attention, therefore, must be focused on the nature, causes, and consequences of institutionalization. Then should follow an exploration of how channels can be opened wider to counter what may be a myopia of those running the institutions so they will be less slow in rectifying injustices. Further, many critics lack a sophisticated knowledge of the requirements for social and political reform. John Gardner, onetime Secretary of Health, Education, and Welfare, aptly observed: "Reality is supremely boring to most social critics. They are extremely reluctant to think about the complex and technical processes by which the society functions. And, in the end, their unwillingness to grapple with those processes defeats them."[17]

A growing number of social scientists are turning their attention to matters on which they may contribute solutions, which will call for more focus on the impact of public policies and on policy outcomes. It calls for concern with normative questions and ecology as well as with who gets what, why, and how. It involves the study of the efficacy of various techniques of conflict resolution and reorganization of aspects of pluralist politics. Systems analysis is being used to gain perspective on interrelationships of the parts of the political system and to assess outcomes and to analyze feedbacks. Evaluation can try to ascertain why current processes result in outcomes unsatisfactory to certain classes of citizens. However, many scientists back off from advancing suggestions designed to improve the processes—these are presumably to be left to public men and lay persons. But some social scientists are venturing into this area and brave the charge of being "reformers."

Professional social scientists, like politicians and political activists, need to evaluate the relevance of what they are doing. The academics are being asked by students and some of their colleagues to scrutinize the significance and relevance of their research and classroom endeavors. If the modern attack on the social, political, and educational institution is doing nothing else it is causing soul searching.

[16] Nelson W. Polsby notes that this is happening in Congress. See "The Institutionalization of the U.S. House of Representatives," *American Political Science Review*, vol. 62, p. 166. Other references show this happening in many settings.
[17] Quoted in *Saturday Review*, Aug. 23, 1969, p. 33.

IN CONCLUSION

Incremental, piecemeal adaptation of political processes and institutions continues to take place and probably suffices in many areas. Where this is done, values and lives need undergo only minimal change. Moderate legislative and judicial reform, expanding the electorate through lowering age and residence requirements afford examples of this kind of change. But in other areas, a more radical approach may be called for, affecting both values and life styles of many persons. New types of public transportation, the "clean" automobile, abolition of ghettos, legalized abortion, guaranteed annual income, are but a few widely considered measures that, if adopted, will mean for many a sharp change in values, outlook, and mode of living. Yet they may be necessary in one degree or another if certain major problems are to be combated successfully. The world has yet to find a satisfactory incremental or piecemeal answer for outlawing war and armament races.

If one will look at the great changes, reforms, and experiments instituted at all levels of government and in the culture, it must be admitted that the social and political system is responding to protest. Public authorities at all levels are tackling environmental problems and creating new mechanisms to focus on community ecology. Whether the response is rapid enough, bringing enough of the *right* kind of changes in the *right* ways is at the heart of the dialogue. What people want is a sense of movement toward equitable and effective solutions. By generating a feeling of moving in the right direction, there will be excitement with politics and a strengthening of faith in the efficacy of popular institutions. Many of the new politicians hold the belief that the system can be made both more effective and more democratic—one need not be at the expense of the other.

FOR FURTHER READING

Bushane, Robert H.: *The Black Vanguard: Origins of the Negro Social Revolution 1960–1966,* 1970.
Brown, Richard M. (ed.): *American Violence,* 1970.
Graham, Hugh D. (ed.): *The History of Violence in America,* 1969.
Harrington, Michael: *The Other America: Poverty in the United States,* 1962.
Howe, Irving: *Steady Work: Essays in Democratic Radicalism, 1953–1966,* 1966.
Huntington, Samuel P.: *Political Order in Changing Societies,* 1968.
Jacobs, Paul, and Saul Landau: *The New Radicals,* 1966.
Jones, J. Harry, Jr.: *The Minutemen,* 1968.
Justice, Blair: *Violence in the City,* 1969.

Litt, Edgar (ed.): *The New Politics of American Policy,* 1969.
McConnell, Grant: *Private Power and American Democracy,* 1966.
Rienow, Robert, and Leona Rienow: *Moment in the Sun,* 1967.
Silverman, Henry (ed.): *American Radical Thought,* 1970.
Teodari, Massino: *The New Left: A Documentary History,* 1970.
Young, James P.: *The Politics of Affluence: Ideology in the United States Since World War II,* 1968.

AUTHOR INDEX

Adamany, David, 393n, 407, 412
Adams, John Quincy, 28, 30, 287
Adams, Sherman, 332
Adrian, Charles, 499, 623n
Agar, Herbert, 60
Agger, Robert, 561n
Agnew, Spiro T., 312–313, 341, 367, 489n
Albright, S. D., 471
Alexander, Herbert, 392, 397, 403–404,
    409n, 415n, 416, 419
Alford, Robert R., 117n, 541n, 542
Allarht, Erik, 96
Almond, Gabriel, 102n, 118n, 445, 561,
    574n
Anderson, Elmer, 462
Anderson, Totten J., 109n
Anderson, Walt, 390
Applegate, A. A., 471

Babchuck, Nicholas, 573n
Backstrom, Charles, 462n
Bailey, Charles W., 321
Bailey, Harry, 515n, 601
Bailey, John, 202
Bailey, Stephen K., 26, 191, 626n, 638n
Bain, Henry, 464
Bain, Richard C., 321
Balch, George J., 481n
Balmer, Donald H., 392
Banfield, Edward C., 127, 199, 445, 499n
Bans, Herbert M. 390
Barber, James D., 244n, 565
Barker, Ernest, 122
Barkley, Alben, 238, 300, 613–614
Barr, Michael A., 644
Bartholomew, Paul, 146n, 150n
Baskoff, Alvin, 499n

Bauer, Raymond G., 633n

Bean, Louis, 48

Becker, Carl, 1

Bell, Daniel, 593n, 601

Benson, Ezra, 211

Bentley, Arthur, 570

Berdahl, Clarence, 271

Berelson, Bernard, 478n, 496n, 503

Berman, Daniel M., 627n

Bernays, Edward L., 605

Bernd, Joseph, 402

Bernstein, Marver H., 639n

Bibby, John E., 297n, 298, 626n, 643

Bienen, Henry, 650n

Binkley, Wilfred E., 28, 225

Birke, Wolfgang, 123n

Black, Gordon, 497n

Blackwell, G. W., 573n

Blaisdell, Donald, 640

Bliss, Roy C., 166, 167, 171, 172n,
185–186, 350

Blum, John M., 6

Blumer, Jay G., 390

Bone, Hugh A., 94n, 111n, 144n, 146n,
162n, 172n, 176n, 283n, 565, 610n

Bowen, Don R., 565

Bowers, Claude, 60, 299–300, 650n

Bowman, Lewis, 141n

Boyer, W. W., 636n

Boynton, G. R., 141n

Bradley, John P., 307n

Breckenridge, John C., 34

Brogan, D. W., 6

Brown, Richard M., 669

Brown, Stuart G., 225

Bruner, S. J., 500

Bryan, William Jennings, 36, 37, 58, 211

Buchanan, James, 34

Buckley, William, 110

Bullitt, Stimson, 150

Bunzel, John, 580n

Burch, Dean, 160

Burdette, Franklin, 60

Burger, Warren E., 247

Burnham, Walter, D., 23n, 27n, 545n,
666n

Burns, James M., 11, 191, 225, 252

Burrow, James G., 601

Bushane, Robert H., 669

Butler, Paul, 168, 184, 186

Byrd, Harry F., 52

Calkins, Fay, 191, 616n

Campbell, Angus, 57n, 113n, 122n, 390,
426n, 468n, 477n, 484n, 502n, 504,
506n, 510n, 513n, 516n, 518n, 522n,
538, 545n, 550n, 553n

Campbell, Christina M., 583n

Cannon, Clarence, 174

Cannon, Mark, 602

Carmichael, Stokely, 591n, 592

Carney, Francis, 140n

Carper, Edith T., 629n

Casstevens, Thomas W., 641

Catlin, Douglas S., 624n

Centers, Richard, 515

Chambers, William N., 23n, 27, 30, 60

Childs, Richard S., 137

Clapp, C. L. 252

Claque, Christopher, 267n

Clark, Joseph, 392

Clay, Henry, 30, 31, 199

Clem, Alan L., 221n

Cleveland, Grover, 196, 198, 205

Cloward, Richard A., 652n

Cohen, Mitchell, 601

Coleman, James S., 118n, 445

Converse, Philip E., 57n, 426n, 468n,
477n, 504, 522n, 550n

Cooke, Edward F., 302n, 612n

Coolidge, Calvin, 16, 206, 294

Cooper, Momer C., 506n, 545n

Corsi, Jerome R., 593n, 650n

Coser, Lewis A., 91n, 652

Cosman, Bernard, 337n

Costikyan, Edward F., 153

Cotter, Cornelius P., 127, 162n, 163–164,
165, 172n, 191

Coulter, Philip, 117n

Cousens, T. W., 29n

Cox, James M., 41, 333

Crane, Wilder, 242n, 633n

Cranston, Alan, 391–392

Crawford, W. H., 289

Crew, Robert C., 98n, 101n, 102n

Crotty, William J., 132, 150n

Crouch, Winston W., 621n

Crowe, Berdyl L., 23n

Cummings, Milton C., 390, 553n

Cutright, Phillips, 103n, 148, 276, 556n

Dahl, Robert, 6, 115, 191, 500, 542n,
602, 643

Dahlgren, Harold E., 503n
Daley, Richard J., 154–155
Dallinger, F. V., 285
Danelski, David J., 252
Daudt, H., 554n
David, Paul T., 287n, 297n, 522n
Davidowicz, Lucy S., 526n
Davidson, Roger, 643
Davies, James C., 191, 500, 526
Davis, James W., 291n, 297
Davis, John W., 42
Davis, S. R., 127
Dawson, Richard, 243, 424n, 443n
Dawson, William L., 104n, 106
Deakin, James, 644
Debs, Eugene V., 89
de Grazia, Alfred, 644
DeLeon, Daniel, 88
Dennis, Jack, 65n, 425n, 426n
De Tocqueville, Alexis, 570
Dewey, John, 48
Dewey, Thomas E., 293
Digman, John M., 517n
Dirkson, Everett, 232, 239
DiSalle, M. V., 223n
Dolbeare, Kenneth, 249n
Douglas, Stephan A., 34
Downs, Anthony, 26, 96, 191, 644
Durkin, Martin, 211
Duverger, Maurice, 66n, 118, 122, 125n,
  132n, 191
Dye, Thomas R., 106n, 127

Easton, David, 425n, 426n
Ebersole, Luke E., 591
Edinger, Lewis J., 282n
Eidenberg, Eugene, 644
Eisenhower, Dwight D., 49–53, 77, 181,
  185, 198, 200–201, 216, 248, 295,
  330–333, 521, 539, 552, 660
Eisenhower, Milton S., 185
Eldersveld, Samuel J., 135n, 141n, 142,
  146n, 150n, 299n, 471, 528, 534, 556n
Ely, Lynn W., 644
Engelman, F. C., 127
Epstein, Edwin M., 602
Epstein, Leon, 149, 269, 543n
Ernst, Henry, 321
Eulau, Heinz, 102n, 428n, 500, 515
Evans, Daniel J., 379
Evans, Rowland, 237n

Ewing, Cortez A. M., 280, 285
Eyre, R. John, 277n

Farley, James A., 167, 191, 212, 390
Feingold, Eugene, 627n
Felknor, Bruce, 368n
Fenno, Richard F., 209n, 212, 627n
Fenton, Richard F., 26, 127, 445, 523n
Ferguson, LeRoy C., 390
Fiellin, Alan, 228n
Fillmore, Millard, 34
Finch, Robert H., 210
Fisher, Joel, 169n
Flanighan, William H., 502n, 530, 549n
Flinn, Thomas A., 150n
Flynn, Edward J., 153, 167
Foltz, W. J., 125n
Ford, Gerald, 232
France, Joseph, 294–295
Francis, Wayne, 252
Frankfurter, Felix, 247
Free, Floyd, 500
Freeman, Howard E., 505n
Freeman, J. Leiper, 636n
Friedman, Jerry W., 502n, 518n
Froman, Lewis A., Jr., 252
Fryer, Peter, 665n
Fuchs, Lawrence H., 445, 521, 566

Gabrielson, Guy, 167, 177
Gaitskill, L. R., 134n
Garceau, Oliver, 228n
Gardner, John, 668
Garrett, Charles, 94n
Gilbert, Charles E., 116, 173n, 267n, 624
Gilbert, Dan, 607n
Glad, Paul W., 60
Glazer, Nathan, 91n, 426n
Glenn, Norvall D., 547n
Gold, David, 103n
Goldman, Ralph, 60
Goldstein, Leon J., 526n
Goldstein, M. N., 561n
Goldthorpe, John H., 515n
Goldwater, Barry, 53–55, 166, 167, 304,
  306, 309, 310, 337–340, 368, 386,
  391, 492, 522
Goldwin, Robert A., 96
Goodwin, George, Jr., 127, 230n, 231n
Gordon, Glen, 117n
Gosnell, Harold F., 138n, 390, 566

Gottfried, Alex, 154n
Gouldner, A. W., 191
Graham, Hugh D., 669
Graham, Otis L., 60
Gray, Wood, 35n
de Grazia, Alfred, 644
Greenhill, H. G., 392
Greenstein, Fred, 26, 426
Greer, Scott, 522n, 573n
Griffin, Clifford S., 34n
Grimes, Michael, 547n
Grodzins, Morton, 126
Gross, Bertram, 252, 631n
Grossman, Joel B., 641n
Gurin, Gerald, 502n, 550n

Hacker, Andrew, 273n, 602, 630n
Hague, Frank, 156
Hale, Dennis, 601
Hall, Donald, 627n
Hall, Leonard, 49, 167, 170, 181
Halleck, Charles, 311
Halloway, Harry, 471
Hamilton, Alexander, 29, 199
Hamilton, Charles, 591n, 592
Hammond, Phillip E., 249n
Harbold, William H., 118n
Harder, Marvin A., 624–625
Hardin, Clifford, 210
Harding, Warren G., 41, 206
Hargrove, Erwin C., 225
Harper, I. H., 471
Harriman, Averill, 521
Harrington, Michael, 669
Harris, Fred R., 166, 167, 182
Harris, Joseph P., 140n, 212, 247n, 278n, 459n
Harris, Louis, 487
Harris, Richard, 628n
Harris, Seymour, 26
Hatfield, Mark, 312
Hathorn, Guy B., 176n, 177n
Haveman, Ernest, 425
Hawkins, B. W., 127
Heard, Alexander, 392, 399, 402, 412n
Hecock, Donald, 464
Hennessy, Bernard C., 162n, 163–164, 165, 172n, 419
Henry, Patrick, 29
Herndon, James, 127
Herring, E. P., 26, 96, 636n

Hesseltine, W. B., 86n
Hickel, Walter J., 210
Hinckley, Barbara, 198
Hinderaker, Ivan, 32n
Hirsch, Herbert, 441
Hirschfield, Robert S., 146n
Hitchner, Dell G., 118n
Hodges, Luther, 211
Hoffman, Paul J., 299n, 557n
Hofstadter, Richard, 60, 96, 602
Holcombe, Arthur, 26, 199n
Hollingsworth, J. R., 60
Holtzman, Abraham, 183n, 303n, 604n, 626n
Hoover, Herbert, 42, 206
Howe, Irving, 91n, 669
Huckshorn, Robert, 337n
Hughes, Charles E., 41, 247
Hughes, Harold, 182
Huitt, Ralph, 237n, 241
Hull, Cordell, 212
Humphrey, Hubert, 55, 109, 126, 186, 282, 292, 293, 309, 312, 333, 340–344, 367, 376, 379, 382, 494
Hunt, Margaret A., 628n, 633
Huntington, Samuel P., 669
Hyman, Hubert, 500
Hyman, Sidney, 225, 424n, 431

Impelletteri, Vincent, 275

Jackson, Andrew, 30, 31, 199, 200, 262, 287
Jackson, Carlton, 198n
Jackson, Henry M., 167, 210
Jacob, Herbert, 98n, 101n, 104n, 106n, 244n
Jacob, Phillip E., 445
Jacobs, Paul, 602, 669
Jacobson, Julius, 602
James, Judson L., 26
Janda, Kenneth, 633n
Janosik, G. E., 441
Janowitz, Morris, 555, 556, 650n
Javits, Jacob, 109, 110, 521, 522
Jefferson, Thomas, 29, 30, 199
Jennings, Kent, 388n, 429n, 498n
Jewell, Malcolm E., 104n, 242n, 273n
Johnson, Andrew, 35
Johnson, Benton, 430
Johnson, Donald B., 60, 203n

Johnson, J. B., 471
Johnson, Lyndon B., 54–55, 186, 206,
 217, 218–219, 236, 239, 295, 312,
 337–340, 453, 492, 522, 639
Johnson, Mrs. Lyndon B., 373–374
Johnson, "Nocky," 155
Johnson, O. M., 88n
Jonas, Frank, 109n, 127, 268n, 445, 538n,
 621n
Jones, Charles O., 60, 172n, 198n, 230n,
 235
Jones, J. H., Jr., 669
Joyner, Conrad, 60
Justice, Blair, 669

Kampleman, Max, 91n
Katz, Daniel, 127, 556
Katz, Elihu, 445, 515n, 566
Katz, Ellis, 601
Katz, Valery, 127
Kaufman, Arnold S., 602
Keech, William, 456
Keefe, William J., 252
Kelley, Stanley, 332n, 357n, 385, 606n
Kendall, Willmoore, 97
Keniston, Kenneth, 595
Kennedy, David, 210
Kennedy, John F., 21, 52–54, 109, 200,
 202, 203, 206, 217–218, 247, 333–337,
 357, 359, 366, 369, 377–378, 462, 522,
 539
Kennedy, Robert, 21, 55, 292, 293, 294,
 295, 351, 379n
Kent, Frank R., 390
Kessel, John H., 337n, 340, 349, 374n,
 487, 491
Key, V. O., Jr., 37n, 264n, 268, 284, 439,
 441, 522n, 544, 553
Keynes, Edward, 237n
Kile, O. M., 584n
King, Martin Luther, Jr., 334
Kingdon, John W., 285, 387
Klapper, Joseph T., 445
Kleeberg, Gordon, 180
Knebel, Fletcher, 321
Knowland, William, 232, 295
Koenig, Louis W., 225
Kofmehl, Kenneth, 235n
Kornbluth, C. M., 321
Kraus, Sidney, 377n
Krislov, Samuel, 642n

Kristol, Irving, 657n
Krock, Arthur, 205
Kuchel, Thomas, 285
Kuhn, H., 88n

Ladd, Everett, 560
La Folette, Robert M., 40, 42, 88, 264
Laird, Melvin, 210, 212
Lamb, Karl A., 252, 337n, 346–347
Landau, Saul, 602, 669
Landon, Alfred M., 46
Lane, Robert, 146n, 432, 481n, 500, 537n,
 558n, 574n, 644
Lang, Gladys, 471
Lang, Kurt, 471, 586
Langton, Kenneth R., 429n
La Palombara, Joseph, 66n
Larson, Calvin J., 586
Lasswell, Harold, 6, 191, 500
Latham, Earl, 602, 647
Lazarsfeld, Paul, 362n, 434n, 445, 478n,
 503n, 566
Lazerwitz, Bernard C., 441
Leavitt, Arthur, 224
Lee, Eugene, 541n, 542, 623–624
Lehman, Herbert, 521
Leiden, Carl, 650n
Leisersen, Avery, 26, 29, 636n
Le May, Curtis, 343
Lenski, Gerhard, 429n, 430
Leuthold, David A., 326, 330, 386
Levin, Martin, 439n
Levin, Murray, 390, 566
Levine, Carol, 118n
Lincoln, Abraham, 35, 197, 199
Lindbolm, Charles E., 647n
Lindsay, John, 109, 110, 312, 552
Lippman, Walter, 181–182, 479–480
Lipset, Seymour M., 34n, 117n, 445,
 488n, 525n, 537n, 604n
Lipsky, Michael, 106n
Litt, Edgar, 586, 670
Lockhard, Duane, 98, 127, 263n, 445,
 615n
Long, Priscilla, 595n
Lowi, Theodore, 648
Lubell, Samuel, 362n
Lucas, Scott, 238
Lyford, J. P., 273

McAdoo, William G., 42
MacArthur, Douglas, 49

McCaffrey, Maurice, 361n, 372
McCarthy, Eugene, 21, 55, 96, 292, 294, 295, 296–297, 305–306, 341, 379n, 492
McCarthy, Joseph, 49
McCloskey, Herbert, 299n, 403n, 557n
McConnell, Grant, 225, 584n, 602, 670
McCormick, Richard P., 28n
McDonald, Neil G., 26
McFarland, Ernest, 238
McGill, Ralph, 445
McGinnes, Joe, 390
McGovern, George, 182, 301n, 305, 320
McGovney, D. O., 471
MacIver, Robert, 363–364
McKay, Douglas, 212, 283
McKean, Dayton, 602
McKeldin, T. R., 307
McKenzie, R. T., 127, 411
McKeough, Kevin L., 297n, 298, 419
McKinley, William, 36, 37, 197
McMurray, Carl, 392, 419
McNeill, Robert J., 419
McPhee, William, 478n, 503n
McQuail, Dennis, 390
Madison, James, 76, 569
Mahood, H. R., 602
Mandelbaum, S. J., 154n
Mansfield, Mike, 237, 238–239
March, James G., 132
Marchi, John J., 552
Maremont, A. H., 582
Martin, Curtis, 277n
Martin, Joseph W., Jr., 167n, 178, 200
Martin, Ralph G., 321
Marvick, Dwaine, 299n, 555, 556
Massotti, Louis H., 593n, 650n
Masters, Nicholas A., 618n
Mathews, George B., 468n
Matthews, Donald R., 237n, 252, 442, 445, 454–455, 456n, 519, 520n
Mayer, George H., 60
Mayhew, D. R., 83n
Mayo, Charles G., 23n
Mazo, Earl, 390
Meany, George, 576
Merriam, Charles E., 285, 566
Merton, Robert K., 158
Michels, Robert, 127, 132n
Milbrath, Lester, 404, 445, 558n, 559, 560, 574n, 628n, 633n, 644

Mill, John Stuart, 564
Miller, Byron, 605n
Miller, Clem, 227
Miller, Jacob, 407n
Miller, Warren, 57n, 113n, 426n, 468n, 477n, 492n, 502n, 504, 522n, 550n
Miller, William E., 167, 339
Minton, Sherman, 247
Mitchell, John, 210, 356
Mitchell, Stephen, 167, 182
Mitchell, William, 445
Moley, Raymond, 303–304
Monroe, James, 28, 30
Monsen, R. Joseph, Jr., 602
Moon, H. L. 451n
Moos, Malcolm, 60, 198n, 321, 358
Morey, Roy P., 644
Morgan, Richard E., 602
Morgenthau, Robert, 521
Morse, Wayne, 379
Morton, Rogers, 167, 172n
Munger, Frank J., 98n, 104n, 627n
Murphy, Walho F., 249n, 252

Nagel, Stuart S., 250–251
Nash, Howard P., 86n
Neuberger, Richard L., 274, 412
Neuman, Sigmund, 66n, 117n
Nichols, Roy F., 60
Nie, Norman H., 574n
Nieburg, H. I., 650n
Nixon, Richard M., 52–53, 56, 169, 181, 198, 200, 205, 206, 210, 219–220, 239, 292, 294, 295, 304, 305, 310, 311, 312, 313, 322–337, 340–345, 367, 370, 376, 377–379, 462, 494, 522, 531, 539, 661
Novak, Robert, 237n

O'Brien, Lawrence, 166, 356n
Odegard, Peter H., 522n
Ogden, Daniel M., 268n, 271, 321, 390
Oglesby, Carl, 595
Ogul, Morris S., 252, 449n
O'Hara, James G., 187
O'Hara, Rosemary, 299n, 557n
Ohlin, Lloyd E., 652n
Olds, Leland, 213
Ostrogorski, M., 175, 191, 313
Ottenberg, James S., 153n

Overaker, Louise, 285, 419
Owens, John R., 392n, 419

Packard, Vance, 390
Packwood, Robert, 379
Parker, Alton B., 37
Patterson, Samuel C., 104n, 149n, 242n, 275
Peabody, Robert L., 234n
Peirce, Ned R., 70n, 71
Penrose, Boies, 154
Percy, Charles, 312
Perry, James M., 390
Peterson, Arthur, 321, 390
Peterson, Svend, 30n
Pettit, Lawrence, 237n, 424n
Pfeifer, David G., 106n
Phillips, Wayne, 158n
Pitchell, Robert J., 359n
Pitkin, Hanna F., 644
Plunkitt, George Washington, 155–156, 361
Pohl, Frederick, 321
Pollard, J. E., 225
Pollock, James K., 471
Polsby, Nelson, 321, 390, 668n
Pomper, Gerald, 149, 287n, 306, 314, 388n, 517n, 550
Pool, Ithiel deSola, 390
Porter, Kirk, 60, 302, 471
Powell, G. B., 574n
Pranger, Robert J., 566
Press, Charles, 127, 419
Prewitt, Kenneth, 574n
Price, H. D., 451n
Pritchett, Herman, 252
Proccoccino, Mario A., 552, 454n, 456, 519, 520n
Prothero, James W., 442n, 445
Pudovkin, V. I., 480
Pye, Lucian, 434n, 437n

Quint, H. H., 88n

Raab, Earl, 488n, 525n
Randolph, A. Philip, 570
Ranney, Austin, 16, 26, 97, 105, 106, 132n, 269, 282n, 500, 543n, 565
Ransome, Coleman B., Jr., 225
Rayburn, Sam, 186, 233–234
Reagan, Ronald, 292, 295, 296–297

Redding, Jack, 191
Redekop, John H., 602
Reichley, James, 560n
Reston, James, 330–331
Rhodes, James A., 223n
Rienow, Leona, 670
Rienow, Robert, 670
Rieselback, Leroy M., 481n
Riordon, W. L., 361n
Ripley, Randall B., 229n, 230n, 239n
Roady, Elston, 392n, 411, 419
Robinson, James, 104n, 106, 234n, 242, 252
Rockefeller, Nelson, 53, 55, 110, 224, 292, 293, 294, 295–296, 304, 305, 309, 310
Roelofs, H. M., 566
Rogers, William P., 210
Rokkan, Stein, 117n
Rolvaag, Karl, 462
Romney, George, 55, 210, 292, 295, 312
Roosevelt, Franklin D., 44–48, 77, 169, 197, 198, 200, 215–216, 284, 303, 361, 521
Roosevelt, Theodore, 38, 40, 41, 58, 86, 96, 197, 200, 205, 294
Rose, Arnold M., 602, 644
Rose, Peter, 515n
Rose, Richard, 419
Roseboom, E. H., 321
Rosenberg, Morris, 561n
Ross, William, 390
Rossi, Peter H., 148, 276, 556n
Rossiter, Clinton, 97, 225
Rourke, Frances E., 173n
Rowe, Leonard, 278n
Rubin, Bernard, 379n, 390
Ruef, Abe, 154
Rusk, Jerrold G., 492n
Rustow, Dankwart, 127

Salisbury, R. H., 141n, 497n
Samish, Arthur, 155
Samuel, H. D., 626n, 638n
Scammon, R. M., 271n
Scarrow, Harry A., 545n
Schattschneider, E. E., 17, 69, 574
Schick, Allen, 649
Schlesinger, Arthur M., Jr., 215
Schlesinger, Joseph A., 104n, 105, 132n, 225, 258–260
Schmid, John R., 301n

Schmidhauser, J. R., 103n, 641n
Schmitt, Karl M., 650n
Schneider, J. G., 390
Schoenberger, Robert A., 602
Schramm, Wilbur, 437n
Schubert, Glendon, 252
Schultz, George P., 210
Schumpeter, Joseph A., 648n
Schwarz, M. A., 127
Scoble, Harry M., 618n, 619n
Scott, Andrew M., 628n, 633
Scott, Hugh, 167, 168, 232, 239
Seligman, Lester, 257
Shadegg, Stephen C., 357n
Shannon, David A., 89n, 90
Shapp, Milton, 392
Sharp, Harry, 545n
Shattuck, Francis M., 302n, 332n
Sherwin, Mark, 593n
Shipstead, Henrik, 582
Showel, Morris, 503n
Sigel, Roberta, 424n
Sikorsky, I. I., 285
Silverman, Corinne, 228n
Silverman, Henry, 670
Simpson, Richard M., 111, 177
Sindler, Allan P., 26, 108
Skolnick, Jerome, 650n
Smith, Alfred E., 42, 46, 369, 375, 521, 524
Smith, Brewster, 500
Smith, Constance E., 463n
Smith, Margaret Chase, 407
Smith, Paul, 337n, 346–347
Smith, Rhoten, 285
Sorauf, Frank J., 26, 97, 275
Spaulding, Charles B., 510–511
Stans, Maurice, 210
Stanton, Frank, 376
Stassen, Harold, 613
Stedman, M. S., Jr., 97, 429n
Stedman, S. W., 97
Steffans, Lincoln, 560
Stevenson, Adlai, 49, 186, 293, 294, 311, 330–332, 333, 375, 539, 613
Stinnett, Ronald F., 462n
Stokes, Carl B., 548
Stokes, Donald E., 57n, 426n, 468n, 477n, 504, 522n, 550n
Stokes, Thomas L., 180
Stone, Harlan, 247

Storing, Herbert J., 500
Stouffer, Samuel A., 500
Strong, Donald S., 445
Swanson, Bert E., 146n

Taft, Robert A., 200, 237, 293, 309
Taft, William Howard, 41, 49, 86, 247
Tanenhaus, Joseph, 249n
Teodari, Massino, 670
Thomas, Norman, 89
Thomas, Norman C., 252
Thompson, "Big Bill," 154, 367
Thompson, C. A. H., 302n, 332n, 390
Thompson, C. S., 287
Thorburn, H. G., 127
Thurmond, J. Strom, 45, 341, 463, 552
Tilden, Samuel J., 36
Tillett, Paul, 153n
Tower, John G., 108, 407n
Truman, David A., 229, 232, 570, 604n, 640n, 647
Truman, Harry, 48–49, 186, 196, 211, 212, 216–217, 382, 552
Tucker, Joseph P., 225
Turner, F. J., 445
Turner, Henry, 33, 359n, 510–511
Turner, Julius, 84
Tuttle, Daniel W., Jr., 462n, 517n

Ulmer, Sidney, 244n

Valin, Henry, 122n
Van Buren, Martin, 200
Verba, Sidney, 102n, 445, 561n
Vincent, W. S., 566
Vines, Kenneth, 98n, 101n, 102n, 104n, 244n
Vinson, Fred, 247
Volpe, John A., 210, 293
Vose, Clement, 640n, 644

Wagner, Robert, 275
Wahlke, John C., 252, 633n
Walker, David, 516n
Walker, Jack, 468n
Wallace, David, 390
Wallace, George A., 46, 48, 55, 86, 294, 342, 344, 379, 493, 494, 530, 539, 594, 658
Wallace, Henry, 16, 552
Wallas, Graham, 500

Warren, Earl, 49, 250, 594
Washburn, P. C., 566
Washington, George, 29, 30
Watts, Meredith W., 242n
Weaver, James B., 36
Weber, Max, 11
Weber, Robert, 104n
Weiner, Myron, 66n
Weisbard, Marvin R., 390
Wells, Henry, 412n
Werner, Emmy E., 458n
West, J., 425
Westerfield, H. B., 252
Westin, Alan, 630
Whalis, Wayne W., 301n
White, John P., 419, 468
White, Robert W., 500
White, Theodore H., 337n
White, William S., 187, 252
Wilder, Philip S., Jr., 188, 191
Wildovsky, A. B., 321, 390

Wiley, Alexander, 248
Wilkins, Roy, 576
Williams, E. J., 127
Williams, Oliver P., 127, 499
Willke, Wendell, 47, 293
Wilson, James Q., 152n, 157n, 191
Wilson, Woodrow, 33, 96, 197, 200, 205, 211, 521
Wirt, F. W., 150n
Wolfe, Arthur C., 492n
Wycoff, Gene, 329n, 380

Yates, W. Ross, 449n
Young, Roland, 573n

Zeigler, Harmon, 388n, 498n, 499n, 570n, 626n, 633n, 640n, 644
Zeller, Belle, 123n, 242n
Ziblett, David, 428n
Zisk, Betty, 602
Zolberg, A., 107

SUBJECT INDEX

Absentee voting, 462–463
Administration, 635–639
  (*See also* Governor; President)
AFL-CIO, 506, 586
Alienation, 560–561
American Bar Association, 588–589, 641
American Brewers Association, 580
American Civil Liberties Union, 590, 642
American Farm Bureau Federation, 583, 584
American Friends Service Committee, 596
American Independent Party, 86, 96
  (*See also* Wallace, George A.)
American Labor Party, 109
American Legion, 590
American Medical Association, 588, 604, 607, 634

American Medical Political Action
  Committee (AMPAC), 578
Americans for Constitutional Action, 506, 578, 595
Americans for Democratic Action, 578
Australian political parties, 117

Ballots, 460–470
  forms, 465–469
  position effect, 463–464
  (*See also* Proportional representation)
Black Liberation Front, 597*n*
Black Muslims, 592
Black Panthers, 593, 597
Black power, 592–593, 595
  (*See also* Negroes)
British Labor Party, 117, 120, 124

British political parties, 117, 120, 124
Brown v. Board of Education, 593
Business, 578–582, 606–608, 620–621
  (*See also* Political interest groups)
Business-Industry Political Action
  Committee (BIPAC), 578

California Democratic Council, 108–109,
  140
California Republican Assembly, 109, 140
Campaigns, 322–419
  communications media in, 375–381
  devices, 364–371
  financing of, 391–419
  major strategies, 323–328
  organization, 345–349, 362
  presidential, 1952–1968, 330–345
  public relations firms, 357–359
  publicity, 371–381
  techniques, 361–385
  uses of, 388–390
Canadian political parties, 118–120
Catholics, 504, 509, 522–526, 547, 548,
  552
Chamber of Commerce, 580, 581, 604
Committee for Economic Development,
  581
Committee on Political Education (COPE),
  578
Committee on Racial Equality, 592
Committee for a Sane Nuclear Policy, 596
Committees (*see* National party
  committees)
Communist party, 90–92, 590
Congress of Industrial Organizations, 91
  (*See also* AFL-CIO)
Conservative party (New York), 110
Conventions (*see* National nominating
  conventions)
County chairmen, 148–150

Democracy, 1–8, 563
  defined, 2–3
  and majority rule, 3–4
Democratic Organizing Committee
  (Wisconsin), 140
Democratic party, 30–37, 44–48, 52–57,
  81–84, 96, 319–320, 486
  under F. D. Roosevelt, 44–48
  under Jackson, 30–34
  1960–1968, 52–57

Direct primary, 264–285, 544, 562
  development of, 264–265
  evaluation, 279–282
  impact on party organizations, 273–279
  nonpartisan, 266–267
  preprimary conventions, 276–279
  types, 265–266
Disabled American Veterans, 590
Dixiecrats, 86, 95

Elections, 57–58, 322–390
  campaigns, 322–390
  classified, 57
Electoral College, 70–71
Electoral systems, 69–71, 122–124
Ethnic politics, 515–518, 552–553, 664
  voting behavior, 515–518
  (*See also* Negroes, voting behavior)
Executive parties (*see* Administration;
  Governor; President)
Extension Service, 585

Factionalism, 72–77, 107–110
Family, political influence of, 424–427,
  549
Farmers, 511–513, 582–585
  voting behavior, 511–513
Farmers Home Administration, 585
Federal Communications Commission,
  635
Federalist party, 28–30
Foreign party systems, 117–127
  electoral systems, 122–124

Gallup Poll, 309, 381, 502, 509, 510, 518,
  521, 522, 527–528, 530, 533, 597
Governor, 220–225
Groups, 431–433, 443–444, 501–526,
  552, 569–578
  classification, 578
  influences on socialization, 431–433
  and party preferences, 507–515
  sociology of, 570–577
  types, 502–507
  (*See also* Political interest groups)

Harris poll, 309, 381, 487, 502
Hatch Acts, 409–410

Initiatives, 498–499, 619–623
International Typographical Union, 604

Inter-University Consortium on Political Research, 485, 488, 547

Jeffersonian Republicans, 28–30
Jews, 504, 507, 521–522, 547, 548
Judicial politics, 242–251, 639–643
  party affiliation and, 249–251

Labor, 504, 511, 547, 585–587, 591, 618–620, 663
  voting behavior, 504, 511, 515
Leadership (*see* Party leadership)
League of Women Voters, 591, 663
Legislative parties, 226–244
  congressional, 227–241
  House of Representatives, 223–236
  Senate, 236–240
  state, 242–244
Liberal party (New York), 109–110, 586
Lobbying, 625–635
Louisiana v. U.S., 453

Middle West (*see* Sectionalism)
Minor parties, 12, 85–96, 120–124, 594
  categories, 86–88
  effects, 92–96
  in Europe, 120–124
  Marxist, 87, 88–92
  right-wing, 92
  (*See also* specific minor parties)

National Association for the Advancement of Colored People, 506, 578, 591–592, 608, 611, 643, 663
National Association of Manufacturers, 580, 581
National Committee for an Effective Congress, 618–619
National Committees (*see* National party committees)
National Council for the Prevention of War, 596
National Education Association, 588, 634
National Farmers Union, 583, 584
National Grange, 583–584
National nominating conventions, 286–321
  composition, 297–421
  criticisms of, 313–315
  defense of, 316–321

National nominating conventions,
  organization of, 299–302
  origin, 286–287
  platforms, 302–307
  presidential nominations, 307–311
  selection of delegates, 288–293, 295–297
  vice presidential nominations, 311–313
National Opinion Research Center, 521
National party committees, 160–191, 302, 347–350, 398, 416–417
  chairmen of, 164, 166–169
  composition, 160–162
  congressional-senatorial campaign, 174–180, 417–418
  functions, 180–181, 188–191
  headquarters activities, 169–174
  organization chart, 171
  power, 180–188
  role of committeemen, 162–164
  staff, 170, 172–174
  (*See also* Party finance)
National Urban League, 500, 578, 592
Negroes, 451–459, 507, 508, 517–521, 527
  suffrage, 451–459
  voting behavior, 507–508, 518–521, 527
  (*See also* National Association for the Advancement of Colored People; various designations under Black)
Netherlands political parties, 118
New Politics (of the 1960s, 1970s), 663–667
Nominations, 255, 285, 613–619
  becoming a candidate, 256–260
  caucus, 261–262
  congressional, 282–285
  conventions, 262–263
  direct primary, 264–282
  preprimary conventions, 276–279
  presidential (*see* National nominating conventions)
Nonpartisan elections, 114–115, 496–498, 517, 520–521, 623–625
Nonparty committees, 351–354, 616–619
  in campaigns, 351–354, 618–619
Nonvoting (*see* Political participation)

Partido Revolucionario Institucional, 119
Party conventions, 134–135, 286–321
  national, 286–321

Party finance, 391–419
    allocations, 395–398
    costs, 391–398
    donors, 398–401
    motivations, 404–406
    party responsibility and, 415–416
    public policy and, 406–408
    public subsidy, 411–414
    regulation of, 408–411
Party government, 15–22
    case against, 18–20
    case for, 16–18
    (*See also* Political parties)
Party identification, 481–486, 493–496,
    550–553
Party leadership, 133, 136–141, 145–159,
    161–169
    bosses, 153–159
    county, 148–150
    incentives for, 150–153
    national, 161–169
    precinct, 145–148
    (*See also* Party organization)
Party organization, 131–191
    auxiliaries, 139–141
    bosses, 153–159
    county, 136
    functions of, 131–132, 141–143
    general characteristics, 132–136
    leadership, 145
    legislative (*see* Legislative parties)
    national, 160–191
    political machines, 153–159
    reform of, 142–145
    state, 136–138
    (*See also* Campaigns; Nonparty
    committees)
Party platforms, 302–307
Patronage, 201–204, 245
Peace societies, 595–597
Policy committees, Senate, 237–240
Political bosses, 153–159
    characteristics, 154–155
    theories of, 157–159
Political interest groups, 569–601,
    603–643, 645–649
    case against, 648–649
    case for, 646–648
    classification, 577–578
    economic groups, 578–590
    electoral activities, 613–619
    functions, 598–601

Political interest groups,
    influencing government, 625–643
    and nonpartisan elections, 623–625
    and political parties, 609–619
    public relations, 605–609
    (*See also* Groups)
Political Left, 595–598, 665
Political participation, 536–565
    alienation, 560–561
    demographic characteristics, 543–549
    by electoral levels, 537–543
    nature, 557–563
    requisites for, 563–565
    (*See also* Voting behavior)
Political parties, 9–25, 27–60, 495–496,
    594, 609–619, 659
    definitions, 9–11
    development of, 27–60
    factionalism, 72–77, 107–110
    financing of (*see* Party finance)
    foreign systems, 117–127
    local, 114–117
    membership, 73–75
    minor (*see* Minor parties)
    organization (*see* Party organization)
    party government, 15–22
    state, 98–117
    study of, 23–25
    tripartite character, 10–11
    uses of, 125–127
    and voter surveys, 495–496
    (*See also* Two-party system)
Political Right, 593–595
Political socialization, 423–445
    church and, 429–431
    communications media, 433–436
    defined, 423–424
    family influence and, 424–427
    group influences on, 431–433
    locale and, 438–443
    school and, 427–429
Politics, 6–9, 58–60
    defined, 6–7
    nationalization of, 58–60
    patterns of, 7–8
Polling, 381–383
    (*See also* Gallup poll; Harris poll)
Populist movement, 36–37, 87, 96
Precinct leaders, 145–148
President, 195–220
    administrative leadership, 207–214
    and cabinet, 209–212

President,
  legislative leadership, 198–205
  national constituency, 196–198
  styles of leadership, 214–220
Press conference, 205–206
Pressure groups (see political interest
  groups)
Professions, 587–590
Progressive Era, 37–41
Progressive party, 41–42, 48, 86–88, 91
Prohibition party, 87
Proportional representation, 122–124
Protest politics, 656–669
Protestant, 522–526, 547, 548, 552
Public relations, 357–359, 608–610
  in campaigns, 357–359
  by interest groups, 606–608

Radicalism (see Political Left;
  Political Right)
Recounts, 461–462
Recruitment (see Nominations)
Referendums, 498–499, 619–623
Regional party associations, 144, 164
Religion, 429–431, 522–526
  and socialization 429–431
  (See also specific denominations; Voting
  behavior)
Republican party, 34–37, 41–42, 49–57,
  81–84, 96, 302, 458, 486
  under Eisenhower, 49–52
Roll-call voting, 81–85
  tables, 82–84

Sectionalism, 438–442
  (See also Factionalism; State parties;
  Voting behavior)
Senate policy committees, 237–240
Socialist Labor party, 88–89
Socialist party, 89–90, 93–94, 571
Socialist Workers party, 90
Soil Conservation Service, 585
Southern Christian Leadership
  Conference, 592
Southern Regional Conference, 458
State parties, 98–117
  classification, 104–107
  factionalism, 107–110
  and national parties, 111–114
Student Nonviolent Coordinating
  Committee, 592
Students Afro-American Society, 597n

Students for a Democratic Society, 597
Suffrage, 446, 470, 564
  administration of laws, 459–470
  legal requirements, 447–451
  Negro, 451–456
  and officeholding, 457–452
  (See also Political participation;
  Voting behavior)
Survey Research Center, 113, 477n, 482–
  485, 487, 490, 492n, 493, 502, 508–510,
  513, 523, 525, 528, 530, 532, 534, 535

Two-party system, 63–85, 121–122
  causes, 68–73
  consequences of, 73–80

United Federation of Postal Clerks, 634
United States Census Bureau, 537, 544,
  545

Veterans of Foreign Wars, 590
Vice President, nomination of, 311–313
Violence, 649–656
Voting behavior, 465–470, 475–535,
  537–558
  and ballot forms, 465–479
  candidate orientation, 489–490
  falloff, 468–470
  independent voter, 527–530
  issue orientation, 486–489
  nonvoting (see Political participation)
  parties and, 481–486, 554–557
  and propositions, 498–500
  psychological influences, 475–500
  participation (see Political participation;
  Suffrage)
  sociological characteristics, 501–528
  split ticket, 530–535
  theories, 477–479

W. E. B. Dubois Club, 597n
Whig party, 30–34
White Citizens Councils, 592
Women in politics, 458, 509–510
Women's Strike for Peace and
  Mobilization Committee, 596

Young Americans for Freedom, 597
Young Socialist Alliance, 597n